NEW SOUTH AFRICAN REVIEW 2

NEW PATHS, OLD COMPROMISES?

NEW SOUTH AFRICAN REVIEW 2

NEW PATHS, OLD COMPROMISES?

EDITED BY JOHN DANIEL, PRISHANI NAIDOO, DEVAN PILLAY AND ROGER SOUTHALL

WITS UNIVERSITY PRESS

Published in South Africa by:

Wits University Press
1 Jan Smuts Avenue
Johannesburg

www.witspress.wits.ac.za

Published edition © Wits University Press 2011
Compilation © Edition editors 2011
Chapters © Individual contributors 2011

First published 2011
ISBN 978-1-86814-541-6

Cover image: Nikki Rixon / Africa Media Online

Project managed by Monica Seeber
Cover design and layout by Hothouse South Africa
Printed and bound by Ultra Litho (Pty) Ltd.

Contents

PART 3: ENVIRONMENT

PART 4: MEDIA

Preface

This second volume of the *New South African Review* is composed of original chapters dealing with contemporary issues in South African politics, economy and society. The new series, drawing upon the tradition of critical scholarship established by its predecessor *South African Review* of the 1980s and 1990s, seeks to present diverse views and perspectives across a range of concerns vital to our country. The present edition brings together contributions from authors from an array of universities and civil society organisations, and while there is much that is complementary between them, there is no intention that the *New South African Review* should assume a particular intellectual 'line': rather, the idea is to promote intellectual debate and diversity.

The *New South African Review* is housed in the Department of Sociology at the University of the Witwatersrand, where three of the editors earn our keep. We should like to thank our colleagues in the Department for their constant encouragement in this project, as well as administrators Ingrid Chunilall and Laura Bloem for their constant willingness to take on the various mundane tasks connected with it. We should also like to acknowledge the vital financial assistance offered by the University's 'SPARC' Funds for special projects, and the support given to our application for that assistance by the Dean of Humanities, Professor Tawana Kupe. In addition, we note the enthusiastic backing and wise publishing advice extended by Veronica Klipp, director of Wits University Press, and the valuable contribution made by Monica Seeber, who served as the technical editor and, finally, we are indebted to all those anonymous referees who dispensed Olympian judgements upon the various chapters in draft form.

John Daniel (School of International Training, Durban), Prishani Naidoo, Devan Pillay and Roger Southall (all Department of Sociology, University of the Witwatersrand).

New paths, old (com)promises?

Prishani Naidoo

THE PROMISE OF LIBERATION

Of the Reconstruction and Development Programme (RDP)'s stated aspiration to 'fundamental transformation' (African National Congress (ANC), 1994), an essay by the late Harold Wolpe (1995) noted that the ways in which the document 'eradicated sources of contradiction and conflict by asserting a consensual model of society' (Hart, 2007) meant that the very notion of fundamental transformation threatened to become a source of contestation. Seventeen years on, not only has this prediction turned out to be remarkably accurate, but politics in South Africa today seems ever more sharply polarised over the content of 'the promise of liberation' (Veriava, 2011).

As the ANC government has attempted to perfect and link its growth and development strategies, increasingly entrenching its neoliberal approach (from the RDP to the Growth, Employment and Redistribution Strategy (Gear) to the Accelerated and Shared Growth Initiative (Asgisa) and now the New Growth Path (NGP)), it has attempted to define the promise and the possibilities for its realisation according to the rationalities and limitations of this model. In so doing, it has come up against community and social movements that have put forward different understandings of the promise and asserted that many of the ANC's claims to realising the promise have been compromises, aimed at

ensuring the reproduction of the fragile coalition between business, labour and government that has determined the nature of the transition (Ballard et al., 2006; Gibson, 2006;
McKinley and Naidoo, 2004).

While in the pre-2006 period the leadership of the ANC Alliance was at pains to
silence any hint of criticism of its policies from within its ranks, by 2007 and the show-
down at Polokwane, differences and conflicts between members and factions of the alliance were being played out in the media, allowing it to re-present itself as a contested
space in which debate and critique are cultivated, permitting change to happen from
within the alliance, a throwback to its critics who had, on the basis of the experiences of
the late 1990s and early 2000s,[1] declared the ANC Alliance to be a space in which dissent
and disagreement is silenced and contained.[2] With the triumph of the 'Zuma-camp'
over the 'Mbeki-camp' at the ANC's national congress in Polokwane, the stage was set
for supporters of the alliance to argue that possibilities had opened up in this moment
for more left-leaning agendas to gain voice. In this volume, Devan Pillay offers a close
analysis of relations within the alliance, pre- and post-Polokwane, posing a number of
questions for the future of the alliance and for left politics more generally, which will be
taken up later in this introduction.

While, as Pillay argues, little has changed in the policies of the Zuma-led government
or party to suggest any dramatic reversal in the macroeconomic principles they hold,
President Zuma's appointment of the former trade unionist, Ebrahim Patel, to the position of minister of Economic Development signalled for many on the left the possibility
of a shift in thinking about the economy, a shift that would prioritise the interests of
a working class experiencing deteriorating life conditions as a result of rising costs of
living, together with rising unemployment and the introduction of more flexible forms
of labour.

NEW APPROACHES TO WORK

But what is 'new' about the so-called New Growth Path? By its own description, its
'newness' lies in its development of a model for economic growth in which 'labour absorption' (in the form of the long-term goal of 'decent work') becomes central. However, as
Eddie Webster points out in his chapter in this volume, decent work is a goal that predates
the NGP, stretching far back in the history of the ANC Alliance and originating in the
policies of the International Labour Organisation (ILO) in the late 1990s. Hardly, then,
something new. However, what is new about its prioritisation in the NGP is its linking
of economic growth to job creation as a new development path and, as such, it calls, for
example, for state interventions to promote private sector investment in job creation, in
particular in sectors of the economy.

Webster also outlines in his chapter the fact that the NGP's proposals for a new growth
model conceptualise 'decent work' as a long-term goal whose only practical realisation will come about through short-term participation by the unemployed in created

'opportunities' for work that will help in developing their skills and discipline for promised 'decent work' some time in the future. Such 'opportunities' will continue to include the short-term contract jobs provided through the Expanded Public Works Programme (EPWP), and new jobs (lower paying, and targeted at youth) to be created through subsidies provided to the private sector, as well as Community Work Programmes (CWP) through which state funds will provide low-paying work opportunities for a hundred days a year per person for the unemployed members of targeted communities.

Webster presents such a model as the only practical alternative, given the present character of the South African economy and labour market, and argues for the union movement and the private sector to accept the logic that the progressive realisation of decent work is the only possible solution to South Africa's crisis of unemployment and low growth rate. In this call, the private sector is asked to concede that certain forms of labour legislation and protection are necessary for the upholding of certain norms and standards of 'decency' and 'dignity'; and organised labour to concede that decent work in its proper sense (that is, full-time, permanent, secure waged employment) is only realisable in the long-term through its 'progressive realisation'. He adds, however, that such an approach has to begin by addressing government inefficiencies in implementing policy decisions.

Some critiques of the 'decent-work' model open the NGP's and Webster's position to debate. Franco Barchiesi (2009: 52), for example, argues that while South Africa's history boasts a rich collection of working-class struggles that 'actively subverted waged work, both through direct refusal or through workers' unwillingness to confine their claims to productivity requirements, a powerful disciplinary narrative has now emerged to celebrate the 'dignity of work' as a disciplinary construct that marginalises, stigmatises and criminalises specific categories identified as disruptive of wage labour discipline'. He argues that after apartheid, a revived discourse of the dignity of work 'came to depict a virtuous condition of active citizenship rightfully enabling the full, practical enjoyment of formal, on-paper constitutional rights'. Barchiesi writes:

> As work becomes the normative premise of virtuous citizenship, it provides an epistemic device with which South African society can be 'known' as an objective, socially ascertainable hierarchy ordered according to the seemingly natural, immutable laws of the labour market ... At the pinnacle of such a hierarchical order stands a by now largely imaginary, patriotic, respectable, hard working, socially moderate, conflict-averse, de-racialised worker as the virtuous citizen of democratic South Africa. Precisely as a creation of official imagination, however, such a subject indicates the practical conducts the poor have to follow, as workers-in-waiting, on their path to actual citizenship: avoid complaining, stay away from social conflicts, and actively seek 'employment opportunities' available in poverty wage schemes of mass precariousness like the EPWP. (Barchiesi, 2009:52).

In this way, the framing of the NGP as a commitment to the progressive realisation of decent work as an ultimate goal for the transformation of the South African economy (and society) could be read as an exercise in producing the discipline and control required for the functioning of a capitalist society in which full-time, waged employment is on the decline.

In this volume, Malose Langa and Karl von Holdt present the experience of a Community Work Programme (CWP) in the poverty-stricken community of Bokfontein in the North West province as a lesson in how work opportunities can shape a collective project through which trauma (related to past and present events) can be addressed and the potential threat of violence averted, while simultaneously providing spaces through which unemployed individuals are able to alleviate their poverty, and gain access to skills and/or experiences that potentially assist them in securing decent work.[3] Langa and Von Holdt argue that the implementation of the CWP in Bokfontein has negated the need for service delivery protests, illustrating how good leadership bolstered by a facilitated process of democratic engagement among community members might have assisted in allowing participants to imagine themselves and their community differently from other communities in which service delivery protests have arisen. They express uncertainty, however, as to whether the tensions and cleavages that persist at the community level can be overcome without the continued assistance of external NGOs, and whether conditions generally will allow for the social cohesion that has characterised the Bokfontein experience to continue over time.

While they raise questions about the long-term sustainability of such projects, they nevertheless propose that the rollout of CWPs throughout poor communities in South Africa would be a worthwhile investment on the part of the state, even at an estimated cost of R10 billion for each one million jobs created. For them, the CWP initiative (currently consisting of fifty-six impoverished communities receiving assistance from the president's office in the form of material resources and the support of NGOs)[4] includes those excluded from waged labour in forms of work through which they are able to continue with the meeting of their basic needs in their everyday lives, and to stay committed to finding waged employment in the long-term, while at the same time contributing to a collective project of community building and development. They also suggest the potential for alternative imaginings of work (and relationships to labour) among those constrained by their lack of access to waged labour. For example, their narration of how some CWP members view their work in the project differently from that done on farms because it is 'work done for the community' signifies a potential for a very different approach to work unfolding amongst these individuals.

What distinguishes the Bokfontein experience from other initiatives such as the EPWPs is that it has been coordinated by NGOs external to the community (such as Seriti) which have been able to develop a methodology for facilitating collective processes of decision making and conflict resolution in relation to the CWP. This seems to have allowed for the collective identification of community needs and priorities, and the collective meeting of these priority needs through different work projects. While there seems to be the potential for such collective discussions and decision-making processes to re-imagine how work is given value, how it is organised, how its products are distributed and so on, the manner in which the CWP is currently structured and framed and the fact that it forms part of a national programme of decent work imagined as waged labour, means that any such potentials are foreclosed as waged labour is already prescribed as the solution to the problem – the problem of how to meet one's basic needs, and not necessarily the problem of not having employment. Langa and Von Holdt, however, note that not all community members chose to participate in the CWP, and the question must be asked how else – outside the CWP and outside formal employment – other unemployed members of the Bokfontein settlement survive. While the experience of Bokfontein, as narrated by Langa and Von Holdt, provides a compelling case for how work can function as a successful means of social inclusion, and as the containment of any threats to social cohesion, it is important to ask what voices, experiences and approaches the imposition of such a work-centred discourse about citizenship and poverty alleviation neglects, and marginalises in so doing. In particular, it neglects the experiences of those who survive outside traditional forms of waged labour.

In their contribution to this volume, Vishwas Satgar and Michelle Williams present a historical account of cooperatives in South Africa. They focus on recent experiences of emerging cooperatives, in particular those owned, managed and controlled by formerly employed workers engaged in alternative ways of approaching and thinking about economic development and work in the context of their lack of access to full-time waged forms of work. Showing the failure, by their engendering of 'business cooperatives', of both the Afrikaner and African nationalist approaches to cooperative development, they argue that the continued use of 'the Afrikaner empowerment approach' in the more recent black economic empowerment (BEE) approach to cooperative development 'eclipses the transformative potential of cooperative development from below'. Through the experiences of three contemporary worker cooperatives in South Africa, Satgar and Williams explore the possibilities and challenges facing those experimenting with alternative forms of ownership, production and distribution. The cases they present relate directly to the choices made by retrenched workers to find ways of surviving and living without access to regular forms of income in the form of their previous full-time jobs that came with proper salaries and protections.

While the NGP presents the notion of 'decent work' as the cornerstone of its 'new' developmental path, the experiences of Bokfontein and of the worker cooperatives presented in this volume suggest that the absence of work in its traditional sense does produce instances in which people imagine their productivity in relation to its collective, emancipatory value. In so doing, they refashion their lives outside the prescriptions of a traditional wage. What is significant about both experiences is that they present alternative ways of thinking about work. Exploring the potentials that exist among such forms of work (outside the traditional frame of the wage) might yield sustainable alternatives to private sector job creation.

While the CWP is clearly an attempt to think beyond the known solutions to the crisis of unemployment, it currently forms only a small part of the NGP's approach to work. Other prescriptions for job creation rely largely on the greater involvement of the private sector, facilitated by incentives and subsidies from the state. Identifying the rate of economic growth and the employment intensity of that growth as two key variables that will affect the five million jobs target, the NGP argues for the maximisation of growth and surety that this growth will create more employment, particularly in the private sector. Aiming to 'grow employment' by five million jobs by 2015, the NGP identifies several 'jobs drivers' (areas with the potential for creating jobs 'on a large scale'), which it predicts will create the required jobs.

These 'drivers' are the development of infrastructure projects; the agricultural value chain; the mining value chain; manufacturing sectors; tourism and 'certain high level services'; and 'the green economy'. While it sets out its own limitations with regard to the realisation of decent work, arguing strongly for a commitment to the progressive realisation of decent work over a time period in which short-, medium- and long-term possibilities are outlined for job creation, when it comes to estimating how many jobs could be created in each prioritised focus area, the NGP does not stipulate into which of these categories new jobs fall. It is thus unclear how the plans to create certain numbers of jobs in each priority area relate to the imagination of these short-, medium- and long-term goals. At a more fundamental level, it results in a lack of clarity about just how much decent work will be created through the NGP, and how many of the jobs created will be short-term opportunities 'preparing' individuals for the experience of decent work.

With such a high level of reliance on the private sector, given that the ultimate goal of business is to realise surplus value and the need to minimise labour costs to this end, it is doubtful that these jobs will reflect the characteristics of decent work. Even the state subsidies outlined in the NGP to support private sector job creation are seen as sustaining short-term, low-wage jobs usually targeted at younger people with less work experience. With flexible forms of work providing employers with greater means to minimise their labour costs, there are no existing incentives for employers to agree to greater protections and benefits for workers in the form of decent work. In fact, there has already been argument from some who fear that the NGP's prioritisation of decent work will result in the enforcement of more stringent labour laws, dissuading job creation (Cloete, 2011; Sparks, 2010).

And, as the Congress of Trade Unions (Cosatu) (2011) has already pointed out, with so many of Gear's principles re-committed to in the NGP, and with Gear having failed to meet its job creation targets, what guarantees are there that the targets so boldly announced for the NGP will be met? Today, 25.3 per cent of the economically active population is unemployed, with the figure rising to 34.4 per cent if the category of 'discouraged workers' is included (that is, those who have stopped looking for waged work) (Statistics South Africa, 2010).

BROAD-BASED INEQUALITY?

While the progressive realisation of decent work focuses on the necessary social inclusion of those most destitute – the unemployed and poor – deracialisation of the higher echelons of the economy continues to be attempted through black economic empower-ment (BEE) and broad-based black economic empowerment (B-BBEE). While the policy shift to B-BBEE, emerging largely in response to criticisms raised by black business and organised labour, has been presented as a means of preventing the process from bene-fiting elites and individuals, the experience has continued to be one through which a minority has gained. Situating the evolution of BEE as an institution in post-apartheid South Africa at the level of the development of the business–state relationship, Don Lindsay's chapter argues that the absence of a proper controlling policy framework has allowed corruption and cronyism to flourish.

Lindsay argues that, coming to be viewed as the vehicle through which good relations between the incoming ANC government and business could be built, the interests of elites and individuals in both spheres have dominated and defined how this process has unfolded. While policy discourse then reflects commitments to economic redistribution among the entire South African population through increasing the access of all groups of black people to economic opportunities, in reality it has been a few individuals and families (with the right political capital, and/or with access to financial capital) who have benefited from the actual policies of BEE and B-BBEE.

Also in this volume, Jane Duncan provides an analysis of the failure of BEE and B-BBEE policies in meaningfully transforming print media in South Africa. She argues that in spite of the newspaper industry being significantly different from what it was twenty years ago – with more racially representative newsrooms and cutting-edge investigative journalism that contributes towards holding those in power to account, and the support of black small business and corporate social responsibility – it 'tends to prioritise the worldviews of those with power and money, who predictably tend to occupy the centre of the political spectrum', with a lack of linguistic and geographic diversity, and women still lacking a significant voice. She writes: 'The fact that newsrooms have more black people and women has not automatically led to a transformation of content on these levels'. Noting a continued lack of diverse forms of journalism or media models, with the professional model of journalism and the commercial model of media remaining the dominant models of media production (even in the community-media sector), Duncan also highlights that BEE and B-BBEE deals that saw the transfer of ownership to black hands (as well as to trade unions and women's organisations) after the end of apartheid, unravelled 'as they were financed through debt rather than equity'. This spelt the with-drawal from the print media industry of BEE companies like Kagiso Media, Dynamo and New African Investment Limited and New Africa Publishers, leaving control once again to the big four companies that have dominated the market – Independent Newspapers, Avusa Ltd, Media24 and Caxton.

Duncan supports the idea of a transformation charter for the print media through which goals, models, and measures set for transformation of the sector are not reduced to a narrow framework of BEE or even B-BBEE. For Duncan, it is not only the deracialisa-tion of the newspaper industry that is necessary, but also a change in the ways in which content is produced, editors appointed, editorial priorities set and determined, audiences defined and prioritised – overall thinking, in other words, about models of media production. Through a close analysis of the industry since 1994, Duncan provides a rich and nuanced case study of the failures of BEE, and of the print media post-apartheid.

Returning to the issue of inequality at the level of individual income, Don Lindsay argues that even where statistics do demonstrate improvements in individual income levels, the post-apartheid period continues to reflect race-based patterns of income inequality, perhaps an argument for why greater emphasis should have been placed on more direct mechanisms for changing patterns of *ownership* in South Africa to form part of programmes such as BEE.[5] Although the per capita disposable income of Africans increased by forty-nine per cent between 1994 and 2007, this amounted to a mere increase from R6 381 to R9 495, while for whites per capita disposable income in the same period increased from R47 674 to R58 926, reflecting an increase of twenty-four per cent. Such changes cannot be attributed solely to BEE and B-BBEE programmes, as many African individuals have benefited from increases in social grant allocations, in particular from 2002 onwards. What is clear, however, is that state policies directed at addressing racialised patterns of inequality, poverty and wealth have not been successful.

In January 2010, researchers from the South African Labour and Development Research Unit (Saldru) released a report on poverty and inequality (in the form of income distribution) since the end of apartheid that made use of national survey data from 1993, 2000 and 2008 (Leibbrandt et al., 2010). The report shows that income inequality increased in South Africa between 1993 and 2008, generally and within each racial group. In addition, it shows that while there was an 'unambiguous increase' (ibid.: 14) in poverty between 1996 and 2001, there has since been a slight decrease in income poverty at an aggregate level. However, it points out that poverty 'persists at acute levels for the African and coloured racial groups' (ibid.: 4). The report also compares poverty in rural and urban areas, highlighting that poverty rates in the former have always been, and continue to be, higher than in the latter. However, it shows that poverty rates 'increased unambiguously in urban areas between 1992 and 2001' and that 'while a much higher proportion of the rural population are poor, the proportion of the poor who are in rural areas is declining' because of the increasing migration from rural to urban areas that happened over this period (ibid.: 15).

The report flags the fact that 'intra-African inequality and poverty trends dominate aggregate inequality and poverty in South Africa', pointing to rising inequality within the labour market (owing to increasing unemployment and rising earnings inequality) as the primary reasons for rising levels of aggregate inequality as they 'have prevented the labour market from playing a positive role in poverty alleviation'. The report confirms that social grants, in particular the child support grant, the disability grant, and the old-age pension, 'alter the levels of inequality only marginally but have been crucial in reducing poverty among the poorest households' (ibid.: 4). In the light of such information, it is significant that the progressive realisation of decent work has been prioritised by the NGP over the provision of alternative forms of access to income, such as a universal grant for all those outside the protections of full-time, permanent, waged employment, especially given the fact that the labour market has been shown to be failing to address the poor economic situations even of a large number of those considered to be working – that is, those who have come to be known as 'the working poor'.

One of the more promising aspects of the NGP, given these levels of inequality, is its call for restraint on earnings for upper income groups. With such intense debate, it will be interesting whether the call for restraint will be enforced in any meaningful way.

A 'GREEN ECONOMY'?

One of the focus areas envisaged as a key site of job creation by the NGP is 'the green economy': those industries and services related to the realisation of profits through the provision of environmentally friendly approaches to different aspects of the functioning of society. In its own words:

> The New Growth Path targets 300 000 additional direct jobs by 2020 to green the economy, with 80 000 in manufacturing and the rest in construction, operations and maintenance of new environmentally friendly infrastructure. The potential for job creation rises to well over 400 000 by 2030. Additional jobs will be created by expand-ing the existing public employment schemes to protect the environment, as well as in production of biofuels. The IRP2 targets for renewable energy open up major new opportunities for investment and employment in manufacturing new energy tech-nologies as well as in construction.
> (NGP Framework, 2010: 13).

While such pronouncements are welcome signs of growing commitments to legitimate concerns about the effects of capitalist production on the environment, the chapter by Khadija Sharife and Patrick Bond in this volume shows that there are other policy choices that the post-apartheid state has made that suggest that such commitments to addressing environmental concerns might be driven by the needs of the market rather than by any ethical stand. For example, state support for Eskom's massive expansion of coal- and nuclear-generated electricity projects suggests a greater prioritisation of the interests of profit generation than of the environmental well-being of the country and the health of its people. In the case of South Africa, it is probably a combination of market forces and the interven-tions of environmental NGOs and activists that determines the final policy choices made by government.

This is quite evident in William Attwell's chapter, which presents a discussion of the different interests at stake in a particular concern related to 'the green economy': that of bio-fuels. Surveying state, business and civil society approaches to the bio-fuels debate in South Africa, Attwell relates how well-intentioned attempts at addressing environ-mental concerns such as climate change, energy security, and rural development through increasing the production and use of bio-fuels, increasingly came under criticism globally as bio-fuels were said to be diverting land and resources away from essential food production, contributing to food price increases across the world: the 'food versus fuel' debate.

Through a close analysis of the South African policy process related to bio-fuels, Attwell shows how strong lobbying from civil society groups helped to shape the final policy, ensuring that maize, one of South Africa's main crops, was excluded from the list of food stocks available for bio-fuel production. However, he also shows more recent shifts in state policy towards bringing together commitments to food security and energy production. Of particular importance is Attwell's demonstration of a renewed commitment on the part of the state, in particular regarding agriculture, to creating jobs and economic growth through increasing its production of bio-fuels, as the market in bio-fuels has shown greater promise of returns.

But while the NGP's (and the broader state's) commitment to 'greening the economy' focuses on the potential for environmental concerns to meet the needs of the market (through job creation and/or more efficient production processes), the existing deleterious effects of capitalist development on the environment continue largely unaddressed. In this volume the chapters by David Fig and by Khadija Sharife and Patrick Bond describe how Johannesburg might literally find its insides outside not too far into the future as polluted water from old mines flows into the surface watercourses and underground aquifers in the surrounding areas of these closed mines, in what has come to be known as acid-mine drainage. This is the term applied to water that becomes contaminated when it comes into contact with sulphide-bearing rocks in the presence of oxygen, and it happens in old mine-shafts when rain water mixes with underground iron pyrite ('fool's gold') and other minerals that break down. Fig points out that the practice of pumping this contaminated water out of the mines stopped with their closure, meaning that the level of acid mine drainage is constantly rising underground at different rates in different parts of the Witwatersrand.

While Fig celebrates the work of civil society activists and NGOs in putting the issue of acid mine drainage on the agenda of the state and big business, he argues that much more must be done in the way of revising policy in an integrated manner that will recognise the urgency of addressing the acid mine drainage, establishing proper legislation and regulatory frameworks, and looking for solutions that protect public health, the natural environment, the built environment, and protected sites such as the Cradle of Humankind. As the NGP searches for opportunities in environmental concerns for job creation, it is equally important that the existing damages inflicted on the natural and built environments by processes of production under capitalism, are also addressed.

CIVIL SOCIETY, COMMUNITY AND THE STATE

Many of the chapters in this volume – Attwell, Fig, Skinner – highlight the continued existence and importance of well-resourced and organised NGOs and other civil society formations in holding the state and private institutions accountable to citizens and in helping to shape and implement policy in certain areas. In cases like that of the

South African Broadcasting Corporation (SABC), described in the chapter by Kate Skinner, the establishment of an independent campaign, Save Our SABC (SOS), worked to ensure the continued functioning of the public broadcaster in the interests of the general public during a period of tremendous crisis and contestation.

South Africa also boasts one of the highest rates of protest in the world, with the Incident Registration Information Service (Iris) recording a total of 10 437 protests for the period 2005–2006; 9 166 for the period 2006–2007; and 7 003 for 2007–2008. Between 2003 and 2008, 34 610 protests were recorded (Alexander, 2010: 26). With a strong and mobilised trade union movement, a well-resourced and organised civil society, and a number of social and community movements, post-apartheid South Africa has seen a number of constituencies mobilise to change their situations or to fight for particular processes of transformation to unfold in particular ways. This has also meant that the ANC government has not always been able to push ahead with the implementation of policies that are seen to have negative effects on the lives of people – and that mobilisation in support of demands that are not always attainable through existing frameworks for engagement, is still possible. This would suggest that the possibilities for 'Zanufication' put forward by James Hamill and John Hoffmann in this volume are rather slim in South Africa. It would also suggest that possibilities exist for the imagination of doing politics differently – that is, in more participatory ways that are not relegated to the realm of the rules, regulations, and constraints of the state.

Imraan Buccus and Janine Hicks present a review of participatory alternatives to democracy that attempts to think beyond the dominance of representative forms of politics in the post-apartheid South African electoral democracy. While they highlight the value of participatory and deliberative models of democracy, other experiences shared in this volume (such as that of cooperatives, the CWP in Bokfontein, and struggles around the bio-fuels debate) also potentially offer ways of thinking about the structuring of decision making, leadership, organisational management, and so on that could shape alternative imaginings of democracy – and indeed of politics.

The chapters by Raji Matshedisho, and by Leslie Bank and Clifford Mabhena offer experiences of attempts at law enforcement and engagements around the law that suggest that issues of governance, the law and democracy are not as simple as contemporary debates make them out to be. In Matshedisho's presentation of his experiences as a participant observer amongst student police officers in a Johannesburg township, the law is given meaning, affect and effect in the everyday interactions between individual police officers and members of the community, with the street-level resolution of conflicts and disputes occurring according to a moral economy and culture of the police and of the community that does not always conform with the law.

Through these experiences, one is given a very clear sense of just how complex are the implementation of policies and the enforcement of laws, especially when one begins to consider particular subjective experiences (past and present) of authority and the law (and life generally) shared by individuals belonging to different groups in post-apartheid society. Matshedisho argues that 'transforming the relationship between the police and communities in South African townships should not just be left to the formal application of democratic law'. Instead, 'we need to understand the tensions and informalities in everyday policing' and 'the hidden transcripts' that are at play if we are to see any positive changes in relations between police and communities. At a broader level, Matshedisho's chapter raises important questions about the ways in which the police and its function in society are viewed by citizens, and about the role of the police in post-apartheid society.

Bank and Mabhena show how the successful opposition to the Communal Land Rights Act (CLRA) by civil society lobby groups and academics on behalf of certain groups of rural communities (in particular from Mpumalanga and North West province) has worked against the interests of similar communities in the Eastern Cape. Highlighting the continued control exercised by traditional authorities over land allocation and administration of communal areas in the Eastern Cape, they argue, based on findings from interviews in thirty-five traditional authorities areas, that the CLRA, it was generally felt by people, would be 'a positive development' because it would: '(1) reduce the power that chiefs, headmen and their advisers have over land allocation, (2) allow families and households to confirm household or family title to land in communal areas, (3) create a framework for better cooperation and interaction between municipalities and traditional authorities, and (4) force government to start to develop meaningful land use and development plans for rural areas'. While people felt that the CLRA was by no means without flaws, it was an important and necessary first step towards establishing clear practices and principles with regard to the powers of traditional authorities over land allocation. With the CLRA gone, Bank and Mabhena argue, there is no legal framework to govern the decisions, actions, and powers of traditional authorities in the allocation of land.

As many of the chapters in this volume argue, when laws and policies are in place to transform institutions and processes, the state repeatedly demonstrates a lack of capacity for implementing them successfully. Haroon Saloojee offers the experience of the crisis in child care in public hospitals as a way of understanding some of the problems being confronted (and sometimes perpetuated from past practices, or created anew) in the public sector. He describes the convergence of the difficulties of resource constraints (as a result of national choices made with regard to the delivery of health care), poor integration between different levels of policy making and sectors involved in delivery, lack of staff, incompetent and/or inappropriately trained managers, and the lack of proper norms and standards for monitoring systems, in the crisis in child care that has come to light in South Africa's public hospitals.

While, as Eddie Webster's chapter points out, the NGP might, then, look like a good plan for the progressive realisation of decent work, the capacity of the state to deliver the processes, institutions, human resources and finances necessary for the plan to work, is lacking and has to be addressed first.

What many of the chapters in this volume point to is a much more complex terrain comprising relations between community, state and civil society than that captured in newspaper reports, one in which the plans of government constantly come up against the critiques and demands of civil society and community organisations, movements and individuals, the differences of context with regard to culture, tradition and custom demand, and the difficulties of the process of governing itself.

LOCAL GOVERNMENT ELECTIONS AND OPPOSITION POLITICS

Since 1994, critics have raised concerns about the lack of opposition to the ANC at a party political level, and the dangers inherent in a *de facto* one-party political system. In this volume, Neil Southern and Roger Southall survey the state of the Democratic Alliance (DA), arguing that the DA's recent absorption of the Independent Democrats (ID) has solidified its position as official party of opposition, putting South Africa on the road to becoming a *de facto* two-party political system. The May 2011 local government election results would appear to confirm this, with one voter in four now voting for a non-ANC political grouping. The implosion of the Congress of the People (Cope), and the internal strife within the Inkatha Freedom Party (IFP), have facilitated the growth of the DA and other opposition groupings. Looking for a more left-leaning alternative, the authors argue that there is little possibility that a split will happen among partners of the ANC Alliance, but that efforts are underway outside the congress movement in the form of the Democratic Left Front (DLF), launched at the University of the Witwatersrand in January 2011. While Southern and Southall admit that the DLF is still an infant, they do not rule out the possibility of the emergence of a left opposition party in the future.

Devan Pillay supports the view that the ANC Alliance will not split, examining how the theory of the NDR has served to hold the three parties together in spite of several conflicts over the years of its existence. He argues that the theory of two stages of revolution has served the function of satisfying the interests of the different class forces that comprise the ANC-Alliance, and he claims that for as long as trade union members have something to gain from being part of the alliance, there is little chance of a split. However, this might, in his view, change with time. Pillay also sees potentials for new political challenges coming from the DLF, a network of activists, academics, NGOs and social movements united in their various struggles against capitalism, and beyond, but only if they are supported by Cosatu and its members.

It is important that the emergence and potentials of the DLF be assessed in the context of a longer trajectory of struggles of post-apartheid social movements, particularly in the light of earlier attempts at similar convergences in the form of the Social Movements Indaba (SMI) and Social Movements United (SMU) that were formed in the course of protests during the World Summit on Sustainable Development (WSSD) in 2002 (Gibson, 2006; McKinley and Naidoo, 2004). In doing this, it would be important to reflect on the various political forms that characterised the organisations and movements composing the SMI and SMU and the relationship of different activists and groups to the question of electoral politics. While for some activists the DLF might hold the potential of becoming a political party worthy of the status of 'official opposition', it is also viewed by some of its members as holding the potential for ways of doing politics beyond the ballot box and the party.

But while much attention has focused on contestation amongst political parties, little has been said about those who for one or other reason do not vote. Close analysis of voting patterns shows that large numbers of South Africans choose not to exercise their democratic right to vote. Commenting on the turnout in the 2009 national election, Schulz-Herzenberg noted (2009: 25–6): 'Despite the growth in the eligible voting population and increases in registration figures, the number of valid votes cast actually decreased by over 3.9 million between the 1994 and 2004 elections. In the 2009 elections, however, the decline in voter turnout halted and increased very slightly from 76.7 per cent in 2004 to 77.3 per cent in 2009. Actual votes cast also increased by approximately 2.1 million … While turnout of registered voters remained relatively high at seventy-seven per cent, turnout as a proportion of the voting age population (VAP) was less impressive at about sixty per cent or less in the past two elections. When these figures are considered against the overall population growth in the VAP, it appears that there are an increasing number of eligible voters who do not for some or other reason cast a vote at election time.'

While the 2011 local government elections have recorded an increase, from 2006, in voter turnout, it is still important to ask why such large numbers of the eligible population do not participate in elections.

The act of voting has come to be seen by many as the granting of greater power and authority to a few to enrich themselves and those close to them.

> Those who are on the top there, their children are fed, they get everything smooth in life, but we on the ground, we have to suffer, I don't know until when. But soon they are going to the elections. So you'll see cars running around, pamphlets will be put all over the place, so that we must just go and vote for them, so they can win again. After that, they'll just dump us again. Empty promises since 1994. I was turning sixty recently, but nothing has been done since 1994. I haven't seen anything being done.' (Female pensioner, Focus Group Discussion, Orange Farm Water Crisis Committee, 26 September 2007)

Politics, seen in its narrowest sense as the marking of an 'X' on a ballot every five years, has come to be viewed by some as the playground of elites and not as a site through which ordinary citizens gain voice. While their choice not to vote may be portrayed, as has often been done, as reflective of a general apathy in society towards issues of government, it could also be taken as a sign of a refusal of a particular way of doing politics in the world. While many South Africans continue to view the ballot box as a means for exercising their voice in politics, for others it has come to represent the failures of traditional politics and politicians.

RE-MAKING THE (COM)PROMISE OF LIBERATION

The struggle against apartheid was significant for its embrace of and experimentation with different political forms – from armed struggle to political theatre to mass marches, demonstrations and stay-aways, and to economic sanctions, and negotiations. This suggests the existence of political imaginaries that were not confined to those circumscribed by the vote, the political party, and the wage. But after apartheid, there seems little left to the imagination of change but electoral politics and the struggle for decent work. While the popular critique of the ANC begins with the adoption of Gear in 1996, missing from these accounts of the transition are the intense struggles that took place within the alliance during the late 1980s and early 1990s over the giving up of armed struggle, the terms of the negotiations with the apartheid state, the protection of the right to private property being included in the constitution, the labour laws (in particular the right to strike versus the right to lock out), and macroeconomic policy generally.

It could, then, be argued that the promise of 1994 was already based on a set of compromises entered into by the ANC that foreclosed the imagination of political possibilities for the transition, limiting it to electoral power and representative democracy, and the promise of full-time, permanent employment. With its adoption of neoliberal policies, each new election has demanded that the party demonstrate its continued commitment to the realisation of 'the promise of liberation', each time this promise refigured according to the limitations and possibilities set by the changing needs of the global capitalist system.

The NGP appears, then, as the latest in the ANC government's attempts at renewing mass confidence in it to continue leading the process towards the realisation of 'the promise of liberation' within the context of its unchanged commitments to a neoliberal macroeconomic policy framework. Having been developed and proposed by a new leadership under the Zuma presidency, the NGP enjoys the support and carries the hopes of millions of working-class people who believe that it must have been developed in their best interests by virtue of its custodianship. Since 1994, the imagination of political possibilities has come to be framed by the nature, characteristics, and commitments of the particular leader in power, from Mandela to Mbeki to Zuma. This is evident not just in the form that politics assumes, but also in the manner in which it is interpreted, with recent academic and other public commentary being driven by the need to write up history in the names of its big men. But perhaps, as the experience of Argentina showed in 2001, and the more recent popular uprisings in the Middle East have shown, politics seems always to return to the people in whose name it claims to speak, who demand accountability and the right to participate in decisions that are made about their lives.

NOTES

1   An earlier period of conflict in the ANC and the Alliance occurred over its adoption of Gear in 1996 and the effects of the implementation of its policies from 1997 onwards. This involved the expulsion of several members from alliance formations, and the formation of new social and

community movements, such as the Concerned Citizens Forum (CCF), the Anti-Privatisation Forum (APF), the Anti-Eviction Campaign (AEC), the Treatment Action Campaign (TAC) and the Landless People's Movement (LPM). While these movements were responsible for a period of heightened censure of the ANC and its adoption of neoliberalism until about 2006, as well as some significant policy changes with regard to the delivery of basic services, many of them no longer exist today, or face internal conflicts. Those that have survived also exhibit a rhythm, routine and predictability with regard to struggle that makes them less threatening to the ANC-led government and less successful in making and winning demands.

2   It should, however, be noted that these conflicts within the alliance have also highlighted levels of intolerance and authoritarianism among its members, and that the very existence of a culture of caucusing, cliques and cabals demonstrates undemocratic practices dominating the functioning of the ANC and the broader congress tradition.

3   Residents of Bokfontein come from two different experiences of forced removals – from evictions from farms in the Hartebeespoort dam area, and from forced removals from land they were occupying illegally in Meloding.

4   Langa and Von Holdt note that the number of sites expanded rapidly, from four pilots to fifty-six, in the space of eighteen months.

5   It should be remembered here that the constitutional protection of the right to private property (a concession by left forces within the ANC and its alliance partners) meant that any conceptualisation of BEE or B-BBEE could not enforce any redistributive measures with regard to racialised patterns of ownership entrenched by apartheid that did not rely on market mechanisms and business rationalities.

REFERENCES

African National Congress (ANC) (1994) *The Reconstruction and Development Programme (RDP)*, South Africa: Umanyano Publications.

Alexander P (2010) Rebellion of the poor: South Africa's service delivery protests - a preliminary analysis, *Review of African Political Economy*, 37: 123, pp. 25-40.

Ballard R, A Habib and I Valodia (Eds) (2006) *Voices of Protest: Social Movements in Post-Apartheid South Africa*. Scottsville: University of KwaZulu-Natal Press.

Barchiesi F (2009) That melancholic object of desire: Work and official discourse before and after Polokwane, *The Johannesburg Salon*, Vol. 1.

Cloete K (2011) Job creation takes centre stage, *The Citizen*, 20 February.

Cosatu (2011) Government's New Growth Path Framework: One Step Forward, Two Steps Backward. A Response from Cosatu http://www.cosatu.org.za/docs/subs/2011/ngp_response.html; accessed 10/3/2011.

Gibson N (Ed.) (2006) *Challenging Hegemony: Social Movements and the Quest for a New Humanism in Post-Apartheid South Africa*. Eritrea: Africa World Press, Inc.

Hart G (2007) Changing Conceptions of Articulation, *Africanus*, special issue, November, pp. 42–72.

Leibbrandt M, I Woolard, A Finn and J Argent (2010) *Trends in South African Income Distribution and Poverty Since the Fall of Apartheid*, OECD Social, Employment and Migration Working Papers No. 101.

McKinley D and P Naidoo (2004) New social movements in South Africa: A story in creation, *Development Update Vol. 5 No. 2*, pp. 9–22.

Naidoo P and A Veriava (2009) Reinventing Political Space in Post-apartheid South Africa http://sacsis.org.za/site/article/281.1; accessed 03/05/2010.

Naidoo P (2010) Indigent management: A strategic response to the struggles of the poor in post-apartheid South Africa. In *New South African Review 1*, pp. 184–204.

Schulz-Herzenberg C (2009) Trends in party support and voter behaviour, 1994–2009. In Southall R and J Daniel (Eds), *Zunami: The 2009 South African Elections.* Johannesburg: Jacana Media, pp. 23–46.

Sparks A (2010) At home and abroad: New Growth Path may fail over 'decent work', *Business Day*, 24 November.

Statistics South Africa (2010) Quarterly Labour Force Survey 4, Pretoria: Statistics South Africa.

Veriava A (2011) (forthcoming). Under the sign of an exception: Post-apartheid politics and the struggle for water, unpublished PhD manuscript.

Wolpe H (1995) The uneven transition from apartheid in South Africa, *Transformation*, Vol. 27, pp. 88–101.

POLITICS AND INTERNATIONAL

1

The Zuma presidency:
The politics of paralysis?

John Daniel and Roger Southall

That the ANC will become another ZANU is possible, but by no means certain,
even if the entrenchment of a one-party dominant system is likely to continue
generating a range of democratic deficits in South Africa.
(James Hamill and John Hoffman in Chapter 2 in this volume)

The intent of the Zuma presidency, according to the Congress of South African Trade Unions (Cosatu) and the South African Communist Party (SACP), both of which played vital roles in bringing about its political ascendancy, was to create a government that would be less remote, more responsive and closer to the people, and which would, above all, implement a shift in economic policy that would create more jobs and be more pro-poor. In short, we were led to believe that Thabo Mbeki's conservative macroeconomic policies would give way to Zuma's more activist, interventionist 'developmental state'. The reality, however, has fallen dismally short of such expectations. Popular anger has been stirred by the personal extravagance of countless government officials, including members of the cabinet. Corruption appears rampant. Key agencies of the state, notably the police, seem unaccountable, if not out of control – an entity as in apartheid days, more to be feared than relied upon. The capacity of local governments in numerous ANC-run councils seems on the verge of collapse. The global recession has bit deeply, causing continuing job losses and spreading indebtedness while a high rand is stimulating higher prices, notably of food. Although some movement towards a significantly different, perhaps employment-creating, industrial path has been presaged by the government's New Growth Path, official policy seems as largely beholden to the market as ever – except insofar as its penchant for ramping up regulations and controls in areas such as mining seems designed to discourage rather than facilitate foreign investment.

Amid this evidence of stasis and looming crisis, Zuma himself appears indecisive and weak. Brought to power by a coalition of those at odds with Mbeki rather than merely of the left, he has seemed to devote more effort to shoring up his position (and promoting the material interests of his family, his friends and his home village) within the ANC than to meeting the challenges of government; he seems so beholden to the diverse constituents of the alliance that enabled him to unseat Mbeki that he seems reluctant to offend any of them. Having, it seems, reneged on his pledge to serve only one term as president, he has plunged the ANC back into a succession struggle, with rivals scheming to unseat him at the ANC's five-yearly conference in December 2012 (although, as ever, the ANC publicly denies what is plain for all to see). So it is that Zuma fiddles while South Africa stumbles along a path of political uncertainty. An unknowing observer studying the recent 2011 local government election campaign of the ANC could be forgiven for concluding that Julius Malema held the party's presidency and not the hapless Zuma, who seems to have lost the brilliant politicking touch he so adroitly displayed in the 2009 national elections.

In 1976, Soweto erupted, taking the then exiled ANC as much by surprise as the then National Party government and fundamentally shifting the terrain of South African politics as, over the following decade and a half, popular resistance was to render the continuance of white minority rule unsustainable. The eventual outcome was the celebrated compromise between popular forces and the white state in 1994, resulting in a liberal democratic constitution which balanced minority protection against majority rule, sought to render government accountable under a system of constitutional rule, and entrenched myriad individual, human and social rights. It has been in many ways remarkable: South Africa has now conducted four free and generally fair general elections; there is freedom of speech and extensive and critical debate; on significant occasions the constitutional and other courts have held government to account; and for all the criticisms of the government's economic strategy there has been a concerted expansion of grants and benefits to the poor. No one seriously questions whether South Africa in 2011 is a better place to live in than in 1976, even though there are many people at the bottom of the social pile who have only seen limited change or no change at all. Nonetheless, there is widespread concern that the ANC, the party of liberation, has become the major problem in regard to the health and prospects of South African democracy.

It is commonplace that the ANC has struggled to transit from a liberation movement to just another political party within a liberal democracy. Nonetheless, the ANC has become the 'dominant party', one which dominates South Africa not only electorally but by setting the national agenda. The fundamental thrust of such opinions is that the ANC views itself as the embodiment of a 'historical project' whereby, as the representative of the popular will as demonstrated by the liberation struggle, it has earned the right to rule irrespective of its performance. With such a worldview, and with party interests having deeply penetrated the functioning of the state (and particularly its security organs), it is hardly surprising that it interprets criticism of the ruling party not as healthy or normal but as originating from reactionary (read racist) motivations or, if from within the popular movement, from treachery or misconception. From such a perspective, ambition and competition for high office is not normal and healthy but treacherous, if not treasonable. And it should not be forgotten that the ANC is a member of that family of African liberation movements-cum-ruling parties – among them Zimbabwe's African National Union Patrotic Front (Zanu PF) and Angola's Popular Movement for the Liberation of Angola (MPLA) – most of which have abrogated democracy and trampled on human rights in their respective domains. The ANC is neither of these two corrupt and authoritarian entities. But the ANC in power (or individual members of the government, notably the minister of Defence, Lindiwe Sisulu) have displayed a disturbing arrogance, a contempt for media criticism and a total disdain for popular opinion and for parliament's role of oversight. Worse, Zuma's own rise to power was in the teeth of evidence that he had been deeply implicated in the corruption of the 1998 arms deal, and was achieved on the back of a populist campaign conducted by his supporters which severely compromised the integrity of the state's security services and undermined the authority of the courts.

Nevertheless, any serious analysis of the ANC in power suggests that it is a much more complicated animal than the assessment of it as a self-justifying liberation movement implies. Overall, in its tenure of seventeen years in power, it has remained true to the tenets of electoral democracy and, as Zuma's displacement of Thabo Mbeki as party president at Polokwane in December 2007 demonstrated, it is to a reasonable degree responsive to popular opinion – or at least that which is channelled through its own structures. But will it stay true to this tradition? How will it respond to that ultimate democratic test – the prospect of, or the reality of, losing political power? Will it follow the catastrophic Kenyan-Zimbabwean path or that of Ghana in more recent times?

The chapters that follow in this section of the *New South African Review* illustrate and explore the character of the ANC while also demonstrating the complexity of South African society. In their contribution, British observers of the African political economy, James Hamill and John Hoffman, discuss the suggestion initially made by Jeremy Cronin (deputy general secretary of the SACP) in 2002: that the ANC had become subject to a condition he dubbed 'Zanufication', meaning that under Thabo Mbeki it had come to display authoritarian and corrupting behaviours and tendencies similar to the ruling Zanu PF in Zimbabwe. Cronin had implied, further, that South Africa under Mbeki was in danger of pursuing a trajectory of political and economic meltdown analogous to what was then occurring in Zimbabwe; from such a perspective, South Africa was in danger of becoming another failing African country, with enormous consequences for the region. Hamill and Hoffman, however, indicate that there are some disturbing similarities within the ANC, notably a tendency towards political intolerance, but they also point out major differences. They note South Africa's strongly democratic constitution 'jealously guarded by its constitutional court … buttressed by a powerful legal profession and a highly critical and feisty media'. They point out that whereas Mugabe has established a highly personalised rule which has brusquely ignored all constitutional constraints, the ANC has not only acted to ensure adherence to its constitutional prescription that no party president should serve more than two five-year terms, but it also has in place – and has used – internal party mechanisms whereby incumbent leaders can legitimately be challenged and overthrown.

Nonetheless, Hamill and Hoffman note that the political prospect for South Africa is not simply either Zanufication or strict adherence to constitutionalism. The ANC is also the focus of Devan Pillay's contribution, in the context of its historic development as an alliance of classes. Taking as his cue the elaboration of the theory of the National Democratic Revolution (NDR) whereby South Africa's diverse classes and races among the politically oppressed came together in alliance under the leadership of the ANC, he argues that the party has very self-consciously become an embodiment of political ambiguity and of the varying interests of different classes. Thus, whereas critics to the left of the ANC-Cosatu-SACP Tripartite Alliance now argue that the theory of the NDR provides a framework for a conservative class alliance of white and black capitalists and a black middle class to pursue market-driven policies contrary to the interests of the impoverished mass of South Africans, supporters of the alliance argue that – despite manifold tensions – it holds the political centre together, and prevents South Africa from becoming victim to a politics of blatant and unprincipled factional struggle for resources. The ANC is many things to many people. Despite its failings and faults, it continues to retain the electoral support of its historic constituencies – with the least advantaged by its policies, the working class and the poor, not yet ready to abandon the 'party of Mandela'.

Pillay argues that, given electoral difficulties which any self-proclaimed party of the left would have in confronting the ANC, Cosatu – although disposed to establishing linkages with civil society organisations, and tendencies critical of the government – remains committed to using its experience in propelling Zuma to power to continue to push the ruling party in a direction favourable to the working class. Again, however, he observes the political ambiguity of the ANC, discussing how the SACP's direct involvement in the Zuma government has placed it much closer to the centre of power and increasingly distant from Cosatu. From this, it is inferred, the struggles for influence, position, and policy will continue within – are indeed inherent to – the ANC. Pillay does not directly link Zuma's personal lack of authority and decisiveness to the historic ambiguity of the ANC as an alliance of contending class forces, yet his analysis does provide an insight into why the ruling party has lapsed into a politics of paralysis, leaning simultaneously to right and left. The danger, as Pillay points out, is that South Africa may soon hit up against the limits to its present development model, and that its present failure to shift away from dependence upon the 'minerals-energy complex' and to develop an alternative path of sustainable industrialisation will lead, in relatively short order, to the inability to fund its extensive provision of social grants to the poor.

Does the focus by Pillay (and the left in general) upon relationships between the working class (or working poor) and the ANC betray an urban bias, one which loses sight of the fact that a huge portion of the ruling party's constituency resides in the country-side, notably within the former bantustans? To what extent, one might ask, are traditional leaders a vital component of the ANC Alliance? And just what is the connection between the ANC and the rural poor? Leslie Bank and Clifford Mabhena, analysing the implica-tions of the overturning of the government's Communal Land Rights Act (CLRA) by the Constitutional Court in May 2010 on the grounds that it made it too easy for the tribal authorities of the former bantustans to reconstitute themselves (and to become, in effect, a fourth tier of government), pose such questions and provide an important insight into basis of ANC rule in rural areas, most particularly the former Transkei region of the Eastern Cape.

The CLRA had sought a compromise between a shift to individual, freehold tenure in communal areas and a retention of communal-tenure regimes, on the grounds that they offered some protection for the poor. After years of deliberation, the CLRA sought to find a balance between giving people real and secure land rights, while recognising that in some areas traditional government had continued to work effectively and that it would be counterproductive to destroy functioning systems. The Act stopped short of giving rural people individual ownership rights, proposing instead the idea of permanent rights, and also allowing for a system of 'commonhold', where groups took control of land as collective units. However, because this was thought by various NGOs, land activists and rural communities to provide for a reassertion of the chiefs' power, the CLRA ended up in the constitutional court and, consequent to a contrary judgment, the government is now having to rework the law so that it conforms to consti-tutional principles.

Bank and Mabhena untangle the strands of this very complicated story. Basing their analysis upon a detailed survey conducted in 2007–2008, they demonstrate that tradi-tional authorities remain firmly in control of rural land allocation across the Eastern Cape, and that most rural households believe that they should continue to direct the process. On the other hand, there is considerable support at household level for more individual title to land within a system of 'commonhold'. Meanwhile, the level of de-agrarianisation within the former homeland areas has reached such a level that an overwhelming number of rural households are heavily dependent upon social grants provided by the government, and herein lies a major reason for the strong support which inhabitants of rural areas continue to give to the ANC. Against that, there lies deep discontent with rural development policies and, in particular, popular anger, directed at the democratically-elected local authorities and councillors who are widely seen as incompetent and corrupt. In contrast, chiefs are seen as far more responsive to their local communities (as indeed, to an extent, they had been forced to be under apartheid), resulting in considerable nostalgia for the era of Kaiser Matanzima, the long-time ruler of the Transkei bantustan. Bank and Mabhena are, however, careful to stress that this does not imply that rural dwellers want to go back to the political authoritarianism of Matanzima's rule. Rather, the nostalgia is an expression of a sense of social marginalisation felt by the rural poor, and the fact that traditional leaders have – under the ANC, and in contrast to local councils – reinvented themselves as community builders, consensus seekers and intermediaries between state and society. Their representative organ, the Congress of Traditional Leaders of South Africa (Contralesa), has proved to be among the most effective of the civil society groupings spawned by the post-apartheid dispensation. Hence the importance to the ANC of Jacob Zuma, a populist of rural origin with strong traditionalist tendencies, who can shore-up or even win new support for the party from the chieftaincy and from their rural subjects.

The analysis of Pillay and that of Bank and Mabhena are conjoined by the apparent contradiction that, despite multiple dissatisfactions and popular disillusion with the ANC government, its constituency continues to vote it back into power. This forces us to examine vital contours of contemporary South African democracy. But how can an electorally dominant party be held accountable? And what are the future prospects for institutionalised political uncertainty; that is, for the development of a political opposition with the capacity to mount a serious electoral challenge to the ANC? And moreover, if there is a disjuncture (as it appears) between electoral democracy and holding the government accountable, what does this say about the content and nature of political participation?

Paul Hoffman approaches the issue of accountability from a robustly liberal basis, arguing that if constitutionalism obtains (imposing limitations upon government; enjoying domestic legitimacy; and protecting, promoting and enforcing human rights), then true democracy or 'people power' will flourish. Without the rule of law and enforcement of property rights, he argues, no country can prosper under present global conditions. However, the ANC, as a former liberation movement, insists upon its historical right to rule, and the majority continue to vote for it. The result is that the ANC has at times, he claims, displayed a dangerous disregard for the constitution and has ignored demands for accountability. It has become the instrument of a political elite and a focus of struggle by factions for perquisites and power.

Although this is his general thrust, Hoffman is at one with Pillay in recognising the manifold and varying tendencies within the ANC. He therefore notes that the ANC's 'theatrics', dressed-up in the ideological clothing of the National Democratic Revolution (NDR), are often at odds not only with the tenets of the constitution, but also with the various exigencies which the ANC faces as a government. The government's actions have therefore often been far more pragmatic than its formal ideologies would seem to allow, and this tendency towards realism and pragmatism accounts for the various successes which the ANC has chalked up in government. He argues that this is no coincidence, for where the ANC has adhered to the values and requirements of the constitution, good governance has ensued; where, by contrast, the values of the NDR have predominated, as in the practice of 'deploying' ANC loyalists to state positions in order to ensure the predominance of the party over the state, there has been consistent government dysfunction and corruption. Overall, the encroachment of party power into all spheres of the constitution, justified by the NDR, is undermining democracy and is at fundamental odds with constitutionalism, not least through an attempted 'transformation' of the judiciary and the erosion of the separation of powers built into the constitution. Ironically, it is the champions of the NDR who are slowing the progress towards a more egalitarian society in which human rights and freedoms for all are to be found. Ultimately, Hoffman finds that the 'crisis of social delivery'which has come to characterise so many departments and levels of government results from a lack of accountability of officialdom to the demands of the constitution. It is therefore up to civil society and ordinary people to keep the politicians in check.

But what of the parliamentary opposition? Classically, in liberal democracies, parliamentary oppositions have two functions. The first is to hold governments to account. The second is to provide institutionalised uncertainty; that is, to be capable of replacing incumbent governments if and when they are unable to summon a parliamentary majority. The problem for democracy in South Africa, however, is that the manner by which the ANC exercises its voter-derived dominance of the polity threatens both of these oppositional roles. On the one hand, ANC control of the parliamentary machinery – and the apparent growing ministerial contempt for parliament – has eroded the capacity of the opposition parties to render government accountable. Often, therefore, it is only when it suits the ANC to allow probing of government departments that opposition parties are allowed free rein. On the other hand, for reasons to do with the legacy of apartheid, opposition parties have hitherto been unable to pose a serious challenge to the ANC electorally, except where the Inkatha Freedom Party (IFP) in 1994 and 1999 in KwaZulu-Natal, the National Party in 1994 and the Democratic Alliance (DA) in 2009 in the Western Cape were able to assert themselves provincially.

The 2009 general election provided further evidence that the IFP is now dying under the twin pressures of Mangosuthu Buthelezi's inability to give up the party's leadership and the inroads made in KwaZulu-Natal by an ANC which championed Jacob Zuma in 2009 as a 'hundred per cent Zulu boy'. The same election revealed the DA as steadily consolidating its role as the only serious locus of parliamentary opposition. From the 1.73 per cent of the total vote taken by its predecessor, the Democratic Party in 1994, the proportion taken by the DA had increased to 16.66 per cent in 2009, so that today it boasts 67 out of the total 136 seats held by opposition parties in the 400-seat National Assembly. Its achievement has been based on a combination of factors, notably vigorous and astute leadership under Tony Leon and, at present, Helen Zille; absorption of rump elements of the former New National Party (NNP); and its drawing on the long experience of parliamentary opposition of its predecessor liberal parties. Even so, for all the DA's gains (including those of the recent 2011 local government elections), the question is whether it can continue to grow. This is the challenge that Southern and Southall analyse in their chapter.

They discuss the efforts of the DA to change its profile in order to appeal to more black, as well as to white, voters. The DP's early mission, they argue, was to establish the legitimacy of opposition, often in the face of ANC liberation movement implications that opposition was illegitimate or disloyal. At one level, this was pursued by adroit use of opportunities in parliament to criticise government policies and to demand answers to awkward questions, a role it has continued to play and in which it outshines all other opposition parties. At another level, it sought to counter numerical weakness by opening itself up to coalition, notably with the NNP when the latter left the Government of National Unity in 1996, and thereby transforming itself into the DA. Later, this alliance with the NNP was to collapse when the latter's leadership, distraught at no longer having its snout in the trough, moved back into government and collaboration with the ANC (although leaving behind many NNP adherents). From there, the DA has consistently worked to forge working alliances with other opposition parties at both national and provincial level, most recently absorbing Patricia de Lille and the Independent Democrats in 2010. The important corollary of this strategy has been to transform its imagery and personnel by variously securing the election of a handful of black politicians to parliament, campaigning aggressively in black areas among those aggrieved by the ANC and, during the recent local government elections, putting up black candidates for mayor in major cities (notably Johannesburg and Cape Town). Having secured control of the Western Cape in 2009 while simultaneously running the Cape Town metropole, and having won control of some eighteen local councils outright in the recent local government elections, the DA has begun to present itself as a party of power, performance and delivery. In short, the DA claims today that it is increasingly able to offer itself as an alternative to the ANC as a party of government.

Southern and Southall suggest that, despite a performance remarkable in many ways, there are limits to what the DA can achieve. Fundamentally, electoral outcomes in South Africa will continue to be determined by what happens among the ANC's historic constituency. The ANC's hold on it appeared to be threatened by the formation of the Congress of the People (Cope) in the lead-up to the 2009 election, but in the end Cope has turned out to be a damp squib. Meanwhile, despite edging closer to social movements, Cosatu remains locked into the ruling Tripartite Alliance and, despite strains therein, seems unlikely to leave to form the core of a party of the working poor. Despite the potential fluidity of this situation, the DA seems an unlikely vehicle to garner the support of that diverse mixture of social groupings which gather behind the new social movements, and which usually espouse a gospel of the left (to which the pro-market DA is unsympathetic). While the DA does claim today to be far more nonracial in composition than an increasingly Africanist ANC; while it may claim increased support from among blacks (across, it says, the class spectrum); and while it appears set to forge a solid alliance across the white/coloured divide around the country, it appears unlikely to appeal to the mass of impoverished

African voters whose support is ultimately needed to give any political party a parliamentary majority.

The theme of first-rate policies and poor implementation is familiar by now. It resonates in Janine Hicks's and Imraan Buccus's discussion of the state of public participation in policy making in South Africa. They note that the constitution and such legislation as the Municipality Structures Act of 1998 provide frameworks operative at all three tiers of government for open and participatory democracy in South Africa; that a variety of instruments has been devised for citizen input – green and white policy papers, town meetings, largely rural-based *izimbizo*, petitions, ward committees, public hearings, access to the parliamentary and provincial portfolio committees, and more. Even so, they talk of the 'significant gap at policy level', the existence of a 'democracy deficit' in the failure of the established representative bodies 'to link citizens with the institutions and processes of the state'. They feel that while the system is not wholly closed to the views of the citizenry, overall they are disappointed at the limited successes the participatory model has had in improving the accountability and performance levels of governance structures in the post-apartheid era.

They acknowledge that this is not entirely the fault of the state sector. For the model to be more effective in this electronic era requires higher literacy and educational skills levels of the people in general, and a far greater degree of internet access than currently prevails. But Hicks and Buccus show that the system has not entirely failed and that there have been successes where government has been forced to retreat from unacceptable policy proposals and intentions. They cite the campaign against the provisions of draconian anti-terrorism legislation in the post-9/11 era, and the current Right2Know campaign which has forced the state to back away from, and dilute, many of the highly restrictive provisions of the spectacularly misnamed Freedom of Information Bill. We would add, however, that such examples are probably less a case of what the participatory framework can achieve and more a testimony to what civil society can achieve if it can put together broad coalitions and stand firm in the face of government's intimidatory tendencies and the sometimes overweening arrogance of portfolio committee chairs, not to mention their sheep-like tendency to vote willy nilly for the ANC position. To be fair, however, it is probably true that the Zuma administration is more willing to listen and give ground than the Mbeki government ever was, headed by a man who believed he 'knew it all' and was oblivious to the cost in human lives of some of his flawed beliefs. It was often only the Constitutional Court which stopped him in his trail of HIV/AIDS deaths and ruined lives. Fortunately, that historical cul-de-sac is a road less travelled under the Zuma administration.

The final contribution in this section is the only article with a foreign policy perspective. Christopher Saunders's chapter looks at South Africa's relations with its neighbours seventeen years into a new era of regional engagement, and at the performance of the regional organ which South Africa opted to join in 1994: the Southern African Development Community (SADC). It is, again, largely a story of promises unkept and of principles conceded. It is impossible to reconcile the Mandela presidency's promise to put human rights considerations at the centre of South Africa's foreign policy with the decision to move into alliance, via the BRICS arrangement, with two of the globe's more authoritarian regimes, China and Russia.

Another of South Africa's foreign policy promises of 1994 was to give priority to the needs of its regional backyard. This has proved largely not to be the case, even though South Africa was, to its credit, party to a renegotiation of the Southern African Customs Union's provisions. From lopsidedly favouring South Africa's interests, the agreement is now more democratic in its decision making and more equitable in the distribution of its tariff revenues but, that said, the Union is now so badly split over its dealings with the European Union that its future may be in the balance. This should not be taken to mean that South Africa has been neglectful of Africa as a whole. It has not. As Saunders notes, President Mbeki's main foreign policy preoccupation was the continent, with his promotion of an 'African renaissance' and 'his own version of Kwame Nkrumah's pan-African dream'. To that end, South Africa has been deeply engaged in peacemaking, peacekeeping and peacebuilding efforts in Africa, contributing more personnel to peace operations than any other African government. It has also been the key player (on behalf of the African Union) in the effort to bring South Sudan to independence in July 2011.

Saunders, however, has little positive to say about SADC. He argues that, geographically, it is too large and amorphous 'for there to be close ties between all its states or even for them to agree on common policies'. Two key members of its most important project, the crafting of a Free Trade Agreement – Angola and the Democratic Republic of Congo – have failed to come on board. But it is not merely its cumbersome size, its inefficiency, and its poor public relations that have rendered SADC ineffective. The larger factor is that collectively it is politically impotent, unable and unwilling to take any of its members to task for flagrant political misbehaviour. Saunders discusses, as a case in point, the failure of SADC to enforce the rulings of its tribunal on land expropriations in Zimbabwe. But it is not the only example. Saunders notes the lack of action by SADC, and bilaterally by the South African government, over Swaziland and correctly describes post-apartheid South Africa's continued collaboration and cosseting of the deeply corrupt Swazi monarchy as a 'betrayal' of principle.

Saunders's conclusion is that SADC is so diverse and supine a body that South Africa's regional interests would be better served if it focused its attention on an inner core of southern African states comprising the Sacu members Zimbabwe, Zambia, Angola and Mozambique. He adds that the prospect of a more effective and enlightened regional arrangement has been enhanced by President Zuma's appointment of Robert Davies as minister of Trade and Industry. Davies has vast experience and knowledge of the region and an enlightened perspective of what needs to be done. On his watch, South Africa is unlikely to pursue policies which put its narrow self-interests first.

South African democracy and its political and economic role in Africa and the world face short- and long-term challenges. Whether an ANC government constrained by internal factionalism and weak leadership can rise to meet the challenge is an open question. While it was once fashionable to be optimistic about post-apartheid South Africa, the reality is that most South Africans are concerned, no longer believing in the inevitability of a happy ever after.

CHAPTER 1

The Tripartite Alliance and its discontents:
Contesting the 'National Democratic Revolution' in the Zuma era

Devan Pillay

———

Despite increasingly shrill public spats between alliance partners since the 2009 elections, was John Kane-Berman, head of the South African Institute of Race Relations, correct to suggest that 'staying in the alliance was the better strategy to push the political centre of gravity of the African National Congress (ANC) further to the left' (*Business Day*, 31 January 2011)? Kane-Berman was lamenting the influence of the Congress of South African Trade Unions (Cosatu) over impending labour legislation, but his fears chimed with broader concerns from within the business community regarding future economic policy. Government's New Growth Path, launched in October 2010, suggests greater state intervention in the economy, and calls for the nationalisation of sectors of the economy are growing within the ANC.

Left critics, by contrast, argue that the alliance, through its National Democratic Revolution (NDR) ideological discourse, fulfils an important legitimating function. It glues together disparate social classes under the hegemony of conservative class interests – a coalition of white and emerging comprador black capital (enmeshed in ever-expanding networks of patronage and corruption), and a professional black middle class that has done rather well out of the post-apartheid dispensation. In other words, the organised working class are being deceived – by their leadership, also implicated in patronage politics – into supporting the ANC against their own class interests, and some believe that the time has come to build a 'left opposition' outside the alliance.

The alliance left, however, insist that since Jacob Zuma assumed the leadership of the ANC at the December 2007 Polokwane conference, space has opened for further contestation within the ANC and the government. To leave the alliance and build a left opposition outside it would, on the one hand, abandon that space to predatory right-wing forces and, on the other, relegate the left to the political fringe, no more than what ANC general secretary and SA Communist Party (SACP) chairperson Gwede Mantashe calls a 'debating society'.[1]

Alliance supporters also argue that, despite slow progress towards reducing inequality and eradicating poverty, the alliance remains essential to holding the centre together by preserving national coherence through an increasingly tension-ridden but nevertheless persistent 'nonracial' discourse, and preventing South Africa from splitting into a dangerously fractious contest over resources. The working class understand that this is in their interests and are influencing their leadership in the unions and SACP, as much as leadership is influencing them.

In other words, despite its class biases and its acknowledged 'sins of incumbency', is the ANC Alliance the only hope for setting the country on an inclusive developmental path? Or does there need to be greater political uncertainty, credible electoral challenges from the left (or, for liberal pluralists, from the right as well) to prevent the ruling party from taking citizens for granted? Indeed, are the two mutually exclusive?

This chapter examines the state of the alliance since the 2007 Polokwane national congress of the ANC, but within the context of the movement's powerful discourse on the national democratic revolution which first emerged in the 1920s. It then considers the various events since the 2007 Polokwane conference that seemingly threaten the stability of the alliance, a recent survey of Cosatu members' political attitudes and, briefly, an attempt by ousted SACP officials and independent socialists to build an alternative pole of attraction outside the alliance.

THE NATIONAL DEMOCRATIC REVOLUTION (NDR)

There has been a long history of alliance-building between the nationalist liberation movement and working-class formations. From 1924, the Communist Party of South Africa (CPSA) theorised that the overthrow of capitalism could not occur through a 'pure' class struggle between the bourgeoisie and the proletariat. The pivotal 1922 white mineworkers strike disabused them of the hope that white workers could be in the vanguard of the class struggle against capitalism because the white mineworkers were too racist, and saw their salvation in white nationalism and the job colour bar (Simons and Simons, 1983). While class exploitation was the 'primary' or 'fundamental' contradiction, the 'dominant' contradiction in the colonial context was that between the colonised people and the white supremacist state. In other words, colonial oppression provoked an anti-colonial and nationalist consciousness within the majority of the population.

The task of communists was to play a leading role in the black nationalist movement to bring about national democracy in the 'first stage' through a multiclass alliance against white rule, and to proceed to socialism in the 'second stage', which would be ensured by building working-class power at the point of production through strong industrial unions and in communities (through various kinds of working-class civic formations). The CPSA did not abandon hope of building a nonracial working-class movement, and continued to organise among white workers, but on the whole their activities during the 1930s and 1940s increasingly involved organising black workers and working within the ANC. Communists wanted to ensure that African nationalism would, at worst, not be anti-communist and would, at best, be modernist, be increasingly nonracial, be anti-imperialist, and have a working-class bias. It would not, however, be explicitly socialist, as this would detract from its broad appeal.

This 'two-stage' character of the NDR attracted much criticism from those to the left of the CPSA, who felt that it owed too much to Joseph Stalin's 'bastardisation' of revolutionary Marxism-Leninism, unlike the Leninist-Trotskyist notion of 'permanent revolution', one 'uninterrupted' socialist revolution led by an independent working class party that was not subordinated to nationalism (for example, see Legassick, 2007).

When the CPSA was banned in 1950 following increased mass mobilisation after the apartheid government came to power in 1948, it disbanded and re-formed underground in 1953 as the SACP. Leading members played a key role in setting up the white Congress of Democrats (COD) and bolstering the South African Indian Congress (SAIC) and Coloured Peoples' Congress (CPC). Communists were also central to the formation of the South African Congress of Trade Unions (Sactu) in 1955. The informal and semi-formal expressions of alliance politics in the 1940s now took on a more formal character with the 1955 Congress of the People at which the Freedom Charter (which served as the binding document of the Congress Alliance composed of the SAIC, CPC, COD, Sactu and the ANC, with the latter seen as the leading component) was launched. This has remained a key reference point for the current Tripartite Alliance.

The Freedom Charter melded together liberal-democratic freedoms and socialistic aspirations such as the nationalisation of the commanding heights of the economy, land redistribution and social welfare. While not a socialist or anti-capitalist document in the hard sense of the term, it had a strong social-democratic flavour in keeping with sentiments popular among post-war ruling parties in northern European countries. This gave it broad appeal. On the one hand, Nelson Mandela could assert that it opened up opportunities for 'non-European' entrepreneurship, while on the other the communists could point to the Charter as a stepping stone towards socialism – but as a result the document could also be denounced by right critics for being 'communist' and by leftists for fudging the question of socialist advance. The influence of white communists in the drafting of the Charter also alienated Africanists, resulting in the splitting-away of the Pan-Africanist Congress (PAC) in 1959. Although this did not remove a narrow Africanism from the ANC, it helped pave the way for a more inclusive nonracial nationalism.

Communists were at the forefront of placing emphasis on an inclusive, cross-class nonracialism within the liberation movement, and while its theory of colonialism of a special type implicated capitalism in the rise of colonialism and apartheid, in practice it de-emphasised class divisions in the interests of nationalism (Wolpe, 1987). However, proletarian assertions coming from an increasingly mobilised trade union movement gave confidence to those arguing for a leading role for the working class in the 'revolutionary alliance'.

After the ANC was banned in 1961, the movement in exile absorbed all sections of the alliance into its ranks, in effect making it a nonracial organisation, although it was only in 1985 at the Kabwe conference that the ANC formally admitted 'non-Africans'[2] into the ANC. At its 1969 Morogoro conference in Tanzania, the ANC recognised the 'leading role' of the working class. However, the ANC remained vague as to whether the working class was 'leading' because of its potentially anti-capitalist, pro-socialist orientation, or because it was merely the majority within the black population. This deliberate fudging was deemed essential to the maintenance of a multiclass alliance, which explains the ANC's broad appeal in later years. Critics argued that it subordinated working-class interests to that of the middle class rather than the other way around.[3] Indeed, former ANC president Nelson Mandela, in his autobiography *Long Walk to Freedom*, remarked:

> 'The cynical have always suggested that the communists are using us. But who is to say we are not using them?' (1995: 139).

These foundational issues, which gave further definition to the binding ideology of the NDR, re-emerged during the turbulent 1980s, and persist today as the ANC continues to undergo intense internal contestation around its future direction.

BETWEEN 'SOCIAL MOVEMENT' AND 'POLITICAL' UNIONISM

After the Freedom Charter was revived in the 1980s, it became the guiding document of the United Democratic Front (UDF) which was formed in 1983 as an ANC-supporting broad front inside the country. The revived nonracial union movement, particular those unions that formed the Federation of South African Trade Unions (Fosatu) in 1979, was initially cautious about its relationship with the ANC and SACP. It expressed strong reservations about being 'hijacked' by middle-class 'populist' politicians, pointing to the experiences of other liberation struggles, and to the subordination of Sactu to the ANC in the 1950s. Fosatu argued that Sactu's demise in the 1960s was due its leading organisers having been detained, killed or sent into exile as a result of their immersion in ANC ativities. Thus the federation wanted to build strong, durable mass organisations at the workplace before entering the dangerous terrain of state-power politics. It flirted with ideas (forming its own working class party, or engaging with state power as an independent union formation and entering into alliances with other groups entirely on its own terms) which its ANC/UDF critics labelled 'workerist' or 'syndicalist'. On this basis, it (and the Western Cape-based General Workers' Union and Food and Canning Workers' Union)[4] refused to join the UDF in 1983, unlike a new generation of smaller, explicitly pro-ANC 'community' unions led by the South African Allied Workers' Union (Pillay, 2008).

By 1984, as township rebellions spilled over into the workplace, pressure built up within Fosatu to become more involved in state-power politics. ANC sympathisers within Fosatu affiliates played a key role in mediating between the 'workerists' and the 'populists' within the union movement (Naidoo, 2010). This led to the formation of Cosatu in 1985, bringing together Fosatu and its allies, the UDF unions, as well as the National Union of Mineworkers (NUM).[5] As the largest affiliate of Cosatu, the NUM would go on to play a key role in championing the cause of the ANC within Cosatu, against more sceptical unions from the Fosatu tradition. Cyril Ramaphosa, the NUM general secretary, moved from black consciousness to embrace the ANC, and became part of its internal leadership group after the release of Govan Mbeki from prison in 1989 (Allen, 2003; Butler, 2007).

At its inception in 1985, Cosatu exemplified 'social movement unionism', where democratically organised workers engage in both 'production politics' at the workplace and the 'politics of state power'. Unlike a narrower form of 'syndicalism', this involved explicit alliances with movements and organisations outside the workplace, but under strict conditions of union independence based on shopfloor accountability. The 1987 adoption of the Freedom Charter as a 'stepping stone to socialism' by Cosatu further entrenched this strategic compromise, which recognised the increasing popularity of the ANC-SACP alliance as well as a strong belief in the independence of the labour movement (Naidoo, 2010). The idea was to combine the best of 'populism' (an emphasis on cross-class solidarity against the apartheid state) and 'workerism' (ensuring working-class independence and democratic shopfloor accountability), such that the working-class led the struggle against apartheid (Pillay, 2008).

Independent socialists who continued to be wary of the SACP for its 'Stalinist' history and subordination to the ANC's nationalism drew comfort from the fact that working-class power was rising during the late 1980s. In effect, with the banning of the UDF in 1987, the labour movement took on the leadership role of the internal resistance movement (Naidoo, 2010). As long as this continued, the possibility of working-class leadership of the anti-apartheid struggle was kept alive.

In its meetings with the ANC, SACP and Sactu in exile, Cosatu stressed that it was an independent formation and not a transmission belt for the ANC. Together with the UDF, it had some influence on the relatively hierarchical ANC and SACP, helping to deepen the lessons learnt during the Gorbachev era about the failures of one-party state 'socialism', and a greater appreciation of the values of mass participatory democracy (Callinicos, 2004; Butler, 2007; Naidoo, 2010). As unionists and independent socialists joined the

SACP in numbers after 1990, it showed signs that it was shedding its adherence to a Stalinised form of Marxism-Leninism. The hope was raised that it could become the non-dogmatic, independent, and counter-hegemonic mass workers' party that many in Cosatu wished for. This promise, however, was largely unfulfilled (Williams, 2008).

When the ANC and SACP were unbanned in 1990, the worst fears of 'workerists' seemed realised, as the ANC took over the leadership of the internal movement and gradually reduced Cosatu to the role of one interest group among many. Ironically, many prominent workerists[6] went on to join the ANC in government and parliament, and some went further, to become wealthy businessmen. Others, however, remained in the union movement to build on Cosatu's heritage as an embodiment of social movement unionism.

Since 1990, when the ANC and SACP dissolved Sactu and formally drew Cosatu into a triple alliance in pursuit of the NDR, Cosatu drifted towards a narrower form of 'political unionism'.[7] While retaining its independence and its commitment to mass action where necessary, and continuing to engage in wide-ranging policy contestation inside and outside multiparty corporatist forums such as the National Economic, Development and Labour Council (Nedlac), Cosatu dared not push too far and forge links with movements outside the triple alliance. This was despite severe misgivings about government's adoption of the market-friendly, economically orthodox Growth, Employment and Redistribution (Gear) policy in 1996 – and particularly without first consulting the ANC or any of its alliance partners (Marais, 2011). The popularity of the ANC was by that stage too great, perhaps, for any alternative path to be feasible for Cosatu.

Although initially supportive of Gear, the SACP soon realised its full implications, and began increasingly to side with Cosatu against the ANC government on policy matters (in particular macroeconomic policy, HIV/AIDS and Zimbabwe). This coincided with Cosatu's commitment to fund the SACP's salary and office expenses around the country in the interests of furthering the working-class struggle and building socialism within the womb of the NDR (Pillay, 2008).

The '1996 class project', as Cosatu and the SACP later termed it, meant that the ANC-in-government was captured by particular capitalist class interests, namely white monopoly capital and its black empowerment allies within the ANC. The ANC's professed bias towards the working class was displaced, but remained at the level of rhetoric in order to keep its left flank happy. This sore festered for eleven years, as the SACP and Cosatu diffused pressure from their own left to leave the alliance owing to the fear that the ANC would lurch to the right if they did. Cosatu did help to form the Anti-Privatisation Forum (APF) in 2000, with groups to the left of the ANC – but the backlash from the ANC was so strong that it backed off, even to the point, in 2002, of kicking the APF out of its building. Cosatu also did not intervene in the dismissal of independent socialist John Appolis as regional secretary of the Chemical, Paper, Packaging, Wood and Allied Workers' Union (Ceppwawu), for daring to initiate a referendum among members on whether or not they wanted to be part of the alliance (Pillay, 2006).

Cosatu was aware that any attempt to leave the alliance would split the federation, and the SACP dared not test its support outside the protective cover of the ANC. Worker surveys conducted before every national election since 1994 pointed to overwhelming, if gradually declining, support for the alliance (Buhlungu, 2006). A better strategy was to 'swell the ranks' of the ANC with working-class members who would reshape policy and ensure that pro-working-class leaders were elected to high office within the party.

Indeed, after the low point of 2001, when Mbeki faced down the left after anti-privatisation strikes (amid increasingly successful new social movement mobilisation), the ANC Alliance left did regroup. It started to make inroads into ANC policy, forcing the ANC to increasingly describe itself as a 'social-democratic' party, and not a 'neoliberal' one (ANC Political Education Unit, 2002). In addition, the ANC government stole much of the thunder of new social movements by partially addressing community concerns over affordable water and electricity provision. The alleged victimisation of deputy president Jacob Zuma, who was dismissed as the country's deputy president in 2005 and later charged with corruption, presented Cosatu and the SACP with an opportunity to shift the balance of forces in the ANC in their favour. When moves were afoot in 2005 to get the ANC, at its June policy conference, to liberalise its labour market policies, the left[8] mobilised to defeat this proposal. Zuma supporters linked the defeat of the proposal to support for the ousted deputy president (who was reaffirmed as the ANC deputy president).

If, in 2004, only three per cent of Cosatu members felt that Zuma represented workers' interests (Buhlungu, 2006), by the time of the 2006 Cosatu congress Zuma had delegates eating out of his hand. Indeed, in 2005, Cosatu general secretary Zwelinzima Vavi said that only a 'tsunami' could stop Zuma from becoming the country's next president. Vavi and SACP general secretary Blade Nzimande campaigned vigorously among workers for Zuma, and sidelined or purged activists who disagreed with this strategy. A climate of fear fell over the working-class movement, and few dared to publicly question the suitability of Zuma. Dismissing critics who queried in what way Zuma, a polygamist Zulu traditionalist charged with corruption in the notorious arms deal, could be seen to be on the left, Cosatu and SACP leaders insisted that Zuma would be more attentive to working-class interests (Pillay, 2008).

THE ROAD FROM POLOKWANE

At Polokwane, the SACP/Cosatu strategy of 'swelling the ranks' of the ANC with working class members – in conjunction with support from the ANC Youth League, among others – paid off, as the Zuma slate received sixty per cent of the vote compared to Mbeki's forty per cent. Resolutions taken at the conference seemed to confirm the drift towards a 'democratic developmental state' and away from neoliberalism.

Nonetheless, this was not a decisive shift. Under Mbeki, Gear's market fundamentalism was steadily being discarded in favour of a more pragmatic policy approach that embraced the concept of an interventionist 'developmental state'.[9] Polokwane may have given it added urgency but there was no overall commitment to move away from a conservative macroeconomic policy stance (although Cosatu (2010a) continues to argue that this was strongly implied).

Where there did seem to be a decisive shift was in a greater commitment to the alliance, and indeed during 2008 the alliance met regularly. There was increasing hope that it, and not the ANC, would become the 'political centre'. This, however, was rejected by the new ANC leadership,[10] which also assured the markets that macroeconomic policy would not change significantly. Indeed – although he was forced to retract after an outcry by Cosatu – Zuma even hinted to the business world that there would be greater labour market flexibility. This trend continued after the ousting of Mbeki as state president in September 2008, with Kgalema Motlanthe installed in his place until elections the following year (Marais, 2011).

Soon after the April 2009 elections, following which Zuma became president, and the appointment of SACP general secretary Blade Nzimande as Higher Education minister and his deputy Jeremy Cronin as deputy minister of Transport, turbulence within the alliance increased significantly. While government dared not talk about labour market flexibility, it became clear that macroeconomic policy was not going to change, for the ANC was too beholden to the minerals-energy-financial complex and its perceived need to attract foreign investment (Mohamed, 2010).

CONTESTATION FROM WITHIN

Cosatu soon realised that there was more continuity with the past than change (Cosatu, 2010a). Indeed, there were ominous signs of creeping social conservatism under Zuma (Butler, 2010), as well as threats to the liberal constitutional order (which Cosatu, in fighting Zuma's corner against corruption charges, assisted by casting doubt on the judicial system, and supporting the closure of the anti-corruption unit, the Scorpions (Pillay, 2007)).

Cosatu, in its September 2010 analysis of the post-Polokwane era, identified three phases of its relationship with the ruling party. First, there was the 'honeymoon' phase from December 2007 to mid-2009, when two 'successful' alliance summits were held; the alliance produced a 'progressive' election manifesto; and Cosatu and the SACP were 'consulted' on the appointment of the new cabinet and won the new post of Economic Development, to 'coordinate economic policy'. There were, however, 'clear signs that the old bureaucracy and leaders of the 96-class project' continued to hold sway in both the ANC and government (Cosatu, 2010a: 20).

Second, there was the 'fight back and contestation' phase from mid-2009 to 2010, when, soon after the national elections which brought Zuma to power, it became clear that conservative class forces were still ascendant in the ANC, particularly around macro-economic policy, and the ANC rejected calls for the alliance to be the political centre.

Third, Cosatu identified the current 'political paralysis' phase, in which the ANC alleg-edly refused to honour all the policy commitments made at Polokwane. For our purposes, the last two phases may be merged into one.

The August–September 2010 public sector strikes stretched tensions considerably. Cosatu embarked on an extended nationwide strike that saw union members hurling insults at the president, questioning his sexual morality and his government's perceived imperviousness to the pain of public sector workers. The strike followed the equally massive 2007 public sector strike, when Mbeki was still at the helm. The Zuma-led ANC had, in its 2009 election manifesto, promised an expanded public sector and 'improve-ments in working conditions and the provision of decent wages for workers' (Hassen, 2010: 4) but, instead, workers have seen high pay increases and excess among the elite. Rising inequality and the conspicuous consumptions of the old and new elite fuelled workers' resolve to demand more out of a government that promised much, but only delivered an eroding real wage and high unemployment. Employed workers (particularly black workers) have stretched their wages to clothe and feed an extended family that includes the large army of unemployed and under-employed.

Although the public potentially had much sympathy for the low pay of public sector workers – particularly health professionals and teachers – there was no attempt to build alliances between striking workers and poor communities and, instead, poor communi-ties bore the brunt of the strike action through neglected essential services in hospitals and schools (particularly in townships). Public sector workers often gave the impres-sion that they were only interested in their own narrow wage and working conditions, and cared little about building a broader working-class unity. This was an opportunity lost for Cosatu to re-ignite its social movement unionism, and build broader solidarity. Eventually, after three weeks of bitter industrial action, a settlement was reached, but not all workers were satisfied (Bekker and Van der Walt, 2010; Hassen, 2010; Ceruti, 2011). While Cosatu's South African Democratic Teachers' Union (Sadtu) felt that it did not go far enough, the Treasury feared the fiscal consequences of the settlement and the govern-ment felt that above-inflation increases should be linked to performance improvements within a public service not known for its efficiency. New rounds of discord between public sector workers and government are pencilled in for the future (Hassen, 2011a).

Cosatu and the ANC were eager to calm things down before the crucial National General Council (NGC) of the ANC in September 2010. By all accounts, the NGC allowed diverse views to be aired, and the ANC came out of it relatively calm and focused (Turok, 2010a). The ANC once again showed skill at orchestrating a wide range of discordant voices into one palatable tune, only for the fragile unity to unravel soon afterwards. Of most concern to the ANC leadership is the issue of nationalisation, supported for different reasons and in different ways by both Cosatu and the ANC Youth League (ANCYL).[11] The ANCYL was particularly irked by the manner in which nationalisation was deflected into a two-year research investigation, and has since ensured that the issue remains on the public agenda.

In September 2010, Cosatu published its own redistributive economic policy pro-posals, which urged greater state intervention in the economy in order to transform its

industrial structure within the context of 'sustainable development' and regional integration (Cosatu, 2010b). These were meant to influence the final New Growth Path (NGP)
eagerly awaited from the new ministry of Economic Development (amid fears that this
department was being sidelined in government and preference given to the more conservative Treasury).

When the NGP was finally released in late October 2010, calling *inter alia* for an
incomes pact between business and labour, and greater attention to increasing green
jobs, its reception by Cosatu was lukewarm (although the SACP endorsed it as a good
starting point, as it emphasised massive job creation and a greater seriousness about
implementing an aggressive industrial policy (Cronin, 2011a))

Despite agreements between the ANC Alliance partners not to criticise each other in
public, there has been little resolve within the ruling party to take decisive action against
powerful dissenters, notably Cosatu's Zwelinzima Vavi. Indeed, Cosatu has won broad
public support for its principled stance against corruption and the rise of a 'predatory
elite' in the ANC, as well as to threats to the civil liberties protected under the constitution.

Unlike the SACP, Cosatu added its voice to that of the media and groups such as the
Freedom of Expression Institute, the Right2Know campaign and SOS: Support Public
Broadcasting when government was seen to be tampering with civil liberties: meddling
in the affairs of the SABC; proposing a media appeals tribunal; and, most worryingly,
proposing a Protection of Information Bill that threatened to restrict access to information deemed critical to the public interest. Ominous voices within the ANC, SACP
and ANCYL seemed bent on muzzling the media and preventing ANC politicians from
being publicly scrutinised; legitimate concerns raised by community media groups about
media concentration and often poor reporting standards were consequently drowned
out in a climate of acrimony.

Eventually, after much public criticism, Zuma dismissed Siphiwe Nyanda as Communications minister. His replacement, Roy Padayachie, calmed fears that the SABC was
about to lose its status as a public broadcaster, and become a state broadcaster (see
Skinner in this volume). Hopes rose that the ANC would back down on the Information
Bill, and the ANC allowed the media to investigate how it could beef up its own selfregulatory mechanisms before considering the tribunal (see Duncan in this volume).
Ominous voices within the ruling party that threaten media freedom, however, remain
strong, and these issues remained unresolved at the time of writing.

Cosatu's voice in all of this served to deflect accusations that it was only the white
middle class that was opposed to the ANC's proposals. It reaffirmed its reputation as
a defender of public rights and democratic freedoms. The SACP's Blade Nzimande, by
contrast, spoke of the media as the 'greatest threat to democracy' (Grootes, 2010) and
warned of journalists being imprisoned or heavily fined if found guilty by the proposed
tribunal for incorrect reporting – although Cronin, his deputy, later reaffirmed the
media's independence, and pointed to the limited intentions of the tribunal proposal,
which was not for a pre-publication but a post-publication *appeals* body. He stressed that
it remained merely an ANC proposal, and not government policy (Cronin, 2011b).

INCREASING SACP-COSATU TENSIONS

Cosatu's criticisms of the ANC and the SACP, and its explicit flirtation with organisations of civil society to the left of the ANC, suggested a return to a more robust, independent social movement unionism. This provoked an unprecedented backlash from its alliance partners, with the SACP openly criticising Cosatu for the first time.

During 2010, Cosatu increasingly raised the question of Nzimande's being in government (as minister of Higher Education) and consequently neglecting his SACP duties. According to Vavi, this is not a personal issue but rather 'a political difference between Cosatu and the SACP in relation to whether it is correct to have amended the constitution of the SACP to allow a general secretary to hold a full-time position in Cabinet' (SABC News online, 1 May 2011). At the Wits University Ruth First memorial lecture on 17 August 2010, Vavi, reflecting on the social crisis facing the country, declared that Ruth First would have asked where her South African Communist Party was, and why it had not led 'a united working class in a struggle to change the direction we seem to be taking' (Vavi, 2010).

Later, Cosatu would more specifically call on Nzimande to leave government and focus on his SACP duties, even offering to pay him a minister's salary. This angered the party, which felt it was an insult to suggest that Nzimande was in government for the money, a sensitive point, given the outcry in 2009 when Nzimande was one of the ministers who spent R1.2 million on a top-of-the range German car.

By late 2010, it was speculated that Vavi himself, who had withdrawn an earlier commitment to leave Cosatu and make himself available for a top position in the ANC at its 2012 national conference, would instead offer himself for the leadership of the SACP (even though he has no profile within the party, and has not himself indicated any interest in becoming leader). This expressed a hope amongst some unionists and SACP members for a renewal of the SACP as a more robust champion of the working class, capable of uniting the broad left.[12]

In late October 2010, Cosatu, in conjunction with the Treatment Action Campaign (TAC) and civil rights group Section 27, held a civil society conference and did not invite its allies (except the South African National Civics Organisation (Sanco)) on the understanding that political parties were not part of 'civil society'. The ANC and SACP were furious. Gwede Mantashe warned Cosatu against working towards 'regime change'; the ANC's National Working Committee (NWC) accused the gathering of attempting 'to put a wedge between civil society formations, some unions, the ANC and its government' (Cosatu, 2010c); and the SACP's Jeremy Cronin (2010) suggested that Cosatu was falling into a 'liberal' trap to upset the NDR. Contrary to popular convention, Cronin defined 'civil society' as including the corporate sector; from his perspective, civil society was suspect, a terrain of anti-state, pro-market liberalism, and because the conference made no reference to the NDR, he proceeded to portray it as 'anti-transformation'. While acknowledging that it would be 'crass' to suggest that those formations present at the conference were 'simply imperialist agents' or part of some 'major conspiracy', he warned

Cosatu that 'we need to be very careful that we are not manipulated into someone else's strategic agenda, particularly when that agenda is itself increasingly hegemonised by a much more right-wing, anti-majoritarian liberalism' (Cronin, 2010).

These harsh criticisms were followed in January by a cutting admonition of Cosatu's criticism of government's New Growth Path. Cronin accused Cosatu of 'entirely missing the bigger picture', and having a 'redistributionist approach to transformation' which, he implied, did not ask 'what is right and wrong about our productive economy'. This 'paradigm shift', Cronin asserted, was implicit in the NGP's emphasis on job creation (2011a).

Cronin seemed to ignore Cosatu's substantial policy document on a new growth path, issued in September 2010. Far from being narrowly 'redistributionist', it is a far-reaching call for decisive intervention in the economy to steer it away from the minerals-energy-financial complex. These proposals were fully endorsed by the civil society conference,[13] underlining its deeply transformative, progressive agenda. Indeed, Cosatu's reservations about the NGP were that it did not take on board Cosatu's proposals (Cosatu, 2011).

In an address to Barometer SA in March 2011, Vavi argued for a 'radically different macroeconomic strategy, based, among others, on lower interest rates, a weaker rand, and more tariff protection for vulnerable industries identified by IPAP2[14] and NGP as potential job drivers'. He also underlined the need for a 'much bigger role to the state in directing investment into the sectors where jobs can be created', including using state-owned enterprises to create jobs (Vavi, 2011).

Cosatu is clearly of the view that the NGP has not shifted government away from a neoliberal paradigm which contradicts the developmental goals set out in the NGP. Vavi asked: 'Even the most developed countries are now abandoning this pro-market approach and taking quite drastic action to try to discipline the private sector, particularly the banks. How much more do developing countries need to build a strong, dynamic, but also democratic public sector and developmental state to drive the agenda of the NGP?'

Cosatu did not publicly attack Minister Ebrahim Patel, nor his ally the SACP's Rob Davies (the minister of Trade and Industry and responsible for industrial policy). These two departments are clearly at odds with more conservative bureaucrats in the Treasury, which has constrained their more heterodox economic perspectives within a macroeconomic strait-jacket. Cosatu was appreciative of the fact that the NGP did contain progressive proposals for job creation, and that Patel's department seemed to have won the battle to become the lead department in economic policy development. Cosatu's difference of opinion with the SACP seems to lie in whether to knock quietly on the door of opportunity, hoping it will open, or to knock loudly, even threatening to break the door down, knowing that there are many on the other side who would rather keep it closed.

CONTINUED, BUT DECLINING, SUPPORT FOR THE ALLIANCE

Cosatu's support for the ANC during the 2011 municipal elections (even while it continued to criticise government policy) underlined its commitment to building the

ANC Alliance. It continues to believe in the strategy of 'swelling the ranks' of the ANC to ensure that in future it elects leaders who truly have the interests of the working class at heart.

A survey[15] of Cosatu members' political attitudes confirmed the continued, if gradually declining, popularity of the ANC and the alliance among workers. Support still remains at sixty per cent (down from eighty-two per cent in 1994, seventy per cent in 1998 and sixty-six per cent in 2004). However, those who are now unhappy about the alliance are more interested in Cosatu being nonaligned (twenty-one per cent), than being part of a new workers' party (nineteen per cent). Most members clearly have no appetite for breaking away from the party of Mandela, despite their unhappiness with aspects of the ANC's policies and performance (particularly those concerning access to nutritional food (fifty-five per cent), higher wages (seventy-two per cent), land (fifty-nine per cent), and jobs (seventy-two per cent)).

Interestingly, despite Cosatu's denunciation of the neoliberal macroeconomic framework Gear, most workers (seventy-five per cent) had never heard of it. Of those that had, only forty per cent believed it was achieving its goals of growth, employment and redistribution. However, only forty-five per cent believed that it was not. Tellingly, sixty-two per cent of the workers vote for the ANC because of its policies or past performance, while only twenty-one per cent vote out of loyalty or because the union told them to (two per cent). It is clear that, despite anger at government for not meeting many working-class aspirations, for most workers this does not yet mean abandoning the ANC or the alliance. If the ANC does not satisfy workers in future, only six per cent of them are interested in forming an alternative workers' party (compared to thirty-eight per cent in 2004, and thirty-three per cent in 1998). Workers prefer ongoing mass action or pressurising unionists in parliament (sixty-two per cent). In other words, worker sentiments are not out of line with those of the union leadership. Working-class aspirations, for most Cosatu members, must be fought for within the ANC and the alliance, rather than outside it – and the post-Polokwane ANC appears more attentive to the working class. Nevertheless, while worker support for the ANC during the May 2011 municipal elections was largely uncontested outside the Western Cape, Cosatu's Vavi revealed that he had to campaign vigorously in Port Elizabeth to ensure that workers came out to vote ANC.[16]

Is this the case of relative 'insiders' (organised workers) being comfortable with a liberation movement that has brought them some benefits such as better housing (fifty-six per cent), access to clean water (eighty-one per cent), electricity (seventy-nine per cent), a telephone (sixty-five per cent), better public transport (fifty-five per cent), better health-care (fifty-three per cent), HIV/AIDS treatment (sixty-two per cent), education and training (sixty-two per cent) and a clean and healthy working and living environment (sixty-one per cent)? While the majority seems relatively satisfied, a sizeable minority is not. The unemployed and underemployed majority are likely to be much less satisfied, as rising 'service delivery' protests indicate.

Nevertheless, the ANC vote increased from 10.9 million in 2004 to 11.7 million in 2009 (less than the 12.2 million votes cast in 1994, but significant nonetheless) (Southall and Daniel, 2009). While much of this support came from organised workers, it is safe to assume that the 11.7 million also included a large number of unorganised workers and the unemployed in urban and rural areas.

However, while voter support generally correlated with increased satisfaction regarding 'national economic' and 'overall conditions' (Schulz-Herzenberg, 2009: 33), 6.8 million of the 30 million entitled to vote in 2009 did not register, while a further 5.3 million who did register did not vote, making a total of 12.1 million voters (40.3 per cent of eligible voters) who did not vote. This indicates significant alienation from the political process among a large section of the population who see little return from voting, particularly within the context of rising 'service delivery' protests. Indeed, while the percentage of *valid* votes for the ANC remained stable at sixty-six per cent, the percentage of *eligible* voters voting for the ANC declined from 53.8 per cent in 1994 to 38.8 per cent in 2009 (Schulz-Herzenberg, 2009).

While the ANC received sixty-two per cent of all votes cast in the 2011 municipal elections, according to Hassen (2011b), using Statistics South Africa's 2010 Mid-Year Population Estimates, 15.6 million eligible voters over the age of twenty did not vote, compared to the 13.7 million voters who did. If eighteen- to twenty-year-olds are included, the 'silent majority' increases, indicating a significant and potentially increasing degree of voter alienation (taking into account that municipal elections normally attract lower voter turnouts).

Does this mixed picture nevertheless give hope to those seeking to build an alternative pole of attraction to that of the ANC?

CONTESTATION FROM THE OUTSIDE

The formation of the Congress of the People (Cope), after the ousting of Thabo Mbeki as president in September 2008, raised expectations that ANC dominance would be challenged, and a realistic opposition would emerge. Cope was led by former ANC chairperson and UDF leader Mosiua Lekota as president, with former Cosatu general secretary and premier of the Gauteng province Mbhazima Shilowa as vice-president. It scored seven per cent of the national vote in the 2009 elections, less than the twelve to twenty per cent predicted before polling started, but a reasonable return for a party that was only a few months old. However, severe internecine squabbles between the Lekota and the Shilowa factions hobbled the party. Repeated attempts in 2010 to hold a congress to resolve the leadership issue failed, leaving the party in complete disarray. In addition, attempts to form an alternative labour movement to Cosatu, led by former Cosatu president, Willie Madisha, proved moribund. By 2011, Cope was clearly not a viable alternative to the ANC Alliance, and the party performed miserably in the municipal elections.

The 2010 public sector strikes, and Cosatu's flirtation with civil society groups, raised hopes among some that the labour federation might leave the alliance earlier than expected. While that hope remains, it was too early for Cosatu to accept an invitation to attend the democratic left conference in January 2011,[17] which launched the Democratic Left Front (DLF), a broad coalition of left formations representing small groups of community activists and intellectuals from around the country. Cosatu had just come out of an ugly spat with its alliance partners over the civil society conference, and the DLF's intention to build an alternative left pole of attraction was too risky politically.[18]

The DLF includes NGOs and social movements that emerged in the late 1990s to fight water and electricity privatisation, home evictions, environmental degradation, and lesbian and gay discrimination, among other social issues – and also includes prominent individuals who had left the SACP.[19] It places emphasis on eco-socialism, participatory-democracy, feminism, gay rights, and a nondogmatic approach to Marxism (DLF, 2011).

However, it is clear that any alternative to the alliance is fraught with difficulty in the absence of a Cosatu breakaway. Whether Cosatu's membership will continue to offer support to the ANC Alliance in the future depends mainly on whether it continues to see benefits accruing from an ANC government – mainly to itself as organised, employed workers in permanent jobs, but also to the larger working communities within which it lives.

CONCLUSION

Is this the same dance as always – fierce quarrels between the battered wife (Cosatu) and abusive husband (the ANC) only to be followed by reconciliation before the next flare-up? Can the battered wife ever leave her husband, despite neglect and abuse, as long as he periodically gives her flowers and a few trinkets? Does she dare blink at the new suitors in civil society, urging her to seek a divorce and ride into the sunset with them? What role does the SACP play in this *ménage a trois*? Is it the older first wife, deeply bonded to the marriage and, despite abuses from time to time, still intent on placating the ANC (and convincing the younger bride that things will get better)?

Whatever view is adopted, recent research among Cosatu members underlines the continued, if declining, popularity of the ANC and the alliance and this seems to reinforce the view that the ANC knows that its partners will continue to line up behind it. However, the argument that this is due to the politics of patronage (Buhlungu, 2010), seems only partially true. Community uprisings involving marginalised, often unemployed residents against ANC councillors and the lack of 'service delivery' also do not seem, ultimately, to question the ANC's legitimacy.

The ANC Alliance has a long history, which is cemented by a powerful NDR ideological discourse that secures its legitimacy among the working class. This has given the ANC, like many other liberation movements, almost mythical (and mystical) status akin to that of a religious authority. It is therefore no surprise that ANC president Jacob Zuma once said that the ANC will rule 'until Jesus comes back' (Mkhwanazi, 2008). In some senses, for many South Africans, the ANC itself can do no wrong – only its leaders can fail the movement.

Unless liberation movements address challenges of underdevelopment, they often start to lose their legitimacy after about twenty years in power, as the cases of India and Zimbabwe illustrate. The Institutional Revolutionary Party in Mexico, however, absorbed the labour movement, and ruled (through corruption and authoritarian practices) for most of the twentieth century. In a different context, the Swedish Labour Party, in close alliance with the labour movement, ruled for most of the twentieth century through free and fair elections – but built a powerful welfare system that has given the working class a 'middle class' lifestyle.

In South Africa there are no signs that the ANC's mystical status as the party of liberation is under immediate threat. Despite some ominous authoritarian tendencies, the movement remains remarkably transparent and internally democratic compared to other liberation movements, allowing dissent from below – whether from the youth or organised workers – to continuously pose a threat to elite aspirations. Indeed, ANC veteran Ben Turok feels that the ANC's 2010 National General Council was the 'most democratic' he had ever attended (2010b). As long as this continues, challenges from the left outside the alliance are likely to remain isolated and parochial.

Although the Alliance will remain in place for as long as the state can manage to appease the aspirations of the working class with relatively protective labour legislation and social grants, ANC support among the broader working class is slowly declining, as is shown by recent surveys as well as election results. Moeletsi Mbeki (*Business Day*, 21 February 2011) is correct to warn that, as long as South Africa remains beholden to the minerals-energy complex (and, I would add, the financial sector) and does not develop secondary industries on a sustainable basis, the point will come when it will be unable to generate sufficient revenue from mining and related industries to provide social grants. At that point the social crisis will deepen. Not only might the alliance fall apart – the country could experience its Tunisian/Egyptian moment.

Attempts to build a left pole of attraction outside the alliance are, consequently, unlikely to have much impact on the political landscape in the near future. However, there is a role for independent socialists to define, in theory and in practice, a more imaginative, more participatory-democratic and 'eco-socialist' alternative. Unless the alliance adapts, and steals its thunder, in the longer term its time might come.

NOTES

1   Comments made at a Society, Work and Development Institute (SWOP) breakfast, Wits University, 5 February 2011.
2   In post-apartheid South Africa the term 'African' has been claimed by all South Africans, resulting in new hybrid terminology such as black African, coloured African etc.
3   See SADET (2006) for different perspectives on this issue.
4   These unions were initially more sympathetic towards the ANC – indeed the FCWU was a former Sactu affiliate (Pillay, 1989).
5   NUM was a former affiliate of the mildly black consciousness Council of Unions of SA (Cusa), which joined forces with the Azanian Confederation of Trade Unions (Azactu) to form the National Council of Trade Unions (Nactu) in 1986.

6   Prominent figures include Numsa's Alec Erwin, Sactwu's Johnny Copelyn and the NUM's Marcel Golding.
7   In extreme form political unionism completely subordinates the unions to political party objectives, and robs them of real independence. Cosatu, on the whole, never quite went that far (Pillay, 2006).
8   This included the broad left within the alliance, not just those supporting Zuma (conversation with Langa Zita of the SACP, November 2005).
9   The presidency's Alan Hirsch (2005) argues that Gear was always mixed with an increasingly redistributive social policy.
10   ANC Kwa-Zulu Natal provinicial secretary Sihle Zikalala (2010) shows that the Polokwane conference clearly affirmed the ANC as the political centre.
11   Cosatu and the SACP are suspicious of the intentions of the Youth League and the 'predatory elite', which it feels want to use nationalisation to increase opportunities for patronage. Nevertheless, unlike the SACP, Cosatu does feel that certain strategic sectors of the economy should come under state ownership, but with democratic control involving workers and consumers (starting with the current parastatals). The SACP wants to see 'socialisation' – democratic control – but believes it does not necessarily imply changes in ownership.
12   Discussions in December 2010 with a union leader in Cosatu (and SACP member) who actively promoted this idea, and in January 2011 with a former SACP official and DLF leader Mazibuko Jara who expressed scepticism about its viability. See also the *Sunday Independent* of 27 March 2011.
13   The conference declaration contains a wide range of far-reaching proposals on social justice, economic growth and rights to health and education – a far cry from Cronin's alleged 'right-wing' liberal agenda.
14   Industrial Policy Action Plan 2.
15   This survey was conducted in 2008 by SWOP as part of a series of surveys done among Cosatu members before each of the past four national elections.
16   http://www.timeslive.co.za/specialreports/elections2011/article1080059.ece/Vavi-wins-over-Nelson-Mandela-Bay.
17   Discussion with Vishwas Satgar, a key organiser of the DLF, February 2011.
18   According to Steve Faulkner of Samwu (discussion, January 2011), had affiliates been individually invited, some, like Samwu, would have attended, even if only as observers.
19   Key figures are Mazibuko Jara (formerly Nzimande's right-hand man in the SACP) and Vishwas Satgar (former Gauteng SACP provincial secretary).

REFERENCES

Allen V (2003) *Organise or Die: The History of Black Mineworkers in South Africa, Volume III, 1982–1994.* London: Merlin.
ANC Political Education Unit (2002) Contribution to the NEC/NWC response to the 'Cronin interviews' on the issue of neoliberalism.
Bekker I and L van der Walt (2010) The 2010 mass strike in the state sector, South Africa: positive achievements but serious problems', *Soziale Gesichte Online* No. 4, pp 138–152.
Buhlungu S (Ed.) (2006) *Trade Unions and Politics: Cosatu Workers After 10 Years of Democracy.* Pretoria: HSRC Press.
Buhlungu S (2010) *A Paradox of Victory: COSATU and the Democratic Transformation in South Africa.* Pietermaritzburg: UKZN Press.
Butler A (2007) *Cyril Ramaphosa.* Johannesburg: Jacana.
Butler A (2010) The African National Congress under Jacob Zuma. In Daniel J, P Naidoo, D Pillay and R Southall (Eds) *New South African Review 1.* Johannesburg: Wits University Press.
Callinicos L (2004) *Oliver Tambo: Beyond the Engeli Mountains.* Cape Town: David Philip.

Ceruti C (2011) 2007 and 2010 public sector strikes. Maturing contradictions, *SA Labour Bulletin* 35 (1) Mar/Apr, pp 2–5.

Congress of SA Trade Unions (Cosatu) (2010a) The Alliance at a crossroads – the battle against a predatory elite and political paralysis, COSATU CEC Political Discussion Paper, September 2010.

Cosatu (2010b) A Growth Path towards Full Employment. Draft Discussion Document (Released September).

Cosatu (2010c) Cosatu's response to ANC statement (Issued by Cosatu spokesperson Patrick Craven, n.d.)

Cosatu (2011) Government's New Growth Path Framework: One step forward, two steps backward.

Cronin J (2010) Whose terrain? *Umsebenzi Online*, Vol 9, No. 22, 17 November.

Cronin J (2011a) Let's consolidate support for the new growth path, *Umsebenzi Online*, Vol 10, No. 2, 19 January.

Cronin J (2011b) What journalists think, *Umsebenzi Online*, Vol 10, No. 6, 16 March.

Democratic Left Front (DLF) (2011) Another South Africa and World is Possible! First Democratic Left Conference Report, 20–23 January, University of the Witwatersrand.

Grootes S (2010) Blade Nzimande's ever-increasing loneliness, *Daily Maverick* 18 October 2010.

Hassen E-K (2010) Public sector strike: Irresistible force meets immovable object, *SA Labour Bulletin* 34 (4) October/November, pp 4–6.

Hassen E-K (2011a) Unsatisfactory strike outcome: Public service agreement, *SA Labour Bulletin* 34(5) December/January, pp 4–5.

Hassen E-K (2011b) The silent majority did not vote! Comparing population estimates with the voter roll. http://zapreneur.com/the-silent-majority-did-not-vote-comparing-population-estimates-with-the-voter-roll/ekhassen/ (accessed 3/6/10).

Hirsch A (2005) *Season of Hope: Economic Reform under Mbeki and Mandela.* Pietermaritzburg: UKZN Press.

Legassick M (2007) *Towards Socialist Democracy.* Pietermaritzburg: UKZN Press.

Marais H (2011) *South Africa: Pushed to the Limit.* Cape Town: UCT Press.

Mandela N (1995) *Long Walk to Freedom.* London: Abacus.

Mkhwanazi S (2008) ANC to rule until Jesus comes back, IOLNews, 5 May. www.iol.co.za/news/.../anc-to-rule-until-jesus-comes-back-1.398843 *(accessed 15/6/11).*

Mohamed S (2010) The state of the South African economy. In Daniel J, P Naidoo, D Pillay and R Southall (Eds) *New South African Review 1.* Johannesburg: Wits University Press.

Naidoo J (2010) *Fighting for Justice.* Johannesburg: Picador Africa.

Nzimande B (2011) Building working class hegemony through the forthcoming local government elections, *Umsebenzi Online*, Vol. 10, No.5, 2 March.

Pillay D (1989) Trade unions and alliance politics in Cape Town, 1979-85. Unpublished PhD thesis.

Pillay D (2006) Cosatu, alliances and working-class politics. In Buhlungu S (Ed.) *Trade Unions and Politics: Cosatu Workers After 10 Years of Democracy.* Pretoria: HSRC Press.

Pillay D (2007) The stunted growth of South Africa's developmental state, *Africanus 37(2)*, pp 198–215.

Pillay D (2008) Cosatu, the SACP and the ANC post-Polokwane: Looking left but does it feel right? *Labour, Capital and Society* Vol 41, No 2, pp 5–37.

Schulz-Herzenberg C (2009) Trends in party support and voting behaviours, 1994–2009. In Southall R and J Daniel (Eds) *Zunami! The 2009 South African Elections.* Johannesburg: Jacana.

Simons J and Simons, R (1983) *Class and Colour in South Africa 1850–1950.* London: IDAF.

South African Democracy Education Trust (SADET) (2006) *The Road to Democracy in South Africa,* Vol 2 [1970-1980]. Pretoria: Unisa.

Southall R and J Daniel (Eds) (2009) *Zunami! The 2009 South African Elections.* Johannesburg: Jacana.

TAC and Section 27 (2010) The ANC should not be scared of independent campaigns against corruption and for service delivery, human rights and public accountability, Statement released on 3 November.

Turok B (2010a) A shift in economic policy, *New Agenda*, Issue 40, Fourth Quarter, p 5.

Turok B (2010b) What the press didn't see: the ANC National General Council, *New Agenda* Issue 40, Fourth Quarter, pp 22–25.

Vavi Z (2010) Ruth First Memorial Lecture, *Links* (http://link.org.au/1851, accessed 12/3/11).

Vavi Z (2011) A growth plan or empty promise? (Input to the Barometer SA debate on the New Growth Path, 9 March).

Williams M (2008) *The Roots of Participatory Democracy: Democratic Communists in South Africa and Kerala, India,* New York: Palgrave.

Wolpe H (1987) National and class struggle in South Africa. In Institute for African Alternatives *Africa's Crisis*, London: IFAA.

Zikakala S (2010) The Alliance Today, *Umrabulo* No. 32, 1st Quarter. www.anc.org.za/show.php?id=2836

CHAPTER 2

The African National Congress and the Zanufication debate

James Hamill and John Hoffman*

———

The unappealing prospect of the Zanufication of the African National Congress (ANC), and by extension of South Africa, has generated considerable discussion in recent years, at both the academic and media levels, as well as having featured in elite discourse within the ANC itself. The term was first used in 2002 by Jeremy Cronin (2008a), then deputy general secretary of the South African Communist Party (SACP) – an organisation in alliance with the ANC – and a strong supporter of Jacob Zuma in his ultimately successful campaign to wrest the ANC presidency from Thabo Mbeki at Polokwane in December 2007. Cronin was subsequently forced by the ANC to apologise for his use of the term and branded, by unattributable ANC sources, a 'frustrated white male who could not come to terms with the loss of white privilege' (Lotshwao, 2009: 906; Suttner, 2008: 136–7). The term has subsequently, however, become more widely popularised in response to the implosion of neighbouring Zimbabwe and the ANC government's ineffectual response to that crisis. It has also served to reflect a mood of pessimism about the direction of the new South Africa.

Although there is no consensus as to the precise meaning of the term, we consider Zanufication to be defined by the following features:
- a conflation of ruling party and state;
- control of the media by the state;

- a tendency to substitute the formal and informal use of violence for the rule of law;
- the prevalence of corruption in state organs;
- the militarisation of society;
- racial demagoguery and a pseudo-militant rhetoric often serving as a smoke-screen for rampant private accumulation;
- a personality cult in political leadership.

In April 2010, the British journalist Fred Bridgland posed the question: 'Is South Africa turning into Zimbabwe?' He pointed to certain factors which he suggested could create the conditions for Zanufication: corruption, the hubris of the dominant party, declining socio-economic performance, and an increasingly racialised rhetoric. He also quoted Barney Mthombothi of South Africa's *Financial Mail* predicting that 'hardly a decade from now Zimbabwe will be our reality' and his view that Zanufication was not a phenomenon unique to Zimbabwe but a regional virus now afflicting South Africa: 'Our politicians have learned from the master's [Mugabe's] knee – the buck passing, blame everything on the imperialists and apartheid, the reckless and incendiary language; the refusal to see reason or deal with reality even as it stares you in the face'.

This theme has been taken up by others. Michael Trapido in the *Mail & Guardian* (15 March 2010) argued that 'the ANC is following the proven disaster that is the Zanu PF on the road to nowhere ... a barren wasteland where citizens are kept in check down the barrel of a gun'. Claims of this kind tap into a view that South Africa has been on the wrong track since Thabo Mbeki became state president in June 1999. In some respects, this provides an oversimplification of the situation by failing to note that Mandela's presidency, bathed though it was in the warm glow of domestic and international approval, also exhibited authoritarian tendencies in its decision-making processes. For confirmation of this, one need only note the introduction of the Growth, Employment and Redistribution (Gear) strategy in 1996 as 'non-negotiable' and the opaque processes which surrounded both the policy *volte face* on Nigeria in 1995 and the diplomatic recognition of China (and de-recognition of Taiwan) in 1996.

That said, it is true that during the Mbeki era, from 1999 to 2008, these autocratic tendencies escalated and took a less benign form as South Africa witnessed growing centralisation of power at both the party and state levels, an intolerance of dissent (from within and beyond the ruling party), and the development of eccentric policy positions – that on HIV/AIDS being the obvious example – which cabinet and party colleagues spinelessly failed to criticise. Mbeki's indulgent response towards the descent of Mugabe's Zimbabwe into brutish tyranny even seemed to suggest that such policies were attractive to him and a potential resource to rely upon in difficult times. Under Zuma, centralisation appears to be continuing (albeit in a slightly more laid-back and consensual mode) with the opposition party, the Democratic Alliance (DA), arguing that attacks on the constitution are likely to intensify. Writing in the *Mail & Guardian* (22 April 2009), the DA leader, Helen Zille, described Zuma as a 'one-man constitutional wrecking machine'.

So is South Africa predestined to take the Zimbabwean path? There is certainly some evidence for the Zanufication thesis, and it does shine a light on some of the more disturbing aspects of contemporary governance in South Africa. However, we argue in this chapter that the Zanufication thesis is a blunt and highly polemical analytical tool which underplays the complexity of the South African polity and ignores a number of crucial differences between the two situations. That the ANC will become another Zanu is possible but by no means certain, even if the entrenchment of a one-party dominant system is likely to continue generating a range of democratic deficits in South Africa.

THE SITUATION IN ZIMBABWE

Robert Mugabe was clearly defeated by Morgan Tsvangirai of the Movement for Democratic Change (MDC) in the presidential elections of March 2008. Then, in June 2008, the world witnessed a second stolen election. After a five-week delay in announcing the result of the first ballot (a delay prompted by a traumatised Zanu PF's search for an alternative to the constitutional option of accepting defeat and transferring power), Tsvangirai was deemed to have won the most votes whilst failing to secure an overall majority, thus necessitating a run-off against Mugabe. Although this episode followed a familiar postcolonial narrative in which oppositions win the vote only to lose the count, this was a particularly egregious example of electoral malpractice. The second poll, on 27 June, was held against the backdrop of an orchestrated campaign of state terror entailing the murder, rape, abduction, and torture of opposition activists and supporters. Indeed, the country witnessed an accelerating decline into something approaching naked fascism, given the scale of the violence meted out by state-sponsored militias to those deemed to have voted for the opposition. Mugabe himself confirmed this trend when he asked rhetorically: 'How can an X on a ballot paper compete with a gun?' and declared that 'only God who appointed me will remove me' (AFP, 2008), statements providing a blend of Hitler (and Mugabe has even described himself as 'Hitler tenfold' (Mugabe, 2003) Mao-Zedong and Charles I of England.

The ferocity of this state-sponsored assault on the MDC and its support base led to Tsvangirai's withdrawal from the second poll and to Mugabe's being re-elected by default, an outcome which only intensified the country's political crisis. In September 2008, a global political agreement (GPA) – brokered by Thabo Mbeki – was signed by Mugabe and Tsvangirai and on 2 March 2009, a government of national unity was formed. Although Mugabe was compelled to make some concessions as a result of the GPA, he effectively retained control of the state and has continued to govern in much the same way as before. In short, while the GPA has brought some respite from the worst excesses of state terror and restored some normality to the functioning of the economy and its financial institutions, it has not transformed the political culture of Zimbabwe nor fundamentally altered its political dynamics, and attention has inevitably turned southwards from this depressing spectacle towards the regional hegemon. The question now posed with increasing frequency is whether Zimbabwe's today is likely to become South Africa's tomorrow.

EVIDENCE FOR THE ZANUFICATION THESIS

In one respect, it is an indictment of the post-apartheid government in South Africa that such a question is posed at all. When Mandela left office in June 1999, South Africa's global standing was high on account of the (relative) peacefulness of its transition to democracy, its discourse of racial reconciliation, and its apparent determination to act as an evangelist for democracy on the African continent. Much, if not all, of that reservoir of goodwill was drained away during Thabo Mbeki's presidency. At no stage – either at home or abroad – did Mbeki command the same aura or inspire the same confidence as Mandela, despite, paradoxically, his superior administrative skills as a head of government.

There were many reasons for this – principally his less accessible personality, the more conspiratorial and secretive political culture he fostered, and his enthusiasm for a highly centralised, top-down style of government (Hamill, 2001). All of this would ultimately sow the seeds of his demise, as he was removed first from the ANC presidency in December 2007 and then from the state presidency in September 2008. Internationally, Mbeki had initially been received favourably as a key figure in the so-called 'new generation' of African leaders who seemed to understand what was required to rescue the continent from its position on the margins of international politics. This 'new generation' had at least mastered the post-Cold War vocabulary of political and economic change, even if their commitment to its substance was yet to be tested. As Mandela's deputy president, Mbeki had championed an 'African renaissance' – central to which was a commitment to clean, open and democratic government – and had spoken of wresting control away from 'petty tyrants who would be our governors by theft of elective positions' (Mbeki, 1998).

In his first two years in office as president, he played a major part, alongside the British prime minister Tony Blair, in constructing the New Partnership for Africa's Development (Nepad), a development contract with the West in which good government, transparency and democratisation were core elements. This was followed in 2002 by the establishment of the African Union (AU), the successor to the widely discredited Organisation of African Unity (OAU). Mbeki was one of the AU's principal architects and he served as its first chair with a more robust – although at this stage still largely theoretical – commitment to democratic governance and a more critical attitude towards the traditional axioms of state sovereignty and non-interference. Here was a leader who seemed attuned to the new post-Cold War orthodoxies and who sought to steer South Africa in particular, and Africa in general, towards a pragmatic accommodation with them. This was evidenced by his pivotal domestic role in fashioning the Gear strategy introduced in June 1996, a more conservative macroeconomic framework and one which was an anathema to the ANC's formal allies, the Congress of South African Trade Unions (Cosatu) and the SACP. This did not make Mbeki an unconditional enthusiast for neoliberal globalisation, as was sometimes charged. It, rather, portrayed him as a reformist globaliser who broadly accepted the prevailing nostrums of globalisation while acknowledging the continuing importance of the state. He also sought the restructuring of the political and economic institutions of global governance to give greater weight to the voice of the global South, and of Africa in particular.

THE SQUANDERED PRESIDENCY

The image of Mbeki the pragmatist and stable technocrat faded as his first term progressed and as he staked out eccentric, even bizarre, positions on particular issues and perhaps sought to overcompensate for the broadly conformist nature of his government's economic policies by a more contrived and laboured militancy in other contexts. His policy of 'quiet diplomacy', introduced following Zimbabwe's descent into state-orchestrated mayhem in 2000, had exhausted its (always) limited potential to stabilise that country and to facilitate democratic change by the time of the fraudulent presidential election of 2002. Persistence with the policy subsequent to that date, in the face of extreme regime violence and an openly stated determination to liquidate the opposition, was an exercise in self-decep- tion on Mbeki's part and a failure comparable in scale to his simultaneous abdication of responsibility in dealing with South Africa's HIV/AIDS pandemic.

Indeed one wonders: was Nelson Mandela's lament (2008) about a 'tragic failure of leadership' directed at least as much towards Mbeki as it was towards the regime in Harare? People inevitably drew the conclusion that if South Africa failed to condemn unbridled state terrorism in its own neighbourhood and could display such scant regard for the flouting of democratic values – and if its own government ministers could offer supportive words to a regime such as Mugabe's – then a replay of the Zimbabwean scenario was a possibility in South Africa. In 2003, the then foreign minister, Nkosazana Dlamini-Zuma (2003), declared that an ANC government would never condemn Zimbabwe, a position which could only have emboldened the Harare regime. In the same year (2003), Membathisi Mdladlana, then labour minister, stated that South Africa had much to learn from the Zimbabwean 'land reform' process. In a similar vein, the ANC Youth League leader, Julius Malema, praised Mugabe's land seizures in Zimbabwe as a model for South Africa to emulate while denouncing the 'Mickey Mouse' MDC (Bridgland, 2010). In June 2009, South Africa's minister of Land Reform and Rural Development, Gugile Nkwinti, announced that the ANC government would scrap its 'willing-buyer, willing-seller' land redistribution policy, which allows the government to acquire land only at a market prices and only with the consent of the land owner, and replace it with 'less costly, alternative methods of land acquisition'. Whether a break with the 'willing- buyer, willing-seller' prin- ciple is an attempt to accelerate land redistribution and thus neutralise Zimbabwean-style populist demagoguery, or whether it is an early symptom of it, remains moot at this stage.

Added to this was a South African rhetoric which tended to focus not on the perpe- trators of human rights abuses and the theft of elections but rather on the easier option of blaming the West or Western racism and which even echoed Mugabe's own vitriol in characterising the opposition MDC – the electoral victors – as Western puppets seeking to reintroduce colonial rule. In a letter to Tsvangirai on 22 November 2008, Mbeki wrote that: 'It may be that, for whatever reason, you consider our region and continent as being of little consequence to the future of Zimbabwe, believing that others further away, in western Europe and North America, are of greater importance'. Such strident criticism was never directed at Mugabe.

There have, over the years, been numerous indications that South Africa has lost its way on the Zimbabwe question and has departed from the values underpinning its own transition to democracy and which informed Mbeki's 'African renaissance' vision and his role in constructing the Nepad. Although 'quiet diplomacy' was premised on the belief that a more punitive approach would cause economic collapse in Zimbabwe, thus triggering a mass influx of refugees, this has paradoxically proved to be the outcome of South Africa's more indulgent policy. At least three million Zimbabweans have now taken refuge abroad, the vast bulk of them in South Africa, and through the first decade of the twenty-first century Zimbabwe had the dubious distinction of recording the highest inflation rate in history and becoming the world's fastest contracting economy.

Instead of intervening to pressurise Zimbabwe, South Africa has rejected any use of its considerable economic leverage against the Mugabe regime and has opposed the imposition of 'smart' sanctions imposed on Zanu's leadership. In 2008, it also used its position as a non-permanent member of the United Nations Security Council to mobilise opinion against any extension of sanctions on Zimbabwe (and indeed any measures against the Burmese junta and the Al-Bashir regime in Sudan), making common cause in the process with China and Russia as guardians of state sovereignty and non-interference in a state's internal affairs. In making this assessment, we do recognise that South Africa finds itself in a quandary in the region; its history of aggressive destabilisation during the apartheid era is an unfortunate backdrop to contemporary debates and its greater economic and military weight *vis-à-vis* its neighbours generates predictable concerns about South African hegemony. Those realities necessitate a pragmatism and sensitivity in South Africa's regional behaviour, but 'quiet diplomacy' is rooted in a culture of over compensation for the past, one which is inhibiting South Africa from playing a more dynamic role as the shaper of a new regional consensus built around democratic values. Instead, as the Zimbabwe case has graphically demonstrated, African peoples continue to be sacrificed on the altar of an African-regime solidarity which is being forged within the supposedly progressive framework of 'multilateralism'.

ZIMBABWE AND THE PATHOLOGIES OF ONE-PARTYISM

In addition to its economic meltdown, there have been three defining features of Zimbabwe's descent into authoritarianism. First is an entrenched political culture of 'liberationism', by which we mean a belief, on the part of those who prosecuted the liberation struggle, that they should now be considered uniquely privileged political actors and able to operate largely unconstrained by the norms and conventions governing competitive, multiparty politics. In this worldview, the liberation movement can never be perceived as 'just another party' in a post-liberation setting. It is entitled to rule and to speak indefinitely on behalf of 'the people'. The popular will is interpreted by the party and not by the people. Voting against the party is intolerable, unacceptable and a sign of false consciousness to be remedied by a programme of 'reorientation' – and the Zimbabwean experience between April and June 2008 underlined the precise meaning of that term to brutal effect. This is, in effect, the politics of divine right and it provides a salutary lesson in the degeneration to which 'liberation politics' and liberation movements can be prone.

The second feature is a militaristic cult of the warrior, prominent in both ANC and Zanu discourses, which takes a masculinist view of the nation and the struggle for national liberation (Suttner, 2010). The struggle is identified as a 'conquest' and violence is viewed not as a regrettable and tragic necessity but as something positive in itself. In Zimbabwe, such a politics is now flouted openly with only token nods in the direction of multiparty democracy or pluralism *per se*. To both Zanu and Mugabe, the MDC is 'a Western project which must be buried' (Jongwe, 2010), effectively a declaration of war on the opposition in which the leader claims for himself the right to stand above the choices made by actual voters and for the ruling party's interests to transcend the verdict of the ballot box (Hamill and Hoffman, 2008).

The third distinguishing feature of Zimbabwe's decline is the extent to which the state itself has become a compliant instrument of the ruling party. The state media is slavish in its veneration of Zanu PF, particularly the *Herald* newspaper which has abandoned even the pretence of independent journalism, while the judiciary has been fully colonised by party loyalists. Most servile of all is the Zimbabwe Electoral Commission, an organisation which delayed the publication of election results for five weeks under orders from a defeated ruling party, and rewrote its own rules at the behest of the same party. The demarcation lines between Zanu PF and the security forces have been eroded, with the army and police required to serve as partisan forces to be deployed against opposition structures (and voters) as well as joining the drumbeat of propaganda against them, an action inappropriate for supposedly neutral servants of the state. It was police chief Augustine Chihuri, and Constantine Chizenda, the most senior commander of Zimbabwe's army, who said that they would never salute a 'sell out' or a 'British stooge' (Sokwanele, 2009), a statement typical of the anti-colonialist invective which has now become an ideological comfort blanket for Zanu PF and its sole means of responding to the country's wider political and social crisis. It was the same security forces who announced in 2002 that they would not accept any result that 'went against the revolution' (Amnesty International, 2006). Currently they have thrown their weight behind Gideon Gono and Johannes Tomana, the reserve bank governor and the attorney-general respectively, unilaterally appointed (or reappointed) in violation of the terms of the September 2008 unity accord between Zanu and the MDC, which clearly states that all senior government appointments must be made with the consent of the three principals (namely, Mugabe, and the leaders of the two MDC factions, Tsvangirai and Arthur Mutambara), and that these appointments include those of the reserve bank governor and the attorney-general.

ZANUFICATION AND SOUTH AFRICA

So, how far are such malign trends visible in contemporary South Africa? Some of the early symptoms of the ideology of liberationism are certainly apparent. The ANC has been able to draw upon a genuine and overwhelming popularity in its four general election victories to date, and has had no need for recourse to the violent intimidation and electoral chicanery of Zanu PF. However, an authoritarian mindset or mode of organisation is still visible in various forms and it has tended to cut across the post-2005 polarisation within the ANC between its Mbeki and Zuma camps. The Mbeki government – and indeed Mbeki as an individual – had a distinctly authoritarian flavour in its attitude to criticism from beyond and from within its own ranks.

The stigmatising of legitimate dissent as 'racist' became a routine response of the Mbeki administration to opposition criticism. While this intolerance was most pronounced under Mbeki, it is not an exclusively Mbeki phenomenon. Jacob Zuma is not free of this contagion. As deputy president he denounced criticism of the government in the media as 'unpatriotic' (*Business Day*, 8 February 2011) and stated that the ANC would rule 'until Jesus comes again' (*Business Day*, 21 June 2009), a clear manifestation of the 'divine right' mindset. He also once described the ANC as more important than the constitution (*Politicsweb*, 2008). In February 2011, while campaigning for the municipal elections, Zuma told an audience that an ANC membership card provided an automatic pass to heaven and that 'when Jesus fetches us we will find (those in the beyond) wearing black, green, and gold; the holy ones belong to the ANC', before adding that to desert the organisation would mean that 'the ancestors of this land ... Hintsa, Ngqika and Shaka will all turn their backs on you' (*Times Live*, 2011).

Another factor reminiscent of the Zimbabwean situation is the growing influence in the Zuma era of the liberation war veterans' associations. This has seen the ANC, like other liberation movements, tending to play 'the struggle' as its trump card in its conflicts with the opposition and the media and it allows the ANC to demonise (and delegitimise) its opponents as seeking a 'return to the past' or for opposing 'transformation' and the 'new South Africa' *per se* when they merely oppose ANC policies and the ANC's model of transformation. The Congress of the People (Cope) party, which broke from the ANC in December 2008 in protest at the Zuma ascendancy and Mbeki's removal, threatened to pose a challenge to this established means of engaging opposition parties because its own leadership had impeccable liberation credentials, and its 7.42 per cent of the vote in the April 2009 election seemed to provide a solid bridgehead from which it might make further electoral advances. However, the post-election period has witnessed the squandering of this historic opportunity as factionalism and leadership disputes have sent Cope into probable terminal disarray.

In the ANC's polemical spats with Helen Zille, the leader of the Democratic Alliance (DA) which now governs the Western Cape , there have been ugly accusations of racism and the gender card is played to grotesque effect. On 1 May 2009, ANC Youth League leader Julius Malema (*Mail and Guardian*, 1 May 2009) referred to Zille as 'a racist little girl' – a sentiment which perfectly captures the unity of the two although some elements in the ANC have gone even further in levelling the most poisonous sexist abuse at Zille.

To certain senior ANC figures the ANC is not 'just another party' in a pluralist setting. Pluralism, by definition, requires an unconditional acceptance that other parties have the right to organise and to compete with the dominant party irrespective of arguments over the historical record. Currently an uneasy tension prevails between the liberal-democratic values embodied in the 1996 constitution and the militant and frequently militaristic liberationist rhetoric emanating from sections of the ruling party. That rhetoric is usually distinguished by its intolerance of dissenting voices and an impatience with the basic ingredients of liberal and popular democracy such as free speech, a separation of powers and the sovereignty, not of the dominant political party, but of the constitution. Julius Malema's infamous statement that he would 'kill for Zuma' was repeated and amplified by the Cosatu general secretary, Zwelinzima Vavi (2008) (who later regretted making the statement). In May 2009, *Umkhonto we Sizwe* (the former armed wing of the ANC) veterans declared that they would make the opposition-controlled Western Cape 'ungovernable'. With regard to the judiciary, the partisan meddling, interference and threats evident from senior ANC figures during the long Mbeki-Zuma conflict (whether from those seeking to bring Zuma to trial on charges of corruption or those campaigning to have the charges dropped) suggested that some in the party did not view the independence of the judiciary as a bedrock principle, but saw it more instrumentally and opportunistically as a temporary expedient to be adhered to (or not) as the occasion and political convenience demanded. The 2008 denunciation by the ANC secretary general, Gwede Mantashe, of the Constitutional Court – itself composed of 'counter-revolutionaries' – is instructive in this regard (Matthews, 2008). One of the defining struggles of South African politics over the next decade will be between the reality of one-party dominance, the liberationist ethos sustaining it (and the morbid symptoms to which it will give rise) and the strength and resilience of the country's liberal democratic infrastructure and the capacity of constitutional values, not merely to survive, but to flourish in a political environment shaped by the hegemony of a single party.

In one significant respect the ANC has emulated its apartheid-era predecessor. In the aftermath of the 1948 election, the National Party populated the higher echelons of the state with its own loyalists. The ANC, through its policy of 'cadre deployment', has followed suit. Not only are key institutions like the South African Broadcasting Corporation, the South African National Defence Force, the Reserve Bank, and South African Police Services presided over by reliable (though not always competent) ANC figures, but the leaks from the intelligence services to make the prosecution of Zuma impossible also shows an alarming ascendancy of party over state. Moreover, as was the case under Mbeki, loyalty to Zuma personally has become the litmus test for senior state appointments. Zuma's appointment of Menzi Simelane as head of the National Directorate of Public Prosecutions, Moe Shaik as head of the Secret Service, and Bheki Cele as National Police Commissioner placed close comrades in strategically important state positions.

Supporters of Zuma suggest in his defence that he has repudiated the authoritarianism of Thabo Mbeki. We are more sceptical, given *inter alia* his pronouncements on the party's electoral immovability and its imagined divine endorsement which suggest, to us, that he too embraces the notion of ANC exceptionalism – and it is that exceptionalist culture which provides the setting in which authoritarian attitudes may thrive.

There can be little doubt that levels of state corruption are rising in the Zuma era. The ANC's ally in the Tripartite Alliance, and therefore a more difficult voice for the leadership to dismiss, Cosatu, argues that the business interests of the South African government pose a real threat to democracy and that if the ruling party does not take a tough stance on this 'We will be en route to Zimbabwe and other failed revolutions elsewhere in the world' (*Mail & Guardian*, 17 April 2010). In June 2010, Cosatu's warnings of the emergence of a crony state were amplified more starkly by its general secretary, Zwelinzima Vavi, previously a staunch Zuma ally, when he stated that South Africa was 'heading rapidly in the direction of a full-blown predator state in which a powerful, corrupt and demagogic elite of political hyenas increasingly controls the state as a vehicle for accumulation' (*The Economist*, 4 September 2010). The disbanding of the Scorpions – a unit set up in 1999 specifically to expose corruption and which incurred the ANC's wrath by its willingness to scrutinise the behaviour of the very highest officials in the land, including Zuma himself – was troubling in this respect. It should also be noted that, in contrast to his later rhetoric, Vavi strongly supported Zuma's decision on the Scorpions.

Writing in *Business Day* (11 February 2011), Moeletsi Mbeki – former President Thabo Mbeki's brother – argued that the post-apartheid state relates to business interests in a corrupt fashion and the easy movement between the ANC and the business world triggered by black economic empowerment (BEE) is a particular concern. In a similar vein, Rapule Tabane (*Mail & Guardian*, 4 June 2010) commented that 'when competent, honest business people have no hope of securing business if they do not endear themselves to the politicians (and share their profits with them) and, more importantly, when our younger brothers and sisters have no chance of finding work unless they lick the arses of politicians, we are no different to the corrupt Kenya Obama wrote about'.

The proposal to shackle the media with a tribunal also represents a potentially sinister development. In the *Mail & Guardian* (30 July 2010), Michael Trapido asked: 'Are we to be told in Mugabe-like fashion when millions are on the brink of starvation that colonialism and apartheid are responsible while a handful of fat cats live like Donald Trump? Is the government seriously expecting the media to condone their hiding of information?' For John Kane-Berman (*Business Day*, 16 August 2010), the proposed media tribunal is essentially an attempt to reduce the media to the status of an instrument of the ANC's 'national democratic revolution'.

Justice Malala (*Times Live*, 30 August 2010), a fierce critic, argues that 'the ANC … has the weakest, greediest, most corrupt and compromised leadership since its birth ninety-eight years ago. These so-called leaders want to shut down the medium that exposes their corruption, looting and hypocrisy'. Equally strident is Rhoda Kadalie (*Business Day*, 31 August 2010) who bemoans a crisis of governance under the ANC: 'Whether it is children killed through reckless driving, corrupt MPs, an unruly SABC, Sisulu or irregular mining deals, they all point to one thing – a creeping anarchic state where things fall apart because the centre is out of control'. The view of much of the media was effectively captured by Lee Hall who, in an open letter to President Zuma (*Mail & Guardian*, 2 October 2010), argued that: 'The African National Congress have signally failed their own people. They have failed the country. And they have failed Africa. It is time now for them either to mend their ways, or else to go – before the Zanufication of South Africa becomes irreversible.'

KEY DIFFERENCES: The experience of liberation

Despite the force and accuracy of at least some of the above commentaries, taken collectively they appear crude, one-dimensional and overstated. South Africa is not Zimbabwe, although we might add the caveat that Zanufication is a process rather than an event and that Zimbabwe was not always as it appears today. The process gives Zanufication a gradual, incremental character, with the symptoms identified above embedding themselves over time, if left unchallenged. Therefore the more appropriate question is not 'has South Africa become the new Zimbabwe?' but, rather, 'in what direction are things moving and do they appear to place South Africa on a Zimbabwean-style trajectory?'

According to his biographer, Mark Gevisser (2007: 433), Mbeki was almost alone among the ANC leadership in his admiration for Zanu in the independence elections of 1980. In general, the ANC was dismayed by the Zanu victory. It had close links to Zimbabwe African People's Union (Zapu) and the ANC's armed wing had fought with Zipra (the armed wing of Zapu) in the Wankie and Sipolilo campaigns in the 1960s. After independence, relations between the Zanu government and the ANC were sensitive, and a number of ANC operatives were detained during the 1983 Matabeleland massacres which cost some 20 000 civilian lives. These massacres provided an early indication of Zanu's authoritarian character and its preference for transacting politics through violence. A badly mauled Zapu was forced into a government of national unity as a junior partner. Although it is tempting to see this as a precursor of the current arrangement with the MDC, the earlier agreement was the product of Zanu coercion and it was able to dictate terms to a broken-backed Zapu. By contrast, the contemporary agreement, although it was the product of Zanu intransigence in refusing to accept electoral defeat, was essentially driven by external forces, particularly the Southern African Development Community (SADC). The GPA was constructed in the face of strong Zanu hostility, even being viewed as an affront to its dignity, thus the reluctance – in some cases, outright refusal – to implement fully its provisions.

If the social character of Zimbabwe is different from that of South Africa, so too are its experiences of white domination. In the 1970s, the overwhelming majority of Zimbabweans were peasants and almost half of Rhodesia's territory was tribal trust land. This contrasts with the scattered and miniscule thirteen per cent of land reserved for black Africans in apartheid South Africa, and the difference is the secret behind the relative success of the Zimbabwean guerrilla struggle, especially in the Eastern Highlands, whereas the guerrilla struggle in South Africa seldom moved beyond the armed propaganda phase.

The epicentre of the South African struggle was the township (both urban and rural), the university campus, the factory shop floor, the faith community and the popular and underground publications, and this set it apart from most Third World liberation struggles in the twentieth century. South Africa developed its anti-apartheid struggle though the wide-ranging democratic movement, the United Democratic Front (UDF) which linked trade unions, civic society organisations, the churches, and women's movements into a formidable force with deep popular roots. This has no counterpart in Zimbabwe's struggle for liberation. It is true that after 1994 the UDF was disbanded, but its legacy has been a powerful civil society and a widespread commitment to pluralism, factors which constitute a powerful antidote to Zanufication. South Africa is not, of course, immune to the ruling party stagnation and bureaucratisation we have seen in Zimbabwe or, for that matter, and in a somewhat different context, in the communist parties of the former Soviet bloc. But after independence in Zimbabwe, the mass base of the liberation struggle was demobilised. Many fighters returned to the countryside while the leaders became cabinet ministers and generals. Raymond Suttner (2010) has eloquently charted the tendency by ANC leaders to use the mass movement as a 'battering ram' rather than a partner (particularly evident during the negotiated transition) and the tendency towards centralisation and aloofness which became so striking under Mbeki was evident even when Mandela was leader. This has inevitably led to dismay and demoralisation among the rank and file. Mbeki's own emphatic defeat by Zuma in the election for the party presidency in 2007, however, confirmed that this demoralisation and demobilisation was much less advanced in the ANC, and that the party grassroots still maintained a vibrancy and assertiveness – and a capacity to overturn elite machinations – which has all but disappeared in Zanu PF.

The strength of South African civil society is evident in the activities of the Treatment Action Campaign (TAC) on HIV/AIDS, South Africans for a Basic Income Grant, and the Anti-Privatisation Forum, as well as the annual strikes by workers against the effects of privatisation. These organisations are new social movements which have introduced new concepts of citizenship and collective action, and most of them operate at the local level. The Soweto Electricity Crisis Committee, or SECC, for example, has campaigned for access to affordable services in that township. The SECC has its roots in the ANC – its leader, Trevor Ngwane, is a charismatic figure who was expelled from the ruling party for opposing restructuring plans for Johannesburg. The SECC has sought to invigorate not only veteran activists and ordinary people, but also young people. It seeks to emulate the ANC's own traditions of defiance by leading marches to councillors and the mayor's house, often cutting off the latter's electricity supply (Egan and Wafer, 2004). The chapter by Buccus and Hicks elsewhere in this volume adds further evidence to our argument in regard to the resilience of South Africa's NGO sector.

The TAC put together the first successful, national-level social movement and fights, as part of the wider Social Justice Coalition, for cheaper anti-retroviral drugs, and to eliminate the stigma associated with being HIV positive. It used the court system effectively and maintains (at times controversially) relations with the ruling ANC, as well as with key elements within the municipal and provincial health bureaucracies. In addition, the TAC has built a movement that includes AIDS sufferers as well as a cross-racial membership and leadership and good ties with the trade union movement (Jacobs, 2008).

THE ANC AND ZANU PF

The ANC was established in 1912 and is Africa's oldest liberation movement. Its commitment to democracy and nonracialism is more powerful than that of Zanu PF, and the Freedom Charter which was endorsed by the ANC in 1955 at the Congress of the People pledged South Africa to a vision of nonracialism and a platform of radical popular democracy.

The ANC's December 2007 Polokwane national conference endorsed Zuma as leader of the ANC and defeated Mbeki and his supporters. This open competition provided a sharp contrast with the national conference held by Zanu PF at the same time and which was a thoroughly orchestrated, top-down affair. The organisational report, for instance, was not discussed; it was not even distributed to delegates. A copy was held up on the podium. 'Here is the organisational report. Does conference adopt it? Thank you very much.'(Cronin, 2008b). In contrast to the liberal, radical democratic and socialist currents of the ANC, Zanu PF has been almost entirely shaped by a bitter military struggle (in which violence was uncritically extolled and practised) and its politics are still strongly marked by ethnicity.

For three decades, Zimbabweans have been held captive by a nationalist project that has become increasingly bankrupt and incompatible with democracy, while it has been estimated that South Africa averages more protests per person than any country in the world – on average at least sixteen every day (Jacobs, 2008). Peter Alexander (2010: 27) suggests that there were some 34 000 protest gatherings between 2004 and 2008. In 2010, delivery protests reached a record high. These 'delivery protests' are a double-edged sword for South Africa: on one level they confirm the existence of a strong culture of protest (of a kind liquidated in Zimbabwe) but they also point towards a crisis of effective governance and place a question mark over the country's long-term political stability.

Although Zuma was regarded by many as a problematic political alternative to Mbeki at the ANC's Polokwane conference, it is true nevertheless that Mbeki respected the fact that he had lost the vote and he ceased to be ANC president. Moreover, in September 2008 when he was 'recalled' by the ANC executive, he resigned the presidency of the state and accepted the committee's view. It is difficult to imagine Mugabe demonstrating such respect for constitutional and democratic processes. In this sense it is important to make a clear distinction between the thoroughgoing authoritarian character of Zanu PF in contemporary Zimbabwe and the real but contained and contested authoritarianism of the ANC in South Africa which still exists within, and is tempered by, the country's broader democratic infrastructure. Just as dominance has an impact upon the strength of a democratic culture so, equally, a democratic culture has an impact upon the character of one-party dominance.

THE WORKING CLASS AND THE TRADE UNIONS

In Zimbabwe, the trade union movement was not involved in the liberation struggle. In South Africa the trade unions are a key component of the Tripartite Alliance. The involvement of Cosatu in the process of liberation and in the current government has no counterpart in Zimbabwe. Nor does the role of the SACP. It is true that the SACP has authoritarian instincts, and like the trade unions (in which it is influential) it played a significant part in bringing the current ANC leadership to power. Both the SACP general secretary, Blade Nzimande, and his deputy, Jeremy Cronin, currently serve in the Zuma government. That said, the SACP has helped to counteract trends towards the type of narrow black nationalism which dominates Zanu PF's politics and which some in the ANC broad church – particularly the Youth League – might otherwise find tempting. The SACP has championed a class analysis which rejects racism and racial categories, although it is true that the theory of 'colonialism of a special type' and the national democratic revolution (each of which the SACP embraced) did recognise the reality of racial division. It has also been a source of significant white involvement in the liberation struggle and its existence reflects the much more urbanised character of the South African struggle. With the trade unions, it will challenge state policies which do not deliver progress for the poorer sections of South African society, although Cosatu is concerned that the SACP presence in government is causing it to mute these protests. The SACP was bitterly opposed to the movement away from redistribution under Mandela and Mbeki and is critical of the neoliberal orthodoxies which investors demand from South Africa. It is also strongly opposed to the Mugabe regime and will doubtless seek to pressurise the Zuma government into adopting a more critical policy towards Zimbabwe.

INTERNAL DEMOCRACY

In a sombre 2009 article, Lotshwao speaks of the ANC as 'internally undemocratic and highly centralised' (2009: 912) and fears this could lead to the slow death of democracy in South Africa. The absence of strong interparty competition to provide a check on the dominant party certainly places greater pressure on the ANC's own internal pluralism to provide a degree of democratic balance, and Lotshwao sees little evidence of this. His argument raises valid concerns but is overstated and requires qualification, given that the ANC has only recently emerged from a process in which it unseated Thabo Mbeki as both party and state president, the rarest of events in Africa. While trends towards centralisation and elitism are real, the aftermath of such important events may seem a singularly inopportune moment to write the ANC off as 'internally undemocratic'. Our judgement is that such a view of the ANC lacks nuance and subtlety and therefore struggles to explain such a groundbreaking event. It is true that the ANC leadership is still too remote from its membership and from the people at large – Zuma's more inclusive persona notwithstanding – and parliament still largely serves as a docile instrument of the ANC leadership. The autonomy of ANC MPs is eroded by both the practice of democratic centralism and by the list system of proportional representation, each of which invests enormous power in party elites. Lotshwao argues that when Mbeki was 'recalled' in 2008, this resulted from his alleged interference in the prosecution of Jacob Zuma, not from pressure by the ANC membership (2009: 912), although this fails to account for his earlier removal from the ANC presidency which was directly attributable to pressure from the mass membership. Although he argues that the executive is virtually free to act as it wishes (2009: 907) it is at least possible that Polokwane has released a democratic genie from the bottle which the ANC leadership will now struggle to return and Zuma's room for manoeuvre in the South African political system is greatly constrained when compared to Mugabe's, even in Zimbabwe's post-GPA era. Although the ANC has an autocratic character which adversely affects the quality of South African democracy as a whole, it still has a more diverse political base than Zanu PF and a degree of internal pluralism which is wholly absent in Zimbabwe. From a bleaker perspective, however, it could be argued that this plurality is increasingly a plurality of rival factions seeking to access and ultimately plunder the state, rather than a genuine clash of rival ideologies (Suttner, 2008).

CONSTITUTIONALISM AND THE LIBERAL TRADITION

South Africa has a strongly democratic constitution which is jealously guarded by its Constitutional Court and compliance with the constitution is monitored by a range of 'chapter nine institutions' – the Human Rights Commission, the Public Protector, the Gender Commission – although their autonomy is invariably encroached upon by the reality of ANC dominance. It is revealing that when Zuma (2006) expressed homophobic sentiments some years ago, he felt compelled to apologise and to acknowledge the constitution's protection for freedom of sexual orientation. The ANC government has also had to accept a number of adverse rulings by the courts, particularly on the HIV/AIDS issue and it has done so without demur although some of the threatening noises made against the courts from sections of the party when Zuma's prosecution was still a possibility were reprehensible. There is, however, a lack of enforcement of the constitution and the adoption of policies, particularly in the international sphere, that tend to be incompatible with the constitution – for example the position it has adopted on gay rights at the UN and, arguably, its policy towards Zimbabwe. It is also true that there is a gulf between an enlightened constitution and grassroots sentiment, as is evidenced in popular attitudes towards capital punishment, women's equality, same-sex unions, gay liberation and the incidence of 'corrective rape' against lesbians. Steven Robins has suggested that those committed to sexual and gender equality constitute a 'relatively small, educated middle class enclave within a sea of sexual and social conservatism' (Robins, 2008: 412). Nevertheless the constitution accepts gay marriage and outlaws capital punishment, and is buttressed by a powerful legal profession and a highly critical and feisty media – comfortably the most vibrant on the continent – which asks awkward questions and fiercely upholds the constitution.

CONCLUSION

There is certainly *some* evidence to support the Zanufication thesis: the liberationist and 'exceptionalist' ideology to which the ANC adheres; the blurred demarcation lines between party and state; the insidious relationship between the ANC and the business community; the overt hostility to much of the print media; the growing levels of corruption; and the frustrations building up over the distribution of land. But, as we have seen, there are also important aspects of the political landscape which differ from that of Zimbabwe – the strength of civil society, the degree of urbanisation, a robust liberal tradition, a liberal democratic polity and constitution, the political role of the trade unions and a relatively influential Communist Party committed to nonracialism. We should also note the role that South Africa's much deeper integration in the global economy than Zimbabwe's, and its aspirations as an emerging power of the 'global South', are likely to have in tempering any drift towards outright Zanufication.

Authoritarian trends are unmistakable, but our overall conclusion is that the Zimbabwean road is a possibility, not an inevitability. Of course it is possible that South Africa may yet follow an autocratic path that is unique in itself rather than one emulating the Zimbabwean 'model', one which is more complex, even chaotic and indefinable, in which the ruling party's authoritarian impulses are contested by opposition parties, the media, civil society and by elements of the ANC itself. Indeed the ANC captures this confusing situation in microcosm as plunderers, and demagogues coexist in its ranks alongside those still committed to the ethos of service and sacrifice which informed the liberation struggle. In short, it may be that South Africa will develop an authoritarian politics resembling certain aspects of the Zimbabwean polity but its complexity is unlikely to be adequately captured by the all-embracing notion of Zanufication.

NOTES

*   The authors wish to acknowledge the help and advice of Raymond Suttner and also of the editorial team of the *New South African Review.*

REFERENCES

AFP (2008) Mugabe says 'only God' can remove him as rivals consider pullout, http://afp.google.com/article/ALeqM5gkh5_FW9U_dXmCiQxDFrKKTT6LpA (accessed 1 March)

Alexander P (2010) Rebellion of the poor: South Africa's service delivery protests – a preliminary analysis, *Review of African Political Economy* 37, 25–40.

Amnesty International (2006) 17 March 2006, http://www.amnesty.org.uk/ (accessed 1 February 2011).

Bridgland F (2010) Is South Africa turning into Zimbabwe? http://www.heraldscotland.com/news/world-news/is-south-africa-turning-into-zimbabwe-1.1022908 (accessed 27 February 2011).

Cronin J (2008a) Thabo Mbeki's downfall, nzcn.wordpress.com/2008/09/21 (accessed 13 January 2011).

Cronin J (2008b) Why South Africa will never be like Zimbabwe, http://www.pambazuka.org/en/category/features/47873 (accessed 4 June 2009).

Dlamini-Zuma N (2003) SA will 'never' condemn Zimbabwe, http://www.news24.com/SouthAfrica/News/SA-will-never-condemn-Zim-20030303 (accessed 5 February 2011).

Egan A and A Wafer (2004) http://ccs.ukzn.ac.za/files/Egan per cent20Wafer per cent20SECC per cent 20Research per cent20Report per cent20Short.pdf (accessed 4 February 2011).

Gevisser M (2007) *Thabo Mbeki: The Dream Deferred*, Johannesburg: Jonathan Ball.

Hamill J (2001) The Conspiratorial Politics of Thabo Mbeki, *Contemporary Review*, April: 12–20.

Hamill J and Hoffman J (2008) Assessing the Zimbabwean elections, *Contemporary Review,* 290: 285–95.

Jacobs S (2008) South Africa is not Zimbabwe, http://www.guardian.co.uk/commentisfree/2008/oct/16/southafrica-zuma-ancsplit?INTCMP=SRCH (accessed 2 June 2009).

Jongwe F (2010) Mugabe's party ready to bury Western NGO, the MDC', http://mg.co.za/article/2010-12-18-mugabes-party-ready-to-bury-western-ngo-the-mdc (accessed 19 December 2010).

Lotshwao K (2009) The lack of internal party democracy in the African National Congress: A threat to the consolidation of democracy in South Africa, *Journal of Southern African Studies*, 35.4: 901–14.

Mandela N (2008) Mandela highlights 'tragic failure' in Zimbabwe, http://zimnewswatch.com/story.php (accessed 5 February 2011).

Matthews A (2008) I am a counter-revolutionary too, www.mg.co.za/.../2008-07-11-anc-shrugs-off-mantashes-stance-on-judiciary (accessed 8 February 2011).

Mbeki T(1998) http://www.dfa.gov.za/docs/speeches/1998/mbek0813.htm (accessed 24 May 2009).

Mbeki T (2008) Letter to Tsvangirai, http://www.newzimbabwe.com/pages/mbeki247.19082.html (accessed 1 February 2010).

Mdladlana M (2003) South African minister hails Mugabe land grab, http://www.guardian.co.uk/world/2003/jan/11/zimbabwe.andrewmeldrum (accessed 3 February 2011).

MK (2009) MK veterans threaten to make the W Cape 'ungovernable', http://www.mg.co.za/article/2009-05-13-mk-veterans-threaten-to-make-w-cape-ungovernable (accessed 2 January 2011).

Mugabe R (2003) 'Let me be a Hitler ten-fold', says President, http://www.shortnews.com/start.cfm?id=29408 (accessed 5 February 2011).

Mugabe R (2010) Mugabe's party ready to bury Western NGO, the MDC. *Mail & Guardian*, 18/12, http://www.mg.co.za/article/2010-12-18-mugabes-party-ready-to-bury-western-ngo-the-mdc (accessed 18 December 2008).

Robins S (2008) Sexual politics and the Zuma rape trial, *Journal of Southern African Studies*, 35, 2: 411–427.

Sokwanele (2009) What's in a salute? http://www.sokwanele.com/thisiszimbabwe/archives/4546 (accessed 5 February 2011).

Suttner R (2008) Where are the alternatives to these harmful voices? http://www.businessday.co.za/
Articles/Content.aspx?id=50373 (accessed 17 February 2011).

Suttner R (2010) The Zuma era in ANC history: New crisis or new beginning? In S Jacobs (Ed.) *The
Politics of Jacob Zuma,* Concerned African Scholars, 84: 12–33.

Vavi Z (2008) Vavi says: 'Kill for Zuma': I regret it, http://www.mg.co.za/article/2008-07-22-kill-for-
zuma-i-regret-it-says-vavi (accessed 2 January 2011).

Zuma J (2006) Zuma apologises, http://www.mambaonline.com/article.asp?artid=546   (accessed
2 June 2009).

CHAPTER 3

Dancing like a monkey:
the Democratic Alliance and opposition politics in South Africa[1]

Neil Southern and Roger Southall

———

Political opposition parties in post-1994 South Africa have always had to confront the electoral dominance of the African National Congress (ANC), perpetually sustained as it is, not only by its firm grip on the state machinery but also by the historical memory it evokes among the majority black population as the party of liberation. Opposition parties have themselves come from a variety of political backgrounds – from alternative liberation traditions (such as the Pan-Africanist Congress and the Azanian People's Organisation); from ethnic exclusivism (the Freedom Front and, many would say, the Inkatha Freedom Party); from non-nationalist ideological perspectives (the Democratic Alliance and the African Christian Democratic Party); and from splits from other parties (the United Democratic Movement). But apart from the daunting prospect of overhauling the ANC, opposition parties have had to confront the continuous dangers of disagreement and disunity among themselves as they seek to share about a third of the total popular vote among the fifteen parties which have – at one election or another – gained representation in parliament. With fragmentation of the vote and a multiplicity of opposition parties and perspectives encouraged by the national list proportional representation electoral system, consolidation of the very diverse opposition vote has always been problematic, despite alliances formed at one time or another between various political parties. Nonetheless, the 2009 general election recorded three significant political developments – two of which, as we shall see, were to be confirmed by the results of the 2011 local government elections.

The first development was the further consolidation of the position of the Democratic Alliance (DA), which increased its share of the vote from the mere 1.73 per cent won by its predecessor, the Democratic Party (DP), in 1994 to 16.66 per cent in 2009; the second was confirmation of the eroding political base of the Inkatha Freedom Party (IFP), from 10.54 per cent of the vote in 1994 to a miserable 4.55 per cent in 2009; and the third was the arrival of what many portrayed as a significant new player on the scene, the Congress of the People (Cope). Formed principally by followers of Thabo Mbeki, who had been defeated as party president by Jacob Zuma at the ANC's Polokwane conference in December 2007 and ejected as state president in September 2008, its emergence from the body of the ruling party was widely presented as a significant threat to the ANC: it was nonracial, yet could simultaneously draw on the ANC liberation tradition and appeal to disaffected African voters. Although performing less well than it had hoped, Cope nonetheless polled a highly respectable 7.42 per cent of the vote after just a few months' existence (Southall and Daniel, 2009).

Hopes were plentiful in opposition circles that Cope would provide for a new era, opening up the prospects for new alliances in opposition politics, as indicated by the appearance at its founding congress in December 2007 of Helen Zille, leader of the DA. Cope, it was argued, could break the logjam of South African politics, potentially providing for the formation of an opposition whose appeal would go beyond race and identity and provide for a more issue-oriented politics. Yet in the two years after the 2009 election events panned out very differently. Cope descended into infighting, and the IFP was embroiled in an internal leadership battle which speeded its decline into irrelevance. In contrast, the DA appears to be further consolidating its position as the undisputed party of opposition, having in 2010 absorbed the Independent Democrats (ID), a small party drawing largely on the coloured vote in the Western Cape, whose leader, Patricia de Lille, is renowned as a feisty and vigorous campaigner and who was to be elected in the 2011 local government elections as the DA's candidate for mayor of Cape Town. These developments would argue for the moment that the South African political system is en route to a *de facto* two-party system – although, as we shall argue in our conclusion, the DA's status as the principal party of opposition could well be challenged in the future if a new political force were to arise to its left, drawing upon disaffection with the ANC among social movements and trade unions.

There is little need to examine the damage which Cope and the IFP have inflicted upon themselves since the 2009 elections. It is sufficient to say that Cope has been riven by a conflict between its principal figures, Mbhazima Shilowa and Mosiuoa Lekota which has led to disputes about leadership and funding, and a hugely embarrassing national conference which saw actual fighting between the principals' supporters. Never before in opposition circles has such intra-party bitterness been generated about so little, with the result that many of those who originally saw in it a new beginning have fled from it, thoroughly disillusioned.

Meanwhile, the IFP has been torn by an internal battle between founder leader Mangosutho Buthelezi and Zanele Magwaza-Msibi, the party's former national chair. As mayor of Zululand district, Magwaza-Msibi established a creditable record for delivery and efficiency, and had seemed the most likely figure to reverse the IFP's decline in KwaZulu-Natal, where the party's vote had collapsed to a mere 22.4 per cent in 2009 compared to 50.5 per cent in 1994. But Buthelezi, aged eighty-two, like many an African leader before him, has been constantly and humbly obedient to the demands of his subservient party heirarchy that he retain the leadership, while Magwaza-Msibi, drummed out of the party by his supporters, proceeded to form her own National Freedom Party. In short, the two parties which presented the major alternative vehicles of opposition in 2009 (securing thirty and eighteen seats in the national assembly respectively, compared to the DA's sixty-seven) are in a state of seemingly irretrievable decline.

That the collapse of Cope and the IFP would offer a new opportunity for the DA to consolidate its position as the principal challenger to the ANC seems to have been confirmed by the results of the 2011 local government elections, in which the party's vote climbed to nearly 24 per cent of the votes cast (in the 2006 local elections it had obtained only 14.7 per cent). In contrast, the third largest share of the vote was taken by the IFP with just 3.6 per cent, followed by the NFP with 2.4 per cent and Cope a miserly 2.1 per cent. The remarkable increase in the DA's vote appears to be principally an outcome of the squeezing by the DA of its opposition rivals but, nonetheless, the party claimed in the wake of the contest to have increased its support among black Africans to five per cent from the one per cent it achieved in the 2009 general elections.

All this raises questions anew about whether the DA is proving able to overcome its image (as sustained by the ANC's harping on its origins), as a party of reaction and racism, unwilling to take South Africa beyond the lingering racial contours of apartheid. This chapter therefore examines the background and prospects for the DA, addressing three themes in particular: first, why white (and particularly Afrikaner) voters have come to favour the DA; second, how the party is attempting to present itself as one which promotes a nonracial South African patriotism; and third, the DA's understanding of political opposition and the obstacles which lie in the way of its making further electoral progress.

THE ELECTORAL RISE OF THE DA

The DA belongs to the liberal tradition in South African politics which was represented during the apartheid era by the Progressive Party (later to become the Progressive Federal Party (PFP) in 1977). From 1961 to 1974 the Progressive Party's only presence in parliament was that robust defender of human rights, Helen Suzman (Giliomee, 2009). The PFP became the Democratic Party (DP) in 1989, following an amalgamation with other liberal parties and splinter groups, and participated in the multiparty talks of the early 1990s which brought apartheid to an end. During these years, the liberal voice was audible if not powerful, yet its presence should not be overlooked as a persistent parliamentary critic of apartheid.

In post-apartheid South Africa, the DP formed an alliance with the New National Party (NNP) in 2000 and became the DA. The NNP was the National Party (NP) of the apartheid era; the addition of 'new' in 1997 was an attempt to dispense with its racist history. The NNP later cut its links with the DA and formed a new alliance with the ANC (with which it had served in the Government of National Unity (GNU) between 1994 and 1996) in 2004. This, however, was not disadvantageous to the DA whose support has steadily increased. If we consider that in the first democratic elections of 1994 the DP's seven seats were swamped by the NP's eighty-two, the party can be seen to have made major progress. In one sense, the 2009 result confirms that the DA, as the vanguard of parliamentary opposition, is numerically less strong than was the NP in 1994. But unlike the NP/NNP which was constrained as an opposition party by virtue of its involvement in the GNU (De Klerk, 1999) the DA was more adversarial in its approach. Certainly, by 2009, after a prognosis following the country's second democratic election that the 'DA now stands to become the home of the majority of whites, coloureds and Indians' (Southall, 2001: 277), it was evident that both the white and coloured community of the Western Cape regarded the DA to be *their* party. But it is worth noting that the DA has not attracted the same level of support from the coloured community in the Northern Cape, a significant regional variation which will be touched upon below.

When apartheid ended and the parties that had traditionally received the support of white voters had to find their way in the new political dispensation it was not immediately evident what the DA's political trajectory would be. Former leader of the DA, Tony Leon, acknowledges that when democracy arrived in 1994 the liberal tradition in South Africa lacked orientation: 'South African liberalism entered the post-apartheid era with a sense of disorientation … under apartheid [it] didn't really need a map. It was anti-apartheid; it opposed the National Party's authoritarian state and the tyranny that upheld it' (Leon, 2006: 38). But Leon himself sent out highly ambiguous messages. On the one hand, after he assumed the party leadership following the first democratic election in 1994 he initially appeared more concerned about attracting support from other traditionally 'white' parties (notably the NNP) than about expanding the party's appeal to black voters; on the other hand, while claiming that 'redressing the imbalances of the past' was one of the two most important challenges facing South Africa (the other was achieving sustainable growth), he vigorously attacked what he termed the ANC's 'race-based' policies without putting in place a serious alternative whereby historic redress might be achieved, save by referring to the necessity of creating an 'opportunity society' and expanding opportunities for all (Leon, 2008: 501). Meanwhile, the party's slogan for the 1999 election campaign, 'Fight Back', might well have proved effective in rallying the white vote but it was far too easily parodied by its critics as sending out the message to its supporters to 'Fight Black', and could also be presented as a coded appeal to coloured and Indian voters on the grounds that they were not really 'black enough' to qualify for affirmative action under the ANC.

The foundation of vocal opposition politics that Leon had laid is one that the current party leader, Helen Zille, has sought to build upon – albeit with a different vision. Although their personalities may be dissimilar, it is possible to observe in the two leaders' different styles a significant shift, away from perceived racial exclusivity and towards more vigorous attempts to embrace racial inclusivity. This complements the DA's contemporary position and strategic needs. Leon's straightforward aggression in the pursuit of strengthening party opposition is no longer the main priority; instead, Zille appears to argue that what is now called for is a pragmatic politics that can cater for the practical needs of ordinary South Africans. Furthermore, as the ruling party within the Western Cape at provincial level, the DA profiles itself as a future party of national government – in coalition form or not.

The protection of individual liberty, which constitutes the core value of liberalism, was embedded in the globally applauded new constitutions of 1994 and 1996. Hence, the fundamental pursuit of the liberal creed – the defence of individual rights – seemed to be secured and, further, the arrival of democracy suggested that the ethnic and racial politics that had defined apartheid South Africa might now become a thing of the past. Hopes were high that South Africa was well on its way to becoming a 'normal' democratic society. Yet, as Giliomee (2009) warns, and of which students of deeply divided societies are well aware, majoritarian democracy is problematic in societies with long histories of ethnic and racial division. We thus need to explore what the case of the DA suggests about race, ethnicity and identity in post-apartheid politics in the country more generally.

It is important, when investigating the reasons for a party's success, to consider the quality of its political competition. A first challenge for the DA was the battle for the white Afrikaans-speaking vote, this competition coming from the Freedom Front Plus (FF+). In 2005, when the NNP, after polling a staggeringly poor 1.7 per cent of the vote in the 2004 elections, opted to disband itself, the Afrikaner constituency had the option of voting for other parties. The parties most likely to appeal were the DA and the FF+. The latter satisfies the criteria laid down by Donald Horowitz (1985) for an ethnic party; thus in its stated ideological defence of Afrikaner interests it might have had wide appeal. But widespread support for the FF+ has not materialised. The most distinguishable policy of the FF+ is its call for an Afrikaner *Volkstaat*, which, although scaled down somewhat in recent years, still forms part of party policy (Southern, 2008). The party's policy prioritises ethnicity over race (demonstrating the limitations of a shared whiteness) and not only does it lack appeal for English-speaking whites but, more significantly, it has failed to gain the support of the vast majority of Afrikaners. As noted by DA MP James Lorimer (private communication to Southern, 25 May 2010), the majority of Afrikaners saw their political future *within the confines* of the new South Africa and not in the unrealistic aspiration of independent nationhood. There has been a de-emphasis on race within Afrikanerdom – at least in terms of political identity – which has allowed Afrikaners to vote for the DA with its non racial message. Afrikaner voters would also seem to vote DA because to do otherwise would place them at the margins of South African political life.

The unrealistic ethnoterritorial policy ambitions of the FF+ provided the DA with the opportunity to address two key issues. First, there was the requirement that the party should focus on winning the support of South Africa's ethnic minority groups. Second, the party needed a new method of operating *vis-à-vis* the ANC. Tony Leon opted for a confrontational style.

Regarding the first of these, Eddy Maloka (2001: 233) was to argue that by the 1999 elections the then DP's ideological restructuring had assumed a thoroughly racial dimension. According to him, 'the DP repositioned itself by opting for a route that led to the abandonment of its liberal ideology' and had come to project itself as a representative of white minority interests. However, in contrast to Maloka's questionable judgement, the DP can be seen to have adopted a strategy which sought support among the country's racial minorities. Indeed, commenting on the success of the DP in the 1999 elections, Davis (2004) points to the party bonding with coloured, Indian and white voters. For Davis, the common denominator of these ethnic groups was their minority position and the fact that each harboured fears of being excluded in a country that showed signs of increasing Africanisation, for by 1999, the interethnic and interracial reconciliatory priorities which had marked Mandela's presidency had given way to the transformation objectives of Thabo Mbeki (Lodge, 2002). Mbeki's racially defined two-nation concept of South Africa led the ANC to emphasise the need for affirmative-action policies and push forward the principle of black economic empowerment. Thus the 1999 elections can be interpreted as a demonstration of the DP's growing capacity to achieve cross-racial appeal, albeit overwhelmingly across racial minorities rather than among the African majority.

Leon gave DP politics an aggressive tone. As noted above, this was most evident in the party's controversial choice of the 'Fight Back' slogan that it used to spearhead its campaign in 1999. Leon (2008: 495–510) argues it was a slogan that was designed to encapsulate the DP's no-nonsense approach to opposition politics. For many, however, this slogan was out of kilter with the reconciliatory needs of the country. Only the year before, the Truth and Reconciliation Commission had presented its report following a truth-searching process that revealed the pain and suffering caused by apartheid. Indeed, Deegan (2001: 183–184) comments that in the DP's attempt to win the coloured vote in the Western Cape in 1999 it 'played on racial scaremongering' and that in order to attract the NNP's Afrikaner constituency the DP had shifted to the right. In contrast, the DP argued that its intention was to link together minority groups who felt alienated. As Louw (2000: 219) suggests: 'Through its "Fight Back" campaign the DP in effect became a de facto "minority front", representing non-blacks alienated by the ANC's black nationalist discourse.'

The central message of the DP in 1999 was uncomplicated: ethnic minority concerns needed to be adequately addressed and it was only by bringing minorities under the political administration of a single party that groups' interests could be effectively safeguarded. By default, the fragmentation and fracture of opposition parties which the results of the 1994 elections confirmed was a contributing factor to ANC dominance (Southall, 1998). Indeed, at one level, the 'Fight Back' slogan can be interpreted as an attempt to counteract any tendency by minority groups to withdraw from politics and, as Lanegran (2001) argues, it worked to attract racial minorities who felt threatened. Additionally, other concerns such as a soaring crime rate, the problematic situation of white farmers and land ownership in Zimbabwe, and the disenchantment many whites felt concerning employment equity undoubtedly made the DP's (and DA's) determination to play political hardball with the ANC an electorally attractive option.

The gains that the DA has made since 1999 can be viewed as a mark of the party's success in marketing itself to a sizeable portion of the country's minority groups. But simply appealing to minority groups can be conceived of as being strategically self-limiting as no party can afford to alienate majority African support. In the next two sections we will explore how the DA has gone about altering its image to the intended end that all South Africans will be able to identify with it yet how certain realities make the achievement of further electoral progress difficult.

POLITICAL OPPOSITION, RACIAL IDENTITY AND OBSTACLES TO ELECTORAL PROGRESS

Regardless of the ANC's massive support base, the DA argues consistently and robustly that South African democracy is dependent upon one crucial factor, namely a strong and committed political opposition. Before handing over the reins of power to Helen Zille in 2007, Tony Leon (2006) referred to the political objectives he and a few others had set out to achieve: 'In 1994 I set out – with a handful of colleagues – with a mission and a purpose: to establish and entrench the concept of opposition as a legitimate and absolutely essential cornerstone of our new democracy.' While the DA cannot be faulted for its efforts to fashion a sturdy opposition, its attempt to make inroads into the African community – the country's richest electoral resource – remains hampered by the fact that race and ethnicity significantly influence voter preferences.

A consistent theme running through DA literature is the political profit enjoyed by the ANC from racially angled policies such as affirmative action. Nevertheless, the DA exhibits confidence that the black/ANC relationship can be challenged.

In the light of the correlation between race and voter allegiance, and a fractured but unbroken ANC, effective oppositional politics in contemporary South Africa requires an openness to building coalitions. The DA-led multiparty coalition governments in the Western Cape and in the Cape Town municipality have generally worked well and demonstrate what can be achieved when smaller parties unite on the basis of a shared minority status.

These experiences will no doubt help bolster the party further. Although the party won the Western Cape in the 2009 provincial elections with 51.46 per cent of the vote, it cannot afford to take electoral support for granted – not least because this province was once a post-apartheid stronghold for the NP. In 1994, the NP won twenty-three seats in the Western Cape before slipping to the point of embarrassment when, as the NNP, it won only five seats. The unpredictability of the province largely derives from parties vying for the non-African vote in the most multicultural and ethnically plural part of the country. The DP went from three seats in 1994 to five in 1999, to twelve as the DA in 2004. The 2009 provincial elections then saw the DA grow yet further to capture twenty-two seats. This was a considerable achievement in only fourteen years (albeit assisted by divisions along African/coloured lines within the provincial ANC) and leaves the Western Cape as the only province that currently is not under the control of the ANC.

The significant concentration of electoral support for the DA in the Western Cape has both positive and negative aspects for the party's prospects. On a positive note, the province allows the DA's performance, in relation to its delivery of services to the people of the province, to be assessed. However, should the politics of racial identity continue to determine how South Africans vote then what happens in the Western Cape might count for little.

As mentioned above, the DA has not drawn the same level of support in the Northern as it has in the Western Cape. The 2009 provincial result for the DA in the Northern Cape indicates that coloured voters in this province were not as convinced as their Western Cape counterparts by the DA's campaign. As leading party strategist, Jonathan Moakes, has pointed out:

> ... the DA has traditionally been more present among coloured voters in the Western Cape than in the Northern Cape. The party has more of a base in the Western Cape from which to start. Furthermore, the platform of being in government in the Western Cape is very significant with voters experiencing DA delivery in very tangible terms. Voters in the Northern Cape have not had that experience yet (Noakes to Southern, private communication, 3 August 2010).

From a strategic perspective, the significance of the Western Cape to the DA's preparation for the next national elections lies in the potential example it can set of good provincial government, but when we compare the vastly different position the DA is presently in from the position it occupied both nationally and provincially following the 1994 elections, it becomes clear that the party has been able to sell its message to an increasing number of South Africans. As mentioned above, Davis (2004) explains the DP's success between 1994 and 1999 as resulting from the party's capitalising on a sense of alienation felt by non-black groups in general. But the DP came under serious criticism from the ANC for its allegedly negative approach to opposition politics. As the 2004 elections drew near the ANC's take on their opponents was that they were nation wreckers, bent on polarising South African society along racial lines. As argued by Mbeki (2004):

> White minority power in our country, in all its forms and manifestations, was necessarily always founded on the division and polarisation of our people and the denial of our common nationhood, sharing one destiny ... This approach finds expression today in the view advanced by some opposition parties that the litmus test defining whether we have a genuine democracy or not is the strength of the Opposition, and therefore the division of our country into permanently antagonistic camps. The

principal task of this Opposition is then defined as opposing everything the government does, with no concern about participating in the effort to address the fundamental challenge our country faces to eradicate the legacy of colonialism and apartheid.

Mbeki equated political opposition with racial opposition. Given the history of South
Africa, the ANC could not attack its political opposition in a more menacing fashion.
From a strategic perspective, it was profitable to convey a message which tethered 'white'
opposition parties to a racist past because to do so would dissuade voters from conducting
a deeper inquiry into the actual policies advocated by the opposition. Mbeki's statement,
however, displays a flawed logic regarding the electoral benefits of racial polarisation. The
DA is far from being backward in calculating the political costs of racial division. So long
as black politics remains a contest among a few 'black' parties (especially if the ANC does
not experience serious fractures) to follow a line that promotes race entrenchment would
spell electoral marginalisation and minority political status in perpetuity for the DA;
whites and other non-African groups are simply too small in number for other possibilities to be countenanced. On the other hand, where a large racial majority exists, to kindle
race consciousness with its inevitably attendant racial political loyalty would work to the
advantage of the ANC.

In essence, a refusal by the DA to bridge the racial divide would be politically unstra-
tegic and the party is going about winning black votes in two ways. First, if race continues
to influence voting patterns and the perceptions of voters are influenced by the racial
profiles of parties, then parties need to consider how they are perceived across the racial
spectrum. It is undeniable that in the long-term a party that claims to stand for racial
inclusivity would probably lose credibility if an electorate sees little evidence of this in its
racial composition. But the racial membership of parties cannot be expected to change
suddenly or instantly. Progressing through the ranks is a gradual process which rewards
hard work and dedication, and also rewards those who are patient and long-suffering of
spirit. So, what can be said about the current racial profile of the DA? According to the
DA parliamentary leader, Athol Trollip:

> We have invested considerable resources in building a body of political representatives
> that reflect the country's racial diversity. The DA's caucus is more diverse than that of any
> other party – which is a testament to the party's efforts. We have put our money where our
> mouth is, so to speak. It is critical that we don't just say we are a party of all South Africans,
> but show that we are (Trollip to Southern, personal communication, 18 May 2010).

According to Trollip and others, ANC propaganda has sought to obscure the multiracial
character of the DA. For rural blacks who have limited access to modern technologies and
little actual contact with members of particular parties there may well be a low level of
awareness of the DA's racial composition, but this is less likely for urbanised members of
the black community. Hence, making all South Africans knowledgeable, not only about
DA policies but also about its racial makeup, becomes a strategic imperative.

A second way the party is choosing to make inroads into the black community is by on-the-ground contact. Grassroots campaigning reinforces the message that the party is serious about its nonracial message. Electioneering can take different forms – door to door contact or mass rallies – but if it is done by parties that are perceived to be 'white', and in places where they have had no historic presence, then this helps add weight to verbal claims of nonracialism. Here, however, the DA is at a disadvantage. In addition to persuading blacks that the DA is nonracial, it has to contend with the black community's political veneration of the ANC as the party that liberated South Africa from apartheid and often at great personal cost to its members. In other words, the ANC suffered with its people and this is particularly significant for older black voters with first-hand experience of the destructiveness of white racism. But attitudes can change with the passing of a generation. A party's credentials as the party of black emancipation will only take it so far. If a new generation of black voters – with only a second-hand knowledge of apartheid – becomes disillusioned with the ANC because of its poor record in addressing such social problems as high crime rates, poverty, insufficient housing and HIV/AIDS, then the historical role the party played in the black struggle is likely to become a less influential factor when votes are to be cast. But will this add up to a better future for the DA?

MONKEY BUSINESS: REMAKING THE PARTY'S IMAGE

In October 2006, the party's main strategist, Ryan Coetzee, put forward a document entitled 'Becoming a party for all the people: A new approach for the DA' in which he indicated the stark realities facing the party. Despite its gradual consolidation of support from racial minorities, it had never polled more than two per cent among black voters. Unless that changed dramatically, the party faced 'irrelevance and slow disintegration over time':

> Our challenge ... is to do what no party in South Africa's history has ever managed: to unite in one political home people of all races ... We must not underestimate the scale of this challenge: it will be very difficult to succeed, because we are taking on all of South Africa's history and the way that history has divided people (cited in *Mail & Guardian*, 20–26 May 2011).

Notwithstanding his rather ungenerous reading of the ANC's historic commitment to nonracialism, Coetzee's analysis stated the politically obvious, however uncomfortably that might sit within the DA's own ranks: that unless the party drive for support among black Africans, it would be limiting the potential for its upward movement in the polls.

The rebranding that Coetzee saw as necessary to the remaking of the party's image was severely constrained as long as Tony Leon, whose aggressive style was widely considered offensive to Africans, remained as leader. The election of Zille in his place provided the opportunity for the party to rebrand itself, to diversify its top leadership structures, and to move beyond the DA's image as a 'white party'. If, in turn, an assertive drive for the African vote would displease right-wingers who had arrived in the party following its 2008 merger with the NNP, then their support was to be regarded as dispensable. The DA, argued Zille, did not have a choice.

The rebranding began in earnest during the lead-up to the 2009 election. The party's electoral campaign began at Constitution Hill on 15 November 2008 when Zille unveiled its new logo, declaring that the DA was launching a new vision for South Africa. The change in image was aimed at increasing the party's internal social diversity and attracting votes from those who, while sharing its values, had not historically supported the DA. 'The specific goal was to wrestle with the party's negative image as a white minority party, to recreate a new DA that would be more diverse, more reflective of South Africa's racial, linguistic and cultural heritage' (Jolobe, 2009: 138) But the DA's 'liberal tradition would remain as embodied in the party's and the country's constitution' (ibid.)

The process of selling the party anew to black communities then began in earnest, helped of course by the increasing levels of political tolerance and lower levels of violence which are becoming a welcome feature of South African elections as time wears on (Daniel and Southall, 2009: 241–243). Even though efforts to secure the coloured vote in the Western Cape dwarfed the party's drive for African votes, Zille made determined forays into African townships, and was at pains to be seen clad in the DA's startlingly dark blue T-shirts, surrounded by African supporters. Yet it was not until the 2011 local government elections campaign that Zille's strategy took off. For one thing, the DA's principal poster which featured photos of three women (Zille herself in the centre, De Lille to her right, and Lindiwe Mazibuko, a black DA MP, to her left), presented the message that the party was for all colours. For another, she took the fight right into ANC territory, interspersing her English and Afrikaans with isiXhosa.

Both symbolically and territorially, the DA appropriated much of the style and imagery of the ANC itself, to the latter's huge annoyance. Zille sang and out-danced even Jacob Zuma, and basked in her disparaging depiction by ANC Youth League leader Julius Malema as 'dancing like a monkey'. And then she launched the DA's manifesto in Kliptown, birthplace of the Freedom Charter, and marked Freedom Day (28 April) in Solomon Mahlangu Square in Mamelodi, Pretoria, while her supporters sang reworked 'struggle songs'. Even more annoying to the ANC was her claim that, while the ANC had become increasingly racialised, the DA had become the party of nonracialism, embodying the vision and values of Nelson Mandela. It was unsurprising that, in the words of Defence Minister Lindiwe Sisulu (2011), the DA was labelled a vehicle for 'perpetuating white privilege', and that Zille's 'parading herself' with a 'few blacks' was dismissed as a political gimmick.

The DA was adamant that the new strategy had paid off. 'South Africans of all backgrounds heard our image,' claimed Zille, and as has been noted above, while the party's support among Africans remained small (five per cent), it increased significantly from the national election in 2009 (one per cent). But will this be enough to achieve the breakthrough that the DA requires?

CONCLUSION

In 1994, it did not seem that the DA had much of a future, but by 1999 the party's fortunes began to change when anxious minority groups were drawn to its bold and committed approach to oppositional politics under Tony Leon. The mantle of an aggressive style of opposition politics is presently being carried by Helen Zille who, like Leon, has no reservations about crossing swords with the ANC. For Zille, it is vital to the future of South African democracy that centralisation of power in the ANC should be vociferously resisted and that dissenting political voices are not silenced. The DA's political rise was helped by the fact that in 1999 its main competitors either lacked a clear vision or offered policies that were thought unrealistic. This proved to be vital to the DA's attracting the Afrikaner vote, a significant achievement given that during apartheid Afrikaners had had little time for the liberal tradition in South African politics.

Perhaps one of the most noteworthy achievements of the DA is its success in keeping the white community politically participative but, following its success in the 2009 national and 2011 local government elections, the strategic objective of the DA is to make inroads into the black community. Embracing the symbols which celebrate South Africanness and ethnoracial inclusivity, elevating blacks to senior positions, and (perhaps above all) having members work in black communities – particularly if they are black themselves – can help to multiply political support. Of themselves, however, these points are unlikely to be sufficient to turn the DA into a more immediate and serious electoral threat to the ANC. Political conditions also have a part to play: the more South African society experiences the socially decaying effects of crime, unemployment, poverty, and chronic health issues associated with HIV/AIDS, the greater the opportunity for the DA to appeal to voters. Against this, the DA's continued espousal of 'free market' economic policies, albeit dressed up as a quest for the 'opportunity society', does little to appeal to a black majority for whom vigorous state intervention in the economy is necessary if greater equalisation and redistribution are to be achieved. There can thus be no automatic assumption that the DA will transform itself into a majority party, even if the ANC's standing among the majority black community were to be undermined. Indeed, it is rather more possible that the DA will be overtaken by new formations of the left.

At its launch, Cope claimed, in essence, to be the 'real' ANC because the mother body had been hijacked by a mix of opportunists and leftists united behind Zuma (Booysen, 2009). It offered little in ideological terms save to say that it would provide more of the same policies as had been pursued under Mbeki, pursued more efficiently. Its present implosion suggests that a party lacking a clear ideological underpinning and which is unable to provide a clear alternative, especially to the African majority of voters, is unlikely to make any significant impact upon South African politics. Similarly, the continuing long-term decline of the IFP suggests the shallowness of any politics located in ethnicity and regionalism, especially if – as is the case of a party which once ruled the KwaZulu homeland and which remained a major player in provincial government in KwaZulu-Natal until 2009 – it becomes divorced from the opportunity to wield state patronage and power. The long-term attention to opposition to the ANC may need to switch to social formations which, at the moment, are outside the formal political arena.

Conventionally, major expectations regarding the inroads that are being made into the ANC's electoral dominance have centred around a breakaway from the Tripartite Alliance with the Congress of South African Trade Unions (Cosatu) and the South African Communist Party (SACP), some believing that this could offer the DA the prospect of coalescing with an openly pro-capitalist ANC. However, this scenario has always been flawed by its various assumptions: that the ANC and the DA, given their mutual differences and hostility, could patch up an ideological alliance; that Cosatu itself is homogeneous (whereas, in the face of a divide, pro- and anti-ANC factions could develop within the federation itself and within individual unions); and that the SACP would necessarily act in harmony with the trade union movement. At the approach of two decades of the ANC in power, the present political situation seems more fluid than at any time since 1994. Granted, despite the various present tensions between Cosatu and the ANC, and indeed between Cosatu and the SACP (which today has senior members in government and is more closely identified with the latter's policies under the presidency of Jacob Zuma) over economic policy (see Pillay, this volume), the Tripartite Alliance seems electorally as firm as ever. Having led the charge within the ANC to displace Mbeki, Cosatu is unlikely for the foreseeable future to abandon a party machinery which places it in a position of considerable influence. Nonetheless, Cosatu is also conscious of growing fractures within the ANC's traditional constituency, and is seemingly edging towards a closer relationship with emerging social movements whereby it may forge a viable political relationship between workers in the formal and informal economies.

Recent years have seen a massive increase in what are broadly (if often misleadingly) referred to as service delivery protests (whose thrust can range from protests against lack of housing, water and other provisions through to struggles against local ANC leaderships, often seen as involved in webs of patronage and corruption). Broadly, community- and issue-based organisations have emerged which, with considerable popular backing from impoverished townships and rural areas, vocally and often violently contest the outcomes of ANC rule. More worryingly for the ANC, these various groupings are groping towards some kind of broad unity, coming together in recent months in first, a major meeting convened in October 2010 and attended by Cosatu in December 2009 (without the ANC being invited), and second, at a Conference of the Democratic Left held at the University of the Witwatersrand in January 2011. Out of the latter came a Democratic Left Front (DLF) which, whilst broadly reminiscent of the United Democratic Front of the 1980s which led the internal assault on apartheid, vowed not to make what one former Robben Islander termed the mistake of collapsing the organisation into branches of the ANC.

At present, the prospects of such a grouping transforming itself into a political party ready to challenge the hegemony of the ANC are limited. The DLF is in its infancy, and the wide ideological differences between various of its groupings could yet reduce it to infantile disorder. Nonetheless, given the steady erosion of the ANC vote as a proportion of the voting age population (Schulz-Herzenberg, 2009), continuing social strains and incessant local protests, the longer-term potential for a new party of the left is evident, especially if – at some point in the future – Cosatu was to forswear the Tripartite Alliance.

What do such present and potential developments portend for the present parties of opposition, and most notably the DA? Our argument here is that, despite recent gains, they promise rather little. It is possible that, even if reduced to electoral rumps, parties like Cope and the IFP might pick up support in local areas – and yet, as recent history has shown, their mobilisational capacities seem in terminal decline (and they could well end up by merging with the DA). In contrast, the DA is making determined efforts to overcome the limits of its past by adopting an aggressively cross-racial appeal and what it presents as its impressive record in governance in the Western Cape. Yet therein lies the rub, for its success in the Western Cape remains bounded by its particular appeal to the coloured community which perceives itself as marginalised by the ANC. Despite its recent inroads into the African vote, and despite the fact that in the recent 2011 local government contest, the DA made gains on the ANC in eight out of the nine provinces, there is no other province which is liable to fall into its hands at the next general election. The DA, in short, despite its best efforts, remains caught in a cleft stick around 'race'. Moreover, its pro-market ideology seems unlikely to appeal to constituencies which provide a foundation for radical social movements, or a nascent party of the left whose emergent rallying calls are for a 'solidarity society' and 'eco-socialism'.

The DA will continue, for the foreseeable future, to provide the ANC with vigorous opposition within the arena of formal politics. In that, its contribution in harrying the ANC regarding corruption, incompetence and poor delivery remains invaluable, but the prospects of its dislodging ANC dominance (save in the Western Cape) continue to appear remote. Such a task can only lie with a political movement drawing upon much wider social foundations among the majority poor and which captures segments of the ANC's own historic constituency. Social movements can go right or left, and the challenge for South Africa in the future is whether they will be able to forge a coherent alternative to the ANC and whether that will deepen democracy or undermine it.

NOTES

1   The present chapter draws heavily upon Neil Southern (forthcoming 2011). Political opposition and the challenges of a dominant party system: The Democratic Alliance in South Africa, in *Journal of Contemporary African Studies*.

REFERENCES

Booysen S (2009) Congress of the People: Between foothold and slippery slope. In Southall and Daniel (Eds) *Zunami! The 2009 South African Elections*. Johannesburg: Jacana.

Daniel J and R Southall (Eds) *Zunami! The 2009 South African Elections*. Johannesburg: Jacana.

Davis G (2004) Proportional representation and racial campaigning in South Africa, *Nationalism and Ethnic Politics* 10 (2): 297–324.

Deegan H (2001) *The Politics of the New South Africa: Apartheid and After*. Harlow: Longman.

De Klerk FW (1999) *The Last Trek – A New Beginning*. Basingstoke: Macmillan.

Ferree K (2006) Explaining South Africa's racial census, *Journal of Politics* 68 (4): 803–815.

Garcia-Rivero C (2006) Race, class and underlying trends in party support in South Africa, *Party Politics* 12 (1): 57–75.

Giliomee H (2009) *The Afrikaners: A Biography of a People*. Capetown: Tafelberg.

Horowitz D (1985) Ethnic Groups in Conflict. California: University of California Press.

Jolobe Z (2009) The Democratic Alliance: Consolidating the official opposition. In R Southall and Daniel (Eds) *Zunami! The 2009 South African Elections*. Johannesburg: Jacana.

Lanegran K (2001) South Africa's 1999 election: Consolidating a dominant party system, *Africa Today*. 48 (2): 81–102.

Leon T (2006) South African liberalism today and its discontents. In M Shain (Ed.) *Opposing Voices: Liberalism and Opposition in South Africa Today*. Johannesburg: Jonathan Ball.

Leon T (2008) *On the Contrary: Leading the Opposition in a Democratic South Africa*. Johannesburg: Jonathan Ball.

Lodge T (2002) *Politics in South Africa*. Indiana: Indiana University Press.

Louw E (2000) South Africa's second post-apartheid elections: A reaffirmation of racial politics but a loosening of ethnic bonds, *Australian Journal of International Affairs*, 54 (2): 217–238.

Maloka E (2001) 'White' political parties and democratic consolidation in South Africa, *Democratisation*, 8 (1): 227–236.

Mbeki T (2004) South Africans of all races will vote for a people's contract. ANC Today 4 (14), http://www.anc.org.za/ancdocs/anctoday/2004/at14.htm (accessed 14 June 2010).

Schulz-Herzenberg C (2009) Trends in party support and voter behaviour. In Southall R and Daniel (Eds) *Zunami! The 2009 South African Elections*. Johannesburg: Jacana.

Sisulu L (2011) The DA is not a success, it's a vehicle perpetuating white privilege, *Sunday Independent*, 15 May.

Southern N (2008) The Freedom Front Plus: An analysis of Afrikaner politics and ethnic identity in the New South Africa, *Contemporary Politics* 14 (4): 463–478.

Southall R (1998) The centralization and fragmentation of South Africa's dominant party system, *African Affairs* 97 (389): 443–469.

Southall R (2001) Conclusion: Emergent perspectives on opposition in South Africa, *Democratisation* 8 (1): 275–284.

Southall R and J Daniel (Eds) *Zunami! The 2009 South African Elections*. Johannesburg: Jacana.

CHAPTER 4

Democracy and accountability:
Quo Vadis South Africa?[1]

Paul Hoffman

———

'What makes modern constitutions work?' The one-word answer to that question, if there is one, is 'accountability'. A society which has the necessary political will to exact accountability from those in charge is one in which constitutionalism has the chance to flourish. Accountability may thus be defined as the obligation of those with power or authority to explain their performance or justify their decisions. This chapter examines aspects of the notion of democratic constitutionalism that have been incorporated as founding provisions of the new dispensation in South Africa.

Democracy in its classical Greek form meant exactly the same as that claimed in the liberation struggles of Africa so many thousands of years later: 'Power to the people' or, in local parlance, 'Amandla awethu!'

The problem with the liberation movements of Africa, including South Africa, is that what starts out as the people's struggle for freedom transmogrifies along the way into the politicians' or ruling elites' struggles for power. This is where constitutional theory and practical politics part company. The yearnings for freedom from the yoke of colonialism, racism and ethnic dominance become subjugated to the power plays of factions within the ruling elite, and the ordinary people often find themselves worse off (as in Zimbabwe now) or not much better off (as seen elsewhere in postcolonial Africa) than they were before receiving the blessing of liberation. Nevertheless, ordinary voters feel a national debt of gratitude towards liberation movements, and these movements continue to draw electoral support (both real and contrived) in the most perplexing of circumstances and often well after their sell-by date. Robert Mugabe only – and only just – lost a general election in March 2008, twenty-eight years after 'liberating' his country. He is not exceptional. Many of the so-called 'big men' of Africa continue to rule their grateful but oppressed followers long after the stated purpose of the liberation struggle has been achieved. The promotion of human dignity, the achievement of equality and the advancement of the various freedoms for which ordinary Africans have struggled are the main casualties of this unfortunate process. In South Africa, the lack of governmental responsiveness to the needs of ordinary people has sparked widespread service delivery protests (or activities dressed up as service delivery protests which are in fact the upshot of faction fighting within the governing Tripartite Alliance).

Without the establishment of the rule of law and respect for property rights, no country has prospered fairly, consistently and sustainably in the increasingly globalised conditions under which most of the population of the planet is now living. It is through the acceptance and application of the rule of law and respect for property rights that foreign investment is attracted, jobs are created and the wealth of nations is augmented. At its lowest, prosperity requires a functioning system of commercial law: known rules recognising property rights and the sanctity of contract, fairly enforced by independent tribunals. And make no mistake about it: wealth is the objective of all too many of Africa's liberators. The notion that entry into politics is for the noble purpose of service to the people is almost, although not quite, unknown in Africa. The spectres of careerism and corruption haunt the corridors of power. A culture of impunity abounds and promotion of human rights and responsibilities is a neglected field of endeavour. South Africa has not escaped these phenomena.

The cure for all this is constitutionalism, the system of government according to a constitution based upon liberal democratic principles. There can be little doubt that if the tenets of constitutionalism are universally embraced and accountably applied in South Africa, or anywhere else, true democracy or 'people-power' would flourish, and with it peace and prosperity.

The notion of constitutionalism is identified according to three interrelated yardsticks:
- Does the constitution impose limitations on the powers of the government?
- Does the constitution enjoy domestic legitimacy?
- Does it protect, promote and enforce human and peoples' rights?

It is appropriate to consider each of these in more detail to examine the situation in South Africa.

LIMITS ON GOVERNMENT POWER

The South African Constitution places limitations on the powers of the government by:
- making its supremacy, and that of the rule of law, founding cornerstones;

- separating power between the three branches of government: the executive, the legislature and the judiciary;
- establishing an independent judiciary whose judgments bind all organs of state and all to whom they apply; and
- establishing independent state institutions supporting multiparty democracy.

The Constitution expressly states that any conduct or legislation inconsistent with it is invalid, and that obligations imposed by the Constitution must be fulfilled. The governing alliance led by the African National Congress (ANC) has committed itself to 'the fundamental provisions of the basic law of the land' which, as it states in its strategy and tactics document, accords with its own vision of a democratic and just society,[2] but it stresses that its commitment to the Constitution should be viewed 'within the context of correcting the historical injustices of apartheid'. In other words, the ANC interprets the Constitution within the framework of its own National Democratic Revolution (NDR) whose central proposition is the elimination of what it regards as the continuing inequalities arising from apartheid. However, there is perennially a mismatch between the theatrics of ANC revolutionary rhetoric and its more pragmatic policies and practices in government. Indeed, it can be argued that its successes in government, which are many, occur when there is consistency with the Constitution. Those aspects of the NDR which are inconsistent with the Constitution afford an explanation for much of the dysfunction found in national government, in provinces and in municipalities in which the governing alliance holds sway. Opposition formations in government in one province and some municipalities, untrammelled by the doctrines of the NDR and with genuine fealty to the Constitution, generally obtain good governance approval from the auditor general, whose function it is to ensure financial accountability in government. The converse applies where the NDR is allowed to muddy the waters of good governance.

The independent judiciary, answerable only to the law and the Constitution, represents the most important limitation on the power of government. The requirements of section 2 of the Constitution [C 2] read: 'This Constitution is the supreme law of the Republic; law or conduct inconsistent with it is invalid, and the obligations imposed by it must be fulfilled.' This, in effect, means that all conduct by anyone, and all legislation emanating from whatsoever source, can be scrutinised on the basis of its compatibility or consistency with the standards of the Constitution and, if found wanting, can be struck down as invalid.[3]

Although, in general, the government accepts and implements the decisions of the courts – even where they conflict with its policies, there are numerous examples of the failure of government departments to carry out court orders. The public service in the Eastern Cape lacks the capacity to pay social security grants to the aged and infirm timeously. It has been described by the Supreme Court of Appeal as 'terminally lethargic' in proceedings aimed at getting it to pay court orders granted against it. In Gauteng, the health department's failure to pay a judgment granted in favour of a man who suffered grievous injuries as a consequence of negligent medical treatment led to the striking down of legal provisions which precluded execution against state assets. More recently, the failure of the transport department in the national government to timeously pay bus subsidies, despite judgments obtained, led to frantic litigation on the part of beleaguered bus operators.

There are also serious concerns regarding moves to 'transform' the judiciary. This transformation operates on two levels: one is the constitutionally sanctioned need for the judiciary to reflect broadly the racial and gender composition of the country and must 'be considered' when judicial officers are appointed. [C 174 (2)] The other, more menacing, level concerns moves to effect executive control of the judiciary. A constitutional amendment and a batch of bills containing amending legislation aimed at making the judiciary 'more responsive to the aspirations of the people' were first gazetted in December 2005. After a huge outcry in which all living chief justices participated, they were withdrawn in July 2006, but at its Polokwane conference in December 2007 the ANC once again called for the implementation of far-reaching reforms to the judiciary before the end of the then government's term of office (in April 2009). These controversial reforms are due to be introduced in a diluted form during 2011 and are certain to be vigorously debated by all who are concerned with the proper administration of justice, which is a cornerstone of democracy.[4]

Another limitation on the power of government is the principle of the separation of powers, which entails each of the three branches of government sticking to its constitutionally ordained area of competence without encroaching upon the territory of the others. The reality, however, is that the borders dividing the executive and the legislature are becoming increasingly blurred. Parliament is firmly under the control of the executive and of the governing alliance, and often fails to carry out its oversight duties in the manner envisaged by the Constitution. As Andrew Feinstein, a former ANC parliamentarian, recently pointed out, this was particularly the case with regard to the manner in which it dealt with questions arising from the notorious arms deal. The seemingly more robust parliament which held the executive to account in the period between December 2007, when Thabo Mbeki lost the presidency of the ANC to Jacob Zuma, and September 2008, when the ANC 'recalled' Mbeki from the state presidency, proved to be a Prague Spring, and the cosy relationship of the past has since been resumed, to the detriment of good governance on issues such as the demise of the Scorpions, an independent corruption-busting unit which got too close for comfort to several leading members of the ANC, and the disciplinary proceedings against the suspended national director of public prosecutions who was pilloried by the executive and legislature in a manner which was resolved only by an out-of-court settlement of handsome proportions. His only misdemeanour would appear to have been that he had taken his responsibility to act 'without fear, favour or prejudice' too seriously for those who would prefer to have a less independent person in his office. The conviction of the former chief of police, Jackie Selebi, on charges of corruption (an appeal is pending), vindicate the brave stance taken by a public servant who was faithful to the Constitution but has now been lost to the private sector.

The government is also encroaching into areas of civil society that should be the preserve of the citizens involved. In terms of recent legislation, the minister of Health will now appoint the board of the association that represents the medical profession. The members of the association will not have the ability to do so themselves.[5]

The dividing line between the governing alliance and the state is becoming increasingly indistinct. This is a feature of the 'Zanufication' dealt with elsewhere in this volume. The Polokwane conference adopted a resolution requiring 'all senior deployed cadres in various centres of power' (presumably including the public service and the security forces) '…to go through political classes to understand the vision, programme and ethos of the movement.'[6] The incoming National Executive Committee (NEC) of the ANC – the party's highest decision-making body – was instructed 'to give strategic leadership to cadres deployed in the state and to improve capacity to hold cadres deployed accountable'.[7]

In addition to the checks and balances inherent in the separation of powers, Chapter 9 of the Constitution creates a phalanx of institutions to uphold constitutional democracy. The most important of these are the South African Human Rights Commission (SAHRC), the public protector (equivalent to an ombudsman in other countries) and the auditor general. All are enjoined to act impartially and to perform their functions without fear, favour or prejudice. Jointly and severally, they constitute a means available to citizens and residents for limiting the exercise of power by government, of holding it to account and of dealing with improprieties as they arise.

However, some of these institutions are under pressure. Although the SAHRC often plays a constructive and independent role in the protection of fundamental rights through, for example, its rigorous research into the failure to deliver on the right to basic education and its interventions on behalf of the oppressed such as immigrants and farm labourers, it is perceived to be riddled with deployed cadres of the NDR. The office of the public protector was also perceived to be executive minded and crippled by inefficiency until it came under the leadership of Advocate Thuli Madonsela in 2009. The scam involving a payment of R11 million to the ANC in the infamous 'Oilgate' saga was unforgivably ducked on the flimsiest of pretexts (even though the ANC subsequently repaid the amount in question) and all efforts to get the outgoing public protector to view his mandate expansively failed, until the Supreme Court of Appeal eventually set aside the 'Oilgate' findings in May 2011, excoriating the former public protector in the process. The auditor general has been accused by Andrew Feinstein (2007) of permitting government interference with regard to the arms procurement scandal, which has been described, as the 'poisoned well' of South African politics. It concerns the payment of illegal 'commissions' or bribes to secure the deals in terms of which a variety of armaments, which are essentially surplus to the country's defence needs, have been acquired at a cost which was announced as R30,3 billion but which now exceeds R50 billion. Proceedings to compel the appointment of a commission of inquiry into the deals have been commenced in January 2009 by the veteran activist Terry Crawford-Browne. They will culminate in a hearing in the Constitutional Court in 2011.

In addition, the Asmal Commission, established under former minister and MP Kader Asmal to examine the effectiveness and efficiency of these Chapter 9 institutions, recommended in 2007 the abolition of several of the other institutions involved – including the Pan South African Language Board and the Commission for the Protection of Cultural, Religious and Linguistic Minorities – and their rationalisation under the aegis of the South African Human Rights Commission.[8] The report of the Asmal Commission has yet to be debated in parliament. While the rationalisation of commissions with arguably overlapping mandates is perhaps logical and economically prudent, this is not what was agreed when the national accord underlying the Constitution was negotiated.

A serious erosion of the powers of the independent institutions has, however, centred on the Polokwane resolution to dissolve the National Prosecution Authority's Directorate of Special Operations (the 'Scorpions'). This independent unit of crime and corruption fighters proved to be the most successful of its kind, to the great discomfort of many powerful people, including senior politicians and the former national commissioner of police, whose corrupt activities were investigated by the Scorpions in the face of hostility from senior police officials loyal to their chief. It has been argued in the Constitutional Court that the dissolution decision is illegal for want of compliance with the requirements of rationality in all government actions; unconstitutional for its emasculation of the National Prosecuting Authority; unreasonable because it would disband a highly successful crime-fighting unit; unfair because the labour rights of individual Scorpions would be violated; in breach of international obligations and unresponsive to the needs of the people at a time when crime is rampant in the country.[9]

The first round of this litigation ended in a finding that the case had been prematurely launched because the executive and legislature should be given the opportunity of curing the criticisms levelled against the proposed dissolution. The two Acts of Parliament necessary to secure the demise of the Scorpions were assented to by the president; notwithstanding the criticisms voiced. The second round of the litigation, in which the same arguments have been raised, ended in victory for those attacking the validity of the legislation in terms of which the Hawks (the replacement of the Scorpions) were established as a part of the police service. The government has eighteen months, calculated from March 2011, to form a new and properly independent anti-corruption unit that is compliant with the international obligations of the country and capable of upholding the constitutional imperatives regarding human rights. The challenge that the abolition of the Scorpions poses to constitutionalism cannot be over-stressed. It was apprehended that if the unit remains disbanded, or is not suitably replaced, the government itself will be left with the final decision as to who should and who should not be prosecuted for corruption. This would constitute a major restriction of the ability of our constitutional dispensation to limit the power of the government. It has been admitted by the secretary-general of the ANC, Gwede Mantashe, that the Scorpions had to be dissolved because of the amount of unwanted attention they were giving to allegations of corruption in high places within his party (the admission was made to Helen Zille, and her affidavit recording it was filed on record in the court proceedings in support of the unsuccessful argument that this rendered it impossible for the relevant legislation to be dealt with rationally by the executive and the legislature).

This, taken together with burgeoning corruption at all levels of government, the dismissal of the national director of public prosecutions on spurious grounds, public attacks on the integrity of, attempts to gain control over, and attempts to gain control of, the judiciary, are all cause for concern.

DOMESTIC LEGITIMACY OF THE CONSTITUTION

Internal features of the Constitution which ensure domestic legitimacy include provision for regular elections; freedom of expression; and freedom of political activity – the rights to assemble, protest and to picket.

There can be little doubt that the Constitution enjoys domestic legitimacy and acceptance by the people. They measure this legitimacy in free and regular elections presided over by an independent Electoral Commission. The fairness of elections can be questioned on the basis that political party funding remains unregulated and the investment arm of the ANC has involved itself in fund-raising in deals that can be described as collusive, illegal, unconstitutional and voidable on the basis of the irresolvable conflict of interests involved. There is a free and fairly outspoken media, dealt with in another chapter of this volume. There is minimal limitation on the ability of people to organise, to form political parties, to assemble, or to protest peacefully in public.

There are, however, some reasons for concern. The Polokwane conference resolved that the media should 'contribute towards the building of a new society and be accountable for its actions'.[10] It also expressed the belief that arts and culture should 'serve the purposes of its National Democratic Revolution' and that the media needed to 'take on a specific responsibility in this regard'.[11] The resolution on the media warned that 'the right to freedom of expression should not be elevated above other equally important rights such as the right to privacy and more important rights and values such as human dignity'.[12] It called ominously for an investigation into the establishment of a media appeals tribunal to 'strengthen, complement and support the current selfregulatory institutions'.[13] This issue has been referred to parliament, hopefully for a decent burial.

It is also disturbing that the ANC does not view itself as a political party 'in the bourgeois sense' but as a revolutionary liberation movement with an uncompleted mandate. It describes itself as a 'hegemonic organisation' that is not just the 'leader of itself, nor just of its supporters'. It believes that history 'has bequeathed on it the mission to lead South African society as a whole in the quest for a truly non-racial, non-sexist and democratic nation.'[14] In constitutional democracies it is the voters, and not history, that give parties the mandate to govern. The clash of values between those set out in the Constitution and those pursued by proponents of the national democratic revolution is a cause of the slow rate of progress towards an egalitarian society in which human dignity and the freedoms guaranteed to all are to be found.

THE PROTECTION, PROMOTION AND ENFORCEMENT OF HUMAN RIGHTS

In terms of C 7 (2), the state is obliged to respect, protect, promote and fulfil the rights contained in the Bill of Rights. On paper, therefore, it can be said that our constitutional dispensation complies with the third test of constitutionalism. Unfortunately, however, full compliance with C 7 (2) has not been the experience of many South Africans. Whether the deficiencies arise from lack of capacity or resources, or from inadequate policies and administration, or because of endemic corruption and cadre deployment in the civil service, are questions discussed elsewhere in this volume and over a wide range of topics.

South Africa's multiparty system of democracy ought to be so effectively and efficiently functioning as to ensure accountability, responsiveness and openness. The rule of law, a foundational value, is supportive of these values. It has been defined by the World Justice Project in its publication 'Rule of Law Index 2011' as conformity to four universal principles:

1. The government and its officials and agents are accountable under the law.
2. The laws are clear, publicised, stable and fair, and protect fundamental rights, including security of persons and property.
3. The process by which the laws are enacted, administered and enforced is accessible, fair and efficient.
4. Access to justice is provided by competent, independent, and ethical adjudicators, attorneys or representatives, and judicial officers who are of sufficient number, have adequate resources, and reflect the makeup of the communities they serve.

The Rule of Law Index 2.0, produced scientifically by the World Justice Project in respect of South Africa, is informative regarding the state of the rule of law and ought to receive the consideration of the government with regard to areas in which scores are low, as these indicate that improved service delivery, as regards the fifty-two sub-factors of the rule of law, is required. The nation's score for accountable military, police and prisons officials is 0.47; our laws that protect the security of the person score only 0.44 and in the efficient, accessible and effective judicial system category our score is an embarrassing 0.48 (a perfect score is 1.0).

Accountability itself is a word often used in the context of service delivery, but the concept is seldom properly understood. When those in positions of political or administrative authority are required (by those who elect or appoint them) to reasonably explain their conduct and to justify their decisions properly, then the conditions for exacting accountability may be said to be in place. The public administration, which is tasked with providing service delivery accountably and transparently, is answerable to the public for what it does, and does not do, in fulfilling its functions. Professionalism and impartiality are basic requirements for proper, constitutionally compliant public administration but both are notably absent in the public administration of South Africa. This has led to deterioration of service delivery in a number of key areas and consequently to protest action by the public, sometimes of a legal nature, and sometimes ranging in its illegality from rent boycotts to violently destructive criminality involving malicious damage to property, assaults, disruption and even loss of life.

The needs of ordinary people are identifiable from the Bill of Rights. It encapsulates the promises of the new South Africa and reflects the aspirations of all who participated in the arduous process of achieving the national accord which preceded the formulation of the Constitution, including the Bill of Rights. Much has been done to 'seek a better life' [C 198 (a)] but much remains to be done. There are tantalising islands of excellence in the public administration – efficient revenue collection and a brilliant climate-change response Green Paper that draws inspiration from and even quotes the Constitution – as well as areas of remarkable improvement, as in Home Affairs, amid a sea of mediocrity and worse. Those departments which have lost their way need to be reminded of the principles and values of the Constitution: they need to engage with their obligations under the Bill of Rights and they must comport themselves accountably. Using the blueprint of the Constitution is the way to construct a sustainable state in which dignity, equality and the various freedoms guaranteed to the people all thrive. Ordinary people must know their rights and claim them.

EXACTING ACCOUNTABILITY: THE BILL OF RIGHTS

Central to the role of all constitutional governments in the social contract between citizens and state is that proper security of persons and property is provided by the state in exchange for the loyalty and support, through taxation, of its people. The groundbreaking first judgment of the Constitutional Court, Makwanyane's case, places the security of persons into proper constitutional perspective in the context of the abolition of capital punishment in accordance with the values that inform our new order. Our Bill of Rights has a variety of provisions regarding security as a fundamental feature: rights to life, dignity, freedom from violence and slavery, a protected environment and to property itself are all guaranteed.

The security of the nation is the responsibility of the security services as against foreign aggression and the police service as regards locally based criminality. Some soldiers rioted at the Union Buildings in 2009; the commission of enquiry appointed to look into their grievances found that the defence force is in disarray. During the debate on the dissolution of the Scorpions the then deputy minister of Justice, Advocate Johnny de Lange (now MP) indicated that the criminal justice system of the country (courts, police, correctional services and social services) is dysfunctional. This submission accords with the poor score of 0.48 for the judicial system on the Rule of Law Index 2.0.

While there is no discernable threat of foreign aggression against the country at present or for the foreseeable future, the level of crime in many provinces is unacceptably high and unnecessarily violent. Far too few criminals are brought to book and far too little is done to address the problems which De Lange identified when he told parliament that the criminal justice system is dysfunctional. The institutional memory built up during his tenure in the ministry has apparently been lost and a new leadership in the security cluster seems to be starting from scratch without proper regard to the information which led to his pronouncement.

South Africa's soldiers are, by and large, hardly fit for purpose and are too ill trained to be of much use to the country. They are also underpaid, sickly and dispirited, according to the findings of a commission of inquiry appointed after some soldiers rioted outside the Union Buildings. The authorities need to consider whether South Africa's true defence needs as a nation have been effectively and efficiently addressed by the acquisition of over-priced and unusable armaments which the flabby military personnel are unable to utilise because the arms in question are not needed and because insufficient numbers are trained in their use. The amount involved in the arms deals, including the effect of inflation and currency fluctuations as well as interest on loans, was estimated by Andrew Feinstein in 2011 at R70 billion. Cancelling the arms deals and reclaiming the money spent on them is an option, if the fraud and corruption alleged in respect of the arms deals transactions are properly investigated.

A key element in the criminal justice administration is an NPA which functions without fear, favour or prejudice. The Constitutional Court, as final arbiter of such matters, has held that this means that the National Prosecuting Authority (NPA) should be independent of the executive. The executive and the current national director of public prosecutions, Advocate Menzi Simelane, have other ideas about this vital feature of the organisation of government. They deny the independence of the NPA and appear to regard it as a part of the ministry answerable to the minister of Justice. While the minister does have final political responsibility, the accountability and policy-making powers in respect of prosecutions are those of the National Directorate of Public Prosecutions (NDPP), and of him alone. Litigation is pending, on appeal, aimed at removing Advocate Simelane from office on the basis that he is not a fit and proper person to be the only public servant with policy-making powers conferred on him in terms of the Constitution.

While crime remains at the current unacceptably high levels, insecurity for ordinary people will continue and the conditions for economic growth in a legitimate fashion will remain hobbled. Correctional services are still dysfunctional and corrupt despite the work done by the Commission of Inquiry into Correctional Services, presided over by Mr Justice Jali. The prisons are overcrowded to such an extent that the human rights of inmates are continuously infringed, and very little rehabilitation takes place, with prisons serving as universities of crime from which inmates emerge as brutalised and antisocial criminals who offend again.

Consideration should be given to depoliticising the Judicial Service Commission (JSC) by replacing some or all of the politicians who serve on it with retired judges and representatives of civil society. Its powers should be extended to recommending the appointment of the NDPP as suggested by Deputy President Motlanthe when he was president. The reconstructed JSC should be encouraged to make appointments to the Bench on merit, with due consideration for gender and race representivity, but not on the basis that race and gender are anything more than factors to be taken into consideration. If there are not sufficient able and worthy judges in the land, the rule of law is placed in jeopardy to the detriment of the criminal justice system, the economy and the security of all who live and work in South Africa.

Equality is the area in which the country has retrogressed most since the dawn of democracy. Equality includes the full and equal enjoyment of all rights and freedoms. Unfair discrimination has been outlawed and everyone is regarded as equal before the law. On the socio-economic side, South Africa is now the most unequal country in the world according to those who monitor the Gini co-efficient, which measures relative wealth.

The levels of inequality are pernicious, and undermine the ethos of freedom and dignity at the core of the value system constitutionally in place. These levels of stark inequality are also not sustainable, as can be seen by the fact that there are some thirteen million welfare recipients and only around five million individual income taxpayers (as well as corporate taxpayers). While all economically active persons are supposed to pay VAT, seventy-five per cent of taxes are paid by only 1.2 million people. The Bill of Rights requires that to promote the achievement of equality, legislative and other measures may be taken to protect and advance persons, or categories of persons, disadvantaged by unfair discrimination. Instead of concentrating on education and training, skills development and mentoring in the ways recommended by Moeletsi Mbeki, a raft of affirmative action and black economic empowerment/broad-based black economic empowerment (BEE/B-BBEE) measures has been adopted by government. These have served to advance the interests of those least discriminated against while leaving those most discriminated against worse off than before in material terms. Worse still, even though there is no reference to race in C 9 (2), race-based criteria for the beneficiaries of affirmative action (AA), BEE and B-BBEE have been set, making a mockery of the nonracial basis of the new order. The provisions of the section read as follows:

> Equality includes the full and equal enjoyment of all rights and freedoms. To promote the achievement of equality, legislative and other measures designed to protect or advance persons, or categories of persons, disadvantaged by unfair discrimination may be taken.

Only in the judiciary and public administration should race be a consideration, but instead it has become a new defining characteristic across the board. This is hardly the way to go about building a nonracial society and the 'unity in diversity' referred to in the preamble to the Constitution.

Many of the types of deals that have been concocted pursuant to the legislation and policy measures taken do not add value to the economy, and some are unravelling in the tough economic climate brought about by the global, greed-inspired, financial crisis. Major banks, through lending and financing, turn out to be the main beneficiaries of BEE, which is hardly the intended consequence. These factors, together with a burgeoning culture of entitlement in the new elite, have led to imprudent calls for nationalisation of mines from some quarters, calls that do immeasurable damage to the international standing of the country and to its attractiveness to foreign investors and their local counterparts, who have the capital necessary to expand the South African economy and thereby create jobs, security and dignity for ordinary people. Because of the (apparently overlooked) provisions of C 25, nationalisation through expropriation would cost a fortune, as it would be illegal and unconstitutional to expropriate without compensation.

Proper service delivery cannot take place in a society riven by the ongoing and worsening inequality present in South Africa. Whether it be capacity constraints, corruption or the unintended consequences of cadre deployment, the conclusion is inescapable that the high standards of delivery required in the Bill of Rights, read with the values and principles for the public administration prescribed in C 195 (1), are not being met. Ability to pay becomes the criterion according to which services are delivered, to the detriment of the poor. So, for example, in the leafy suburbs, private security contractors are engaged to fill the void left by police inefficiency and ineffectiveness and their operatives protect persons and property for a fee. In townships and poor rural areas, the residents cannot afford private security services and are preyed on with impunity by the criminals who are unwilling to take the risk of being apprehended in those areas in which private security companies render services. The same applies to the provision of healthcare, education and other services. This creates a downward spiral which can only be reversed if well-considered measures to promote the achievement of equality are taken, most particularly in education. Constitutionally compliant affirmative action is perfectly acceptable, and is indeed necessary if implemented in a balanced fashion but the policies in terms of which the current manifestations of affirmative action are implemented should be revisited in order to enhance the prospects of a viable and sustainable system which truly promotes the achievement of equality across the board, rather than enriching a few politically well-connected moguls.

Basic education has been guaranteed to all since the dawn of our democracy. Despite what the executive says (in the recent Green Paper put out by Collins Chabane, minister in the Presidency) and does, in all the education departments, this is a right that has been due and claimable in full by all, child and adult alike.

It is not a right subject to progressive realisation in the light of available resources, as is the case with the socio-economic rights to housing, healthcare, food, water and social security in respect of which reasonable measures – within available state resources – are contemplated to achieve the progressive realisation of each of these rights.

There has been a dramatic, sustained and disgraceful failure to deliver on the constitutionally guaranteed right to basic education. Matric results mask the unacceptably high pre-matric dropout rate and the fact that many of those who do get a matric certificate are actually functionally illiterate to the extent that tertiary education is beyond them and jobs in the private sector are unattainable.

It is the obligation of the state to respect, protect, promote and fulfil the right to basic education. This is not happening on a massive scale, and there are deleterious consequences for the youth, the economic development opportunities in the country, the incidence of crime by the unemployable and the desperate dropout underclass. The achievement of equality on a nonracial basis is made unattainable without proper education. The paucity of adult education facilities that are accessible to the illiterate adult population (twenty-four per cent of all adults) thirsty for basic education has the effect of perpetuating poverty.

Radical steps are required to address the inability of some schools to deliver. The organisational structures in place need to be revisited and the teachers and principals in schools need to be properly empowered, rather than regarded as functionaries in a 'production unit' by departmental managers who are denying them their professionalism and a career path that would be attractive to a school leaver with a good matric pass. Urgent steps along the lines recommended in the 'road map' of the Development Bank of SA and those propagated by Mamphela Ramphele should be considered and rapidly put in place. A special effort must be directed towards the 'lost generation' of twenty-something-year-old youths who don't work, don't have an education and don't have any hope for the future beyond casual and sporadic menial work. The system has let them down; they deserve better.

The courts have described the public administration as 'terminally lethargic' and 'at war with its own people'. This is the consequence of employing junior personnel who are incapable of carrying out the tasks assigned to them as effectively and efficiently as the Constitution requires.

Housing is an area in which service delivery has failed to live up to the expectations of millions of shack dwellers still stuck in undignified and inadequate housing. Everyone has the right to have access to adequate housing but the promise of an RDP house to the millions who live in informal settlements around the economic hubs of the country has not been met. Billions of rands have to be spent on tiny houses shoddily built by politically connected contractors appointed pursuant to questionable tender procedures. There is also a need for better coordination between government departments so the necessary services and infrastructure are made available to those houses which are built.

Consideration must be given to the levels of corruption in the provision of state-sponsored housing, as corruption is always inimical to proper service delivery and corruption in the public administration has the effect of stealing from the poor. Means of dealing effectively with the corrupt through an institutionally and personally independent unit must be put in place – and soon.

Nor are healthcare services above criticism. The legacy of AIDS denialism apart, (too many sufferers still go untreated) there are causes for concern in the manner in which the public healthcare sector is organised and structured. The minister of Health publicly admitted on 8 January 2010 in a radio interview that management in his department 'frightens' him, and later confessed on television. during the illegal industrial action of 2010, that he was 'shocked' by the misconduct of striking health workers. As it has with teachers, the essential professionalism of the doctors and other healthcare professionals in the public healthcare sector has been undermined so seriously that state hospitals are regarded as 'production units' without due regard to the professional status which these qualified medical professionals ought to be entitled to enjoy if the system is to function effectively and in a constitutionally compliant manner.

Food and water are classified as socio-economic rights to which all should have access. The rights of children, and in particular their best interests, are of paramount importance. It is unfortunately true that there are children in South Africa who go to sleep hungry.

Water quality is being adversely affected by failure to maintain sewerage treatment plant and equipment, and by irresponsibility on the part of municipal officials. Beaufort West has run out of water. Rivers polluted by raw sewerage and industrial pollutants feature in the news with monotonous regularity. The pollution left by mines that are closed is a serious problem (as is their illegal exploitation). In some areas, notably on the Garden Route, the water supplies are under stress. The effect of water policy is that water is made available to those who can afford it – which is effectively anti-poor and can hardly be what the founders of the Constitution had in mind.

If the predictions of scientists who study global climate change are reliable, then the ability of the state to provide food and water must be carefully stewarded for water and food security to be maintained, and it is a serious dereliction of duty – and of proper service delivery – for municipalities to do anything prejudicial to water and food security. South Africa became a net importer of food for the first time in 2007; this is not an encouraging development.

THE BASIC VALUES AND PRINCIPLES GOVERNING PUBLIC ADMINISTRATION

South Africa's public administration is required to be governed by the democratic values and principles enshrined in the Constitution – including the principles of public administration set out in this chapter. The centrality of all of these values and principles should be considered afresh, and constructively, because they hold the key to improving service delivery and, with it, the lot of the people still in search of a better life. However, for present purposes, only some of the principles will be highlighted to illustrate the problems and challenges.

The first principle is that a high standard of professional ethics must be promoted and maintained in the public service. Far too many public servants are corrupt, uninterested, dispirited or downright lazy; these are the adjectives used, quite justifiably, by the president in his 8 January 2010 report. They are the antithesis of what is required and explain the lack of proper service delivery at every level. In far too many departments of state, at every level from national to municipal, telephones go unanswered, correspondence is ignored or perhaps acknowledged and then forgotten, piles of unsorted files stand in passages and the smell of fried chicken hangs in the air from around 11 am to well past 3 pm. These are not indicators of a professional, efficient and effective public service. The structures of the public administration ought to be supportive of the professionalism necessary to have a well functioning public service. They are not.

There is instead an informal, illegal and unconstitutional system of cadre deployment grafted on to the structures created by law, a system that has been implemented by the governing alliance in pursuit of its avowed intention to have loyal party hands on all of the levers of power in society. While some deployed cadres in the public administration are able to function at an acceptable level, far too many are there to do the bidding of the cadre deployment committee that appointed them to national, provincial or local-level positions. This undermines the accountability structures in the public service. Deployed cadres who succeed do so despite their deployment, not because of it.

The cadres feel accountable not to their employer but to the committee of the alliance that assigned them to the position in question. Not surprisingly, the High Court has struck down cadre deployment as illegal and unconstitutional in a case concerning the appointment of the municipal manager in the Amathole district of the Eastern Cape, but cadre deployment continues, with scant regard to the judgment of the court.

The government should take on board the judgment, *Mlokoti v Amathole Municipality and Another*, and see to it that the practice of cadre deployment in the public service is discontinued. Professor Kader Asmal, speaking at a conference on ethics in the public administration in October 2010, called for the scrapping of the NDR under which deployment is effected. The premier of the Free State, Ace Magashula, has condemned cadre deployment in the public administration there, according to a report in the *Mail & Guardian*. If a high standard of professional ethics is to be maintained then the legally prescribed methods of appointing staff on merit must be scrupulously observed. President Zuma has already indicated, in his 8 January 2010 statement, that he does not want party political office bearers to be deployed at municipal level and the necessary legislation is being created, but in point of fact party political officer bearers should not be deployed at any level because the public administration is constitutionally required to be impartial, fair, equitable and without bias. [C 195(1)(d)]. Party political office bearers cannot live up to these requirements and loyally serve their party simultaneously.

It is impossible to comply with these requirements and be true to the sectional interests of a political party. The conflict of interests is both obvious and intractable. How, for example, could Jimmy Manyi be impartial as director general of labour and serve the sectional interests of the Black Management Forum at the same time? Yet he was allowed to do so, in clear conflict with the case law and the Constitution, until he was dismissed by the former minister of Labour – only to pop up as government spokesman. How can Menzi Simelane regard himself as capable of functioning without fear, favour or prejudice while simultaneously advocating the sectional interests of the ANC, in particular its decision to disband the Scorpions? He even took leave when he was director general of the department of justice so that he could sell the idea of dissolving the Scorpions to party members in KwaZulu-Natal. This does not cure his pro-ANC bias, nor is it appropriate that he sees himself as the implementer of the ANC's vision for the NPA. He should be independently creating his own vision, without fear, favour or prejudice.

There are many other examples of cadre deployment in the public administration that should be ended, simply because they are illegal and have the effect of debasing the public administration which is meant to be built on personnel management practices based on ability, objectivity, fairness and the need for redress of past imbalances. The deployed cadres, although employed in the public service, feel answerable to the party cadre deployment committee that landed them the positions they occupy. This undermines accountability, which is split between the employer and the cadre deployment committee in a manner which creates an intractable conflict of interests. The secretary-general of the ANC, Gwede Mantashe, has called this type of procedure, in relation to directors general, a 'recipe for disaster', and quite rightly so.

CONCLUSION

If the basic requirement that all conduct and laws must be consistent with the Constitution is respected by those in the majority and enforced by the state on behalf of the minority, the dispossessed and the downtrodden; if accountability and responsiveness to the needs of the people, the foundational values of constitutionalism, are taken seriously and claimed by all the people; then all in society will enjoy enhanced prospects to be free of oppression and able to enjoy their human rights in dignity, peace and prosperity. This is the way to prevent a 'winners and losers' scenario; it requires a vigilant civil society, a willingness to challenge abuse of power and a well developed capacity to exact accountability whether on behalf of oppressed minorities or of forgotten masses. It is in this way that constitutionalism best serves the cause of progress in an 'era of responsibility' to use the phrase of US President Obama. The Chapter 9 institutions exist for, and should be used to achieve, this purpose.

South Africa has an exemplary constitution which can be used as a template for measuring its compliance with the tenets of constitutionalism. It is a constitution worthy of implementation. Any constitution that does not pass the three tests identified (proper limitations on the exercise of power, legitimacy and respect for human rights) may be regarded as suspect. However, the Constitution is not perfect: its proportional representation system and the control of party bosses over parliamentary representatives could be improved upon so as to make public representatives more accountable to the people and less beholden to their parties. Fostering a culture of accountability is certainly preferable to blindly toeing the party line regardless of the irrationality of the party bosses' positions. It is apparent that, while the structures of the Constitution remain in place and theoretically comply with the three tests posited, there is much work to be done before it can be said that the Constitution has taken root and is flourishing. While the courts and the media remain free and independent there is still hope that this can be achieved. A culture of justification, in the sense used in the definition of accountability suggested above, is the best way of addressing all that ails the system at present. With the necessary political will, it can be done.

Fortunately, it is not only politicians who determine the fate of nations. Religious and traditional groupings, civil society organisations, academics, the business sector and the international community all have a role to play in promoting constitutionalism. While the politicians are at least paying lip service to the values of constitutionalism and to the rule of law, it is incumbent upon all persons of goodwill to join in promoting constitutionalism as the best means available for achieving a prosperous and peaceful future for all who live in this vast continent of unfulfilled potential. This is achievable if ordinary people claim their rights, demand responsiveness to their needs and exact accountability from those who govern them.

NOTES

1   This chapter is derived from an updated combination of a paper I presented to an SA Institute for International Affairs conference held in November 2008, and a submission by the Institute for Accountability in Southern Africa to the ad hoc parliamentary committee on service delivery in 2010.

2   African National Congress, Strategy and Tactics: Building a National Democratic Society, as adopted by the 52nd National Conference, Polokwane, 16–20 December 2007. See www.anc.org.za.

3   Section 2 of the Constitution of the Republic of South Africa.

4   None of the new bills is finalised yet; the wording in quotations is taken from those withdrawn in July 2006.

5   South African Government, Health Professions Amendment Act (No 29 of 2007), signed into law by the president on 17 January 2008.

6   African National Congress, ANC 52nd National Conference Resolutions, as adopted by the 52nd National Conference, Polokwane, 16–20 December 2007, paragraph 47.

7   Ibid.

8   Parliament of the Republic of South Africa, Report of the ad hoc Committee on the Review of Chapter 9 and Associated Institutions – A report to the National Assembly of the Parliament of South Africa, Cape Town, South Africa, 31 July 2007. http://www.info.gov.za/view/DownloadFileAction?id=72517.

9   *Hugh Glenister v The State President and Others*, unreported judgment available at www.concourt.org.za.

10 African National Congress, 'ANC 52nd National Conference Resolutions', as adopted by the 52nd National Conference, Polokwane, 16–20 December 2007, paragraph 92.

11 African National Congress, 'ANC 52nd National Conference Resolutions', as adopted by the 52nd National Conference, Polokwane, 16–20 December 2007, paragraph 104.

12 African National Congress, 'ANC 52nd National Conference Resolutions', as adopted by the 52nd National Conference, Polokwane, 16–20 December 2007, paragraph 125.

13 Ibid.

15 African National Congress, 'ANC 52nd National Conference Resolutions', as adopted by the 52nd National Conference, Polokwane, 16–20 December 2007, paragraph 126.

REFERENCES

Agrast MD, JC Botero and A Ponce (2011) World Justice Project Rule of Law Index 2011. Washington DC: The World Justice Project.

Feinstein A (2007) *After the Party: A Personal and Political Journey inside the ANC* Cape Town: Jonathan Ball.

CHAPTER 5

Civil society and participatory policy making in South Africa:
Gaps and opportunities

Imraan Buccus and Janine Hicks

———

The National Assembly must facilitate public involvement in the legislative and other processes of the Assembly and its Committees (section 59 (1) of the 1996 Constitution).

The National Council of Provinces may: make rules and orders concerning its business, with due regard to representative and participatory democracy, accountability, transparency and public involvement (section 70b).

A provincial legislature or any of its committees may: receive petitions, representations or submissions from any interested person and institutions (section 115a).

The focus of this chapter is public participation in policy making in South Africa, exploring how participation and deliberation can overcome the shortcomings of a purely representative democracy by connecting citizen voice with state decision making, thereby transforming broader social power relations and enabling responsive policy making. The chapter provides an overview of policy and legislative provisions for participation, existing mechanisms and practice and, through highlighting civil society experiences of these processes, it presents a case for the need to open up executive policy-making processes to engagement by affected communities.

THEORETICAL FRAMEWORK FOR PARTICIPATION

Participatory policy making and the democratic 'deficit'

Many authors have written about the notion of a 'democracy deficit' – the failure of established, liberal notions of representative or participatory democracy to link citizens with the institutions and processes of the state, affecting the quality and vibrancy of democracy and resulting in reduced accountability (Gaventa, 2004; Luckham et al., 2000). Many democracies are characterised by a sense of disappointment as to how little elections improve government accountability and performance.

Carothers (2005) notes that political participation declines where poverty, inequality and corruption increase and where citizens become increasingly sceptical and distrustful of political parties and institutions. This widening gap between citizens and state institutions results in what Skocpol (2003: 11) has called a 'diminished democracy'. Where political parties focus on electoral processes to the detriment of effective representation, links between citizens and the state are eroded. The result, in most cases, is a weakened democracy with poor representation (Carothers, 2005).

Around the world, governance actors, analysts and activists are grappling with this issue and exploring how best to engage citizens in government decision making, especially the policy-making processes. The reality is, however, that currently citizen participation in policy-making is primarily reduced to participation by the elite, organised civil society in the form of predominantly non-governmental organisations (NGOs), and business and other interest groups with access to resources. Crenson and Ginsberg (2002) refer to this monopoly of participatory processes by elite forces as 'downsized' democracy.

Participation mechanisms that are established to channel citizen input are not accessible to the majority population (particularly marginalised communities and sectors) in societies characterised by inequality, and typically do not 'automatically benefit poor people and groups that have long faced social exclusion' (Manor, 2004: 5). The question then is how mechanisms can be developed to enable the poor and unorganised to influence policy making, to build 'democratisation with inclusion' (op. cit.: 6).

Deepening democracy

Some authors argue that the solution to low levels of citizen participation lies in strengthening or deepening democracy: focusing on governance institutions, the capacity of civil society, and the interface between the two. This, it is argued, enables a greater level of participation by communities in governmental decision making, deepening the reach of marginalised groups to participate. To do so requires a strengthening of representative democracy and participatory mechanisms; building civil society as an external counter-force to government; bringing civil society into the state in a form of co-governance and service delivery; exploring deliberative policy making through models such as citizens' juries and other 'deliberative inclusionary processes' (Holmes and Scoones, 2000: 24), bypassing traditional policy formulation processes; and exploring empowered participatory processes through debate and consensus-based fora (Fung and Wright, 2001; Cohen and Fung, 2004).

Some argue that representative democracy is the only truly legitimate means of representing the interests of the marginalised and unorganised. For instance, while agreeing that democratic mechanisms need to promote opportunities for citizens to demonstrate 'which ideas have majority support', Friedman argues that the 'only mechanism yet devised which is capable of doing that is representative democracy, because only it is able to establish how all citizens feel about particular ideas or interests' (2004: 23).

But how effective is the representative democracy model in tapping into the interests and needs of the poor? In contexts of corruption and domination by elites, and political funding by wealthy interest groups, this is questionable. Critics of purely representative models of democracy argue in addition that in inequitable societies representative systems will inevitably reproduce social, economic and political inequities in terms of who can engage with, and influence, decision making. They claim that participatory democracy, a term denoting citizens' participation in decision-making processes outside the structures of elected government institutions, provides an opportunity to break this mould and offers scope for 'fundamentally redressing these inequities through the participatory and deliberative process itself' (McGee et al., 2003: 9–10).

A slightly deeper or expanded notion of representative democracy is that of deliberative democracy, replacing 'voting-centric democratic theory' with 'talk-centric' democratic theory (Chambers, 2003: 52). With an emphasis on the quality of citizens' debate about problems, it is perceived as a 'mechanism that enriches participatory democracy' (McGee et al., 2003: 10) while enhancing civic engagement (McCoy and Scully, 2002).

Each of these approaches, however, is based on the assumption of the existence of a functional state and empowered civil society. Empowered participatory processes, in particular, require a relative equity of power between citizens, and imply 'voice and agency, a feeling of power and effectiveness, with real opportunities to have a say' (McCoy and Scully, 2002: 118). This latter notion, particularly in the South African context, has to be scrutinised to assess whether meaningful, effective participation is possible – and operational.

Participation or co-optation?

If we are to explore strengthening participatory mechanisms to deepen democracy, then the notion of participation must itself be examined, as this has various interpretations and application. Sisk et al. posit that participation is 'intrinsic to the core meaning of democracy' (2001: 147), yet it seems that sometimes government's view it as important only where it 'reduces government costs and responsibilities ... when governments can offload service delivery to ... NGOs and community groups or convince local residents to donate volunteer labour or materials' (Ackerman, 2004: 447). This approach fails to take cognisance of the fact that 'the opening up of the core activities of the state to societal participation is one of the most effective ways to improve accountability and governance' (op. cit.: 448).

Others see citizen participation in governance as having the potential to 'reduce poverty and social injustice by strengthening citizen rights and voice, influencing policy making, enhancing local governance, and improving the accountability and responsiveness of institutions' (Taylor and Fransman, 2004: 1). It has largely been assumed that as governments develop expertise in facilitating greater levels of participation, services tend to improve and things get better for those in poverty. More and more, participation is seen as critical to the goals of poverty reduction and social justice, but it is seen from varying perspectives.

Experience shows, however, that there are degrees of participation and their impact on policy outcomes. At one end of the spectrum, citizens are viewed as beneficiaries of development processes, involved only to a limited degree in planning and assessing predetermined development projects, to increase the effectiveness of projects. Here, a government agency might open up a process for citizen input with the sole purpose of seeking support for its pre-planned initiatives. Similarly, it might seek legitimacy through such a process, increasing citizen ownership of, or support for, a predetermined agenda. In such instances, citizens may be given the opportunity to obtain information on a proposed state intervention, and air their views, but where participation is limited to a 'tokenistic' process, it will 'lack the power to ensure their views are heeded by the powerful' (Arnstein, 1969: 216). Where there is no genuine empowerment of citizens, the participation process simply becomes an 'instrument for managed intervention' (Cornwall, 2002: 3). Discussing the consequences of superficial or cosmetic processes, Manor notes: 'If ordinary people find that what at first appears to be an opportunity for greater influence turns out, in practice, to be a cosmetic exercise – if they gain little or no new leverage – then they will feel conned and betrayed' (2004: 9).

In the middle ground, citizens are taken on board as stakeholders to share control of development initiatives, to broaden ownership. Here, the government agency might engage its citizens in planning and implementing programmes to increase their efficiency, cost-effectiveness and sustainability. Such instances can enable citizens to 'negotiate and engage in trade-offs with traditional power-holders' (Arnstein, 1969: 217).

The progressive end of this spectrum reflects a rights-based approach, recognising participation as a right in itself, and an entry point to realising all other rights (Eyben, 2003). As Cornwall (2002: 16) notes, this 'recasts' citizens as 'neither passive beneficiaries nor consumers empowered to make choices, but as agents: the 'makers and shapers' of their own development'. Here, the participatory process might transform underlying social and power relations (Gaventa, 2003) and grant citizens 'full managerial power' (Arnstein, 1969: 217).

Innovations and approaches to participation

The extensive literature on participatory policy making reveals an array of models and designs used by many state institutions to deepen their consultation and engagement with citizens, and ensure more deliberative policy making. These include: elected multipurpose councils, user or stakeholder committees, joint management of development programmes, participatory auditing, town hall gatherings, citizens' juries, deliberative workshops, citizens' forums, deliberative polling, consensus conferences, sample surveys, preference polling, participatory research, citizen monitoring programmes and participatory appraisals, citizen advisory councils, community budgeting, and many more. Smith has classified these into six design types: electoral innovations; consultation innovations; deliberative innovations; co-governance innovations; direct democracy innovations; and E-democracy innovations (2005: 8-10).

THE SOUTH AFRICAN CONTEXT

Legislative and constitutional framework for participation

As the references at the head of this chapter reflect, there are a number of sections in South Africa's Constitution (1996) which deal directly with the concept of public participation, charging both houses of the national parliament and all provincial legislatures with the responsibility of facilitating public participation in their processes.

In addition to those sections cited above, section 118 (1) makes provision for the public to have access to provincial legislatures and to be involved in legislative processes. It states that provincial legislatures must facilitate such public involvement, and conduct their business in an open manner. Finally, section 59 (2) provides that legislatures may not exclude the public and media 'unless it is reasonable and justifiable to do so in an open and democratic society'. However, having rules for public participation in the legislative process does not by itself guarantee that the take-up of this right by citizens will ensure more responsive policy making, nor bring about the levels of deliberation and engagement envisaged by public participation literature.

Significantly, the obligations at local government level to engage with citizens are more developed. Section 152 (1) of the Constitution states that 'local government must encourage the involvement of communities and community organisations in the matters of local government'. This implies going beyond merely consulting communities as an aid to deliberation. The Municipal Systems Act, 2000, section 16, obliges municipalities to 'develop a culture of municipal governance that complements formal representative government with a system of participatory governance, and must for this purpose (a) encourage, and create conditions for, the local community to participate in the affairs of the municipality, including in: (i) integrated development planning; (ii) the performance management system; (iii) performance; (iv) the budget; and (v) strategic decisions relating to services'. If this were vigorously employed, this could lead to highly engaged communities such as those evident in Porto Allegre[1] and other situations where democracy and planning are closely linked.

In addition to requiring that local councils consult communities on key municipal processes, the Municipal Structures Act of 1998 establishes ward committees. Consisting of ten people and chaired by the ward councillor, ward committees are intended to act as the main means of communication between the council and local communities. Notably, however, as with the national and provincial spheres, legislation makes it clear that decision-making powers rest with council alone, and that public participation in key council processes, or through ward committees, really only means community consultation to aid the deliberations of municipal councils.

We turn now to reflect on the implementation of these provisions, and evaluate the effectiveness of mechanisms put in place to enable South Africans to influence policy making.

EXISTING MECHANISMS FOR PARTICIPATION IN POLICY MAKING

The national and provincial spheres
Since 1994, all legislatures have established some form of programme or plan of action to encourage public participation. Recent research (Buccus, 2008) into the form and extent of such participation interventions reveals the following:

Public hearings
In the most common form, written and oral comments are invited from interest groups, stakeholders and individuals. Legislatures usually give the public between five days' and three weeks' notice, sending invitations, placing advertisements in newspapers, public places and on radio (even so, the complexity of the issue often means that this notice period is too short for effective preparation). The venues for public hearings are generally accessible to rural communities, with hearings often held in local centres other than capital cities, but when the hearings are held during working hours they become available primarily to the retired and unemployed, unless there is a political party with an agenda to follow. In some cases, transport is provided for rural communities. Some legislatures (for example, the Free State, Northern Cape and Gauteng provincial legislatures) undertake pre-hearing work in the form of community briefing sessions where bills and policy documents are simplified and explained. The Free State legislature also claims that it organises community briefing sessions when the legislature is considering new legislation. These sessions are chaired by the chairperson of the relevant committee, who explains the process for making submissions, and the impact that the proposed legislation would have on the community. In addition, the Gauteng legislature claims to provide information on how to prepare submissions. All legislatures also claim that they make provision for public hearings to take place in the indigenous language of the region.

The provision for public hearings should enable direct, formal input by community groups into the refining of legislation, and many groups have indeed taken advantage of making submissions and have seen their recommendations taken up in legislation. On the other hand, the turnout at hearings is often disappointing, and submissions are often not relevant to the subject matter at hand, which exposes the lack of interest and capacity of civil society to engage at this level. The reality is that both legislatures and civil society must do more for the public-hearings process to become truly effective and productive in promoting participation in the national governance process.

There are, however, examples of civil society taking advantage of this provision to press for policy reform. A recent example is the considerable public response to, and input into, the planned Protection of Information Bill, currently before parliament, by the Right2Know Campaign (R2K), a nationwide coalition of people and organisations who are opposed to this Bill, known also as the 'Secrecy Bill'. Civil society has argued that the Bill will threaten hard-won constitutional rights, including access to information and freedom of expression. R2K believes that a responsive and accountable democracy, able to meet the basic needs of people, is built on transparency and the free flow of information. Civil society organisations argue that the Bill should be drastically rewritten to bring it in line with constitutional values, or it should be thrown out. The coalition has tabled a submission with parliament and has established working groups in the Western Cape, Gauteng and KwaZulu-Natal. Mobilising for this campaign proved to be a huge success – 12 000 individuals endorsed the campaign, and sixty-two civil society organisations attended a recent summit to voice their support for the campaign.[2]

Public access to portfolio committee meetings

All portfolio committee meetings at both national and provincial levels are open to members of the public, although they are not always publicised and so the public is not necessarily encouraged to attend. Records and minutes of meetings and other legislative documents, particularly from committee processes, are often difficult to access. Some legislatures have initiated 'Taking Parliament to the People', a process whereby some committee meetings, and even formal sittings of a legislature, are held in towns in the more rural parts of their provinces but the problem is that these are often quick-fire, dash in-and-out gatherings, and staff organisers have told the authors that it would be far better if politicians remained within the community for a while after the meeting, to enable members of the public to engage with them and raise issues of concern. They are also high-cost events, and the return probably does not justify the expense.

A number of these meetings have taken place in KwaZulu-Natal and most have been dismissed by civil society as public relations exercises. There are exceptional cases, however, as the following excerpt from parliament's reports reveals:

> Mimi Makhanda of Lady Frere recently said, Parliament has come as a beacon of hope to help end her hardship.
>
> During the public hearings on safety and security, she broke down in tears as she told panelists including Safety and Security Minister Nathi Mthethwa of the constant fear that she and her fellow residents of Exeni Village lived under. The women especially, felt as if they were under siege from criminals.

She cried as she remembered the misery she has had to endure. A victim of domestic violence, Ms Makhanda was forced to leave her partner and flee with her three children. She could not find a stable job, and often had to do laundry for neighbours in order to provide for her family. That changed when she got sick two years ago and could no longer find employment. Two of her sons were forced to drop out of school. With tears in her eyes, she said: 'I became depressed especially after my son could not go into Grade 10 this year because I could not afford to buy him a school uniform. He was my hope for a better life.'

With Parliament coming to the people of Lady Frere, the Department of Health and the Department of Social Development intervened. Both have promised to meet with Ms Makhanda and assess how they could help her. Soon after she left the public hearings, she was taken to the social development stall where officials promised to enter her into the database of those eligible to receive food parcels. With a smile, she said: 'It's not much, but it's a start.'

After completing all the necessary documents needed for the food parcels, she thanked Parliament. 'We often think that we're neglected, and that everyone has forgotten us, but this really proves that parliamentarians are caring people, and we thank them for coming here, and giving us a chance to raise our grievances.'

Had she known that Parliament had passed laws to force partners to be financially liable for their spouse's children, even if they were not the fathers of the children, she would have asked for child maintenance from her partner.

For 64-year-old Nozukile Cimani, the Parliamentary initiative had just bought joy to her heart. 'We often vote, but half the time we don't see the people that we've voted for, so I am happy that they have come to us, and more importantly (we can) question the Departments on how money was spent.'

Like many residents in the area, Mrs Cimani's wish is for Parliament to put pressure on the government to provide her village – kuRhantswana - with basic services like water and electricity. [3]

At times, legislatures also convene sectoral parliaments for young people, women and other special interest groups. These generally take place at provincial level and are seen as educational opportunities to raise the profile of matters, such as policy, affecting these groups, and to facilitate an understanding of the role and function of legislatures. While these events generate huge interest and excitement, and are generally marked by high levels of participation, civil society stakeholders have commented that better use could be made of this initiative, through better selection and preparation of participants, and by following up the very serious issues raised by them in mock parliamentary debates.

Most legislatures also facilitate committee on-site tours of relevant state facilities and visits to communities to assist in the gathering of information, deepening of committees' understanding of community issues and establishing linkages between committees and communities. As part of a public relations exercise, most legislatures also facilitate parliamentary tours by interest groups and schools.

Outreach programmes and information dissemination

Legislatures in South Africa generally have some form of outreach programme, with rural communities particularly targeted. Strategies include educational workshops and information dissemination through focused use of media, with some legislatures innovatively making use of community radio stations. The Western Cape legislature uses a website, and the Northern Cape, KwaZulu-Natal and Eastern Cape legislatures are known to have made effective use of community radio to disseminate information about some of their provincial programmes (Buccus, 2008).

Some legislatures have also developed programmes to target people who do not belong to organised civil society structures, although organised structures and groups are more likely to be included in workshops and discussions, and therefore more successful in making submissions. As significant pockets of the public do not understand how legislatures are structured and function, or the significance of the work of portfolio committees, most legislatures produce pamphlets, other materials and educational tools to supplement outreach programmes. These increase interest in and awareness of legislative processes, strengthen relationships between legislatures and communities, and build capacity of community groups to understand and engage with legislative processes.

Petitions

Some legislatures, such as KwaZulu-Natal and Gauteng, have passed legislation providing for the submission of petitions by members of the public, and have established, dedicated petition-standing committees to receive petitions and deliberate on them. It is also their responsibility to make decisions on forwarding the matters raised to relevant government departments. However, in recent years various sectors, including HIV/AIDS, women and youth, have submitted petitions but have not received any feedback.

As a recent example, the community of Manyiseni, in northern KwaZulu-Natal, together with the Commission for Gender Equality (CGE), tabled a petition with the KwaZulu-Natal Legislature in January 2010. Their complaint related to the failure of several provincial government departments to respond to their requests for assistance and information regarding socio-economic rights. Despite the intervention of the CGE, a statutory body empowered to monitor state compliance with gender equality obligations, it took more than a year for this community to receive feedback from the standing committee, which eventually indicated that the delay was occasioned by initial investigations to ascertain whether the petition did in fact comply with the provisions of the Petitions Act. In the face of threatened protest action by the community of Manyiseni, the committee has since arranged for a site visit to this community, raising the hope that this will provide leverage in holding the provincial executive to account for service delivery.

Izimbizo

Although this form of public gathering was much favoured by former president Mbeki, particularly during his first term (1999–2004), its frequency has declined in recent years and where such gatherings have been convened, they have usually been at the provincial and municipal levels. These gatherings often draw thousands of community members together to raise issues of concern in the presence of the premier and departmental representatives, who are expected to respond to and attend to the concerns raised, to the satisfaction of the premier. While it is not without its uses, limitations to this include the sheer size of the gatherings, which make the forum often unsuitable for deliberation on the issues and the possible solutions. They are also often unfocused, resulting in a catch-all process for all community problems. Dates and venues set for *izimbizo* are often changed, and they are set at inconvenient times like 17h00 so that participants are not given the chance to eat an evening meal before attending the *izimbizo*.

Green/white paper processes

Policy making in South Africa often takes the form of the publishing, in government gazettes, of a 'green paper' which outlines a set of policy intentions, and a 'white paper', or actual policy proposal. Public comment is invited to each paper, but the document is written in convoluted and legalistic English, making it inaccessible to most. In some instances, these papers are also circulated among relevant interest groups for feedback, or consultative processes are facilitated to engage stakeholders on the proposals. However, critiques of these processes allege significant shortcomings: the reach and depth of consultation is limited to existing networks of sectoral stakeholders as opposed to representative groups of affected communities; and consultant-driven workshops on policy recommendations fall short of a truly deliberative forum where stakeholders develop and negotiate policy alternatives.

Timeframes for comment and the uptake of civil society input is also limited, as demonstrated by a recent example concerning some twenty NGOs in the gender-based violence (GBV) sector, which sought to engage with the national policy framework developed for the implementation of the Sexual Offences Act. Civil society organisations in this sector feel the policy document is inherently flawed, as it does not speak to the progressive realisation of services as envisaged by the Act: it does not stipulate the services that will be made available to victims of sexual offences, a costing of these services, details of who will provide them, and a timeline. The drafting of this policy document provides an opportunity for policy clarity on these issues, and the clear allocation of resources – without this information, the policy framework as it stands does not offer anything more of substance than the Act itself.

Tshwaranang, a local NGO focusing on gender-based violence (GBV) and providing legal services to victims of sexual offences, reports that there was a brief window for consultation with civil society but that it was not adequate. Tshwaranang and a group of NGOs in this sector is in the process of developing a set of recommendations on strengthening the policy framework, and is resorting to appealing directly to parliament and the minister of Justice and Constitutional Development to stay the policy process to enable civil society input. It has further sought the assistance of the CGE to secure a meeting with the minister and the opportunity to engage more meaningfully with the policy document.[4]

The apparent trend of state departments to not engage with affected community groups and sectoral NGOs at the outset of the policy process, in the identification of objectives and approaches and in the development of policy recommendations, gives rise to the situation reported by Tshwaranang. The failure of departments to make policy documents available in plain language and in local languages, and to distribute them widely for comment, raises questions about the participatory nature of these processes and does not create meaningful opportunities for broad consultation and for input by civil society into policy making.

The local sphere
Two main participatory mechanisms operate at the local government level: integrated development planning (IDP) and the budget process. The IDP is a plan developed by each local and district municipality identifying programme priorities and expenditure over a five-year period. As noted at the outset of this chapter, local government legislation requires municipalities to engage directly with citizens on the development of these plans. Research by Buccus (2008) reveals that there is no standard approach to public participation in the IDP process, with municipalities developing varying mechanisms to consult with community stakeholders. All municipalities report adherence to the requirement of consultation in planning, although the substance of that consultation may be questionable. For example, all municipalities claim to have had at least some *izimbizo* on the IDP and budget at both district and local levels. In all cases, the ward committee is used in some form as the vehicle for community consultation on the IDP.

Ward committees
In the main, participatory processes take place at the ward level. Ward committees are created by legislation and policy as the institution to link communities with municipal representatives and processes. Chaired by ward councillors, they are the foundation stones for community participation in development processes and municipal decision making. But despite their promise, ward committees are often dysfunctional, being inadequately resourced to fulfil their function, with limited capacity of members to undertake the work required of them, and vulnerable to political manipulation.

Overall, there appears to be no common understanding of how ward committees can feed into municipal development planning and decision making. There are also no resources made available for the functioning of ward committees, nor any stipend made available for travel, or administration costs covered for ward committee members, many of whom lack a meaningful understanding of municipal processes and how to ensure that developing planning takes account of community needs. In fact, these ward commitees simply become areas of patronage and a first stepping stone to a hoped-for career in politics.

CIVIL SOCIETY PERCEPTIONS OF POLICY MAKING IN SOUTH AFRICA

So what does civil society make of the public's role in policy making? Research conducted in 2007 (Buccus and Hicks, 2007) reveals that the predominant view is critical; the policy-making process is seen as driven by an elite and as functioning largely to the exclusion of the public and affected stakeholders. Attempts to facilitate community input into policy making are perceived as largely superficial, and not connected to the real power base where decisions are made, whether at a political or bureaucratic level. Most processes are assessed as presenting predetermined positions and programmes for limited feedback or information-sharing purposes only, or creating limited opportunities for communities to raise concerns – and as a result they make very little substantive difference to policy decisions. The co-opting of civil society stakeholders into such compromised processes is regarded as having a demobilising effect, channelling the relative power of civil society mass-mobilising into apparently consultative processes that do not deliver on substance.

Our research also indicates that among both marginalised and middle-class civil society groupings there is an increasing perception of being sidelined and marginalised, excluded and disempowered by the policy-making process; a perception caused by, for example, not receiving feedback on inputs made, not seeing recommendations being taken up, and not deriving the sense of having had any noticeable effect on the policy in question. Some stakeholders raise real concerns of having been co-opted into participating in a process with a predetermined outcome, and of being excluded from an 'inner circle' enjoying privileged access to decision makers.

Our research also reveals a widespread concern at government's tendency to call for community input only in the advanced stages of policy formulation, rather than at the outset when needs are identified and solutions developed. Participation interventions are therefore perceived as an attempt by the state to obtain community buy-in for implementation purposes. The use of primarily print media in government communication and information dissemination excludes certain groups and communities with limited access to these forms of media.

Also, language used in policy processes, predominantly highly complex, technical and in English, further alienates communities, and notice of opportunities to make submissions tends to 'come late', as expressed by communities. As a result, community-based organisations (CBOs) report that they are largely excluded from policy making. Across the sectors surveyed, representatives stated that CBOs need to be involved by the state from the outset of the policy process.

NGOs and CBOs reported being particularly struck by power relationships at play in the policy process, among policy makers themselves and also between policy makers and civil society stakeholders. These are unequal power relationships between politicians and bureaucrats, government and civil society representatives; between those with access to information and resources and those without; between those belonging to organised structures and those not; between those who are viewed as educated and those not; between urban and rural residents; between men and women, and people with differing abilities.

Participants reflected that these unequal power relationships tend to play themselves out in the policy arena, resulting in some issues not making it onto the agenda, the exclusion of some stakeholders, the rendering invisible of others, and the exclusion of many from that critical juncture where decisions are made. Participants noted that unless these power issues are addressed through careful planning, collaboration and facilitation, they will continue to undermine participatory initiatives seeking to gain civil society input and buy-in.

An examination of power in the policy-making arena itself reveals a complex territory, characterised by contestation. Policy has been defined as constituting the 'decisions taken by those with responsibility for a given policy area, and these decisions usually take the form of statements or formal positions on an issue, which are then executed by the bureaucracy'. It is a political, 'ongoing process of negotiation and bargaining between multiple actors over time' (Keeley and Scoones, undated: 4), and reflects 'conflicts and alliances between economic interest groups' (Robinson, 2003: 7). Participants from a group working in the children and women's sector noted in addition that, as a starting point, power resides with political parties. There is power in the process of setting the agenda for discussion itself, and participants questioned how issues get onto the political agenda and attract sufficient support and attention. When it comes to the implementation of policies and programmes, power is devolved to government agencies, and is not monitored by or made accountable to civil society.

Participants from the HIV/AIDS discussion group which we interviewed in the late Mbeki era distinguished between the power base of political and bureaucratic actors, and national government actors as opposed to provincial and local actors. While politicians deliberate ideas and make decisions, bureaucrats have the final power of implementation. The implication of this distinction is that most policy processes are formulated at the national level, which is perceived as being far removed from communities and difficult to access, with provincial and local governments then tasked with merely implementing these policies.

Representation and voice

Writing on the policy-making process in Brazil, Shankland (2005) uses a term which we believe could equally be applied to South Africa: 'representation dressed up as participation', a flawed notion of political representation of citizens' interests through civil society organisations, which ignores the fact that debates in 'new democratic spaces' occur in the absence of some (indeed most) citizens and with the presence of others who may be speaking in their name (op. cit.: 2).

In looking at the South African policy arena, it is important to assess who participates, and whose voice is heard. Our view is that the relative inaccessibility of information on governmental decision making and the resources and abilities required to engage in participatory processes result in the domination of such spaces by a middle-class elite, in the form of NGOs, business and other similar interest groups. These civil society organisations (CSOs) often bypass, or fail to connect with, the much broader grassroots sector of community-based organisations (CBOs), which they often purport to represent.

Our research suggests something of a class divide among CSOs, with CBO groups expressing the view that organised CSOs dominate policy processes where there are spaces for civil society to engage with government. CBO groups characterised by a lack of resources articulated challenges they experienced in influencing these processes. Although they did have a voice, it was often used to little effect. Children's and women's groups added a gender dimension, as they noted that participatory processes at community level tend to be dominated by men, or powerful women, and they stressed the importance of questioning which stakeholders are present at these processes, and whom they represent. CBO research participants concurred, stating that men tend to set the agenda and to dominate discussions and processes, with women excluded from certain discussions. Groups representing people with disabilities noted, in the main, limited opportunities to express their concerns. Overall, the experiences reflect that those who have access to power and information tend to hold onto these resources.

Tensions were particularly apparent between organised network bodies such as the South African National Civics Organisation (SANCO), the South African NGO Coalition (SANGOCO), CBO network bodies and the CSOs and communities they claim as membership bases. There is a perceived level of competition and struggle for dominance between these structures which have diverse identities, yet a shared membership base. CBOs at a discussion forum we observed challenged network representatives, claiming that they were not accountable to them or representative of their needs and interests, yet had access to information, recognition and resources, all in the name of the membership interests they claimed to represent. They appeared wary of networks' agendas, and suspicious of their perceived and sometimes overt political affiliation, which they stated discouraged many CBOs from identifying and engaging with them.

Clearly, the question arises: how can these tensions and power imbalances be brought to the surface and addressed so that these issues do not play themselves out in participatory policy-making spaces, thereby rendering them ineffective? It is more than apparent that CSOs and representative umbrella bodies need to be challenged on issues of mandate and representation. Consideration also needs to be given to how marginalised groups enter the policy arena motivated, empowered and equipped to engage with a greater sense of equity with government and other civil society actors. But these are important issues beyond the scope of this paper.

Learning from successes

What these experiences and reflections from civil society suggest to us is that although there is legislative provision for participatory mechanisms, and many such mechanisms have been put in place, this is not enabling civil society to participate meaningfully in policy making. The existing mechanisms are largely inadequate, inaccessible and disempowering, and new, innovative approaches to participatory policy making are required

– particularly if inherent power and class inequalities are to be overcome to ensure equitable participation.

There have been some notable civil society interventions which have had a significant impact on policy making. These, however, are distinguished in that they move beyond the formal state participation channels, and entail multiple strategies and civil society stakeholders across class and political affiliations. Often quoted instances include successful interventions by the Treatment Action Campaign to ensure state provision of anti-retrovirals to those infected with HIV. This campaign drew on a range of interventions: mobilising a massive groundswell of support from communities, organised civil society, academics and faith-based organisations; litigating against the state; and working in partnership with state institutions for the successful implementation of prevention measures.

The following case study identifies how leveraging political support for a policy position, in the form of the powerful allegiance of the largest union body in South Africa, the Congress of South African Trade Unions (Cosatu), can affect policy making.

The public versus the Protection of Constitutional Democracy against Terrorism Act of 2004

The mobilisation of opposition to the above legislation, initially referred to as the 'Anti-Terrorism Bill' (ATB), illuminates several useful strategies in engaging with a policy process. The civil society response to the Bill shows that public participation in resisting a controversial bill appearing before parliament for consideration can be effective. A vast cross-cutting section of South African society participated in numerous ways in resisting the Bill, with resistance coming from two distinct categories: the Muslim community on one side and a loose coalition of journalists, unionists, NGOs and activists on the other. The participation here was unprecedented in the post-apartheid context, as never before had there been such a concerted effort by civil society to reform or reject a particular piece of legislation, with relative success.

Attacks on the United States on 11 September 2001 served as a catalyst for many countries, particularly the United States and the United Kingdom (and South Africa at a later stage) to consider introducing additional legislation to deal with terrorism. In the case of South Africa, the government's argument that the then ATB would bring our country in line with similar international legislation was met with public anger and discontent from the time the draft Bill was introduced in 2002. The resistance stemmed primarily from the fact that draconian powers would be given to our law enforcement agencies to investigate and deal with acts of terror. The vague description of 'terrorism' further fanned fears that the ATB would seriously limit civil liberties such as the freedom of association, expression, assembly and demonstration. The experiences of the Muslim and other minority communities in the United States, in the wake of such legislation, further illustrated the dangers of these laws being effected, and the South African public was understandably nervous about having its own civil liberties curtailed yet again, after years of such treatment under apartheid.

These events in the United States and elsewhere clearly provided sufficient motivation for those groups feeling most vulnerable to act. As a result, South African Muslims, together with a range of interest groups such as Cosatu, were propelled to undertake a sustained campaign to challenge and engage the government on this Bill. What followed was a rare and intriguing partnership forged between faith-based and other non-governmental interest groups, to tackle an issue of common concern.

In September 2002, the Department of Safety and Security introduced the draft ATB for comment and scrutiny. At this point, a number of human rights organisations opposed the Bill, arguing that it was fundamentally flawed. At issue were the many archaic provisions that would significantly curtail civil liberties guaranteed in the Bill of Rights. The initial demand by some, including the Muslim community, was that the Bill be completely shelved – which the government did not deem feasible. A revised Bill, with shortened content and the removal of some problematic clauses, was then placed before parliament in March 2003. This version was also not viewed favourably by civil society.

A number of organisations challenged the need for new legislation, arguing that the state already had twenty-two pieces of legislation to cover crimes and activities covered by the ATB. This argument effectively informed and shaped the foundation of the objections to the introduction of the Bill. On the face of it, it seemed, in the latter part of 2003, that government – obviously under severe pressure from the United States government – would fast-track the Bill through parliament. Cosatu's intervention, however, disrupted the process with the argument that even basic strike action would be classified as an act of terrorism in terms of the Bill's provisions. The April 2004 elections halted any progress on the Bill, but thereafter it was once again revised, taking into account Cosatu's concerns, and reintroduced to parliament. A compromise was reached with Cosatu, and the Bill was renamed and passed unanimously in November 2004.

The most prominent faith-based group in the coalition was the Muslim community. The horror of the experiences of the Muslim community in the United States and in other parts of the world was an indication to South African Muslims that they could not allow such legislation to be passed without challenging its draconian measures. They managed to draw in a broad range of the Muslim community, to present a united front across the ideological spectrum in its submissions in opposition to the Bill.

In addition, a number of progressive interest groups undertook to resist the Bill. While some of the resistance involved a limited number of public meetings and protests, oral and written submissions to the relevant parliamentary portfolio committee were the more notable forms of resistance. For example, in its June 2003 submission to parliament, the Institute for Democracy in South Africa (Idasa) supported the intention of the Bill and acknowledged the need for legislation to deal with terrorism in South Africa and internationally, but was concerned that in addressing terrorism, the Bill might be making provisions that could contravene the Constitution.

The Law Society of the Cape of Good Hope (LSCGH) also voiced resistance to the Bill, arguing in its submission that existing legislation was more than adequate to deal with the threat of terrorism and that the proposed Bill's provisions were unconstitutional.

The South African Human Rights Commission (SAHRC) was also not convinced of the need for the Bill. In its submission, the SAHRC proposed a number of technical changes, and expressed concern at limitations on the right to silence. The SAHRC did, however, explain that it understood that the international environment was difficult and thatSouth Africa had obligations to meet.

Another notable submission was that made by the Unemployed and Social Activists Committee (Usac) which rejected the Bill as unconstitutional and oppressive. In a number of statements, the Freedom of Expression Institute (FXI) argued that the Bill would seriously affect individual civil and political liberties. The FXI was also concerned about the impact the Bill would have on progressive formations, particularly the social movements, in the country. Journalists were also among those who resisted the introduction of the ATB. In January 2003, the South African National Editors Forum (Sanef) called for the withdrawal of the ATB, saying that it was a serious threat to media freedom because the legislation could be used against journalists (Buccus and Nadvi, 2004).

In the face of this concerted onslaught, the government backtracked; the Bill was revised, and renamed the Protection of Constitutional Democracy against Terrorist and Related Activities Bill. A compromise was reached, primarily with the trade union movement, with the significant change being that legislation now stipulates that 'a struggle waged by peoples … in furtherance of their legitimate right to national liberation, self-determination and against colonialism shall not be considered as terrorist activity'.

While the submissions from the Muslim community played a very significant role in resisting the Bill in its original state, it was the intervention by Cosatu that probably swung the balance of power. The point, however, is that government wavered in the face of a broad front, and that is the lesson to be learned. Such coalitions in post-apartheid South Africa have been rare. Nonetheless, the indication is that when such coalitions come into being they augur well for the project of democratic consolidation and participatory democracy.

CONCLUSION AND RECOMMENDATIONS

Participatory policy making is realistic, desirable and achievable – it works for citizens and government alike. There is, however, a significant gap at policy level relating to public participation in policy and decision-making processes themselves within the realm of South Africa's executive. While the Constitution provides a framework for an open and participatory democracy, it provides specific references and creates particular obligations in this regard only within the realms of national and provincial legislatures, and local government.

The ensuing policy and legislative framework relating to public participation is similarly silent on the issue of opening up decision-making processes at executive policy level to citizen participation. When one considers the fact that not all policy processes result in legislation that would come before the scrutiny of legislatures – and be open to public debate and input – it is apparent that legislative processes provide citizens with a limited vehicle to engage with policy processes themselves, and then perhaps only marginally through oversight powers exercised by legislatures. This, coupled with the significant impact, for instance, of the formulating of national economic policy and poverty reduction strategies, and the absence of opportunities for public deliberation and engagement on these topics, reveals the significance of this lacuna within our democratic architecture and processes. Executive policy-making processes need to be made more accessible – and accountable – to affected communities.

A fundamental emerging issue is the need to critically assess how participation and deliberative democracy can fundamentally transform inherently unequal social power relations, so that marginalised and vulnerable groups are brought into governance processes in a meaningful, empowering way. This requires careful design and facilitation of participatory mechanisms, drawing on comparative experiences and examples from the international community and local experiments, coupled with capacity building and support for government institutions tasked with driving these processes, and the civil society structures seeking to engage with them.

Above all, the focus should be placed on enabling the voices and interests of marginalised communities to influence policy making, from the framing of policy issues to the deliberation of policy options. Without such significant and meaningful opportunities, civil society and marginalised communities and groupings will disown the processes for engagement and will remain active within the 'invented spaces' reflecting greater legitimacy and expression of power.

NOTES

1   Port Allegre, a city in Brazil, is credited with having successfully implemented participatory budgeting at the municipal level.
2   Right to Know Campaign (2010). www.r2k.org.za (accessed 22 March 2011).
3   Parliament of South Africa. www.parliament.gov.za (accessed 21 March 2011).
4   Tshwaranang complaint to, and e-mail correspondence with the CGE, 25 March 2011.

REFERENCES

Ackerman J (2004) Co-governance for accountability: Beyond 'Exit' and 'Voice', *World Development*, Vol 32, No 3: 447–463.
Arnstein SR (1969) A ladder of citizen participation,' *JAIP* 35(4): 216–224.
Buccus I (2008) Towards developing a public participation strategy for SA's legislatures, *Critical Dialogue: Public Participation in Review*, Vol 3, No 1: 48–58.
Buccus I and J Hicks (2007) Crafting new democratic spaces: Participatory policy making in KwaZulu-Natal, South Africa, *Transformation* 65.
Buccus I and L Nadvi (2004) Civil society and the anti-terrorism bill, *Critical Dialogue: Public Participation in Review*, Vol 1, No 1.
Carothers T (2005) What really lies behind challenges of deepening democracy and establishing the rule of law? Presentation at the Centre for the Future State conference New Challenges in State Building, 21 June 2005, London: 36–49.

Chambers S (2003) Deliberative democratic theory, *Annual Review of Political Science*, Vol 6: 307–326.

Cohen J and A Fung (2004) Radical democracy, *Swiss Political Science Review,* Vol 10, No 4: 23–34.

Cornwall A (2002) Making spaces, changing places: Situating participation in development, *IDS Working Paper 170*, Brighton, CDRC, IDS: 3–19.

Constitution of the Republic of South Africa, Act 108 of 1996.

Crenson M and B Ginsberg (2002) *Downsizing Democracy: How America Sidelined its Citizens and Privatised its Public.* Baltimore: Johns Hopkins University Press.

Eyben R (2003) The rise of rights, *IDS Policy Briefing*, issue 17, May.

Friedman S (2004) A voice for all: Democracy and public participation, *Critical Dialogue: Public Participation in Review*, Vol 1, No 1: 22–6.

Fung A and E Wright (2001) Deepening democracy: Innovations in empowered participatory governance, *Politics and Society*, Vol 29, No 1: 5–41.

Gaventa J (2003) Perspectives on participation. Paper presented at symposium Developing Participation: Challenges for Policy and Practice, Stockholm.

Gaventa J (2004) Deepening the deepening democracy debate, background paper prepared for Ford Foundation seminar, December.

Holmes T and I Scoones (2000) Participatory environmental policy processes: Experiences from North and South, *IDS Working paper 113.*

Keeley J and I Scoones (undated) Understanding environmental policy processes: A review, *IDS Working Paper 89.*

Luckham R, A Goetz and M Kaldor (2000) Democratic institutions and politics in contexts of inequality, poverty, and conflict: A conceptual framework, *IDS Working Paper 104.*

Manor J (2004) Democratisation with inclusion: Political reforms and people's empowerment at the grassroots, *Journal of Human Development,* Vol 5, No 1: 5–29.

McCoy M and P Scully (2002) Deliberative dialogue to expand civic engagement: What kind of talk does democracy need?, *National Civil Review*, Vol 91, No 2:117–135.

McGee R, B Nyangabyaki, J Gaventa, N Rose, M Rai, R Joel, S Nelson, W Emma and S Zermeño (2003) Legal frameworks for citizen participation. Synthesis report, Logolink, University of Sussex.

Republic of South Africa, Municipal Systems Act, No 32 of 2000.

Robinson M (2003) States in transition? Frameworks of analysis and determinants of change. Background paper for workshop entitled The Changing State, Hanoi, Vietnam.

Shankland A (2005) Speaking for the people: Representation and health policy processes in the Brazilian Amazon. Paper for DPhil Research Outline Seminar, Institute for Development Studies, University of Sussex.

Sisk T, J Demichelis and J Ballington (2001) Expanding participatory democracy', Chapter 5 in *Democracy at the Local Level: The International IDEA Handbook on Participation, Representation, Conflict Management, and Governance*, International Institute for Democracy and Electoral Assistance.

Smith G (2005) Power beyond the ballot: 57 democratic innovations from around the world. A report for the Power Inquiry, London.

Taylor P and J Fransman (2004) Learning and teaching participation: Exploring the role of higher learning institutions as agents of development and social change, *IDS Working Paper 219*, March.

CHAPTER 6

Bring back Kaiser Matanzima?
Communal land, traditional leaders and the politics of nostalgia

Leslie Bank and Clifford Mabhena

Had I known how the ANC would handle the rural question after apartheid I would not have joined the liberation movements in the 1960s, but supported Kaiser Matanzima and his version of development for the Transkei.
(Former PAC activist in Cala, Transkei)

We miss the old days, when there was still farming here and we got support from the tribal authority. When it rained the tractors came and ploughed our land. It was easier for us then to plant crops. It was Matanzima who organised that for us, he cared for the rural people
(Elderly woman, Ketani, Transkei)

There is always the misunderstanding that the Matanzimas were not popular with the people. This is untrue, Kaiser Matanzima had a massive following in the Transkei
(Mda Mda, anti-apartheid activist and advisor to King Sabata Dalindyebo, the Thembu paramount)

On 10 May 2010, the Constitutional Court of South Africa declared that the Communal Land Rights Act (CLRA), which had been passed in 2004, was unconstitutional and could no longer be implemented in its current form. The court found that inadequate consultation had taken place with communities and provincial structures prior to the adoption of the Act, and that the Act did not fully address tenure insecurity among rural residents, specifically single women. It was also found that the way the notion of 'community' was used in the Act was problematic because it potentially reproduced apartheid-style tribal authorities as 'new communities', placing too much control of land in the hands of existing traditional leaders. In fact, part of the case against the state was based on the assertion that CLRA, together with the Traditional Leadership Governance Framework Act of 2003 and a proposed new law that expands the role of traditional courts in law enforcement, would effectively create a fourth tribal tier in the judicial system that was at odds with the democratic constitution of the country. In ruling on the CLRA matter Justice Ngcobo disagreed with this assertion, but felt that the Act made it too easy for the old tribal authorities of the Bantustan era to reconstitute themselves through the legislation. In response, the incumbent minister of land affairs, Gugile Nkwinti, said that his department would not contest the judgment and would revisit the law (SABC News, 10 May 2010).

The May 2010 judgment brought to an end a protracted and highly contested process which started in the mid-1990s with attempts to devise a law that would address Section 26 (5) of the South African Constitution, which states that: 'a person or community whose tenure of land is legally insecure as a result of past racially discriminatory laws or practices is entitled … either to tenure which is legally secure or to comparable redress'. The debate was initially dominated by disputes between those who favoured individual, freehold tenure in communal areas and those who argued that communal tenure regimes should not be discarded because they offered flexibility and protection for the poor (Bernstein, 2005; Cousins, 2008). After four years of deliberation, a Draft Land Rights Bill was produced in 1999 that, as Weideman (2003: 321) suggests, 'tried to find a balance between giving people real and secure land rights, while recognising that in some areas traditional government works quite effectively and that it would be counterproductive to destroy functional systems'. The Bill stopped short of giving people ownership rights, proposing the idea of 'permanent rights' while also allowing for a system of 'common-hold' where groups took control of land collectively. In the conversion of the Bill into an Act the issue of individual rights was downplayed and a new version of community came to the fore, resulting in the court case against the Department of Land Affairs led by NGOs, land activists and rural communities.

We now need to ask what the setting aside of the law has meant for rural development and land reform in the former homelands. How long will it take for the minister of Land Affairs to reformulate the Act, and what will be the content of the new Act? Will the minister move away from a policy of titling communities towards a system of individualised forms of tenure and title? And how will land rights be managed? Is it conceivable and realistic that responsibility for land administration in communal areas can be taken away from traditional authorities? Do rural communities share Judge Ncgobo's view about the 'threat' of traditional leaders? Are local municipalities or other structures better equipped to manage land and rural development? And what if it was found that the relationship between rural people, traditional leaders and elected officials varied considerably across the country? What would the solution be then? Would it be possible to develop different legislative frameworks for tenure security and land management on communal land in the different provinces and regions? Furthermore, how can tenure reform be linked directly to development in rural areas? In short: is it possible to rewrite CLRA in such a way that it directly stimulates new investment, encourages development through new and innovative land use practices and helps to strengthen food security in rural areas?

In this chapter we engage with these issues by reflecting on the results of a study undertaken in 2007/8 in the Eastern Cape for the then Department of Land Affairs to establish the level of readiness of rural communities for the implementation of the CLRA. The study was concerned with rural livelihoods, land use and management practices, and the attitudes of rural households and stakeholders to tenure reform and to the CLRA in particular. It aimed to provide a rapid survey of a range of issues in the communal areas, and it involved research teams visiting households, traditional leaders and local authorities in thirty-five traditional authority areas in the former Ciskei and Transkei. The findings of the study were immediately embargoed by the Department of Land Affairs because of the ongoing court case against the CLRA, but now that the case has been resolved it is useful to reflect on this study and consider what its findings might mean for rural development and tenure reform.

One key finding was that traditional authorities remained firmly in control of rural land allocation across communal areas in the Eastern Cape, and that most rural households believed they should continue to play a dominant role in land allocation. It was also discovered that there was a strong demand at the household level for more permanent, individualised title to land within a system of 'commonhold', such as that imagined in the original Bill. Local residents were more interested in having their own rights to land endorsed than in securing those of the outer boundaries of their communities. Beyond specific tenure issues, the study showed that de-agrarianisation had reached alarming levels in the Eastern Cape with rural households intensely dependent on social grants for survival. Development in rural areas was found to be hampered by the mismanagement of development funds and by intense conflict and mistrust between traditional leaders and local authorities.

In this context, we found that the possibility of CLRA's being implemented was viewed by many as a potential 'game breaker', a mechanism that could not only bring additional resources into the rural areas but also unblock the political stand-off that existed between local authorities and traditional leaders. More than anything else, though, the study showed a deepening sense of disillusionment with the current format and content of rural development policy and practice. The most severe criticism was reserved for democratically elected local authorities and councillors attached to municipalities, who were widely presented as self-serving, disconnected and corrupt. Chiefs and traditional authorities, by contrast, were viewed in a much more positive light, as potentially helpful, consensus seekers, and desirable intermediaries in community development. We also encountered a school of thought that proclaimed that 'things were better' under Kaiser Matanzima and his Transkei National Independence Party (TNIP) than they are under the African National Congress (ANC). What should we make of these claims? Why do some rural residents, especially older ones, now remember the homeland era with such fondness? Do they not recall how the Matanzimas ruled with an iron rod and how they were bullied by 'decentralised despots' (chief and headmen) in the old tribal authorities? What was it about that time that provokes positive memories? Why do the rural poor of the Eastern Cape continue to support the ANC when, at the same time, they express high levels of dissatisfaction with government and development? Finally, what do the attitudes of the rural poor tell us about the reformulation of the CLRA and the reconfiguration of rural development in South Africa?

The first aim here is to reflect on the historical context of land management and cooperative governance in the Eastern Cape; the second aim is to present some of the main results of our 2007/8 enquiry into rural livelihoods and land use practices in the Eastern Cape; the third aim is to explore the current politics of nostalgia in the region by probing the deeper reasons and meanings that lie behind rural dissatisfaction with the state and its policies, its elected personnel, and its style of operation. In his book *Native Nostalgia*, Jacob Dlamini reminds us that 'the irony of nostalgia is that, for all its fixation with the past, it is essentially about the present' (2009: 16). The challenge, then, is to find an explanation for the current politics of nostalgia in the former Transkei. Why for example, is there a growing demand for chiefs and traditional leaders to play a more active role in development? Is this a sign of the re-emergence of ethnic nationalism? Do people really want to go back to Matanzima-style rule, where liberal democratic rights and privileges are limited? Is this a case of what Dlamini calls 'restorative nostalgia', or is it something more fragmented that has less to do with old social forms than with the current political style and the manner in which the state engages people on the rural fringes of the South African political economy?

We adopt a historical perspective that starts by analysing the origins of traditional authority control over land and the roots of cooperative governance in the Eastern Cape, before moving on to our recent Eastern Cape CLRA survey and the politics of nostalgia. We conclude with suggestions as to how the CLRA might be re-imagined as the department goes about the work of assembling a new Bill for the country and the province.

CLRA AND THE GHOST OF CECIL JOHN RHODES

The province of the Eastern Cape covers an area of 169 875 square kilometres and has a population of approximately 6.7 million, sixty-five per cent of whom are classified as rural. The most densely populated districts are those of the former Transkei, reaching as many as 93.9 persons per square kilometre in some districts. The Eastern Cape is, by most indicators, the province with the highest incidence of poverty in South Africa; it has the lowest mean monthly household expenditure, and forty-eight per cent of the population is classified as living in poverty. Approximately ten million hectares of land (fifty-nine per cent of the province) is in the hands of an estimated 6 500 commercial farmers, who employ approximately 70 000 farm workers. This land is used (in descending order of area) for sheep, beef cattle, mixed farming, dairy cattle and vegetable production (Bank and Minkley, 2005: 10). The rest of the land in the province, about five million hectares of it, is located in the former Ciskei and Transkei homelands. Almost all of this land is communally owned and has been held in trust by the state on behalf of its residents. Nationally, it is estimated that about fifteen million people live on communally owned land in the former homelands, about four million of whom live in the Eastern Cape (Koelble and LiPuma, 2011: 7). The aim of the CLRA was first to transfer this land into the hands of communities and then to explore the possibility of devolving title down to smaller groups and individuals. Now that the Act has been set aside, however, communal land will remain under the direct control of the state for the foreseeable future.

The communal lands of the former homelands were acquired by the state through warfare and colonisation in the nineteenth century. The territory known as British Kaffraria, which included the former Ciskei homeland, was annexed by the British in 1866. Six years later, full responsible government was established, resulting in the appointment of white magistrates to manage districts with between twenty and thirty African rural locations in each. Over the next twenty years, the Cape Colony extended its borders eastwards, finally reaching Pondoland in 1894. In the Ciskei and new Transkei territories, headmen were appointed in all the locations to work with magistrates to keep order, implement government policy and raise taxes. Headmen became lowly paid government officials and were advised locally by an *inkhundla*, consisting of adult men from the area (Southall and Kropiwnicki, 2003: 49–54; Hammond-Tooke, 1975: 43–6). In much of the former Ciskei and southern Transkei, where missionary activity was strong and traditional authority weak, the magistrates often appointed educated men to the headman position because they could help with administration and keep written records. But this was not the case in all areas, as Monica Hunter (1936 [1963]: 421) explained in the 1930s:

> Subordinate to the magistrate in each district, are headmen appointed and paid by the government. Those appointed as headmen at the annexation were usually the district chiefs and headman then in authority, and their places have in most cases been filled by their eldest sons or nearest male heirs. The government is anxious to have literate and progressive headmen, and may refuse to appoint the heir of a deceased headman if he is considered personally unsuitable, but the general policy is to appoint the heir of the last headman.

David Hammond-Tooke (1975) claims that the colonial position of headman was unlike the pre-colonial positions of *isiduna* (ward-heads) or *inkosana* (sub-chiefs) and was therefore given its own name, *isibonda* ('those who carry a pole') implying collaboration with the state. It seems that the model of governance with headmen was established first in areas where traditional leaders had been crushed, setting up a system of patronage where magistrates exercised considerable power (they were less powerful in areas where headmen had a strong and independent following). In the period prior to the 1930s, rural district councils were formed with representation from both local taxpayers and traditional leaders, creating an embryonic form of cooperative governance (ibid). Southall and Kropiwnicki (2003: 51) argue that the system at this stage actually undermined the power of chiefs by elevating headmen at their expense.

This all changed with the passage of the 1927 Native Administration Act which brought chiefs into the administrative system, giving them civil jurisdiction over disputes arising within their areas. It also placed the white governor general in the position of 'supreme chief' (Bennett 2004: 109). The governor general had full authority to create and divide tribes and to appoint any person he chose as a chief or a headman (ibid.). This change set in motion a process of designating new tribal areas within and beyond district boundaries; in fact, it marked a shift from the hybrid 'liberal' Cape tradition to a uniform system based on what is called 'Natal traditionalism', in which chiefs had always been more central to the colonial administration (see Southall and Kropiwnicki, 2003: 52). The Act laid the foundation for the Bantu Authorities Act of 1951, which further empowered chiefs and tribal authorities in the governance of communal areas. Headmen now reported directly to chiefs, who were accountable to tribal authorities that were in turn connected to regional authorities and territorial authorities as the homeland system evolved. In terms of land allocation, headmen still played a central role. But, with Bantu Authorities, headmen were prevented from allocating sites without the permission of the tribal authority. The new system provoked widespread resistance, some of which was actually led by dissident chiefs (Mbeki, 1964; Mqotsi, 1990; Mager, 1999; Ntsebeza, 2006; Redding, 2006), in the former Transkei and Ciskei.

Despite resistance, the Bantu authority system was swiftly accepted by traditional leaders in the Transkei in the mid-1950s, presumably because the new system placed much more power in the hands of chiefs and headmen, moving away from an earlier cooperative system where district councils advised the magistrates and native commissioners. The roots of the earlier mixed representation system lay in interventions by Cecil Rhodes, who feared that African voters from the newly incorporated Transkei territories would become too influential in the Cape parliament if an alternative system of representation was not found for them. This resulted in the Glen Grey Act of 1894, which proposed the district council system with representatives from elected as well as tribal structures, offering a kind of compromised democracy for Africans while at the same time keeping them off the Cape voters roll. This governance system evolved into the *amaBunga* council system that operated in the Transkei until the 1950s. The Glen Grey Act also advocated that African households be given individual title to land in communal areas to encourage economic development and a more liberal economic system (Hammond-Tooke, 1975: 83–5).

In some ways, then, the CLRA and the other Acts which surround it, such as the Traditional Leadership Governance Framework Act (TLGFA) passed in 2003, represent a return to the older colonial mode of cooperative governance advocated by Rhodes. In fact, in terms of the TLGA of 2003, new traditional councils were to be established in communal areas with sixty per cent of the representatives being tribal officials and forty per cent elected from the community. Overall, a third of all representatives had to be women. These new councils were imagined to play a critical role in the implementation of CLRA, as well as in other aspects of rural governance and administration. It is in some ways ironic, then, that Ntsebeza (2006) and others, such as Jara (2011), argue that the arrival of the CLRA and the TGFA marked a reactionary return to the 'tribal authority model' based on Natal traditionalism, when they actually reinvent the hybrid Cape model of rural governance that predated Bantu authorities. This is a crucial point for the understanding of the CLRA, which was conceptualised and imagined as part of a shift in policy (back) towards forms of cooperative governance. When the CLRA was enacted in 2004 it was part of a multilayered effort to affect a workable system of rural local government and land management based on a model first conceived by Cecil Rhodes, who wanted traditional leaders to come in as weak partners in a modernising colonial state. But how has the system come to work in the Eastern Cape? Have the new traditional councils actually been established since 2003, and do they play a role in land allocation?

TRADITIONAL COUNCILS, HEADMEN AND THEIR *AMAPHAKATHI*

In the latter half of 2007, we visited thirty-five traditional authorities and fourteen local municipalities in the Eastern Cape with a team of students from the University of Fort Hare, to assess the views of rural people on land, livelihoods and their readiness for the rollout of the CLRA. The results of our enquiry endorsed the court's finding that there was limited consultation at the local level concerning the legislation prior to its adoption in 2003. It also suggested that where communities were informed about the CLRA there was not an unequivocal rejection of the law. Many people who knew about the legislation actually said that they were eagerly awaiting the introduction of the CLRA because it would lead to more resources coming to their areas. They also said that it would enforce cooperation between elected leaders and traditional authorities and act as a way of *limiting the power of chiefs* in land allocation. Many felt that if the implementation of the CLRA was done properly it could help resolve the tension between traditional leaders and elected officials that prevented rural development from taking place (cf. Koelble and LiPuma, 2011; Williams, 2010).

By 2007, most traditional authorities in the Eastern Cape had already registered their traditional councils as required by the TLGF Act of 2003. The speed with which these councils were formed was reminiscent of the acceptance of Bantu authorities in the mid-1950s. Traditional leaders realised that it would be in their interest to form councils in order to get their hands on a larger share of the development action in their areas. The councils were registered with the department of local government and traditional affairs in the province. In most cases, the so-called elected representatives were simply appointed to the councils by traditional leaders. Descriptions of this process were remarkably similar to the way in which white magistrates allegedly constituted their councils during the colonial era. Many people complained that the so-called elected members on the councils were 'too close' to the chiefs and that the women on the councils were usually the 'wives and close associates' of traditional leaders. In the Gibisela Traditional

Authority, we heard that although women do attend traditional council meetings, their participation in deliberations was limited. The traditional council, we discovered, only started with 'serious business' once women had left. In parts of Pondoland, women were excluded entirely from attending the deliberations of the new councils. The argument made by male members was that women are not, traditionally, at liberty to question decisions of men in issues pertaining to custom. These observations confirm the objections raised by feminists who argued that the traditional councils and the CLRA would not necessarily benefit women in rural areas (Cousins, 2008; Walker, 2008).

Traditional councils were not fully functional in many areas we visited; they existed in name only and played little part in land allocation. Many people did not even know that they had been constituted, even though traditional leaders showed us the registration papers, and this meant that, in practice, land continued to be administered by headmen and their trusted advisors (*amaphakathi*). We found the process described for allocation of sites and arable land in 2007 almost exactly the same as that presented by Hammond-Tooke for the Transkei in the 1970s in which he states that headmen and chiefs allocated land to individuals and families following consultation with their *amaphakathi* or councillors, whom he described as follows:

> These councillors or *amaphakathi* (lit. 'those inside'), attained their position through personal qualities of loyalty and intelligence. One or two may have been councillors of the late chief; other boyhood friends of the present chief, whose advice and probity had been found valuable. They were sometimes referred to as *abahluzi*, 'sifters', stressing their function of sifting and evaluating evidence. Formerly they tasted the chief's food to guard against poisoning (1975: 175).

Our study revealed that it was not the traditional councils that controlled land in 2007, but local headmen and their *amaphakathi*. Of 2 045 households visited, ninety-three per cent said that chiefs or headmen were still responsible for allocating residential and arable land in their areas. Only three per cent said that land was allocated by elected ward councillors or other officials from the local municipalities. Local civics or residents' associations were said to control land allocation in less than one per cent of cases. In many neighbourhoods, sub-headmen (*iibhodi*) would make the allocations with advice from male elders. Land allocation was also still associated with gift-giving or payment of bribes, as was the case in the 1960s and 1970s. Generous gifts to the *isibonda* or *iibhodi* could influence the location, size and speed of a land transaction. It was not possible, we found, to secure land through a headmen without offering some gift. The vast majority of household heads understood the allocation system well and were reasonably happy with the way it worked. If gifts were paid and people were known to be locals, land was usually made available. Despite complaints about gift transactions, most householders said the system was more or less fair, but supported the idea that corruption and unfair land allocations needed to be monitored. This is where, some felt, the structures proposed by the CLRA had a role to play.

When asked who in their view *should* control the allocation of land in their areas, eighty-four per cent of households said that this responsibility should rest with traditional institutions, while twelve per cent said that local municipalities, civic bodies, [or] government departments should administer communal land. When residents were asked to respond to the statement that 'the current system for the allocation of land is fair and works well', seventy per cent of households endorsed the statement, while ten per cent were neutral and twenty per cent – mainly female-headed households – disagreed. The research showed that seventy-five per cent of the household heads had received their land from the tribal authority structures, twenty-three per cent had inherited their plots and the remaining three per cent either bought or rented them. The latter figure is quite low by comparison to other provinces, where more plots are bought, sold or rented. In the Eastern Cape, this practice is most prevalent on communal land on the fringes of the larger urban centres of East London, Mthatha and Queenstown. With over ninety per cent of households having accessed land through traditional authorities, it is not surprising that the traditional leaders we spoke to regard the allocation of land as an incontestable right and that some community leaders and municipal officials expressed the view that the CLRA would help curb the enormous power that traditional authorities wielded over land allocation.

What was also clear from our study was that men still dominated rural governance, including land allocation and administration, despite the fact that women constitute over fifty per cent of the rural population. Women did not have easy access to land in rural areas, especially if they were single. In most traditional authorities (TAs) married women were not allocated residential land in their own right. Married women were regarded as part and parcel of the male household and denied access to a separate plot for their own use. In almost all TAs married women were seen to 'access' residential land through their spouses. An *iphakathi* in one TA even stated that: *Hayi asizoze simnike umafazi othstileyo inxiwa lakhe, kaloku loo nto ingathetha ukuba siqhawula umthsato* (We cannot give an individual site to a married woman because this might mean we are breaking the marriage). Chiefs and headmen differed in their approach to the allocation of land to these women. Some accepted the need for women to independently access land, while others were more resistant to the idea. One headman noted that the practice of giving land to women is new and they are still in the process of learning to accept it hence there is no consensus even within his area. He stated that: *Kusenzima ke bantu bakarhulumente kwezinye iibhodi apha kwezilali zethu ukuyamnkela into yokunika oomama ingakumbi amantombi umhlaba, kodwa ke kule yam ilali sivumelene ukuba simnike umntu nokuba yintombi nje ukuba uneminyaka eyi 18 kwaye uyasebenza* (It is difficult for government people in some villages to give women or young girls land, but in this village we have agreed to give a woman a site if she is above eighteen years and is working). We generally found that once women had access to residential land in the village, they would qualify to apply for arable land which was often made available to residents after three years of settlement (if such land was still available in the area).

In areas where South African National Civic Organisation (Sanco) structures were in existence it was found that women generally had acquired land – and other rights – more easily, although in some of these areas women were allocated smaller pieces of land than their male counterparts. In most of the former Transkei, unmarried women had access to land provided they had children and provided they approached the traditional structures accompanied by male relatives who, it is assumed, would act as guarantors and negotiate on their behalf. There were very few instances where single women without children had access to land in communal areas. Access to arable land by women often depended on where and with whom they stayed. Local practices were quite diverse in this regard.

IDLE LANDS, RURAL LIVELIHOODS AND TENURE PREFERENCES

One of the most shocking findings of our 2007 survey was the very low level of participation of households on communal land in agricultural production. Fewer than two per cent of households in these areas said that they made their living from farming. There are complex debates about how, when and why de-agrarianisation occurred in the Eastern Cape, beginning with discussions of the 1913 Land Act and its impact on rural communities. But it is generally agreed that the 1950s were watershed years and that the rural revolts against Bantu authorities and betterment planning in the region represented final gestures of resistance from the collapsing peasantry to inevitable proletarianisation (Mbeki, 1964; Mayer, 1980; Delius, 1996). What happened after this is usually depicted as a steady and progressive decline into poverty and cash dependence for rural households in the former Transkei and Ciskei (Simkins, 1981). What is less well understood is how rapidly this decline occurred during the homeland era and how much the absence of a rural development strategy after apartheid has aggravated the situation.

There are conflicting reports on how different aspects of the agrarian system have responded to change. Ainslie (2005), for example, argues that livestock numbers in the communal areas of the Eastern Cape are today at similar levels to those of the 1930s and that they have remained much more constant than the literature indicates, suggesting that the linear decline thesis might need to be revisited, at least to accommodate drought and variations in climate. On the crop production side, Andrews and Fox (2004) argue that the critical shift from field production to reliance on household gardens coincided with the growth of migrant labour in the apartheid years. But McAllister (2001) points out that the abandonment of fields did not necessary mean reduced homestead output as gardens were now expanded and used more intensively than fields. It seems possible to conclude that, while less maize from the homestead sector reached the market during the homeland era, the output of households might not have fallen quite as much as analysts predicted. In trying to maintain rural production, tribal authorities and local agricultural officers played a critical role in securing access to resources such as seed, dip, tractors and even fertilisers for homesteads, through their networks into the homeland state and its agricultural services (Gibbs, 2010). Access to this sort of support depended on the quality of local-level social relations, as well as the ability of chiefs and local officials to extract favours within local patronage networks. Many chiefs still wanted to be respected by their people and did what they could to ensure that they could maintain a role as patrons in their communities.

In the Transkei, Matanzima knew that if people did not continue to produce food to survive he could face rural revolt. He encouraged people to produce crops, insisting that the Transkei was fundamentally an agrarian country that needed to be food secure, and he supported families on the land, even in difficult circumstances. He also placed agricultural production at the core of the rural development strategy for the homeland. Since the end of apartheid, agricultural extension services have fallen away and the focus has shifted to a urban-centred service delivery model where 'the poor', as a generic category, are seen to require the same basic services, namely square houses, on-site domestic taps, flush toilets and electric lights. The modalities of rolling out these services have also made development a largely technical affair which is less reliant on interaction and participation from locals. Although the framework for service delivery stresses the need for 'civic engagement' and citizen empowerment it is well known that sessions with communities are infrequent and mainly focus on what they are being given rather than on what they want or need. Most basic services are delivered on a once-off basis, in any case. In essence, it is a top-down model that has been very largely focused on urban communities; even in rural municipalities most of the delivery has gone into the small towns. By ignoring rural areas and the agrarian needs of its rural subjects, the ANC has greatly accelerated de-agrarianisation in the former Transkei and other areas over the past fifteen years, perhaps doing more to undermine homestead production than forty years of gruelling apartheid planning had done. Through the removal of agricultural extension services, the disempowerment of tribal authorities as development agencies, and relegation of the rural poor to a non-agrarian constituency, the Transkei countryside has been urbanised in ways that are plain to see. RDP-style houses are popping up everywhere as the rural economy flounders and households shift their focus from production to a low-level consumption lifestyle based on grants and on free land and services.

This general change was clearly revealed in our household survey, which found that by 2007 forty per cent of households said that they had no access to land anymore, while fifty-two per cent claimed to have access to household gardens (usually less than half a hectare in size) and twenty-four per cent said that they had access to a field (of, usually, between one and three hectares). Of the twenty per cent of households that had access to arable fields of between one and three hectares, fewer than five per cent used this land on a regular basis. In most communal areas, unused fields were not generally reallocated to other households which were able and willing to use them and traditional authorities did not place pressure on households to 'use their fields' or 'lose them'. Gardens were more frequently used, and crops grown in gardens and fields were seldom sold on the market. Production was for own consumption and sometimes for village-level exchanges. In relation to livestock, we found that about forty per cent of households still had access to cattle, and slightly fewer had access to goats and sheep. The average number of beasts owned by cattle owners was seven, but the majority of owners only held between one and four animals (the high average was partially caused by urban entrepreneurs and businesspeople running large herds in the location, although they no longer lived there permanently, and we noted that this created severe pressure on communal grazing areas).

So how did locals view tenure security and reform? The results showed that household tenure security was not generally under threat in communal areas. There were high levels of residential stability in most of the communities surveyed: seventy-three per cent of the households interviewed said that they had always lived in the same settlement, and a further twelve per cent had grown up in another village in the same tribal authority area. Data from interviews with traditional leaders indicated that 'outsiders' were easily identified and generally only granted access to residential plots if they could provide a letter of recommendation from their chief or headman in the area from which they came. Families seeking land were expected to offer a beast as 'a token of appreciation' (*urhafa*) to stimulate the negotiation process with traditional leaders (mostly headmen). But despite the fact that very few households felt threatened or insecure on the land, there was a very strong demand for individualised title and most households said that they were less concerned about confirming the 'outer boundaries' of their communities than getting legal papers proving that they owned the land on which they lived. They wanted 'happy letters' like people in the city got, saying that they were the rightful owners of their houses and land. Part of the reason for this demand might be related to the fact that only a third of rural households in the Eastern Cape have the old permission to occupy (PTO) certificates indicating their right to the land while a further twenty per cent had letters or other documents associating their families with the land they occupied, and this meant that almost half the residents on communal land in the Eastern Cape had only verbal commitments from tribal authorities giving them the right to occupy land.

RIVAL CHIEFTAINCIES: TRADITIONAL LEADERS AND LOCAL COUNCILS

In 2000, Jeff Peires wrote that the introduction of a new democratic local government system, which denied traditional leaders a developmental role in rural service delivery, was creating considerable conflict and confusion in the former Transkei. Prior to the local government elections in 2000, Thabo Mbeki had rejected a central role for traditional leaders in rural local government. In a 1998 White Paper it was proposed that elected and traditional leaders should cooperate in governing rural areas, but that the mandate for development should be left in the hands of elected officials (Peires, 2000; Southall and Kropiwnicki, 2003: 71). So while chiefs and headmen control land allocation in communal areas, elected officials in the new municipalities are responsible for development planning and delivery through the construction of an integrated development plan which is supposed to be devised in consultation with local citizens. In the Tsolo and Qumbu districts, where Peires worked in 1999, he detected intense hostility between traditional leaders, who mainly supported the Bantu Holomisa's United Democratic Movement, and newly elected municipal councillors, most of whom were members of the ANC. He wrote:

Numerous attempts have been made to bring the chiefs and councillors together. Each blames the other side for mutual hostility. The chief says that the councillors deliberately by-pass and ignore them. The councillors say that chiefs continue to cling to the undemocratic old order where they did what they pleased. The bottom line, however, was well expressed by one of the Langa royal family of Tombo at a meeting with the MEC for local government in September 1999: 'The chiefs and the councillors are fighting over the people' (Peires, 2000: 110).

By the late 2000s, the ANC had eradicated United Democratic Movement (UDM) opposition in the Transkei by combining a strategy of co-opting chiefs with enlarged benefits and stipends on the one hand, and ensuring that rural households had easy and regular access to social grants on the other. By 2007, over seventy-five per cent of rural households in communal areas had access to one or other monthly grants from the state. Our 2007 survey found that fifty-one per cent of households reported cash income of less than R1 100 a month, where the largest part of household income was clearly derived from social welfare grants and pension payouts. The figure below provides an estimate of household income levels in communal areas in 2008.

Figure 1: Estimated monthly household income (CLRA Survey, 2008)

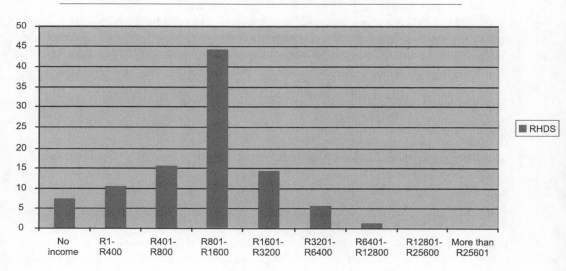

Households in these areas were much more dependent on grants than they were on local employment, migrant remittances or agricultural production. Grants were associated with the ANC and did much to consolidate the ANC's rural power base. In fact, in the run-up to the 2011 local government elections, grants were used as a political tool, with the ANC informing its rural support base that opposition parties would not honour the grants the ANC had provided. Local chiefs are also careful not to be too outspoken against the ANC lest they lose their increasingly cushy perks, which some say is a pay-off for keeping quiet (*Daily Dispatch*, 14 February 2011).

These developments, however, have not diluted the intense rivalry and competition between elected councillors and traditional leaders at the local level and the demise of the UDM has actually done little to dampen the mutual disregard of chiefs and councillors for each other. In many areas, traditional leaders deliberately make it difficult for elected officials to enter their domains, and frustrate development at the local level. It is equally common for municipalities and councillors simply to ignore the tribal authority areas. From the point of view of villagers, elected councillors seem to exist in splendid isolation of rural realities, appearing arrogant, aloof and distant. One villager explained that 'the municipality really does not care for the people out here, they are only interested in developing the towns'. Another stated: 'Look at the housing that is being developed in the towns, the flush toilets and electricity they get. Here we get nothing.' One man depicted municipal officials as drive-by developers, people who 'occasionally passed through the district in government cars with other officials' in tow, but 'never stopped to ask local people what they wanted or needed'. Another respondent said that elected councillors behaved like 'urban chiefs' who preferred cars to cattle. This image of local municipalities as disconnected, urban-style chieftaincies where the mayors, senior officials and their town-based *amaphakathi* call the shots and dispense favour to enrich themselves, is common in the rural areas.

Stripped of their former powers, chiefs have tried to present themselves as conciliators, interpreters of grievances and consensual leaders. Evidence collected on the CLRA project suggests that the ordinary people in the villages want traditional authorities to play a larger role in development in the rural areas. It appears that the grassroots popularity of traditional leaders, and the fond memories locals now have of traditional leaders and the Matanzima years, has more to do with their exclusion from local government than anything else. As Southall and Kropiwnicki (2003: 78) have noted, 'if chiefs are to recover their legitimacy, it is less likely to be the result of mixed government, than … because of their exclusion from power'.

The literature on rural local government usually explains the tension between traditional leaders and local municipalities in terms of a clash of incompatible systems of government – a modernist, liberal version in collision with a traditionalist reactionary form (Mamdani, 1996; Ntsebeza, 2006). Neoliberalism is often blamed for the poor performance of local municipalities because they are said to be cash starved by a stingy, urban-centred state that leaves rural municipalities with 'unfunded mandates' and a nonexistent tax base (Ruiters, 2011; Koelble and LiPuma, 2011). The logical response of local councillors would be to turn their back on service delivery to avoid the trap of increasing debt and dysfunction but they have done quite the reverse and have chased development funds by marketing the poverty of their districts and localities to donors, the central fiscus and the provincial government. Significant resources do flow down into the region from the centre and they are invested in all kinds of projects and programmes, many related to poverty relief, infrastructural development and integrated development, making their way to or through rural local and district municipalities. The provincial budget is also always in some sense an equity budget in the Eastern Cape, since it tries to build political consensus by ensuring that everyone gets a piece of the pie. By contrast, traditional authorities do not have the same access to public funds and lack power in the places where funds are located. While there can be no doubt that neoliberal forms of government have left their mark on the region, more money is flowing into the rural areas from state coffers than is often acknowledged.

But our point here is about *governmentality*, understood as the culture and style of governance and the expectations of the governed. In local practice and understanding, rural municipalities in the Eastern Cape are perhaps better understood as urban chieftaincies, as suggested above, than as resource-squeezed modernist, Weberian bureaucracies. They are not accountable in any real democratic sense to their constituencies and are still locally based patronage machines which, unlike the old rural chieftaincies, circulate resources and opportunities to urban residents (as services) and elites (as tenders), rather than the rural poor. Networks of inclusion and exclusion block out rural people on communal land – which brings us finally to what we have called the politics of nostalgia.

THE POLITICS OF NOSTALGIA

In the rural Transkei, we encountered a deepening sense of nostalgia, reflected in some of the extracts quoted at the start of this chapter, where people in communal areas now look back to the Matanzima years as 'better times'. When one objectively compares what rural households have received from the ANC and what they were given as subjects of the Transkei state, it is clear that they are better served by the ANC than the TNIP. In those days, there were no regular social grants and monthly pensions for the aged and the needy; there was limited access to electricity or to communal taps; and there were fewer schools and clinics in rural areas. So why, when new household and community services have been delivered and grants have taken the edge off desperate poverty, do some families think back to the homeland era with such fondness? One obvious reason is that most men of working age were employed then as migrants and were able to send home remittances on a monthly basis. People recall how Matanzima advocated education and literacy for all and said that no child who completed matric in the Transkei would be denied a job in his bureaucracy. Today, they observe that there are no jobs, not even for matriculants. This exclusion of the rural poor from the labour market has generated a profound sense of betrayal, even though many of those who were employed were exploited as migrant labourers or as cheap labour in border industry sweatshops (Bank and Minkley, 2005). One woman explained that 'even our children, who travel to the cities in search of work, sit in shanty towns for years without work, sending back nothing'. 'We only see them again', another women said, 'when they are sick or come back in coffins', concluding that they missed the old days when there was a rhythm to rural life, a clear sense of the comings and goings of household members and the income that would come from remittances at the end of the month.

The second sense in which many we spoke to felt more connected in those days was in their relationship to the state. Tim Gibbs (2010) has argued that the Matanzima regime was predicated on a locality politics, where different localities were made to compete with one another for favours and resources. It was a state that encouraged a kind of tribal authority 'boosterism' in which good localities were rewarded and bad ones punished. In this system, those who resisted, as the Ntsebeza (2006) book on the Xalanga district shows, got next to nothing. Gibbs's argument is that during the Matanzima years the homeland state and the tribal authority system operated as a patronage machine, not merely as a mechanism for elite enrichment and class formation (Southall, 1982; Streek and Wicksteed, 1981). It is clear to us that, while Matanzima eliminated his opponents and promoted his own interests, he was also deeply concerned about his political popularity at the grassroots level inside the Transkei, and viewed himself as a patron chief who filtered down state resources and agricultural services to the rural poor through projects and the tribal authorities. The state provided deserving communities and projects with tractors to plough, fertiliser to plant, dip for cattle, and other resources. Local chiefs and headmen acted as intermediaries in this system. Rural areas were also conceived of as agricultural spaces where development initiatives were locally organised and often implemented with the participation of local people. With rural municipalities operating at some distance from the everyday lives of rural people, it is not surprising that people want development to have a human face again, where known gatekeepers and go-betweens deliver goods and connect local people to the state. The return to traditional leaders as beacons of hope is a direct product of the failure of the current municipal development model.

The third factor driving the politics of nostalgia relates to what one might call the social 'thinning out' of rural places. Kolb (2008: 72) makes a distinction between dense and diluted spaces, where dense spaces have multiple layers of memory, routine and shared experience, while diluted spaces tend to be defined by single-stranded relations and a certain shallowness of experience. He associates diluted spaces with American theme-parks such as Disneyland and goes on to suggest that a place is 'historically dense insofar as its social norms involve reference to a history that has been sedimented', but emphasises that social density is not just a matter of age or tradition. It ultimately depends, he argues, on how the marks of 'sentiment and age are taken up into the contemporary texture of action in place' (2008: 73). The fact that many of the social norms of tradition that relate to agrarian practices no longer operate in rural areas in the Eastern Cape has certainly contributed to a dilution of place. Another key aspect of this experience has been the collapse of the village general dealer store. In the 1950s, the general dealer stores scattered across the Transkei were centres of community life, where people gathered to buy and sell maize; to find out about local rituals, beer drinks and jobs; to meet friends; to collect post; and to get their weekly supplies. In the 1960s and 1970s, these stores were handed over to new Xhosa entrepreneurs, who continued the tradition, making them places of social density and significance in the countryside, and they remained incubators of social networks and service provision until the 1990s when large-scale, national retail capital penetrated the region and sank the stores, pushing their customers into Shoprite, Spar and Build-It on the main roads of Idutywa, Butterworth, Mount Frere or Mthatha (Du Toit and Neves, 2008). This loss of sociality at the store and in other public social spaces around the locations has helped to thin out locations and villages as social spaces, contributing to the general sense of nostalgia for what has been lost.

The experience of household life has also been diluted by the persistent out-migration from the rural areas, which has continued to gain momentum during the 2000s. The Eastern Cape is now defined as the province with the highest rural out-migration rate in the country (ECSECC 2010). The average size of rural households has shrunk steadily over the past fifteen years as young men and women have headed for the towns and cities. Many still stay behind in the rural areas, but their brothers and sisters are no longer at home – they have their own shacks in the towns or cities and phone and 'sms' their siblings and friends, encouraging them to follow suit. The experience of household life has changed during this time. It is much quieter at home, and life is more focused on occasional events, such as funerals and rituals, and the periodic visits of missing household members. Families regroup at home at Christmas and Easter time to socialise and reconnect with kin, initiation mates and friends before heading off swiftly for the cities. When they leave, people say that the homesteads and the locations feel empty and deserted, 'socially barren', as if frozen, until the absentees return for another period of conspicuous consumption, socialising and customary interaction. In this mode, rural households and locations seem remarkably similar to Kolb's description of 'themepark-type social spaces', places of single-stranded relations, where custom is performed rather than lived and where people no longer feel connected in complex overlapping, multistranded social relations. This sense of social emptiness and domestic entrapment, in the in-between times, provoked many to recall better times in the past, when the homestead had a 'sense of purpose' and people were 'busy with productive activities'. People complained that rural life was boring and isolated, suggesting other reasons for urban migration besides lack of economic opportunities at home.

This image of the Eastern Cape as a 'themepark' is reinforced when one reads in the press of the endless squabbles and politicking among Xhosa kings and paramount chiefs over land, the ranking of chiefs and the recognition of new kingdoms and great places in 'Xhosaland'. These disputes are fuelled by chiefly prestige and the government stipends in the regional House of Traditional Leaders (George, 2010), while at the local level this politics circulates as African pride and is reformulated by traditionalist intellectuals such as Chief Patekile Holomisa, as hidden histories of identity that have been denied by colonialism and more recently quashed by the ANC's post-apartheid fascination with Western modernity. The local Department of Arts and Culture has developed projects that seek to reify local tribal histories and cultures into heritage products, about which the Comaroffs (2009) argue that ethnic identities in South Africa are being refashioned as commodities to be sold as heritage, fashion or tourist products which circulate in capitalist markets with minimal returns for local people who become complicit in the reconstruction of their own identities. The Comaroffs conclude that local people buy into what they call 'Ethnicity Inc' because their rural economies are so depleted that they have little other option. In the communal areas of the Eastern Cape, capital investment in tourism is limited and cultural villages are few and far between; even local beadwork and garments circulate mainly within the village economy. The cultural tourism sector has thus not had the kind of impact it has had in KwaZulu-Natal, where 'Zuluness' is for sale everywhere, or in the Cape where ethnic entrepreneurs have fashioned a multitude of products around San and Bushman identities. So, while these forces feed into the changing notions of Xhosa identity, they are seemingly not nearly as influential here as in other parts of South Africa and have little impact on everyday identity politics in the region.

In our observations, re-engagements with tradition in rural villages and locations where 'sentiment and age are taken up into the contemporary texture of action in place' (Kolb, 2008: 73) is most evident in the contemporary politics of death and misfortune in the communal areas. The toll of HIV and AIDS on rural households in the Eastern Cape has been enormous, as Steinberg's (2008) work in Pondoland shows, and our latest figures suggest that something like one in three households now buries family members in the rural locations every year (Bank and Kamman, 2010: 10). These practices have had a major impact on the flows of people and resources into rural homesteads that are seemingly now endlessly preparing for the next ritual. As rural areas reshape themselves into ritual landscapes, soaking up family capital and emotional resources, they ask new questions of community and identity. The social economy of death, as argued more fully elsewhere (Bank, 2009: 15–20), tests social networks and commitments, while reconnecting people to localities, reconfirming who they are, where they come from and where they will choose to die. Rituals, as McAllister (2006) demonstrates in the Transkei context, always pose fundamental questions about belonging to places, clans and kinship groups. The social thinning or hollowing out of households as a result of migration and de-agrarianisation is being counteracted by the social and symbolic economy of death, which reinscribes the rural landscape and infuses tradition with meaning. To be sure, tradition in this everyday sense is constructed and owned by all those who live in these places, and is constantly being reworked to suit local needs – cows are no longer slaughtered for certain rituals because they are too expensive, beer replaces brandy and chickens are sacrificed in the place of goats. In acknowledging death, men and women also reassert their relationship to place and to other people through narratives of belonging that invoke chiefs and ancestors. The feelings of loss and trauma that cuts across the Eastern Cape, touching almost every family, provoke their own politics of nostalgia, of longing and loss, where the time before AIDS is associated with social wholeness, coherence and cohesion in their lives. It is in this context that the social power and presence of tradition and chieftaincy has come to stand for continuity and integrity, suggesting processes that go beyond what the Comaroffs (2009) call Ethnicity Inc.

CONCLUSION

There has been a shift in attitude in favour of traditional leaders in rural governance in South Africa since the late 1990s when Mbeki left no space for their involvement in local-level development. The Zuma administration has pushed cooperative governance and policies that see traditional leaders playing a larger developmental role in future. Cynics argue that this shift has been necessitated by the neoliberal agenda which has found traditional leaders to be a more cost-efficient and politically secure means of controlling the excluded rural poor than democracy and real development. From this point of view, Judge Ngcobo's decision on the CLRA is good news because it will block traditional authorities from going back to the bad old days of 'decentralised despotism'.

In this chapter, we have seen how women are denied rights to land and how male traditional leaders work with their *amaphkathi*, by-passing the limited democracy of the traditional councils, to exclude community participation so there is no evidence to suggest that traditional authorities would have used the Act as an invitation to share their power unless they were forced to do so. However, at the same time it is clear that local authorities in the Eastern Cape are not doing their jobs and are ignoring the plight of the rural poor. Government departments, rather than local municipalities, are credited with having delivered something to the poor whereas, ideally, there should be functional, cooperative governance structures at the local level, where land could still be formally allocated through traditional structures but with appropriate checks and balances to ensure that rural people's constitutional rights are protected in the process. For local people to have more power in these interactions, there needs to be a much stronger emphasis on confirming permanent, individualised rights and entitlements to land, to keep the collective forces in check and to allow households a stronger sense of agency in crafting their own livelihoods and futures. Local people should be able to use their land as an asset to raise collateral and develop their homesteads as they desire. The power of the collectives, tribal authorities, government departments and local municipalities, has generated struggles 'over the people', as Peires (2000) puts it, but also over the heads of local people, who feel disconnected from participation in their own futures. Rural residents either feel a sense of passive entitlement (which limits agency) or view themselves as victims or objects of development, rather than as participants in development. This sense of social exclusion, we have argued, is one of the central driving forces behind the politics of nostalgia.

Jacob Dlamini (2009) makes the distinction between restorative and reflective nostalgia, where the latter engages the past with fondness without wanting to return there, and the former yearns for the restoration of something that has been lost. We found that the two forms exist more as a continuum than as clear opposition in the former Transkei. We would also want to emphasise that expressions of nostalgia were certainly not confined to a handful of old men, as is sometimes alleged, and were quite widely and critically expressed in the rural areas, even by women. But does this mean that the rural people are drifting away from an allegiance to the ANC and shifting back into ethnic nationalism? Our argument is that what people are expressing through nostalgia is essentially not a desire for a return to the old ethnic nationalism of the Matanzima regime because if this were the case it would be very difficult to explain why there is in the Eastern Cape such widespread support for Zuma, the current South African president of Zulu ethnicity. Nor is it simply a call for chiefs to resume the all-powerful position they had under apartheid. In the 1970s, Hammond-Tooke (1975: 123) tried to defend the institution of chieftaincy in the Transkei against anti-apartheid detractors by suggesting that traditionally:

> The Cape Nguni chief was never a despot. As we have seen he could not generally go against the wishes of his people, he could not move faster than the pace of the majority of his tribesmen. He was always a conservative element, the interpreter, the upholder of tradition, seldom a legislator. He was only in rare, and sometimes spectacular, instances an initiator of social change.

His work stressed that the command mode of chiefly power and control in the Transkei in the 1970s was at odds with older cultural narratives of the role and function of this institution in society. In this chapter, we have suggested that, even in the 1960s and 1970s, chiefs did not completely jettison the desire to satisfy local expectations of them as facilitators, patrons and leaders through consent. The use of state resources to fulfil this function, we argue, has been underestimated in the critical scholarship of rural class formation in the Bantustan era. In the late 2000s, in a context where traditional leaders lack formal power, we have suggested that they have reinvented themselves, and have been reinvented, as community builders, consensus seekers and essential intermediaries between state and society (Koelble and LiPuma, 2011; Holomisa, 2010). It is precisely their exclusion from a clear developmental role within the state, as Southall and Kropiwinicki (2003) suggest, that has allowed them to regain credibility after apartheid. One would, however, also want to be very careful, given the history of the Eastern Cape, not to underestimate the continued power of Africanist politics, identities and ideologies in rural areas and to recognise the difficulties an urban-centred ANC has historically faced in winning popular support in the Transkei. As the opening quote from the well-known Transkei lawyer and anti-apartheid activist, Mda Mda suggests, Matanzima's version of ethnic nationalism and African self-reliance was not without local support in the former Transkei. Many more believed, as Mda Mda went on to state, that 'riding with the devil' (the white regime) was a better way of 'getting to the other side' than fighting against it. None doubted that Matanzima was a genuine Xhosa nationalist who saw no role for whites in the longer-term future of his region, and many liked this message after a century of being bullied by white magistrates, native commissions, policemen and agricultural officers. Others felt that genuine liberation required a broader pan-African nationalism. The truth be told, the ANC has always been much weaker and more vulnerable in the rural Transkei than the party and its pundits would have us believe and this is precisely why the populist Africanism of a figure like Zuma is so critical in shoring up ANC support in the region today. Zuma's support for chiefs and chieftaincy, as was Mandela's before him, is based on a keen understanding of the political constituency and ecology of this region.

The real problem for rural development in the Eastern Cape is that there are currently no enabling narratives of cooperative governance and productive rural development for the region. One of the critical differences between the Eastern Cape and KwaZulu-Natal is that cooperative governance has never effectively worked in the former Transkei or Ciskei where there are very few cases in which traditional leaders and democratically elected officials have worked together around common problems. The history of the *amaBunga*, with its limited functionality as an experiment in cooperative governance, is forgotten in a way that the cooperative structures established by the Inkatha Freedom Party in KwaZulu-Natal are not (Williams, 2010). What people remember in the Eastern Cape is the oppositional politics between chiefs and democratically elected structures of the 1980s – and also the anti-betterment struggles of the 1960s, which continue today in the lingering conflicts between traditional authorities and local government. The current scholarship on the region reflects this divide, with authors either being intensely opposed to traditional leaders (Ntsebeza, 2006; Jara, 2010) or strongly in favour of them (Holomisa, 2010). Finding a cooperative system for people-centred development in which Africanists and democrats can work together remains a fundamental challenge for the region. The new comprehensive rural development programme, with its emphasis on participation and local-level cooperation, provides a potential template for new efforts to be made in this regard (Kariuki, 2010), but in reality the conflict between traditional leaders and local authorities in the Eastern Cape is making meaningful development impossible. It has become a yoke around the neck of the rural poor that is weighing them down. One way of removing it is to loosen the control chiefs have over land and to increase their involvement in development, where they have a positive role to play, while at the same time making local government more accountable in rural areas.

What people at the local level seem to desire is for rural development to be *re-socialised* in new ways – but they also want the state to come up with meaningful plans and projects for rural economic development rather than merely taps and toilets. The inability of local and district municipalities to construct clear, production-orientation integrated development plans – and to implement them – has meant that there has been no locality-specific vision for *rural* development. This has to change, and it is not a job that should be outsourced to consultants; it must be done with very high levels of local involvement and with clear commitments to fund local agendas.

In conclusion, then, the politics of nostalgia is essentially a response to social exclusion and the difficulties people face in connecting to the state and to each other. For the state to address this concern it must reimagine the practice and content of rural development, creating visions for improvement that are embedded in relations of cooperation at the local level. If a return to decentralised despotism is to be avoided, new kinds of local democratic projects, social movements and institutions, depending less on the old subject-citizen divide than on building development from below in novel and cooperative ways, will have to be built in the Eastern Cape.

REFERENCES

Ainslie A (2005) Farming cattle, cultivating relationship: cattle ownership and politics in the Peddie District, Eastern Cape *Social Dynamics* 31 (1): 50–68.

Andrews M and R Fox (2004) Under-cultivation and intensification in the Transkei: A case study of historical changes in the use of arable land in Nompa, Shixini. *Development Southern Africa* 21 (4): 687–706.

Bank L (2002) Beyond red and school: Gender, tradition and identity in the Eastern Cape. *Journal of Southern African Studies*, 28 (3): 34–56.

Bank L (2009) 'Between the *umzi* and the *ndlu*: Land, livelihoods and the ritual economy of death'. Unpublished paper, African Studies seminar, University of Stanford.

Bank L (2011) *Home Spaces, Street Styles: Contesting Power and Identity in a South African City*. London: Pluto Press.

Bank, L and E Kamman (2010) *Changing migration patterns and basic service delivery in the Eastern Cape*. Eastern Cape Socio-economic Trends Series, Vol. 3, Fort Hare Institute of Social and Economic Research (FHISER), University of Fort Hare.

Bank L and G Minkley (2005) Going nowhere slowly? Land, livelihoods and rural development in the Eastern Cape, South Africa, *Social Dynamics*. 31, 1: 1–38.

Bennett T (2004) *Customary Law in South Africa*. Cape Town: Juta.

Bernstein A (2005) *Land reform in South Africa: A 21st century perspective*. Research Report 14, The Centre of Development and Enterprise, Johannesburg.

Comaroff J and J Comaroff (2009) *Ethnicity Inc*. Chicago: University of Chicago Press.

Cousins B (2008) Contextualising the controversies, dilemmas of communal tenure reform in post-apartheid South Africa. In Classens A and B Cousins (Eds) *Land Power and Custom: Controversies generated by the Communal Land Rights Act*. Cape Town: UCT Press.

Daily Dispatch newspaper (various editions)

Dlamini J (2009) *Native Nostalgia*. Johannesburg: Jacana.

Delius P (1996) *A Lion amongst the Cattle*. Johannesburg: Ravan.

Du Toit A and D Neves (2008) *Vulnerability and social protection at the margins*. Working Paper, Institute for Poverty, Land and Agrarian Studies (PLAAS), University of the Western Cape.

Eastern Cape Socio-Economic Consultative Council (ECSECC) (2010) *Eastern Cape fact sheets*, East London: Eastern Cape Government.

Gibbs T (2010) From popular resistance to populist politics in the Transkei. In Beinart W and M Dawson (Eds) *Popular Politics and Resistance Movements in South Africa*. Johannesburg: Wits University Press.

Hammond-Tooke D (1975) *Command or Consensus: The Development of Transkei Local Government*. Cape Town: David Philip.

Holomisa, Chief Patekile (2010) *According to Tradition: A Culturalist Perspective on Current Politics*. Somerset West: Essential Books.

Hunter M (1936 [1963]) *Reaction to Conquest: Effects of Contact with Europeans on the Pondo of South Africa*. Oxford: Oxford University Press.

Jara M (2011) *Ubukhosi, amalungelo*, democracy & rural development: A return to tribal authorities? Seminar paper, University of Fort Hare, 24 March 2011.

Kariuki S (2010) The Comprehensive Rural Development Programme (CRDP): A beacon of hope for rural South Africa. In Daniel J, P Naidoo, D Pillay and R Southall (Eds) *New South Africa Review 1*. Johannesburg: Wits University Press.

Koelble T and E LiPuma (2011) Traditional leaders and the culture of governance in South Africa. *Governance: An International Journal of Policy, Administration and Institutions* 24 (1): 5–29.

Kolb D (2008) *Sprawling Places*. Athens: Georgia University Press.

Mager A (1999) A *Gender and the Making of a South African Bantustan: A Social History of the Ciskei*, 1945–1959. Oxford: James Currey.

Mamdani M (1996) *Citizen and Subject: Contemporary Africa and the Legacy of Colonialism.* Oxford: James Currey.

Mayer P (1980) The origins of two rural resistance ideologies. In P Mayer (Ed.) *Black Villagers in an Industrial Society.* Cape Town: Oxford University Press.

Mbeki G (1964) *South Africa: Peasant's Revolt.* London: Penguin.

McAllister P (2001) *Building the Homestead: Agriculture, Labour and Beer in South Africa's Transkei.* Aldershot: Ashgate.

McAllister P (2006) *Xhosa Beer Drinking Rituals: Power, Practice and Performance in the South African Rural Periphery.* Durham, NC: Carolina Academic Press.

Mqotsi L (1990) *House of Bondage: A Novel of Collaboration in South Africa.* London: Karnak House.

National Department of Land Affairs (2008) *Report on Communal Land Rights and Rural Livelihoods in the Eastern Cape.* Unpublished report compiled by the Fort Hare Institute of Social and Economic Research, East London.

Ntsebeza L (2006) *Democracy Compromised: Chiefs and the Politics of Land in South Africa.* Cape Town: HSRC Press.

Peires J (2000) Traditional leaders in purgatory: Local government in Tsolo, Qumbu and Port Saint John's, 1990–2000. *African Studies* 59, 1: 97–114.

Redding S (2006) *Sorcery and Sovereignty: Taxation, Power and Rebellion in South Africa, 1880–1963.* Athens: Ohio University Press.

Ruiters G (Ed.) (2011) *The Fate of the Eastern Cape: History, Politics and Social Policy.* Scottsville: UKZN Press.

Simkins C (1981) Agricultural production in the African Reserves of South Africa, 1918–1969, *Journal of Southern African Studies* 7 (2): 256–83.

South African Broadcasting Corporation (SABC) News (various editions).

Southall R (1982) *South Africa's Transkei: The Political Economy of an 'Independent' Bantustan.* London: Heinemann.

Southall R and Z De Sas Kropiwnicki (2003) Containing the chiefs: The ANC and traditional leaders in the Eastern Cape, South Africa. *Canadian Journal of African Studies* 37 (1): 48–82.

Streek B and R Wicksteed (1981) *Render Unto Kaiser: A Transkei Dossier.* Braamfontein: Ravan.

Steinberg J (2008) *The Three Letter Plague.* Cape Town: Jonathan Ball.

Weideman M (2003) *Land Reform, Equity and Growth in South Africa: A Comparative Analysis.* PhD Thesis, Department of Political Science, University of the Witwatersrand, Johannesburg.

Walker C (2008) *Landmarked: Land Claims and Land Restitution in South Africa.* Athens: Ohio University Press.

Williams M (2010) *Chieftaincy, the State and Democracy: Political Legitimacy in Post Apartheid South Africa.* Bloomington: Indiana University Press.

CHAPTER 7

South Africa and 'Southern Africa': What relationship in 2011?

Chris Saunders

South Africa is the only African country to take the name of a geographical part of the continent, and therefore it is customary to speak and write of 'Southern Africa' to distinguish the region from the country formed in 1910. Those who founded the Union of South Africa chose that name for the country in part because they expected the Union to expand to embrace much, if not all, of the southern half of the continent. In the event, the expected expansion of South Africa to the north to incorporate, at a minimum, Southern Rhodesia and the then High Commission Territories of Basutoland, Bechuanaland and Swaziland, did not happen, and what is now Namibia was never formally annexed, so the boundaries of the South Africa of 1910 remain today virtually the same as they were then (Chanock, 1997; Hyam, 1972).[1] Nevertheless, the history and prospects of South Africa remain closely bound up with those of the neighbouring countries in the region of which it is part, and for that reason the first number of the *South African Review*, published in 1983, began with a section on 'South Africa and Southern Africa' (South African Research Service, 1983).

Long before 1910, people living in the area encompassed by the state called South Africa had been involved, in many different ways, with those living further north in Africa, not least through the extensive migrant labour routes that criss-crossed the continent. Such ties continued, and were extended, after 1910. For a decade, from the late 1970s, South Africa engaged in a war of terror against its neighbours to try to prevent largely ANC-aligned guerrillas based in those countries from undertaking operations in the struggle to end the apartheid regime. The death and destruction wreaked on the region by apartheid South Africa in that period stands as one of the lesser acknowledged crimes of the twentieth century. The Truth and Reconciliation Commission's final report found that this campaign of military aggression 'constituted violations of the sovereignty of the countries involved and an infringement of the principles of international law' (TRC, 1998: Vol. 2, 154). Since 1994, a quite different set of relations has developed between South Africa and 'Southern Africa', and it is some of these that this chapter explores.

THE RELATIONSHIP OVER TIME

If, in early 2011, one accessed the website of South Africa's Department of International Relations and Cooperation (Dirco) to find out about South Africa's relations with the countries of the region, one read the following:

> Since 1994 the South African government has regarded the Southern African region as the most important priority of its foreign relations. To illustrate the importance attached to this region, the first foreign policy document adopted by this government was in fact a 'Framework for Cooperation in Southern Africa' approved by Cabinet in August 1996. In terms of this 'Framework', our vision for the Southern African region is one of the highest possible degree of economic cooperation, mutual assistance where necessary and joint planning of regional development initiatives, leading to integration consistent with socioeconomic, environmental and political realities.

Reading on, however, one noticed, with surprise, mention of restructuring 'expected to be completed by December 2002', and then that the webpage as a whole had not been updated since 2004.[2] What has happened to South Africa's interest in the region since then?

Soon after Thabo Mbeki became president in 1999, it became clear that his focus was continental rather than regional and that he wished to promote his own version of Kwame Nkrumah's pan-African dream. Reflecting this, much of the recent academic literature on 'South Africa and Africa' has discussed South Africa in relation to Africa as a whole, or at least the rest of sub-Saharan Africa, blurring the distinction between 'Southern Africa' and the rest of the continent (for example, Solomon, 2010).[3] Such an approach is justified when, say, South Africa's participation in the African Union (AU) and its institutions such as the Pan African Parliament or the AU's Peace and Security Council are analysed. It is justified when, say, the economic ties between South Africa and countries north and south of the equator, or South Africa's politico-military involvement in Burundi, the DRC, Darfur and Sudan are examined.[4] The potential importance for South Africa of the creation, in recent years, of a continental African security and institutional architecture, or (as will be mentioned below) the beginnings of sub-regional consolidation, should not be discounted, but South Africa's interests surely lie – as the official statement from the Dirco website suggests – more in relation to the countries next to it, or relatively nearby, than further afield.

What, then, is South Africa's 'neighbourhood'? How is 'Southern Africa' to be defined? There are different ways to answer these questions. In 2011, 'Southern Africa' is often thought of in terms of the Southern African Development Community (SADC), possibly the most important regional organisation to which South Africa belongs. The development of a tightly knit SADC bloc has been conceptualised by some as a step towards eventual continental unity. Since 1997, SADC has included the Democratic Republic of the Congo (DRC), so that in this usage the region reaches from Cape Town to north of the equator. And besides the DRC, SADC includes the island countries of Mauritius, Madagascar (since March 2009 suspended from membership) and the Seychelles, which rejoined SADC in 2008. While its geographic extent is impressive, the downside is that because SADC is made up of countries that differ so greatly in size, history and political and economic systems, it is, as a regional grouping, too large and amorphous for there to be close ties between all its states – or even for them to agree on common policies. When SADC launched arguably its most important project of the past decade, the free trade agreement of August 2008, Angola and the DRC did not sign on.

Whether the sprawling DRC, or Tanzania, or the countries that lie in the Indian Ocean should be in SADC at all may be queried, for they have close ties with countries in other regions, as indicated by their concurrent membership of other regional organisations, most notably the Common Market for Eastern and Southern Africa (Comesa) and the East African Community (EAC).[5] The DRC, Malawi, Mauritius, the Seychelles, Zambia and Zimbabwe are all members of both SADC and Comesa, while Tanzania is a member of both SADC and the EAC. South Africa chose to be only a member of SADC but has in recent years been one of the main drivers of the idea of a free trade area that would join the SADC countries with those in Comesa and the EAC to form a twenty-six-state bloc that would cover half the entire continent (Madakufamba, 2008).[6] Such a goal is, in 2011, far from realised, and such a tripartite sub-regional grouping is even more amorphous than SADC. While this larger grouping may be seen as a way to deal with the problem of overlapping membership, the logic of the arrangement is not clear. Does South Africa necessarily have closer ties with the countries on the eastern half of the continent than the western, other than those that go back to the history of British colonial expansion and even to the Cape to Cairo dreams of Cecil Rhodes?

A glittering new SADC headquarters was officially opened, with much fanfare, in Gaborone in November 2010, but SADC as an organisation is cumbersome and unwieldy, with an inefficient bureaucracy – and it is poor in its public relations. Anyone who has tried to find material on its website will be acutely aware of its inadequacies, and key SADC officials are often almost impossible to contact. Not surprisingly, some academic commentators have referred to SADC as 'sad' SADC (Vale and Sachikonye, 2010), or even as a joke.[7] But, on the other hand, one commentator has called it 'Africa's most successful regional community', the most efficient and effective of the regional economic communities in Africa (Ford, 2010: 52). It may be that, but this is not necessarily a strong commendation, given the competition. While it may well be true that it is better to have SADC than not to have it, precisely what value does it add to bilateral relations between its component countries?

Effective regional institutions are not, of course, created overnight. It took decades for the European Community to become the European Union (Phinnemore and Warleigh-Lack, 2009). SADC did, however, choose to refer to its 2010 summit as its thirtieth jubilee one, even though it was the Southern African Development Coordinating Council (SADCC) that was born in 1980, not SADC itself, which did not come into existence until 1992. The organisation might well have done better not to have emphasised three decades of existence, for there is all too little to show for having existed for so long.

In the 1980s, the main concern of SADCC and its *de facto* ally, the Frontline States group, was bringing down apartheid rather than regional integration. In pursuit of the latter, SADC has, since 1992, produced a set of ambitious goals but the bulk of them remain unrealised and most of its many protocols remain unimplemented in any real sense. The SADC Standby Force, envisaged as part of a continental African standby force, was launched with some fanfare in August 2007 in Lusaka, Zambia, and was supposed to be operational in 2010, but is still bedevilled with many problems, not least of interoperability between very different armed forces (Mandrup, 2009; Cilliers and Potgieter, 2010; Franke, 2010). And instead of using limited resources to make existing institutions more effective, there is talk in SADC of adding new ones, most recently a SADC parliament. This was proposed by the current chair, Namibia, at the August 2010 SADC summit in Windhoek, and explored further at a SADC meeting at the Victoria Falls in November 2010 (Musemwa, 2010).[8]

SADC has a history of deep divisions. South Africa and Zimbabwe contested the status of the SADC Organ on Politics, Defence and Security Cooperation (OPDS) in the 1990s; Zimbabwe, Namibia and Angola sent their armies to the DRC in 1998 when other SADC countries opposed such military intervention; and the South Africa-Botswana military incursion into Lesotho that year was only retrospectively given a SADC imprimatur. Militarily this was an inept operation which resulted in numerous casualties, but it did set in motion a process of negotiated constitutional reform to prevent the almost ritualistic infighting that accompanied elections conducted under the old 'first-past-the-post' electoral system (Southall, 1999).

Zimbabwe is of course, the prime example of SADC's failure as an organisation to take decisive action when a member country becomes, in effect, a failed state because of the tyrannical rule of its leader. When SADC's judicial institution, the Tribunal, which began work in Windhoek in November 2005, issued a judgment in the case of *Mike Campbell vs. the Republic of Zimbabwe*, challenging the expropriation of agricultural land in that country by its government, Zimbabwe rejected the judgment and refused to compensate the farmers concerned (*The Zimbabwean*, 2010; Cowell, 2010). Then SADC itself, at its 2010 heads of state summit, decided to review the role and functions of the tribunal to ensure that it did not 'overstep its jurisdiction' and this has, in effect, rendered the tribunal toothless (see for example *Southern Africa Today*, 2010).[9]

While SADC has occasionally wielded suspension of membership as a threat, the suspension of Madagascar's membership, and then the mediation of the former president of Mozambique, Joaquim Chissano, to try to restore constitutional normality in that island nation, had by the end of 2010 achieved nothing, for the SADC mediated agreement of November 2009 was ignored by the government of Andry Rajoelina; it went ahead with its own constitutional referendum, and in early 2011 it remains in power.[10]

The reality is that, for all the talk of regional integration, bilateral relations between SADC states are often more important than intra-regional ones, the political will to cede any sovereignty to SADC is not there, and the economic and other national interests of individual SADC countries still trump such commitment as they have to the regional project. How long, one wonders, will the EU and other international donors, who largely fund SADC's many meetings, put up with SADC's failure to deal effectively with the Zimbabwean and other crises? The Windhoek summit in August 2010 called on Western countries to lift sanctions on Zimbabwe – as if that would help resolve the situation in that country! Past experience suggests that SADC will not be able to ensure that the Principles and Guidelines Governing Democratic Elections that it adopted in August 2004 are observed in the Zimbabwe election expected to be held in 2011 or 2012, for SADC was not able to prevent violent election-related conflict erupting in Zimbabwe in 2008.

For all its weaknesses, however, SADC clearly has some uses. Not only does it hold out the prospect of eventual regional integration but it has practical application in, say, the way it promotes regional development corridors and transfrontier conservation areas.[11] Ordinary residents in SADC countries may benefit from, for example, the common standards that SADC has recently set for digital television (Marais, 2010a), or the preferential rates for SADC residents at certain game parks (*Southern African Times*, 2010). Students from the SADC region pay far lower tuition fees at South Africa's universities than non-southern African foreign students, and, in most cases, the SADC students acquire a superior training to that available to them in their own universities and colleges. The Southern African Power Pool, which operates under SADC's umbrella, is, by one assessment, 'the most successful example of regional energy sector cooperation in Africa' (Ford, 2010: 54).[12] And SADC gives South Africa useful cover to hide behind: when asked why South Africa is not taking action on Zimbabwe, President Zuma has often said that it is an issue for SADC as a whole to deal with (see for example *New Age*, 2011).

TOWARDS A MORE EFFECTIVE RELATIONSHIP

While SADC may be seen as a building block for eventual continental integration, should the first step not be to build the blocks that will eventually create a more effective SADC? In the remainder of this chapter I shall be concerned with a narrower concept of 'Southern Africa' than that of SADC, one that more closely resembles the concept in the first *South African Review*. In other words, I focus on aspects of the relationship between South

Africa and what might be called the core or inner periphery of other southern African countries: the former British High Commission territories that became Botswana, Lesotho and Swaziland (the BLS states); Zambia; Zimbabwe; Namibia; Mozambique and Angola.[13] (Whether Malawi, the only black-ruled state now in SADC to have had diplomatic relations with apartheid South Africa, should be included in this core group may be argued, but its relations with South Africa now are not as close as South Africa's relations with the other countries in the core group, in part because of its role in the apartheid era. By early 2011, President Mutharika had not paid an official state visit to South Africa under President Zuma, even though he had been AU chair for a year.)

When the first *South African Review* was published in 1983, the story of South Africa and the countries of the southern core zone was mainly one of brutal destabilisation for, unlike Malawi, they all suffered attacks from apartheid South Africa. The first *Review* did, however, include a piece on the way in which some of these neighbouring countries (including far-removed Tanzania, because of its role in hosting the Organisation of African Unity's Liberation Committee and its past support for Frelimo in Mozambique and other liberation movements) had combined into a new organisation, then called SADCC (Jaffee, 1983). Three decades later, the story of South Africa and the core Southern Africa states is of course dramatically different. South Africa's destabilisation – which included, in its most extreme form, the war that South Africa fought in southern Angola from 1975 to 1988 – ceased with the ending of apartheid, and with the advent of democracy in 1994 South Africa became a member of SADC. As the official Dirco statement quoted above suggested, Southern Africa as a region became a key priority for South Africa's foreign relations. Until that time South Africa had exerted its military power to dominate the region; from the early 1990s the question became the form its new role in the region would take. Would it continue to dominate, and if so, in what ways?

In 2011, South Africa still has the strongest military force in the region, now equipped with some highly sophisticated weaponry, although the effectiveness of the South African National Defence Force has been queried, so much so that it has been suggested that it would not be able to deal with the Zimbabwe army if South Africa were ever to invade that country. And of course South Africa still dominates the region economically. While Angola now has the third largest economy in sub-Saharan Africa, thanks largely to its oil, and while Botswana, Namibia and Zimbabwe have extensive mineral deposits, only South Africa has an extensive commercial agricultural sector and a significant manufacturing base as well as such deposits, and South Africa produces over sixty per cent of the region's gross domestic product (Draper et al., 2010: 1).[14] And South Africa dominates not only because of its advanced economy but also because it has a global presence quite different from that of any other country in the region, in part because of its history of moving from apartheid to democracy in the early 1990s. In 2011, South Africa is again a non-permanent member of the United Nations Security Council and that it has now been invited to join the BRIC (Brazil-Russia-India-China) group of countries is largely because of its dominance in the region and its potential as a gateway into the rest of

Africa. It can be argued that the gap between South Africa and most of the other states in the core region has not shrunk in recent years but grown.

It may be that South Africa's awareness of its dominant position has been one reason why, in recent years, it has not wanted to be seen to be focusing more attention on its immediate neighbourhood. Other countries in the core region have not forgotten how the apartheid regime destabilised them before 1990, even if in 2011 the idea of reparations by South Africa for destabilisation – initially sought especially by Angola post 1994[15] – is no longer talked about. And though suspicions of South Africa remain alive, both for its historic role in the region and its present economic dominance, there are common bonds, especially among the liberation movements now in power in South Africa, Namibia, Zimbabwe, Angola and Mozambique. In these countries (unlike in Zambia and Malawi, where the political parties that came to power at independence and could claim to have played the key role in achieving that status have long since been removed from office), the movements that emerged victorious at the end of armed struggles are now in government. Although the armed struggle was not the main cause of apartheid's collapse, all these governments, including South Africa's, claim legitimacy, at least to some extent, from their roles in armed struggles, and view themselves as the 'sole and authentic' representatives of the people of their countries.[16] It may not be stretching things too far to say that an 'old boys' club' of liberation struggle veterans controls the core region.

The relatively small BLS countries, which moved to independence without armed struggles, have relatively little weight. Since independence they have had very different histories: in Botswana one party has dominated the political scene for almost as long as the forty-six years that the National Party ruled South Africa; Lesotho has had a history of coups and political tensions; and in Swaziland a brief immediate post-independence flirtation with the Westminster system of multiparty democracy gave way to an absolute monarchy which remains in place after nearly forty years. Despite Swaziland's open collaboration with the apartheid regime in the 1980s and its betrayal of many leading ANC leaders and cadres, post-apartheid South Africa has cosseted the despotic and deeply corrupt Swazi monarchy, and it would be true to say that apartheid's collaboration with the Swazi monarchy has been more than matched by South Africa's post-apartheid rulers. When President Ian Khama of Botswana stepped out of line on Zimbabwe, showing his support for Prime Minister Morgan Tsvangirai in his battle with President Robert Mugabe, pressure was exerted to bring him back into line with the spineless SADC consensus, in the making of which South Africa took the lead.

Another regional organisation links South Africa, the BLS countries and Namibia: the Southern African Customs Union (Sacu). In 2010, Sacu celebrated its centenary and proudly said that it was the oldest customs union in the world. South Africa has always dominated Sacu, from which it has greatly benefited. In recent decades, however, South Africa has subsidised the other members (which from 1990 included Namibia), and lately it has been demanding that Sacu's revenue-sharing formula should become more equitable. This is already having a negative impact on the smaller countries, especially Swaziland, which is virtually bankrupt (Bertelsmann-Scott, 2010). Ignoring the concerns of the majority of members in Sacu, South Africa under Thabo Mbeki went ahead unilaterally in forging new trading arrangements with the outside world, in 1999 signing its own Trade Development and Cooperation Agreement (TDCA) with the EU. And in recent years, the countries in Sacu have been divided over the issue of the Economic Partnership Agreements (EPAs) that the EU wanted to sign with them, to bring trading relations into line with World Trade Organization (WTO) requirements.[17]

The EPAs led to such new tensions that for a time the very continued existence of Sacu seemed in doubt. When, after November 2008, the EU approached Sacu countries individually, Botswana, Lesotho, Mozambique and Swaziland saw it to be in their economic interest to sign interim EPAs. South Africa and Namibia, on the other hand, refused to sign such agreements,[18] with South Africa insisting that any new trade agreement to replace the TDCA should deliver additional benefits, in particular in regard to trade in agricultural products.[19]

In the course of 2010, however, the Sacu countries began to work more closely together. Although the deadline of the end of 2010 for an agreement with the EU was not met, South Africa's minister of Trade and Industry, Rob Davies, said in December 2010 that he was hopeful a unified position would soon be reached and a final regional EPA agreement would be signed by mid-2011 (Van der Merwe, 2011).[20] When Davies had worked as an academic at the *Centro dos Estudos Africanos* (Centre for African Studies) at Eduardo Mondlane University in Maputo, Mozambique, he and his colleagues had argued for closer regional ties on a non-hegemonic basis, and while he remains a cabinet minister it is unlikely that South Africa will undermine the larger interests of the region. With SADC's goal of achieving a customs union in 2010 not met, and not likely to be met for a long time to come, the new idea advanced by South Africa is to enlarge Sacu to include at least some of the other countries in the core region.

In his first year in office, President Zuma devoted much more attention to South Africa's neighbours, including Angola, than had his predecessor. This was in part because Mbeki had been so focused on his continental ambitions and in part because of Zuma's personality and his own involvement in the liberation struggle in the region. The first international visit of his presidency was to Angola, where *Umkhonto we Sizwe* had been based until 1989 and where he was warmly received by President Jose Eduardo dos Santos, who reciprocated by making, in December 2010, his first state visit to South Africa since 1994. And when President Rupiah Banda of Zambia made a state visit to South Africa in the same month, President Zuma emphasised the close ties that had existed between South Africa and Zambia since the ANC had had its exile headquarters in that country. By the end of 2010, Zuma had visited almost all the core states since becoming president – some of them a number of times.[21] And as the SADC-appointed facilitator to deal with the problems thrown up by the coalition government formed as the result of the earlier SADC mediation of Mbeki, he played a special role in relation to Zimbabwe.

As long as Zuma is president, then, South Africa seems likely to return to the vision set out in the official statement issued soon after 1994, and to focus particularly on the

Southern African core, with liberation credentials and other ties helping to cement rela-tions between these countries. There would seem to be good reasons for such a focus, rather than on countries further away in Africa, even if the continuing Zimbabwe crisis keeps eating away at the potential for the economic development of the core states. It seems unfortunate that this focus was lost for much of the period since 1994, for it would surely have been more advantageous for South Africa if the African Renaissance Fund (now being transformed by South Africa's Dirco into the South African Development Agency) had prioritised projects in the country's neighbourhood, rather than in far away West Africa, as happened during Mbeki's presidency (Games, 2010).

IN CONCLUSION

SADC as now constituted is too large and diverse and too politically supine to be an effective sub-regional organisation. It has failed to respond at all adequately to the state violence in Zimbabwe. Though it is hardly likely that the Southern African region as a whole will 'dissolve' 'as a result of Chinese involvement and other alternatives to regional integration presenting themselves' (Martin, 2008:131), South Africa should pay greater attention to its relations with the countries of a smaller core of neighbouring states. Because they are close neighbours, the impact of developments in any one of them has a direct and immediate impact on the others, as seen, for example, by the flood of Zimbabweans into Botswana and South Africa in recent years. Present-day relations with these states are shaped in part by past relations, including South African destabilisation in the 1980s and more recent deep divisions relating to South African hegemony in the region. It seems, however, that such divisions are now a fading memory, and that South Africa is overcoming its hesitation at being seen to dominate the region (cf. Landsberg, 2003; Alden and Le Pere, 2009).

The core region may today appear relatively peaceful and stable (at least compared to many other parts of the continent, even with Swaziland collapsing into bankruptcy (Hall, 2011) and state violence again taking hold in Zimbabwe), but there is of course the potential for further instances of violent upheaval within one of the states in the region or for future intra-state conflict – let us say between Botswana and Namibia for scarce water resources, or resulting from xenophobic attacks on the citizens of another SADC state. Liberation struggle veterans cannot remain as heads of governments in the more important states for much longer, and the transition to a new generation of leaders may bring instability, even if the liberation parties themselves remain in power. Intra-regional migration flows between the countries of this core are likely to increase in the future, especially as a result of the impact of climate change, but also possibly as a consequence of economic collapse in one of the component countries. The more effective regional integration of the core countries in the southern part of the continent, whether through an enlarged Sacu or in some other way, could help to deal with the advent of failed states, economic decline or the consequences of major natural disasters. South Africa's relations with other countries in Southern Africa, however that is defined, are bound to remain fluid and changing, and it is important for these changes to be studied and made known to an informed public. The relationship between South Africa and the rest of Southern Africa deserves closer academic and other attention than it has been given to date, for no detailed and continuing work has followed Peter Vale's pioneering attempt to consider that relationship (Vale, 2003). This chapter has only been able to touch briefly on some of the issues but it may help to provide a springboard for more sustained and comprehensive research in future.

NOTES

1   Walvis Bay, the best natural harbour along the Namibian coast, was annexed by the British and then transferred to the Cape Colony. It therefore became part of the new united South Africa in 1910. The South West Africa People's Organisation always argued that Walvis Bay belonged to Namibia but it remained South African territory when Namibia became independent in March 1990. It was only during the multiparty negotiations in South Africa that it was decided that it should be transferred to Namibia, and this happened at the end of February 1994. After Nelson Mandela became president, South Africa agreed to write off Namibia's debt, incurred when it had been a *de facto* colony of South Africa.

2   http://www.dfa.gov.za/foreign/Multilateral/africa/sadc.htm, (accessed 22 January 2011).

3   South Africa has built a museum in Timbuktu, Mali, to preserve ancient manuscripts. President Mbeki's pan-African ambitions were rooted in a long history of a pan-Africanism strand within African nationalism. Most of the essays in Adebajo and Landsberg (2007) concern South Africa's relations with Africa north of the neighbouring states; the only one to focus explicitly on Southern Africa is K Matlosa's, 'South Africa and regional security in Southern Africa'.

4   In 2010, for example, South Africa was chair of the AU Committee on Post Conflict Reconstruction and Development in Sudan.

5   An example of confusion: the map highlighting the SADC countries on the cover of Cawthra (2010) does not include the DRC.

6   A Tripartite Summit in October 2008 in Kampala, Uganda, 'agreed on a programme of harmonisation of trading arrangements amongst the three RECs [Regional Economic Communities], free movement of business persons, joint implementation of inter-regional infrastructure programmes as well as institutional arrangements on the basis of which the three RECs would foster cooperation.' The then SADC chairperson and South African president, Kgalema Motlanthe, said the region 'believes the time has come for Comesa, Mesa, EAC and SADC to bring together our respective regional integration programmes in order to further enlarge our markets, unlock our productive potential, increase the levels of intra-Africa trade, and enhance our developmental prospects.' A second tripartite summit was to have been held in 2010 but did not take place. It is now expected in 2011.

7   Ian Taylor of St Andrews in discussion with the author in Oxford in August 2010. One of the best studies of SADC is Derblom and Hull (2009).

8   Such a parliament was proposed by the SADC Parliamentary Forum, first established in 1997, which held its 28th plenary assembly from 29 November to 4 December 2010 in Swakopmund, Namibia.

9   The SADC tribunal did rule, on 9 December 2010, in *Gondo and 8 others vs. the Government of Zimbabwe* (case no SADC (T) 05/2008) that the government of Zimbabwe had violated the SADC Treaty by failing to compensate the applicants for organised violence and torture, but there was no sanction if such a ruling was ignored.

10   An extraordinary SADC summit held in November 2010 in Gaborone, at the same time as the official opening of the new SADC headquarters, resolved not to recognise the referendum held in Madagascar on a new constitution but did nothing to give effect to this decision beyond calling for the establishment of a SADC mediation office in Madagascar. On the background see Cawthra, 2010. My thanks to Andre du Pisani for giving me a copy of this document.

11   For the way regional development corridors and spatial development initiatives may boost economic growth see, for example, Mutambara (2009) and Caholo (2010).

12   South Africa, for example, imports electricity from the Cahora Bassa hydroelectric scheme in Mozambique, and exports it to Namibia and other neighbouring countries.

13   This is called 'the HCTs and an outer periphery' in Daniel et al.(2003) p. 369.

14   Flemes (2009) says that South Africa's GNP is twice that of the rest of SADC: p. 141.

15   The need for reparations from South Africa was stressed to me by the first Angolan ambassador to South Africa after 1994, Kito Rodriques, in an interview I had with him c1995.

16   'Sole and authentic' comes from the UN General Assembly resolution relating to Swapo of Namibia. For the assertion of a similar idea in the ANC see Suttner (2011).

17   Until the end of 2007, African, Caribbean and Pacific countries traded with the EU under the Cotonou agreement, a preferential agreement not in line with WTO rules.

18   Namibia did provisionally initial an EPA. The SADC EPA group was originally made up of Angola, Botswana, Lesotho, Namibia, Mozambique, and Swaziland, with South Africa an observer, but South Africa became an active negotiating party in February 2007.

19   South Africa opened eighty-one per cent of its agricultural market to EU imports, but the EU opened only sixty-one per cent of its market to South African exports. (Marais 2010b).

20   One of the sticking-points was the Most Favoured Nation clause that would force signatories to extend trade preferences negotiated with other countries to the EU.

21   He visited Namibia in April 2010 (mainly on Sacu business), in August for the SADC summit, and again in November for bilateral discussions. He visited Lesotho in August and Mozambique in October.

REFERENCES

Adebajo A and C Landsberg (Eds) (2007) *South Africa in Africa. The Post-Apartheid Era.* Scottsville: UKZN Press.

Alden C and G Le Pere (2004) South Africa's post-apartheid foreign policy: From reconciliation to ambiguity?, *Review of African Political Economy*, Vol 31. (100): 283–197.

Alden C and G Le Pere (2009) South Africa in Africa: Bound to Lead? *Politikon: South African Journal of Political Studies*, 36 (1), April: 145–170.

Bertelsmann-Scott, T (2010) *SACU – One Hundred Not Out: What future for the Customs Union?* Johannesburg: SA Institute of International Affairs, Occasional paper 68 (September).

Caholo JS (2010) Status of Regional Integration in the SADC Region. http://www.un.org/africa/osaa/speeches/SADC_Presentation_18Oct2010.pdf

Cawthra G (2010) *The Role of SADC in Managing Political Crisis and Conflict. The Cases of Madagascar and Zimbabwe.* Maputo: Friedrich-Ebert Stiftung.

Chanock M (1997) *Unconsummated Union.* Manchester: Manchester University Press.

Cilliers J and J Potgieter (2010) The African Standby Force. In U Engel and J Gomes Portes (Eds) *Africa's New Peace and Security Architecture. Promoting Norms, Institutionalizing Solutions.* Farnham: Ashgate.

Cowell F (2010) The Suspension of the Southern African Development Community Tribunal: A Threat to Human Rights. www.polity.org (accessed 3 November 2010).

Daniel J, V Naidoo and S Naidu (2003) The South Africans have arrived: Post-apartheid corporate expansion into Africa. In J Daniel, A Habib, and R Southall. (Eds) *State of the Nation, South Africa 2003-2004*. Cape Town: HSRC Press.

Derblom M and C Hull (2009) Abandoning frontline trenches? Capabilities for peace and security in the SADC region, Available at http://www2.foi.se/rapp/foir2768.pdf.

Draper P, S Kiratu and C Samuel (2010) The role of South African FDI in Southern Africa. Berlin: German Development Institute, Discussion paper 8/2010.

Flemes D (2009) Regional power South Africa: Cooperative hegemony constrained by historical legacy'. *Journal of Contemporary African Studies* 27 (2) April.

Ford N (2010) SADC: Africa's most successful regional community, *New African*, November 2010: 51.

Franke B (2010) Steady but uneven progress: The operationalisation of the African Standby Force. In H Besada (Ed.) *Crafting an African Security Architecture*. Farnham, Surrey: Ashgate.

Games D (2010) Renaissance fund's random spending should be more strategically focused', *Business Day*, 13 December.

Hyam R (1972) *The Failure of South African Expansion 1908–1948*. London: Macmillan.

Jaffee G (1983) The Southern African Development Coordination Conference (SADCC). *South African Review I*. Braamfontein: Ravan.

Landsberg C (2003) Hegemon or pivot: Debating South Africa's role in Africa, http://www.sarpn.org/documents/d0000620/P611-Pivotalstate.pdf (accessed 5 February 2011).

Madakufamba M (2008) Giant step toward a single SADC-COMESA-EAC market, *SADC Today*, 11 (3), December.

Mandrup T (2009) South Africa and the SADC Standby Force. *Scientia Militaria: South African Journal of Military Studies*.

Marais J (2010a) Digital TV standards up in the air, *Sunday Times*, 28 November.

Marais J (2010b) EPAs high on EU-Africa agenda, *Sunday Times*, 28 November.

Martin WG (2008) South Africa's imperial futures: Washington Consensus, Bandung Consensus, or People's Consensus, *African Sociological Review*, 12 (1).

Musemwa M (2010) SADC parliament on the cards, *ZimEye*, 25 November.

Mutambara TE (2009) Regional transport challenges within the Southern African Development Community and their implications for economic integration and development. *Journal of Contemporary African Studies*, 27 (4) October.

New Age (2011) President Zuma speaks his mind, 13 January, p. 11.

Phinnemore D and A Warleigh-Lack (Eds) (2009) *Reflections on European Integration. 50 Years of the Treaty of Rome*. Basingstoke: Palgrave Macmillan.

Solomon H (2010) South Africa in Africa: A case of high expectations for peace. *South African Journal of International Affairs*: 131–7.

South African Research Service (SARS) (1983) *South African Review 1: Same Foundations, New Facades?*. Braamfontein: Ravan.

Southall R (1999) Settling old scores: From authoritarianism to dependent democracy in Lesotho. In Daniel J, R Southall and M Szeftel (Eds) *Voting for Democracy. Watershed Elections in Contemporary Africa*. Aldershot: Ashgate.

Southern African Times (2010) SADC Breakaway Deals, 25 November, p. 7.

Southern Africa Today (2010) 12 (6), October, p 4.

Suttner R (2011) The National Democratic Revolution, *Business Day*, 12 January.

The Zimbabwean (2010) SADC called to act, 12 August, p. 5.

Truth and Reconciliation Commission (1998) Truth and Reconciliation Commission Report, Volume 2. Cape Town: Juta.

Vale P and T Sachikonye (2010) Sad SADC lacks the creativity to serve its people, *Business Day*, 25 November.

Vale P (2003) *Security and Politics in South Africa. The Regional Dimension.* Boulder, Colorado: Lynne Rienner.

Van der Merwe C (2011) Davies sees SADC trade deal with Europe by mid-2011. www.polity.org.za. (accessed 6 January 2011).

ECONOMY AND SOCIETY

2

Continuing crises, contradictions and contestation

Prishani Naidoo

The chapters in this section provide a glimpse into the complicated, difficult and contested worlds of policy making and the implementation of policy (and laws) in an economy and society that continue to be characterised by high levels of racialised inequality, unemployment and poverty. Through analyses of the ongoing crisis in childcare in South African public hospitals and an experience of street-level policing in a South African township, some insight is gained into the relationship between economic choices and social outcomes; into the difficulties of government; and into the very real ways in which existing social relations and meanings, and/or problems and tensions at the level of communities and groups can contribute to how laws and policies are able to be enforced and implemented. The remaining chapters hone in on different economic models and choices that have been adopted and made post-1994, looking at their successes and failures or potentials for success, from different forms of cooperatives, to black economic empowerment, to strategies for decent work currently being experimented with by national government in the form of community work programmes, and proposed in the New Growth Path (NGP). Individually and together, the chapters in this section confirm that problems such as the crisis in healthcare and conflicts between communities and police are both 'social' and 'economic', requiring approaches that bring together 'social' and 'economic' solutions. Recent debates about economic policy and its social effects are also shaping the political realm, with Cosatu and the ANC Youth

League differing with the ANC on the New Growth Path and prospects for nation-alisation respectively.

Haroon Saloojee's chapter on the crisis of childcare in South African public hospitals opens a window onto a catastrophe facing the entire health system, a crisis explained to be the result of 'a national healthcare system designed to prioritise treatment over prevention'. This crisis is one characterised by 'rampant diseases such as HIV/AIDS and tuberculosis; excessively high maternal and child mortality; poorly motivated health professionals; shut-down of critical units in hospitals; and perennial shortages of vitally needed supplies and equipment'. Acknowledging the contribution of apartheid poli-cies and practices to this crisis, Saloojee offers an in-depth assessment of attempts at implementing policies aimed at addressing these problems in relation to child health since 1994. He argues that while 'excellent child health policies now exist, there has been less success in transforming these into measurable actions and outcomes'. While funding for primary healthcare has increased substantially since 1994, for example, it has not produced improvements in healthcare for children. Saloojee demonstrates how, in many cases, money has been spent on the development of infrastructure rather than on enhancing care and service delivery for children directly, and often too few resources (both material and human) are made available for processes of change in the interests of redress. Through careful presentation of cases and analyses of statistics and policies, Saloojee offers a detailed and nuanced understanding of the problems facing the health sector and their causes, as well as some recommendations for addressing them.

Raji Matshedisho provides an experience of the difficulties and complexities involved in enforcing the law at the level of the street. Through participant observation with student police officers in an urban South African township, Matshedisho is able to apprehend certain 'hidden transcripts' that come to figure in the ways in which relations between the police and members of the community unfold and are given meaning and effect, ways that are not always within the limits of the law. Matshedisho also points out that it is only a minority of community members who relate without antagonism to the police, in the main those who belong to the community policing forum. Outside the community policing forum, community members hold little or no respect for the police, often preferring to take the law into their own hands, administering their own forms of justice. Matshedisho points to continuities in such practices with those of angry mobs during apartheid (for example, the practice of 'necklacing' — placing a tyre around a person's neck, dousing it with petrol, and setting it alight, thereby burning the person while she or he was still alive). Matshedisho argues that the root of the problem lies in the fact that the building of relations between the police and the community has been approached and imagined within the narrow frame of crime fighting. Without addressing the historical relation-ship of black communities and individuals to the police under apartheid, Matshedisho argues that present-day attempts at building positive partnerships between the police and communities are destined to fail as members of communities seldom overcome the negative stereotypes and perceptions that they have of the police, for example, that they are themselves criminals, and the police seldom overcome similar prejudices, based on stereotypes, about members of the community. His chapter suggests that the current approach of the South African state to community policing requires serious attention.

Many would argue that these problems could easily be solved by making a few macro-economic policy changes, in particular those that would assist in creating jobs and in making more resources available for the redress necessary to correct the inequalities and injustices entrenched by apartheid capitalism. As the introduction to this volume has already argued, the adoption of neoliberal policies by the ANC government has only been cemented in the New Growth Path (NGP), suggesting that there is little possibility for the kind of changes that would result in 'a better life for all'. But, recent public spats in the ANC Alliance, in particular between leadership of the ANC Youth League and its parent body, have led some to suggest that there is still a possibility that more redistributive approaches to the economy, such as nationalisation, could be adopted by the ANC government, given that the ANC Alliance is a space for contestation, and the fact that Cosatu and the SACP have also spoken in favour of nationalisation in relation to the mines, the banks, and land.

Even among those who speak in favour of nationalisation there is disagreement. SACP leaders, for example, have rejected the ANC Youth League's most recent calls for nationalisation of the mines on the basis that they serve only to bolster the interests of a black elite in society, bailing out failing black businesses rather than serving the interests of the working class. The debate about nationalisation in the Alliance must, then, be understood within and according to the context of the existing conflicts and histories of differences within the Alliance, and will, in all likelihood, be resolved according to the organisational and ideological rationalities operative within this Alliance. At present, the upcoming battles over the leadership of the ANC tend to dominate all debates and disagreements within the Alliance, and will probably continue to determine the nature and content of mobilisations by different groups in the ANC in the run-up to the next national election in 2012. While the ANC has deferred resolution of the nationalisation debate to the outcomes of a research process, it will be important to reflect on the concrete possibilities for socio-economic change in post-apartheid South Africa through different approaches to nationalisation outside the highly politicised sphere in which the debate has unfolded until now. Beyond the rhetorical mobilisations of slogans such as 'economic freedom in our lifetime' and calls for greater state ownership and management in and of the economy, is an important and necessary discussion about the potentials for nationalisation as an economic alternative that offer solutions to the growing socio-economic problems faced by South Africans. This could perhaps be a challenge for a future volume of the *New South African Review*.

The remaining chapters in this section survey different attempts at changing aspects of the economy, and their effects on society more broadly. The introduction to this volume has already made reference to most of them in relation to the debates about decent work and job creation.

Don Lindsay looks at the ways in which black economic empowerment (BEE) has developed into an institution for the benefit of a few politically connected elites in spite of policy commitments to extending its reach, in the form of broad-based BEE (B-BBEE), for example. Michelle Williams and Vishwas Satgar survey the history of cooperatives in South Africa. Based on interviews, field visits, and existing literature, the authors examine the shift from apartheid cooperative development to post-apartheid cooperative development, focusing on 'the use and appropriation of the white cooperative development experience in the contemporary BEE context'. They argue that this approach, led by the post-apartheid state, has resulted in the promotion of a business approach to cooperatives, an approach that has failed. Through an exploration of three case studies, they explore the importance of worker ownership and control in the development of cooperatives, and highlight a new trend in trade union-linked worker cooperatives. Malose Langa and Karl von Holdt, and Eddie Webster, explore possibilities for addressing the decline of full-time, waged, formal-sector employment in South Africa today. While Langa and von Holdt assess the successes and failures of a community work programme, a pilot project of national government aimed at providing unemployed individuals with short-term 'work opportunities' through which to gain a small income, skills, and the discipline necessary for a job, Webster looks supportively at the NGP's proposals for addressing what he calls 'the decent work deficit'.

CHAPTER 8

'The wages are low but they are better than nothing':
The dilemma of decent work and job creation in South Africa

Edward Webster

In August 2010, government officials began closing down clothing and textile factories in Newcastle, in the KwaZulu-Natal Midlands, in the face of angry protests from the workers because the owners were paying less than the statutory minimum wage of R324 a week. Dudu Mabaso, who works in one of these factories, said that as much as she wanted conditions to change at her company, closing down was not an option. 'People will revolt against closure. It's their source of survival and working for these textile companies is the only way to survive. The wages are low at R250 per week but they are better than nothing.' (Olifant, 2010:10). The factory owners said that they could not pay more, and survive, in the face of cheap Chinese textile imports. As Alex Liu, chairman of the Newcastle Chinese Chamber of Commerce, asserted, 'It is impossible for us to pay the minimum wage because we are competing with imports from China and the cut, make and trim price from our customers will not sustain us if we paid the minimum wage of R324 a week' (Khanyile, 2010a: 3).[1]

South Africa has a sophisticated collective bargaining and dispute resolution system, and by December 2010 agreement had been reached between the South African Clothing and Textile Workers' Union (Sactwu) and employers' organisations that manufacturers paying less than minimum wages would have until 2012 to get their houses in order. Manufacturers were granted a further sixteen-month extension in which to resolve their noncompliant status. They would have to be at least seventy per cent compliant by the end of March 2011, with further phase-ins over the following thirteen months, culminating in full compliance by the end of April 2012 (Khanyile, 2010b:1). By the end of March 2011, fifty-nine per cent of the inspected factories were complying with the target of paying seventy per cent of the minimum wage, effective from April (Khanyile 2011).

But from the employers' point of view this was a reluctant agreement. 'Our view remains,' commented Johann Baard, director of the Apparel Manufacturers' Association (Amsa), 'that many noncompliant factories, and currently compliant factories, cannot afford the current wage structure' (Marais, *Sunday Times*, 2011). Renato Palmi, director of the Redress Consultancy, described the agreement as 'upsetting and worrying'. It was likely, he said, to lead to retrenchments, factory closures and relocation to South Africa's neighbours – Lesotho, Swaziland and Mozambique – whose governments are wooing investors and where minimum wages are lower.[2] 'Provided the workers are happy with the wages being paid,' Alex Liu said, 'the bargaining council should not have the right to shut down factories' (Marais J, 2011).

The clothing and textile industry is controlled globally by an oligopolistic group of large retailers and branded manufacturers who stipulate their supply specifications in terms of low price, high quality and short lead times (Pretorius, 2010: 45).[3] But owing to the strengthening rand since 2003, the end of the Multifibre Agreement (MFA) in 2004 and relatively high labour costs, South Africa no longer has a comparative advantage in an integrated and global economy.

The figure below illustrates what I call the decent work deficit logic that is eroding decent work. The dismantling of barriers to trade and capital flows has opened up a cost-cutting competition between and within countries and companies, with the result that employers bypass the labour laws, triggering a process of informalisation either through outsourcing or retrenchment. Theron (2010) calls the former informalisation from above, the latter, the creation of survivalist-type jobs, informalisation from below.

Figure 1: The decent work deficit logic

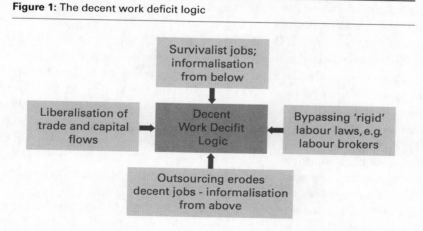

As Barchiesi argues, wage labour has not fulfilled its promise of social emancipation. Instead, wage labour has declined in the face of retrenchment and it has also become more precarious and insecure in the face of growing casualisation and outsourcing of work. This has led to the growth of the 'working poor' where workers remain poor even though they are in formal employment (Barchiesi, 2011).

South Africa's labour regime is at a crossroads: does it abandon labour standards to become globally competitive or does it try to balance decent work with enterprise efficiency? The veteran journalist, Alistair Sparks, has gone as far as to argue that it is 'the government's commitment to Cosatu's insistence on "decent work" which compels employers to pay industry-wide minimum wages in each sector and apply a range of specified working conditions to all workers regardless of whether they are skilled or not that has driven South Africa into an economic cul de sac (Sparks, 2010: 1).

At stake, labour believes, are the hard-won labour rights introduced by South Africa's first democratic government in 1994. But from the beginning those gains by labour were contested by employers and, from time to time, inside the ruling party, triggering a major ongoing and unresolved debate over labour market reform which continues into the present with proposed changes to the Labour Relations Act, the Employment Equity Act, the Basic Conditions of Employment Act and the introduction of an alternative to private labour brokers, the Employment Services Bill, designed to create greater security in employment, under discussion in parliament during 2011. The response from employers has been hostile (Phakathi, 2011: 1); they argue that the current labour relations regime runs against the global trend of labour market flexibility, raises the costs of labour, and inhibits job creation (SAIRR, 2009: 31). P-E Corporate Services MD, Martin Westcott, has said that restricting the use of temporary workers in the economy, as proposed in the latest raft of labour legislation, would go against international employment trends and add to the rigidity of the labour market (Ensor, 2010: 9). Contrary to these opinions, extensive *de facto* flexibility exists in a labour market that increasingly is characterised by 'shell' agreements 'where labour wins high standards on paper that apply to fewer and fewer workers in reality' (Webster and Bezuidehout, 2005: 25).

A recently commissioned ILO study on micro and small enterprises (MSEs) in the clothing, footwear and metal sectors concluded that employers often comply reluctantly with the labour law and that they continue to believe that labour law inhibits the expansion and growth of their businesses (Bischoff, Roskam and Webster, 2010). The result is that noncompliance continues in four key areas: some MSEs continue to pay below the minimum wage; some do not adhere to the overtime provisions (hours of work); many do not register all of their employees with the bargaining council; and most feel that the bargaining council-administered benefits and the contributions are onerous for small business. Employers complain that exemption from the bargaining council is difficult or even impossible, as it involves a lot of paperwork.

Labour's response is that this drive by employers for greater labour market flexibility is an attempt to reduce labour costs and undermine the core rights won by the labour movement during the anti-apartheid struggle. Labour argues that flexibility is re-segmenting the South African labour market and creating greater insecurity and unemployment for both core and peripheral workers – and that employers are either not complying with the labour regulations or are by-passing them through outsourcing and subcontracting the work to a third party, *a labour broker*. The result of this flexibility is that real individual incomes declined between 1995 and 2000, with the drop steepest among the lower half of income earners, especially younger workers, women and Africans (Marais, 2011:179). Marais summarises the recent wage trends by arguing that the average real wage in South Africa is propped up by the improved fortunes of comparatively small numbers of high-skilled, high-salary workers. 'Even then,' he concludes, 'the median wage in 2009 stood at a paltry R2 500 (US$310) per month' (Marais H, 2011).

In addition to declining incomes, job creation has been slow in the core sectors of the economy. In the period 1970–1995, 211 000 jobs in the mining sector were shed. While the manufacturing, utilities and construction sector gained 400 000 jobs over the same twenty-five-year period, Bhorat and Hodge argue that for a key sector of the South African economy such as manufacturing to gain so few jobs was an early sign of 'an undynamic if not a struggling sector' (Bhorat and Hodge, 1999: 350). Over the same period, the highest increase in jobs was in the financial and businesses services sector and the wholesale and retail sector; both these sectors gained approximately 1.2 million workers.

Over the following ten years, jobs in the manufacturing industry declined slightly and employment increased marginally in the mining sector. The most significant changes were the increase in employment in the financial services sector, where jobs more than doubled and in the wholesale and retail sector; the latter, which had shown significant increases in the preceding twenty-five years, grew by more than fifty per cent in the ten-year period from 1995 to 2005 (Development Policy Research Unit Data Corner, 2005).

In spite of the progress South Africa has made in the struggle for decent work, a key feature of the apartheid workplace remains in place – that of insecurity in the workplace and in society. Indeed, with 25.3 per cent of the economically active population unemployed, the goal of the right to work and security seems as elusive as ever. If we were to include those who do not have work but have stopped looking for it (the so-called discouraged worker) the figure is at least 34.4 per cent (South African Labour Force Survey, Third Quarter, October 2010). This is illustrated in the diagram below.

This dilemma is not peculiar to South Africa. There is a widespread view that the concept of decent work has no relevance to developing societies. Indeed, all three dominant theories of globalisation – neoclassical liberalism, the anti-globalisation movement, and development statism – treat the struggle for decent work as either an obstacle or an add-on (Bowles, 2010). There are, in fact, governments in the global South that see decent work as a Eurocentric concept designed to protect jobs in the North. By insisting on certain labour standards, it is argued, these countries are taking away the only comparative advantage the poor have – their cheap labour (Hensman, 2010). After all, it is argued, is it not on the back of labour exploitation, including child labour, that the North industrialised? Some, indeed, ask: 'Is the demand for decent work not a form of non-tariff protection?' (Chang, 2002).

Figure 2: The structural unemployment challenge

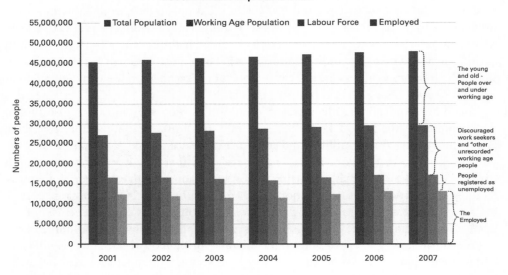

Source: T Scott, DBSA 2010.

Interestingly it is not only developing societies which see decent work as an obstacle to economic growth. In the heartland of social democratic Europe, employers and governments – including labour governments – have responded to global competition by lowering the cost of labour through introducing precarious employment and eroding the gains hard won by working people through the welfare state (Webster, Lambert and Bezuidenhout, 2008: 50–77). This hyper-commodification of labour, however, is not happening without resistance from workers. In Germany, the Harz reforms that reduced welfare benefits led to a split in the Social Democratic Party and the formation of De Linke, a coalition of ex-communists, labour movement activists and left social democrats.

This chapter challenges the false dichotomy between decent work and job creation, arguing that the potential exists within South Africa's policy discourse for the implementation of a new employment-oriented paradigm where decent work is not seen as an obstacle or add-on to development but is integrated into an alternative developmental path. Such a path involves difficult policy choices and political trade-offs. To date, the South African government has responded ambiguously to this challenge, as if unable to make up its mind as to whether decent work is an obstacle, an add-on or central to a new developmental path.

In part one, the origin of the concept of decent work is analysed, and its introduction into the post-apartheid policy discourse identified. In view of the growing informalisation of work – or what we have called the decent work deficit logic – the question is raised as to whether the adoption of the concept of decent work is mere rhetoric, or whether it opens up possibilities of reducing the decent work deficit. In part two, it is argued that decent work is not something that can be immediately realised in a developing country such as South Africa. Through such policy initiatives as the New Growth Path and the Community Work Programme (CWP), the question is raised as to whether South Africa is developing a strategy for the progressive realisation of decent work. I conclude by arguing that unless the state is able to orchestrate a concrete national project, and begins to address the inefficiencies in government, this potential paradigm shift will be stillborn.

PART ONE: The origins of decent work and its adoption in post-apartheid South Africa

While the demand for better working conditions was deeply rooted in the struggle for democracy in South Africa, the use of the concept of decent work in the policy discourse of the government is relatively recent. The concept has its origins in a 1999 report of an International Labour Organisation (ILO) conference, where a discussion paper by Dharam Ghai explained it:

> The notion of decent work emphasises four elements: employment, social security, workers' rights and social dialogue. Employment refers to work of all kinds and has both quantitative and qualitative dimensions. Thus the notion of decent work is applicable not just to workers in the formal economy but also to 'unregulated wage workers, the self-employed, and the home workers'. Further, it refers to both adequate opportunities and remuneration for work (in cash or kind). Decent work also embraces safety at work and healthy working conditions. The social security component of decent work is intended to protect against the risk of losing income (Ghai cited by Cachalia, 2009).

The principles underlying decent work have been expressed well by Juan Somavia, director general of the ILO. He has highlighted three principles that bring the value of work to the fore. Firstly, labour is not simply a commodity with a cost that is bought and sold on the market; it is, first and foremost, human activity, which cannot be reduced to something bought and sold like any other good or service. Secondly, the notion of decent work has to come from how people themselves define it within their own social context, because decent work in an impoverished developing country is not the same as decent work in an affluent developed country. Thirdly, work is a source of dignity, and is linked to a person's sense of identity and self-worth. The value that people contribute to society is determined by the work they perform (Somavia, 2004: 5–6).

In other words, employment brings benefits, not only for the employed, but also for their community as a whole. In addition to income, employment provides useful production and recognition for doing something worthwhile. While economists usually focus on the economic multipliers, there are also social multipliers associated with job creation – decreased crime; enhanced family and community cohesion; strengthened security; better education, healthcare and childcare (Forstater, 2006).

The problem with the term 'decent work' has always been its inherent vagueness. To some, that was seen as an advantage. To others, it left too much room for vague platitudes. Both words are difficult to define – *decency* is a normative concept, and *work* as a focus of public policy and research has been transformed over the past three decades from a mainly male activity involving stable, full-time, unionised employment to a variety of precarious forms of formal and informal employment as well as unpaid care work.

The concept of decent work has been criticised by those on the left, who see it as a 'reformist' strategy designed to restore capitalism (both materially and ideologically), and by neoliberals on the right who see it as an unwarranted attempt to intervene in the market. However, the strongest challenge to the ILO's notion of decent work has come from a senior ex-employee, Guy Standing, who notes that:

> The pursuit of flexible labour relations at the centre of emerging labour markets all over the world posed a particular difficulty for the ILO – that of identifying employers and employees. Unless these are clear, labour law and regulations become hard to apply. Flexibility has meant a growing fuzziness, with labour externalisation and a global resurgence of labour broking, employment 'agencies' and labour sub-contracting. ILO conventions began to look inapplicable for rather a lot of work statuses (Standing, 2008: 365).

A difficult challenge with the concept is how to measure it and assess the progress of decent work in the world (Ghai, 2003). The one comprehensive attempt to measure decent work and present indices for over a hundred countries was shelved when it was attacked by employers (ILO, 2004; Standing, 2008).

In September 2008, a tripartite meeting of experts on the measurement of decent work was held in Geneva (ILO, 2008: 1–3). The indicators shown in Table 1 were agreed upon at the tripartite meeting.

Decent work in South Africa

The African National Congress (ANC), in alliance with the South African Communist Party (SACP) and the Congress of South African Trade Unions (Cosatu), contested the 1994 elections on the Reconstruction and Development Programme (RDP). The RDP identified the interconnection between the challenges facing South African society: the lack of housing and jobs, inadequate education and healthcare, and a failing economy. It proposed job creation through public works programmes linked to the provision of basic services such as water, sewerage and roads. This targeted the poor and the rural areas. The idea was to create jobs and at the same time improve the life of the people by providing them with basic services. By 1999, 240 000 job opportunities had been created through public works, on road construction schemes, sewerage installation, water supply and sanitation (Lodge, 2002).[5]

Table 1: Decent work indicators

Indicator	Examples
Employment opportunities	Labour force participation rate Employment-to-population ratio Unemployment rate Youth unemployment rate Wage employment Non-agricultural (per cent)
Adequate earnings and productive work	Average earnings in selected occupations Recent job training
Decent hours	Excessive hours Under-employment
Stability and security at work	Tenure less than one year Temporary work
Balancing work and family life	Employment rate of women with children below school age Children in wage employment
Equal opportunity and treatment in employment	Occupational segregation by gender Female share of managerial posts Share of women in employment in the non-agricultural sector
Safe work environment	Occupational injury rate Fatal injury rate (per 100 000 employees) Number of inspectors per 100 000 employees Occupational injury insurance
Social protection	Public social security expenditure (per cent of GDP) Share of population aged 65 and above benefiting from a pension Healthcare expenditure not financed out of pocket by private households Public expenditure on needs-based support (child grant, disability grant and pension) as a per cent of GDP
Social dialogue and worker representation	Union density rate Number of enterprises belonging to employer organisations Collective wage bargaining coverage Strikes and lockouts (per 1 000 employees)
Socio-economic context of decent work	Growth rate of GDP per person employed (labour productivity) Inflation Adult literacy rate Poverty (per cent): proportion of people living below US$1 (PPP) per capita

Source: ILO (2008).

The adoption of the RDP was an attempt by the new government to fulfil and reassert the vision projected in the 1955 Freedom Charter, a vision that clearly embraces the notion of decent work. It achieves this by linking poverty alleviation to job creation and service delivery.

The presidential commission to investigate labour market policy 'was charged with developing the labour market policies necessary to meet the RDP's employment-related objectives and that are consistent with the requirements of productivity enhancement and macroeconomic stability' (Presidential Commission, 1996: xiii). In particular, the commission was required to investigate 'the role of public sector employment policy in achieving the employment-related objectives of the RDP' (Presidential Commission, 1996: xiii).

The report recommended the establishment of a National Public Works Programme (NPWP):

> ... to encourage and advocate, through the Department of Public Works, the use of labour-intensive methods of production in the provision of infrastructure by the public sector, and by those tendering for public sector contracts. Ancillary goals of the NDWP included the acquisition of skills on the job, intensive community participation, the creation of necessary assets, and finally the promotion of involvement of small-scale black contractors in the provision of infrastructure (Presidential Commission, 1996: 132).

In large part, the focus was on the construction industry, including a move toward more flexible methods of production, particularly that of labour-only subcontracting (LOSC) which enables firms to avoid the costs of providing benefits, training, health and safety, and minimum-wage protections. Indeed, concern was raised by some commissioners that the 'informalisation of the labour market may be accelerated' (Presidential Commission, 1996: 132–133). The commission proposed an 'accord process' where:

> ... unions may concede greater flexibility in the method and level of remuneration, in return for greater and more secure employment. They could be offered a more stable labour relations environment where the use of labour brokers and casual labour would be curtailed. The private sector would, in return for a flow of public projects, offer to undertake labour-intensive construction methods and take over facilitation of industry accredited training (Presidential Commission, 1996: 135).

The report concluded by proposing that a national accord for employment and growth be negotiated through the recently established National Economic Development and Labour Council (Nedlac). The aim of the accord would be three-fold:

- First, an accord can enable the reconciliation of the twin objectives of steadily rising labour productivity and rapid employment creation.
- Second, an accord provides a more employment-friendly means of fighting

inflation than do the relatively blunt instruments of fiscal and monetary austerity.
- Third, an accord provides a forum in which the optimal sequencing of economic policy decisions can be debated and co-ordinated responses formulated (Presidential Commission, 1996: 193).

The first national jobs summit was held in October 1998, and was convened by Nedlac. The social partners accepted that increased investment and economic growth would not, on their own, generate employment growth unless yoked to a comprehensive job creation programme. There was agreement at the summit on the main elements for job creation:
- industrial policy measures and programmes to directly address unemployment and increased investment;
- public works programmes;
- a social plan to avoid job losses and employment decline and, where job losses are unavoidable, to manage retrenchments and ameliorate their effects on individuals and companies;
- a comprehensive social security system, aimed especially at the unemployed and those living in poverty (Webster and Adler, 1999: 374-375).

A second growth and development summit was called by Nedlac in June 2003 to address urgent challenges that were having a negative effect on the economy. One of the major challenges was the growing rate of unemployment (Mbeki, 2003). To address the challenges of employment, the social partners at the 2003 growth and development summit made a commitment to 'work for more jobs, better jobs and decent work for all'. They agreed on a number of strategies, including public investment initiatives, the introduction of an expanded public works programme (EPWP), and sector partnerships. The government described the summit not as an isolated event but as a step forward in the protracted process that would in time culminate in a people's contract for development and growth.

Although these agreements were hailed as significant, post-summit assessment by different social partners was less enthusiastic. The first major weakness was that the summit did not deliver the social accord on growth that President Mbeki had spoken about. Instead, unhappy with not succeeding in amending labour legislation in 2000, Mbeki announced in his State of the Nation address in February 2005 that a comprehensive review of the regulatory environment faced by small and medium enterprises would be undertaken with 'the aim of introducing a simpler and streamlined system for all businesses' (Webster and Sikwebu, 2010: 198). Research was commissioned and presented at a round table with the social partners in April 2006. The research confirmed the concept of 'regulated flexibility' that underpins the fundamentals of the labour relations system, and suggested a number of minor amendments to the current legislation to deal with some of the 'rigidities in the South African labour market' (Webster and Sikwebu, 2010: 198).

Of particular concern for trade unions was the *de facto* highly flexible labour market that had emerged through the rapid growth of the labour broker sector. 'Liberalisation', argued Webster and Von Holdt in 2005, 'has polarised the labour market by increasing the resources of some of the 6.6 million people in the core while at the same time reducing the resources of the 3.1 million in the intermediate category of the non-core (or atypical work) and those in the periphery, consisting of the 2.2 million workers in informal work and the 8.4 million unemployed' (Webster and Von Holdt, 2005: 27).

Increasingly, Mbeki came under attack inside the ANC, culminating in his ousting as president, in favour of Jacob Zuma, in December 2007 at the ANC's 52nd national conference in Polokwane. With strong support from Cosatu and the SACP, expectations were high for a significant shift to the left through an Alliance-led political process. In his inaugural State of the Nation address in June 2009, President Jacob Zuma stated: 'It is my pleasure and honour to highlight the key elements of our programme of action. The creation of decent work will be at the centre of our economic policies and will influence our investment attraction and job creation initiatives. In line with our undertakings, we have to forge ahead to promote a more inclusive economy' (quoted in the New Growth Path: The Framework, 2010: 10).

In 2010, the adoption by Nedlac of South Africa's own decent work country programme (after a series of consultations between government, the social partners and the ILO), seemed to be further evidence of this commitment.[6] In an audit undertaken during the formulation of the programme, it was concluded that 'the primary problem in relation to decent work in South Africa is not the failure to ratify conventions, nor the failure to enact proper laws, but the enforcement of those laws by the department of labour (Brand, 2011).

Three priorities were identified:
* strengthening fundamental principles and rights at work through, *inter alia*, improved labour inspection;
* growing levels of employment with particular focus on the expanded public works programme and labour absorbing sectors;
* strengthening and broadening social protection coverage strengthening tripartism and social dialogue, including the formalisation of the informal economy.

However, in terms of new, more progressive policies, as Marias observes, the Alliance had, by 2011, very little to show for its pro-Zuma exertions, except for some changes made to industrial policy (Marais, 2011: 441). Many of the policy improvements and institutional adjustments pursued by the government, he argues, originated in the Mbeki era:
* Attempts to refurbish industrial strategy started well before Mbeki's departure.
* A more flexible monetary policy capable of spurring 'job creation, investment and poverty eradication' had been ANC policy since 2002.
* A prescribed investment proposal seeking to tighten a voluntary commitment was made at the 2003 growth and development summit.
* The creation of a planning commission was an extension of Mbeki's 'style' of governance, with decisions and coordination centralised in the presidency.
* The expanded public works programme was conceived and implemented by the Mbeki administration.
* Substantial expansion of the social grant system began during Mbeki's second term (Marais H, 2011).

To this list of policy continuity I would add decent work, which emerged in the Mbeki policy discourse in 2003. Is the adoption of the concept of decent work by the Mbeki/Zuma adminstrations simply an electoral ploy adopted on peak-level social dialogue occasions designed to garner support, particularly from Cosatu, or does it signal a significant shift in government thinking and policy implementation to reduce the decent work deficit? I turn now to an examination of the progress made under the Zuma administration towards the goal of decent work for all.

PART TWO: Towards the progressive realisation of decent work

A central challenge facing South Africa is how to integrate decent work into a new developmental path. An important part of the problem is that, in the eyes of neoliberalism and its model of market-led growth, trade unions are an obstacle, as they push up the costs of labour by creating a 'rigid' labour market. What is required, it is argued, is greater labour market flexibility so that employers can hire and fire with minimal restrictions. This is a deeply entrenched argument. The impact of labour market policies and regulations on employment creation is an ongoing and unresolved issue in South Africa (Webster and Sikwebu, 2010: 200–203). Importantly, these divisions exist inside the ANC itself where, from time to time, proposals have been made to relax labour laws. 'The analytical wellspring of the labour market flexibility proposals,' writes Marais, 'lies in the "two economies" schema. Reducing the costs of labour and capital, it is argued, would help bridge the gap between the "two economies". The thinking is freighted with World Bank dogma, particularly the refurbished competiveness approach adopted after the collapse of the Washington Consensus. In rough, this calls for the optimal operation of market mechanisms, while a strong state ensures a stable, low-cost and productive environment (by investing, for example, in infrastructure and skills development and social schemes designed to assist the indigent)' (Marais H, 2011).

To reduce the decent work deficit, I argue, South Africa will need to develop a longer-term vision of the policy-making process. In other words, the goal of decent work should be seen as an objective to aspire to that can be progressively realised over a number of years. Quite simply, this involves accepting that decent work is not an immediately achievable goal. Each country has to take into account its specific social and economic context and set itself a series of immediate, medium- and long-term goals.

The process of attempting to integrate decent work more directly into a new employment-generating development path began in 2010, when the cabinet adopted the New Growth Path. In describing this new path, it needs to be recognised that the NGP does not yet constitute solidly grounded policy: it is not yet clear how the state is to support 'labour-absorbing activities', especially as employment is expected to be created in sectors – such as agriculture, mining and manufacturing – that have been shedding jobs over the past thirty years. Above all, it is not clear what incentives there are for capital to engage in such activities or what kinds of concessions the social partners will have to make if a 'deal' is to be reached.

With these provisos in mind, the NGP suggests three phases of employment creation:

- **In the very short term** the state can accelerate employment creation primarily through direct employment schemes such as the Expanded Public Works Programme (EPWP) and the Community Work Programme (CWP).
- **In the short to medium term** it can support labour-absorbing activities, especially in the agricultural value chain, light manufacturing and services, to generate large-scale employment.
- **In the longer term**, as increased employment is achieved, the state must increasingly support knowledge- and capital-intensive sectors in order to remain competitive (NGP, 2010: 7).

'This inherent phasing', the NGP argues, 'means that in the medium term the state must focus on facilitating growth in sectors able to create employment on a large scale. But it should not neglect more advanced industries that are crucial for sustained long-run growth.' (NGP, 2010: 7).[7]

The aim of the growth path is to increase employment by five million jobs by 2020 and to narrow unemployment by ten percentage points from twenty-five per cent to around fifteen per cent (NGP, 2010: 8).[8] In order to reach its annual employment and growth targets, the strategy focuses on areas that have the potential for creating employment on a large scale – what they term 'jobs drivers'. Most of the projected new jobs are planned to come from the private sector.[9] Two key variables will affect the target of five million new jobs: the rate of economic growth and the employment intensity of that growth – that is, the rate of growth in employment relative to the rate of growth in the GDP (NGP, 2010: 9).

Five jobs drivers are identified:

- Substantial public investment in infrastructure both to create employment directly, in construction, operation and maintenance, as well as the production of inputs, and indirectly by improving efficiency across the country;
- Targeting more labour-absorbing activities across the main economic sectors – the agricultural and mining value chains, manufacturing and services;
- Taking advantage of new opportunities in the knowledge and green economies;
- Leveraging social capital in the social economy and the public services;
- Fostering rural development and regional integration (NGP, 2010: 9–10).

As a first step, the NGP will prioritise efforts to support employment in the key sectors of: infrastructure; the agricultural value chain; the mining value chain; the green economy; manufacturing sectors, which are included in IPAP2; and tourism and certain high-level services (NGP, 2010: 10).

The most difficult task will be to develop job strategies for each phase, and to rank the decent work indicators in terms of what is achievable in each phase. The ANC's annual national executive committee *lekgotla* in January 2011 began such an exercise when it identified a list of jobs that could be created by 2020 (Phakathi, 2011: 1) but they quickly ran into the dilemma of whether they were trying to create jobs or whether they were also creating decent jobs. The secretary-general of the ANC, Gwede Mantashe, was interpreted as toning down the party's commitment to 'decent work' when he commented publicly after the *lekgotla* that to insist on jobs being 'decent' was 'putting the cart before the horse'. There was 'nothing more degrading then being unemployed', he said (Phakathi, 2011: 1). Mantashe was quite right to emphasise the importance of job creation, but by omitting to mention that job creation was the first step in the long-term goal of decent work he opened himself up to allegations of back-sliding.

BUILDING A COMMON VISION

A key process in the implementation of the New Growth Path will be to build a common vision with the social partners – labour, employers, the community and government departments – around the idea of a social or developmental pact. What the trade-offs would be in such a pact are best developed by the key actors, but the institutional precon-ditions for successful social dialogue already exist in South Africa through the structures of Nedlac, a peak-level social dialogue institution (Webster and Sikwebu, 2010). The chal-lenge will be managing the trade-offs between the social partners. This will require that 'the state (a) facilitate national and workplace productivity accords, (b) support community organisation, including through the Community Work Programme and other delivery mechanisms that build community and collective action, and (c) strengthen existing insti-tutions for social dialogue, including Nedlac, sectoral and local forums' (NGP, 2010: 30).

How have the social partners responded to the NGP? The authors of the NGP believe that the key to its successful implementation is the development of more constructive and collaborative relations between state and business (NGP, 2010: 29). They maintain that this will require the state to minimise unnecessary economic costs such as need-less regulatory requirements and delays, inadequate infrastructure, weak education and training; and it will require business to support critical and innovative initiatives for a more inclusive and equitable economy, especially projects that can generate employment on a much larger scale through investment, technical support and mentoring, and appro-priate pricing policies (NGP, 2010: 29).

Employers are concerned over the proposals to cap pay and bonuses for senior managers earning over R550 000 a year and over moderate price increases, especially on inputs and wage goods (NGP, 2010: 25). While labour remains sceptical of how this will be monitored, evidence drawn from research is that the greater the employment-creation orientation of policies, the stronger the stimulus for the real economy. Indeed, there are economists who argue that, by making government *the employer of last resort*, it would be possible to offer a job to anyone willing to work – in other words, full employment – in developing countries (Randall Wray, 2007).

The initial response of Cosatu, the largest trade union federation, was that the NGP 'fell far short of the comprehensive and overarching development strategy ... that will fundamentally transform our economy and adequately address the triple challenges of extraordinary high levels of unemployment, poverty and deepening inequality'. These criticisms continue to be articulated by Cosatu in the structures of the ANC and are part of the process of political exchange. At the January 2011 ANC *lekgotla*, Cosatu argued that the NGP monetary policy framework places emphasis only on inflation targeting, does not give enough attention to the unemployment rate, and is not addressing the 'over-valued' currency (Ndlangisa and Mboyisa, 2011: 5).

The NGP document acknowledges this challenge: 'A critical challenge lies in maintaining union commitment to policies that support employment creation and equity even when it requires some sacrifice from union members. In order to achieve this, the New Growth Path must ensure that economic and social policies demonstrably reward any sacrifice by members with real gains for the working class as a whole' (NGP, 2010: 29).

COMMUNITY WORK PROGRAMME

Labour may see the public employment schemes as a dilution of their commitment to labour standards. Government argues that such a view misunderstands the aim of the EPWP and CWP: namely, poverty alleviation and an opportunity for first-time job seekers to gain work experience and training, while contributing to the community. That the jobs created accept the minimum wage in the given sector removes the threat to existing jobs from this form of employment. Indeed, in October 2010, a ministerial determination establishing conditions of employment for employees in EPWPs came into effect (Basic Conditions of Employment Act, 1997, Ministerial Determination 4; Expanded Public Works Programmes, No 949, Government Gazette, 22 October 2010).

The determination lays down a number of employment conditions. At the start of employment, workers must be given a contract containing details of the expected duration of the contract, the rate of pay and the training they will receive. An employer must ensure that the terms of the contract are explained in a suitable language to any employee who is unable to read the statement, and the employee must be supplied with a copy of these conditions of employment (BCEA, Ministerial Determination 4, 2010: Section 12.1–3). The determination lays down a minimum wage of R60 per day and workers must be given a pay slip (ibid., Section 14.8). Workers do not have to give notice but if they are away from work for more than three days without informing their employer, then the contract is terminated (ibid., Section 18.1–5). On termination of employment, a worker is entitled to a certificate stating what the conditions of their employment were (ibid., Section 19.1).

The state is experimenting with the idea of the state as the employer of last resort (ELR) through introducing Phase 2 of the Expanded Public Works Programme (EPWP): the Community Work Programme (CWP). This pilot project was initially located in the presidency under the Second Economy Project but is now under the Department of Cooperative Governance and Traditional Affairs (Cogta) (Trade and Industry Policy Strategy, 2009). The CWP is 'an experiment in key municipalities of an employment safety net providing a minimum level of regular and predictable work, usually two days a week, while wider policy processes to create sustainable employment take effect' (Philip, 2010).

Although it does not meet all the indicators identified in the concept of 'decent work', the CWP provides work opportunities, some income although not a living wage and, through a regular income, some degree of social protection. It has already created 100 000 work opportunities and is a step in what I identify as the first phase of the progressive realisation of decent work.

There are five key features of the CWP that distinguish it from the EPWP. The work is regular and predictable, not temporary; the work undertaken must be useful (it must contribute to the public good and the quality of life in poor communities); members of the community must identify and prioritise work; a reference group of key stake-holders in the community must be established; and the work undertaken must be aligned to the government's Integrated Development Plans (IDPs) at local level (Philip, 2010). In research undertaken in two CWP sites, Westonaria and Keiskammahoek, between November 2010 and February 2011, the programme was seen to be making a significant socio-economic impact on the lives of the participants (Webster, Metcalfe, Fakier and Cock, 2011). Four economic multipliers were identified:

- The programme provided a predictable and regular income of R480 per month to the participants. In addition, ninety-three per cent (Westonaria) and ninety-two per cent (Keiskammahoek) received R250 from the child support grant.
- The programme facilitated work searches. Twenty-four per cent of the participants from Westonaria and thirteen per cent from Keiskammahoek had looked for work over the previous seven days. Of those who had looked for work, fifty per cent (Westonaria) and fifty per cent (Keiskammahoek) had used their CWP income to facilitate the search, to pay for transport or for cell phone usage.
- Twenty-one per cent of the participants in Westonaria and twenty-five per cent in Keiskammahoek claimed to have been able to save some of their CWP money. Thirty per cent in Westonaria and forty-four per cent in Keiskammahoek saved on average over R100 month.
- In almost all the sites (eighty-nine per cent in Westonaria and eighty-seven per cent in Keiskammahoek), communal vegetable gardens had been built by partici-pants. Fifty per cent of the respondents in Westonaria and seventy-seven per cent in Keiskammahoek had built vegetable gardens at their homes and were now able to provide their families with vegetables on a daily basis.

In addition to the economic multipliers, four social multipliers were identified that are contributing to social cohesion in these communities.

- Participants in the programme had made new friends (eighty-two per cent in

Westonaria and seventy-four per cent in Keiskammahoek) where they were able to share personal problems and gain social support.

• The programme encourages an ethic of care and support to the vulnerable in the community. Examples given by participants were cooking and cleaning for the elderly and sick, collecting medicines for the bedridden, food parcels and clothing for child-headed households, and vegetables for crèches.

• The programme has improved community safety through the creation of community police forums.

• The community is taking greater care of their natural resources through clean-up campaigns, tree-planting activities, clearing the environment of alien vegetation, repairing dams and water harvesting.

A more difficult goal is for the CWP to facilitate sustainable self-employment. In spite of limited resources, the Hluma Development Cooperative in Keiskammahoek employs seventeen former CWP participants but the enterprise remains precarious because of a lack of capital to invest in a new equipment (interview with Zukisa Ngudle, manager, 17 February 2011).

The CWP is an example of grassroots organisational innovation that contributes to the progressive realisation of decent work through building a social floor. The concept of a basic social floor of social security benefits could be introduced, the ILO believes, as a matter of priority in developing countries where there are wide coverage gaps (Cichon, Behrendt and Wodsak, 2011: 3). The crucial step in advancing this debate was the demonstration that a basic set of social security benefits, or at least parts therof, is affordable in developing countries (ILO, 2008). The realisation that, in the short term, it is possible to imagine building a global social floor – a basic pension, child benefits, access to healthcare, temporary employment guarantee schemes or income transfers for the long-term unemployed – broke the spell of the 'non-affordability myth' (Cichon, Behrendt and Wodsak, 2011: 3). But, as these authors go on to show, the argument for the progressive realisation of decent work and social security cannot be used 'as a pretext for non-compliance' and 'resource scarcity does not relieve states of certain minimum obligations in respect of the implementation of the right to security' (ibid.: 3). Social security systems, they argue, 'have to grow in sync with economic and social development' (ibid.: 12). The metaphor that emerged is that of a social security 'staircase', with the bottom step comprising a set of basic guarantees for all, and a second level and third level of ascending 'staircases' where rights are strengthened (ibid.). Importantly, they maintain,'without investment in a social protection floor, many people will not reach a level of skills and productivity which would enable them to enter the formal economy but will remain trapped in informality and low productivity. Investing in a basic level of social protection that triggers a virtuous cycle of improved productivity and employability will ensure the sustainability of statutory schemes by enabling more and more people to move into contributory schemes' (ibid.).

CONCLUSION

Laying the foundations for reducing the decent work deficit

Slowly and unevenly, the institutional foundations are being laid in South Africa to bridge the decent work deficit. In sum, four initiatives can be identified:

- Bridging the employment gap through the adoption of a New Growth Path (NGP) that foregrounds employment;
- Bridging the rights gap through the concept of regulated flexibility, giving workers rights but allowing for a degree of flexibility in the implementation of regulations to ensure that labour market institutions play a more active role in preventing the abuse of vulnerable workers through, for example, labour brokers;
- Bridging the social protection gap (progress has been made in building a social floor through the introduction of the CWP (Phase Two of the EPWP));
- Bridging the social dialogue gap through Nedlac, an established peak-level social dialogue institution.

Let me illustrate my argument with Figure 3, reducing the decent work deficit.

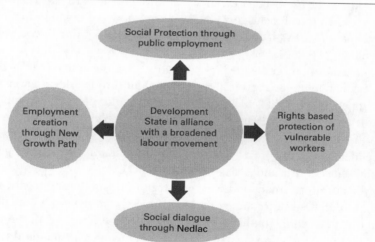

Figure 3. Reducing the decent work deficit

I have suggested in this chapter that the potential exists for the emergence of a new paradigm to progressively achieve decent work; to realise this potential will require a national shift from a narrow individualism towards short-term sacrifices in the interests of long-term national gains. Strategies of future-oriented growth will only succeed if they are 'credible and inclusive, reassuring people that they or their children will enjoy the full fruits of growth' (Keeton 2011: 8)[10], but what is clear is that the construction of a democratic and efficient developmental state is required.

There is an extensive body of literature on the key features of a development state and whether South Africa has the potential to become one (Ediigheji, 2010; Marais H, 2011). As Evans has shown in his path-breaking research, 'the idea of a developmental state puts robust, competent public institutions at the centre of the development matrix' (Evans, 2010: 37). This requires, he insists, two conditions: bureaucratic capacity and 'embeddedness'. The first condition requires that states approximate the ideal-typical Weberian bureaucracy.

> Meritocratic recruitment to public service careers offering long-term rewards commen-surate with those obtainable in the private sector were institutional cornerstones of the East Asian economic miracle. Meritocratic recruitment was important, not only to promote competence but to give state employees a sense of *esprit de corps* and belief in the worthiness of their profession. Long-term career rewards based on performance kept competent individuals from deserting the public service' (Evans 2010: 45).

Von Holdt has shown, through his ethnographic research on public hospitals, that the post-apartheid bureaucracy differs significantly from that described by Weber. The obstacles to bureaucratic efficiency are: affirmative action targets which are leading to high vacancy rates, high mobility, and many employees who lack the requisite skills; an underestimation of the importance of, and an ambivalence towards, skill; an exaggerated importance attached to rules and procedures; a breakdown of organisational discipline; and a preoccupation with black class formation that may legitimate corrupt practices (Von Holdt, 2010: 241–260).

The second condition, embeddedness, requires that the state be in a position to orchestrate a concrete national project of development through drawing on 'a dense set of concrete impersonal ties that enable specific agencies and enterprises to construct joint projects at the sectoral level' (Evans 2010: 46-47). Being able to avoid capture by capital and being able to discipline entrepreneurial elites is, Evans concludes, a defining feature of the 'embedded autonomy' of East Asian development states, distinguishing them from less successful states in Asia and Africa (Evans 2010: 47).

While key institutions remain under the nominal control of the South African state, the state has failed to 'orchestrate a concrete national project'. Instead it finds itself distant from capital, and often locked in conflict with militant public-sector unions. Informalisation has opened up a representational gap between union members in standard employment relationships and the growing numbers of outsourced, temporary and casual workers without a voice. To date there are no signs that the labour movement has the political will to bring together wage labour and the great swathes of informal and precarious labour.

Instead of meeting Evans's conditions of 'embedded autonomy', the evidence of post-apartheid governance suggests, with few exceptions, the opposite, as local governments and national departments fail to deliver services because of loss of skills, numerous vacancies and endemic corruption (Southall, 2007). This is the challenge South Africa faces in 2011; these are the pitfalls that confront us.

NOTES

1   It is worth noting a fascinating study done in 1995 on purchasing parity power which takes into account domestic prices of goods and services between China and South Africa. South African real wages in the clothing industry in Newcastle were found to be 30 per cent lower than the Chinese wage. The secret of East Asian competitiveness, the author argues, lies in the way industrial wages are effectively subsidised by other forms of social and economic security. Instead of broadly based systems of access to land, brutal dispossession in South Africa has stripped people of the associated social and economic security. (Hart, 1995; see also Hart, 2002) For Arrighi et al., China's developmental advantage 'must stem from differences in public transport, educational, health and social security facilities, policies and investments' (Arrighi et al., 2008: 11).

2   It is worth noting that the difference in monthly income between South African garment workers and those in Swailand is a relatively modest R53.16: R1064.80 per month in South Africa and R1015.64 in Swaziland (Bezuidenhout and Jepperson, 2011).

3   On 31 May 2011, South Africa's Competition Tribunal approved Wal-Mart's $2.4 billion bid for control of retailer Massmart with minimal conditions, which will accelerate South Africa's integration into the global economy.

4   The anti-globalisation movement covers a range of responses from codes of conduct, international labour standards, global unionism through to bulding a global counter-hegemonic movement. Politically, it ranges from social reformist to anti-capitalist/autonomist.

5   An important semantic shift has taken place in the discource around job creation. The government now prefers to talk about jobs, the vast majority of 'opportunities' created by the public works programmes, as temporary jobs that are supposed to provide 'bridges' toward more secure long-term employment. Although these jobs provide a much needed source of income, there is little evidence that they are leading to long-term employment.

6   Although a document was produced, it is vague and the participation of key actors such as Cosatu was episodic.

7   It is not clear how this goal relates to the ongoing dominance of the minerals-energy complex.

8   It is not clear whether 'jobs' means job opportunities (short-term employment), or whether this means standard employment, i.e. decent work as defined by the ILO.

9   The document does not say exactly how the state is to pursue this objective and what incentives it has to leverage the cooperation of capital.

10 Keeton cites the 2008 Report of the Commission on Growth and Development which argues that only those countries that were 'future oriented, forgoing consumption in the present in pursuit of a higher level of income in the future' sustained growth of more than seven per cent a year for a period of at least twenty-five years. Current consumption was sacrificed in favour of investment and higher future consumption; real growth was postponed in favour of job creation and future wage growth supported by productivity improvements; and current profit margins were sacrificed to increased turnover and higher future profit (Keeton 2011: 8)

REFERENCES

Barchiesi F (2011) *Precarious Liberation: Workers, the State and Contested Social Citizenship in Post-Apartheid South* Africa. Scottsville: University of KwaZulu-Natal Press.

Bezuidenhout A and S Jepperson (2011) Between the state, market and society: Labour codes of conduct in the southern African garment industry. Paper presented at University of Johannesburg, Department of Sociology Seminar, 23 February.

Bhorat H and Hodge J (1999) Decomposing shifts in labour demand in South Africa, *South African Journal of Economics* 67(3): 348–80.

Bischoff C, A Roskam and E Webster (2010) Report on compliance to labour law by micro and small enterprises in South Africa. Society, Work and Development Institute, University of the Witwatersrand, Johannesburg.

Bowles P (2010) Labour and globalisation, *Global Labour Journal* 1 (1).

Brand J (2011) Decent work has solid basis in law, but lacks application' *Business Day*, 9 May 2011.

Cachalia F (2009) Department of Economic Development 2009/2010 Budget Vote Speech (Vote 3), Gauteng Legislature, Johannesburg, 7 August.

Chang H-J (2002) *Kicking Away the Ladder – Development Strategy in Historical Perspective*. London: Anthem Press.

Cichon M, C Behrendt and V Wodsak (2011) The UN Social Protection Floor Initiative: Turning the Tide at the ILO Conference 2011. Friedrich Ebert Stiftung.

Development Policy Research Unit Data Corner (DPRU) (2005) Employment by sector. http://www.commerce.uct.ac.za/Research_Units/DPRU/DataCorner15.htm (accessed 26 September 2006).

Edigheji O (Ed.) (2010) *Constructing a Democratic Developmental State in South Africa: Potentials and Challenges*. Cape Town: HSRC Press.

Ensor L (2010) Labour law changes would buck international trend, *Business Day*, 21 December.

Evans P (2010) Constructing the 21st century developmental state: Potentialities and pitfalls. In Edigheji O (Ed.) (2010) *Constructing a Democratic Developmental State in South Africa*. Cape Town: HSRC Press.

Forstater M (2006) Full employment and economic flexibility, *Economic and Labour Relations Review*, 11: 69–88.

Ghai D (2003) Decent work: Concepts and indicators. *International Labour Review* 142(2): 113-145.

Hart G (1995) 'Clothes for next to nothing': Rethinking global competition, *South African Labour Bulletin*, Volume 19, Number 6, December.

Hart G (2002) *Disabling Globalisation: Places of power in Post-Apartheid South Africa*. Berkeley, CA: University of California Press.

Hensman R (2010) Labour and globalisation: Union responses in India, *Global Labour Journal*, 1 (1): 112–131.

International Labour Organisation (ILO) (2004) *Economic Security for a Better World*. Geneva: ILO Socio-Economic Security Programme.

International Labour Organisation (ILO) (2008) Measurement of Decent Work. Discussion Paper for the Tripartite Meeting of Experts on the Measurement of Decent Work.

Keeton G (2011) Wage restraint is New Growth Path's lesser evil, *Business Day*, 31 January.

Khanyile S (2010a) Low wages put 8 000 clothing jobs at risk, *Business Report*, 21 August.

Khanyile S (2010b) Clothing firms get wage extension, *Business Report*, 22 December.

Khanyile S (2011) More clothes plants meet wage targets, *Business Report*, 23 May.

Lodge, T (2002) *Politics in South Africa. From Mandela to Mbeki*. Bloomington: Indiana University Press.

Lieuw-Kie-Song M and K Philip (2010) Mitigating a jobs crisis: Innovations in Public Employment Programmes (PEP). Employment Sector, Employment Report No 6. Geneva: International Labour Office.

Marais J (2011) Sactwu stays firm on wages, *Sunday Times*, 16 January.

Marais H (2011) *South Africa Pushed to the Limit: The Political Economy of Change*. Cape Town: UCT Press.

Mbeki T (2003) Speech of the President to the Growth and Development Summit, Johannesburg, 7 June.

Ndlangisa S and C Mboyisa (2011) Allies outgun Vavi at NEC, *Sunday Times*, 16 January.

Olifant N (2010) Labour trapped in the cracks, *Sunday Independent*, 24 November.

New Growth Path (2010) Department of Economic Development, Pretoria.

Phakathi B (2011) State 'open' to changing contentious labour laws, *Business Day*, 19 January.

Presidential Commission to Investigate Labour Market Policy (1996) Report: Restructuring the South African Labour Market. Pretoria: Department of Labour.

Pretorius L (2010) A hypercompetitive industry, *Financial Mail*, 26 November.

Philip K (2010) Towards a right to work: The rationale for an employment guarantee in South Africa, TIPS. December.

Randall Wray L (2007) The employer of last resort programme: Could it work for developing countries? Economic and Labour Market Papers, 2007/5. Geneva: ILO.

Southall R (2007) The ANC State, more dysfunctional than developmental? In S Buhlungu, J Daniel, R Southall and J Lutchman, *State of the Nation: South Africa 2007*. Cape Town: HSRC Press.

Sparks A (2010) New growth path may fail over 'decent work', *Business Day*, 24 November.

Trade and Industrial Policy Strategies (TIPS) (2009) Second economy strategy: Addressing inequality and economic marginalisation.

Temkin S (2010) SA executives income streets ahead of their overseas peers, *Business Day*, 25 November.

Lindell I (Ed.) (2010) *Africa's Informal Workers: Collective Alliances and Transnational Organising in Africa*. London: Zed.

Somavia J (2004) The ILO Decent Work Agenda as the Aspirations of People: The Insertion of Values and Ethics in the Global Economy. In P Dominique (Ed.) *Philosophical and Spiritual Perspectives on Decent Work*. Geneva: ILO.

South African Institute of Race Relations (SAIRR) (2009) Liberation of the Poor: Fifteen Years of Freedom and Democracy in South Africa. Policy Conference, Johannesburg, 27–28 May.

Standing G (2008) The ILO: Agency of globalisation, *Development and Change*, 39(3): 355–84.

Theron J (2010) Informalization from above, informalization from below: The options for organization, *African Studies Quarterly*, Volume 11, Issues 2 & 3: 87–105.

Von Holdt K (2010) The South African post-apartheid bureaucracy: Inner workings, contradictory rationales and the development state'. In O Edigheji (Ed.) *Constructing a democratic developmental state in South Africa: Potentials and challenges*, Cape Town: HSRC Press.

Webster E and G Adler (1999) Towards a class compromise in South Africa's double transition: Bargained liberalisation and the consolidation of democracy. *Politics and Society* 27(3): 347–385.

Webster E and A Bezuidenhout (2005) Debating the flexible world of work in South Africa. In Edigheji O (Ed.) Trajectories for South Africa : Reflections on the ANC's Second National General Council's discussion documents, Special Edition of Policy: Issues and Actors, Vol. 18, No 2, Johannesburg: Centre for Policy Studies, pp.22–6.

Webster E and K von Holdt (2005) *Beyond the Apartheid Workplace: Studies in Transition*. Scottsville: University of KwaZulu-Natal Press.

Webster E, R Lambert and A Bezuidenhout (2008) *Grounding Globalisation: Labour in the Age of Insecurity*. Oxford: Blackwell Publishing.

Webster E, D Phoskoko, J Machaka, C Bischoff, C Chinguno, T Guliwe and A Metcalfe (2009) A policy framework for the progressive realisation of the goal of decent work in Gauteng. Johannesburg: Society, Work and Development Institute, assisted by the Department of Economic Development, Gauteng.

Webster E and Sikwebu D (2010) Tripartism and economic reforms in South Africa and Zimbabwe. In Fraile I (Ed.) *Blunting Neoliberalism: Tripartism and economic reforms in the Developing World*. Basingstoke: Palgrave Macmillan/ILO.

Webster E, M Metcalfe, K Fakier and J Cock (2011) Building a social floor: Perspectives from two community work programme sites, Society, Work and Development Institute, University of the Witwatersrand.

CHAPTER 9

The crisis of childcare in South African public hospitals

Haroon Saloojee

The words 'crisis' and 'healthcare' follow each other in sentences so often in South Africa that most citizens have grown numb to the association. Clinicians, health managers and public health experts have been talking about a crisis in access to healthcare for more than half a century, and the advent of democracy has not alleviated the situation.

The subject of this chapter is childcare in public hospitals, where there is undoubtedly a crisis. However, in truth, there are multiple simultaneous healthcare crises – rampant diseases such as HIV/AIDS and tuberculosis; excessively high maternal and child mortality; poorly motivated health professionals; the shut-down of critical units in hospitals; and perennial shortages of vitally needed supplies and equipment. The ill-health of, and dismal health services offered to, children at public hospitals is but the most prominent and painful tip of a predicament that extends beyond child health to adult and geriatric medicine and pervades all levels of the health system, including primary healthcare. Patients – young and old – are dying unnecessarily because South African public hospitals are over-burdened, under-staffed, poorly managed and failing to deliver.

Decades of discriminatory apartheid policies resulted in marked racial disparity in children's health. In 1994, the new democratic government inherited a highly fragmented health service consisting of fourteen health departments (each of the ten Bantustans had its own health department) plus a private sector mainly serving a white minority and funded predominantly through medical insurance. Seventeen years of democracy have yielded varied success for child health and well-being, and the public health system, overburdened from its inception, has yet to catch up with the health needs of the country's children. Excellent child health policies now exist, but there has been less success in transforming them into measurable actions and outcomes. Nine provincial health departments, organised under a single national health department, continue to provide disparate services, with poorer, more rural provinces offering the least care to its children despite significant improvements in their budgetary allocations. Simultaneously, the devastating effects of the AIDS pandemic have rapidly eroded hard-earned child mortality gains.

South Africa's inability to respond adequately to its many crises is also the result of a national healthcare system designed to prioritise treatment over prevention. The over-dependence on hospital-based care not only makes the healthcare system expensive and inefficient, but also precludes much-needed investments in effective primary and preventative care. The health minister, Dr Aaron Motsoaledi, concedes that the public health system faces 'very serious challenges' (Philip, 2009). Despite the funding for primary healthcare having increased more than three-fold since 1994, this has not resulted in an improved ability of clinics to serve children, mainly because most of the money was spent on infrastructure development rather than on service delivery expansion and on quality-of-care improvements.

In this chapter I describe the crisis in childcare and its consequences for the health of children, characterise the underlying reasons for the crisis, examine current interventions, and explore some medium- and long-term solutions.

HOW SEVERE IS THE CRISIS?

It is not surprising that the public's perceptions of health services are often determined by stories in the media about the care offered to children. For instance, in one week in May 2010, two stories dominated newspaper and media headlines in Gauteng: one was the death of seven newborn infants and the infection of sixteen others as a result of a virulent infection (subsequently identified as a norovirus) acquired by the infants at the Charlotte Maxexe Johannesburg Academic Hospital; at Natalspruit Hospital in Ekhuruleni, ten children similarly succumbed to a nosocomial (hospital acquired) infection (Bodibe, 2010).

These types of events – large numbers of children acquiring infections simultaneously in hospitals – are not uncommon, although only a fraction grab the headlines. Outbreaks occur at regular intervals at hospitals throughout the country – an outbreak of Klebsiella infection was responsible for 110 babies dying at Mahatma Gandhi Hospital in Durban according to the organisation 'Voice' that threatened a class-action case against the KwaZulu-Natal Department of Health. The national Department of Health itself has identified infection control as one of six key areas that need improvement in the public health sector (Department of Health, 2010).

Poor healthcare at several Eastern Cape hospitals resulted in 140 children dying in the Ukhahlamba district within three months in 2008 (Thom, 2008). A task team investigating these deaths in one of South Africa's poorest districts concluded that they were not the result of exposure to contaminated water, as initially suspected, but the consequence of a vulnerable group of children being served by a poorly responsive and inadequate health system (Report on childhood deaths, Ukhahlamba District, Eastern Cape).

The Ukhahlamba task team, comprising three experienced public-sector paediatricians, offered a disheartening and bleak analysis of Empilisweni Hospital children's ward, where most of the deaths occurred. Problems identified included the following:

- The ward and cubicles were overcrowded with no provision for lodger mothers, who paid R30 to sleep on the floor next to their children.
- The basic structure was grossly inadequate with no oxygen and suction points, few electrical sockets, no basins or showers and too few toilets in the patient ablution blocks.
- The structure and layout of the physical facility was inappropriate – no nurses' station or work surfaces, no separation of 'clean' and 'dirty' areas, no play or stimulation facilities, and a ward kitchen with old furniture and minimal equipment, with infant feeds prepared there with water brought from another building. Clinical equipment was extremely limited.
- Staffing deployment and rotation did not promote effective care, with few nurses dedicated to the children's ward and doctors changing wards every two months, leaving the ward devoid of experienced personnel.
- There were limited policy documents and no protocols or access to appropriate clinical reference material or guidelines.
- Clinical practices were ineffective or dangerous, particularly those regarding infection control and the preparation and distribution of infant feeds and medicines.
- The majority of the children were never weighed and their nutritional status was not assessed; nor was their HIV status established.
- Not a single hospital record included details about the prescribing or administration of infant feeds. Fluid management was badly documented. Three of the children appeared to have died from fluid overload owing to inappropriate and unregulated fluid administration.

The task team's audit of forty-five of the deaths revealed that most had occurred within the first forty-eight hours of admission to hospital and had occurred in infants who were self-referred. The main diagnoses were diarrhoeal disease, pneumonia and malnutrition. The task team concluded: 'These deaths are more likely the result of poor care of a vulnerable impoverished community with high rates of malnutrition among the infants and poor utilisation of the available health services' (Report on childhood deaths, Ukhahlamba District, Eastern Cape).

The pathetic situation at Empilisweni Hospital is not unique; similar abject conditions can be found in some of the paediatric wards of the 401 hospitals in the country.

While the extent of the problem is undocumented, the consequences of the crumbling infrastructure at state hospitals is an ongoing concern for clinicians nationally. The explanation offered in reports of adverse events occurring at public hospitals country-wide is remarkably similar. Uniformly, there is a combination of overcrowded wards, understaffing, overwhelming workloads, a breakdown of hygiene and infection-control procedures, and management failure – with a lack of auditing or monitoring systems to identify and respond timeously to problems.

INCREASING CHILD MORTALITY

What is not contentious is that South Africa is one of only twelve countries in the world where childhood mortality increased from 1990 to 2006 (Children's Institute, 2010), with a doubling of deaths in children under the age of five in this period (from approximately 56 to 100 deaths per 1 000 live births). The 2010 Unicef *State of the World's Children* estimates South Africa's under-five death rate to be 67 per 1 000 for 2008 (Unicef 2009). This high rate ranks South Africa 141st out of 193 countries. The national statistic also hides marked interprovincial variations; from about 39 per 1 000 in the Western Cape to 111 per 1 000 in the Free State (McKerrow and Mulaudzi, 2010). A single disease, HIV, is largely responsible for the increased mortality, accounting for more than half of all child deaths at public hospitals between 2005 to 2009 (Stephens et al., 2011).

Countries with economic profiles similar to that of South Africa, such as Brazil and Turkey, boast under-five mortality rates (U5MR) about four times lower. South Africa's high U5MR is even more disconcerting when compared to poorer countries such as Sri Lanka and Vietnam with child mortality rates roughly five times lower (15 and 14 per 1 000 respectively) despite having a Gross National Income less than one-half to a third of South Africa's (Unicef, 2009; World Bank, 2010).

Although it is classified as a high middle-income country, South Africa has high levels of infectious diseases such as diarrhoea, pneumonia, HIV, tuberculosis and parasitic infections normally found in poorer countries. Similarly, there has been little success in reducing undernutrition in children: a quarter of South Africa's children are stunted (short). As a result of increased urbanisation and economic development, the country is also experiencing increasing levels of traumatic injuries and chronic diseases of life-style such as obesity, diabetes and cardiovascular disease that are more typical of better resourced countries – diseases that mainly affect adult populations but are increasingly being identified in children.

The deterioration of child health has occurred despite significant improvement in children's access to water, sanitation, primary healthcare and social services. Almost 3 000 new clinics have been built or upgraded since 1994, healthcare is provided for free to children under five and pregnant women (Saloojee and Pettifor, 2005), and the child social support grant is reaching 10.5 million children (more than half of all children in the country) (Dlamini, 2011). But these achievements have been marred by several shortcomings: many new clinics and the district health systems are not yet properly functional because of a lack of personnel and finances, poor administration, and expanding demands, and public tertiary healthcare (academic hospital) services have severely eroded. It is the crushing burden of HIV, however, that has overwhelmed the health system's ability to cope with the existing disease load, and has displaced the resources available for preventing and controlling other important childhood illnesses such as malnutrition and infectious diseases.

CHARACTERISING THE CRISIS

In 2000, the World Health Organization ranked South Africa's healthcare system as the 57th highest in cost, 73rd in responsiveness, 175th in overall performance, and 182nd by overall level of health (out of 191 member nations included in the study) (World Health Organization, 2000). What explains this dismal rating? Despite high national expenditure on health, inequalities in health spending, inefficiencies in the health system and a lack of leadership and accountability contribute to South Africa's poor child health outcomes.

INSUFFICIENT EXPENDITURE ON HEALTH, HOSPITALS AND CHILD HEALTH

Between 1998 and 2006, South African annual public per capita health expenditure remained virtually constant in real terms (that is, accounting for inflation). Although spending in the public sector increased by 16.7 per cent annually between 2006 and 2009 (National Treasury, 2009), this has not kept pace with the greatly increased burden of disease and with population growth (including the massive influx of foreign migrants). In 2009, the country spent 8.9 per cent of the gross national product (GDP) on health (Day and Gray, 2010), and easily met the World Health Organization's informal recommendation that so-called developing countries spend at least five per cent of their GDP on health (World Health Organization, 2003). However only 3.7 per cent of GDP was spent in the public sector, with 5.2 per cent of GDP expended in the private sector (Day and Gray, 2010). In per capita terms, R9 605 was spent per private medical scheme beneficiary in 2009, while the public sector spent R2 206 per uninsured person (Day and Gray, 2010).

Although the health of mothers and children has been a priority in government policy since 1994, including in the latest Ten Point Plan for Health (Department of Health, 2010), it has not translated into movements in fiscal and resource allocation. Children comprise nearly forty per cent of the population (Statistics South Africa, 2009), but it is unlikely that a similar proportion of the health budget is spent on child health (no reliable data exist, as government departmental budgets do not specifically delineate expenditure on children, easily allowing this constituency to be shortchanged or ignored).

INEQUITY

Inequities and inequalities abound in South African healthcare spending generally, and specifically regarding children's health. Of the R192 billion spent on healthcare in 2008-2009, fifty-eight per cent was spent in the private sector (Day and Gray, 2010). Although this sector only provides care to an estimated fifteen per cent of children, two-thirds of the country's paediatricians service their needs (Colleges of Medicine of South Africa, 2009). Of the R90 billion provincial public health sector budget, about fourteen per cent is spent on central (tertiary) hospital services (Day and Gray, 2010), which primarily benefits children residing in urban settings and wealthier provinces such as the Western Cape and Gauteng. Similarly, marked inequities exist in the number of health professionals available to children in different provinces with, for example, one paediatrician servicing approximately 8 600 children in the Western Cape but 200 000 children in Limpopo (Colleges of Medicine of South Africa, 2009). This differential exists among most categories of health professionals.

The current health system claims to provide universal coverage to children, which means that all services are available at no cost for children who cannot afford to pay for healthcare. Yet, from a resourcing, service delivery and quality perspective, the availability and level of service is inequitable, with many patients and communities experiencing substantial difficulty in gaining access to the public health system. Rural and black communities remain most disadvantaged.

Apartheid-era differentials continue in present-day healthcare. For instance, while the formerly 'whites only' Charlotte Maxexe Johannesburg Academic Hospital now mainly serves a black urban population, its resources (including ward facilities, staff-patient ratios and overall budget) are still better than those available to the Chris Hani Baragwanath Academic Hospital located in Soweto (a former 'black' hospital) (Von Holdt and Murphy, 2007). Nationally, the most stressed hospitals are those with the lowest resources per bed while the least stressed continue to be those with previous reputations as high-quality institutions (mostly previously 'whites only' hospitals) that provide them with a kind of 'social capital' (Von Holdt and Murphy, 2007).

CHANGING HEALTH ENVIRONMENT

Some of the increasing stresses faced by the public hospitals may be attributed to the changing health environment in which they operate. Two factors are most responsible for the change: the AIDS epidemic and increasing urbanisation. About a third of children at most South African hospitals are HIV infected. HIV-positive children are hospitalised more frequently than HIV-negative children (17 per cent compared to 4.7 per cent hospitalised over one year) (Shisana et al., 2010). Children with AIDS tend to be sicker and often require longer admissions, despite suffering from the same spectrum of illnesses as ordinary children. Urban, township hospitals are particularly affected by the burden of increased patient loads, and are barely coping with the demand.

Greater numbers of patients, higher disease acuity levels and complications, and slower recovery rates all affect limited resources. High mortality rates take an emotional toll on doctors and nurses. Hospital paediatrics, which has always been a popular and rewarding choice for newly qualified doctors because of modern medicine's ability to quickly restore desperately ill children to health, has now become much more about chronic care delivery because of the high number of HIV-infected children in the wards, many of whom are readmitted regularly because of recurrent infections. In recent years, young doctors have also been dissuaded from selecting primary care disciplines, such as paediatrics, and have moved instead to pursuing specialities where contact with patients is limited – such as radiology – for fear of acquiring HIV from needle-stick injuries. However, the improved coverage of mother-to-infant HIV transmission prevention strategies, and the availability of highly active anti-retroviral therapy to an increasing number of children nationally, though still limited to fewer than half of all eligible children, have the potential to return paediatrics to its previous status as a rewarding and fulfilling speciality.

Although a national strategic plan for HIV/AIDS exists, the ability to implement it is constrained by the enormous demands it will make on human and fiscal resources. The budget allocated to HIV/AIDS has increased from R4.3 billion in 2008 to an estimated R11.4 billion in 2010 (thirteen per cent of the total health budget) (Mukotsanjera et al., 2009). New initiatives aimed at strengthening the HIV/AIDS response include a national HIV counselling and testing campaign and the decentralisation of anti-retroviral treatment from hospitals to clinics, with nurses now providing the drugs.

The greatest improvement in reducing child mortality and a reduction in the number of hospitalised children lies in the successful implementation of the prevention of mother-to-child transmission of HIV (PMTCT) programme. It was dogged with controversy from its inception, and was the subject of a successful Constitutional Court defeat in 2002, by civil society advocacy groups, of the health ministry's stubbornly slow nevirapine implementation strategy. Despite a court order instructing it to improve access, the ministry continued to frustrate PMTCT expansion efforts for another five years. Only in the last three years have PMTCT activities accelerated, although the deficiencies in antenatal care provision and labour ward services has hindered universal implementation. Nevertheless, there is exciting, albeit weak and anecdotal, evidence that HIV infection rates in infants are now decreasing, with fewer hospital admissions of children, and the prospects of an HIV-free generation of infants in five to eight years are more promising.

HOSPITALS OPERATE WITHIN A DYSFUNCTIONAL HEALTH SYSTEM

Poor hospital care is but one marker of a dysfunctional health system that comprises blotches of disconnected services rather than a coherent, cooperative approach to delivering healthcare. Ideally, few children should require curative care because of the high uptake and effectiveness of preventative services such as immunisation and growth monitoring, and good parental practices such as breastfeeding, hygiene and the provision of simple, appropriate care at home for sick children (such as oral rehydration solution for children with diarrhoea).

The vast majority of sick children, more than ninety-five per cent, should have their illness managed at the primary care level, at clinics staffed by nurses, and by family practitioners (for private patients). The remaining children require services available at a district hospital, where there are doctors, but sometimes at a regional hospital where there is a paediatrician, if the disease is complicated. Fewer than 0.1 per cent of children should ever require care at a tertiary (or sub-specialist academic) hospital. The reality, however, is that many parents by-pass the primary care level, opting to immediately visit a hospital, and in urban settings this is often an academic hospital, such as Red Cross or Chris Hani Baragwanath. There are a number of reasons for this behaviour. Most primary healthcare services for children are only offered during office hours, with some clinics restricting new patients' access to services by early afternoon – a waste of available and expensive human resources (explanations offered for this behaviour include the need for the clinic to clear queues by 16h00 or the need for nurses to complete administrative tasks and paperwork in the afternoon). Some clinics lack basic diagnostic tests and medication. Consequently, many hospital emergency rooms are flooded with children with relatively minor ailments because their caregivers choose not to queue for long periods at poorly functioning local clinics, or prefer to access health services at hospitals after returning from work.

The referral system in which patients are referred from clinics and community health centres to district, regional or tertiary hospitals, depending on the severity of their illness, is malfunctioning in many parts of the country. Children who require additional or more specialised care often cannot get it either because they get stuck within a dysfunctional system or because there is no space for them at the next level of care. Transport to secondary and tertiary level hospitals is problematic, resulting in delays or non-arrival; patients' abscond (return home) and the child's condition is not attended to until it worsens, increasing the severity of the disease and treatment costs when the child does arrive. On the other hand, clinics are often guilty of referring children elsewhere when they should be managed at the clinic.

District hospital services are the most dysfunctional (Coovadia et al., 2009), with patients, and clinics, often by-passing this level of care where access to secondary (regional) or tertiary care (specialist) services are available. Despite cut-backs in budgets, tertiary care settings continue attempting to provide 'first-class' services; although this is commendable it could result in over-investigation and treatment, and denial of essential care to children who reside outside immediate catchment areas because the tertiary hospital is 'full'.

Further contributors to the crisis of childcare in South African hospitals are explored below. These include crises in management capacity, particularly in determining who is responsible for hospital services; the rationing of care and poor fiscal management; limited human resources for delivering adequate childcare and the inattention to the needs of these individuals; and the inability to extract accountability for poor service delivery to children.

MANAGEMENT CAPACITY CRISIS

The battle for the control of hospitals

South Africa has embraced the concept of health services delivered within a three-tiered national health system framework: national, provincial and district. Provinces are charged with the responsibility of providing secondary or tertiary hospital services; district services have responsibility for district hospitals and clinics. Existing legislation allows hospital chief executive officers considerable powers in the running of their own hospitals. There is, however, a dysfunctional relationship between hospitals and provincial head offices, which often assume authoritarian and bureaucratic control over strategic, operational and detailed processes at hospitals – but are unable effectively to manage them. There is a blurred and ambiguous locus of power and decision-making authority between hospitals and head offices (Von Holdt and Murphy, 2007). Hospital managers are disempowered, cannot take full accountability for their institutions and are mostly unable to determine staff numbers and appointments, design their own budgets or assume responsibility for the procurement of goods and services.

The structural relationship between province and institution is a disincentive for managerial innovation, giving rise to a hospital management culture in which administration of rules and regulations is more important than managing people and operations or solving problems, and where incompetence is easily tolerated. Hospital managers' lack of control undermines management accountability and promotes subservience to the central authority.

SILOS OF MANAGEMENT

Most South African hospitals have essentially the same management structure in which authority is fragmented into separate and parallel silos. Doctors are managed within a silo of clinicians, nurses within a nursing silo, and support staff by a mesh of separate silos for cleaners, porters and clerks. The senior managers in the institutions have wide spheres of responsibility but little authority to make decisions or implement them (Von Holdt and Murphy, 2007).

As an example, a clinical department such as paediatrics is headed by a senior paediatric specialist who has no control over the nurses in the paediatric department. In the wards, nursing managers are responsible for effective ward functioning but have little control over ward support staff such as cleaners or clerks. A senior clinical executive (superintendent) has responsibility for the paediatric (and other) departments but can exercise little substantial authority because power lies within each of the silos (doctors, nurses, support workers), and as a result, the clinical executive has to attempt to negotiate with all parties. Doctors and nurses do not determine budgets, or monitor and control costs. In essence, those responsible for using resources have no influence on their budgetary allocation, while those responsible for the budget assume no responsibility for the services that the budget supports. Most clinical heads have no idea what their budgets are and costs are not disaggregated within the institution to individual units or wards.

What should be managed as an integrated operational unit – for example, a ward or clinical department – operates instead in a fragmented fashion with little clear accountability. In this situation all parties are disempowered, and relationships oscillate between complaint, angry confrontation, persuasion, negotiation and withdrawal. In the process few problems are definitively resolved, with negative consequences for patient care. Where institutional stress is high, the fragmented silo structures generate the fault lines along which conflict and managerial failure show up (Von Holdt and Murphy, 2007).

FINANCIAL CRISIS

Financial governance and poor fiscal discipline

National economic policy has rationed the resources available for transforming the health system and imposed 'the overriding imperatives of fiscal restraint and crowding out of other goals' (Schneider, 2007). A lack of accountability extends throughout the health service, and includes poor and sometimes misguided financial governance and the lack of fiscal discipline. In 2009-2010, provincial departments of health collectively overspent their budgets by more than R7.5 billion (Engelbrecht and Crisp, 2010); they frequently fail to budget adequately, resulting in the freezing of posts and the restriction of basic service provision – for example, routine child immunisation services were seriously disrupted in the Free State in 2009 (Kok, 2009). Every year, budgetary indiscipline results in critical shortages of drugs, food supplies and equipment in many provinces, particularly during the last financial quarter from January to March, and during April when new budgetary allocations are being released.

'Stock-outs', the temporary unavailability of pharmaceutical agents, medical supplies such as disinfectants or gloves or radiological material, and food or infant formula may annoy staff but may have devastating consequences – including death – for patients. Most 'stock-outs' are the result of suppliers terminating contracts because accounts have not been paid. In Gauteng, medical suppliers were owed more than half a billion rand by the Auckland Park Medical Supplies Depot in early 2011, the central unit from which medicines are distributed to provincial hospitals and clinics. The largest amounts owed by the depot, some R130 million, were to two pharmaceutical companies (Bateman 2011).

A recent embarrassing occurrence is the return by the Department of Health of R813 million in unspent funds to Treasury at the end of the past financial year (Bateman, 2011). Most of the money was budgeted to revive collapsed and unfinished infrastructure at hospitals but this function belongs to the Department of Public Works, and hospitals have little influence on the functioning of this separate department – a further example of fragmented services. Treasury has nevertheless allocated billions for the revival or construction of five academic hospitals by 2015, mainly through public-private partnerships. These are Chris Hani Baragwanath in Soweto, Dr George Mukhari in Pretoria, King Edward VIII in Durban and Nelson Mandela in Mthatha, as well as a new tertiary hospital for Limpopo.

Provincial health departments are beginning to show modest success in rooting out fraud and corruption but their efforts have revealed widespread swindling costing taxpayers billions of rands, much of it deeply systemic (Bateman, 2011). The bulk of endemic corruption involves dishonest service providers with links to key health department officials, looting through ghost and multiple payments loaded onto payment systems. In the Eastern Cape, an external audit of 'anomalies' in four health department supplier databases revealed R35 million in duplicate or multiple payments in 2010 (Bateman, 2011). Some 107 suppliers had the same bank account number, 4 496 had the same physical address and 165 suppliers shared the same telephone number. Less sophisticated fraud involved the bribing of district ambulance service directors to transport private patients. Theft of equipment, medication and food is pervasive, aggravating existing bottlenecks in supply-chain management. Almost R120 000 worth of infant formula destined for malnourished babies or the infants of HIV-positive mothers was stolen in the Eastern Cape in 2010, for which three foreign businessmen and four health department officials were arrested. Eight nurses at Mthatha's Nelson Mandela Academic Hospital were arrested in 2010 for allegedly stealing R200 000 worth of medicines (Bateman, 2011). Ten health department officials in Mpumalanga, including its chief financial officer, have appeared before a disciplinary tribunal on charges of corruption. Three separate probes uncovered massive fraud and corruption in the department, including irregularities with tender procedures and the buying of unnecessary hospital equipment. Sibongile Manana, the health MEC, was removed from her post by the provincial premier, and given the sports, recreation, arts and culture portfolio. The premier justified this decision by claiming that the reshuffle of his executive council was to rectify 'instances of mismanagement and wrongdoing' uncovered by a series of forensic audits (Bateman, 2011). In KwaZulu-Natal, a report to the finance portfolio committee revealed twenty-four 'high priority' cases involving irregularities, supply-chain and human resource mismanagement, overtime fraud, corruption, nepotism, misconduct and negligence, amounting to nearly R1 billion. The former health MEC, Peggy Nkonyeni, was one of those who faced charges of irregular tender awards amounting to several million rands (Bateman, 2011).

HUMAN RESOURCES CRISIS

Staff shortages
Staff shortages are a critical problem in most public hospitals, and are the result of underfunding and a national shortage of professional skills. Almost forty-three per cent of health posts in the public sector countrywide are vacant, and the trend is deteriorating, as the figure was thirty-three per cent in 2009 and twenty-seven per cent in 2005 (Lloyd,

Sanders and Lehmann, 2010). Rural and township hospitals suffer disproportionately, with more than two-thirds of professional nurse posts and over eighty per cent of medical practitioner posts in Limpopo unfilled (Lloyd, Sanders and Lehmann, 2010). Shortages of support workers, such as cleaners and porters, exacerbate the problem, because nurses and doctors end up performing unskilled but essential functions.

It is shortages of nurses, in particular, that are generating a healthcare crisis in South African public hospitals (Von Holdt and Murphy, 2007) as nurses have a wide scope of practice, and bear the brunt of increased patient loads, staff short-ages and management failures. Primarily the consequence of the closure of nursing colleges in the 1990s as a cost-cutting measure by government, the shortage is now being addressed with recognition of the need for more nurses and more doctors to be trained. However, the constricted resources available limit a speedy or meaningful response, and considerable investment in new facilities and trainers is required over the next decade to make up the current deficit.

Throughout the country, doctors and nurses constantly make decisions about which patients to save and which to withhold treatment from, based on available staff and physical resources rather than medical criteria. Because of the pressure on beds, children are sometimes denied admission to hospitals, not referred appropriately or discharged prematurely, facing the dangers of deterioration, relapse or death.

CONDITIONS OF SERVICE

Understaffing, and vacant professional posts, result from a number of factors which vary in different locations but include failure to establish new posts despite the increased demand for services; 'frozen posts' because of insufficient funding being available; and lack of suitably qualified staff. This last-named may be because of 'pull' or 'push' factors: 'pull' factors attract staff away from the public service and include emigration and move-ment to the more lucrative private sector. 'Push' factors, such as poor salaries, the inability of hospitals to satisfy the simple creature comforts of staff, particularly in rural or town-ship settings, and blatant disrespect by hospital administrators of the professional status of staff, induce staff to leave the public service. The high death rate of health workers from AIDS has further exacerbated the skills crisis, although no objective data are avail-able about the extent of this.

The occupational specific dispensation was a measure introduced to specifically address the poor salaries paid to nurses and doctors. Although the intervention has been successful in retaining some staff in public sector hospitals, and even enticing private sector nurses and doctors back, the financial incentive was insufficient to prevent national strikes by doctors in 2009 and by the entire health sector in 2010. Much of the dissent and unhappiness related to conditions of service rather than to the declared dispute about the size of the annual increase of the pay package. The long and bruising six-week strike was a sad indictment of the poor levels of professionalism of health workers; wards full of newborn and young infants in many hospitals were abandoned instantly and completely, with no interim plans for their feeding or care. This necessitated emergency evacuations or alternative arrangements by practitioners who were willing to place their little patients' needs above those of the strike action, and by concerned members of the public. It is likely that many children's lives were lost during this industrial action, but the failure to document these deaths has prevented any consequent punitive action.

ABERRANT STAFF BEHAVIOUR

Widespread absenteeism among health professionals is common, even at well-run institutions. In one study of maternity services at fifteen hospitals and twenty-seven clinics in three South African provinces, eleven per cent of available professional nurse staff days in one month were lost to unplanned periods of leave, mostly as isolated days rather than prolonged sick leave (Penn-Kekana et al., 2005). This is often the result of stress, but nurses 'moonlighting' in private hospitals to augment their state salaries is also believed to contribute. Senior doctors are allowed to spend some time in private practice but abuse of this 'privilege' is widespread, and there are many documented instances of doctors leaving hospitals by mid-morning to pursue private practice. At poorly managed hospitals, doctors and nurses turn up late, leave early, and often neglect patient care (Cullinan, 2006). Disciplinary action by hospital managers is constrained by the centralised nature of provincial health bureaucracies. In some provinces, the provincial head of health is the only person authorised to dismiss staff.

SERVICE DELIVERY CRISIS

Inadequate patient care
There is a crisis of caring at hospitals throughout the country. Evidence of poor service delivery at hospitals is disputed, ignored, and mostly tolerated by the ready acceptance of the excuses of low staff morale, staff or resource shortages and 'no money' (Saloojee, 2010). In overburdened care environments, it is challenging for nurses and other health professionals not only to meet the daily demands of clinical care but also to maintain the emotional work of caring. The caring ethos that characterises the health profession has eroded to the degree that most patients are grateful for any acts of kindness directed towards them. Many patients can recount how their most basic needs, such as assistance with feeding, using the toilet, or pain control, have been ignored by health staff, even in situations where wards have been quiet and adequately staffed. The well-known Batho Pele (People First) and Bana Pele (Children First) principles are prominently displayed in health centres, but few staff appear to be committed to their implementation. The apartheid-era service mentality was that patients were viewed as subjects that need to be disciplined rather than citizens with rights, and this mentality is still dominant.

The consequences of such a lack of caring and accountability are predictable and inevitable for children – higher morbidity and death. Hospitalised children are the most vulnerable, because they cannot demand services or advocate for their own needs – and missed feeds, failure to receive prescribed medication timeously or missed doses, inattention to monitoring vital signs and delays in responding to sudden clinical deterioration are daily occurrences in children's wards countrywide. Researchers who conducted an eight-month observational study (including video documentation) at a large tertiary hospital in KwaZulu-Natal found that nursing staff were reluctant to become involved with caregivers and children. They performed routine and other procedures but otherwise left the children alone. Children fluctuated between states of fretful sleep, distressed crying and withdrawn immobility. Toys, visual stimuli and pacifiers were noticeably absent in the paediatric ward (Richter, Chandan and Rochat, 2009).

The evidence for inadequate paediatric care is well documented and substantial. The Saving Children 2009 report reviewed 19 295 child deaths at 101 hospitals in all nine provinces of South Africa (Stephen et al., 2011). The sites represented different levels of paediatric healthcare serving rural, peri-urban and urban populations. One-quarter of the deaths was considered to have been avoidable. For each child who died during this time there were, on average, more than two occurrences of sub-standard care, one of which could be attributed to clinical personnel. One-third of deaths occurred during the first twenty-four hours in hospital, which reflects problems with initial assessment and with the emergency care of children on admission, as well as the dire state in which children arrive at hospital because of factors such as delay in seeking care or poor nutrition. Nevertheless, the review identified problems in all areas of clinical care: assessment, management and monitoring. In the wards, staff shortages worsened progressively during the years under review.

In 2007, only fourteen of 380 public sector hospitals met and maintained standards set by the internationally accredited not-for-profit quality improvement and accreditation body, the Council for Health Service Accreditation of South Africa (Cohsasa) (Bateman, 2007). This organisation has pioneered a quality improvement programme to encourage and help hospitals to achieve compliance with its quality standards, leading ultimately to accreditation. While many hospitals (243) were supported in achieving accreditation over the previous decade, only thirty-two achieved accreditation status. Some (thirty-six) made insufficient progress or withdrew from the programme, while others (seventeen) achieved accreditation but subsequently 'backslid' as a result of not maintaining standards.

LACK OF ACCOUNTABILITY

Insufficient accountability at all levels of the health system may be the best explanation for why inept performance has been tolerated for so long. Accountability requires public officials to be answerable to the public (from whom they derive their authority) for specific actions, activities or decisions. Accountability also means establishing criteria to measure performance, as well as oversight mechanisms to ensure that standards are met. Focusing on accountability is therefore important for promoting capacity development and performance.

In the absence of any provincial or district-level monitoring of deaths or quality of care, the poor or negligent performance of some health institutions continues unchecked. A 'culture of mediocrity' dominates. Only the occasional patient or problem attracts media attention, usually because of a calamity sufficient to raise major concern from health authorities, who habitually act to punish the 'guilty party' rather than to correct or address the underlying causes and problems inherent in the system.

It is not only health professionals who are prone to ill discipline. Underperforming support workers are also able to get away with it because of the power of trade unions to protect them. Von Holdt and Murphy argue that the primary reason for the unions' 'disruptive' influence (according to nurses interviewed) was that the old apartheid disciplinary regime has crumbled in the face of worker militancy and has not been replaced with a mutually embraced new workplace order, and there is an absence of a strategic human resource function with the capacity to proactively establish a new post-apartheid disciplinary order appropriate for a constitutional democracy (Von Holdt and Murphy, 2007).

A disturbing but important set of pronouncements on the performance of the health sector was provided by the consolidated national and individual provincial reports of the Integrated Support Teams commissioned by the then minister of Health, Barbara Hogan (Barron et al., 2009). Although they were ready in May 2009, the reports were only publicly available after being leaked in late 2010. The consolidated report was scathing about many issues noting a lack of:

- national guidelines, norms and standards;
- alignment between planning, implementation and monitoring and evaluation;
- managerial accountability for the attainment of service-related targets; and
- clarity regarding roles and responsibilities (between monitoring and evaluation, strategic planning and programme divisions [for example, HIV, TB, maternal and child health]).

The national Department of Health has been loath to establish clear norms and standards for a number of key areas such as human resources (for example the number of nurses per paediatric bed), equipment or budgets. This is probably related to a fear of the real possibility of a court challenge if it is found wanting in its own standards. The consequence is a further lack of accountability, as no one can be held accountable for not delivering to a standard that does not exist. This situation is now being addressed through the establishment of an office of health standards compliance at the national level.

SOLUTIONS

From the description presented, it should be clear that a solution to the health crisis in general, and for hospital care of children in particular, requires the intervention of multiple actors and activities, demands new and reallocated resources, and will inevitably be a long-term process. Many health professionals despair, not knowing how to influence or effect change in such a complicated and dysfunctional system, and prefer to do nothing, hoping that some saviour (such as the minister of Health) will fix everything. The health minister himself recognises the need to 'overhaul the whole health system' and considers the healthcare system unsustainable, 'extremely expensive', curative and 'hospicentric' (*The Star*, 2011). But despite there being no quick fixes, a number of short- and medium-term solutions could significantly ameliorate the situation. The limited scope of this chapter prevents an in-depth exploration of these ideas. Many should be obvious, from the detail presented earlier, but even obvious solutions can be impossible to implement in some environments. Below, I summarise some of the key interventions required.

IMPROVED HOSPITAL AND WARD GOVERNANCE

A major impediment to adequate care at state hospitals is managerial disempowerment. Considerable investment in management capacity and systems is required to overcome current management paralysis, and optimise scarce financial and human resource usage. A restructuring of the relationship between provincial head offices and public hospitals is a priority, as is the empowering of hospital management and augmentation of their competencies. There is recognition and agreement at the highest levels, including the presidency, about the need for this.

Provincial head offices must relinquish their stranglehold on hospitals and an insistence on micromanagement, and concentrate instead on policy, strategy and the monitoring of management performance. Hospital managers should have the authority to run their own hospitals and should be held accountable for this without undue interference from head offices, according to agreed business, budget and performance plans. Hospital organisational structures should be based on clear operational units. A unit such as paediatrics should have clear lines of authority and accountability and silo functions should be disintegrated.

IMPROVED STAFF AVAILABILITY, RETENTION AND DEVELOPMENT

Equally disabling is the lack of competent staff. In his 2011 State of the Nation address, Jacob Zuma emphasised the need for the appointment of appropriate and qualified health personnel. Nurses' training colleges are being reopened and medical schools are being encouraged to increase admission numbers, with a clear preference for students originating from rural or remote settings because they are more likely to return there on completing their training. Equally important is the training of specialists such as paediatricians. A doubling of paediatricians in the public sector is warranted, and possible, within the next decade.

The occupational-specific dispensation has made public sector salaries much more attractive and competitive. Task shifting, where tasks that can be performed by fewer trained staff with specific skills are allowed to manage some conditions within their competency, is acknowledged to be a useful way of dealing with the skills deficit, but a more difficult problem to overcome is the inability of hospital and provincial administrators to manage health professionals – not as dispensable and readily replaceable commodities, but as valuable assets whose needs (such as decent living quarters or receiving salaries on time) must be respected.

APPLICATION OF NORMS AND STANDARDS

Better service delivery can be promoted through the generation and application of norms and standards, including monitoring of compliance. The new office of health standards compliance will need to be adequately resourced to develop a national repository of norms, standards and guidelines, and should oversee the development and implementation of more effective and affordable service, quality and clinical care guidelines. Extending the Child Healthcare Identification Programme (CHIP) system of auditing deaths to all hospitals in the country offers another mechanism for quality control, even though this approach only scrutinises those children with the worst outcome, death.

DISCIPLINE AND ACCOUNTABILITY

Measures and procedures that extract accountability from support staff, health professionals, managers and administrators are desperately needed, but few have succeeded to date. Civil society has played a prominent role in promoting action for HIV/AIDS and could play a more powerful role in demanding and contributing to healthcare delivery. However, even the highly successful AIDS advocacy group, the Treatment Action Campaign, were able to achieve only very limited success in the mid-2000s when they attempted to extend their role to mobilise and organise individuals and communities to tackle broader health system issues.

DISTRICT (REGIONAL) PAEDIATRICIANS

A promising recent development is the acceptance by the Health ministry of the need to create a committed layer of senior clinicians (paediatrician, obsterician and family physician) to oversee the function of the various major specialties in each of the fifty-two districts in the country. The regional paediatrician, for instance, would be required to oversee the development and implementation of norms and standards for the physical infrastructure and equipment of children in all hospitals in his or her district. This individual would be required to organise training, to address issues of inequity, to improve synchronisation between clinics and hospitals, and to remove bottlenecks in the referral system.

MORE RESOURCES FOR CHILDREN'S HEALTH

The specific requirement for paediatrics is a commitment to greater resource allocation for children's health. A recent exercise conducted in Gauteng estimated that an additional (marginal) investment of just R4 billion over five years (or R70 per capita) in maternal and child healthcare could save the lives of 14 283 children and reduce the under-five mortality rate by half, almost meeting the target of the provincial Millennium Development Goal 4 for 2015. This additional investment would require less than five per cent of the current provincial health budget (Gauteng Department of Health, 2009). Not all of this has to be 'new' money – much, but not all, of the money could be obtained through reducing present inefficiencies.

The government will introduce a new national health insurance in 2012. Details are still sketchy and its impact on childcare at hospitals is difficult to predict. It is primarily a healthcare financing mechanism, raising funds from taxpayers and private health sector users to subsidise healthcare benefits for the general population. The minister of Health has argued that the NHI could deliver 'universal coverage and better healthcare in one united healthcare system' (*The Times*, 2009). Sceptics argue that it can and will do little to address the inherent flaws in the health delivery system outlined in this chapter. The benefit for children is difficult to predict.

Many of the recommendations made in this section are not new; they are well recognised and some have been accepted by health departments in the past, although there is limited evidence of their implementation and even less evidence of their successful implementation. Even so, islands of excellence remain in the public health service, with many hospitals continuing to provide good care in the face of the same financial and logistical constraints as evidenced elsewhere. The challenge for health practitioners countrywide is to turn around a health service that appears to be in a spiralling decline. Children's lives depend on stopping the rot and finding new solutions promptly.

REFERENCES

Barron P, H Gouws, B Loots, G Mistry, L Rispel and A Snyman (2009) Consolidated Report of the Integrated Support Team: Review of health overspending and macro-assessment of the public health system in South Africa. DFID Rapid Response Health Fund. http://www.hst.org.za/indicators/DoH/IST_reports/

Bateman C (2007) Izindaba: Hospital standards – private expertise virtually unused, *South African Medical Journal* 97 (9): 821–825.

Bateman C (2011) Izindaba: Health corruption busters reveal the monster in our midst, *South African Medical Journal* 101 (1):1155.

Bodibe K (2010) Why children died still unclear. Cape Town: Health-e News Service.

Children's Institute (2010) *South African Child Gauge 2009/2010*. Cape Town: University of Cape Town.

Colleges of Medicine of South Africa (2009) Project: Strengthening academic medicine and specialist training. [Unpublished data].

Coovadia H, R Jewkes, P Barron, D Sanders and D McIntyre (2009) The health and health system of South Africa: historical roots of current public health challenges, *Lancet* 374(9692): 817–834.

Cullinan K (2006) South Africa: Hospitals in crisis. Cape Town: Health-e News Service.

Cullinan K (2009) Zim crisis 'A threat to SA AIDS success', *Saturday Argus*, 4 April 2009, p. 13.

Day C and A Gray (2010) Health and related indicators. In Fonn S and A Padarath (Eds) *South African Health Review*. Durban: Health Systems Trust.

Department of Health (2010) *Strategic plan 2009/10–2011/12*. Pretoria: DoH.

Dlamini B (2011) Under 18s now eligible for child support grant – Minister. Politicsweb: http://www.politics web.co.za/politicsweb/view/politicsweb/en/page71656?oid=219530&sn=Detail&pid=71656.

Engelbrecht B and N Crisp (2010) Improving the performance of the health sector. In Fonn S and A Padarath (Eds) *South African Health Review*. Durban: Health Systems Trust.

Gauteng Department of Health (2009) Marginal budgeting for bottlenecks. [Unpublished report].

Kok D (2009) Entstofkrisis in Vrystaat, *Volksblad;* 5 August.

Lloyd B, D Sanders and U Lehmann (2010) Human resource requirements for national health insurance. In Fonn S and A Padarath (Eds) *South African Health Review*. Durban: Health Systems Trust.

McKerrow N and M Mulaudzi (2010) Child mortality in South Africa: Using existing data. In Fonn S and A Padarath (Eds) *South African Health Review*. Durban: Health Systems Trust.

Mukotsanjera V, K Mwenge and G Giya (2009) *HIV and AIDS: Analysis of the South African National Budget (2009/10)*. Cape Town: Institute for Democracy in South Africa.

National Treasury (2009) Provincial Budgets and Expenditure Review 2005/06 - 2011/12. Pretoria: National Treasury. http://www.treasury.gov.za/

Penn-Kekana L, D Blaauw, KS Tint, D Monareng and J Chege (2005). Nursing Staff Dynamics and Implications for Maternal Health Provision in Public Health Facilities in the Context of HIV/AIDS. http://www.popcouncil.org/pdfs/frontiers/FR_FinalReports/SA_QOC.pdf

Philip R (2009) Hospital hell, *Sunday Times*, 24 May.

Report on childhood deaths, Ukhahlamba District, Eastern Cape. http://www.health-e.org.za/documents/7f3 d48106e60e6e5d164698624c5efb3.pdf

Richter L, U Chandan, T Rochat (2009) Improving hospital care for young children in the context of HIV/AIDS and poverty, *Journal of Child Health Care* 13: 198–211.

Saloojee H and JM Pettifor (2005) International Child Health: 10 years of democracy in South Africa; the challenges facing children today, *Current Paediatrics* 15: 429–36.

Saloojee H (2010) 'No we can't': What will it take to change the 'lack of' chant? *South African Journal of Clinical Nutrition* 23: 7–8.

Schneider H, P Barron and S Fonn (2007) The promise and the practice of transformation in South Africa's health system. In Buhlungu S, J Daniel, R Southall and J Lutchman (Eds) *State of the Nation: South Africa 2007*. Cape Town and East Lansing: HSRC Press and Michigan State University Press.

Shisana O, L Simbayi, T Rehle, N Zungu, K Zuma and N Ngogo (2010) *South African National HIV Prevalence, Incidence, Behaviour and Communication Survey, 2008: The health of our children*. Cape Town: Human Science Research Council.

Statistics South Africa (2009) General Household Survey 2008. In Hall K (2010) *Demography – Children in South Africa*. Children Count – Abantwana Babalulekile website, Children's Institute, UCT. www.childrencount.ci.org.za/indicator.php?id=1&indicator=1

Stephen CR, LJ Bamford, ME Patrick and DF Wittenberg (Eds) (2011). *Saving Children 2009: Five Years of Data. A sixth survey of child healthcare in South Africa*. Pretoria: Tshepesa Press, Medical Research Council, Centres for Disease.

The Star (2011) Motsoaledi: Health system needs overhaul, *The Star*, 27 January.

The Times (2009) State counts on private health facilities, *The Times*, 6 June.

Thom A (2008) 140 baby deaths due to poor health services. Cape Town, Health-e News Service.

UNICEF (2009) *State of the World's Children 2010. Special Report. Celebrating 20 Years on the Convention on the Rights of the Child.* New York: UNICEF.

Von Holdt K and M Murphy (2007) Public hospitals in South Africa: Stressed institutions, disempowered management. In Buhlungu S, J Daniel, R Southall and J Lutchman (Eds) *State of the Nation: South Africa 2007.* Cape Town and East Lansing: HSRC Press & Michigan State University Press.

World Bank (2010) Gross national income 2008, Atlas method. World Development Indicators database, 1 9 April 2010. http://siteresources.worldbank.org/DATASTATISTICS/Resources/GNI.pdf

World Health Organization (2000) The World Health Report 2000. Geneva: WHO.

World Health Organization (2003) How much should countries spend on health? Discussion paper no. 2, 2003. EIP/FER/DP.3.2. Geneva: WHO.

CHAPTER 10

The worker cooperative alternative in South Africa

Vishwas Satgar and Michelle Williams[1]

Modern cooperatives have existed for over 150 years and are found in nearly every corner of the globe. Although cooperative trade only registers at one per cent of world trade, a 2007 International Cooperative Alliance (ICA) study shows that the top 300 cooperatives are equivalent to the tenth largest economy, and while they make up a small fraction of global trade, cooperatives have continued to survive in the difficult global capitalist conditions that prevail today. While their survival is impressive, cooperatives are extraordinary not for their economic success but rather for the principles and values that constitute their inherent character. Of these values and principles, democratic owner-ship, one-member-one-vote, collective decision making, and an ethic of cooperation and solidarity (as opposed to individualism and competition) lie at the heart of genuine worker-owned cooperatives.

Cooperatives also have a long and multifaceted history in South Africa. From the racially determined apartheid cooperatives to the post-apartheid black economic empowerment approach to cooperatives, they have featured prominently in the economy for much of the twentieth and beginning of the twenty-first centuries and have been instrumental to development over the last sixty years. There have been markedly different approaches to cooperatives over this period. Today there is a sharply defined duality: on one side the emerging black cooperatives and on the other the older and established (mostly white) 'cooperatives'. This duality also reflects their impact on the economy. Emerging coop-eratives have tended to target poverty alleviation and local-level development, while the established cooperatives have been concentrated in the agro-processing sector and have significant assets and turnovers. We focus primarily on the emerging cooperatives in this chapter.

Using interviews, field visits and existing literature, we look at the shift from apartheid to post-apartheid cooperative development, and focus on the use and appropriation of the white cooperative development experience in the contemporary black economic empowerment context. Instead of providing a narrative history of cooperative devel-opment, we concentrate on how the past shapes the present and what is at stake. We argue that emulating the Afrikaner empowerment approach does not engender genuine cooperative development, but rather abuses the cooperative form for perverse forms of economic development. Post-apartheid South Africa has gone this way with disastrous consequences. Instead of engendering genuine cooperatives grounded in values, prin-ciples, cooperative identity and advantage, a business approach to cooperatives has been promoted. In quantitative and qualitative terms the state-driven business approach to cooperatives has not worked.

A long view of the history of cooperatives illustrates a double failure of cooperative development, in both the past and the present. This provides a point of departure for discussing alternative approaches, particularly worker ownership. In this chapter we discuss the general theoretical case for such an approach and illustrate the importance of worker ownership, as a new form of work and property relations, in relation to contem-porary trade union practice. Using three case studies, we illustrate how unions have utilised the worker cooperative alternative in the context of the current economic crisis. We highlight a new trend in trade union-linked worker cooperatives as opposed to the more established community-based worker cooperatives.

COOPERATIVE HISTORY OF DOUBLE FAILURE: Apartheid to post-apartheid cooperatives

The South African historical narrative on cooperative development is complex. The racial duality of cooperative development engendered by early twentieth-century segre-gation, and later apartheid, utilised the cooperative form in a perverse way to empower and enrich a minority.[2] At its height in the twentieth century, the racialised cooperative economy buttressed agricultural modernisation and financial diversification through mutuals and building societies, and fostered various forms of service-based coopera-tives (Van Niekerk, 1998).[3] The state provided enabling conditions through financial, regulatory, and technical support. Some economists suggest that a few hundred 'whites only cooperatives' in the early 1990s contributed close to two per cent of national GDP, translating into billions of rands. In white-controlled agriculture the structural economic power of cooperatives was starkly evidenced.

In the early 1990s, 250 white agricultural cooperatives had approximately 142 000 members, total assets of R12.7 billion, turnover of R22.5 billion and annual pre-tax profits of more than R500 million (Amin and Bernstein, 1995). Agricultural cooperatives handled all exports of citrus and deciduous fruit, processed the entire wool clip, and marketed ninety per cent of dried fruit. On the input side, they provided and/or financed ninety per cent of fertiliser, eighty-five per cent of fuel, sixty-five per cent of chemicals, and a significant proportion of the machinery and implements used by white farmers. They also provided twenty-five per cent of credit used by white farmers (Amin and Bernstein, 1995: 5). At the heart of this white-owned agricultural complex were eleven summer grain cooperatives of which the two largest, OTK and SWK, had annual turnovers of R2.374 billion and R2.22 billion respectively. This suggests ostensibly impressive development and provides an important insight into the role cooperatives played in the apartheid political economy.

Notwithstanding its racialised dimension and duality, apartheid cooperative development was successful. It was, however, only a qualified success. It is ironic that post-apartheid cooperative development is understood through the success of that racialised system, from which it follows that post-apartheid cooperative development must benefit the previously oppressed majority in the same way, and that Afrikaner empowerment through cooperatives has its inverse in post-apartheid South Africa: black economic empowerment (BEE). In other words, African nationalism seeks to achieve what Afrikaner nationalism attained through cooperative development. In policy terms, this nation-building rationale is entrenched in the Black Economic Empowerment Act (No. 53 of 2003), which provides an ideologically loaded, prescriptive discourse for cooperative policy and legislation.[4] The BEE discursive emphasis on cooperatives has been buttressed through significant policy and legislative developments over the past sixteen years; this includes the Cooperative Development Policy for South Africa (2003), the Cooperatives Act (No.14 of 2005) and the Cooperatives Bank Act (No. 40 of 2007), which are crucial policy and legislative pillars for promoting cooperative development. The BEE approach has, however, politicised cooperative development, to the extent that cooperatives are a central instrument for the achievement of black economic empowerment rather than of cooperative empowerment, and suggests a nationalist-driven capitalist and racialised approach to cooperative development.

The appropriation of cooperatives by Afrikaner and by African nationalism has influenced how cooperatives are understood in development. This raises a number of questions. Is replicating an Afrikaner empowerment model to cooperative development in post-apartheid South Africa the appropriate way forward? To what extent does a hegemonic Afrikaner/African nationalist discourse undermine alternative cooperative development approaches such as bottom- up-worker-owned cooperatives? Central to answering these questions is whether or not Afrikaner and BEE-driven cooperative development have been 'successful'. From a normative point of view, success comes down to two issues. First, what is the definition of a 'genuine' cooperative? Genuine cooperatives are universally understood as enterprises that institutionally and practically embody the values and principles of the international cooperative move-ment. Second, the logic of member-driven cooperative development determines its content. Is it building an alternative cooperative economy or is it integrating with existing capitalist structures?

Based on the two foregoing criteria we argue that South Africa's apartheid and post-apartheid history of cooperative development is based on a *double failure*: failure of the past and failure of the present. Two issues stand out. First, both Afrikaner and BEE cooper-atives reproduce a racialised duality. Afrikaner cooperatives were consciously established as 'whites only', and while the racial character of BEE cooperatives may not be intentional, it has not deracialised cooperatives because BEE discourse evokes racial exclusiveness and engenders an unintentional form of racial discrimination. This discriminatory dimension is contrary to the non-discriminatory approach of the international coopera-tive movement. Second, while Afrikaner empowerment initially promoted cooperative forms to meet members' needs through collective ownership and democratic member control, these qualities were eroded over time. As South African capitalism developed, Afrikaner empowerment cooperatives increasingly began to behave like typical capitalist businesses. A values-based practice gave way to profit maximisation, and member-driven cooperatives were replaced with management hierarchies. Power slipped from member control. The size of these cooperatives and widening geographic operations also played a role in undermining member control.

On the other hand, BEE-led cooperative development shows an attempt by the state to promote a market-centred approach. The almost instant registration of cooperatives without proper planning, generic start-up financing and supply-side attempts at coop-erative education have not led to genuine cooperative consciousness and understanding. Instead, cooperatives have been treated as just another business form and understood in quantitative terms as part of outcomes-based management within the state bureaucracy. This translates into a numbers game – the more cooperatives registered the better, and as a result there has been a rapid growth in numbers. For example, in 1994 there were 1 300 registered cooperatives, which grew to 4 061 by 2007. Then, remarkably, between 2007 and 2009 the number of cooperatives jumped to 22 030 and again soared further to 31 898 formally registered cooperatives by 2010[5] (see Table 1). The majority are located in four provinces – KwaZulu-Natal, Limpopo, Gauteng and the Eastern Cape – and are mainly found in villages, townships, and on farms (DTI, 2009: 3). The promotion efforts of cooperative development have spanned national departments, provincial and local government and state-linked institutions, with the state providing large fiscal injections. For example, the total financial outlay between 2005 and 2010 for cooperative develop-ment within these institutions amounts to R923 million.[6]

The lack of bottom-up cooperative development centred on member education has produced dismal outcomes. In 2009, the DTI baseline study established that out of a total of 22 030 cooperatives, an overwhelming majority of 19 386 were no longer functioning: an eighty-eight per cent failure rate. In KwaZulu-Natal, with the highest spend (R454 million) and highest number of cooperatives (8 697), the mortality rate of eighty-eight

Table 1: Cooperative numbers by province

Province	Current data from Cipro register	National picture: No. of surviving co-ops	No. of dead co-ops	Survival rate	Mortality rate
KwaZulu-Natal	8 697	1 044	7 653	12 per cent	88 per cent
Eastern Cape	4 124	287	3 957	7 per cent	93 per cent
Western Cape	1 003	69	934	7 per cent	93 per cent
Northern Cape	798	20	778	2.5 per cent	97.5 per cent
Limpopo	1 779	405	1 474	22 per cent	78 per cent
Mpumalanga	1 396	187	1 309	12.5 per cent	87.5 per cent
Gauteng	2 265	394	1 971	17 per cent	83 per cent
Free State	850	71	829	8 per cent	92 per cent
North West	1 208	167	1 090	13 per cent	87 per cent
National Total	22 030	2 644	19 386	12 per cent	88 per cent

Source: DTI Baseline Study 2009.

per cent mirrors the national trend such that only 1 044 cooperatives are surviving.[7] Nationally, only 2 644 have survived out of 22 030. However, survival does not necessarily equate with the ability to realise cooperative objectives and meet member needs. For example, in the Amathole region of the Eastern Cape most cooperatives are marginal or barely managing to be self-developing (COPAC, 2010). Out of twenty case studies only one cooperative was commercially viable and grounded in institutional cooperative practices that ensure values and principles exist in its everyday world. Many of the cooperatives were given government financial support through grants, and had built up assets, but were not able to effectively utilise these resources, partly because while the government provided funds to cooperatives, it did not facilitate education and training to evolve them in a member-driven manner.

Under apartheid, member-driven cooperative development was not a priority. Instead, Afrikaner empowerment was integral to a racialised model of capitalist development, which reached its apogee in the 1990s when many large white farming cooperatives converted into companies.[8] This trend has continued into the present, the most recent being National Clover Dairies (*Sunday Times*, 2010). Cooperative conversion into companies dismisses any attempt to build a cooperative economy through strategic choices. At the same time, 'white cooperatives' that have remained so are in fact only nominally cooperatives, but behave in practice as any other capitalist business. In other words, they are 'business cooperatives', and are not concerned with grounding their economic activities within cooperative identity and practice. In structural terms, both forms of white cooperative experience (converted into companies and business cooperatives) reflect the liberalisation of the South African economy.

In the post-apartheid context emergent black cooperatives are simply treated as another business form similar to the white business cooperatives that seek a place in the 'first economy'. Two things stand out. First, while the push from the state is about leap-frogging these institutions into viable businesses, the squeeze from the market creates a 'push back' pressure – in other words, the market does not facilitate cooperative development into viable cooperative enterprises, but rather encourages the members to see themselves as BEE entrepreneurs and as a result many cooperatives end up in the arms of the state or are pushed back into poverty (Satgar and Williams, 2008). Clearly, this type of state approach does not build a cooperative economy with backward/forward and horizontal/vertical linkages through a movement. Instead, it is about a failed state-supported business approach to cooperatives.[9] Second, through a qualitative study of successful cooperatives in Africa, we found that strategic and enabling state-cooperative relations contributed to more positive development conditions for cooperatives (Satgar and Williams, 2008). However, in South Africa the state has not pursued such a strategic and enabling state-cooperative relationship, but has, rather, relied on a top-down, market-led approach.

This failure of the state to build genuine relations with cooperatives has reverberated into the 'cooperative movement'.[10] The two failed attempts of cooperative movement building, which began in 1996, were top down, and the more recent effort (2000–2004) was undermined by bureaucratic state control, vanguardism emanating from the South African Communist Party (SACP), and corruption. Today the National Cooperative Association of South Africa (Ncasa) is a moribund organisation, but despite these experiences the state continues to drive cooperative development from above. The current state strategy and proposed amendments to the Cooperative Act suggest a number of support organisations such as a Cooperatives Development Agency (for financial and non financial support), a Cooperative Training Academy, a Cooperative Tribunal (for adjudicating disputes, enforcement of the act and investigation), a Cooperative Advisory Council, a grant and loans-based financing model, and a new tax regime for cooperative promotion.[11] While still in the policy-making process, these institutions should be celebrated in that they potentially provide vital institutional support, but there is also the danger that they will further entrench relations of dependency on the state, given the existing mould of state practice.

THE EMERGENCE OF THE WORKER COOPERATIVE ALTERNATIVE

The demographic makeup of emerging cooperatives contrasts markedly with the established white cooperatives. Emerging cooperatives tend to be small and rooted in villages and townships, with a majority of women members and a significant presence of youth members. For example, sixty-five per cent of cooperatives have fewer than ten members and twenty-three per cent have between eleven and twenty members; only twelve per cent have over a hundred members (DTI, 2009: 4). The majority are primary cooperatives with a much smaller number of secondary cooperatives and three tertiary cooperatives.[12] What this suggests is that primary cooperatives have not been able to form secondary and tertiary cooperatives that coordinate and support each other within and across sectors. Agricultural cooperatives (including white business cooperatives) continue to be the largest sector at 29.71 per cent, with service cooperatives registering the next largest at 14.84 per cent, and multipurpose and construction at 9.55 per cent and 9.37 per cent respectively (DTI, 2009 and 2010).

Cooperatives are deeply rooted in communities in South Africa. For example, the DTI 2009 survey found that more than seventy-five per cent of those surveyed were formed through community initiatives. Interestingly, the survey also found that worker cooperatives only represent 1.03 per cent, although this low number is misleading for two reasons. First, the study asked cooperatives to identify themselves without reference to their legal standing based on the Cooperatives Act of 2005 (that is, it did not ask under which legal classification the cooperative was registered).[13] Second, self-identification was done in a context in which there were low levels of understanding – a worker cooperative might, in practice, not be able to recognise itself as such because the worker owners do not have in-depth knowledge of cooperatives in general, and their cooperative in particular. Ironically, one of the study's findings was that many aspirant cooperatives did not understand the cooperative model.

Whether there are large or small numbers of worker cooperatives in South Africa today is not the crucial point. What is important is that worker cooperatives have an important contribution to make, as an alternative economic form, to national and local development but for this role to be fulfilled two important aspects of worker cooperatives must be clearly understood. First, the normative case for worker cooperatives, derived from international and historical experiences spanning more than two centuries, must be made. The main arguments are the following:

- **Worker owner-based work** is fundamental to a worker cooperative, which is characterised by worker owners who work in their enterprise under conditions determined by them collectively. The worker owners own the enterprise and collectively share in the benefits and losses. In short, a worker cooperative organises work differently than other forms of work such as self-employed or wage earning forms of work.[14]
- **Economic democracy** refers to the practice in which all decisions about production, distribution, and the redistribution of surplus are made democratically

by members of the cooperative. The importance of economic democracy goes beyond the workplace as it has positive implications for political democracy by inculcating democratic skills, an appreciation for values, and human capabilities-centred development. In other words, economic democracy enhances citizen participation in practising democracy in the political sphere. It also lends itself to incorporating ecologically centered production. This stands in contrast to the capital-managed firm in which the labour process is based on hierarchy, control, subordination, ecological destruction, and lack of transparency.

- **Equality** refers to the value that worker cooperatives have for society in terms of ensuring and promoting greater equality of income and wealth distribution. This is partly a function of worker-controlled decisions, information sharing and values-based practices. Worker cooperatives tend to have flatter income scales, even if labour market pressures for scarce skills have placed pressure on worker cooperatives to properly compensate skilled labour. This stands in contrast to capital-led firms, which generally distribute income upwards and engender deep inequalities in society.

The secondary aspects of worker cooperatives that must be understood are conceptual and legal, and are constantly evolving from practice. We have identified four primary categories of worker cooperatives: worker owned, worker producer, worker managed and worker supported. While worker control and ownership is central to all four forms, there are interesting variations that fit different sectoral needs. The variation relates to how internal relations are organised through membership, degrees of worker control (over strategic, policy and operational decisions) and, finally, the structure of ownership. While the classic worker cooperative is what we have thus far referred to, the other three forms – worker producer, worker managed and worker supported – also exist, although they are not as well known.

Worker producer cooperatives most often exist in agriculture, but can also be found in sectors that lend themselves to a degree of individual ownership. In agriculture, individual members often own their own plots of land, but collectively farm, harvest, process, and market the production from the land through a worker producer cooperative. In other sectors, such as information technology (IT), there exist worker producer cooperatives in which individual operators combine into a cooperative in order to provide a service. The cooperative allows for individual members to own their own means of production such as computers (or plot of land in the case of agriculture), but to collectively provide the service (or harvest, process, and market the produce in the case of agriculture).

Worker managed cooperatives, on the other hand, exist in a nationalised enterprise where the state owns the means of production, but the enterprise is managed through worker control. In such cases the cooperative often owns property, such as equipment and raw materials, within the enterprise. For example, in Argentina the Zanon tile factory is owned by the state but managed and controlled by the worker members in a worker managed cooperative.

The fourth type, the worker supported cooperative, is a relatively new form that has recently taken root in parts of Europe and Canada in an attempt to utilise worker cooperatives for the disadvantaged in society. In Trento, Italy, for example, worker supported cooperatives for the physically disabled have been very successful in the restaurant and handicraft sectors. The physically disabled are the main worker members, but there are other categories of membership such as volunteer members who provide skills training, and finance members who provide a regular financial contribution to assist the cooperative with operating capital. Table 2 provides an overview of the four types of worker cooperatives.

Table 2: Typology of worker cooperatives

Type of worker cooperative	Membership	Degree of worker control	Ownership
Worker owned cooperative	Worker owners	Worker control of strategic, policy and operational decisions (all decisions)	Individual and/or collective ownership of all cooperative property
Worker producer cooperative	Worker owners	Worker control of all decisions	Individual ownership of land or other means of production but also collective ownership of cooperative property
Worker managed cooperative	Worker owners	Worker control of all decisions	Individual and/or collective ownership of cooperative property but state ownership of means of production
Worker supported cooperative	Worker owners, other kinds of members	Worker control of operational decisions	Individual and/or collective ownership of cooperative property with other members

All four types of worker cooperatives are normally governed by national laws and internal legal arrangements embodied in a constitution. In South Africa, the Cooperatives Act (2005) is very narrow and does not elaborate on the different kinds of worker cooperatives identified above but, rather, it collapses all of them into the worker owned cooperative model.[15] The Act does, however, provide guidelines for worker owned cooperative constitutions to ensure provision for membership conditions; rules for organising work; termination of membership; provisions for temporarily laying-off members; and for the exemption of worker cooperatives from the Labour Relations Act and the Basic Conditions of Employment Act (the reason for this exemption is that worker cooperatives are made up of worker owners and not employees). In cases where employment is provided it must be in accordance with the Act and the constitution of the cooperative. Essentially these provisions ensure that a worker cooperative does not lose its identity by exploiting paid labour. In most instances, genuine worker cooperatives are extremely conscious of the labour standards and conditions of work for non-worker owner employees (and, in fact, rarely engage in such employment relations).

In the following section of this chapter we explore the role of trade unions in worker cooperative development.

TRADE UNIONS, THE ECONOMIC CRISIS AND WORKER COOPERATIVES

The worker cooperative alternative emerged out of movements searching for alternatives in the nineteenth century. Utopian socialists, Marxists, anarchists, Christian socialists and various other political traditions championed worker cooperatives in various contexts. At the same time, moments of economic crises brought the worker cooperative alternative to the fore. In the twentieth century, during the great depression and the aftermath of the Second World War, worker cooperatives played a crucial role in reconstructing societies and providing a new kind of work. More recently the crisis of the neoliberalised economies has also brought the worker cooperative alternative to the fore. For example, in response to the economic collapse in Argentina in 2001, over 200 enterprises were taken over by workers and run as worker cooperatives, and with the more recent systemic shock, another wave of worker takeovers is happening in different parts of Latin America, and the world.

South Africa also had an experience of worker cooperatives during the apartheid era, including community-based worker cooperatives and trade union-linked cooperatives. In many ways these initiatives were inspired by the radicalism of the national liberation struggle. The trade union-linked cooperatives emerged in the context of retrenchments, but many of these experiences failed.[16] Both internal and external factors explain the failures; there were organisational, financial, technical and trade union dynamics that posed serious challenges. In the case of the National Union of Mineworkers (NUM), for example, the late 1980s and early 1990s saw the union set up the Mine Workers Development Agency as an independent vehicle to support NUM cooperatives. However, many of these cooperatives failed because of bad planning, a lack of proper education on worker cooperatives, financial constraints and donor-driven approaches to cooperative development.[17] Moreover, the trade union in the post-apartheid context has increasingly moved away from transformative approaches to property relations and has chosen employee stock-option schemes and employment equity struggles as a means of deracialising capitalism.

Post-apartheid South Africa has witnessed two waves of worker cooperatives. The first wave has been mainly community based, with one trade union-linked example (discussed below). More recently, there has been a second wave, of community-based cooperatives and a few hopeful signs of emerging trade union-linked worker cooperatives (also discussed below).

Table 3: Trade union-linked cooperatives in post-apartheid South Africa

Trade union	Date	Context	Approach	Level of worker cooperative development
Nehawu	1998	Outsourcing	Collective bargaining	Growth and expansion
Numsa	2009	Distressed enterprise	Buy out	Start-up
Mewusa	2010	Insolvent enterprise	Workplace occupation	Ground work

In the following sections we discuss each of these experiences of trade union-linked worker cooperatives.[18] All the examples continue to face serious challenges and are at different stages of development. We chose to showcase these examples, not for their shining success, but to illustrate the way in which trade unions are experimenting with worker owned cooperatives and to explore the way in which cooperatives are part of trade unions' strategic responses to retrenchments, outsourcing and layoffs.

NOMZAMO GARDENING AND GROUNDS WORKER COOPERATIVE

The Nomzamo Gardening and Grounds Cooperative maintains the gardens and grounds at the University of Fort Hare in Alice, Eastern Cape. The cooperative emerged in the context of a fiscal squeeze on the university through the imposition of conservative macroeconomic management in which universities were forced to restructure and bring down running costs in order to be become viable 'business entities' that depend less on government support. In the case of Fort Hare, when the university outsourced its cleaning and grounds-keeping services in 1998, the workers decided to form a cooperative and tender for the new contract. The National Education, Health and Allied Workers Union (Nehawu) played a pivotal role in assisting the workers and negotiating with the university to secure the contract.

After long and difficult negotiations, the university agreed to the union's proposal, although it still took a couple of years before the tender was received. One cooperative, the Nomzamo Worker Cooperative Limited, was formed in July 1998, bringing together the gardening and grounds and the cleaning staff. The cooperative received important support from students and the rector of the university. In 2002, the gardening and grounds workers broke away from the cleaning cooperative and formed its own separate cooperative with fifty-three members (forty-five per cent of whom were women and fifty-five per cent youth). By 2010, the cooperative, having gone through many difficult times, was tightly run, guided and motivated by an innovative and enterprising former mining trade-union shop steward. While Nehawu was vital in forming the cooperative, over time it became less involved.

The cooperative provides grounds and garden services to the university by maintaining grass and flower gardens, landscaping, cleaning hard elements (sweeping pavements; maintaining tarred roads and gravel areas; dust bins and refuse removal), looking after irrigation systems, and maintaining sports fields. Because the cooperative sees its role as providing employment to its members and as an instrument to meet its members' other needs, another important objective is to promote the economic interests of its members in a wider context and the cooperative has mobilised its members to join the Amandla Savings and Credit Cooperative. The cooperative is also developing policies to address the retirement of older members and has decided to have a pension fund.

The cooperative also holds member education and training in high regard and supports skills development opportunities for its members through job rotation, the provision of adult basic education and training (ABET) and computer literacy, as well as courses on horticulture, composting and permaculture. The cooperative has also been able to rely on the advice and short-term training provided by the university's Community Business Development Support Centre (CBDC) for ongoing opera-tional challenges – however, this has not included extensive and ongoing education and training on how cooperatives work, and how to consolidate cooperative identity, culture and practices.

Nomzamo provides a useful example of the structure of a worker cooperative. The general manager coordinates official administrative duties between the cooperative and the university. There are five distinct sub-areas, each with its own coordinator: grass cutting and flower decoration, refuse management, irrigation, sports fields and grounds, and general workers. There is also a part-time horticultural expert. To facilitate rela-tions with the university, the cooperative proposed a university gardening and grounds committee composed of different members of the university community chaired by either the chief operations officer or the contracts manager. The committee oversees and advises on the maintenance of the garden and grounds. It has improved communica-tion between the cooperative and the university, and it facilitates proactive approaches to problems and challenges. It also acts as a complaints-handling mechanism and a quality assurance system, and provides advice on landscaping and the preservation of natural resources within the institution as required by environmental laws.

The cooperative has faced many challenges, including from within its own struc-ture. Its most serious challenge was between 2003 and 2005, when it was taken over by a rogue committee. After the gardening and grounds cooperative separated from the cleaning cooperative, it employed a general manager and elected a board of worker directors, which became the rogue committee in collusion with the general manager. This rogue committee was involved in fraudulent activities and embezzled R200 000 of the cooperative's money. During this period, the members of the cooperative felt as if they were living under a reign of terror; they felt powerless and some were forced to condone the criminal activities. The rogue leadership became a serious crime syndicate using the cooperative's office to steal university property (copper and other metal) for resale on the black market. The members of the group were eventually arrested and convicted (the cooperative also laid charges of fraud against them), and this provided an opportunity for the members to finally convene a proper annual general meeting (AGM), elect a new board and start to put the affairs of the cooperative in order. Although this took a few years, it was an important step for the cooperative, and the experience reinforced the cooperative's commitment to work with cooperative values and principles.

Its internal structure is similar to that of most worker cooperatives: members constitute the base and, through the AGM, elect a board of directors who manage the organisation. The cooperative holds regular general meetings at which the five department coordinators inform the membership of what is going on in their departments. This structure allows internal democratic control. The AGM is the highest decision-making structure and where all strategic decisions are made.

In 2008, Nomzamo secured its best contract yet. Previously, the highest contract was R1.06 million per annum which translated into average monthly salaries of between R1 000 and R1 500, with a small bonus at the end of the year if a surplus was made. In 2008, however, the cooperative won a tender for R2.106 million for the 2008–2009 financial year, increasing to R2.280 million for 2009–2010 and to R2.509 million for 2010–2011 (a total of R6.949 million over three years). The cooperative consequently raised the monthly salary to R2 366 then to R2 638 and finally to R2 862 in the third year. It has also been able to recapitalise its assets and buy additional equipment – it has four tractors, a van, a refuse truck, and other specific equipment for each of the functions it undertakes.

This cooperative seeks to position itself as one of the beneficiaries of the provincial government's decision to locate a provincial cooperatives institute at the university. Its relative success is in part due to the university's willingness to support such a venture, demonstrating that wider community and institutional support is extremely important. By all accounts, given its skills and assets, this is a successful, viable and sustainable cooperative – but its sole reliance on the university contract, and the limited private market for gardening and grounds services in Alice and Fort Beaufort, are a serious threat, and diversification will be crucial for the future growth and sustainability of this worker cooperative.

SIHLAHLA MURI RECYCLING WORKER COOPERATIVE

The Sihlahla Muri recycling worker cooperative emerged through an attempted buy-out of a distressed recycling plant in the Johannesburg inner city. The National Union of Metalworkers of South Africa (Numsa) supported the initiative to break new ground in union strategy, a strategic shift that emerged through its recognition of the failure of black economic empowerment and the impact of the economic crisis on the union, with 36 000 jobs lost in the automotive sector alone.[19] While the union was reluctant to use the worker cooperative option, given its failed experiences in the 1980s (with the BTR Sarmcol cooperative and Panama Texas supported by Ford in the Eastern Cape when it disinvested from South Africa), its March 2009 conference prompted a strategic shift in two respects.[20] First, the 'bail outs' that employers were pushing were only considered important and necessary by the union if they saved jobs. Second, Numsa adopted the slogan 'how can we turn the crisis into an opportunity?' which prompted it to think about the production of socially useful products as a way to save jobs in the metal industry. At this conference, the union began envisioning the conversion of car production into tractor and bus production and began championing the training lay-off scheme as part of its response to the crisis. The conference also entertained the idea of organising work differently, in worker cooperatives, and discussed worker takeovers after having watched a documentary on worker takeovers in Argentina.[21]

Later that year Numsa had an opportunity to take over Split Rock, a waste collection and recycling business, through a buy-out. Split Rock operated a cash business that bought waste from street collectors and sold it to metal, plastics and paper companies. The company had been badly mismanaged and the workers were keen to save their jobs by taking it over and converting it into a worker cooperative. In late 2009, the owner showed keen interest in the workers buying it out, but set difficult deadlines. After several workshops and strategising meetings the union engaged several potential sources of government financial support to assist the buy-out and to ensure that the business was converted into a cooperative. But in January 2010, two important developments undermined the worker buy-out. First, a worker was killed at the recycling plant owing to a faulty machine and electrical problems, and as a result the labour department closed the plant because of its unsafe conditions – to which the employer responded by retrenching all thirty workers. The situation became even more complicated at this point. The 'employer' had leased the machines from another company, thus making it very difficult to ascertain who the actual employer was and as a result Numsa struggled to claim retrenchment benefits from the owner who sat behind several holding companies. Nevertheless, the union continued to organise the workers into a cooperative and secured financial management training for the workers in the hope that the buy-out would go through.

The second development that undermined the worker buy-out was that the owner leased the business to a new 'employer' who then selectively re-employed some of the workers. This divided the workers. Some chose to work for the new employer, while ten workers pressed ahead with forming the cooperative (but no longer as a buy-out). After several months of preparation, the cooperative was formally registered with the registrar of cooperatives and leveraged the money for a DTI incentive scheme together with a grant from Numsa to capitalise the cooperative. The City of Johannesburg was engaged to also contribute to finding a work space and to assist with capitalisation. This process took up most of 2010, and by 2011 the Sihlahla Muri Workers Cooperative was in the start-up phase. One of the important innovations that emerged through this process was a cooperative support committee, which provided a space for workers to sit with government and non-government support institutions to solve problems and build the cooperative. Numsa has strongly supported this initiative. With union support, the workers have continued waste collection in the city from offices of unions affiliated to Cosatu. The cooperative has been given office space at the regional union office, equipment has been procured through the DTI incentive scheme, and the cooperative's assets are insured by the union. This experience has important implications for Numsa, but also more broadly for trade union-linked worker cooperatives. One of the lessons for the union is the need to build internal institutional capacity to support worker cooperatives. The experience has also taught the union important lessons about the responsiveness of state institutions to the challenge of developing the worker cooperative alternative, and that state institutions carrying mandates to support cooperative development are not effective. For instance, there is no dedicated financing mechanism in government for worker cooperatives, which could have assisted the Sihlahla Muri worker owners in buying out Split Rock quickly. The cooperative and the union had to lobby hard to secure support from the DTI and the City of Johannesburg. Finally, this experience has shown the union a development path beyond BEE. Groundwork has been done and the cooperative is poised to utilise its assets, advantages and member-driven capacities to actively develop.

THE MINE-LINE TAP ENGINEERING WORKER COOPERATIVE

The Mine-Line factory is an engineering and fabrication company located in the West Rand, near Soweto. In 2010, it employed 110 workers who produced valves, underground trains for mines and other customised metal products. In August 2010, Mine-Line experienced a tragedy; three workers were killed when a boiler machine exploded and it was revealed that the owner had not contributed to the pension fund (despite making deductions from the workers' wages) and had stolen workers' unemployment benefits. As a result, the union representing the workers, the Metal Electrical Workers Union of South Africa (Mewusa), threatened to sue the company, which led the owner to file for bankruptcy and unilaterally close the factory. According to the liquidator, the employer created the financial crisis by borrowing R35 million from ABSA bank and then siphoning off R15 million from the business.[22]

The unfair dismissals and the failure to pay death benefits to the families of the deceased workers enraged the workers. In response the union brought in a liquidator to wind down the company and secure wage and non-wage benefits for the workers. At the same time, the union and workers began discussing the possibility of taking over the company and forming a worker cooperative. Events quickened in October-November 2010, when the workers discovered that the liquidator had sold off finished products and allowed the employer to remove machinery from the factory without consulting the union and workers. The workers' only compensation (the machines and finished products) was quickly disappearing through the collusion of the owner and the liquidator. It came to a head on 20 October 2010, when Mine-Line workers gathered at their factory to demand an explanation from the liquidator about machinery taken and proceeds from finished products. The liquidator was unable to provide proper verification of assets taken and explanations for the asset stripping, and the workers decided that the only way to secure their benefits and future jobs was to occupy the factory.

Although the case is still unfolding, it provides an interesting example of a trade union-linked worker cooperative through a factory occupation. The occupation of the Mine-Line factory is both defensive and offensive, defensive in trying to ensure that benefits such as pension funds and wages owed are secured for workers from the liquidation process, offensive in that it is trying to create a different form of factory, one run by the workers. The workers immediately began practising democracy in the occupation, and collectively set up the Mine-Line tap engineering worker cooperative, with the help of the support organisation COPAC. All decisions are made by the worker members, with a committee elected to facilitate the day-to-day process of the occupation such as dealing with the liquidation and leveraging support from DTI; and in promoting solidarity from other workers, unions, support organisations and communities. The cooperative's main task at the moment is to defend the occupation and secure state support for their attempt to save their jobs and turn the enterprise around.

There are two important implications, which highlight the wider significance of the Mine-Line factory occupation. First, in the context of the global economic crisis, the Zuma government placed on the national agenda an initiative called Framework for South Africa's Response to the International Economic Crisis. This framework committed the state to support stressed sectors of the economy through financial support for turn-around strategies through the Industrial Development Corporation (IDC) and training linked to layoff schemes. Engineering is a key sector in this framework and provides an opportunity for the retrenched Mine-Line workers. However, in assisting the Mine-Line workers to set up a worker cooperative, COPAC discovered that both the IDC stress fund and the training layoff scheme have not supported insolvent enterprises and have not assisted worker takeovers of distressed enterprises. The Mine-Line workers' conversion of the factory into a worker cooperative lies outside the framework, as a stressed enterprise is different from one that has stopped production. The insolvency laws, however, provide an option for the workers to buy out the company but for the cooperative to access this option will require state support and a political struggle to ensure the state is responsive to the needs of the Mine-Line workers through the IDC and the training layoff scheme. The Mine-Line workers have been challenging the state to adapt the framework so that it supports worker cooperatives, and not simply capital, but they have not succeeded in time to save their factory. By June 2011, Mine-Line workers reported that IDC promises for financial assistance in a turnaround strategy did not materialise. According to the workers, at the same time as they were promised financial support and given undertakings by the IDC to stop the liquidation, the IDC let the factory assets be auctioned (when the workers queried these actions, the IDC gave further assurance that it would still assist with the capitalisation of the cooperative, despite the auction). But it is clear that the situation is highly uncertain for the workers.

Despite this setback, there is a second important implication of the historical experience of the Mine-Line occupation and worker cooperative: it shifts the property relations debate. This will be an issue for other factory occupations that will be inspired by this experience. Post-apartheid South Africa has not developed a transformative approach to property relations; land reform has been mired in a market-driven approach, black economic empowerment has emphasised deracialising existing capitalist structures to produce an elite, and the more recent debate on nationalisation has degenerated into factional battles inside the ANC. The Mine-Line factory occupation takes us beyond the polemics of the ANC-led Alliance and gives primacy to the voices of workers. Through debates and deliberations as part of the build up to the factory occupation, two approaches emerged to secure ownership of the factory as part of defending workers' jobs. The first was partial socialisation through a worker-managed cooperative in which the state pays out creditors so that the machines are secured for the Mine-Line workers; the machines and the factory would then be run through a worker-managed cooperative. State ownership plus worker control was understood as one way forward.

A second approach was full socialisation, in which the stolen machinery is returned by the owner, and the state pays out creditors their proportionate share as per the liquidation and provides working capital to restart production through a worker cooperative. This route requires that the worker cooperative reaches an agreement with the state (and perhaps repays some of the state loan) and the assets are placed in the hands of the workers. In this option, worker ownership and control prevails over the means of production. A variation on this option is still possible, despite the auction, if the IDC capitalises the Mine-Line tap engineering worker cooperative.

In both approaches, property relations are transformed, either through partial or full socialisation. This has been a central objective of the factory occupation.

CONCLUSION

Cooperatives have played an important role in the development of modern South Africa. However, the Afrikaner and African nationalist approaches to cooperative development show failure rather than success; they have not engendered genuine cooperatives but, rather, 'business cooperatives'. These approaches have not facilitated the development of an alternative cooperative economy but have merely linked cooperatives with capitalist development. The historical uses of Afrikaner empowerment discourse for cooperative development and as a basis to rationalise a BEE business approach to cooperative development eclipses the transformative potential of cooperative development from below, particularly through worker cooperatives. However, in the deepening structural crisis of the South African economy and the impact of the global economic crisis this marginalisation of alternative cooperative approaches is being challenged.

This trend is best witnessed in the context of new trade union practices to discover alternative approaches to work and new understandings of property relations. Worker cooperatives lie at the forefront of these experiments in alternative forms of production and new forms of ownership. The three cases of worker owned cooperatives illustrate many of the potentials and challenges of pursuing an alternative within the harsh economic climate in which we find ourselves. While all the cases are defensive reactions to outsourcing, retrenchments, and factory closure, they are also offensive efforts by workers to regain control and ownership of their lives through establishing worker cooperatives. All the examples demonstrate how trade unions are exploring new strategic approaches to the capitalist economic crisis and advancing transformative practices from below.

NOTES

1   This chapter draws on the authors' current book project focusing on cooperative alternatives to capitalist globalisation.

2   The first formally registered cooperative was formed in 1892 as the Pietermaritzburg Consumers Cooperative. Subsequently, Gandhi, Dora Tamana and Govan Mbeki also promoted cooperative development.

3   Some of the more commonly known Afrikaner empowerment-based cooperatives and mutuals were KWV wine farmers, Old Mutual and Volkskas.

4   See section 1 and 1 (b) dealing with definitions and section 2 (b) regarding objectives of the Broad-Based Black Economic Act, 2003, which defines a role for cooperatives.

5   Interview, Patience Gidongo, DTI Cooperatives Unit, 21 October 2010.

6   This includes the DTI cooperative incentive scheme, the South African Micro Apex Fund (SAMAF), Small Enterprise Development Agency, National Youth Development Agency, National Empowerment Fund, Department of Agriculture, Department of Cooperative Governance and Traditional Affairs, Department of Minerals and Energy, Department of Arts and Culture, Department of Public Works, Department of Labour, National Treasury, Social Development, KZN Department of Economic Development, Gauteng Province, Northern Cape, North West, Eastern Cape, Free State, Mpumalanga, Limpopo, Western Cape. Contained in DTI (2010).

7   KZN has channelled these large quantities of finance to cooperatives through the Ithala Bank. Recent newspaper reports have revealed widespread corruption in the Ithala Bank.

8   Interview Rector Rapoo, Registrar of Cooperatives, CIPRO, 21 October 2010.

9   Such linkages have been achieved in successful cooperative movements in the world, from Mondragon in Spain, throughout Brazil, various regions of Italy, Quebec in Canada and to some extent in Kenya.

10 The question of failed cooperative movement building has been documented by COPAC and has formed the basis of a conference held on this issue in 2006.

11 Interview, Geoff Nduma, Head of DTI Cooperatives Unit, 22 August 2010.

12 The DTI 2009 baseline study found eight tertiary bodies, but only three that provide tertiary services — the Savings and Credit Cooperative League of South Africa (SACCOL), the South African Housing Cooperative Association (SAHCA), and the South African Federation of Burial Societies (SAFOBS).

13 The Cooperatives Act (2005) makes provision for cooperatives in general, but provides for four kinds of cooperatives: worker cooperatives, housing cooperatives, financial services cooperatives and agricultural cooperatives. Contained in Schedule 1.

14   To be clear, worker owner-based work is distinct from self-employed and wage-earning work. Self-employed work generally involves an individual attempting to foster a livelihood through a particular kind of economic activity, while wage-earning work requires a worker to sell his/her labour power to an employer in a capital-managed and owned firm.

15   Schedule 1, Part II of the Cooperatives Act of 2005.

16   For a case study of the Mineworkers Development Agency see Kate Philips (1987) *Producer Cooperatives in South Africa: Their Economic Potential and Political Limits.* SWOP: WITS.

17   Interview Sifiso Ndwandwe, Head of the Mine-Workers Development Agency, October 18, 2010.

18   COPAC has played a role in setting up all of these cooperatives. It has also documented Nomzamo Gardening and Grounds Cooperative in two of its research reports (COPAC 2008 and 2010).

19   Interview with Dinga Sikwebu, NUMSA national education officer, 8 October 2010. DTI and ILO Seminar Report, Placing Worker Cooperatives on the Agenda: Opportunities and Challenges, May 14th, 2009, pp. 5–6.

20   Ibid.

21   COPAC was invited to this conference and screened the documentary *The Take,* which documents the takeover of a metal works company in Argentina.

22   Discussion with the liquidator on 20 October 2010.

REFERENCES

Amin N and H Bernstein (1995) The role of agricultural cooperatives in agriculture and rural development. LAPC: Policy Paper 32.

Cooperative and Policy Alternative Centre (COPAC) (2006a) Cooperative support institutions in the Gauteng cooperative sector (case studies): Enabling support or dependent development? Research Report.

------(2006b) Cooperative alternatives to capitalist Globalisation – Building human solidarity to sustain life, Johannesburg, 8–10 June. Conference publication.

------(2010) Cooperating for transformation: Cooperative case studies from Amathole District, Eastern Cape. Johannesburg: COPAC Research Report, 20010a.

Department of Trade and Industry (DTI) (2009) The DTI Baseline Study on Cooperatives in South Africa. Johannesburg: The Growth Laboratory. http://www.dti.gov.za/Co-operative/baseline_study_of_co-operatives.pdf (accessed 11 October 2010).

------Briefingonthedevelopmentandsupportprogrammesforcooperatives:EmpowermentandEnterprise Development Division. Presentation to the Select Committee on Trade and International Relations, 25 August 2010. http://www.pmg.org.za/files/docs/100825dti-edit.pdf (accessed 11 Oct-ober 2010).

Department of Trade and Industry (DTI) and International Labour Organisation (ILO) (2009) Placing worker cooperatives on the agenda: Opportunities and challenges. Seminar Report, 14 May.

International Cooperative Alliance (ICA) (2007) *Global 300.* www.ica.coop.

Philips K (1987) *Producer Cooperatives in South Africa: Their Economic Potential and Political Limits* SWOP: WITS.

Satgar V and M Williams (2008) The passion of the people: Successful cooperative experiences in Africa. Johannesburg: COPAC Research Report.

-------(forthcoming) The politics of cooperative development in post-apartheid South Africa. In A Webster, A Brown, D Stewart, J Walton, L Shaw and G Lonergan (Eds) *The Hidden Alternative*, Manchester: Manchester University Press.

Van Niekerk JAS (1998) *Cooperative Theory and Practice.* SAAU: Pretoria.

CHAPTER 11

Policing in the streets of South African townships[1]

Knowledge Rajohane Matshedisho

—•—

INTRODUCTION

Police reform forms part of the debate in transitional societies that are moving from colonialism, communism, conflict and various forms of authoritarianism, to democracy. Bruce (2009) argues that post-conflict African countries are characterised by uneven state and non-state partnerships in policing, concluding that police and community partnerships should be strengthened and should focus on crime prevention rather than on police using communities as tools for state policing. In the same breath, Albrecht and Buur (2009) recognise the tensions in state-civilian policing partnerships in security and development reform programmes in sub-Saharan Africa. They partly attribute the tension to lack of an understanding of the context by policy makers and bureaucrats. Ivkovic (2009) outlines police transition in Croatia and concludes that recent research shows improved but uneven and uneasy reform from police servicing communist governments to servicing civilians. Kešetovic (2009) addresses the requirement for Serbian police to exert control in the context of multicultural minorities. Even though the context and priorities are different in transitional societies, the commonality is that police reform research (as in South Africa, cf. Rauch, 2000) typically focuses on crime reduction and prevention (Cf. Marks and Shaw, 2002), police accountability (Cf. Leggett,

2002), community policing, the law of policing (Cf. Brogden, 1994), and public relations with the police.

It is the relationship between police and public (in the context of transformation) that form the subject of this chapter, which tries to bring forth the daily experiences of police and community as they encounter each other at street level. The encounters are analysed in the context of transforming the South African Police Service from its previous apartheid and militaristic orientation into community policing in which the objective of policing is not only to fight and prevent crime but also to make communities feel safe.

The chapter argues that transforming the relationship between the police and communities in South African townships should not be reduced to the formal application of democratic law. Rather, we must also understand the tensions and informalities in everyday policing (Hornberger, 2004) and both the hidden and public transcripts that are embedded in the social history and practice of policing in South Africa and which have implications for democratic policing and the post-1994 generation of police. Moreover, they add to Marks's and Wood's (2010) argument for minimalist policing. Marks and Wood warn that the re-militarisation of the South African Police Services is regressive and puts further strain on police-public relations. They suggest that some policing should, and can, also be done by the community, and that the police should rather focus on the serious interventions, when such interventions are needed.

The chapter is arranged in four parts. I first discuss democratic policing, and then explain the concept of the hidden and public transcript. I give instances of the tensions in police and community encounters and, finally, I suggest implications for democratic policing in South Africa as a society in transition.

Unlike sociodemographic and non-sociodemographic correlation studies such as those of O'Conner (2008) and Gau (2010) on public attitudes toward police, this chapter is based on observation of the police during their patrols, over a period of five months. It derives its data from police narratives, and the interaction of police with civilians in one of Johannesburg's townships. I was observing student constables' visible (street-level) policing under the guidance and authority of their commanders, senior constables. However, even though this study is different from the sociodemographic norm, all studies on policing have practical implications for street-level policing, especially for the public's support of police in different multicultural, democratic and transitional societies.

DEMOCRATIC POLICING

Rauch (1993) and Shaw (2002) sketch the political context within which police reform took place in South Africa during political liberalisation. Rauch mentions problems such as the political origins of the South African Police (SAP) in which policing was about protecting the interests of government, business and, later, racial domination; the lack of comprehensive policy on law and order within liberation movements where an organisation such as the ANC did not have a clear and coherent policy on the nature of policing in post-apartheid South Africa; a militaristic tradition in government and ANC discussions on security; lack of accountability and abuse of power by the SAP; and crisis intervention orientation in policing discussion whereby policing is seen as responding to crime rather than preventing it and making communities feel safe. Shaw mentions similar problems, but he focuses on increasing levels of crime during the transition period between the 1990s and 2000. Rauch concludes that after a series of police reform discussions and planning:

> The model of 'community supported policing' is based on a rather simplistic interpretation of British and North American models of community policing. SAP policymakers have managed to ignore the differences between South Africa and these advanced democratic states where citizens have rights, political representation, mechanisms of accountability at all levels of government, etc. The aspect of inter-agency cooperation is also underdeveloped. This problem is exacerbated by the absence or collapse of many state bureaucracies (e.g. education and local authorities), especially in black residential areas. They have also failed to take into account the various organic traditions of self-policing, such as 'people's courts', and to draw from these some important aspects of indigenous community policing'. (Rauch, 1993: 8)

SO HOW SHOULD POLICING HAPPEN IN A DEMOCRATIC STATE?

In a democratic state the police should be guided and bound by the rule of law, which unfortunately is often in conflict with the values of a democracy. 'The police of a free country is to be found in rational and humane laws – in an effective and enlightened magistracy – and in the judicious and proper selection of those officers of justice ... yet the institutions of the country being sound, its laws well adjusted, and justice executed against offenders, no greater safeguard can be obtained without sacrificing all those rights which society was instituted to preserve' (Reith, 1938: 188).

The tension between the rule of law and the values of democracy has created public controversy, and a dilemma for the police. In a democracy, police cannot maintain order without regard of the law, for the law is the instrument of order. The rule of law controls matters such as the searches, arrests, handling of suspects, and what constitutes lawful accusation and the right to legal representation (Skolnick, 1975). Yet in everyday policing the rule of law often has to be maintained without regard for the law. The disregard, or sometimes ambiguity, of the law causes tension and controversies that lead to police abuse of power: police brutality, arbitrary or unlawful arrests, improper searches and contaminated crime scenes.

Skolnick (1975: 6) observes: 'the police in democratic society are required to maintain order and to do so under the rule of law. As functionaries charged with maintaining order, they are part of the bureaucracy. The ideology of democratic bureaucracy emphasises initiative rather than disciplined adherence to rules and regulations. By contrast the rule of law emphasises the rights of individual citizens and constraints upon the initiative of legal officials. This tension between the operational consequences of ideas of order, efficiency and initiative, on the one hand and legality on the other constitute the principal problem of police as a democratic legal organisation.' These tensions and dilemmas have led to several ways of understanding policing.

Lipsky (1982: xi) sees police as street-level bureaucracies, which he defines as organisations and agencies whose workers (police, welfare departments, schools, hospitals and lower courts) interact directly with the public and have wide discretions over the dispensation of benefits or the allocation of public sanctions. He argues that the decisions, routines and devices of the street-level bureaucrats (such as the police) that they use to cope with the vicissitudes of their work become public policy that they execute daily. The strictly followed rules of policing give way to the dynamic of the encounter between the police and the public on the streets and which leads to whatever course of action the police decide to take.

Reiner (1997) outlines three approaches that explain police discretion. The first is an individualistic approach, which focuses on the personalities of police or recruits. He demonstrates that, contrary to other claims, there is no evidence that police have more authoritarian personalities than do the civilian population, and he condemns the view that police have an inherently authoritarian personality which makes them choose a career in policing. The second approach is cultural: a 'set of informal rules, rites and recipes for coping' (Reiner, 1997: 1016). The final approach is a contextual explanation which supplements cultural explanations by suggesting that the context within which the police work presents countervailing factors that might inhibit the translation of police values into expected practices. Reiner argues that even though the police might create their own ways of policing and dealing with citizens, these ways are themselves a product, and counter-product, of the context in which police do their work. Reiner does not necessarily dispute the discretion of the individual police, but, rather, says that police are also influenced by their wider context.

Chan (1996) employs the concept of police culture in analysing the impact of police reform, arguing that static and structural concepts of culture cannot help us understand police culture, and observing that there are multiple cultures – and levels of cultures – in policing, and that acculturation is not passive but includes structure-agency mediation. She concludes that the craft of policing is constituted by the relationship between the social, legal and organisational contexts of policing, together with their discursive practices. Loftus (2010) agrees with this observation, but he disputes claims that orthodox conceptions of police culture (maintaining law, order and discipline by the book) are outdated, concluding that: 'The timeless qualities of police culture endure because the basic pressures associated with the police role have not been removed and because social transformations have exacerbated, rather than reduced, the basic definitions of inequality. Unless there is a marked refashioning of that role stemming from wider social change, it would seem there is little hope of achieving any radical reconfiguration of police culture' (Loftus, 2010: 17).

In South Africa, Hornberger (2004: 227) observed police at work in the Johannesburg inner city and concluded: 'I want to maintain the notion that the police force is informally managed and transformed through an imaginary to fit the conflicts that are played out in the inner city. State power is redirected and renegotiated for a purpose removed from its formal application. At the same time, this way of managing police interventions and its incoherence cannot guarantee security. Rather, it provides an improvised and provisional security that may backfire and contradict itself. Insecurity is not eliminated, only framed.'

Faul (2010: xiii) sums up the above discussion: 'The expectations placed on the everyday cop are enormous, often bordering on the impossible, while a progressive constitutional framework is interpreted as overly limiting police powers to act. In order to survive the weight of these competing forces, police develop their own informal rules, codes and systems to deliver on their mandate …These informal systems are not taught at police college but rather learnt on the job … even to the new student entering SAPS, familiarity with the informal culture [grows] as their post develops over time, through experience, observation and storytelling.'

In Township Z, police culture is reflected by much of what Faul argues. The interactions between constables and student constables seems to be partly characterised by power relationships, in which the student constables' success depends partly on accepting the daily 'teachings' of the senior constables. In many instances, student constables would talk about their admiration of how certain senior constables would violently force out confessions from suspects and how they themselves copied such 'strategies'. In parades and during informal lunchtime conversations, some senior constables would encourage the student constables to fight the criminals in the township and never to forget the bond of being a 'member of the force'. Therefore, above all the formal rules of policing, student constables would observe, listen and copy some of the ways of their seniors; but they were also aware of the changes that they are required to represent, as members of the police in a new democratic South Africa.

PUBLIC AND HIDDEN TRANSCRIPTS

On one of my days of participant observation in the township, I was driven around in a police vehicle by a senior constable. As we drove down the main road we saw a minibus obstructing traffic. He stopped next to it and asked the driver to move. The driver apologised. As we proceeded he said, 'Driving is bad in this township. Sometimes one spends the whole day dealing with bad drivers. Did you see that he [the driver] raised his right hand as a gesture of apology? As soon as I drive away he would use the same hand to sneer at me and say "this fool thinks he is clever!"'.

The above observation introduces the concepts of public and hidden transcripts between the police and the community in this township. The constable is aware that he has power and authority over the citizen driver, who has to obey the command to let road traffic flow freely. However, he is also aware that there may be a hidden transcript behind the driver's public transcript of obedience. So what are the public and hidden transcripts?

> With rare, but significant, exceptions the public performance of the subordinates will, out of prudence, fear, and the desire to curry favour, be shaped to appeal to the expectations of the powerful. I shall use the term public transcript as a shorthand way of describing the open interaction between subordinates and those who dominate. The public transcript, where it is not positively misleading, is unlikely to tell the whole story about power relations. It is frequently in the interest of both parties to tacitly conspire in misrepresentation.
>
> If subordinate discourse in the presence of the dominant is a public transcript, I shall use the term hidden transcripts to characterise discourse that takes place 'offstage', beyond direct observation by powerholders. The hidden transcript is thus derivative in the sense that it consists of those offstage speeches, gestures and practices that confirm, contradict or inflect what appears in the public transcript. We do not wish to prejudge, by definition, the relation between what is said in the face of power and what is said behind its back. Power relations are not, alas, so straight forward that we can call what is said in power-laden contexts false and what is said offstage true' (Scott, 1990: 4-5).

My chapter does not seek to critically discuss the concepts of hidden and public transcripts. It uses them, instead, as a framework for understanding the tensions in the context of the hierarchies operative in street-level policing. The concepts are meant to highlight what often transpires when civilians encounter police at street level, and the tensions embedded in the unequal power relations between them. In the case of democratic policing, the tension stems from police authority to suspend civilians' rights and freedom in the interests of law, order and security. These tensions are evident in township policing. It is a case of mutual mistrust and constant discretion outside the boundaries of the law.

POLICE AND COMMUNITY TENSIONS IN A TOWNSHIP[2]

In a rather unusually sombre parade one day, an inspector said to student constables: 'If a suspect points a gun at you or any officer you must shoot the suspect. Don't wait for the suspect to shoot and then arrest him and take him to the police station. Don't think that will make you look proper by adhering to the law. You must shoot them! You see, in Township Z, it's a big thing to shoot a police. If you shoot a police you become a hero in the township. We can't let that happen. We must fight them.' The inspector was making this point as part of a painful and emotionally charged parade address, the night before which a policeman had been shot by a suspect. The suspect was arrested and the policeman was said to be alive and recovering. This utterance not only shows police intolerance for firearms in a civilian's hands, but also reveals that the police are aware of the public's attitude towards them – and it is a negative attitude. However, as I will suggest, the attitude has its paradoxes.

The police see the community of Township Z as extremely violent and criminal. In my conversations with the police, none spoke about sociological variables such as poverty. Instead, they see alcohol abuse as the primary cause of crime and disobedience in Township Z, and as a consequence police attitudes during patrols are also influenced by their perception of the community. In one conversation with a student constable, I asked him what the problem was in Township Z. He answered enthusiastically and at length: 'Township Z is very hectic over the weekends. Alcohol, robberies and domestic violence are very widespread. Sometimes, someone comes to report broken entry and stolen property from his shack – that person would be drunk and have no knowledge of suspects or any information that might help us. Then the next day he forgets everything. People here have no respect for the police so we sometimes teach them a lesson just for the sake of it. For example, sometimes if I find you holding a sealed bottle of beer, I can arrest and charge you for public drinking even though I know you were not drinking in public'. 'Why do you do that?' I asked, amused. He replied, 'It's about the suspect's attitude. If I see that you are arrogant then I will find something to arrest you. However if a suspect is apologetic and respectful then I forgive him. If people show respect or are apologetic and say, "Sorry officer I did not mean to do this, forgive me,"[3] then I will forgive them because I have a heart and I am human too.'

Thus, from the police perspective, Township Z is a place to teach criminals and the stubborn community some harsh lessons. Police work becomes primarily that of discipline.

This nature of police work also seems to influence how the police view the 'absence of crime'. In the absence of crime, patrol officers feel they are wasting time. In my early days of participant observation they would say, 'Thursdays are very boring, quiet. You see nothing. You must come on Friday, Saturday or Sunday; then you will see real action. Today it's just for you to take a tour of the township ... we on the other hand will be honking at ladies!'

Comments like this make it seem as if the only relationship that the police have with the community is over fighting crime or attending to matters that involve crime prevention. The visibility of the police does not seem to count, as a tactic, from the patrol officer's point of view. They do not think of their visibility as something that might make the community feel safe; it is, rather, a threat to criminals. Police seem to view their work as something that should be quantifiable by the numbers of arrests and 'stop and searches', and their mere visibility is not enough to qualify as work. They want action, which, of course, includes arrests and searches with the possibility of disciplining the criminal in the public gaze. This, they hope, reminds the public of the consequences of disobeying the law and the police.

The public gaze is not silent, though. Community members voice their disregard for the police. This is evident during arrests when civilian onlookers insult the police, directly or indirectly. The insults are meted out in at least four categories: the first is that police are generally illiterate or functionally illiterate, which means that they did not pass matric and do not have tertiary education qualifications. In one instance, a shack stood burning while the police stood observing the flames. Although the police had called the fire brigade, the latter did not come because they were on strike (as were the doctors and ambulance workers). The burning shack was an excruciating sight and some of the onlookers could not understand why it was only the neighbours who were trying to extinguish the fire. In a callous tone one man shouted, 'What do these tenth or eighth graders know anyway?' He was suggesting that it did not come as a surprise that the police were not helping because they were invariably incompetent and uneducated.

The following incident exemplifies the next three categories of insults. One evening about twenty police were taking turns in beating three suspects. As the drama unfolded, a student constable asked the onlookers to move away from the scene in case shots were fired; they resisted and the student constable started shouting at them to move away. Other student constables backed her up and told them to move back. There followed the usual altercation between police and the group of civilians. The police were told how rude, illiterate and useless they were. They were told to go and attend to more serious cases.

As the civilians were dispersed I was among them, and as I moved around I eaves-dropped on their conversations and heard comments such as: 'These people did not resist arrest. So why are they beating them?'; and 'She would not say these things if she was on her own. She is doing this because she has the backup of other police. They are very silly when they are in a group'; and 'It serves them right. Their Zuma said that we must like the xenophobia.[4] Now look what these xenophobia people are doing'; and 'We know our rights. They won't tell us what to do'; and 'How can so many police come and attack just three people?'; and 'They [police] are just as corrupt as anybody else. You will find them drinking inside police cars too!'

In the middle of these confrontations, one of the student constables despondently and angrily said, as he left the civilian crowd, 'I don't understand these people. We are helping them but they are fighting us. We are helping them so that they don't get mugged by these thugs [pointing at the three suspects as the police continued with the beatings]'. Struggling to hear what was being said, as almost every group in the crowd seemed to be quarrelling with a member of the police, I witnessed a policeman hit a drunken man twice, causing him to fall to the ground.

This brings me to the second category of insults: that police are useless because they are afraid of serious crimes and instead harass harmless people. Like the above example, this is often observed in motorists' sarcasm at road blocks, or the overt insults from onlookers during an arrest. Public drinking warnings and arrests also evoke this category of insults. Civilians feel that public drinking is harmless. They rebuke the police and tell them to go and fight real crime in the streets. This insult is conflated with the complaint that police never arrive on the crime scene on time. The perception is that they don't care. They are afraid of serious crimes and arrive late because they wish to avoid confrontation with real criminals.

The third category of insults is that police have no right to arrest or beat crimi-nals because they are just as corrupt and criminal as the suspect(s). In so saying, the community does not of course refer to the police at any particular crime scene but, rather, to members of the South African Police Services in general. In this category of insult the morality of policing is questioned. The police are not seen as neutral enforcers of law and order; instead they are viewed as moral agents who hypocritically enforce ethical standards rather than the actual laws. In the community's eyes, the police, being moral agents, must feel guilt and shame for punishing people for offences which they (police) have probably themselves committed in the past. Onlookers, and even suspects, believe that the police should be understanding and let them go instead of arresting, warning or beating suspects for 'minor' offences.

The final type of insults refers to the police as cowards. They are cowards because they are usually arrogant and prone to violence if there are many of them on the scene. What the community members mean is that police need backup in order to be confident and arrest or beat suspects. On several occasions, onlookers were amazed at the number of police officers at a crime scene. They also expressed their disgust at police officers who take turns in beating suspects who are defenceless against so many.

UNDERSTANDING THE CONTEXT OF THE COMMUNITY'S VIEWS

The first defining feature of this context is the level of education of the police. It is true that most of the police are functionally illiterate, and the community members feel intellectually superior to them. There is, however, some historical context to explain the view of the police as poorly educated. In the 1980s, black police performed 'surrogate policing' as municipal police or special constables, to augment the SAP strength and also to dissociate the SAP from white police violence in the townships. Like municipal police, special constable recruits:

> required no educational qualifications, and included many illiterates. Equipped with shot guns, and dressed in functional blue overalls, they were allocated the tasks of foot patrol and riot control the work of black police men did not need a senior certificate. In fact black police men under apartheid could not be promoted beyond the rank of sergeant and constable because they were non-commissioned officers. It was also after the 1976 uprisings that black auxiliary police were allowed to carry firearms. Moreover a lot of officers who were recruited in the 1990s did not have a national senior certificate (Brogden and Shearing, 1993: 83).

The second contextual issue relates to police avoiding serious crimes. According to the police, serious crimes are indeed dangerous and need backup. They are often reluctant to attend to serious crimes if they do not have the necessary resources such as appropriate patrol vehicles and backup from colleagues. At other times, police feel too tired to attend to these calls, especially if they are not working within the sector in which the crime is being reported. However, in the streets, police also choose which crime interventions are important to them – for example, most find domestic violence intervention a waste of their time because the complainants usually drop the charges.

The third contextual issue relates to police corruption. The community sees police as corrupt and not worthy of arresting others. This evokes the argument about the principle of accepting to be policed in a democratic liberal state. By agreeing to be policed, the community accepts the authority and power of the police irrespective of the police's moral virtues or vices. In a democratic liberal court the arresting officer is innocent of corruption, but the community adds another dimension – that the police themselves must be morally upright before they are entitled to enforce the law. Such ideas were acceptable during apartheid, and the police were chased out of Township Z by self-defence units. The return of police to Township Z since the early 1990s means that the community has accepted to be policed and thereby is expected to be cooperative. Cooperation, however, also demands that police should have virtues such as honesty, and this creates further tensions in street-level policing. The ideal of democratic policing, and the experiences of real policing in this context, are worlds apart.

The final contextual issue relates to police cowardice. In one of their patrols, the police in Township Z came across a brawl in the street. The suspect ran away, into a yard. It turned out that he was hitting his girlfriend. There was a crowd of about twenty people in the yard. The officers stood outside the yard and did not pursue the suspect. When they returned to their car they said that they did not pursue the suspect because the girlfriend did not seem in need of their intervention; they also said that they did not want to enter the yard because there were few of them and they could be easily disarmed by the crowd. In their training and parades, the officers are told that in every intervention they should consider their safety and lives first. Although the strength of the police lies, in reality, in their legal authority, member backup, and the Constitution, the community seems to view reliance on such factors as cowardice.

POLICE VIEWS

Police have their own views about how the community sees them. In addition to participant observation, I conducted interviews with ten student constables, who all gave almost the same answers about the animosity between the police and their communities. Police think that the community lashes out for three reasons: the first is that the community is ignorant of the law. If people don't know how the law operates then they will always hate those who enforce it. All the officers said that they were not bothered by public insults during an arrest, as part of their training has socialised them and helped them to develop 'thick skins' to shield them from emotional abuse. The only time that police have to deal with the onlookers is when they are interfering with police duties, and at that point they are allowed to use 'minimum force' or to arrest a civilian for interference.

The second reason that the community insults the police is that police understand their duties as simply enforcing the law, regardless of the community's feelings about it, whereas the community, on the other hand, think that the police make the law as well as enforce it. The police, who think of themselves as 'agents of the state', shrug at this display of what they consider simple ignorance. This reminded me of one public-drinking arrest incident. The perpetrator pleaded with the police not to arrest him but they refused, and got him into the vehicle. On the way to the station he continued to plead with them to let him go but they refused, and one of them said, 'We can't. He is our *success*! You know public drinking is wrong yet you do it. You don't respect the police.' Then a student constable said, 'We have already forgiven you. Now we are just doing our job!' They returned to the station to open a case against the arrestee.

The third reason, police observe, for communities to attack them, is that the onlookers who insult them are likely to be close to the suspect. On my first day of fieldwork, as a dagga arrestee was taken to the patrol vehicle, a civilian lad asked, 'Why are you arresting him?' One of the women constables retorted, 'Why do you want to know? What's in it for you? What are you going to do with that information?' The lad kept quiet. Then suddenly an old man appeared at the street corner, demanding to know why they were arresting his son. He shouted: 'This is my son. He does not smoke dagga. Why are you arresting him? Don't arrest him! Leave him alone!' The police explained that the boy was being taken to the police station but the old man continued to protest and police told him that if he carried on he would be charged with interference. A woman arrived, and also protested. She claimed it was her son. They were both told to keep quiet and go to the police station if they had any problems with the arrest, or else they would both be charged for interference. The vehicle left and the police continued with the patrol.

The patrol team were very angry about the civilians' responses and talked about the incident as they drove. The senior constable said, 'These parents are very silly. They know that their children use drugs and do nothing about it. When their children are arrested they defend them. They should tell them to stop taking drugs and we will not arrest them!' The team members all agreed.

Police say that friends and family members of suspects usually defend the suspect and view the police actions as unfair. Police understand that friends and family members don't want their relatives to go to jail, but they usually do not sympathise with any civilian who tries to defend a suspect during an arrest. In most cases, the police enter into a verbal altercation with the onlookers – in fact, it often happens that when the suspect resists arrest most of the onlookers cheer in favour of the suspect, and the scene turns into a wrestling tournament.

Police are also aware that, inasmuch as the community disregards them, they sometimes think of them as superhuman. The community can also, at times, see police as male, macho, and brave. They are supposed to fight crime and arrest criminals; they are supposed to save lives. At one moment civilians think of police as 'scumbags' and at another moment they think of police as saviours – heroic, compassionate and merciful.

Police brutality is a contested concept and practice. The community think the police use brutal force too often, but the police themselves say that they use 'minimum force' and are forced to be brutal only when suspects resist arrest or pose a threat. For the purpose of this chapter, what caught my attention was that in one vehicle patrol the student constables spoke of a mother who called the police in to discipline her unruly daughter. One of them seemed to have savoured the moment when he hit the girl with a belt. They spoke of how ill-mannered the girl was towards her mother and the police. This presents one of the paradoxes of police work: the community hates the police for alleged police brutalities, yet when they feel powerless they invite the police in to use physical force.

The effect of this relationship on both the community and the police is negative. Even though the police say that they shrug at the insults and negative perceptions, these seem to have an emotional impact. On one evening after parade, and while waiting for the patrol vehicles to arrive, one of the student constables said, 'I wish I could work at the community service centre. I hate patrols. I hate getting into altercations with people in the streets. They are just bad luck!' On the other hand, civilians are often afraid of the police because a police presence might mean trouble instead of feelings of safety. The tension builds up.

POSITIVE ASPECTS OF THE POLICE-COMMUNITY RELATIONSHIP

Even though the relationship between the police and the community in Township Z is tense and paradoxical, there are two aspects of the community about which the police feel positive. The first is that crime has decreased in Township Z. During patrols and interviews, the police would acknowledge that there was crime in the area but then emphasise that it had decreased. In an interview, one reservist recalled: 'There is a place called Mike's. It was very notorious. About seven police vehicles were damaged by the patrons. In one incident a police firearm was lost. Police used to be afraid to pass by that place on Sundays but we fought back and patrolled that area, even inside it … and now sometimes when we pass by there on Sundays we even forget it's Mike's place. They respect us now and they are no longer unruly.' In ensuing conversations with the student constables, and judging by their facial expressions and gestures in the conversation, it was clear that they felt that the 'order' in Mike's place means that the police were able to discipline the patrons. In effect they were trying to say that the patrons now feared the police and hence were no longer rowdy and disrespectful.

The second positive development that police see is the Community Police Forum (CPF). They view the CPF as community members who understand police work and who help police in preventing and fighting crime. Although the CPF did not feature in their usual conversations during patrols and parades, it featured prominently in the interviews as the positive aspect of the relationship between the police and the community.

In thinking about the relationship between the police and the Township Z community one can see that it is a relationship primarily based on crime. The police are suspicious of community members because they see Township Z as a criminal hub. The community hates the police because they think they are not doing enough to fight crime – and that police are criminals themselves. The community's attitude towards the police is positive to the police only insofar as they attend to crime and complaints; the police's attitude towards the community is positive only in regard to the CPF. In this relationship there is no room for building trust and civility.

THE HISTORICAL CONTEXT

The historical relationship between the police and Township Z[5] has also been riddled with tensions. As was the case in many South African townships in the early twentieth century, in Township Z police embarked on raids for illicit liquor trading, and the community complained about these raids which took place at ungodly hours and were even conducted on 'innocent' households. The community regarded such raids as police harassment. In 1944, police were involved in demolishing illegal shelters erected by squatters in Township Z. In 1947, police estimated that there were 7 000 shacks in Township Z and then formed a force of thirty men to control theft and drunkenness in the area. Police were also involved in enforcing influx control, through which they prevented Township Z residents from working in Johannesburg, forcing them to work on the farms. Police were also accused of colluding with gangs in the township.

At one point authorities regarded Township Z as noisy and rowdy and as drinking excessively, and wanted to discipline the community to be orderly at night and, in particular, at weekends. More than fifty years later, a policewoman in Township Z said, 'Do you see what is happening? In South Africa the Bill of Rights will never work. We can't do what we were taught in college. Yes, I agree that we have to respect people's rights but in South Africa you just can't. There is too much crime and violence and you have to beat the hell out of these criminals for the truth to come out. There is nothing like rights here.' The student constable was referring to a crime scene. Two men were suspected of mugging at gunpoint, hijacking a car and carrying an illegal firearm. One suspect was arrested and held in a police van; the police were searching for the second. There was commotion between police and civilians as police tried to find out what had happened – some civilians were giving different versions of the story while others were demanding justice or damning the police. In effect, the police were arresting, assaulting, listening, solving a crime and acting as magistrates at the same time and at the same crime scene.

So, if police view the Township Z community as people to be punished and disciplined, and if the community members of Township Z 'give' police reasons to punish and discipline them, a vicious circle of crime, violence and mistrust is perpetuated.

IMPLICATIONS FOR POLICING

When we think of policing we often understand it within the framework of the formalities of the law and the Constitution, but we should understand the context, subtleties and

informalities that are involved in everyday policing, for these considerations are important in shaping a community's views about police. Understanding street-level policing,
and the community's discourse of policing, is one way of doing so. The public and hidden
transcripts give us some idea of mutual distrust (because the police are convinced that
people do and say the right things only to avoid confrontation with the police when in
reality they hate the police and flaunt the law when it suits them. The public transcript is
therefore a lie in the face of authority. The hidden transcripts are the true feelings about
the police and the law, revealed in private conversations).

Police-community tensions have to be minimised, in the interest of fighting and
preventing crime in the country. If communities do not trust the police, then they are
unlikely to cooperate in helping to prevent crime and to solve it. Moreover, police must
make communities feel safe instead of threatening them. Community police forums are
some of the structures that point towards this direction. In neighbourhoods that can
afford private security companies the relationship between police, private security and
residents is another way of making communites feel safe.

Finally, whatever the requirements of policing laws, street-level policing often devi-
ates from them within both the current and the historical context of policing, and this
has implications for a new generation of police. Spending time with student constables
revealed the impact on them of police culture and of street-level policing. Policing in a
democratic country not only requires revision of policing laws (such as the South African
Police Services Act) and some understanding of the nuances of street-level policing, it
also requires a change of attitude from both the police and the communities.

NOTES

1   The research on which this paper is based was conducted under the auspices of the Forced Migration
     Studies Programme (now the African Centre for Migration and Society) at the University of the
     Witwatersrand, Johannesburg, with the permission of the South African Police Services and a
     research grant from the Open Society Foundation. This chapter is developed from the initial Open
     Society Report 'Beyond 'Good'/'Bad Cop': Understanding Informality and Police Corruption in
     South Africa', edited by Darshan Vigneswaran and Julia Hornberger (October 2009).
2   As per contract with the SAPS Gauteng Head Office, the names of the township and police station
     are withheld for publication.'Township Z' will henceforth replace the real name.
3   As he said this, he made gestures mimicking a humbly apologetic person who would usually display
     praying hands, lifted shoulders and an almost bowing head and trunk.
4   By 'xenophobia', the drunken man meant 'foreigners'. The three suspects were said to be from
     Maputo.
5   Some material in this paragraph cannot be referenced because it will reveal the name of the town-
     ship and the police station and will breach the agreement between the South African Police Service
     and the Forced Migration Studies Programme (now the African Centre for Migration and Society).

REFERENCES

Albrecht P and L Buur (2009) An uneasy marriage: Non-state actors and police reform, *Policing &
     Society* 4(19): 390–405.

Baker B (2009) A policing partnership for post-war Africa? Lessons from Liberia and southern Sudan, *Policing & Society*, 4(19): 372 –389.

Brogden M (1994) Reforming police powers in South Africa, *Political Studies* 17 (1): 25–44.

Brogden M and C Shearing (1993) *Policing for a New South Africa*. London: Routledge.

Chan J (1996) Changing police culture, *British Journal of Criminology*. 36(1): 109–32.

Faul A (2010) *Behind the Badge: The Untold Stories of South Africa's Police Service Members*. Cape Town: Zebra Press.

Gau JM (2010) A longitudinal analysis of citizens' attitudes about police, *Policing: An International Journal of Police Strategies & Management*, 33(2) 236–252.

Hornberger J (2004) My police your police: The informal privatisation of the police in the inner city of Johannesburg, *African Studies*, 63(2): 213–230.

Ivkovic SK (2009) The Croatian police, police integrity and transition toward democratic policing, *Policing: An International Journal of Police Strategies and Management*, 32(3): 459–488.

Kešetovic Z (2009) Understanding diversity in policing: Serbian perspective, *Policing: An International Journal of Police Strategies and Management*, 32(3): 431–445.

Leggett T (2002) Performance measures for the South African Police: Setting the benchmarks for service delivery, *Transformation*, 49: 55–58.

Lipsky M (1982) *Dilemmas of the Individual in Public Services*. New York: Russell Sage Foundation.

Loftus B (2010) Police occupational culture: Classic themes, altered times. *Policing & Society*, 20(1): 1–17.

Marks M and M Shaw (2002) Point of order: Police and crime in South Africa. *Transformation*, 49: i–x.

Marks M and J Wood (2010) South African policing at a cross-roads: The case for 'minimal' and 'mini-malist' public police, *Theoretical Criminology*, 14 (3): 311–329.

O'Conner CD (2008) Citizen attitudes toward the police in Canada, *Policing: An International Journal of Police Strategies and Management*, 31(4): 578–595.

Rauch J (1993) State, Civil Society and Police Reform in South Africa. Paper presented at the International Society of Criminology conference, Budapest.

Rauch J (2000) Police Reform and South Africa's Transition. Paper presented at the South African Institute for International Affairs conference.

Reiner R (1997) Policing and the Police. In M Miguire, R Morgan and R Reiner (Eds) *The Oxford Handbook of Criminology* (Second Edition). Oxford: Clarendon Press.

Reith C (1938) *The Police Idea: Its History and Evolution in England in Eighteenth Century and After*. Oxford: Oxford University Press.

Scott J C (1990) *Domination and the Arts of Resistance: Hidden Transcripts*. New Haven and London: Yale University Press.

Shaw M (2002) *Crime and Policing in Post-Apartheid South Africa: Transforming Under Fire*. Cape Town: David Philip.

CHAPTER 12

BEE reform:
The case for an institutional perspective

Don Lindsay

'Theory is important ... because how we understand our world enables us to direct our actions in a manner that is most fruitful and more likely to achieve the results we seek.'
(Suttner, 2011)

This statement sums up the fundamental challenge affecting black economic empowerment (BEE), namely, that there is little agreement as to what it is. To some people, BEE is a programme to facilitate change in society. To others it is a vehicle for building relations between business and the state. Still others see BEE as an instrument for the advancement of black people, while many people perceive it as a vehicle for elite enrichment.

Nor has it been clarified what BEE is supposed to be doing. The name would suggest that BEE operates across the economy and involves the economic empowerment of black people. If so, why are there different programmes in different sectors, dealing with different people? Is the employment equity project not about empowering black people? Because there is land reform and BEE, does that mean that agriculture is not considered to be an economic activity or that rural people are not black? How is it that everyone ostensibly agrees that BEE is a worthwhile endeavour yet it is proving almost impossible to achieve the desired results for the programmes associated with it?

To paraphrase Suttner, the problem is that there is no body of theory that adequately informs the BEE project and, therefore, little to direct our actions and help us to achieve the results we seek. This chapter seeks to address this shortcoming by advancing the case for BEE to be understood as having evolved into a powerful institution that transcends its origins and the interests of those who gave rise to it.

OVERVIEW

South Africa evolved over more than three centuries as a country wherein the majority of its citizens were prejudiced against on the basis of race (Terreblanche, 2002). As a result, the new government in 1994 faced the task of addressing centuries of discriminatory practice that had become rooted in the socio-economic structures of the country and in the values and beliefs of its citizenry (MacDonald, 2006). This task has come to be referred to as the transformation of South African society and it is not only premised on the need for moral justice but also on the socio-economic imperative of making South Africa a stable, efficient and productive society (ANC, 1992).

In the economic sphere, the process of transformation has come to be known as BEE. This term was adopted in the early 1990s as a name for a project of big business, aimed at building relations with the new ANC government (Gqubule, 2006). It gradually evolved to become recognised as a programme of social change, although this development was more the result of lobbying by powerful interest groups than any attempt at coordinated policy formulation by government.

The heritage of this evolutionary process is that BEE has never been adequately conceptualised or defined and has thus developed as a collection of uncoordinated policies and programmes that have proven difficult to implement and which have not achieved their stated objectives (CEE, 2010; Nkwinti, 2010; Zuma 2010).

But why BEE came about and how it has developed is of less importance now than the phenomenon it has become. The evidence would suggest that BEE has evolved a unique identity and power that transcends the influences that gave rise to it and the programmes that constitute it. In short, it would appear to have become an institution.

Institutions are the medium through which societies function and they come about in response to perceived shortcomings in the social order (Hodgson, 2006; North, 1990). The most apparent manifestation of the institutional nature of BEE is the industry of financiers, lawyers, consultants, rating agents, lobbies and NGOs that has sprung up around it, and it can also be seen in the policies and programmes of government and the resulting strategies and tactics implemented by business. It exists in the widespread commentary on BEE and even in the belief systems of ordinary people.

Institutions are an integral part of everyday life. However, the recent collapse of the international financial system serves to demonstrate the effects of inadequate monitoring and control of everyday institutional entities. The failure in that instance came about as a result of mortgage company lending practices not being considered in the broader context of the socio-economic system. The short-term benefit to the banks that made these loans and sold them on was the overriding consideration.

The current programmatic approach to BEE has similar failings. It positions BEE as a policy of government that is operationalised through the programme of broad-based black economic empowerment (B-BBEE) (DTI, 2003). This perspective does not take account of the complementary nature and influence of other empowerment programmes (such as employment equity or land reform) or the extent to which the various BEE policies have become ingrained in the social, political and economic fabric of society.

BEE is a highly controversial and emotional issue and it is not the intention of this chapter to apportion any blame for the manner in which it originated or for the form that it has subsequently taken. The 1990s were a time of great upheaval and uncertainty in South Africa. The established business community and the new government had to find one another, and BEE played a key role in facilitating that relationship. Its subsequent development has been driven by the changing interests and needs of these and various other groups in society, responding, in turn, to the demands of their constituencies.

Now, however, almost twenty years since the first big BEE transaction, much knowledge has been amassed on the subject. Government has announced its intention to revisit B-BBEE policy, which it views as having been subverted to serve narrow interests rather than the broader community, and President Zuma has even called on the academic community to assist (Magubane, 2010).

In responding to this call, the case is presented here for BEE to be reviewed on the basis of its having evolved into an institution. In pursuit of this objective, the chapter will first explore the nature of the BEE phenomenon, its development path and performance record to date. The question will then be posed as to whether it matters that BEE has developed as it has, and this will lead into a discussion on the relationship between business and the state, and the impact of BEE at this nexus. Consideration of BEE in this context will then lead to an analysis of BEE as an institution and the implications thereof.

CONCEPTUALISING BEE

While BEE is regularly referred to as a policy of government, even by the state president (Zuma, 2009), there is, actually, no policy or programme of that name. Rather, there is a collection of projects and programmes aimed at addressing the issue of transformation in the economic sphere and these are often referred to, generically, as BEE programmes. The term is also widely used as a convenient alternative to the awkwardly titled B-BBEE programme.

The transformation project in the economic sphere has developed along a number of paths that today include programmes such as B-BBEE, employment equity, land reform, programmes focused within the mining and energy sectors and programmes of government designed to facilitate the financing and development of black business, to name but a few. Each of these programmes has a specific set of objectives, although there is considerable overlap between them. They are administered by different ministries and each has developed a substantial presence and power within the polity.

The B-BBEE programme is an attempt to centralise the process of economic transformation within one project (BEECom, 2001). It is governed by the B-BBEE Act which is intended to 'provide a legislative framework for the promotion of black economic empowerment' (RSA 2003). Yet the Act does not define what BEE is; in the preamble, the term BEE is subtly replaced by the term B-BBEE which the Act goes on to define as the 'economic empowerment of all black people including women, workers, youth, people with disabilities and people living in rural areas through diverse but integrated socio-economic strategies' (Ibid.). The phrase 'diverse but integrated socio-economic strategies' suggests recognition that BEE is a complex phenomenon requiring a multifaceted approach; yet the evidence is that government is keen to advance the B-BBEE programme as the central repository of transformation policy, and in pursuit of this objective huge resources are being put into collapsing a wide range of transformation initiatives and industry-specific programmes into this one overarching framework – despite the poor performance record of the programme to date (*Financial Mail*, 2010b) and the controversy that swirls around attempts to bring the IT, mining and financial services sectors under its sway (Claasen, 2010; Ensor, 2010; Gqubule, 2010). The chapter by Duncan, in this volume, gives deep insight into the challenge the project presents in the print media sector.

BEE is simply too broad a phenomenon to be discussed only within the narrow ambit of the B-BBEE programme, and any such discussion must view BEE as the collectivity of efforts to effect economic reform. It could be argued that such a broad interpretation of BEE should then include education, welfare and housing policies as these also play a key role in the empowerment of black people. While they do, such policies provide only indirect support to a policy framework focused on the business world and it would complicate matters hugely to try to incorporate them.

Many important BEE projects and programmes have been established that operate independently of government BEE structures, for example, the Business Trust and the small business development programme operated by the International Finance Corporation, but it is the job of government to provide leadership in the area of economic development and to create a suitably enabling policy framework (Evans, 1995). Much of the problem with BEE is that, up to now, its development has been driven from outside government, and readjusting roles must, therefore, be a key element of future BEE strategy.

THE ORIGINS AND EVOLUTIONARY PATH OF BEE

It is important to appreciate the diverse influences that have driven the development of BEE policy so as to better appreciate the nature of the phenomenon.

Gqubule (2006) notes that the term BEE first emerged in the late apartheid era as a rallying cry for those few black people who were able to access commercial opportunities under the reform programmes of the apartheid government. These reforms are rarely discussed in the context of BEE, and are often written off as a cynical attempt to undermine the political aspirations of black people or as a strategy of the apartheid government to strengthen its alliance with the business community (Terreblanche, 2002).

However, many leading figures in business today, such as Patrice Motsepe, Sizwe Nxasana and Don Mkwanazi, got their start during this time, which also saw the establishment of several of today's major black businesses and the listing of the first black-owned company, National Sorghum Breweries. The business doyen, Lot Ndlovu, notes that black business associations such as the National African Federated Chamber of Commerce (Nafcoc), Foundation for African Business and Consumer Service (Fabcos) and the Black Management Forum (BMF) were founded, or grew greatly in stature, during this pre-democracy period (Ndlovo; 2007). Of great significance, also, was the fact that restrictions were lifted on the operations of black trade unions under these reforms – which effectively legitimised a key instrument for the economic advancement of black people (Terreblanche, 2002).

Although the term BEE was widely used in the discourse on societal change from the late 1980s onwards (Edigheji, 1999), it came to have a very specific meaning when it was adopted by big business as a term for its response to the transformation imperative.

In the early 1990s, the insurance giant Sanlam initiated a wide-ranging project to find ways in which the company could facilitate the advancement of black people through the medium of its business operations and its influence in the economic sphere (Verhoef, 2003). A key impediment to economic participation by black people at the time (and even today) was the fact that they lacked the wealth to acquire business assets (Marais, 1998); as part of its project, therefore, Sanlam developed an innovative financing model to overcome this problem and a key principle of this model was that such transactions should serve to 'establish closer links with black leaders in business and community affairs, especially those anticipated to control the direction of South Africa in the future' (Verhoef, 2003: 32).

In the circumstances prevailing at the time, this requirement to include politically connected individuals in business deals set the stage for cronyist relations to develop between the institutions of business and the state. Nevertheless, the Sanlam model was widely adopted and is still in use today despite its being frequently cited as an attempt by white business to capture the state, or as a project of elite formation (Bond, 2005; Mbeki, 2009). To be fair to big business, in the early 1990s the incoming ANC administration was not only advocating redistributionist policies that greatly threatened commercial prospects for the business community (ANC, 1990) but the state was already a very major source of business and this was expected to increase as a result of spending on black communities in the post-apartheid era. It would, therefore, have constituted a serious dereliction of duty for business leaders not to have attempted to address such risks and opportunities. It is also a matter of record that powerful people within the Alliance leadership acceded to these advances of business with alacrity. Southall (2006) contends that the notion of BEE fitted quite well with aspects of ANC ideology, notably the creation of a patriotic bourgeoisie that would gain control of the commanding heights of the economy from whence it would effect change in favour of the party and the ideals of National Democratic Revolution.

It was inevitable that this early BEE model would cascade through the economy as the circumstances that gave rise to it amongst elites were reflected throughout society (Marais, 1998). However, such was the concentrated form of the South African economy at the time and the paucity of desirable BEE partners, it soon became apparent that a few well-connected individuals were being accorded all the opportunities under BEE. This gave rise to widespread dissatisfaction and calls for reform of the policy, led by organised labour and black business associations (Tangri and Southall, 2008).

While it is possible to trace the origins of post-apartheid BEE to the initiative and influence of big business, it would be inappropriate to suggest that the state itself did not initiate any programmes or policies. However, government was somewhat hobbled on the legislation and policy front. There existed huge structural impediments to change (Marais, 1998; Terreblanche, 2002) and the ANC had acceded to a neoliberal orthodoxy that accorded it a facilitatory rather than a leading role in matters of economic policy (Marais, 1998). The party was in an alliance with Cosatu and the SACP; both of whom challenged this form of economic orthodoxy (Turok, 2008) and, to complicate matters further, the three Alliance partners had to share power with the National Party and other old-order parties for the first three years of the new administration. On top of all this, government was committed to also consult widely with civil society on policy matters.

In such a context, the ANC government could never have been expected to implement comprehensive policies such as the New Economic Policy implemented by the Malaysian government (Gomez and Jomo, 1999) or the programme of Afrikaner advancement undertaken by the National Party government (O'Meara, 1996). Nor did it want to, a position it makes quite clear in its own strategy document on BEE, subsequently issued in 2003 (DTI, 2003). It did have two avenues open to it though. One was to effect change in the private sector, over time, through the medium of policy and legislation, and the other was to fast-track transformation in the public sector over which it exerted total control – and which it set about doing almost immediately.

On the policy front, the alliance partners saw to it that the new Constitution made particular provision for the advancement of those disadvantaged by apartheid (Sachs, 2007) and legislation was subsequently enacted on a wide range of issues that served to advance the cause of BEE.

This legislative framework was again influenced by lobbying from within the business sector, although this time by the black business community. In 1993, representatives of black business met with the senior leadership of the ANC to discuss challenges facing this largely emergent sector. History has shown that the meeting had little immediate effect on their circumstances but the resulting Mopani Memorandum of Understanding cites agreement on the need for intervention in eleven areas, including affirmative action; restructuring of organs of state; competition law; small business financing; and state procurement policy, all of which subsequently became major policy projects of the new government (ANC, 1993).

Cosatu has also had a major influence on the nature of BEE policy. Tangri and Southall (2008) note that the organisation never approved of BEE, which it perceived as a project of elite formation with no meaningful benefit to its membership. The organisation, therefore, lobbied for a broader interpretation of BEE and this action resulted, *inter alia*, in the passing of the Employment Equity Act, a major pillar of the BEE project.

Marais (1998) notes that Cosatu was behind the formation of the National Economic Development and Labour Council (Nedlac)[1] which has played a major role in the development of the transformation charter concept. The first charter to appear within the BEE legislative framework was the outcome of a Nedlac summit on transformation in the financial services sector (FSCC, 2004). The mining sector was also busy at this time with its transformation project and it too adopted the transformation charter concept. These two charters became models for other business sectors and, ultimately, for the central measurement mechanism of the future B-BBEE Act.

The most significant lobbying effort on BEE since the creation of the project in the early 1990s also came from within the black business community. At its annual conference in November 1997, the Black Management Forum called for the establishment of a commission to investigate the concept of BEE and to propose a more effective policy framework on the issue (BEECom, 2001). The work of this commission resulted in the first policy document issued by government to focus specifically on the subject of BEE (DTI, 2003) and this was quickly followed by the B-BBEE Act.

The conflicting and uncoordinated framework of BEE policies stands as evidence that, throughout these various key stages in the development of BEE, government seemed not to recognise the need for a more strategic approach to transformation policy. This is quite surprising considering the strong historical commitment of the ANC to economic transformation and subsequent statements on the matter that indicate appreciation of the strategic nature of the challenges involved (ANC, 1992).

It has been speculated that the original transformation agenda of the ANC was undermined with the move from the Reconstruction and Development Programme (RDP) economic policy framework to the neoliberal Growth, Employment and Reconstruction (Gear) policy in 1996 (Terreblanche, 2002). Even so, while the ANC could not act in the dictatorial manner of the Malaysian or National Party governments, it would surely have been within its power to create cross-ministry clusters, or even a dedicated ministry to oversee and coordinate its various transformation efforts.

The result of this patchy evolutionary process is that, today, the peak transformation programme, B-BBEE, is administered by the Department of Trade and Industry and it overlaps the requirements of the Employment Equity Act, administered by the Department of Labour. It also overlaps the transformative elements of the Minerals and Petroleum Resources Development Act which governs BEE in the mining and energy sectors and which is administered jointly by two other government departments.

The Preferential Procurement Policy Framework Act of 2000 was established specifically to facilitate the transformative potential of government spending. However, certain of the provisions of this Act, administered by the Department of Finance, are in conflict with the provisions of the newer B-BBEE Act. This has led to great confusion in government procurement circles and the Act is, therefore, to be reviewed (Paton, 2010).

In the agriculture sector, research has shown how the focus on the acquisition of business ownership by black people, tacitly encouraged by government in the context of BEE, has served to undermine the broader objectives of land reform policy (Du Toit, Kruger and Ponte, 2008). Also, the sheer bureaucratic burden of BEE compliance is such that it undermines government transformation policies aimed at advancing entrepreneurial activity in the small and medium enterprise (SME) sector.

A BEE advisory council was established under the B-BBEE Act (2003). Its job is to assist in the formulation and implementation of policy. It is chaired by the state president and members are drawn from diverse positions within the ranks of government, business, labour and civil society. However, it is symptomatic of the myopia that pervades BEE that this council has been established within the framework of the B-BBEE Act and so falls under the auspices of the Department of Trade and Industry yet it is chaired by the president, and the panel includes two other ministers responsible for competing empowerment programmes. Several members of the council also represent lobbies with vested interests in particular policy outcomes.

The potential for this forum to exacerbate the current problems facing BEE was exemplified by contradictory statements put out within a week of one another by its chairman, President Zuma, and a sub-committee member, Sandile Zungu. Referring to the narrow base of BEE beneficiaries, President Zuma called for a 'decisive shift to meaningful economic transformation … deepening the empowerment of black South Africans in general' (ANC, 2010: 1). Within the B-BBEE framework, such a strategy would be accommodated by focusing on issues such as employment creation, training, small business development and social responsibility, rather than the ownership and management of business by black people. Yet, just days before the president made this speech, Zungu issued a statement in which he announced that his sub-committee was conducting a review of existing policy such as would expand opportunities for ownership and management control in the small and medium business sector (Salgado, 2010). This statement not only contradicted that of the president but demonstrated a substantial lack of insight into the nature of the small and medium business sector.

THE PERFORMANCE OF BEE POLICY

The case for reform of BEE policy is supported by the performance and outcomes of the various programmes aimed at transforming the economy. While there have certainly been success stories, they have been relatively rare. Cargill (2010) notes, for example, how empowerment provisions entrenched in the requirements for the awarding of new telecommunications, broadcasting and casino licences were particularly effective in creating new enterprises that met the requirements of the B-BBEE Act.

For the most part, however, none of the various programmes has come close to achieving their stated objectives and the reliability of the data supplied is frequently the subject of dispute (McKaiser, 2009; Radebe, 2010b; Solidarity, 2009).

No comprehensive system for reporting on the performance of the B-BBEE programme has yet been established. Several surveys are conducted within the private sector but none professes to meet high standards of rigour and validity. One such survey that has been running annually for ten years reports on levels of B-BBEE compliance among listed companies. A trend can be seen in this report that does indicate increasing, albeit low, levels of compliance (*Financial Mail*, 2010b). However, in a telling commentary in the preamble to the 2010 report, the editor in charge questioned the value of the report findings, stating that 'BEE has developed some coded language that has a scant relationship with the experiences of its designated beneficiaries ... a language that seems to be developing a meaning of its own, parallel to the observed real world' (Radebe, 2010a).

Little data is available on the actual cost of the B-BBEE programme but a report by the Presidency (2009) shows that R497 billion was absorbed in the acquisition of shares by black people in the period from 1995 to 2008. The B-BBEE programme comprises seven elements and this spending satisfies only one of them. Huge resources would equally have been absorbed in achieving compliance with the other six.

The minister of Rural Development and Land Reform is on record as advising parliament that 'the land reform programmes implemented to date have not been sustainable and have not provided the anticipated benefits.' (Nkwinti, 2010: 8). In support of this assertion the minister reported that much of the six million hectares of land that had been redistributed was unproductive and had not contributed to the economic upliftment of its recipients and, further, that the land reform programme had led to a worrying decline in the general level of agricultural productivity which in turn raised the spectre of problems with food security (ibid.).

In its 2010 annual report, the Commission on Employment Equity (CEE) found that 'the slow pace of transformation and the general resistance by employers to change has necessitated the need to amend the Employment Equity Act in order to strengthen its implementation and enforcement' (CEE, 2010: 36).

The biggest BEE project to date was that implemented in the state sector in the mid 1990s. This project sought to bring the demographic profile of all agencies operating under the auspices of the state into line with the demographic profile of the broader population. The project is credited with contributing to a consumer-driven economic boom, and opportunities were created that many people might not otherwise have had. However, this initiative carried a large cost burden and led to a huge reduction in the efficiency of the state (*Financial Mail*, 2010a ; Ramphele, 2008) which, in turn, damaged the image of BEE and created secondary challenges, many of which contributed directly to impeding the transformation objectives of government.

Considering the lack of coordination and effective management of these policies and programmes, the effectiveness of BEE can perhaps best be assessed on the basis of national socio-economic performance data. BEE is concerned with 'the economic empowerment of all black people' (RSA, 2003) and, because black people constitute more than ninety per cent of the population (SAIRR, 2010), national performance statistics can provide a reliable measure as to the overall performance of the BEE project.

The greatest challenge to BEE lies in the relatively low level of economic growth that has been experienced in the post-apartheid era. The minister of Finance recently stated that a growth rate of over six per cent per annum would be required in order to bring about a marked reduction in the level of poverty and inequality (Gordhan, 2010). As can be seen from Table 1, this level of growth has not been achieved in the period since 1994 and the minister is of the opinion that it is unlikely to be achieved in the near future (ibid.). If the economy is not growing, the process of economic empowerment inevitably becomes one of redistribution from the haves to the have-nots.

Table 1: Gross domestic product 1994–2009

	Real Total GDP	
Year	Rbn	Change
1994	1,100	3.2%
1995	1,135	3.1%
1996	1,183	4.3%
1997	1,215	2.6%
1998	1,221	0.5%
1999	1,250	2.4%
2000	1,302	4.2%
2001	1,338	2.7%
2002	1,386	3.7%
2003	1,427	2.9%
2004	1,492	4.6%
2005	1,571	5.3%
2006	1,659	5.6%
2007	1,750	5.5%
2008	1,815	3.7%
2009	1,782	-1.80%

Source: SAIRR (2010) South Africa Survey 2009/10: The Economy. p. 10.

Even where the statistics do reflect improvements in individual income levels, traditional race-based patterns of income inequality are shown to have endured in the post-apartheid era. It can be seen from Table 2 that although the per capita disposable annual income of Africans increased by forty-nine per cent in the period from 1994 to 2007, this only amounted to an increase from R6 381 to R9 495. By comparison, the per capita income of whites increased from R47 674 to R58 926 in the same period, reflecting a reasonable twenty-four per cent increase, off an already high base.

The increase in black income levels should also be seen in the light of increases in government welfare spending, most of which would have gone to black people. In 2007–2008, such spending amounted to R69 billion (Presidency, 2009).

Table 2: Real disposable income per head by race 1994–2007

	African	Coloured	Indian	White	Average
YEAR	R	R	R	R	R
1994	6,381	11,114	21,040	47,674	12,361
1995	6,629	11,412	22,295	48,014	12,585
1996	6,962	11,845	23,863	48,994	12,974
1997	7,165	12,129	24,354	49,493	13,166
1998	7,208	12,153	24,357	49,042	13,076
1999	7,335	12,324	24,735	49,170	13,146
2000	7,591	12,690	25,541	50,645	13,502
2001	7,818	12,955	26,253	51,755	13,750
2002	8,076	13,331	27,041	52,892	14,076
2003	8,259	13,581	27,574	53,514	14,276
2004	8,508	13,935	28,321	54,534	14,591
2005	8,771	14,310	29,111	55,619	14,933
2006	9,123	14,827	30,192	75,233	15,421
2007	9,495	15,370	31,330	58,926	15,939
Change 1994–2007	49%	38%	49%	24%	29%

Source: SAIRR, South Africa Survey 2009/10: Employment and Incomes. p. 81.

Terreblanche (2002) also points to the fact that while income levels have risen greatly for some black people, they have fallen greatly for most. Inequality has thus increased within the black, and especially within the African, community. Taking this into account, along with the twenty-four per cent increase in income enjoyed by whites, it becomes immediately apparent that increases in income levels among blacks have been achieved by the loss of income to other blacks rather than by a loss of income to whites.

On the employment front, the picture has also been disappointing. Table 3 shows how unemployment among all race groups has risen. However, it has been African South Africans who have been especially hard hit, with the loss of more than two million jobs.

In summary, the performance record of BEE has been poor when examined at the level of national economic performance indicators. There is little prospect of South Africa's achieving the six per cent GDP growth rate considered necessary to make an

Table 3: Unemployment numbers[†] by race 1994–2010

Year	African	Coloured	Indian	White	Total
1994	1,637,000	260,000	48,000	42,000	1,988,000
1995	1,336,000	229,000	41,000	38,000	1,644,000
1996	1,714,000	191,000	58,000	57,000	2,019,000
1997	1,895,000	229,000	52,000	62,000	2,238,000
1998	2,793,000	220,000	59,000	89,000	3,163,000
1999	2,751,000	232,000	72,000	99,000	3,158,000
2000	3,748,000	339,000	98,000	148,000	4,333,000
2001	3,447,000	395,000	70,000	170,000	4,081,000
2002	3,886,000	468,000	85,000	165,000	4,603,000
2003	4,136,000	439,000	95,000	173,000	4,843,000
2004	3,681,000	357,000	77,000	116,000	4,231,000
2005	3,437,000	364,000	37,000	125,000	3,993,000
2006	3,439,000	372,000	46,000	127,000	3,984,000
2007	3,565,000	407,000	52,000	95,000	4,119,000
2008	3,645,000	367,000	62,000	117,000	4,191,000
2009	3,632,000	384,000	68,000	100,000	4,184,000
2010	3,704,000	428,000	49,000	129,000	4,310,000
Change 1994–2010	126.3%	64.6%	2.1%	207.1%	116.8%

Source: SAIRR : South Africa Survey 2009/10: Employment and Incomes. p.41.
[†]Definition of unemployment excludes discouraged work seekers.

impact on current levels of poverty and inequality (Gordhan, 2010). Income inequality is rising across the board but mostly within the African demographic group and the trend in overall employment is downward (SAIRR, 2010). While government has introduced the New Growth Path economic policy framework to address these and other macroeconomic challenges, response to this initiative has been lukewarm while organised labour is of the opinion that the policy does not go far enough (*Business Day*, 2011; Du Plessis, 2011).

THE PROBLEM OF UNINTENDED OUTCOMES

Thus far, this chapter has explored the failure of BEE to achieve its intended outcomes. Much of the criticism levelled at the BEE project, however, is levelled on the basis of its supposedly unintended outcomes, primarily the narrow base of beneficiaries (BEECom, 2001) and the role BEE has played in facilitating cronyism and corruption between the institutions of business and the state (Butler, 2010; Friedman, 2010).

In this vein, much is made of projects such as those involving Arcelor Mittal and the ICT empowerment investment company but this, and other such projects, vary little from the first major post-apartheid BEE project which involved Sanlam and a coterie of politically connected individuals. That foundational project was premised on linking business and political elites (Verhoef, 2003). The exchange of rents in return for political influence, therefore, has been a fundamental element of the BEE project since 1993, and it was always inevitable that there would be a narrow base of beneficiaries because those with the appropriate level of political influence are few.

This is not to suggest that the model is not problematic. There is an extensive body of literature that addresses the potentially corrupting influence of business on the institutions of government (Evans, 1995; Krueger, 1974; Maxfield and Schneider, 1997). Such influence can subvert prospects for long-term economic development, particularly in developing countries such as South Africa, where the institutions necessary to counter such influence are often very weak (Handley, 2008; Taylor, 2007).

Several studies have been conducted on business-state relations in the southern African region, highlighting the common colonial histories of the countries involved and noting the limited capacity or willingness of these states to initiate coalition formation with their business communities (Brautigam et al., 2002; Taylor, 2007; Sen and Te Velde, 2009). In her study, Handley (2008) notes how this has often resulted in business communities taking the lead in coalition formation – as indeed was the case here in South Africa. However, Handley also notes that in such instances, coalition sustainability has been dependent upon the capacity of business to ensure the continued utility of the coalition relationship to political elites (ibid.). It is noteworthy, therefore, that both Handley (2008) and Taylor (2007) have expressed concern as to the narrowness of the post-apartheid business-state coalition and the extent to which its currency is dependent upon political elites benefiting through BEE.

THREE IMPORTANT REASONS FOR BEE REFORM

To summarise, there are three compelling reasons for the reform of BEE policy:

- First, as the government and many others have noted, there are structural impediments to making South Africa as productive as it needs to be. These are deeply rooted in the racial profile of society and so are not going to go away without some form of change management programme such as BEE (Kotter, 1966; Marais, 1998; Chang and Evans, 2005; ANC, 2007)

- Second, as demonstrated elsewhere in this chapter, BEE currently absorbs a huge amount of scarce financial resources, with little to show in the way of results. South Africa cannot hope to achieve its development objectives while using its resources so unproductively.
- Third, and, arguably of greatest strategic importance, the current BEE model is having a potentially negative impact on the business-state relationship which has negative connotations for long-term development prospects.

THE RATIONALE FOR AN INSTITUTIONAL APPROACH TO BEE REFORM

So how does this justify an institutional approach to BEE reform and why will it not help to tweak specific policies? The answer lies in the manner in which BEE has become rooted in the business-state relationship and the centrality of this relationship to the functioning of society.

Diagram 1 demonstrates the link BEE initially facilitated between business and political elites, providing the business community with political influence and government elites with rents and, ostensibly, the opportunity to effect change from the commanding heights of the economy.

Diagram 1: The early BEE project

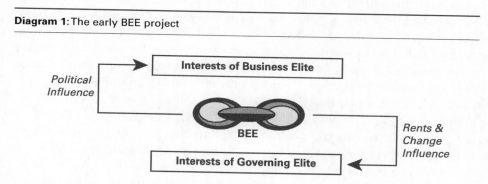

Diagram 2 shows how this initial relationship has evolved. The narrow interests of business and state elites have expanded to become the interests of a wide variety of agents operating collectively under the banners of business, the state, labour and civil society. The creation of access to rents has expanded into open corruption as agents have increasingly used unscrupulous means to acquire their share of influence and rents.

However, a more significant development can be seen as having emerged in this second diagram. BEE is no longer just a linking mechanism. The volume, cost and complexity of the transactions associated with BEE have become such that they have necessitated the development of an administrative framework complete with its own infrastructure, rules, organisations and systems of belief. BEE has thus become much more than a pivot in relations between business and the state. It has now developed its own unique institutional form and thus its own unique power and influence, demonstrated by the arrows that run in both directions between BEE and the various agents. In short, BEE has become an institution that mediates the business-state relationship (North, 1990; Hodgson, 2006).

Diagram 2: Contemporary BEE
_____

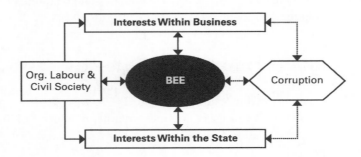

WHY DOES IT MATTER THAT BEE HAS EVOLVED INTO AN INSTITUTION?

Institutions are hubs that serve to bring together the various elements that constitute social and economic activity (Chang and Evans, 2005). They are variously defined as 'systems of established and prevalent social rules that structure social interactions' (Hodgson, 2006: 2) and 'humanly devised constraints that shape human interaction' (North, 1990: 1). Institutions can emerge naturally or they can be the intentional creation of one or more agents (Hodgson 2006). In either case they come about as a result of there being some need or shortcoming in the social order which coalesces with the interests of agents and wider environmental factors (Chang and Evans, 2005; North, 1990).

Institutions are complex social phenomena – which makes them inherently difficult to manage (Hodgson, 2006). An agent may initiate the founding of an institution to address a particular need but, in the process of normal operations, the institution is influenced by inputs from other agents and sundry environmental factors (North, 1990). The originating agent must, therefore, monitor these diverse influences and manage them so as to avoid subversion of the original objective.

A key feature of institutions is that they can exert an upward influence on those agents and forces that gave rise to them in the first place. As Chang and Evans (2005: 103) note, 'institutions have a symbiotic dimension and therefore inculcate certain values, or world views, onto the people who live under them'. An iterative process exists, therefore, which impedes the accurate forecasting of particular outcomes.

Diagram 3 demonstrates this institutional form applied to BEE. As previously discussed, BEE has evolved into an institution through the interaction of agency and environmental factors. It has thus developed a character and influence of its own which not only transcends its formative influences but now also exerts its own unique influence over them.

Diagram 3: The institution of BEE

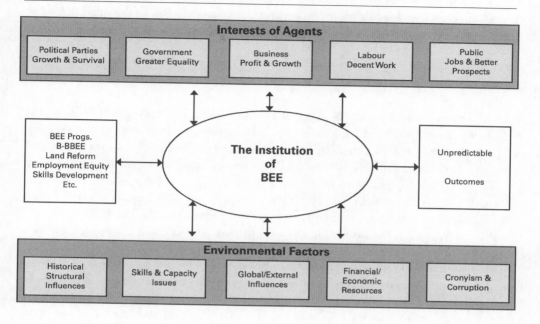

BEE was created as a vehicle to link business and government elites (Verhoef, 2010). In 1990 there was no government policy on BEE and no rules or guidelines as to how it should be done. There were no specialised consultancies that could advise on BEE transactions and innovative financing structures had to be created by sponsors to facilitate BEE ownership transactions.

Today, there are laws and complex rules governing BEE and no major decision is taken in business or government without considering its BEE implications. Every bank and major legal and accounting practice has a team of specialists to handle BEE, such is the lucrative nature of this work. A new industry has even emerged that specialises in assisting businesses and government departments with the implementation and measurement of their BEE performance rating.

Yet, despite all the evidence as to the evolution of BEE into an independent and powerful institutional entity in society, it is still viewed by many as something that can be managed at the level of bureaucratic interventions. The futility of this perspective becomes immediately apparent when BEE is viewed in the context of Diagram 3. The model demonstrates how the outcomes of the various transformation programmes of government are mediated by the very structures and rules that have been created to facilitate their implementation. It can be seen how the institution that BEE has become is, itself, mediated by diverse environmental and agency factors and is thus a highly volatile phenomenon. It is hardly surprising that corrupt and cronyist influences take advantage of such an uncontrollable environment.

To have any prospect of success, BEE policy must be informed by such a wider institutional perspective. Specific programmes and initiatives can then be designed in a more informed context and thus have greater prospects of success.

SUMMARY

This chapter set out to address some of the confusion that pervades BEE policy by advancing the case for it to be interpreted as having evolved into an institution in society. In pursuit of this objective, the chapter first addressed the lack of theoretical clarity that characterises the issue of BEE and the challenge this presents to discourse on the subject. It was argued that this is a result of the fact that BEE policy has been influenced more by diverse agents, acting in their own self-interest, than by any coordinated, planned action on the part of government. The chapter showed how this has resulted in BEE becoming a multifaceted project, administered under a conflicting array of policies and programmes, none of which has come anywhere close to achieving its stated objectives.

It was argued that reform of BEE policy is necessary for it to be able to address impediments to change that are deeply rooted in the structures of the South African economy and, also, to stem the hugely inefficient use of resources consumed in the course of implementing contemporary BEE policies. The chapter argues, however, that the main justification for reform lies in the influence that BEE exerts at the nexus of business-state relations and thus on prospects for long-term economic development.

In exploring this connection between BEE and the business-state relationship, the chapter showed how BEE has evolved into a complex phenomenon that mediates, and is mediated by, a wide array of socio-economic factors. In short, it shows how BEE has evolved into an institution. The conclusion is that the current programmatic approach to transformation fails because these programmes cannot address the complexity inherent in the institutional entity that BEE has become.

NOTES

1   Nedlac is a forum for dialogue between government, labour, business and community organisations.

REFERENCES

ANC (1990) Recommendations on post-apartheid economic policy: Report from workshop on economic policy for a post-apartheid South Africa, Harare, 28 April to 1 May 1990. *Transformation* (12): 2–15.

ANC (1992) Ready to Govern: ANC Policy Guidelines for a Democratic South Africa. Johannesburg: African National Congress.Available at: http://www.anc.org.za/227 (Accessed 12 June 2009).

ANC (1993) Historic ANC/Black Business Summit. Johannesburg: African National Congress.Available at: http://www.anc.org.za/show.php?doc=ancdocs/pr/1993/pr1101a.html (Accessed 9 March 2009).

ANC (2007) Strategy and Tactics of The ANC: Building a National Democratic Society. African National

Congress. Available at: http://www.anc.org.za/ancdocs/history/conf/conference52/ (Accessed 30 May 2009).

BEECom (2001) *Report of The Black Economic Empowerment Commission.* Johannesburg: Skotaville.

Bond P (2005) *Elite Transition.* Scottsville: University of KwaZulu-Natal Press.

Brautigam D, L Rakner and S Taylor (2002) Business associations and growth coalitions in sub-Saharan Africa. *Journal of Modern African Studies* 40 (4): 519–547.

Brummer S (2010) Zuma jnr heading for first billion, *Mail & Guardian*, 13 August, p2.

Business Day (2011) ANC cannot wish jobs into existence, *Business Day* [Online], 11 January. Available at: http://www.businessday.co.za/articles/Content.aspx?id=131179 (Accessed 11 January 2011).

Butler A (2010) From sports reporter to connected enforcer, *Business Day* [Online], 7 June. Available at: http://www.businessday.co.za/articles/Content.aspx?id=111076 (Accessed 7 June 2010).

Cargill J (2010) *Trick or Treat: Rethinking Black Economic Empowerment.* Auckland Park: Jacana.

CEE (2010) Employment Equity Annual Report 2009-2010. Pretoria: Commission for Employment Equity.

Chang H and P Evans (2005) The role of institutions in economic change. In De Paula S and GA Dymski (Eds) *Reimagining Growth: Towards a Renewal of Development Theory.* London and New York: Zed Books.

Claasen L (2010) All talk and no action, *Financial Mail* [Online], 22 January. Available at: http://secure.financialmail.co.za/10/0122/moneyinvest/amoney.htm (Accessed 22 January 2010).

DTI (2003) South Africa's Economic Transformation: A Strategy for Broad-Based Black Economic Empowerment. Pretoria: Department of Trade and Industry. Available at: http://www.dti.gov.za/bee/complete.pdf (Accessed 10 March 2009).

Du Plessis C (2011) New economic plan 'needs to be overhauled', *Business Report* [Online], 17 January. Available at: http://www.iol.co.za:80/business/business-news/new-economic-plan-needs-to-be-overhauled-1.1012544 [Accessed 17 January 2011].

Du Toit A, S Kruger and S Ponte (2008) Deracialising exploitation? 'Black economic empowerment' in the South African wine industry. *Journal of Agrarian Change* 8 (1): 6–32.

Edigheji O (1999) Rethinking black economic empowerment in post-apartheid South Africa. Glenburn Lodge, Muldersdrift.

Ensor L (2010) Finance sector warned on empowerment goals, *Business Day* [Online], 16 August. Available at: http://www.businessday.co.za/articles/Content.aspx?id=118055 (Accessed 16 August 2010).

Evans P (1995) *Embedded Autonomy: States and Industrial Transformation.* Princeton, NJ: Princeton University Press.

Financial Mail (2010a) Editorial: BEE should uplift, not corrupt, *Financial Mail* [Online], 26 August. (Accessed 26 August 2010).

Financial Mail (2010b) Special report: Top empowerment companies 2010, Johannesburg: *Financial Mail.*

Friedman S (2010) The worst threat to democracy that money can buy, *Business Day* [Online], 27 January. Available at: http://www.businessday.co.za/articles/Content.aspx?id=92123 (Accessed 27 January 2010).

FSCC (2004) Financial Sector Charter. Johannesburg: Financial Sector Charter Council.

Gomez ET and KS Jomo (1999) *Malaysia's Political Economy: Politics, Patronage and Profits.* Cambridge: Cambridge University Press.

Gordhan P (2010) Medium Term Budget Policy Statement. Pretoria: Department of the Treasury. Available at: http://www.dha.gov.za/PDF/speech.pdf (Accessed 13 January 2011).

Gqubule D (2006) *Making Mistakes Righting Wrongs: Insights Into Black Economic Empowerment.* Jeppestown & Sandton: Jonathan Ball & KMM Review.

Gqubule D (2010) Shabangu fires blanks on BEE mining targets, *Sunday Independent*, 31 October, p. 17.

Handley A (2008) *Business and the State in Africa: Economic Policy-Making in the Neo-Liberal Era.* New York: Cambridge University Press.

Hodgson GM (2006) What are institutions? *Journal of Economic Issues* 40 (1): 1–25.

Krueger AO (1974) The political economy of the rent-seeking society, *American Economic Review* 64 (3): 291.

Macdonald M (2006) *Why Race Matters in South Africa*. Scottsville: University of KwaZulu-Natal Press.

Magubane T (2010) Zuma: Business not the BEE-all of empowerment, *The Witness* [Online], 30 December. Available at: http://www.witness.co.za/index.php?showcontent&global[_id]=53088 (Accessed 7 January 2011).

Marais H (1998) *South Africa, Limits to Change: The Political Economy of Transition*. Cape Town, London & New York: University of Cape Town Press & Zed Books.

Maxfield S and B Schneider (Eds) (1997) *Business and The State in Developing Countries*, Ithaca and London: Cornell University Press.

Mbeki M (2009) *Architects of Poverty*. Johannesburg: Picador Africa.

McKaiser E (2009) Case for affirmative action not black and white, *Business Day* [Online], 23 October. Available at: http://www.businessday.co.za/articles/Content.aspx?id=84803 (Accessed 23 October 2009).

Ndlovu L (2007) Placing black business on the agenda. In Mangcu X, G Marcus, K Shubane and A Hadland (Eds) *Visions of Black Economic Empowerment*. Auckland Park: Jacana Media.

Nkwinti G (2010) Speech by the Minister of Rural Development and Land Reform at The Debate on the Budget Vote of The Department of Rural Development and Land Reform. Cape Town: Department of Rural Affairs and Land Reform. Available at: http://www.ruraldevelopment.gov. za/DLA-Internet//content/document_library/Ministry/Ministry_Minister_Speeches/Speech2.pdf (Accessed 22 October 2010).

North DC (1990) *Institutions, Institutional Change, and Economic Performance*. Cambridge, New York: Cambridge University Press.

O'Meara D (1996) *Forty Lost Years: The Apartheid State and The Politics of The National Party, 1948–1994*. Randburg: Ravan Press.

Paton C (2010) Making it local, *Financial Mail* [Online], 3 June. Available at: http://www.fm.co.za/ Article.aspx?id=110826 (Accessed 3 June 2010).

Presidency (2009) Development Indicators 2009. Pretoria: The Presidency of The Republic of South Africa.

Radebe S (2010a) Food for thinking minds, *Financial mail* [Online], 4 May. Available at: http://www. fm.co.za/Article.aspx?id=107765 [Accessed 22 July 2010].

Radebe S (2010b) The spotlight is on real players, *Financial Mail* [Online], 3 May. Available at: http:// www.fm.co.za/Article.aspx?id=107764 [Accessed 22 July 2010].

Ramphele M (2008) It is not just the taking of the money, *New Agenda* Second Quarter, 6–14.

RSA (2003) Broad-Based Black Economic Empowerment Act. No. 53 of 2003. Pretoria: Government of The Republic of South Africa.

Sachs A (2007) The constitutional principles underpinning black economic empowerment. In Mangcu X, G Marcus, K Shubane and A Hadland (Eds) *Visions of Black Economic Empowerment*. Auckland Park: Jacana Media.

SAIRR (2010) South Africa Survey 2009/2010. Johannesburg: South African Institute of Race Relations.

Salgado I (2010) Zuma's team moots BEE overhaul, *The Star* [Online], 10 January. Available at: http:// www.thestar.co.za:80/zuma-s-team-moots-bee-overhaul-1.1009857.

Seekings J and N Nattrass (2006) *Class, Race, and Inequality in South Africa*. Scottsville: University of KwaZulu-Natal Press.

Sen K and DW Te Velde (2009) State business relations and economic growth in sub-Saharan Africa, *Journal of Development Studies* 45 (8): 1267–1283.

Solidarity (2009) A rebuttal of Manyi's statements regarding the latest CEE report. Pretoria: Solidarity.

Southall R (2006) Ten propositions about black economic empowerment in South Africa, *Review of African Political Economy* 34 (111): 67–84.

Suttner R (2011) Democracy: National democratic revolution is an ever-evolving concept, *Business Day* [Online], 11 January. Available at: http://www.businessday.co.za/Articles/Content.aspx?id=131164 (Accessed 11 January 2011).

Tangri R and R Southall (2008) The politics of black economic empowerment in South Africa, *Journal of Southern African Studies* 34 (3): 699–716.

Taylor SD (2007) *Business and the State in Southern Africa: The Politics of Economic Reform.* Boulder, Colorado: Lynne Rienner.

Terreblanche S (2002) *A History of Inequality in South Africa 1652–2002.* Scottsville & Sandton: University of Natal Press & KMM Review.

Turok B (2008) *From The Freedom Charter to Polokwane: The Evolution of ANC Economic Policy.* Mill Street: New Agenda.

Verhoef G (2003) 'The Invisible Hand': The roots of black economic empowerment, Sankorp and societal change in South Africa, 1995–2000, *Journal For Contemporary History* 28 (1): 27–47.

Verhoef G (2010) Savings for life to build the economy for the people: The emergence of Afrikaner corporate conglomerates in South Africa 1918-2000, *South African Journal of Economic History* 24 (1): 118–163.

Zuma J (2009) We remain committeed to taking the economic transformation forward, *ANC Today* [Online], 45 (9). Available at: http://www.anc.org.za/ancdocs/anctoday/2009/at45.htm (Accessed 16 November 2009).

Zuma J (2010) Statement of the National Executive Committee on the occasion of the 99th anniversary of the ANC. Johannesburg: African National Congress. Available at: http://www.anc.org.za/7123 (Accessed 10 January 2010).

CHAPTER 13

Bokfontein amazes the nations:
Community Work Programme (CWP) heals a traumatised community[1]

Malose Langa and Karl von Holdt

INTRODUCTION

At our very first meeting with King George Mohlala and Patrick Ledikwa, two community leaders of Bokfontein, a small and poverty-stricken informal settlement near Brits in North West Province, they told us that theirs had been a community traumatised by the violence of evictions. 'Eviction robs you of your dignity, respect and self-esteem,' said Mohlala. 'It robs you of your history. Your children do not know where you come from. You feel shame in front of other communities.' They then went on to talk about how the Community Work Programme (CWP) and a community-building programme called the Organisation Workshop (OW) have helped them overcome this trauma: 'It brought back our humanity, we understood we were part of South Africa. It built us so that we can stand on our own without waiting for help from elsewhere.'

We chose Bokfontein as a site in our research into collective violence in South Africa after hearing that the leadership in this community had prevented a threatened outbreak of xenophobic violence in 2008, at a time when violent attacks on foreign nationals were taking place in many similar communities. At the time, we were told that the state-sponsored CWP had played a part in strengthening the community to resist the apostles of xenophobic pogroms. Bokfontein sounded like the ideal research site in which to investigate the factors of resilience in a community which may reduce or prevent violence.

In this chapter, we describe the origins of Bokfontein and the impact of trauma due to the forced removals, which generated an ongoing cycle of intra-community violence. We then describe the implementation of OW and CWP and how this has helped to transform the community. We go on to discuss community responses to collective trauma and intra-community violence, to the threat of xenophobic violence, and to the multiple local government service delivery failures which, in other communities, have led to community protests. We conclude with an argument that the CWP – which incorporates OW as one of the community development approaches used in the inception stage of new sites – is able to respond to collective histories of traumatic violence as well as to socio-economic challenges of poverty and joblessness. The programme has already been rolled out in some sixty-four communities nationally, where a total of about 90 000 people are employed for a minimum of two days a week in providing public goods at a local level; with a further eighteen communities targeted by mid-2011. Overall, this kind of intervention holds promise for the wide-scale healing and development of hundreds of marginalised communities across South Africa.

Methodologically, the research for this chapter consisted of community participation and observation over a period of two months, combined with in-depth interviews with key informants such as community leaders, the local councillor and municipal officials, as well as the designers and implementers of CWP and OW.[2] The researcher stayed in Bokfontein every weekend for a period of two months in late 2010, attending meetings and soccer matches, accompanying participants in the CWP on their work rounds, chatting to residents on street corners, and interviewing them in their homes about the impact of OW and CWP on their community.

BOKFONTEIN: A tale of two traumas

Bokfontein is an area which includes various farm plots near Hartebeespoort Dam in the North West province. Bokfontein settlement, which is the subject of this chapter, consists of about 5 000 residents. It is the product of the removals of two separate communities from the vicinity of Hartebeespoort Dam and is therefore, in its origins, a place of violence, trauma and division.

The residents of the first community were evicted from nearby farms at Hartebeespoort Dam in 2005 and taken to Bokfontein. Many reported that they had been staying on these farms for many years until it was bought by a new owner who wanted to develop new up-market housing on the land. The new owner and municipal officials promised that new land would be bought for the community in Bokfontein, but this never happened. Community members feel betrayed by the municipality, and there are suspicions that some municipal officials may have received bribes for this community to be forcefully evicted.

Many of the residents described their eviction as reminiscent of forced removals under apartheid. Their homes were bulldozed. Their building materials and graveyards were also destroyed. Some residents complained that due to forced eviction, they are not able to appease their ancestors. They attributed some of their difficulties (for example, lack of job opportunities) to angry ancestors. They felt that the only way to appease their ancestors was to go back to the farm and collect their ancestors' remains, but this was not possible as new up-market houses had been built on their graves.

Others narrated that their eviction was very traumatic and humiliating. They felt that the current ANC-led government did not care about them because they were forcefully removed and dumped in the middle of nowhere with no access to water and other basic services. In terms of the existing case law,[3] alternative accommodation including access to basic services should be provided when people are evicted from their homes, but in the case of Bokfontein this requirement was never met. Their removal also violated other basic human rights as enshrined in the Bill of Rights. For example, following the eviction, many children were not able to continue with their schooling because of the long distance between Bokfontein and Hartebeespoort Dam. Many people also lost their jobs as domestic and farm workers owing to lack of money to commute between Bokfontein and Hartebeespoort Dam every day. Many residents asserted that eviction had destroyed their lives. There were no roads, toilets or access to water when they arrived in Bokfontein. The place had nothing. People had to start from scratch, with no help from the state, to rebuild their lives.

In August 2006, another neighbouring community in Meloding was also forcefully removed by the municipality to Bokfontein because they had been illegally occupying private land that was earmarked for low-cost housing. Again, this group of people described their forced removal as humiliating and traumatic. Neither of the two communities that were evicted to Bokfontein resisted their evictions.

The two communities were forced to live together and to share a small piece of land in Bokfontein. The first group, which was evicted in 2005, saw the new group that arrived in 2006 as intruders who were not welcome on 'their' land – so the community was divided into two sides. We were shown the line which demarcated the two communities, and told that during that period it was extremely dangerous for a member of one community to cross the line and enter the space of the other community. We were told that, for two years, there was bloody violence between members of these two communities; people in one community could not socialise with people in the other; it was a situation of 'us and them'. It is reported that levels of crime were also very high owing to the violence that existed between the two communities, and some participants described the situation at that time as being like a 'war-zone'.

The violence between the two communities was partly a power struggle over limited resources such as water (which was being provided by the municipality on an *ad hoc* basis) and the limited space to build their shacks, and partly an expression of anger in response to the trauma of forced removal. Seedat, Lau and Suffla (2010) follow Franz Fanon's work in noting that violence amongst marginalised community members themselves generally 'represents the spillover of repressed trauma, manifest through the transfer of anger and hatred of the former "colonial masters" onto an equally or more vulnerable "other" through physical acts of denigration' (Seedat, Lau and Suffla, 2010: 10). It was clear in Bokfontein that the trauma of eviction had produced a collective psychological experience of brutalisation and dehumanisation in the community, whose feelings of anger were now being displaced and projected onto each other. The level of violence was high until both the OW and CWP were implemented in the area.

THE COMMUNITY WORK PROGRAMME (CWP)

It was in 2008 that Bokfontein was chosen as one of the four sites to pilot the implementation of the newly developed Community Work Programme (CWP). This programme, inspired by the National Rural Employment Guarantee Act (NREGA) in India, was conceived by Kate Philip, then heading the strategic assessment for the Presidency of what was at the time referred to as the 'second economy'. The concept was then developed and operationalised in partnership with a range of key players, including Gavin Andersson of the Seriti Institute and David Cooper of Teba Development, and officials from the Department for Social Development, which played a key leadership role in the development of the CWP.

The CWP was designed against the backdrop of a review of the first phase of the Expanded Public Works Programme (EPWP). The logic of the EPWP was that access to temporary full-time job opportunities for unemployed people would act as a stepping stone into formal sector jobs, or to self-employment in an enterprise, and yet too many beneficiaries were instead cast back into unemployment on the expiry of their contracts. In a context in which the wider economy was not creating jobs, short-term employment in the EPWP helped while it lasted – but its effects on poverty beyond the employment period were limited.

In this context, the CWP was instead designed to be an ongoing form of 'employment safety net' in the most marginal areas, where economic alternatives of any kind are the most constrained. Rather than offering full-time work on a short-term basis, the CWP is designed to offer 'regular and predictable' access to work on an ongoing basis: two days of work per week – or a hundred days per annum – to provide an earnings 'floor' for participants. In the period covered here, CWP paid R50 a day; a ministerial determination of R60 a day has since been set for this sector.

The CWP's primary goal was to offer work opportunities for the most marginal communities, on the understanding that formal sector jobs would take a long time to come and that opportunities for self-employment were extremely limited. The programme aimed to make an impact on poverty, not only through creating access to income, but also 'to instil the practices and disciplines of work, to institutionalise and embed the causal link between work and remuneration – currently often absent; to give people access to the dignity of being productive rather than being dependent, and to rebuild their sense of economic agency' (Philip, 2010: 7).

Because the work priorities would be decided, organised and led by community members, it was essential that the project in each community be initiated in a collective process of community-building and training through which local project leadership, as well as the coordinators of work teams, would emerge. Seriti, one of the two NGOs appointed to drive the pilot projects, uses a particular format of community building, called the Organisation Workshop (OW), for this part of the process.[4] As the implementation of OW featured so prominently in accounts by interviewees, it is important to give some sense of what it entails.

ORGANISATION WORKSHOP (OW) AS A COMMUNITY-BUILDING MODEL

OW is rooted within the participatory action model of consciousness-raising informed by the work of Paulo Freire, and developed by the Brazilian sociologist and activist, Clodomir Santos de Morais. OW was conceived by De Morais, drawing on the social psychology of Lev Vygotsky, as an active process of learning through collectively organising production, in which those who have no experience of formal sector workplaces learn the cooperative practices, collective orientation, division of labour and work discipline to develop self-managing organisations. The OW, which lasts for four weeks, starts with participants deciding on, and then organising, a collective production project of some sort, which becomes the basis for actively learning new ways of working together (Carmen and Sobrado, 2000: 16–17). De Morais sees the OW as a form of 'social engineering' in which 'all inclinations towards individualism, spontaneity, voluntarism, self-sufficiency and so on' are reduced and replaced with a 'mass organisational consciousness' among a group of people who work collectively (ibid.: 35).

The OW model has in turn been adapted by the Seriti Institute. The Seriti director, Gavin Andersson, writes that the the key principles of the OW are consultation, people-centred development, social justice, equality, capacity-building, empowerment, and citizen participation (Andersson, 2000). This is in line with De Morais's argument that the OW is aimed at helping the 'excluded' and 'hard-to-reach' citizens who are marginalised through existing economic structures. The success of the OW is also attributed mainly to the fact that it gives priority to empowering communities to create work opportunities for themselves rather than to wait for state intervention. In this way, according to the proponents of OW, communities genuinely become more self-reliant.

In Bokfontein, all community members were invited to attend the OW over a period of a month. Participants decided to establish a large cooperative vegetable garden, and collectively organised their work to fence the large plot, to plough, to sow and to tend the vegetables. Some of the themes covered in the OW lectures and discussions included dealing with the past and grappling with the problems of xenophobia, crime, alcohol abuse, community tensions and domestic violence, helping community members to see their community with new eyes and imagining an alternative future. Participants began concretely reshaping their community. A borehole was sunk and storage tanks installed, providing a reliable source of water for the first time, forty-three shacks were moved to create an access road through the community, space was set aside for a recreational park and for netball and soccer fields, 500 trees were planted, and the small existing crèche was expanded to cater for more than a hundred children.

Many participants interviewed in this research quoted the organisation workshop as the turning point of life in Bokfontein: 'The OW was an eye-opening experience for us as the people of Bokfontein on how to deal with issues of development'; 'The OW gave us some skills on things that we can do for ourselves to create job opportunities.'

After the completion of the OW process of community building, the broader community went through a process of discussing what projects should be undertaken by the CWP workers; team leaders were selected from among the OW participants, and work teams were allocated to each project. More than 800 people are employed in the Bokfontein CWP. Any community member may join the work programme, as long as they have an identity document, and foreign nationals submit their asylum papers to be employed in the project. Those who do not have relevant papers are assisted by community leaders to apply for them in Pretoria.

Our observation is that young and old, males and females work in the CWP.[5] It is open to everyone. In Bokfontein, people work on Wednesdays and Saturdays; the working hours are from eight in the morning to three in the afternoon. People work in various projects such as road maintenance, gardening, home-based care, after-school care, cutting grass, installing pipes for water, and establishing a park. Each group has one or two coordinators who take the register every day, allocate duties and supervise the work; the register is then sent to the managing agency, Seriti, for cash payment at the end of the month.

THE MEANING OF WORK FOR CWP PARTICIPANTS

The view that the CWP was relieving poverty and hunger was shared by all the participants we interviewed, one of whom said, 'I hate to imagine where we would be if we did not have the CWP. Many of us would be dead of hunger.' There are no job opportunities in the area as it is surrounded by farming plots, and the CWP is the main source of employment. Other participants said: 'The CWP is better than to work on farms where many workers are exploited and forced to work many hours for nothing,' and 'I have not been working since we got here, until the CWP came. I can say the CWP has really helped us. Now everyone is working.'

Many people mentioned that they work in the CWP (for two days per week) and use other non-working days to look for other work opportunities at the mines and other companies in Brits. Some succeed, while others still struggle to find permanent jobs. Some people with full-time jobs work from Monday to Friday, and on Saturdays they work in the CWP to supplement their income. Some participants mentioned that with the little money (R400 per month) they receive they are able to support their families:

> 'The money (R50 per day) obviously is not enough but it is better than nothing. With this little money, believe me, I'm able to buy few things and support my family. Yeah, I wish they can increase our working days.'

> 'Yeah, I agree that the money is too little but it is better than to stay at home … You now feel like a human being that at least you are working and are able to send some money back at home.'

As these comments show, many community members wished they could work for more days so that the money would be enough for them to support their families in Bokfontein and still to send money home to the rural areas. The complaint in all the interviews was not about the money that they earn per day, but the wish to work for at least ten to fourteen days a month because they would then earn R800 to R1 000 a month – many thought that this amount of money would be enough for them to meet all their economic needs. As an example, CWP participants mentioned the high cost of transport for their children to attend school, as there is no school in Bokfontein and the nearest school is more than thirty kilometres away. As a result, only children whose parents can afford to pay the transport fee of R150 per month can go to school. Community leaders recently negotiated for the transport to be reduced to R120, but many parents still cannot afford this.

Nonetheless, working in the CWP was giving people a sense of achievement in doing something for their community:

> 'Even though the money is not good, but you feel good that you are doing something good for your own community.'

> 'For me it is not about money. I feel happy that I'm helping my community. Look at us [referring to his fellow CWP workers], we are one happy family. We all work together to solve our community problems.'

These interviews reveal that the meaning of work in the CWP resides not only in work as a source of income, but also as a social contribution to the community. Many found the experience of working together and learning by doing to be empowering and strengthening interpersonal relations in a community that was once divided along ethnic lines and residents' community of origin. The CWP also helped a great deal in raising awareness about possible projects that could be undertaken in this community to meet some of its requirements.

SOME CWP PROJECTS IN BOKFONTEIN

Road construction

There was no access road to Bokfontein when people were evicted in 2005 and 2006. During the rainy seasons, it was difficult for vehicles to move in and out of the area. Road construction was chosen as one of the CWP projects, following the demarcation of the road and initial grading during the OW. With CWP funds, workers were given road construction tools such as hammers, tape measures, wheelbarrows, hardhats, and spades, and the leadership of the community managed to negotiate the donation of stones from a neighbouring mine to be used in road construction.

With the road now built, access has improved for residents who have cars, but also for emergency vehicles such as ambulances and police vans, a key concern for the community's leadership.

Food gardening

As part of the CWP, the community was provided with shade nets to start a food gardening project. There are three vegetable gardens, and the vegetables produced are supplied to other CWP projects.

Water supply

In Bokfontein, people did not at first have access to water. Initially, the municipality used to deliver water on trucks, but delivery was very erratic and the community used to spend days and even weeks without water. During the OW, the community managed to sink a borehole to pump water, and it is carefully managed by a committee drawing in management of the CWP, charging 50 cents for twenty litres in order to cover the costs of diesel and maintenance of the pump.

Care workers

The only health services in Bokfontein are provided by a monthly mobile clinic. As part of the CWP, home-based care services are provided to families of the sick, and to child-headed households. Patients who are too sick to do any work receive vegetables grown in the community food gardens. Home-based care workers cook, clean and bathe some of the patients (the main challenge is that home-based workers do not have the necessary equipment, such as gloves, cotton wool, and bandages to clean and wash their patients). The CWP has also established a drop-centre where a group of women prepares and cooks nutritious meals every day for the children of vulnerable households, making use of produce from the community food gardens.

THE STRUCTURE OF CWP

The CWP has put in place local project capacity in every community where it is established, together with a reference committee comprising local leaders such as the councillor, municipal officials, school principals, civil society leaders, and so on. For example, in Bokfontein, Mohlala is the site manager who, together with two administrators, sixteen work team coordinators (of whom Ledikwa is one) and a storekeeper, are employed full-time by Seriti as the local implementing arm for the CWP. Seriti, as the implementing agent, manages and accounts for the finance, and the local staff are accountable to it. However, the quality of leadership that has emerged in Bokfontein is such that the Bokfontein Development Forum (BDF), an organisation formed by Mohlala and Ledikwa before the arrival of the CWP, has been reconstituted as an NGO which will be contracted by Seriti as the local implementing agent. Half the board of the reconstituted BDF consists of members from outside Bokfontein with no specific stake in the community, to ensure impartiality, and the BDF employs Mohlala as the CWP manager and Ledikwa as a project development officer with the task of investigating and overseeing new community projects. This development, with its improved governance structures and institutionalising of local capacity and initiatives, is seen as a pathbreaking innovation which could be replicated in other communities, according to Andersson.

OW, CWP AND RESISTANCE TO VIOLENCE

Much of the literature on development and violence makes the point that development initiatives in poor communities frequently exacerbate violence: the influx of new resources and opportunities may destabilise existing social hierarchies, and may also intensify competition over the control of resources and projects, stoking conflict.

In Bokfontein, the experience of development has had the opposite effect – namely, the formation of strong community leadership, increased social cohesion, and a collective approach to problem-solving. We explore these issues in relation to the cycle of violence between the two evicted communities, the mobilisation against xenophobic violence, and the preference for adopting strategies of community development rather than engaging in community protests directed against government authorities.

Breaking the cycle of violence

As mentioned earlier, the OW engaged community members in collective introspection about the trauma of their evictions and life histories, establishing a new identity and enabling them to address the violent divisions that afflicted them:

> 'We were angry after we were evicted but the organisation workshop helped us to deal with our anger. It has helped to restore our dignity.'

> 'The organisation workshop helped us deal with the pain of our eviction and also the lines that were dividing us communities.'

'Yes. That workshop made it possible for us to know each other. And it brought us together to accept each other as human beings.'

A sense of solidarity was also fostered amongst community members in breaking divisions and bringing peace and unity in Bokfontein. Mohlala explained that, prior to the OW, they were angry with the government; they had had some ideas about community development, but were unable to engage with government because of their 'hatred' for government officials as a result of the experience of forced removals. Many residents said that OW 'comforted us, and helped us forget the past and move on.'

As a result, the conflict between the two communities fell away, and they now regard themselves as a single community oriented towards a future of development through the CWP.

Mobilising against xenophobic violence

It was evident in this research that the OW also involved challenging people's attitudes and stereotypes about each other. Many residents also cited the OW as a tool that helped to prevent xenophobic violence in the area. The OW process was coming to an end just at the point in April 2008 when waves of xenophobic violence were spreading in various communities across Gauteng and the rest of South Africa. Ledikwa and Mohlala related how, at this time, some members of a nearby community came to Bokfontein in an attempt to encourage the community to mobilise against foreigners:

'They wanted us to expel the foreigners living amongst us, as they had done in their community. We called the whole community to confront them – we were a mob, and they were few so they could do nothing.'

Interviewees told us that it would not have been possible to prevent xenophobic attacks without the experience of the OW. Because numerous foreigners live in the community, it was argued that they should be included in the OW and CWP-related projects. In the course of the OW, Seriti gave lectures on slavery and on the Rwandan genocide, opening up a discussion of 'othering', discrimination and violence. Participants decided they needed to understand more about each other's culture, for instance by teaching each other to sing each other's songs (Andersson, interview). Many residents cited the OW as an intervention that had helped them to understand identities and respect for diversity. According to Ledikwa, 'We're all people of Bokfontein. We don't use words and categories such as Tswana, Zulu, or Zimbabweans. We are just Africans. We are one. We are all human beings.' This view that 'we are all Africans' was shared by many people we interviewed. The impact of the OW was reinforced by the access to jobs and incomes provided by CWP, through which foreign nationals and South Africans worked side by side.

There may be other factors, besides the explicit attempt of the OW process to address xenophobic attitudes, that mitigated the potential for xenophobic violence in Bokfontein.

Many respondents, for example, felt that xenophobic violence was unlikely to occur because, they thought, half or more of the community are foreign nationals. Others said that many foreign nationals are fluent in local languages such as Zulu and Tswana (probably because they were long-standing residents in the pre-eviction communities), and it is therefore not so easy to identify them. Finally, others mentioned that xenophobic attacks would not happen because their leaders were against them, and 'there is no one who could instigate it', which returns us to the OW, and the way it strengthened the local leaders to deal with issues of violence prevention and development.

Despite this, xenophobic attitudes tied to material interests remain a source of tension in the community, as illustrated by the conflict over a new shop that was opened by a Somali foreign national. A public meeting was called to discuss the Bokfontein Business Forum (BBF)'s unhappiness about this. The main complaint by the business forum was that the new shop sold cheap items and as a result they had been losing their customers. The community was divided, because many community members wanted the shop to continue operating as they were happy with the low prices, but it was agreed that the community and the BBF, with the help of the Bokfontein Development Forum (BDF) and the local municipality, should deal internally deal with the matter without resorting to violence. It was also suggested that new shop owners should give groceries every month to the drop centre which cooks for vulnerable children in the community, as part of their contribution to social responsibility.

The dominant sentiment expressed by community members was that members of the business forum should compete with the new Somali shop owners by also reducing their prices. Other community members said, 'If the new shop owner leaves, all shop owners must also leave, because they are also not South Africans. All the shops belong to the Shonas, but we did not make it an issue and we are supporting their businesses. But today they come and say the Somalis must go.' The community was deeply divided over this issue. Some residents, in fact, were happy when the South African government announced that the special dispensation to allow Zimbabweans to move in and out of South Africa would come to an end on 31 December 2010. Some (mainly South Africans) privately said to the researcher that 'these people' (meaning Zimbabweans) must go back to their country because 'they come and all of a sudden they want to control us'. Some were using the government's announcement to justify their views that foreign nationals come to South Africa to commit crime and take their jobs.

This incident demonstrates that xenophobic attitudes are existent in Bokfontein, but they are not overt and visible. Although the implementation of the CWP and OW in Bokfontein has substantially reduced violent xenophobia, such attitudes are unlikely to disappear as long as the economic status and living conditions of the poor remain unchanged. The Bokfontein case shows that xenophobia is not simply a hatred of foreign nationals; it provides an axis of mobilisation in the struggles between different interests among the poorest of the poor. The CWP has established sufficient leadership structures, livelihood support and social capital to contain xenophobic conflict in Bokfontein over the short term; whether it can do so over a wider set of communities and a longer time-frame remains to be seen.

WHY WERE THERE NO COMMUNITY PROTESTS IN BOKFONTEIN?

Community protests have been spreading like wildfire in the last few years (Alexander, 2010). Many of these community protests are blamed on lack of services, allegations of corruption, and power struggles among political leaders to gain power and access state resources. The local councillor agreed that the municipality has dismally failed the people of Bokfontein in terms of service delivery. In 2009, the former premier of North West Province, Maureen Modiselle, ordered an investigation into allegations of corruption in Madibeng municipality. As in other towns,[6] it was found that the municipality was also characterised by allegations of corruption, political infighting and nepotism.

In Bokfontein, however, the two key community leaders, Ledikwa and Mohlala, were vehemently opposed to violent community protests, arguing that *toyi-toyi* teaches people to be violent. According to Ledikwa, 'Children need good role models. So when we *toyi-toyi* we become violent. What are we teaching our children? Are we not teaching them to also be violent?'

Our ongoing research into violence and community protests reveals that in many communities collective violence is regarded as the only effective way of challenging the exclusion and lack of consultation with residents and ensuring improvements in service delivery. In sharp contrast to Ledikwa's comment, a participant in violent protest in one of our other research sites said, 'Violence is the only language that our government understands. Look, we have been submitting memos, but nothing was done. We became violent and our problems were immediately resolved. It is clear that violence is a solution to all problems.'

But in Bokfontein the community leaders asserted that service delivery protests do nothing but destroy public property. They mentioned that they believed in nego-tiations to solve community problems. They have had countless meetings with Madibeng municipality, and although nothing has happened they asserted that they would continue to explore other avenues rather than wait for the municipality to bring changes to their community.

What accounts for this? Their own answer is that what they learned in the OW process has empowered them and the community to take charge of their own future, and not wait for delivery from government. For example, they mentioned that they had been emboldened to approach companies in the area to get formal sector jobs for the community, as well as to seek sponsorship for community projects. As a result, nearby mines have employed more than forty-five workers from the community and a chrome washing plant has also employed some. One of the mines is in the process of funding a sophisticated vegetable tunnel for the Youth Forum, the products of which can be sold to supermarkets. They mentioned that the same mine had now also promised to help them buy their current residential land so that all their developments could continue, and they also mentioned that they plan to open their own supermarket as an income-generating project. All relevant documents have been completed for the supermarket to be opened and the stock has already been bought. All these activities are carried out under the auspices of the Bokfontein Development Forum (BDF).

It is also true that the CWP itself constitutes a highly visible and effective delivery on the part of government, as the CWP is a government initiative that combines national government policy and funding with local municipality involvement and oversight, so that even where the municipality fails to provide other services it does provide evidence of government activity to support poor communities, and this in itself can be expected to reduce tendencies towards community protest.

The opposition to protest and *toyi-toying* was not shared by everyone in the community, however. In fact, some residents felt that protest would benefit the community, and accused the community leaders of being a stumbling block for the people of Bokfontein to also *toyi-toyi* like the many other communities that have done so.

POVERTY ALLEVIATION, THE DECOMMODIFICATION OF LABOUR AND SOCIAL CAPITAL FORMATION

The primary motivation for the mobilisation of state resources behind the CWP is that it is an effective poverty alleviation programme in the most marginal and impoverished communities. However, what struck us most forcefully was that its impact in Bokfontein is not limited to improving the incomes of impoverished households; it has significantly transformed the community's sense of itself and its place in the world.

Ledikwa and Mohlala exemplify a kind of independent and visionary leadership we have not seen in other communities. They are convinced that through working collectively with the community, and engaging with companies, NGOs and state institutions, they can initiate projects, create job opportunities, and leverage resources that will set the community on a path of development, and so far they have achieved remarkable successes in doing this. They themselves emphasise the way their experience of the OW expanded their consciousness of possibilities and of the role of leadership. Indeed, Mohlala told us that without the OW, the CWP would have failed, as various leaders in the community, including themselves, would have approached it with the aim of benefiting themselves rather than the community. He himself saw the CWP as a temporary poverty-alleviating measure; more important than this was the process of collective empowerment through the OW, which, he argued, provided the platform for longer-term development and job opportunities which would provide better wages and a more sustainable future than the CWP.

Our interactions with the community, however, made it clear that the CWP was a crucial factor in transforming community relations and providing a material basis for the vision of an alternative future. A striking feature of the work provided by the CWP – despite its part-time and low-wage character – is that it entails the decommodification of labour and focuses on providing public goods as defined by the community itself. CWP work is provided for an indefinite period, is available to any member of the community who desires to participate, and neither the work nor the wages is decided by the market. Indeed, the work projects are decided by the community collectively, and provide public goods that are collectively defined as important for improving the lives of those who live there. CWP workers emphasised that the work differs from employment on nearby farms because it is work for the community, and this makes them feel differently about the work as well – they know it has an intrinsic value for the community, and they therefore do not resent the low wages in the way they would if they were working for a private employer.

At the same time, the CWP establishes social capital in communities often charac-terised by low levels of social capital formation, a point made by Philip. The regular meetings of work team coordinators, the twice-weekly participation of more than 800 residents in work teams where work is planned, organised and implemented, and the public visibility of the work process, create new networks and social interactions which strengthen community solidarity, provide forums for discussion and decision making, establish participant leadership, and generate a vibrant sense of community. These forms of social capital, as the Bokfontein case illustrates, provide a social resiliency against intra-community violence and crime, including xenophobic violence.

Overall, both the OW and CWP privilege citizen participation in which community members themselves play a significant role in identifying problems, priorities and also projects that need to be initiated to solve all community problems. This has helped to give community members in Bokfontein a sense of ownership and empowerment to network and mobilise more resources to achieve their ideal future goals.

These characteristics distinguish the CWP from other kinds of poverty alleviation and job creation projects currently on offer. Social grants such as the child support grant provide a crucial poverty alleviation mechanism, but do not include grantees in produc-tive work relations or incorporate them as agents in the formation of social capital. In many senses, grantees remain outside society. While public works programmes, like the CWP, also provide public goods, the fact that these are decided and organised by the central state that might not deliver those goods that are most pressingly desired in poor communities, means that they continue to generate high levels of alienation in workers. Grassroots cooperatives, on the other hand, tend to compete in the marketplace with the private sector and so, while they might exhibit the kind of collective initiative and control evident in the CWP, they are compelled to provide goods for which there is a market demand; at the same time, market competition means that cooperative jobs are always under threat. With the CWP, the wages are guaranteed by the state, and the finances are managed by an external agent in the form of an NGO, taking the complexity, anxiety and insecurity of financial sustainability and management out of the equation.

These qualities of the CWP mean that it provides a material basis for the community to collectively imagine a different future for itself. The *choice* of what public goods should be provided is highly significant, and provides a fresh insight into what marginal communi-ties most desire for themselves. In Bokfontein, there is a strong emphasis on reimagining a divided, impoverished and violent community as a *caring* community: the emphasis on home-based care, on ensuring that children in vulnerable families have daily access to a cooked and nutritious meal, and on establishing a creche, provide the evidence for this.

Apart from the more predictable emphasis on the material infrastructure of the community – a road, piped water – the Bokfontein community values a pleasant public space. Their new road is lined with young trees that will provide shade and soften the harsh impression made by the broken stone and glaring heat of the road surface. The new park provides a wide green space for a marginal and impoverished community, to 'enjoy nature', in Mohlala's words, like any other more prosperous community.

Through these and other public goods, established with resources provided by the state, the Bokfontein community has been able to concretely imagine itself as a different kind of place, providing material evidence that they can work towards an alternative future, at the same time as the households of some 800 CWP workers are able to experience a new degree of income security. The importance of the symbolic dimension of the CWP impact is illustrated by the way the participants in the OW decided to rename Bokfontein *Ditshaba Dimaketse* , 'the nations will be amazed'.

The Bokfontein case suggests then, as Philip (2010) argues, that the CWP is more than a straightforward poverty alleviation programme. The decommodification of labour, the provision of desired public goods, the formation of social capital, and the concrete imagining of alternative futures have a profoundly transformative impact in the community, empowering active layers of leadership to work towards development.

It is also clear that in Bokfontein the CWP and OW played complementary roles in empowering and transforming the community. The CWP depends on an empowered and well-organised community for its implementation, so the OW or similar collective community-building programmes are a necessary condition for CWP implementation; on the other hand, community building without access to material resources may be experienced as ultimately disempowering, so the CWP provides a strong material foundation to the OW intervention.

ADDRESSING COLLECTIVE TRAUMA AND POVERTY

In the Bokfontein case, what made the CWP/OW intervention so powerful was its ability to simultaneously address the collective trauma of the community and its poverty and marginalisation. All the participants interviewed in this research agreed that development would not have been possible in Bokfontein if people had not been assisted collectively through the OW to deal with their anger and the effects of collective trauma resulting from forced removals and intra-community violence. It was evident that the OW increased social cohesion, strengthening local community leadership and a collective approach to problem-solving. This case suggests that developmental initiatives that only address socio-economic issues, while neglecting socio-psychological issues, are unlikely to achieve great success and may only reproduce lines of conflict in communities.

However, this case study also shows that real collective healing needs to go beyond the psychosocial needs of the community to address their socio-economic needs. The employment and social capital provided by CWP projects has broken the cycle of violence and crime, improved household livelihoods, and provided public goods and services that are actively reshaping the community, materially and symbolically. It is unlikely that, on its own, the attitude-changing processes of the OW would be able to make a lasting impact on the community. Implemented together, though, the OW and CWP have empowered this community both psychologically and economically to believe that they can create opportunities and contribute meaningfully to their own process of reconstruction and community development. In this way, the Bokfontein community has created a collective narrative of dealing with past traumas and transforming them into a new narrative about the future and about collective agency to make a different future.

CHALLENGES OF IMPLEMENTING CWP

The Bokfontein experience is not unique. According to Philip, Andersson and various CWP documents and reports, the programme is having similarly transformative effects in many sites. But notwithstanding these remarkable achievements, our research suggests that implementing and sustaining CWP will entail some profound challenges.

First, it is clear that despite its new-found cohesiveness, community tensions and cleavages persist. The dispute over the Somali shopkeeper brought to the surface tensions between existing traders and newcomers, between customers and traders, and between South Africans and Zimbabweans. In other words, the potential for xenophobic and other forms of conflict remains. Likewise, the stance of the community leadership against community protests is not shared by all residents, and given the poor performance of local government, this tension could also spill over into open conflict. In the period of our fieldwork, such tensions remained muted, and were resolved through meetings and collective discussion; however, over the longer term the persistence of poverty and marginalisation may stoke them into open conflict.

Second, the question remains whether the CWP is sustainable over a longer term. Currently, the CWP/OW intervention is relatively fresh, and many in the community are strongly aware of its benefits. Over time, though, enthusiasm may pall. Once the road, the park and the laying of water pipes has been completed, it may be difficult to continue conceiving of large-scale labour-intensive infrastructural projects. While the community currently decides on socially useful projects, it is not inconceivable that once they are finished there might be a slow drift towards 'digging holes to fill them in', or simply pretending to work so as to lay claim to an income. Considerable energy and hope is invested in mobilising external resources and assistance for new projects and job creation; if these are not successful, leadership and community may become demoralised. The frugality of CWP incomes may also become a source of resentment and grievance. Under such circumstances, it may be difficult to sustain community solidarity as the harsh reality of poverty reasserts itself, and different interest groups compete for scarce resources.

Third, and considering the rollout of CWP more broadly, it is not only possible but likely that in some communities CWP interventions become subject to elite struggles for control, in the same way as access to local government resources and positions have become fiercely contested. Although the CWP finances are externally controlled, there are a myriad ways in which the ability to allocate work and projects and dispense incomes could be shaped by patronage and corruption. Indeed, the Seriti director, Gavin Andersson, described two cases in which local elites attempted exactly this. Bokfontein may be fortunate in the quality of its leadership; nonetheless, we did come across allegations of corruption levelled by a handful of community members against Ledikwa and Mohlala. These are implausible in the light of government audits which found them to be scrupulously careful in their financial management, but the latent popular discourse about corruption points towards the kind of conflict that may erupt in future.

Finally, up until April 2010, CWP was run from outside government, as a form of special project, with strategic oversight from a steering committee including the Presidency and the Department for Social Development. The innovative strategy of using highly experienced and capable NGOs to drive implementation created the necessary momentum to expand the four initial pilot projects to fifty-six sites nationally, an expansion that took place over the short timespan of eighteen months. The CWP has since been relocated into the Department of Cooperative Governance to become a full-blown government programme. However, its change in status generates new problems. Government inertia, lack of expertise and flexibility, and the pressure of competing programmes initially stalled expansion, and evidence suggests that it may place the target of establishing a CWP programme in every municipality nationally in jeopardy. It is not clear that a programme that was innovative, vigorous and vibrant when driven as a special project and implemented by NGOs can retain these qualities when embedded in a large-scale and relatively ineffective bureaucracy in the South African state.

On the evidence of Bokfontein and the other CWP sites established so far, CWP appears to hold considerable potential for poverty alleviation, work creation, healing community trauma and social capital formation in the traumatised and marginalised communities of South Africa. Philip advocates that once the CWP is established in every municipality in the country (a goal set for 2014), it becomes a national work programme for all those who cannot find alternative employment, along the lines of NREGA in India, a goal that was built into the CWP from the beginning (Philip, 2010: 26–7).[7] The fiscal implications are not excessive. Philip estimates an annual budget of R12 billion per million jobs created. This kind of budgetary allocation is certainly feasible, and it is necessary if South Africa and its government are to demonstrate a serious commitment to reducing the poverty and unemployment that blight our society with misery, hopelessness, depression and crime. The CWP may bring with it new problems and challenges, as described above, but these are the challenges of progress.

NOTES

1   The authors would like to thank Kate Philip and Gavin Andersson, as well as the editors and fellow contributors to the *New South African Review 2*, for comments on earlier drafts of this chapter. The case study of Bokfontein is part of a larger research project into collective violence conducted by the Centre for the Study of Violence and Reconciliation (CSVR), and the Society Work and Development Institute (SWOP) at Wits University. Malose Langa is a CSVR psychologist and Wits academic, and Karl von Holdt is a senior researcher at SWOP. We would also like to thank the people of Bokfontein who were so keen to share their stories with us, as well as Andersson and Philip for making the time to discuss their work and facilitate our entry into the community.
2   After our first visit to the community together, all fieldwork was conducted by the first author, Langa.
3   See *The Government of the Republic of South Africa vs. Grootboom* in which the Constitutional Court ruled that people should be provided with accommodation when evicted from their homes.
4   The second NGO was Teba Development.
5   Nationally, CWP participation is split equally between 'youth' and 'non-youth', and about seventy per cent of participants are women (Philip, 2010: 22).
6   This refers to other municipalities in which we conducted research about causes of service delivery protests. In these studies, we have found that corruption was cited as one of the reasons for the violent service protests.
7   See Webster (2010) for a similar argument.

REFERENCES

Alexander P (2010) Rebellion of the poor: South Africa's service delivery protests – a preliminary analysis, *Review of African Political Economy*, 123: 25–40.

Andersson G (2000) Organisation Development (OD) and Morais's Organisation Workshop (OW) – South Africa and Botswana. In Carmen R and M Sobrado (Eds) *A Future of the Excluded: Job Creation and Income Generation by the Poor*. London and New York: Zed.

Carmen R and M Sobrado (2000) Setting the scene: 'Those who don't eat and those who don't sleep'. In Carmen R and M Sobrado (Eds) *A Future of the Excluded: Job Creation and Income Generation by the Poor*. London and New York: Zed.

Philip K (2010) Towards a right to work: the rationale for an employment guarantee in South Africa. Unpublished paper, Trade and Industrial Policy Strategies (TIPS).

Seedat M, U Lau and S Suffla (2010) Collective Violence in South Africa: Explaining the explanations. Paper presented at School of Graduate Seminar, UNISA, June 2010.

Webster E (2010) There shall be work and security: Utopian thinking or a necessary condition for development and social cohesion?, *Transformation* 72–73.

ENVIRONMENT 3

Ecological threats
and the crisis of civilisation

Devan Pillay

———

The interrelated triple threats of rising pollution, the rapid depletion of natural resources and declining biodiversity are increasingly being acknowledged as threats to the survival of the earth as we know it. There is little doubt that human intervention, in the form of industrial (or 'fossil') capitalism, has brought us to this point.[1]

Despite international efforts such as the Brundtland Commission on environment and development in 1983, the Rio Summit in 1992, the 1997 Kyoto Protocol on climate change and the 2002 UN World Summit on Sustainable Development (or Rio+10) in Johannesburg, among many other interventions, the process of environmental degradation in recent decades has accelerated, rather than receded. The notable exception has been the partial restoration of the ozone layer, after international efforts to ban ozone-depleting substances contained, *inter alia*, in aerosols and refrigerators.

As the world approaches the next round of climate change talks – known as the Conference of the Parties 17 (COP17) – in Durban in December 2011, there is scepticism that the rich countries of the world, whose corporations over the past two centuries have primarily been responsible for environmental degradation, will agree to significant action to stem the impending disaster.

Developing countries in turn have adopted the view that they cannot move off the path of rapid fossil fuel-based industrialisation to 'catch up' with the developed world, if the rich countries do not first commit to transforming their own economies (including, for some, the question of 'degrowth', or shrinkage), as well as sufficiently compensate developing countries. It is a question, it seems, of who blinks first – with only a few countries in Latin America, such as Bolivia and to an extent Ecuador, prepared to make bold moves and grant the Earth constitutional rights (meaning moving towards a more balanced, holistic, sustainable human development path). In the meantime, environmental destruction in the world, including increased carbon emissions, continues unabated, with more talk but little action.

In South Africa the minerals-energy complex, which since the discovery of minerals subordinated all economic activity to the needs of the mining and energy sectors, remains pivotal to the economy. Efforts to diversify into sustainable manufacturing have been lame. Instead, the mining industry has left a legacy of acid mine drainage contaminating the environment, first in the West Rand, and then spreading to the East Rand and the central basin, potentially causing land instability and threatening the foundations of buildings in Johannesburg, as is shown in the chapters of David Fig and of Khadija Sharife and Patrick Bond.

As Fig argues, this is a story of over a century of inadequate governance, regulation and corporate accountability, with the current government's efforts possibly fatally flawed by the division of responsibility's spread across multiple institutions which lack political will. The slow response to this impending disaster has already made farming unviable in parts of the West Rand.

Parliament's Water and Environmental Affairs committee finally held a hearing on the matter in June 2011, when government experts confirmed the scale of the problem, and also revealed that seismic events in the affected regions have almost doubled since acid mine drainage filled derelict mines in 2008. According to government, the mines chiefly responsible include Rand Uranium, Durban Roodepoort Deep, Mintails, ERPM and Grootvlei mines (*Business Day*, 22 June 2011). However, the problem goes beyond Gauteng and includes mines in Mpumalanga, KwaZulu-Natal and the Northern Cape. Persistent public exposure and compelling scientific evidence have moved government to finally take action, including, possibly, a new environmental levy on polluting mines to help pay for cleaning up the toxic water, the cost of which could run into billions of rands (*The Times*, 23 June 2011). It remains to be seen whether this is too little, too late.

The Green Economy Summit of May 2010, which led to the New Growth Path (NGP), promised a dramatic move out of the stranglehold of the minerals-energy complex, and towards a 'green economy'. This includes a renewed interest in bio-fuels as an alternative energy source and creator of green jobs – a highly contested and still unresolved policy process unearthed by William Attwell's chapter. However, as Sharife and Bond argue, the NGP, as well as the National Climate Change Green Paper, are tepid responses to the challenges. The Green Paper is technicist, and relies on market mechanisms such as carbon trading to reduce emissions, as well as dangerous technologies such as carbon capture and storage, and nuclear energy.

Corporate-led efforts to 'greenwash' the problems of environmental degradation, and the subordination of 'sustainable development' to economic growth (and corporate profits), continue to dominate global and national discourse and action. Can 'green capitalism' address the needs of humanity as well as preserve the planet, or will it lead to the intensification of global inequality, where green gated communities consume an unfair share of increasingly limited resources, while the vast majority of humanity continues to sink deeper into polluted poverty? In the latter scenario, increased social instability will be met by increased state repression, leading to an even more unstable planet.

Unless governments and citizens understand the common roots of environmental threats – incessant industrial growth and rampant consumerism – and take concerted action by subordinating economic growth to social need and ecological sustainability, it is not alarmist to say that we all face a crisis of civilisation.

NOTES

1   This does not negate the fact that some climate change is also caused by natural phenomena – however, scientists have pointed to a direct correlation between rising carbon emissions and climate change.

CHAPTER 14

Above and beyond South Africa's minerals-energy complex[1]

By Khadija Sharife and Patrick Bond

INTRODUCTION

The South African minerals-energy complex is now widely understood as a barrier to the society's balanced development and also a threat of great magnitude to the local and global environment. By early 2011, with a New Growth Path (NGP) document stressing a green economy, a Green Paper on climate, and a new national energy plan under debate, and following the March 2011 meltdown of a Japanese nuclear power plant, a great many potential routes opened up for sensible policy changes. However, the inherited legacies of apartheid-era and post-apartheid 'developmental state' projects have made a U-turn extremely difficult.

Dating back to the discovery of Kimberley diamonds in the 1860s and Witwatersrand gold in the 1880s, a handful of corporations gained power over South Africa's development policy. At one point, Anglo American and De Beers – run mainly by the Oppenheimer family dynasty – controlled almost half the country's gold and platinum, a quarter of its coal, and virtually all its diamonds, and held critical stakes in banking, steel, auto, electronics, agriculture and many other industries. The Truth and Reconciliation Commission determined after the 1996 hearings that the South African mining industry's 'direct involvement with the state in the formulation of oppressive policies or practices that resulted in low labour costs (or otherwise boosted profits) can be described as first-order involvement [in apartheid] … The shameful history of subhuman compound [hostel] conditions, brutal suppression of striking workers, racist practices and meagre wages is central to understanding the origins and nature of apartheid' (TRC, 1998: 34).

By the 1980s, however, South Africa's internal accumulation crisis – brought on by social resistance as well as internal contradictions in the capitalist system (Bond, 2006) – began to compel both political and economic changes. As the chairman of Anglo, Harry Oppenheimer, stated, in 1985: 'Nationalist policies have made it impossible to make proper use of black labour' (cited in Sharife, 2010c). The result, from 1994, was a 'liberated' nation accurately described by Ali Mazrui in a speech in Cape Town where he stated of the thriving legacy: 'You were the crown, we'll keep the jewels', referring to black political domination – the crown of the state – and white control of intellectual, economic and other 'jewels' (Mazrui, 1998).

Could South Africa's economic jewels be snatched back by the masses and refashioned into something more socially and environmentally appropriate? Minister of Economic Development Ebrahim Patel's keynote address at the May 2010 Green Economy Summit acknowledged: 'There is now broad acceptance that 150 years of industrialisation that started in Europe, based mainly on fossil driven energy, has impacted on the climate and environment in very profound ways.' The future could be different, he predicted, for if South Africa was able to capture two per cent of the estimated global green economy in the next five years, 'we can expect to create up to 400 000 jobs in energy, manufacturing, agriculture, mining and services'. But how serious is Pretoria about the needed shift from a minerals-energy complex to a genuinely sustainable economy?

GREEN ECONOMY OPPORTUNITIES FOR A U-TURN?

At the Green Economy Summit, the government undertook to define a green economy path by integrating a 'supportive regulatory framework' (South African Planning Institute, 2010) to develop green industries through instruments such as sector action plans and market instruments to incentivise the use and production of cleaner and low carbon products. Other focuses included: a) greater localisation of manufacturing of materials (solar, nuclear, wind, hydro power and electronics industries); b) the expansion of green jobs employment opportunities through the public works programmes; and c) acceleration of programmes supported by the Clean Technology Fund ($500 million from the World Bank) to meet renewable energy targets. Led by the Department of Environmental affairs, other Pretoria agencies meant to support the Green Economy included the Departments of Economic Development, Science and Technology, Trade and Industry, Energy, and Public Works as well as the Department of Agriculture, Forestry and Fisheries (Green Economy Summit, 2010). (It is notable that the role of the Department of Water Affairs was insignificant.)

The DTI had already begun implementing potential 'green' industry growth in various job-intensive sectors such as organic produce, solar water heating and manufacturing. South Africa's manufacturing industry, currently operating below 2005 levels, was hard hit by liberalisation, by China's expanding footprint and, more recently, by the global economic meltdown. The DTI's Industrial Policy Action Plan 2 (IPAP 2), described by the minister of Trade and Industry, Rob Davies, as a living document that would be realised in 'bite size chunks', will allegedly generate 2.5 million indirect jobs and over 825 000 direct jobs in several strategic areas, including agro-processing, green economy and energy jobs. For example, the tax incentive programme known as a '12i' will see government forego R5.6 billion in much needed taxes, in the hope of motivating corporations to engage in energy efficiency, expansions and upgrades, cleaner production technology, and skills training, designed to have a positive impact on upstream and downstream industries. 'One of our key criteria is energy efficiency through technologies geared for more efficient processes. It would be easier for new companies than those that are upgrading existing businesses,' according to Moeketsi Marumo (2011), head of the 12i tax incentive programme.

Yet a genuine turn to green economic activity has not yet been made. To illustrate: the domestic solar industry currently produces a mere 35 000 units per annum worth R220 million. The most appropriate technology, solar water heating, is a relatively labour-intensive form of energy generation with more than half the workers involved in installation, yet currently only 400 employees work as installers, 200 in manufacturing and the remainder in administration. The domestic market is perceived as potentially huge, with 11 million households, although only a small fraction can afford the capital costs (around R10 000 per unit), and the majority of black South Africans are still not consuming electricity at the level required to achieve savings from switching from geysers (which most do not have) to solar water heating. Still, if the DTI has its way, domestic solar water heating promotion will increase investments in local manufacture and skills development. Employment could be created rapidly, as it takes a mere six months to train an employee in installation services. Targeted increases in installations would increase to 250 000 units annually, and manufacture would rise to 200 000 units each year. Given the huge potential, a much more rapid and expansive rollout should be possible if subsidies are made available and building codes changed, so that staged conversion can be started on all existing and new houses.

The Industrial Development Corporation has allegedly earmarked a budget of R11.7 billion for green industries over a five-year period, including R33 million on feasibility studies for wind farms, solar and thermal electricity generation and R800 million on resource and waste management (Patel, 2010). However, many such 'green initiatives' are dubious, including the R800 million approved for bio-ethanol, which will transform South Africa's limited water resources and arable land into fuel-utilising, expensive (and ecologically destructive) inputs.[2] The bio-ethanol project has a potential budget of R20 billion, almost a quarter of the total 'green budget'. Patel's NGP promises to cut unemployment from twenty-five to fifteen per cent by generating five million jobs in manufacturing, infrastructure, agriculture, tourism and mining. In addition to the establishment of a sovereign wealth fund, the NGP proposes capped salaries for those earning over R45 000 a month, and the creation of a state-owned bank and mining company to ensure that 'the developmental state is not simply hostage to market forces and vested interests' (ibid.).

While Cosatu has claimed that the NGP does not go far enough, for Investec analyst Annabel Bishop, the NGP U-turns the South African economy: 'The NGP aims to increase labour intensity, weaken the rand and cap wages for high income earners. But it shifts even more of the burden of employment onto government and the cost onto the private sector, of which the business sector is a major contributor to tax revenue, which is used to pay for the increased employment in the government sector' (Bishop, 2011). In contrast, Riaz Tayob of the Southern and Eastern African Trade Information and Negotiations Institute maintains that: 'Job creation in the NGP is essentially about leaving things to the market. When the private sector is doing its job, it should really be left alone, but the market has given us decades of jobless growth, if evidence is to count for anything. The NGP largely remains a fiscal austerity policy reminiscent of the old strategy, Gear, pro-cyclical at precisely the wrong time' (Tayob, 2011).

CLIMATE CHANGE AND CARBON MARKETS

Another potential site of U-turning would be through the national climate change response Green Paper. The potential for a new climate policy is vast as a result of South Africa's November-December 2011 hosting of the Kyoto Protocol's Conference of the Parties (the Durban 'COP 17'). But the legacies of the minerals-energy complex's power are formidable, as witnessed by the 2010–2011 multi-billion rand financing decisions on Eskom coal-fired mega power plants (with more price increases), the conclusion of the Energy ministry's multi-decade integrated resource planning exercise – run by a committee dominated by electricity-guzzling corporations – and Pretoria's contributions to four global climate debates in 2010–2011. These four debates are: President Jacob Zuma's co-chairing of a UN sustainable development commission; Planning Minister Trevor Manuel's role within the UN Advisory Group on Climate Finance seeking $100 billion a year in North-South flows; the G8-G20 meetings in France, and the COP 17 preparatory committee meetings.

Unlike his predecessor, Zuma had no obvious capacity to wax eloquent on sustainable development, so his appointment to chair a UN committee could be seen as tokenistic – or as a chance to make a mark on the world if he so desired. Not only did Manuel win a co-chair of the team designing the Green Climate Fund in April 2011, he was also a candidate in June for the post of managing director of the International Monetary Fund (IMF), so his ability to weigh in on climate financing could have been decisive. But the IMF post was predetermined by the G8's power structure in the wake of the demise of the misogynist Dominique Strauss-Kahn, and while Europe faced a quadruple sovereign financing crisis (Greece, Ireland, Portugal and Spain) it was evident that a European would keep the top job. Finally, all indications at Bangkok in April 2011 and at Bonn in June 2011 were that the overall emissions reduction targets at Durban would not be ambitious, yet huge decisions on climate finance would be made. Instead of paying reparations for 'climate debt', the new fund would aim to codify existing power structures. Instead of raising revenue from major polluters in the North to deter their emissions, Manuel supported the notion that fifty per cent of the climate fund would come from carbon trading.

The Green Paper revealed the narratives that Pretoria would deploy at the COP 17. Primary authors included the Department of Environmental Affairs official, Joanne Yawitch, from a struggle-era background in land reform NGOs, and once dedicated to far-reaching social change. But Yawitch moved to the National Business Initiative in 2011, confirming the state-capital revolving door through which so many other politicians and bureaucrats have tread since 1994. At the Copenhagen COP in December 2009, the lead G77 negotiator, Lumumba Di-Aping, accused Yawitch of having 'actively sought to disrupt the unity of the Africa bloc', a charge for which she forced him to publicly apologise, even though within days Zuma proved it true by signing the Copenhagen Accord (whose implications for much of Africa include a seven-degree centigrade rise in temperature this century).

The Green Paper's initial premise is not incorrect: 'South Africa is both a contributor to, and potential victim of, global climate change given that it has an energy-intensive, fossil-fuel powered economy and is also highly vulnerable to the impacts of climate variability and change.' But this allows an all too predictable Pretoria formula: talking left, so as to more rapidly walk right. Thus: 'South Africa, as a responsible global citizen, is committed to reducing its own greenhouse gas emissions in order to successfully facilitate the agreement and implementation of an effective and binding global agreement' (National Climate Change Response Green Paper). The reality, however, could be retyped as: South Africa, as an irresponsible global citizen, is committed to rapidly increasing its own greenhouse gas emissions by building the third- and fourth-largest coal-fired power plants in the world (Kusile and Medupi) mainly for the benefit of BHP Billiton and Anglo American which get the world's cheapest electricity thanks to apartheid-era, forty-year discount deals, and to successfully facilitate the agreement and implementation of an ineffective and non-binding global agreement – the Copenhagen Accord – which is receiving support from other countries only because of coercion, bullying and bribery by the US State Department, as WikiLeaks has revealed.

The Green Paper claims that South Africa will achieve an 'emissions peak in 2020 to 2025 at thirty-four per cent and forty-two per cent respectively below a business as usual baseline'. But Earthlife Africa's Tristen Taylor had reminded Yawitch in 2009 that the 'baseline' was actually called 'Growth Without Constraints' (GWC) in an earlier climate policy paper: 'GWC is fantasy, essentially an academic exercise to see how much carbon South Africa would produce given unlimited resources and cheap energy prices' (Earthlife Africa: 2009a). Officials had already conceded that GWC was 'neither robust nor plausible' in 2007, leading Taylor to conclude that 'the SA government has pulled a public relations stunt' (ibid.).

The Green Paper admits that, 'economic risks emerge from, among others, the impacts of climate change regulation, the application of trade barriers, a shift in consumer preferences, and a shift in investor priorities.' Already, Europe's 'directive on aviation and moves to bring maritime emissions into an international emissions reduction regime could significantly impact' on South African tourism, air freight and shipping. If this analysis were to be taken seriously, a city like Durban would have to fundamentally rethink its massively subsidised economic development strategies reliant upon revived beach tourism; mega-sports events to fill the Moses Mabhida stadium (one of several white elephants); port widening and a new dug-out harbour at the old airport site (along with more auto manufacturing); a competing Dube trade port next to the King Shaka Airport; new long-distance air routes; expansion of south Durban's dangerous petrochemical complex; and a massive new Durban-Johannesburg oil pipeline (and hence doubled refinery capacity). Yet the Green Paper passes the buck downwards to the officials currently engaged in business-as-usual planning: 'Most of our climate adaptation and much of the mitigation efforts will take place at provincial and municipal levels.'

Another danger, so poignant after the March 2011 meltdown of the Fukushima Daiichi nuclear reactor, is the Green Paper's commitment to 'a nuclear power station fleet with a potential of up to 10 GWh by 2035 with the first reactors being commissioned from 2022' and, just as dangerously, a convoluted waste incineration strategy that aims to 'facilitate energy recovery' through 'negotiation of appropriate carbon-offset funding'. Indeed, the Green Paper repeatedly endorses 'market-based policy measures', including carbon trading and offsets, at a time when Europe's Emissions Trading Scheme had collapsed owing to fraud, hacking and an extremely volatile carbon price, and the main US carbon market in Chicago had all but died. The Green Paper claims that attempting to 'kickstart and stimulate the renewable energy industry' requires Clean Development Mechanism (CDM) projects. Yet the miniscule R14 per tonne being paid in 2011 by investors for the Durban methane-electricity conversion at three local landfills shows the futility of that mechanism, not to mention the historic injustice of keeping the Bisasar Road dump open in spite of residents' objections to environmental racism.

This strategy suggests a more general problem, because carbon trading is strongly endorsed by corporations of the minerals-energy complex. Eskom and Sasol have been most active in trying to continue fossil-fuel investments, such as the Medupi coal-fired power plant and the Mozambique gas pipeline, with CDM funds. The UN advisory group on finance states that carbon trading is expected to provide as much as fifty per cent of the funds available from the North (US$100 billion a year by 2020) to mitigate climate change globally, even though as much as ninety per cent of emissions traded by some European countries in the EU's emission trading system are considered to be fraudulent (Europol, 2009). By 2008, the world emissions trading market was valued at US$130 billion, and while the economic recession undercut the market's growth, it was projected to increase to US$3 trillion by 2020, provided the US came on board (Bond, 2010).

Given the global and South African power relations, it should come as no surprise that the 'privatisation of the air' is considered a solution to pollution. Carbon trading, largely developed by multinational corporations like Goldman Sachs, threatens to create another manipulated, gamed 'derivatives' market. For the Third World, the current 'under-exploitation' of the atmospheric commons is the source of profits and ongoing emissions licences for industrialised countries and multinational corporations. These Annex 1 countries[3] pledged at the Copenhagen COP 15 to reduce greenhouse gas (GHG) emissions to between twelve and eighteen per cent of 1990 levels by 2020. But instead of making cuts at home, the carbon markets and offsets allow allegedly equivalent GHG sequestration or mitigation in the Third World. This is an open door for gaming the system using CDMs. A 2009 paper by Benjamin Sovacool and Marilyn Brown revealed a 4.7 billion scam to make apparent cuts in trifluoromethane (HFC-23), a GHG used as a refrigerant (Sovacool and Brown, 2009). More than seventy per cent of CDM projects in 2009 were based on HFC-23, which was deliberately produced in excess by corporations that then claimed to 'offset' it in order to receive financial benefits through certified emissions reductions credits. A moratorium was only placed on this technique in February 2011.

How does such CDM gaming play out in South Africa, especially in the context of the Green Economy Summit's proposed move to support the idea that 'transition to a low-carbon and sustainable economy can create large numbers of green jobs across many sectors of the economy, and indeed can become an engine of development'?[4]

GREENWASHING ENVIRONMENTAL RACISM

The example of Durban's Bisasar Road dump is instructive, in part because the landfill, located in the black residential area of Clare Estate, is Africa's largest. One of three fully permitted landfill sites in Durban, Bisasar was opened for business in 1980 by the apartheid regime. The Group Areas Act, a crucial pillar of the apartheid government's segregation agenda, meant that Bisasar Road would 'import' waste from privileged white areas to impoverished and working-class black areas deprived of basic human rights. Bisasar was emblematic of the 4 000 disposal dumps created across the country (of which, the government claimed, only 200 met minimum environmental standards).

Residents of Clare Estate – classified as an 'Indian' and 'coloured' area but with a large African shack settlement from the mid-1980s – lacked access to political, economic and legal recourse. Their attempts at mobilising dissent against the regime were ignored, although the African National Congress pledged in 1994 that the new democratic municipal government would close the racist dump. Despite ongoing opposition to the dump from residents, and promises by the government to close and rehabilitate the dump, Durban Solid Waste supported the continued use of the dump, as two other sites – in wealthy Umhlanga and impoverished Umlazi township – were shut instead. Described by the municipality as 'favourably placed with respect to central Durban, close to a major artery connecting the city to the west, north and south' (Durban Municipality, 2011), the dump processes 3 000 to 5 000 tonnes of waste daily, including hazardous waste such as sewage sludge and healthcare risk waste. In spite of vehement calls for closure, of the dump's significant leachate and of respiratory problems in the community, the national Department of Water Affairs and Forestry extended the landfill's life cycle in 1996.[5] Although the permit issued was for general waste only, a meeting between the municipality and national water officials in 1995 resulted in the site's operators being 'granted a permit without a buffer zone' even though (as Condition 5.7 of the permit put it), 'the permit holder shall accept obnoxious sewage sludge'. Hosting nineteen million cubic metres of waste, the dump was described by Carl Albrecht, research director of the Cancer Association of South Africa, as a toxic 'cancer hotspot' where residents 'are like animals involved in a biological experiment' (Bond and Dada, 2005). Bisasar holds a further four million 'available' cubic metres of fully permitted landfill space before critical mass is reached, hence there is potentially another decade and a half of dumping in the black neighbourhood.

Given this potential, in 2002, Ken Newcombe of the World Bank – later a managing director of carbon at Goldman Sachs – promised his institution's prototype carbon fund would provide R100 million for keeping the dump 'open for business', rather than resorting to closure and rehabilitation. The reason was that the methane coming from the vast landfill could be collected, flared and used to run a set of small electricity turbines, hence generating 3.1 million Certified Emissions Reductions (CERs). In spite of its environmentally racist past and present, Newcombe declared Bisasar to be 'operated and maintained on a world-class level' (groundWork, 2010). Replied Sajida Khan, the activist who was instrumental in bringing the issue of the dump to the city's and the world's attention – for example, on the front page of the *Washington Post* in February 2005 – 'Unlike me, he does not live across the road from Bisasar' (ibid.). As Khan argued, 'The community would not have: marched and demonstrated; blocked the entrance to the site; handed a petition with 600 signatures to the mayor; written press articles and voiced our dismay on national television if we had accepted the Bisasar dumpsite'(ibid.). The World Bank was apparently intimidated, and it pulled out of the Bisasar Road project, although two other much smaller methane-electricity CDM projects were funded at the same time. But by July 2007, having been twice struck by the cancer she believed came from particulates that floated across the road into her life-long home, Khan had died.

The municipality then went to the markets, without the World Bank. As said by the Durban city manager, Mike Sutcliffe, 'Landfill gas offers a viable renewable energy source only when linked to carbon finance or CDM' (Sutcliffe, 2010). By March 2009 the municipality registered the initiative on the United Nations list of CDM projects as active until 2014 at least. The French Development Bank assisted with a US$8 million loan, and municipal officials soon constructed the full system of extracting methane, burning and flaring it (with associated incineration hazards given the GHGs and heavy metals that coexist with the methane, including CO_2, nitrogen oxide, lead, cadmium and other toxics), powering the turbines, and connecting the generated electricity back into the municipal grid. John Parkin, deputy head of engineering at the city's waste department stated, 'What makes it worthwhile is the revenue that can be earned from carbon credits' (*Financial Mail*, quoted in Schneider, 2008), and as of April 2010, this monthly revenue totalled US$600 000 (*Impumelelo*, 2010). The CDM financing justifies utilisation of the remaining landfill space, a toxic site based in a residential area under the guise of environmental protection against climate change.

The chequered history of Bisasar Road, South Africa's most important CDM pilot, corresponds to the externalisation of pollution so typical of free market economics. When economists do attempt to internalise such externalities, as did John Dales (Dales, 1968) they inevitably turn not to regulation but to a market for pollution rights and trading. The transferable property rights were an allowable quota of pollution emissions that could be bought and sold, and this conceptual apparatus would be used to justify the privatisation and propertisation, by financiers, of natural resources and ecosystems. As Lawrence Summers so evocatively put it in 1991: 'I think the economic logic behind dumping a load of toxic waste in the lowest-wage countries is impeccable and we should face up to that' (Summers, 1991). It is this trajectory – the commodification of every-thing – that logically takes the South African government from its own minerals-energy complex past through to another form of environmental racism – carbon trading. The next ecological crisis associated with the minerals-energy complex is being handled with similar sensitivity to planet and people: acid mine drainage.

WITWATERSRAND WATER CATASTROPHE

After climate change, acid mine drainage (AMD) has been described as the single most dangerous threat to South Africa's environment. Gold mining acted as primary pillar of South Africa's emergence as a 'resource colony' capable of supplying cheapened labour and cheap resources. The Witwatersrand region, mined since the mid-1880s, is the world's largest gold and uranium mining basin, yielding an estimated 43 500 tons of gold and 73 000 tons of uranium (Earthlife Africa, 2009b). The externalities of this legacy include a mine tailings dam composed of waste material, measuring 400 square kilometres next to six billion tons of iron sulphide, 'one of the substances, which, when exposed to air and water, produces acid mine water'(ibid.). Already, the Cradle of Humankind has been affected by as much as 40 million litres of AMD, according to Anthony Turton (2011), a leading water resources management expert: 'Johannesburg is the world's largest city that is *not* on a river, a lake or a seafront. It is a city on a watershed, both literally and figuratively … a city on a major continental divide, because flowing from a massive dolo-mite aquifer system underneath Johannesburg are the headwaters of the tributaries of the Limpopo and Orange River basins … seen in this way, Johannesburg can be described in one sentence as being a city that has grown out of the chaos of the gold rush, sitting on top of one of the largest karstic aquifer systems in the world, underlain by the one of the largest non-alluvial gold deposits in the world.'

Like the porous dolomite aquifer, acting as a sponge, the multinationals of the minerals-energy complex sponge off economies, peoples and ecologies. The Western

Basin began decanting in 2002, near Black Reef Incline, at fifteen million gallons a day, and unless it is addressed immediately the Central Basin will begin decanting in two and a half years at sixty million gallons a day, and the Eastern Basin (currently maintained by Pamodzi Gold) will decant eighty-two million gallons per day in three years unless water-pumping operations continue (Western Utilities Corporation, 2010). Even partial treatment costing R11 million per month, financed by the mines, was considered an exorbitant internalisation of externalities.

But the cost of AMD will be far higher; it is incalculable. Some of the worst pollution is generated by coal mines which are located, ironically, on South Africa's best agricultural land (*BusinessLive*, 2011). These mines could be 'inherited' by the government if nationalisation of the type proposed by the ANC Youth League takes place. But in its climate Green Paper, the government proposed the policy of 'polluter pays', stipulating that 'costs of remedying pollution, environmental degradation and consequent adverse health effects, and of preventing, controlling or minimising further pollution, environmental damage or adverse health effects must be paid for by those responsible for harming the environment (Department of Environmental Affairs, 2010).

These lofty sentiments are, however, unlikely to be realised, given that historically and currently AMD remains the direct consequence of free-riding by multinationals. The expense for mitigating AMD has been projected at R360 billion (Aeon, 2010), mainly for specialised water treatment plants, over the next fifteen years. Although South Africa's agricultural sector utilised ten times the volume of water used by mining houses, the latter represent the most lethal, mobile (able to relocate should government not appease demands) and systemically powerful polluter.

In fact, these very multinationals have been seeking 'closure certificates' exonerating them from environmental reparations and liabilities. Through a reverse listing on the AIM board of the London Stock Exchange under the name of Watermark Global PLC via the Western Utilities Corporation (WUC), it seems that this exit route has become possible. The main WUC owners are the mines eagerly vying for closure certificates, asserts Turton (2011). 'The WUC deal will give all the mine owners their closure certificates, and because of the way that government has fumbled the ball, it will also give them a guaranteed sixteen per cent return on investment (much larger than many operating mines enjoy), so that not only will the mines evade the legal requirement of the 'polluter pays principle' enshrined in our internationally acclaimed water law, but they will actually profit from that evasion and, what is more, that profit is all but guaranteed because it will be underwritten by the state in the form of a mooted public-private partnership,' he argues.

The public-private partnership involves a sixty per cent mandatory deal, said Turton (who, because of his critical assessment, was suspended from the Council for Scientific and Industrial Research (CSIR) in 2008). The WUC would hold forty per cent of the remaining equity. The core of the company's business, with a capital value of R3.5 billion with no tendering process, will be treating hazardous waste, thereafter sold to Rand Water and its eleven million users.

So far, WUC has raised £1.5 million in working capital, and is awaiting the South African government's decision on the project (Balashov, 2011).

André Botha, spokesman of Agriculture South Africa (AgriSA), an agricultural trade association representing 70 000 large- and small-scale farmers, argues:

> My problem with this is that there is legislation in South Africa that requires mines to ensure to rehabilitate water, to prevent or mitigate any contamination. We know that South Africa is a water-scarce land and if we allow for contamination of our ground water resources, we are heading for serious trouble (Botha, 2011).

Botha claimed that part of the problem included intimate ties between the ANC (directly or indirectly) and mine ownership. He cited the case (dismissed in May 2011) of the nearly submerged Grootvlei gold mine, managed by Aurora Empowerment Systems. The company, headed by President Jacob Zuma's nephew Khulubuse Zuma, is also known as 'Mandela's mine' for its connection to former president Nelson Mandela's grandson, Zondwa. Botha said that contamination of agricultural land 'is already occurring in the Krugersdorp-Boksburg stretch. They stopped pumping the water at the Grootvlei mine, which then seeps through, contaminating the ground water. This is the same water used by vegetable farmers for irrigation' (ibid.). Grootvlei's Shaft 3 mine alone seeped ninety megalitres of water each day, equivalent to 2 000 Olympic sized swimming pools, during the first four months of 2010 alone.

According to Stephanie de Villiers, co-author of the Africa Earth Observatory Network report 'H_2O-CO_2 Energy Equations for SA':

> The proposals by corporations such as WUC to step in with their proposed solutions have apparently been shot down, because they wanted to sell the cleaned water back to Rand Water, making a profit in the process. I'm not sure why mining houses are allowed to pollute while making a profit, and corporations who want to clean up are apparently expected to do so without the benefit of making a profit. What I find even more confusing is why the government is not using this as an opportunity to set up a state-owned enterprise that actually will have the potential to make some money that can be ploughed back into state coffers. This is one aspect of the country's water crisis that appears to be totally bogged down by politics (De Villiers, 2011).

Such costs of mitigation, budgeted by the South African government at a cost of R1.2 billion should be classified as 'ecological reparations' when contextualising the activities of major mining companies (chiefly entities like Anglo-American) over a period of 120 years, notably during apartheid. Recent studies by respected scholars such as Chris Hartnady, a former geology professor at the University of Cape Town, revealed that pollution and environmental degradation far outweigh the value of remaining resources (such as gold, which is ninety-five per cent exhausted):

Given the energy and environmental problems associated with ongoing ground water control, water-resource contamination by acid mine drainage and the possibility of widespread mercury and other factors of pollution caused by illicit underground ore-processing by the *zama-zamas* (illegal miners), the glory days of South African gold mining appear to have arrived finally at an ignominious end (Hartnady, 2009).

The United States Geological Survey cites existing South African gold reserves at just 6 000 tonnes, some 30 000 tonnes less than South Africa's own estimates, which would be forty per cent of the global total (Umvoto Africa, 2009). Much like the potentially over-inflated estimates of gold, the justification behind Eskom's R400 billion expansion plan, largely structured around coal, operates on the premise that coal reserves, estimated at 30 billion tonnes (downsized by the Department of Minerals and Energy during 2003–2004 from 50 billion tonnes) will last for 200 years, vindicating the initiative's drastic expense on the public purse (*Mail & Guardian*, 2010). A report published in the *SA Journal of Science*, (Hartnady, 2009) estimates that coal, currently generating as much as ninety per cent of South Africa's electricity, may in fact be capped at 15 billion tonnes and would become increasingly difficult to excavate four decades from now, with coal production peaking at 285 million tonnes in 2020.

The financial burden of AMD mitigation, extending far into the future, is similar to that of Eskom's new coal expansion plan, which will generate yet more AMD and place severe strains on crucial catchment systems. Bobby Peek of groundWork (the leading anti-pollution NGO) stated: 'The environmental and social cost of this development will impact on all South Africans as three major water catchments, the Limpopo, Vaal and Senque (Orange) Rivers are all going to have their water diverted for Medupi and future power stations' (groundWork and Earthlife Africa, 2010).

Pretoria's Department of Water Affairs has identified AMD as the biggest threat to South Africa's limited water resources. South Africa is, after all, one of the world's most water-scarce nations, with over ninety-eight per cent of the country, representing four per cent of Africa's overall land mass, classified as arid or semi-arid. As with most nations, water resources are 100 per cent allocated. Yet even in the context of Africa, the driest of the world's seven continents, the country receives just 40 millimetres in annual run-off, compared to the continent's annual run-off of 114 millimetres, against a global average of 266 millimetres. In Africa, over eight per cent of rainfall precipitation is lost to evaporation; in South Africa, the figure is ninety per cent, with under ten per cent converted to river run-offs.

The government estimates that future water shortages will be in the range of between two and thirteen per cent of available water resources in South Africa. But De Villiers argues that water demand will exceed availability by thirty-three per cent in 2025, because government's projected water shortages deliberately or incidentally fail to factor in reduced availability from pollution and climate change. 'If you look at the water management areas in which the new coal power plants will be established,' argues De Villiers, 'and where the coal mining will take place, you'd see that these water management areas are already "red" zones, areas where water demand already exceeds availability' (De Villiers, 2011). De Villiers states that the water that will be used by power plants will come at the expense of existing water users: 'It is just a matter of time before groundwater pumps across Limpopo province start to dry up.'

The government's 2010 Green Paper emphasises the importance of water and water-use, such as accelerating the 'development and/or capacity of effective and account-able catchment management agencies; water-use pricing schedules including effluent charges'; and investments in waste-water treatment capacity so as 'to safeguard public health, river health and ecological services and to minimize environmental disasters and treatment costs'. But the realities of minerals-energy complex residual power and pollu-tion are potentially debilitating negations of this fine rhetoric, as Eskom proves with its expansion plans.

ESKOM'S COAL-FIRED ELECTRICITY EXPANSION

South Africa's current capacity, inclusive of industry and consumers, is 36 000 MW (Eskom, 2008). In the context of the extreme historical damage by the minerals-energy complex to South African air and water quality, Eskom's dramatic expansion of coal-fired electricity generation in coming years is breathtaking. Globally, coal is the preferred source of elec-tricity-generating fuel, supplying forty per cent of energy. A recent study by Paul Epstein of Harvard Medical School's Center for Health and the Global Environment revealed that the public health and economic burdens of coal are US$500 billion annually, including mercury and greenhouse gas emissions, toxic spills, land and agricultural damage, and respiratory diseases (Schwartz, 2011). It is sometimes claimed that the emissions damage of coal-fired plants can be mitigated by carbon capture and storage (CCS) systems and, moreover, the World Bank claims that Eskom's Medupi plant will be the first power station in Africa to use supercritical clean coal technology, reducing emissions by five per cent. Paradoxically, Eskom's managing director, Steve Lennon, confirming the utili-sation of use of CCS technology, disclosed that 'one of the plants we are building is CCS ready ... [but] to be quite frank no one really knows what that is at the moment' (Earthlife Africa 2009c). CCS technology could reduce Medupi's real output to a capacity of 3600 MW (groundWork 2010). Moreover, despite the supercritical cooling system, approximately ten per cent of the cost of Medupi will come from water transfers for traditional cooling.

The cooling of Eskom's coal-fired stations, especially in Mpumalanga, makes the power company South Africa's single largest water customer. Projections for future coal-cooling water requirements suggest that new dams will be needed more rapidly within the Lesotho Water Highlands Project (LWHP), Africa's largest dam network and the world's second largest water transfer scheme. Formulated by the apartheid regime and the World Bank, and characterised by notorious corruption, socio-environmental impacts and sanctions busting, the LHWP's collaborators included the compliant regime in Lesotho installed by Pretoria during the 1980s, as well as a number of multinationals that would later be prosecuted for corruption and bribery. While LWHP was opposed by the African National Congress during the apartheid era, it was subsequently endorsed by Kader Asmal, the first post-apartheid water minister.

The planned power plants will continue providing the world's cheapest electricity to the world's largest mining and metals houses, for some of Africa's most capital-intensive and export-oriented smelters. Medupi will be the world's fourth largest coal plant, and is pegged to generate 4 800 MW of electricity after it begins operations in 2012. Emissions of around 30 million tonnes of carbon dioxide per year will put this plant ahead of the annual emissions of 115 countries. There are thirteen other coal-fired stations in South Africa, and the next one, Kusile, will be even larger. The government's struggle to finance the R125 billion Medupi project is ironic, given that the government's Upington solar project, valued at R150 billion, is seeking funds largely from private investors, and when built is anticipated to supply 5 000 MW of electricity (National Public Radio, 2010).

Eskom plans to invest R440 billion in new plants over the next seven years, for which funding has begun to flow from international institutions. Emblematic was a US$3.75 billion loan from the World Bank in April 2010, and in an opinion editorial published by the *Washington Post*, just prior to the Bank shareholders' vote on Medupi, the South African minister of Finance, Pravin Gordhan, justified the expansion based on 'strong new demand for electricity from millions of previously marginalised South Africans … now on the grid' (Gordhan, 2010). He did not mention that paying for Medupi will require a 127 per cent real price increase from 2007 to 2012 for South African household electricity consumers. With prices soaring, many more residents were being disconnected, and of Eskom's four million customers, one third registered zero electricity consumption. Many had reconnected illegally and, as Eskom and the municipality clamped down, the result was more social strife in a country with what is probably the world's highest rate of community protest over a five-year period.

As noted, the source areas of the coal for Medupi are highly contaminated by mercury and acid-mine drainage, with air, land, vegetables, animals and people's health at much greater risk. Forty new coal mines in impoverished areas of Limpopo and Mpumalanga provinces will be opened to provide inputs to Medupi and its successor, Kusile. This will create a few coal sector jobs (hence receiving endorsement from the National Union of Mineworkers), but a great many jobs in agriculture and tourism will be lost as a result of the invasive mining activity and downstream degradation. Medupi itself will be built in a water-scarce area where communities are already confronting extreme mining pollution and, even though an air-cooled model (Africa's first) was chosen, the cost of supplying an additional water-cooling supply amounted to hundreds of millions of dollars, given the long transport and pumping costs.

Once the coal is burned and electricity generated, the winners and losers become even more divergent. Medupi's main beneficiaries will be the world's largest metals and mining corporations, especially BHP Billiton (Melbourne based) and various Anglo-

American subsidiaries (most reporting to London), which already receive the world's cheapest electricity thanks to multi-decade deals. Anger soon grew about the huge discounts made when secret, forty-year 'special pricing agreements' were offered by Eskom during late apartheid, when the firm had a third too much excess capacity owing to the long South African economic decline. These agreements were finally leaked in March 2010, and disclosed that BHP Billiton and Anglo were receiving the world's cheapest electricity, at less than $0.02/kWh (whereas the overall corporate price was around $0.05/kWh, still the world's cheapest, and the consumer price was around $0.10/kWh). In early April, just before the World Bank decision, Eskom announced that a small modification was made to BHP Billiton's contract price but it was reportedly to the firm's 'advantage'. Finally, however, the Australian-based mining house was sufficiently intimidated by the glare of publicity that, in October 2010, Deutsche Bank mining analysts predicted BHP would dispose of Richards Bay assets. *Business Day* believed that: 'The reason for selling the aluminium smelters would be the scrutiny under which BHP's electricity contracts have come amid demands for resource companies to use less power' (*Business Day*, 2010b).

An additional problem with BHP and Anglo as beneficiaries is the outflow of profits to Melbourne and London, at a time when South Africa's current account deficit made it the world's most risky middle-income country, claimed *The Economist* (25 February 2009). Moreover, South Africa had an existing US$75 billion foreign debt, which would escalated by five per cent with the World Bank loan. The 1994 foreign debt was just US$25 billion, and First National Bank projected that the ratio of foreign debt to GDP would by 2011 rise to the same level as was reached in 1985, when a debt crisis compelled a default (on US$13 billion), a signal that business and banking were finally breaking ranks with the apartheid regime.

Another controversial aspect of the loan was the World Bank's articulation of the privatisation agenda. The confirmation that Eskom would offer private generating capacity to independent power producers was established in loan documentation, in relation to the renewable component, advancing Eskom's desire to privatise thirty per cent of generating capacity (including a forty-nine per cent private share in Kusile, although no private interest had been expressed for Medupi). This component attracted explicit opposition from trade unions – especially the National Union of Metalworkers of South Africa (Numsa) – and consumers.

Corruption was another feature that generated criticisms of the World Bank by South African opposition political parties (especially the centre-left Independent Democrats and the liberal Democratic Alliance, which subsequently merged) and the influential liberal *Business Day* newspaper. These organisations opposed the loan because, contrary to supposed World Bank anti-corruption policies, it will directly fund African National Congress (ANC) ruling party coffers. Medupi will be built with Hitachi boilers that in turn kick back between $10 and $100 million (the amount is still unclear) thanks to an ANC investment in Hitachi. As the Eskom-Hitachi deal was signed, Eskom chairperson Valli Moosa was also a member of the ANC's finance committee. A government investigation released in March 2010 found his conduct in this conflict of interest to be 'improper'. The ANC promised to sell the investment stake, but this dragged on for several months. Finally, in May 2010, Chancellor House managing director Mamatho Netsianda relayed by text message to the media: 'The official position is that Chancellor House Holdings is not selling its stake in Hitachi Power Africa … (SAPA, 2010). Ironically, in February 2010, the World Bank had issued a major statement at the same time as its annual African Development Indicators, entitled 'Quiet Corruption', in which it blamed African teachers and healthcare workers for moonlighting (a result of World Bank structural adjustment policies).

As in the case of the Bisasar Road CDM, the matter of historic racial injustice should not be ignored. The World Bank's financing of apartheid began just three years after the 1948 election of the Afrikaners' National Party, lasting until 1967, and including $100 million for Eskom. During that period, the Bank financed the supply of electricity to no black households (which only began receiving electricity in 1980), and instead empowered only white businesses and residences (Bond, 2003).

Curiously, Gordhan has argued that 'South Africa, in sixteen years of democracy, never has had to take any loans from the World Bank …This is an opportunity for the World Bank to build a relationship with South Africa' (Gordhan, 2010), yet the Bank's 1999 and 2008 Country Assistance Strategy documents show conclusively that Medupi is the fifteenth credit since 1994. As for 'building a relationship', Gordhan also neglected to mention that the Bank co-authored the 1996 Growth, Employment and Redistribution (homegrown structural adjustment) programme, whose orthodox strategies failed and which led South Africa to overtake Brazil as the world's most unequal major country, as black incomes fell below 1994 levels and white incomes grew by twenty-four per cent within fifteen years, as was claimed by official statistics.

Still, the World Bank was the obvious financing choice for Medupi, because even though it has embedded itself deeply within the climate-change discourse, over eighty per cent of the Bank's oil-related Third World projects are geared for export to the North. Since Kyoto, the Bank has invested in more than 128 fossil-fuel projects, with an increase of 256 per cent for coal and coal-related project during 2007–2008 alone. Nor do the industrialised economies whose governments run the Bank, and which are on the receiving end of cheap benefits from foreign-owned multinationals, care to consider socio-economic and environmental externalities. The Bank's role in climate-change financing has been aggressively promoted by its president, Robert Zoellick, whose track record on financing, environment and the US military-industrial complex is, simply, shocking (Bond and Dorsey, 2010).

Each year, the world's governments (mainly in the North) supply over $700 billion in fossil-fuel subsidies, including through the World Bank, the African Development Bank and others of their ilk. In contrast, by 2009, almost two decades after the non-binding United Nations Framework Convention on Climate Change was adopted at the Rio Earth Summit, Northern governments channelled a mere $3 billion in climate mitigation and adaptation funding to the Third World. The fossil-fuel subsidies that do trickle down into Southern elite pockets are often siphoned out to offshore financial centres. Since the early 1960s, Nigeria's political and military elites have engaged in over $400 billion of capital flight (UNODC, 2011). Overall, more than sixty per cent of Africa's illicit capital flight is siphoned by multinationals through corporate mispricing, much of which is related to oil, gas and other mineral resources (Sharife, 2010b). Ironically, more than half of the small islands on the frontline of climate change are economies 'outsourced' as tax havens (Sharife, 2010c). In South Africa, meanwhile, capital flight has been estimated in 2007 as high as twenty-three per cent of GDP, amounting to R450 billion in 2007 (*Business Day*, 2010a).

This is a continuation of capital flight during the apartheid era, which has been projected at seven per cent of national GDP, smaller in part because of a more 'patriotic' minerals-energy complex elite and the existence of exchange controls from 1985 to 1995. For South Africa, then as now, exploitation of resources therefore constitutes a double-edged form of economic theft. And it raises the question of how to gain compensation for the enormous damage done by the minerals-energy complex, beyond even the extreme crisis presented by acid mine drainage.

CONCLUSION

The minerals-energy complex has had a devastating impact on South Africa's society and environment. Its continual renewal through new waves of crony-capitalist tycoons is remarkable: first there was Cecil Rhodes and his allies who accumulated wealth in the Kimberley diamond mines through taking over (or forcibly evicting) competitors. They were followed by the randlords of the era from the 1890s to the 1910s, and especially the Oppenheimers, who ensured consolidation of white English mining capital from the 1920s to the 1990s (by 2001, most had successfully externalised their cash and sold off their worst assets via Black Economic Empowerment schemes). They were followed in turn by Afrikaners who, from the 1960s were allowed entry via cheap purchase of Gencor (later to become BHP Billiton, when the last apartheid finance minister, Derek Keys, relaxed exchange controls for the very purpose of Gencor's asset externalisation). And they were followed first by those deemed suitable for accumulation by the Mandela-Mbeki governments (Patrice Motsepe, Mzi Khumalo, Bridget Radebe, Cyril Ramaphosa and Tokyo Sexwale) in the 1990s–2000s, and finally by the Zuma regime (including the latter's family and their allies in the Gupta family).

The revolving door between state and capital has been impressive, with leading politicians and bureaucrats such as Keys (BHP Billiton chief executive after 1994), Mick Davis (formerly Eskom treasurer when early 1990s' special pricing agreements were made and then Billiton chief operating officer), Xolani Mkhwanazi (first post-apartheid chief executive of the National Electricity Regulator of SA, then chair of BHP Billiton Southern Africa), and Vincent Maphai (leading state research official in the Mbeki camp, then chair of BHP Billiton Southern Africa).

The antidote to the continuation of the minerals-energy complex, short of Tunisia/ Egypt-style bottom-up democracy, is louder civil society demands for genuine solutions not found in the Green Paper or other state initiatives:

- turning off BHP Billiton's aluminium smelters (and saving around ten per cent of electricity) so as to forego more coal-fired plants;
- direct regulation on the biggest point emitters, starting with Sasol and Eskom, compelling annual declines until SA cuts emissions by fifty per cent (from 1990 levels) by 2020;
- strengthening the Air Quality Act to name greenhouse gases as dangerous pollutants (as even the US Environmental Protection Agency now does); and
- dramatic, urgent increases in investments for public transport, renewable technology and retrofitting of buildings to lower the emissions and to create a million genuine green jobs, such as in solar hot water heater construction and installation.

These are the obvious solutions, but there is only one way to achieve them: grassroots activism. Such activism exists in isolated, fragmented forms, such as the myriad township battles with municipalities and Eskom over electricity access and pricing; or labour struggles against asbestosis and silicosis (successful in a March 2011 Constitutional Court judgment against Anglo); campaigns to close the south Durban petrochemical complex and Bisasar Road dump (both still under way); or struggles against multinational corporations' plans for resource extraction in the platinum fields of Limpopo and North West, the titanium sands of the Wild Coast, and the gas-fracked Karoo, to mention a few examples.

A fully connected civil society project to link demands for renewable energy, household electricity, climate change mitigation and adaptation, anti-pollution, protection of the Witwatersrand water table, occupational safety and health, reparations for climate damage, return of capital flight, and an end to crony-capitalist political-corporate corruption, and the need to leave minerals in the soil (especially coal in the hole), is yet to catalyse. If South Africa is to overcome the vast economic, social and environmental problems associated with the minerals-energy complex, this kind of multi-issue front had better emerge above and beyond the society's gaping cracks, and very quickly indeed.

NOTES

1   We are grateful for financial support for this research from the Research Council of Norway.
2   See Africa Centre for Biosafety (http://www.biosafetyafrica.net/) for more information.
3   Annex 1 countries are the developed countries constituting the biggest greenhouse gas polluters.
4   Green Economic Summit 18–20 May 2010. This appeared to be copied verbatim from the UNEP's website (cached): 'A global transition to a low carbon and sustainable economy can create large numbers of green jobs across many sectors of the economy, and indeed can become an engine of development. Current green job creation is taking place in both the rich countries and in some of the major developing economies.' http://www.unep.org/greeneconomy/LinkClick.aspx?link=1377 &tabid=1350&language=en-US.
5   Bisasar Permit. http://www.sawic.org.za/sawis-license/documents/download/57 (accessed 21 February 2011).

REFERENCES

Africa Earth Observatory Network (AEON) (2010) 'H$_2$)–CO$_2$: Energy equations for South Africa' 22 November http://www.aeon.uct.ac.za/content/pdf/annualreps/2010-Energy%20Report%20series%202%202010%20LoRes.pdf (accessed 21 February 2011).

Balashov S (2011) Watermark Global raises £1.5mln, still waiting for SA decision on AMD, 1 June. http://www.proactiveinvestors.co.uk/companies/news/28874/watermark-global-raises-15mln-still-waiting-for-sa-decision-on-amd-28874.html (accessed 30 May 2011).

Bishop A (2011) Interview with K Sharife for *The Africa Report*.

Bond P (2003) *Against Global Apartheid: South Africa meets the World Bank, IMF and International Finance*. London and Cape Town: Zed and UCT Press.

Bond P (2006) *Talk Left, Walk Right: South Africa's Frustrated Global Reforms*. Scottsville: University of KwaZulu-Natal Press.

Bond P (2010) Climate change: From renewed climate hope to absurd market expectations, 31 December http://www.businessday.co.za/articles/Content.aspx?id=130625 (accessed Web 21 February 2011).

Bond P and R Dada (2005) Putting a price on fresh air, 17 January. http://www.mg.co.za/article/2005-01-17-putting-a-price-on-fresh-air (accessed 21 February 2011).

Bond P and M Dorsey (2010) Anatomies of environmental knowledge and resistance, *Australian Journal of Political Economy*, 66, Dec, pg. 286–316.

Botha A (2011) Telephone interview with K Sharife for *The Africa Report*.

Business Day (2010a) Answers needed on bank's policy by stealth, 10 August. http://www.businessday.co.za/articles/Content.aspx?id=117524 (accessed 21 February 2011).

Business Day (2010b) Assets may be on block in BHP Billiton's bid to buy potash, 25 August. http://allafrica.com/stories/201010250137.html (accessed 8 March 2011).

BusinessLive (2011) Acid mine drainage part of a bigger problem, 16 February. http://www.businesslive.co.za/incoming/2011/02/16/acid-mine-drainage-part-of-bigger-problem (accessed 21 February 2011).

Dales J (1968) *Pollution, Property and Prices*. Toronto: University of Toronto Press.

Department of Environmental Affairs (2010) National Climate Change Response Green Paper, 25 November. http://www.info.gov.za/view/DownloadFileAction?id=135920 (accessed 21 February 2011).

De Villiers S (2011) E-mail interview with K Sharife for *The Africa Report*.

Department of Water Affairs and Forestry (2010) Report to the Inter-Ministerial Committee on Acid Mine Drainage, December. http://www.dwaf.gov.za/Documents/ACIDReport.pdf (accessed 8 March 2011).

Durban Municipality (2011) Landfill disposal http://www.durban.gov.za/durban/services/cleansing/gastoelec/disposal?-C=&plone_skin=eThekwiniPrint.

Earthlife Africa (2009a) Copenhagen: The End Days. http://www.earthlife.org.za/?p=743 (accessed 8 March 2011).

Earthlife Africa (2009b) Acid Mine Drainage Fact Sheet August. http://www.earthlife.org.za/wordpress/wp-content/uploads/2009/08/pdf16-Aug-09-draftAMD-fact-sheet-no-2.pdf (accessed Web 21 February 2011).

Earthlife Africa (2009c) Sustainble Energy News. http://www.earthlife.org.za/?p=572 (accessed 8 March 2011).

Earthlife/groundWorks (2010) Press release on Medupi 19 April. http://www.sustainactmoveorg/2010/04/19/earthlifegroundwork-press-release-on-medupi/ (accessed Web 21 February 2011),

Eskom (2008) Eskom Transmission Development Plans in the Waterberg Coal Fields Area (2008–2028) – Appendix A. http://www.eskom.co.za/content/Appendix%20I-1%20Development%20Plans%20in%20Waterberg%20Coal%20Fields%20Area.pdf/ (accessed May 30 2011).

Europol (2009) Carbon credit fraud causes more than 5 billion euros damage for European Taxpayer, 9 December. http://www.europol.europa.eu/index.asp?page=news&news=pr091209.htm (accessed Web 21 February 2011).

Gordhan P (2010) Why coal is the best way to power South Africa's growth. http:/www.washingtonpost. com/wp-dyn/content/article/2010/03/21/AR2010032101711.html (accessed 21 February 2011).

Green Economic Summit (2010) 'SA Green Economy Summit' 18-20 May. http://www.sagreecono-mysummit.co.za/2about.html (accessed 11 February 2011).

groundWork (2010) Response to the World Bank. Web 21 February 2011 http://www.groundwork.org. za/Publications/EskomFinalDocs/ResponsetotheWorldBankpanelreportandFactSheet.pdf .

groundWork and Earthlife Africa (2010) Press release: World Bank's Climate and Governance Disaster, 10 April.

Hartnady CJH (2009) South Africa's gold production and reserves. *S. Afr. j. sci.* [Online] Vol. 105 (9–10). http://www.scielo.org.za/scielo.php?script=sci_arttext&pid=S0038-23532009000500004&lng=en &nrm=iso (accessed 12 July 2011).

Impumelelo (2010) Who We Are: Annual Report. http://www.impumelelo.org.za/who-we-are/annual-reports/2009_2010.pdf/download (accessed 21 February 2011).

Mail & Guardian (2010) SA is nearing peak coal, say scientists, 25 September. 1 http://www.mg.co.za/ article/2010-09-25-sa-is-nearing-peak-coal-say-scientists/ (accessed 21 February 2011).

Marumo M (2011) Telephone interview with K Sharife for *The Africa Report.*

Mazrui A (2008) In conversation with Ali Mazrui, Nelson Mandela Foundation. 30 March. http://www. nelsonmandela.org/index.php/news/article/in_conversation_with_ali_mazrui/.>(accessed 21 February 2011).

National Public Radio (2010) South Africa plans huge solar farm. http://www.npr.org/templates/story/ story.php?story Id=130878478 (accessed 21 February 2011).

Patel E (2010) Keynote address by minister of Economic Development, the Green Economy Summit, Johannesburg, 20 May. http://www.info.gov.za/speech/DynamicAction?pageid=461&sid=10977&t id=10994 (accessed 21 February 2011).

Reuters (2010) Fact Box: South Africa's power generation plans, 23 November. http://www.necsa.co.za/ Article/8afc4d91-b1f5-42d8-8e52-22811f361f00/6/Factboxsouth-africas-power-generation-plans. aspx (accessed 21February 2011).

Reuters (2011) South Africa to spend $168 million on gold cleanup, 24 February. http://www.reuters.com/ article/2011/02/24/us-safrica-mining-acid-idUSTRE71N2LI20110224 (accessed 8 March 2011).

SA Press Association (2010) ANC closes shop on Hitachi stake inquiries, 13 April. http://allafrica.com/ stories/ 201004130983.html (accessed 30 May 2011).

Schneider M (2008) Landfills: Hope for recovery purpose, 17 October Web 21 February 2011 http://free. financialmail.co.za/report08/green08/qgreen.htm.

Schwartz A (2011) Coal costs the US $500 billion annually in Health, Economic, Environmental Impacts, 16 February. http://www.fastcompany.com/1727949/coal-use-costs-half-a-trillion-dollars-each-year-in-health-economic-environmental-impacts?partner=rss (accessed 21 February 2011).

Sharife K (2010a) Climate change's secret weapon, 24 February Web 21 February 2011 http://www.fpif. org/articles/climate_changes_secret_weapon.

Sharife K (2010b) Mauritius Treasure Islands, 20 July Web 21 February 2011 http://mrzine.monthly review.org/2010/sharife200710.html.

Sharife K (2010c) The Flying Dutchman, 17 November Web 21 February 2011 http://hir.harvard.edu/ blog/khadija-sharife/sabmiller-flying-dutchman.

South African Planning Institute (2010) Draft statement of conclusion http://www.sapi.org.za/index.php? option=com_content&view=article&id=39%3Adraft-statement-of-conclusion-green-economy-summit&Itemid=23.

Sovacool B and M Brown (2009) Scaling the policy response to climate change, *Policy and Society* 27 (4) March pp. 317–328.

Summers L (1991) The Memo, 21 December. http://www.whirledbank.org/ourwords/summers.html (accessed 21 February 2011).

Sutcliffe M (2010) eThekwini Case Study, Landfill to Gas Electricity project, 27 September. http://www.energy.gov.za/files/esources/kyoto/Web%20info/Capetown%20workshop/Case%20study;%2Ethekwini%20Landfill%20Gas%20to%20Electricity%20Project.pdf (accessed 21 February 2011).

Tayob R (2011) Email interview with K Sharife for *The Africa Report*.

Truth and Reconciliation Commission (1998). Report. Volume 4, Chapter Two. http://nelsonmandela.org/ omalley/index.php/site/q/03lv02167/04lv02264.htm.

Turton A (2011) Interview with K Sharife for *The Africa Report*.

Umvoto Africa Company Announcement (2009) 'SA's gold reserves dip well below official estimates'. http://www.miningweekly.com/attachment.php?aa_id=24543 (accessed 21 February 2011).

United Nation Office on Drugs and Crime (UNODC) (2007), Nigeria's corruption busters, 20 November.http://www.unodc.org/unodc/en/frontpage/nigerias-corruption-busters.html (accessed 21 February 2011).

Western Utilities Corporation (2010) Water Security Seminar, 26 March 2010. http://www.h2o4life.co.za/pdf/26-03-2010_AMD.pdf (accessed 21 February 2011).

WikiLeaks (2010) Addis Ababa Cable http://213.251.145.96/cable/2010/02/10ADDISABABA163.html.

CHAPTER 15

Corrosion and externalities:
The socio-economic impacts of acid mine drainage on the Witwatersrand

David Fig

————

'Problems related to mining waste may be rated as second only to global warming and strato-spheric ozone depletion in terms of ecological risk. The release to the environment of mining waste can result in profound, generally irreversible destruction of ecosystems.'
United States Environmental Protection Agency, 1987. [1]

'Amongst the many things I learnt, as a president of our country, was the centrality of water in the social, political and economic affairs of the country, continent and indeed the world. I am, therefore, a totally committed "water person". [2]
Nelson Mandela, 2002.

INTRODUCTION

For over 125 years, the area around Johannesburg has been at the centre of the mining of the richest underground gold and uranium bearing reefs in southern Africa. Mining has occurred over an arc of approximately seventy-five kilometres, along a geological ridge of 'white waters', the Witwatersrand, or 'Rand', which also constitutes the continental divide: to the north of the ridge surface water flows into the Limpopo catchment and out into the Indian Ocean; to the south, surface water flows into the Vaal and subsequently via the Orange/Gariep River into the Atlantic (Turton et al., 2006: 316).

By the turn of the second decade of the twenty-first century, the gold is mostly no longer viable to be mined and, with a few exceptions, the mines have closed down. Although many of the companies which exploited the resource have disappeared, they have left an expensive legacy of environmental pollution, without having internalised these costs in their balance sheets or having been required by the state to pay them. Until recently, the state imposed little obligation on the mining companies, or their share-holders, to account for cleaning up the damage.[3]

Because of the deep level of the gold-bearing ore, the Witwatersrand goldfields could only be exploited by means of huge capital investments, mostly from abroad, in the late nineteenth century. The mining industry demanded that African peasants be alienated from their land and taxed in order for them to seek paid work on the mines. This was the start of the migrant labour system which drew on the whole region of southern Africa for its manual workforce. Contradictions between the mining industry and the Kruger state led to the South African war of 1899–1902 in which the Transvaal republic was defeated and recolonised, and after which a British dominion consisting of all of current South Africa was established in 1910. Under this Union, mining interests were seen as a vital source of tax and other revenue for the state. This led to the state privileging the 'minerals-energy complex' (Fine and Rustomjee, 1996), allowing racist employment practices to endure, and allowing the industry to escape financial responsibility for its negative impact on the environment.

Part of the damage to the environment is the result of mismanagement of tailings dams, the huge piles of solid and liquid waste which, for the most part, lie above ground. Increasingly, however, attention is having to be paid to the problem of acid mine drainage, which consists of liquid flows of polluted water from the mines into the surface water-courses and underground aquifers in the areas surrounding the former mines. These water resources have sustained life in the area for hundreds of years, including the provi-sion of drinking, washing and cooking water, agricultural use (watering of crops and cattle), supporting biodiversity, heritage, tourism and leisure activities and, indeed, also supplying water used in industrial and mining enterprises.

Fresh water in South Africa is scarce and the supply is fully accounted for in terms of existing use. Much of the country is semi-arid, and only fourteen per cent of its surface is available for arable farming. Cities are facing water stress and in some cases, due to drought, municipalities have had to recycle sewerage or institute expensive desalina-tion projects.

Johannesburg and its environs serve the bulk of the country's industry, as well as a population of approximately nine million (eighteen per cent of the country's people). It is one of the seven per cent of the country's municipalities to have competent water management facilities. If, however, the surrounding catchments become badly polluted, this would represent what the Department of Water Affairs (DWA) has called a 'poten-tial environmental catastrophe' (DWA, 2009: 22). All kinds of industrial and agricultural processes would be compromised, contingent jobs could be lost, people and animals would experience health problems, and huge structural damage would be done to the built and natural environments, including to the Johannesburg city centre – and to a significant world heritage site, the Cradle of Humankind.

Is this alarmist? Many water scientists and geologists are already warning that the need for government action is urgent if the problem is to be forestalled. Some have argued that time for action is running out. Government has been slow to act; despite years of publicity, the issue was only considered at cabinet level for the first time in February 2011 (Pressly, 2011b).

This chapter will try to define the problem in general and then outline the specific experiences in different mining basins in the Witwatersrand gold-uranium complex. It will look at some of the technical solutions offered by science and business, and it will raise questions about the policy arena in which this issue is being played out. It will conclude with observations about the management of complex environmental issues in contemporary South Africa in the context of a constitution which guarantees environmental rights to its citizens.

ACID MINE DRAINAGE: The problem

Acid mine drainage is the name given to water which becomes contaminated when it interacts with sulphide-bearing rocks in the presence of oxygen. There are vast amounts of underground iron pyrites (fool's gold, Fe_3S_4) in the Witwatersrand basin and when these interact with oxygenated water, sulphuric acid is formed. Other minerals break down in the acidic conditions, causing their metals to enter into the solution and further contaminate the water. These conditions occur when neglected old mine shafts and the underground cavities that have been mined out start to fill with rain water, or with groundwater flowing from other areas. With the closure of many mines, the practice of pumping out the contaminated acid mine drainage has more or less ceased, and the underground cavities and shafts have started to fill up. Because there is almost no pumping at present, the level of acid mine drainage is constantly rising underground, at different rates in the different basins on the Witwatersrand.

Since August 2002, the acid mine drainage has been decanting (flowing uncontrollably from underground) and entering the watercourses on the surface of the West Rand basin. Because the acid mine drainage is highly corrosive (pH of around 2–3 makes it very acidic), toxic (owing to dissolved heavy metals) and often radioactive (uranium and its daughter products are present underground), it has the ability to contaminate the catchment areas not only at the point of decant, but for kilometres downstream (Naicker et al., 2003: 40). It also has the capacity to dissolve dolomitic geological formations, creating the possibility of increased sinkholes, and the potential to destroy the cave systems and archaeological sites linked to the Cradle for Humankind, which is one of South Africa's and the world's most important areas for the conservation and future excavation of hominid finds. The danger is compounded by the prediction that unless urgent action is taken, the Central Rand basin, which straddles an area from Boksburg to Roodepoort, including the central Johannesburg business district, will begin to see a decant, and this may cause immeasurable damage to an area of much higher population density and economic activity.

Gold and uranium mining wastes were calculated at 221 tons per year, or forty-seven per cent of the 468 tons of mining waste per year measured in 1997, and thus form the largest single source of waste and pollution in the country (DWAF, 2001). Much of the waste from the mined-out ores was placed in 270 tailings dams across 400 square kilometres of the Witwatersrand, for the most part unvegetated and unlined. These, too, have become a source of seepage, as oxygenated rain water has interacted with the pyrites and other sulphides and metals in the waste. Not only is there acid mine drainage in the run-off, but wind erosion results in air and further water contamination, and some catastrophic dam failures (for example Merriespruit, Westonaria) have had severe consequences for the environment and human health (Oelofse et al., 2007: 1–2).

Faced with the potential decant in the Central Wits basin, government has been tardy in providing a solution. It has, moreover, continued to allow the decant to occur in the Western Basin without undertaking significant remediation. It faces a huge task, and needs huge resources to tackle the problem, which will not be short-lived. The damage is being caused due to closure and/or abandonment of mines by companies that may no longer be in existence. Until the 1990s, there were no enforceable closure plans, and companies which had benefited from mining the gold failed to leave any funds for post-closure remediation.

The companies that continue to mine have not been able to fund the prevention of the decant of an entire basin, which includes the acid mine drainage emanating from all the other mines in the basin. It is left to the state to finance the bulk of the remediation, with some expectations of private-sector involvement. The Cabinet finally released the report made to an inter-ministerial committee by its technical task team (South Africa Council for Geoscience, 2010), simultaneously allocating R225 million for remediation in the 2011 budget. This response has been deemed 'lukewarm' and 'extremely modest' by concerned environmentalists (Biyase, 2011).

The hydrogeology of the Witwatersrand is such that there are distinct basins, composed of collections of gold mines in the West, Central and East Rand, as well as the Far Western, Free State and KOSH (Klerksdorp, Orkney, Stilfontein and Hartebeestfontein) basins. Each of these basins comprise interconnected mining tunnels and underground cavities in which the acid mine drainage occurs, each basin having its own water flow patterns, and levels to which the contaminated water has risen. As the basins on the Rand each have a distinct experience of acid mine drainage, they will be discussed in turn.

West Rand basin

Because the decant of acid mine drainage in the West Rand basin has been under way since 2002, this basin has received by far the most extensive publicity and public attention. The basin is located beneath Krugersdorp/Mogale City and Randfontein. It includes, on the surface, the Wonderfonteinspruit,[4] which flows south into the Vaal, and the Tweelopiespruit, which flows north into the Crocodile. The sizeable township of Kagiso is located close to Krugersdorp, and an array of informal settlements has sprung up within the Wonderfonteinspruit catchment. Their inhabitants are negatively affected, as well as those who draw water from local boreholes, as are the residents of the Potchefstroom area, who rely on the watercourse to supply their household water and may be exposed to higher levels of leukaemia (Winde, 2010c).

In the 1950s, the Chamber of Mines Research Organisation produced a report to the Council for Scientific and Industrial Research (CSIR) noting the potential problems associated with mine closure. These included the deterioration of water and air quality, increasing seismic activity and the formation of sinkholes (Frost, 1957). Further concerns were raised in technical and scientific reports throughout the 1960s (Adler et al., 2007: 33; Jordaan et al., 1960; FSE, 2010a), but it was only in the 1990s, once many mines had closed, that attention was once again drawn to the problems arising from mine closures. In 1996, mine consultant Garfield Krige was involved in predicting that the decant from the mines would occur around 2002 (JCI, 1998). As mines developed and became deeper, so the practice of pumping relatively clean groundwater (which had not yet acidified) out of the mines was instituted. However, with closures, and to avoid taking on post-closure financial burdens, the mining companies in the Krugersdorp/Randfontein areas ceased pumping, allowing the old mine tunnels to fill up with groundwater. By 1998, when the last company, Harmony Gold, stopped pumping operations at its central ventilation shaft, the underground cavity, or void, started to fill up with contaminated water. Mine ownerships changed, responsibilities were not regulated, and the predictions of 1996 were slowly forgotten.

When the decant occurred in August 2002, the specialists, mining houses and authorities were astounded by the magnitude of the event, with an outflow of twenty million litres per day. Contaminated water entered the surface watercourses of both the Wonderfontein and Tweelopiespruit. In a recent interview Krige noted:

> The Department of Water Affairs was completely aware that the voids would start filling up. The fact that the department did not take proper decisions over that period, from 1996 to now, gave all the mines time to get rid of their liability. The department should have said 2002 is the deadline. Instead, in 2002 the water started to decant, and it caught everybody off guard, even though everybody knew about the whole thing. It is now 2010 and nothing has been done (Kardas-Nelson, 2010: 20).

The failure to prevent the decant has led to serious pollution problems in the two catchment areas, arising from deposits of sulphates, heavy metals and radioactive metals. All these pose serious health risks to organisms, to ecosystems and to human beings. Sulphate concentrations have been measured at around 5 000 mg/litre, way beyond the point at 600 mg/litre where human health will be affected. The metals, largely manganese, aluminium, iron, nickel, zinc, cobalt, copper, cadmium, arsenic, and lead, are toxic and potentially carcinogenic. As a result of the decant they are present at levels well above those of regulatory concern (Van Eeden et al., 2009: 55).

Of serious concern is the impact of the radioactive metals, such as uranium, thorium, radium and polonium, which are chemically toxic in addition to their radioactivity. Annually around fifty tons of uranium are discharged into the catchments of the West and Far West Rand. Radioactive materials have been leaching out of the tailings dams and through the decant, and accumulate in the sediments of the watercourses. (Coetzee, Winde and Wade 2006). These sediments can have their radioactive content mobilised by animals drinking from, or by children playing in, the streams. Through ingestion of water or contaminated plants and animal products, they enter the food chain. The effects of these materials include genetic and reproductive damage, blood diseases, kidney disease, compromise of immunity, organ failure, and cancers (Winde, 2010b).

When pumping was still going on, much of the mine effluent from the West Rand basin ended up being directed into the Robinson Lake, the source of the Rietspruit, the main tributary of the Tweelopiespruit. At one time, property developers were keen to sell lakeside properties for their leisure value but the lake was declared a radiation area by the National Nuclear Regulator, having a uranium concentration of 16 mg/litre. This should be compared against a background concentration of uranium in water at 0,0004 mg/litre, and means that the load in the lake is 40 000 times higher than background. A site inspection on 30 January 2010 revealed that there was no vestige of organic life left within the lake. The same holds for the entire Tweelopiespruit, now designated as a Class 5 river, one that is acutely toxic (Fourie, 2006).

In the West Rand basin, human settlements have been built on radioactive land, and in some cases people in informal settlements on this land, such as those close to the Tudor Dam,[5] have been cultivating crops such as maize for sale and consumption in the area. Housing materials have been made out of bricks fashioned from reclaimed tailings materials. Even an upmarket Tuscan-style retirement village, Amberfield, was constructed within 500 metres of a tailings dam, on land contaminated by radioactive dust. It is now an abandoned ghost town, surrounded by billboards advertising the lavish life once promised there. On private farms in the vicinity of the Wonderfonteinspruit, farmers have been prevented from allowing their cattle to drink water from local streams and dams by order of the National Nuclear Regulator, for fear that they would disturb the sediments and mobilise the radioactive materials in the water.

The decant flowing into the Tweelopiespruit has already contaminated the dams in the Krugersdorp Game Reserve, especially in the Hippo Dam, where the acidity and radioactivity have become a threat to the many species of fish, amphibians and mammals, including the resident hippopotami (Hobbs and Cobbing, 2007a).

One of the most serious potential threats caused by acid mine drainage in the area may be to the integrity of the Cradle of Humankind, declared a world heritage site by United Nations Educational, Scientific and Cultural Organization (Unesco) in December 1999. Known principally for the Sterkfontein caves complex, the Cradle is one of the richest hominid fossil sites in the world, and is the longest continuous palaeo-anthropological excavation.

It recently yielded important new finds such as Little Foot, probably the most complete hominid fossil yet discovered, as well as an extraordinary discovery of examples of a new hominid species, *Australopithecus sediba*. Many of the fossils are preserved in dolomitic limestone rock formations, which when eroded, for example through the percolation of rain water, leave a series of chimney-like openings, revealing where bone remains have accumulated, often through the activities of scavenging animals (Clarke and Partridge, 2010: 15).

Should a large-scale decant of acid mine drainage enter the underground caverns in the Cradle of Humankind world heritage site, the limestone of the dolomitic rock may be so decisively eroded by the acidity that it is eaten away, or collapses in sinkholes near the surface. This could destroy the use of the area for further scientific research and excavation, badly compromising South Africa's undertakings to Unesco to preserve the site for global humanity. Moreover, the destruction of the possibility of new finds that reveal the origins of humanity and further establish our common ancestral heritage (important in a country whose history is marked by racism), will be a serious blow to the construction of a new vision for humankind, of a sense of our continent's place in pre-history and history, and of a common identity. Tourism establishments in the area account for 7 000 permanent and 2 200 casual jobs (Durand, Meeuvis and Fourie, 2010: 85). The management authority of the Cradle has been monitoring the impact of the decant on the Cradle (see Gauteng Government, 2010) without detecting much damage at yet. However there is a need for the management authority to be far more proactive and precautionary in helping to solve the overall problem posed by the decant. This can be achieved by working more effectively with other officials and civil society stakeholders.

The extensive summer rains experienced over the seasons of 2009–10 and 2010–11, and attributed to the La Niña phenomenon, have resulted in much more elevated underground water levels and extended the magnitude of the decant in the West Rand basin. In the other basins, the danger is that the decant may arrive more suddenly than predicted and shorten the time period in which a solution must be found.

Despite the intensification of the decant in the West Rand basin, government and its many agencies and regulatory bodies have failed to implement an adequate remediation strategy. In April 2009, a remediation action plan for the Wonderfonteinspruit catchment area was drafted (Van Veelen, 2009) and later that year issued for public comment by the commissioning bodies, the Department of Water Affairs – at the time Department of Water Affairs and Forestry (DWAF) – and the National Nuclear Regulator (NNR). Together with the Chamber of Mines, the Mining Interest Group and the Federation for a Sustainable Environment, the DWAF and NNR had formed a cooperative initiative to support the crafting of the action plan. The plan was, however, criticised by Earthlife Africa's Acid Mine Drainage Working Group, *inter alia* on the grounds that inadequate recognition was given to the danger of uranium, and to how the polluted material removed from the sites would be managed (Earthlife Africa, 2010). Criticism also came from Professors Stoch, Winde and Cohen, scientists attached to the specialist task team.

It seems as if the state's response to the intensified decant after January 2010 was to spend R6, 9 million on neutralisation, adding lime to the affected watercourses in order to elevate the very acidic pH (Adatia, 2010) but this has been seen as a highly inadequate response to the need for a broader and more sustainable solution because although some sulphates are removed by the neutralisation, the remaining levels are still extremely high (3 700 parts per million compared with the regulatory limit of 600). Liming precipitates the heavy metals, which enter the sludge in the rivers, and the metals can be mobilised (dissolved again) in the water if the residues are disturbed. Liming also adds to the huge salt load in the water, requiring further treatment to remove dissolved contaminants (FSE 2010b). It is feared that neutralisation, despite its problems, may be advocated as one of the recommendations presented to Cabinet by the inter-ministerial committee as a part-solution to the decant problem in the West Rand basin.

East Rand basin

The Grootvlei gold mine lies on the edge of the town of Springs, at the eastern end of the Witwatersrand. It is the only mine in the East Rand basin still pumping water out of the shafts in order to prevent flooding and the disruption of mining activities. Because all the abandoned mines in the East Rand basin are linked underground, the pumping at Grootvlei mine is essential for preventing the decant of the entire basin's acid mine drainage. Grootvlei is located adjacent to the sensitive Blesbokspruit wetland which includes the nearby Marievale Bird Sanctuary. The Blesbokspruit has, since 1986, been recognised globally as a wetland of international importance under the Ramsar Convention, the only such site in Gauteng province (see www.ramsar.org).

Alarm bells rang when the mine started discharging its untreated pumped-out water into the adjacent wetland in the mid-1990s. Randgold and Exploration Co. Ltd, the then owners, consistently refused to install filters to remove the contaminants from its effluent. As a result, there were mass deaths of fish, crabs and other life-forms. Birds were driven away from the wetland, one of their key habitats.

The then minister of Water Affairs, Professor Kader Asmal, took action in June 1996 by ordering the mining company to switch off its pumps. Randgold claimed that this would mean that its shafts would fill with water, and that the jobs of 6 000 workers would be jeopardised. Asmal responded by insisting that Randgold should invest R10 million in sediment settling ponds for receiving the water, rather than discharging it raw into the neighbouring wetland. Without the plant, Asmal claimed that there were no long-term prospects for the mine. He claimed that the department would be assessing not only the technology, but whether or not the jobs the mine created were worth sustaining, balanced against environmental pollution and the high costs of the remediation (US Water News Online, 1996). Cabinet instructed Grootvlei to develop a pilot plant by November 1998 and a full desalination facility by December 1999 (Van Wyk and Munnik, 1998: 7).

Within a decade, Grootvlei had been acquired by a company called Pamodzi Gold, which claimed to be 'the only JSE-listed gold mining company in South Africa to be owned and controlled by historically disadvantaged South Africans (HDSAs)' (Boyd, 2007: 188–9); a spate of acquisitions of mines on the East and West Rand and in the

Free State goldfields by this company followed. However, by 2008, Pamodzi had run out of capital, and was beginning to default on its payments to employees, contractors and loans. An envisaged R200 million loan failed to materialise, and the company was forced to go into liquidation.

The liquidators gave preference to bids from a company called Aurora Empowerment Systems, possibly because the company chairman was listed as Khulubuse Zuma (the president's nephew), its CEO was Zondwa Gadaffi Mandela (the former president's grandson, eldest son of his daughter Zindzi) and a third board member was Michael Hulley (the lawyer who had represented president Zuma in his corruption suit).[6] None of these had any mining experience. They were able to convince the liquidators that they would raise the necessary R597 million for Pamodzi's Grootvlei and Orkney mines, and took control of these mines in October 2009. The liquidators accepted a R10 million deposit, and set a date for the rest of the payment to be made. This date has been extended continually, and even the 'final' deadline set at 28 February 2011 was further extended in order to ensure that a firm investment commitment by a Chinese investor (the Shandong Gold Mining Company) be approved by the Chinese state council (Seccombe, 2011a). On three previous occasions, Aurora had made claims of having backing from foreign investors (Malaysian, Swiss and Chinese in succession). None of these had materialised, and the company has imitated Pamodzi in its failure to pay miners, contractors and the liquidators. The difference has been that the Department of Mineral Resources has been reluctant to press for the company's liquidation on the grounds that the state would be saddled with the mine's considerable environmental liabilities.

Within four months of taking control over the mines, Aurora began to default on its liabilities. In February 2010, workers were paid only a portion of their salaries, and from March payments ceased entirely. The company also failed to pay its employees' medical expenses and their unemployment insurance. It allowed acid mine drainage to be deposited in the Blesbokspruit, attracting a visit, on 10 March, from the Blue Scorpions, the enforcement arm of the Department of Water Affairs. On 19 March, 2 000 workers, distraught by their failure to be paid, downed tools, leaving only one hundred workers involved in essential care and maintenance, including workers staffing the water pumps.

In early April 2010, it was reported that angry workers had converged on management offices, throwing stones and harassing mine officials, who were escorted off the mine in a motor convoy with the assistance of the police. Five miners were injured by police firing rubber bullets at them.

Pressures on the care and maintenance workers to join the strike became overwhelming by the first week of June; they had remained on duty to pump water from Shaft 3, and within days of their stoppage, water began to flood the underground pump station room. Had this continued, the entire mine would have been flooded. Suddenly the maintenance workers were offered the chance to receive their pay, and although this was not realised, they returned to their posts an hour before catastrophe was averted.

For the majority of workers at Grootvlei, housed in nearby company hostels, life began to become desperate. The hostel electricity and water supply was cut, catering services were terminated, toilets started to malfunction, and medical attention ceased. This posed acute problems for the striking workers, who were left to forage and seek handouts in order to survive. Some reported that they were living on a diet of thin maize porridge and tea. Diabetic workers complained that they were eating so little food that their medication was not working. The lack of sanitary facilities was forcing workers to defecate in the nearby bush, and there was insufficient water for bathing. Many of the workers spoke of having to take their children out of school because they could no longer pay fees and transport. Others suffered from breakdowns of their marriages, because they were no longer in a situation to support wives and children. Workers from other African countries said they could not afford to go home because it cost too much to get passports renewed.

The mine started to be invaded by 'illegal' miners, working on their own account to extract the small amounts of gold still available, largely using mercury to extract the metal. Many of these illegals stay underground for months on end, supplied with food and drink at exorbitant prices by smugglers. It is not clear whether the illegals were unemployed residents of nearby informal settlements, or whether some of the desperate striking workers had begun to engage in mining on their own account as a means of survival. As the tensions mounted, six workers were charged with theft by Aurora for allegedly stealing R16 million worth of underground cables – at the same time there were reports that the company was stripping its own assets. In August 2010, there was an incident underground which remains murky, but which resulted in outsourced mine security shooting between four and twelve illegal workers. The security guards claimed that one of their colleagues had been shot the previous day and another held hostage while the company claimed that the deaths had mostly resulted from faction fighting amongst the illegal miners. The police placed a number of the mine security guards under arrest.

Since February 2010, most miners had received no pay and their unions, the National Union of Miners, and Solidarity, initiated a case in the labour court in late November 2010 to obtain payment for their members. The court decided that the miners should be paid, and nothing further has occurred, prompting the unions to call for mine management to be arrested for contempt of court.

Criminal charges were laid against the company by the Blue Scorpions, acting for the Department of Water Affairs, in mid-May 2010. The legal liability of management is that they can be fined R10 million for causing serious pollution, and can face jail sentences. However, Aurora has not yet been required to answer to any of these charges, perhaps because of the political protection which its board members might receive. Throughout most of this debacle, management has acted with impunity, arguably violating the 'code of ethics' which the company claims to aspire to on its website (see www.aurora empowerment.com).

Khulubuse Zuma embodies all the contradictions of black empowerment, leading an ostentatious and lavish lifestyle, owning multiple luxury vehicles and turning up at the wedding of South Africa's police commissioner in a rare gull-wing Mercedes sports car, to the delight of the paparazzi. During the April 2011 municipal elections he donated a million rand to the African National Congress (Anderson, 2011). Most recently he has been reported to have consorted with a Taiwanese ex-criminal, who served a sentence for murder in South Africa, in order to persuade Shandong Gold, a Chinese public corporation, to invest in Aurora (Sole, 2011: 2–3). His starving unpaid workforce remains witness to Aurora's reputation as being immune from regulation owing to nepotism and political connections.

The Shandong Gold offer to invest in Aurora seemed plausible, and the media was informed that the company was simply awaiting final state approval, but gradually it became clearer that even the possibility of the Shandong Gold investment was imaginary, because the company seemed more interested in adding gold reserves to its balance sheet and not in the costly rehabilitation of Grootvlei (Matomela, 2011). The master of the North Gauteng High Court lost patience and, on 23 May, sacked Enver Motala, who had been the principal liquidator in the matter and an avid protector of Aurora's interests (Seccombe, 2011b). With Motala out of the picture, the courts could cancel Aurora's claims to Grootvlei and Orkney (Speckman, 2011). The company has been berated for asset stripping, ending the pumping, flooding local Ramsar wetlands and neighbouring mines with acid mine drainage, and starving its workers. Litigation against Aurora may be one of the outcomes (Masondo, 2011).

Under Aurora's watch, the destruction of Grootvlei, a once prosperous mine, has been immense. None of the former seven shafts is in operation any longer, and the stripping of the headgear means that there is now an extra hole in the ground. Not only has Aurora done physical damage to the mine, probably making it too expensive to rehabilitate, but it has also stripped the workforce and their dependents (14 000 people in all) of their livelihoods. While the pumping in the mine has ceased, the acid mine drainage will continue to rise and then decant into the environment, possibly with the first appearance of the acid mine water in the streets of Nigel.

Central basin

Predictions vary among scientists as to the exact date of the potential decant, should too little action be taken to prevent it. Some scientists believe that the decant will start as early as February 2012, while others claim it could take a further two or three years, giving a better margin of time for its prevention.

Should the decant occur, it is likely to start in Boksburg, but could also occur in downtown Johannesburg. McCarthy identifies the most important risk zone as extending along, and 500 metres to the south of, the Main Reef Road, and along the northern side of the M2 highway (McCarthy, 2010: 20). Because of its corrosive nature, the acid mine drainage would eat at the city's limestone foundations, seriously corroding pipes and the steel that reinforces concrete in buildings, causing subsidence and potential collapse. Should this be allowed to happen, there will be high bills resulting from serious structural damage, costs of relocation, and costs of treating waterborne diseases and the higher costs of doing remediation after the event. Government has made little provision to cover such damages. These costs will be exacerbated by the higher population density and the concentration of the built environment in the area of the Central Basin. This could have implications for the health impact of the decant, because far more people may be exposed to the contamination.

Meanwhile the acid mine drainage in the Central Basin continues to rise steadily at an average level of 15, 2 metres a month (McCarthy, 2010: 17), at which rate the decant can be expected in under three years.

POLICY QUESTIONS

Regulation

In view of the magnitude and potential consequences of the problem of acid mine drainage, and of regulating pollution from the mining industry more generally, we have to ask whether we are being well served by current legislation and administrative practice. Clearly, one of the issues is that for over a century our economy has favoured mining and has been prepared to allow the industry to pass on the costs of environmental and public health protection to others. Their costs have generally been externalised and either borne by the state or taxpayers in general or inscribed in affected human bodies and ecosystems. The industry has justified this by claiming that the high tax regime it faces means that the state benefits from mining revenues and can hence afford to bear the externalised costs. In turn, the state has been complicit with the industry in order to secure and enhance this revenue stream.

With the advent of a new Constitution, and legislation reflecting a post-apartheid reality, we are entitled, as citizens, to a 'clean and healthy' environment as a matter of enshrined right (section 24 of the Bill of Rights). Recent laws have made clear two key principles: the precautionary principle (which speaks to avoiding predictable harm or potential harm where there is uncertainty) and the principle that the polluter should pay for any harm caused to people and the environment (as enshrined in chapter 2 of the National Environmental Management Act No 107 of 1998).

What has prevented these principles from being enforced? Part of the answer lies in the question of the state's continued complicity with mining capital. During the years of segregation and apartheid, the state wilfully turned a blind eye to the industry's damaging impact on the environment. While some of this analysis has focused on the behaviour of current mine owners, the heaviest responsibility lies with the major mining houses which profited from South African gold and uranium during the boom years. Key gold mining companies like the Anglo-American Corporation, Gencor, Goldfields, and Johannesburg Consolidated Investments have largely been transmuted into new legal structures, but clever corporate forensics could establish the extent to which they were beneficiaries over the lifetime of their mining operations. It is clear that this would require a good deal of political will, which is unlikely to be forthcoming. For example, the state has not supported the efforts by civil society organisations to obtain restitution from key transnational corporations which benefited from apartheid, and the same reluctance to take on the mining industry still applies – instead, the state and its taxpayers are likely to be saddled with any remaining bills for mining pollution. Moral culpability should remain squarely with those companies and shareholders who benefited from ownership during the most productive cycle of gold mining.

Even the post-apartheid governments have witnessed overlapping interests between the political elite and the mining industry. Instead of the change of regime being a new opportunity to radically reform mining to reflect a new balance between the interests of the market and protecting ecological integrity, the new laws simply tried to expand opportunity for new entrants into the field of mining as an attempt to redress past racial economic inequities. The new elites saw environmental protection as a barrier to their entry into new areas of the economy. Mining has always been exempt from the practice, compulsory in other industries, of holding an environmental impact assessment of new projects; instead, for mining, there is an environmental management reporting system, administered by the Department of Mineral Resources, and mining is not subjected to more stringent regulation by the Department of Environmental Affairs. A flaw of both these regulatory systems is that they only regulate individual sites, and do not examine the accumulated impacts on a region of new developments.

The question of state complicity has meant that the state has failed to regulate effectively. Statements by former minister Buyelwa Sonjica that the problem of acid mine drainage has been 'exaggerated' (I-Net Bridge, 2010), or the outburst in parliament by the planning minister, Trevor Manuel, that unspecified private sector interests were dominating the agenda[7] (SAPA, 2010; De Lange 2010b: 6–8) are reflections of the state's inability to respond adequately to the urgency of the problem after years of neglect. The former director general of Water Affairs, Mike Müller, who currently has a seat on the National Planning Commission, has stated that the problem has been one constructed by the mining and water treatment industries in order for them to gain from selling proposed solutions. 'Media coverage of the issue is heavily influenced by interests in the mining and water treatment industries, which stand to profit by exaggerating the problem,' Müller wrote in *Business Day* on 1 July 2010, and he repeated the sentiment at the AgriSA water conference the following month (Prinsloo, 2010).

Perhaps the test of the state's decisiveness was the raid of the Blue Scorpions on the premises of Aurora's Grootvlei mine on 10 March 2010. The subsequent criminal charges that were laid against the Aurora management for deliberately allowing the pollution of the Blesbokspruit seem not to have been taken up by the courts, probably because of management's familial relationships with key members of the political elite.

The national nuclear regulator has entirely failed to protect the public from the radio-activity associated with acid mine drainage. A recent report on the impacts of uranium and other radioactive substances in the Wonderfonteinspruit catchment which did not note any immediate danger to communities (NNR, 2010) has been decisively challenged by a number of radiation experts. Professor Chris Busby, a member of the International Society for Environmental Epidemiology and the European Committee on Radiation

Risk subsequently visited some of the tailings dams and informal settlements in the Wonderfontein catchment during December 2010 and, warning that radiation levels were fifteen times higher than normal, recommended that the question of radiation exposures to the public in this area be addressed properly, and scientifically overseen by an independent committee of experts. Busby felt that some informal settlements subject to radioactive contamination should urgently be relocated (Mammburu, 2010). Dr Rianne Teuel of Greenpeace Africa has questioned the scientific accuracy of the NNR report's methodology and criticised its study as being unprofessional. She has further drawn this to the attention of the International Atomic Energy Authority in Vienna (personal communication, 27 January 2011). These are damning critiques of the regulator, whose entire *raison d'être* is protection of the public from the ill effects of radioactivity, and which is facing the future expansion of the nuclear industry in South Africa with questionable scientific approaches and methodologies.

Liability

The companies whose shareholders profited from their gold and uranium mining holdings on the Witwatersrand over the past 125 years were clearly responsible for the consequences of mining waste on the environment and on human health and livelihoods. These mining companies have never been required to assume legal liability for the damage they caused. Without a very thorough forensic study, it would be extremely difficult to assign the proportion of damage to each mining company. And given that many of the original companies are no longer in operation, assigning liability to them retrospectively might prove fruitless.

Because liability cannot easily be enforced against companies that have gone out of business or been liquidated, there should be clear demarcations in law about what liabilities the state should assume. Where liability is established under current legislation (Van Eeden et al., 2009: 58–62), it is essential that the rule of law operates to penalise transgressors. The Department of Mineral Resources (DMR) should oversee more scrupulously the post-closure plans of all existing mine owners; this monitoring should include a prior determination of realistic funds that should be lodged in advance for dealing with mine waste and pollution, adjusted at regular intervals to reflect changes in circumstances affecting the mine during the course of its operation. The state – through the inter-ministerial committee or the DMR – should also establish a broader fund for addressing the problem of acid mine drainage. Where feasible it should demand that – along with current mining houses – former mining companies which profited from Witwatersrand gold and uranium should make retrospective contributions to such a fund proportionate to the extent of their many years of profits as part of redress and of corporate social responsibility.

In the June 2011 hearings of the parliamentary portfolio committee on water and environment, the Treasury mentioned that it would be exploring the idea of an environmental tax on mines, and sending a team to the United States to look at the workings of the Superfund arrangements (Matji, 2011; Pressly, 2011c).

Disputes over solutions

Various solutions have been put forward towards tackling the problem of acid mine drainage on the Witwatersrand. It should be noted that the problems of mining waste management (historic and current) will be present for many years ahead (Oelofse, 2008: 6). Solutions should be sustainable, use resources efficiently and have an eye on the long term.

Neutralisation, or adding lime to watercourses, reduces acidity in the short term, but has long-term implications for the mobilisation of salts, as well as toxic and radio-active substances in the water. It is therefore not a sustainable or holistic solution. The pollution load in the Vaal catchment is already extremely critical (Tempelhoff et al., 2007).

Pumping and subsequent treatment of the acid mine drainage is one of the key solutions advocated in the medium term (McCarthy, 2010) but this is an extremely expensive and energy-intensive process. The regional director of Water Affairs, Marius Keet, claimed in evidence before the parliamentary portfolio committee that a single pump station on the East Rand would cost R185 million to install (Masondo, 2010).

Mining companies that formed the Western Basin Environmental Corporation have established the Western Utilities Corporation which has put forward a plan to offset costs of remediation (*Noseweek*, August 2009: 13). It proposed setting up a treatment plant to turn seventy-five million litres of acid mine drainage a day (later expanding to 300 Ml/day) into water for industrial use (grey water) or, if the economics allow, to class 1 drinking water standard. The purification process would be the CSIR's alkaline-barium-calcium process which, through precipitation, removes heavy metals and sulphates from contaminated water, converting the by-products into marketable raw materials, the sales of which would offset the costs (De Lange 2010a: 4–5).

This proposal has been treated by the state with scepticism, and although it was ready to be implemented (with Rand Water as a potential customer), it was vetoed by the inter-ministerial committee, for reasons articulated by ministers Sonjica and Manuel. Their objection was to private capital making profits from the pollution it had caused.

Others have supported non-pumping solutions. Professor Anthony Turton of Free State University has proposed that, after pumping out the contaminated water, the underground voids be utilised for storage of fresh water resources. This, he argues, would prevent the acid mine drainage from forming underground, and would also solve the huge problem of water evaporating from open-air dams under South African conditions. Evaporation is the largest contributor to water loss, and can be overcome by storing water in old mines. Other scientists have argued for more intensive use of passive solutions, such as running acid mine drainage through wetlands which have the capacity to remove the toxic matter.

Most recently, researchers at the University of Cape Town have developed a technology that freezes acid mine drainage in order to enable the extraction of useful salts and potable water. If they used it, mines would be able to market the salts commercially. The research team has teamed up with an industrial engineering company to pilot the technology. It claims that the freezing process will be much cheaper than using evaporative crystallisation (Bugan, 2011).

The variety of solutions point to the need for an impartial evaluation process, and it was expected that the inter-ministerial committee's team of experts would perform such a role. However the team of experts reported its findings to Cabinet in October 2010 and these remained outside the public domain prior to a Cabinet meeting in late February 2011 which adopted the findings (Pressly, 2011a, 2011b). The Department of Water Affairs set aside R225 million for implementation in Gauteng. This amount has proved to be derisory, and even the body charged with putting the solution in place – the parastatal Trans Caledon Tunnel Association (which has previously been responsible for inter-basin transfers of water from the Lesotho Highlands to the Vaal catchment) – claims it needs around R750 million to implement the minimum programme. It has later transpired that the Department of Mineral Resources has also allocated R328 million to the process (Matji, 2011).

The document accepted by Cabinet and coordinated by the Council for Geosciences, has, *inter alia*, recommended that the state:
- implement control measures to reduce the rate of flooding and the eventual decanting and pumping volume;
- improve water quality management, including neutralisation and metal removal in the short-term;
- undertake research to inform decision making and managing, and monitor other acid mine drainage sources within the Witwatersrand basin (South Africa. Council for Geosciences, 2010: x)

This programme has been heavily criticised by civil society representatives for being inadequate, relying in the short-term on the process of neutralisation in the Western basin which removes much of the acid but adds considerably to the salt load. Hundreds of tons of salt will be added to the waters of the catchment, ending up in the Vaal river system, needing subsequent dilution despite shortages of fresh water for this purpose. Attempts by civil society to engage with the Department of Water Affairs on the question of implementation have only resulted in the most anodyne of responses (Govender, 2011).

Public participation and activism

Without the activism of non-governmental organisations, the extent of the problem would not have been highlighted and constantly brought to public attention. Foremost is the work of Mariette Liefferink of the Federation for a Sustainable Environment, who has worked tirelessly for a number of years. Not only has she been a public advocate of the need for solutions, but has personally kept the media and affected communities informed, mobilising resources to draw attention to the problem in new and creative ways. Most serious news reports will contain comment by Liefferink. She has appeared before a number of parliamentary committees, informed ministers and worked with some of the key players to ensure that the problem comes closer to resolution. Her approach has also been to make the science intelligible to ordinary people, and to that end she has worked with academic and scientific experts; her own expertise is recognised through awards and an honorary associateship from North-West University in Potchefstroom. Non-governmental organisations helped to get her appointed as the community representative on the board of the national nuclear regulator, and becoming an insider has given her insights into its shortcomings. It is clear from the record that Liefferink's activism has been extremely important in raising public awareness of the acid mine drainage problem (Christie, 2010: 17; Liefferink and Van Eeden, 2010).

Another non-governmental organisation that plays an active role in addressing the issues is the Johannesburg branch of the membership-based Earthlife Africa, which has an acid mine drainage working group and operates an active website with reliable information (see for example Earthlife Africa, 2010a and 2010b). Recently the formation of the Centre for Environmental Rights in Cape Town has begun to work with the Federation for a Sustainable Environment, Earthlife and other non-governmental organisations to craft potential litigation strategies for making progress on the problem. As information on the problem increases, so it is likely that activism will spread to other areas affected by acid mine drainage, especially to the Northern Cape and Mpumalanga (Salgado 2011). The latter is the site of large coal deposits and thousands of new applications for mining rights to exploit the coal.

Public activism creates the political space to demand a place for the public in the decision-making processes, and for it to be consulted by government prior to the setting of policy. During the Mandela presidency, public participation in policy processes became the norm, and this was a fruitful time in which new legislation was being contemplated in almost every sphere of government. As the post-apartheid government consolidated its power under the Mbeki presidency, so it became more opaque, resenting public participation in ways that set the democratic process back. Although it is important for the NGOs and activists concerned with acid mine drainage to realise the complexity of the issue and the fragmentary way in which it is being dealt officially, it is only by activists expanding the political space for deeper participation that solutions will find public acceptance. It is incumbent on the activists to keep stressing the urgency for government action, and to challenge notions of the problem being seen as exaggerated or ridiculous.

CONCLUSION

It is time for an integrated policy overhaul which will recognise the urgency of the acid mine drainage, correct the regulatory deficit, establish the rule of law, and actively seek solutions that protect public health, the natural environment and the integrity of precious sites such as the Cradle of Humankind – as well as safeguarding the built environment and the livelihoods of millions of citizens. While it is important to use overarching processes like the National Planning Commission to play a coordinating function in this regard, the outburst of scepticism from the minister is not helpful in building public confidence in the new commission's neutrality.

The inter-ministerial committee currently charged with developing policy solutions to the crisis also seems cumbersome and lacking in transparency. Its sluggish approach to releasing the report of its team of experts does not augur well, as the time-frame for implementing appropriate solutions is narrowing daily.

Public confidence in the ability of the National Nuclear Regulator to undertake its mandate is rapidly evaporating. This points to a need for a radical overhaul of this institution, so that it accommodates public concerns, a vital component of re-establishing its social licence to operate as a public protector and discontinuing its role as an apologist for industry.

The management authority of the Cradle for Humankind also needs to come to the party in a more proactive and precautionary fashion.

If the issue of mining pollution is, as the United States Environmental Protection Agency frames it, second only in importance to climate change, we must ensure that it receives the same kind of public attention. It should be incumbent on the inter-ministerial committee to convene a national public summit at which these matters can be discussed transparently by all the stakeholders, with a healthy amount of public participation. This would have the broad objective of establishing policy ground rules, upholding the rule of law, assigning appropriate and effective institutional responsibilities, and crafting sustainable solutions to the problem.

NOTES

1   Manders et al., 2009: 1.
2   Address by former president Nelson Mandela during the opening of the Waterdome, World Summit on Sustainable Development, Johannesburg, 28 August 2002. Downloaded from http://www.info.gov.za/speeches/2002/02091711461003.htm on 24 January 2011.
3   The National Environmental Management Act, No. 107 of 1998 established the legal principle that the polluters should pay for damage caused by their actions.
4   Also known as Mooi River. The term *spruit* is the Afrikaans for stream or rivulet. The name *Wonderfontein* means miraculous spring. The water in its catchment forms the basis of the municipal supply for the town of Potchefstroom further downstream.
5   On 3 March 2011, the responsible municipality, Mogale City, announced that it was seeking to resettle many of the families at the Tudor Shaft informal settlement. This was a result of years of lobbying by civil society organisations.
6   In a telling interview with the liquidator, Enver Motala, Chris Barron of the *Sunday Times* asked: 'How can you give mines to a company with no track record whatsoever in mining?' Motala: 'We had nobody else at the time' (Barron, 2011).
7   In response to a statement on 10 August 2010 made by Independent Democrat MP Lance Greyling that decisive government action was necessary on the question of acid mine drainage, Manuel responded: 'What we need is a rational discussion ... informed by an empirical basis, because the idea that there will be acid mine drainage running through the streets of Johannesburg next week, and that we should all walk around in gum boots, is completely ridiculous'(SAPA, 2010).

REFERENCES

Adatia R (2010) Inadequate treatment of acid water flowing into the Tweelopiespruit, 13 June. www.earthlife.org.za/?p=989 (accessed 16 February 2011).

Adler RA, M Claasen, L Godfrey and A R Turton (2007) Water, mining and waste: An historical and economic perspective on conflict management in South Africa, *Economics of Peace and Security Journal* 2(2): 33–41.

Anderson A (2011) National Union of Mineworkers wants Aurora donation to African National Congress to go to workers, *Business Day*, 12 April.

Barron C (2011) Interview with Enver Motala, liquidator of Pamodzi. *Sunday Times*, 13 March.

Biyase L (2011) Acid mine plan underwhelms, *Sunday Times*, 27 February.

Boyd M (Ed.) (2007) *Deep South Africa: A Celebration of Mining*. Cape Town: Nelida.

Bugan D (2011) New treatment freezes acid mine water, *Business Day*, 1 February.

Christie S (2010) Our lady of the mines, *Mail & Guardian*, 17–23 September: 17.

Clarke R J and TC Partridge (2010) *Caves of the Ape-men: South Africa's Cradle of Humankind World Heritage Site*. Pretoria: SE Publications.

Coetzee H, F Winde, and P W Wade (2006) An assessment of sources, pathways, mechanisms and risks of current and potential future pollution of water and sediments in gold mining areas of the Wonderfonteinspruit catchment (Report 1214/06). Pretoria: Water Research Commission.

De Lange J (2010a) Acid attack. The Green Book 2010: Jo'burg's toxic time bomb. Johannesburg: FinWeek, 4 November: 4–5.

De Lange J (2010b) Acid mine water: Reasons to worry. The Green Book 2010: Jo'burg's toxic time bomb. Johannesburg: FinWeek, 4 November: 6–8.

Department of Water Affairs and Forestry (DWAF) (2001) Waste generation in South Africa (Water Quality Management Series). Pretoria: DWAF.

Department of Water Affairs (DWA) (2009) Water for growth and development framework (Version 7). Pretoria: DWA.

Durand JF, J Meeuvis, and M Fourie (2010) Environmental management and the threat of mine effluent to the Unesco status of the Cradle of Humankind World Heritage Site, *Journal for Transdisciplinary Research in Southern Africa* 6 (1): 73–92.

Earthlife Africa, Johannesburg branch (2009a) What is acid mine drainage? (AMD Fact sheet 1), Johannesburg, 16 August.

Earthlife Africa, Johannesburg branch (2009b) Acid mine drainage on the Witwatersrand (AMD Fact sheet 2), Johannesburg, 16 August.

Earthlife Africa, Johannesburg branch (2010) Correspondence with Department of Water Affairs, Gauteng Regional Office responding to the Remediation Action Plan of the Wonderfonteinspruit Catchment Area, 27 January.

Federation for a Sustainable Environment (FSE) (2010a) Chronological timeline of government efforts regarding the treatment of acid mine drainage: West Rand goldfields. Johannesburg: FSE. www.fse.org.za (accessed 4 January 2011).

Federation for a Sustainable Environment (FSE) (2010b) Cabinet to decide AMD solution. 18 December 2010. Johannesburg: FSE. www.fse.org.za (accessed 5 January 2011).

Fine B and Z Rustomjee (1996) *The Political Economy of South Africa: From Minerals-Energy Complex to Industrialisation*. Boulder: Westview.

Fourie J and Associates (2006) Environmental impact document: Impact of the discharge of treated mine water, via the Tweelopiespruit, on the receiving water body, Crocodile River system, Mogale City, Gauteng province (DWAF 16/2/7/C221/C/24). Krugersdorp: Johan Fourie and Associates.

Frost M (1957) Report on an investigation into mine effluents. Johannesburg: Chamber of Mines Research Organisation.

Gauteng Government, Management Authority, Cradle of Humankind World Heritage Site (2010) Press release: Cradle of Humankind not yet affected by decant, says CSIR. Johannesburg.

Govender B (2011) Letter from the Gauteng Regional Office of the Department of Water Affairs to the Centre for Environmental Rights, in answer to a request for information on the implementation of the recommendations of the inter-ministerial committee on acid mine drainage team of experts, Pretoria, 11 May.

Hobbs PJ and JE Cobbing (2007a) The hydrogeology of the Krugersdorp game reserve area and implications for the management of mine water decant. Proceedings of the Groundwater Conference, Bloemfontein, 8–10 October.

Hobbs PJ and JE Cobbing (2007b) A hydrogeological assessment of acid mine drainage impacts in the West Rand basin, Gauteng province (Report CSIR/NRE/WR/ER/2007/0097/C). Pretoria: CSIR/THRIP.

I-Net Bridge (2010) Sonjica: Acid mine drainage flooding exaggerated, 19 August. www.miningmx.com/news/markets/Sonjica-Acid-mine-drainage-flooding-exaggerated (accessed 24 January 2011.

Johannesburg Consolidated Investments (JCI) Inc. (1998) An integrated strategic water management plan (SWaMP) for the Gauteng gold mines (3rd revision). Johannesburg: SWaMP Steering Committee.

Jordaan J M, J F Enslin, J P Kriel, A R Havemann, L E Kent, and W H Cable (1960) Finale verslag van die tussendepartmentele komitee insake dolomitise mynwater: Verre Wes-Rand. Pretoria: Department of Water Affairs.

Kardas-Nelson, M (2010) Rising water, rising fear: South Africa's mining legacy, *Mail & Guardian*, 12–18 November: 20-21.

Liefferink, M (2010) Water pollution of the Witwatersrand catchment. Presentation to the Amandla forum, Johannesburg, 19 February.

Liefferink M and Elize S van Eeden (2010) Proactive environmental activism to promote the remediation of mined land and acid mine drainage: A success story from the South African goldfields, *Journal for Transdisciplinary Research in Southern Africa* 5 (1) July: 51–71.

Manders P, L Godfrey and PJ Hobbs (2009) Acid mine drainage (Briefing note 2009/2). Pretoria: CSIR.

Masondo S (2010) Acid water rescue plan, *The Times*, Johannesburg, 7 September.

Masondo S (2011) Mine bosses face charges, *The Times*, Johannesburg, 31 May.

Matji MP (2011) Acid mine drainage funding and recommendations. Presentation by the Director of Public Finance in the National Treasury to the Parliamentary Portfolio Committee on Water and Environment, Cape Town, 21–22 June.

Matomela D (2011). Aurora pins last hope on Chinese, *Business Report*, 25 May.

Mammburu L (2010) Dangerous radiation levels endanger communities – expert. *Business Day*, 11 December.

McCarthy TS (2010) The decanting of acid mine water in the Gauteng city-region. Johannesburg: Gauteng City-Region Observatory.

Naicker K, E Cukrowska and TS McCarthy (2003) Acid mine drainage arising from mining activity in Johannesburg, South Africa and environs, *Environmental Pollution* 122 (1): 29–40.

National Nuclear Regulator (2010). Surveillance report of [sic] the Upper Wonderfonteinspruit catchment area (Report TR-NNR-10-001). Pretoria: NNR.

Noseweek (2009) Joburg's poisoned well. Issue 118, August: 12–13.

Oelofse S (2008) Mine water pollution – acid mine decant, effluent and treatment: A consideration of key emerging issues that may impact the state of the environment (Emerging Issues paper). Pretoria: Department of Environment and Tourism.

Oelofse S, PJ Hobbs, J Rascher and JE Cobbing (2007) The pollution and destruction threat of gold mining waste on the Witwatersrand: A West Rand case study'. Paper presented at the 10th International Symposium on Environmental Issues and Waste Management in Energy and Mineral Production (SWEMP), Bangkok, 11–13 December.

Pressly D (2011a) Cabinet mum on acid mine drainage report, *Business Report*, 27 January.

Pressly D (2011b) Acid water report in cabinet today, *Business Report*, 16 February.

Pressly D (2011c) Treasury to research mining levy for acid mine drainage, *Business Report*, 23 June.

Prinsloo L (2010) Interim acid mine solution to cost R218 million – minister, *Mining Weekly*, Johannesburg, 11 August 2010.

Salgado I (2011) Mines threaten water catchment areas, *Business Report*, 21 February.

Seccombe A (2011a) Chinese mining group gets nod to buy Aurora. *Business Day*, 1 March.

Seccombe A (2011b) Motala in court plea to remain Pamodzi liquidator, *Business Day*, 24 May.

Sole S (2011) Ex-con is Khulubuse's link to Chinese deals, *Mail & Guardian*, 7–13 January: 2–3.

South Africa Council for Geoscience (2010) Mine water management in the Witwatersrand gold fields with special emphasis on acid mine drainage (Report to the Inter-Ministerial Committee on Acid Mine Drainage). Pretoria: Council for Geoscience, December.

South African Press Association (SAPA) (2010) Johannesburg acid mine water ridiculous, 10 August. http://acidminedrainage.wordpress.com/2010/08/10/jhb-acid-mine-water-ridiculous/ (accessed 28 January 2010).

Speckman A (2011) Aurora ordered to leave mines, *Business Report*, 30 May.

Tempelhoff J, V Munnik and M Viljoen (2007) The Vaal river barrage: South Africa's hardest working waterway: an historical contemplation, *Journal of Transdisciplinary Research in Southern Africa* 3 (1) July: 107–133.

Turton AR, C Schultz, H Buckle, M Kgomongoe, T Malungani and M Drakner (2006) Gold, scorched earth and water: The hydropolitics of development in Johannesburg, *Water Resources Development* 22 (2) June: 313–335.

US Water News Online (1996) South African gold mine shut down for pumping polluted water into wetlands, June. www.uswaternews.com/archives/arcglobal/6goldmine.html (accessed 24 January 2011).

Van Eeden ES, M Liefferink and J F Durand (2009) Legal issues concerning mine closure and social responsibility on the West Rand, *Journal for Transdisciplinary Research in Southern Africa* 50 (1) July: 51–71.

Van Veelen M (2009) Wonderfonteinspruit catchment area: Remediation action plan (Final draft report). Pretoria: Department of Water Affairs and Forestry and National Nuclear Regulator.

Van Wyk JJ and R Munnik (1998) The dewatering of the Far East Rand mining basin: A critical evaluation of the government's approach towards solving the associated environmental problems. www.ewisa.co.za/literature/files/1998%20-%20-20151.pdf (accessed 18 January 2011).

Winde F (2010a) Long term impacts of gold and uranium mining on water quality in dolomitic regions: examples from the Wonderfonteinspruit catchment area in South Africa. In Merkel B J and A Hasche-Berger (Eds) *Uranium in the Environment: Mining Impact and Consequences*. Berlin: Springer.

Winde F (2010b) Uranium pollution of the Wonderfonteinspruit, 1997–2008. Part 1: Uranium toxicity, regional background and mining related sources of uranium pollution, *Water SA* 36 (3) April: 239–256.

Winde F (2010c) Uranium pollution of the Wonderfonteinspruit, 1997–2008. Part 2: Uranium in water – concentrations, loads and associated risks, *Water SA* 36 (3) April: 257–278.

CHAPTER 16

Food versus fuel?
State, business, civil society and the bio-fuels debate in South Africa, 2003 to 2010

William Attwell

INTRODUCTION

Bio-fuels have been hailed as a potential panacea for a host of pressing issues including climate change, energy security and rural development. In recent years, however, initiatives aimed at increasing the production and utilisation of bio-fuels have faced harsh criticism from many quarters, including multilateral agencies and human rights groups from around the world. They argue that the production of bio-fuels diverts land and resources away from vital food production, ultimately contributing to global food price inflation. This has become known in the literature and in the news media as the 'food versus fuel debate'. The chapter explores how the food versus fuel debate played out within the context of the post-apartheid South African political economy and examines how opposing interest groups sought to influence the state's policy towards this controversial source of renewable energy. For (mainly white) commercial farmers and their counter-parts in the nascent bio-fuels processing sector, the prospect of a supportive incentives regime for the industry was very attractive because it promised to revive the fortunes of a sector in decline by creating additional markets for agricultural produce, especially maize. The Mbeki administration at first appeared to support their position and singled out bio-fuels production as a key pillar of his new targeted economic growth strategy, the Accelerated and Shared Growth Initiative for South Africa (AsgiSA). However, under pressure from civil society groups and, perhaps more significantly, the ruling ANC's main political ally, the Congress of South African Trade Unions (Cosatu), this support proved to be short-lived.

Criticisms levelled by these groups varied widely and were not limited to discussions about the relationship between bio-fuels production and rising food prices (which, given South Africa's regular maize surpluses, was an economic relationship that was not entirely clear). Submissions received during the public consultation process also included, for instance, concerns for the negative health implications of an increased distribution of genetically modified (GM) seeds, concerns about the retreat of rural communities' diverse 'natural farming methods' and criticisms regarding the overall economic rationale underlying AsgiSA itself. What they all had in common, however, was that they drew on the growing 'anti-bio-fuels consensus' that was gaining momentum around the world by using the language of the debate to articulate concerns emanating from a characteristically South African domestic political and economic context. The food versus fuel debate, coinciding as it did with soaring food prices at home and abroad, provides critical insights into how an international discourse played out in a national political context and how this, in turn, affected domestic policy making. As we shall see, the results were mixed. Bio-fuels industry lobbyists received more incentives than had existed before, but not to a degree that would enable them to compete internationally. Civil society activists ensured that the country's main food crop, maize, was dropped from the list of available feedstocks, but the reduced incentives regime also meant that many of the rural development projects envisioned as part of the government's AsgiSA initiative were now no longer viable. More recently, however, a focus on the job-creating potential of 'green industries' as part of the Zuma administration's New Growth Path (NGP), suggests that the bio-fuels debate is still far from over.

HISTORICAL BACKGROUND

Official interest in bio-fuels was not entirely new. From the 1970s, under the National Party government, the increasing international isolation and protectionist policies of the apartheid regime meant that bio-fuels became part of the government's strategy, 'promoting energy security, reducing import burdens and supporting national agricultural sectors' (Cartwright, 2007: 5). In recent years, however, the primary impetus behind the promotion of the domestic bio-fuels industry came with the launch of AsgiSA in 2006. Formulated by President Mbeki's office in conjunction with a team of international economists, AsgiSA aimed to maintain the government's fairly orthodox economic policies while simultaneously promoting targeted initiatives that would achieve 'accelerated growth' while attending to the structural imbalances that underpinned the country's widespread poverty and unemployment (AsgiSA 2006: 2). One of the initiative's key aims was to use the formal or 'first' economy to leverage the informal 'second' economy through large-scale public and private investments as well as through state subsidies promoting links between the two. The specifics of these targeted initiatives were to be contained in a number of sector strategies that would 'harness the energy of government and its partners' (South Africa, 2006b: 6). The country's nascent bio-fuels industry was singled out as offering a particularly fruitful arena for encouraging such investments owing to increasing local and international interest in renewable energies as well as the opportunities it presented for rural development through the creation of additional markets for agricultural produce.

AsgiSA was not, however, the only factor driving formal interest in bio-fuels. A number of international agreements, including the Kyoto Protocol (which created incentives for developing countries to reduce carbon emissions) and the Johannesburg Plan of Implementation (formulated at the Earth Summit 2002) laid the groundwork for renewable energies in South Africa by obliging the government to seek out alternatives to the country's over-reliance on increasingly expensive as well as environmentally damaging fossil fuels.[1] Further impetus was provided by a study released in 2004 by the Food, Agriculture and Natural Resources division of the Southern African Development Community (SADC) recommending that governments in the region take measures to develop domestic bio-fuels industries in response to rising international oil prices and the concomitant decline in regional energy security (Sugrue and Douthwaite 2007: 3). South Africa was the first country in the region to respond to the call for renewable energies and, after consultation with Brazil, the European Union (EU) and Britain – and with generous funding from the EU – in December 2005 announced the establishment of a bio-fuels task team to be made up of representatives from industry, agriculture and relevant provincial government departments. Its mandate was to investigate the viability of promoting a modest bio-fuels industry in the country that could, with minor regulatory interventions, create jobs and bridge the gap between the first and second economies (*Engineering News*, 1 November 2006).

INTERESTED PARTIES

Private sector interest in bio-fuels had already been steadily growing since 2003 when the national treasury announced that it would make significant reductions to the fuel taxes levied on bio-fuels. This reduction had initially taken the form of an exemption to the value of thirty per cent of the fuel tax levied on liquid fuels. In 2004, this was increased to forty per cent. Incentives for the nascent industry were again expanded in September 2005 when the Treasury approved the implementation of a renewable energy subsidy scheme to provide further financial assistance to the country's renewable energies sector. Administered by the Department of Minerals and Energy, the scheme subsidised the bio-fuels industry to the value of 16.7 cents per litre for bioethanol and 27.3 per litre for biodiesel, with a maximum subsidy cap of R20 million – a fair incentives regime for a small industry (South Africa, 2006b: 6). This early state support, together with the news that the government had set up a task team to advise on future state intervention to promote the industry, sent a message to investors and other interested parties that the future of bio-fuels in South Africa looked very promising indeed. At the annual conference of the National African Federated Chamber of Commerce, the (then) minister of Minerals and Energy, Lindiwe Hendricks, stated that, 'this industry, ladies and gentlemen, has the potential to be a significant creator of enterprises and jobs, and is one of the most exciting developments emerging from my department at present' (Hendricks, 2005).

Among the interest groups most directly affected by future bio-fuels policy were South Africa's (predominantly white) commercial farmers, especially those who produced potential bio-fuel feedstocks such as maize, wheat and sugar. White farmers had been amongst the principal beneficiaries of the National Party's policy of keeping whites on the land through generous state subsidies. They had also enjoyed guaranteed markets as a result of the apartheid state's elaborate system of agricultural marketing boards (Lodge, 2001: 71). This was to change with the coming to power of the ANC-led government in 1994. Although limited deregulation had begun to take place during the waning years of the apartheid regime, this process accelerated under the new government. Citing high costs and high levels of debt, the ANC announced a retreat from direct marketing and subsidies for commercial agriculture in favour of limited interventions to assist small-holder agriculture in disadvantaged rural areas (ANC, 1994). This was to the extent that 'from being one of the most highly protected and regulated sectors of the South African economy agriculture has experienced almost total liberalisation and state deregulation in the post-apartheid period' (Mather and Greenberg, 2003: 394).

This approach was consistent with broader trends in economic thinking at the time, notably the government's overarching post-1994 economic policy agenda, the Growth, Employment and Redistribution policy (Gear), adopted in 1996. In short, Gear was a set of economic reforms that sought to restructure the economy through orthodox budgeting, tight control of inflation, the promotion of exports and the freeing of the money market (Davenport and Saunders, 2000: 570). For the agricultural sector, however, the shift away from state regulation and support had decidedly negative implications for the sector's long-term financial situation, a trend borne out by declining production and employment figures. Whereas 4 706 000 hectares of maize was planted in 1975/76, for example, this had declined to 2 032 000 in 2005/06. Agricultural employment decreased from 1 433 500 to 628 200 during the same period (South Africa, 2009: 4–7). According to Wessel Lemmer, senior economist at Grain South Africa, an organisation representing commercial maize farmers, the appeal of a supportive bio-fuels policy was that, by encouraging the development of a domestic bio-fuels industry it would stimulate a second, parallel market for agricultural goods which would promote demand security and ease price volatility while also ensuring the long-term commercial well-being of the agricultural sector in the country (Lemmer, 2009).

The government's main priority was, however, the emerging class of black, mostly small-scale commercial farmers. From 1999, following the appointment of Thoko Didiza as the minister of Agriculture and Land Affairs, the department set in motion a plan to spend R1 billion a year on settling farmers on what was then state-owned land while a complementary grant distribution scheme would assist aspirant farmers to establish their own commercial operations (Lodge, 2001: 79).[2] Despite this initial state assistance, and, crucially, owing to their exposure to the same market risks as their more established white counterparts, many black farmers struggled to remain commercially viable. This was especially the case for farmers in the former homeland areas where the 'kinds of help the homeland administrations previously offered to commercial farmers within their borders are no longer available' (Lodge, 2001: 72). For this group, the prospect of producing feedstocks for bio-fuels presented an opportunity to overcome their structural disadvantages; however, according to Motsepe Matlala, president of the National African Farmer's Union (Nafu), overcoming barriers to entry such as access to irrigation, poor organisation at farmer level, production finance, and only having access to unviably small, marginal plots of land, would have to involve a good deal of private sector assistance. In addition to creating additional demand, first economy 'leveraging', according to Matlala, also meant that 'bio-fuels companies must facilitate access to machinery and must be placed within the farmer's reach for the realisation of potential harvests, build farming enterprises, expand operations [and] operate profitably and sustainably' (cited in *Nafu Farmer*, April 2007).

Given the incentives provided by the thirty per cent fuel levy exemption, the support provided by the Renewable Energy Subsidy Scheme and the formal endorsement of bio-fuels as part of Mbeki's AsgiSA initiative, it seemed certain that the necessary private sector investment would be forthcoming. Indeed, media reporting at the time was characterised by a certain 'triumphalist inevitability'. According to *Engineering News*, a prominent business publication, 'while today's Middle Eastern wells will eventually run dry, South Africa's farmers will enjoy infinite supply horizons, courtesy of their renewable crops' (14 August 2006). Both local and international investors seemed to share this confidence in the future. In 2005, the South African company Ethanol Africa unveiled plans to build a one billion dollar bioethanol factory in Bothaville in the Free State, making it among the largest operations of its kind in Africa. An ambitious joint venture between the state-owned Energy Development Corporation, a black economic empowerment (BEE) consortium led by the former environment and tourism minister, Valli Moosa, the Belgian bio-fuels company Alco and a consortium of four hundred maize farmers called Grain Alcohol Investments, the project was to receive significant funding from Sterling Waterford, a securities company listed on the Johannesburg Stock Exchange (*southafrica.info*, 12 September 2005).

The Bothaville plant was presented to the state and the general public as a catch-all development panacea. With maize prices slumping from R1000 per ton in 2004 to R700 in 2005, the establishment of a ethanol-from-maize plant promised to restore commercial farmers' profits while an emerging farmer programme, to be managed by Ethanol Africa's crop securitisation division, proposed to assist small-scale farmers with 'detailed grower plans, budgets and cash flows, financing and mentorship'(*Engineering News*, 14 August 2006). Ethanol Africa CEO Johan Hoffman, for one, placed special emphasis on the venture's BEE contribution, stating that 'it allows the company the opportunity of access to the top tiers of black business in South Africa' (*Business Day*, 22 February 2007). Elsewhere in the country, the Industrial Development Corporation (IDC) and the Central Energy Fund (CEF), both state-owned entities, planned even larger bio-fuels investment projects as part of the government's AsgiSA initiative. At Hoedspruit and Ogies in Mpumalanga, the IDC announced the construction of two bio-fuels plants (at a cost of R3.2 billion) that would make 100 and 150 million litres of bio-fuel from sugar cane and maize respectively (*southafrica.info*, 13 April 2009). Further projects were envisaged for the Eastern Cape and KwaZulu-Natal. What farmers and investors eagerly awaited were the findings of the bio-fuels task team and the announcement by the Department of Minerals and Energy of the draft bio-fuels industrial strategy, both sure indicators of the kind of regulatory environment and state support the industry could expect in the near future.

SUPPORT FOR THE DRAFT STRATEGY

The bio-fuels task team announced their findings in the National Bio-fuels Study, published in October 2006. For investors and for commercial farmers, its recommenda-tions appeared to herald a highly supportive regulatory framework that would create additional markets for agricultural commodities while also ensuring a decent return on investment through price regulations and various financial incentives and supports. These supports included provision for the mandatory uptake of bio-fuels by liquid fuel wholesalers (which would have made the procurement of bio-fuels a condition for the issue of a wholesale licence), further tax reductions, and a supportive producer price regime that would regulate bioethanol and biodiesel selling prices at 95 per cent and 100 per cent respectively of the basic fuel price.[3] The study noted that such supports were justified, 'at least in the short-term to establish a sustainable bio-fuels industry' (South Africa, 2006: 101). Although the promotion of certain sectors through carefully planned 'sector strategies' had formed part of the AsgiSA initiative, it should be emphasised that this supportive regulatory environment, complete with price supports and market protection, represented something of a departure from the established neoliberal ortho-doxy enshrined in Gear.

The study furthermore emphasised the potential for bio-fuels to stimulate demand for agricultural commodities, noting its potential to create commercial opportunities that would assist beneficiaries of the government's land reform and restitution programme as well as small-scale farmers in the former homeland areas (South Africa, 2006c: 51). To realise these opportunities, however, emerging black farmers would require addi-tional supports (for example, irrigation schemes and energy crop subsidies) to help them overcome the structural disadvantages associated with chronic poverty in the coun-try's underdeveloped rural areas, especially in the former homelands. Significantly, the task team found 'no cause for concern' with regard to food security. It stated that 'the cultivation of energy crops does not pose a substantial threat to food security or food prices; as the industry matures, it is even expected that the impact on food prices will diminish even further' (South Africa, 2006b: 54). The substance of the study was largely carried over into the draft bio-fuels industrial strategy, released in November of the same year. While maintaining the highly supportive regulatory environment envisaged in the national bio-fuels study, the rhetoric of the draft strategy went further, to coordinate its stated aims with those enshrined in AsgiSA, namely the potential for the bio-fuels industry to create jobs and stimulate growth in the rural areas through linkages between the first and second economies.

As far as business and agriculture were concerned, there was little that was surprising about the draft strategy. The Agricultural CEO's Forum, a group of business leaders from the agricultural sector, had been part of the bio-fuels task team from the very beginning and, together with representatives from provincial government structures, industry and academics from the universities of Missouri and Pretoria, had been part of an initial consultation process that pre-dated the announcement of the draft strategy itself (*Engineering News*, 20 October 2006). Nevertheless, interested parties from business and agriculture were quick to respond with statements reinforcing the positive virtues and economic value added by South Africa's bio-fuels industry. In addition to creating a larger market for grain and oilseed producers (a point of mutual interest for both commercial and emerging farmers), it was claimed that the emergence of a healthy bio-fuels industry would also reduce the country's dependence on imported crude oil (thus reducing pressure on South Africa's foreign exchange reserves) as well as assist in the fight against global warming (*Sapa*, 8 January 2009). Employment, a key priority of AsgiSA, was also set to expand, with predictions that 'the production of biodiesel could create 38 500 farm-level jobs by 2015', and that 'ethanol-from-maize production could result in 17 000 farm-level jobs by 2015' (*Engineering News*, 20 October 2006). The only potential deal-breaker – the impact of increased feedstock demand on food prices and food security – was minimised. The business media reiterated claims made in the draft strategy that food security would not be adversely affected and that, at most, prices for maize and sugar (both primary feedstocks) could be expected to rise by approximately 7.7 per cent and 5.9 per cent respectively.[4] During the coming months, however, global events would make these claims appear very hollow indeed.

RISING FOOD PRICES

At the 2006 meeting in Rome of the committee on World Food Security of the UN Food and Agriculture Organisation (FAO), it was predicted that global food prices were likely to increase by a couple of percentage points in the coming months, owing to a variety of factors ranging from natural disasters to energy price increases. By May the following year, the situation had deteriorated significantly. From being a matter of incremental increases over a period of months, the total cereal import bill for low income food-importing countries was, as a group, expected to increase by fifteen per cent – and it was reported that the most prominent feature of this food and feed market volatility was the dramatic surge in the price of cereals which, by November, 'had reached levels not seen for a decade' (FAO, 2007). Within expert circles, and in the media, the growth of the global bio-fuels industry was singled out as a key factor contributing to rising food prices – a trend that would affect the poor and aid-dependent in Africa the hardest.

> 'The surge in demand for agrofuels such as ethanol is hitting the poor and the en-
> vironment the hardest. The UN World Food Programme, which feeds about ninety
> million people mostly with US maize, reckons that 850m people around the world
> are already undernourished. There will soon be more because the price of food aid
> has increased by twenty per cent in just a year' (*The Guardian*, 29 August 2007).

In a report commissioned by the FAO, it was stated that 'food and fuel compete. The grain required to fill the fuel tank of a sport utility vehicle with ethanol (240 kilograms of maize for 100 litres of ethanol) could feed one person for a year' (FAO, 2008: 6). Amid reports of rioting in Haiti, Cameroon and elsewhere over the unaffordable cost of food, the image of middle-class car owners using grain-based ethanol to fuel their cars while the poor in Africa went hungry became a persistent image in the development of a growing international 'anti-bio-fuels consensus' (*Der Spiegel*, 27 April 2007). The apparent trade-off became characterised in the media and among aid agency circles as the 'food versus fuel debate' (*The Washington Post*, 12 December 2007). A sense of scandal permeated the language of the debate; for example, the UN special rapporteur for the right to food, Jean Ziegler, was reported to have exclaimed on a German radio station that using cereal crops for bio-fuels production was tantamount to a 'crime against humanity' (*Der Spiegel*, 16 April 2008). *The Guardian* commented that 'if governments promoting bio-fuels do not reverse their policies, the humanitarian impact will be greater than the Iraq war' (6 November 2007).

In South Africa, the food security situation steadily worsened during the months immediately following the announcement of the draft strategy. The first six months of 2007 saw a marked increase in the price of staple foods, averaging 10.89 per cent in urban areas and 7.97 per cent in rural areas. The price of maize, an important staple in much of the country, increased most of all, averaging 24.2 per cent in urban areas and 13.84 per cent in rural areas (NAMC, 2007: 12). Although the National Agricultural Marketing Council (NAMC), in an assessment released in August 2007, identified rising energy costs and increasing demand for bio-fuels as key factors underlying price increases on the global food market, it noted that bio-fuels did not pose an imme-diate threat to food security in South Africa itself.[5] Nevertheless, food security came to dominate the bio-fuels debate as it played out in South Africa – a crucial point consid-ering that the food price hike coincided with the public consultation process that followed the publication of the draft industrial bio-fuels strategy (*Engineering News*, 12 February 2007).

With President Mbeki eager to have the official bio-fuels industrial strategy finalised as soon as possible, all interested parties were required to submit their comments for appraisal by 10 March 2007. The final strategy would then be released shortly afterwards. The ensuing tussle to influence the outcome of the government's final policy on bio-fuels not only reveals how the global bio-fuels debate translated into a national political and economic context, but it also provides insights into how various constituencies pursued their own particular sector interests and concerns by attempting to influence the terms of the debate itself. Moreover, as the submissions process and media campaign waged by pro and by anti bio-fuels lobbies reveals, the 'bio-fuels debate' touched a nerve that ran right to the heart of political and economic tensions within South Africa during the waning months of the Mbeki presidency.

For the non-governmental organisation (NGO) sector and representatives of organised civil society, the bio-fuels debate provided an opportunity to voice their concerns about more specific issues to do with GM crops, the dominance of big business within the agricultural economy, the insufficient attention paid to traditional farming practices and sensitivities in the formulation of government policies. Standard issues that had come to characterise the international bio-fuels debate such the industry's impact on food security and its questionable contribution to greenhouse gas emission reductions also circulated in South African civil society circles, albeit with variable emphasis. These concerns were vehemently articulated at a workshop organised in Durban on 5 March 2007 by the African Centre for Bio-safety (ACB), the University of KwaZulu-Natal, and various NGOs. The workshop brought together academics, environmental and social rights activists and community organisers to discuss and plan a coordinated response to the draft strategy. At the workshop, delegates expressed dismay at the lack of public consultation during the formulation of the draft strategy (dominated as it was by business leaders and government officials). Furthermore, they remained sceptical about the supposed poverty reduction potential of bio-fuels, finding it to be 'preoccupied with economic instruments that will facilitate large corporate involvement in bio-fuels with trickle-down benefits to the poor at best, and potentially disastrous consequences due to the expansion of industrial agriculture into new areas' (ACB and UKZN, 2007: 2).

It was feared, for example, that this 'expansion of industrial agriculture' in the form of commercial mono-cropping for feedstocks such as maize and sugar would signal the retreat of rural communities' diverse 'natural farming methods' – a development that, it was claimed, would have detrimental environmental and social consequences (Earth Harmony, 2007: 5). Delegates also expressed concern that small-scale farmers were not in a position to negotiate favourable contracts with feedstock wholesalers and bio-fuel producers. One delegate, Nelwisa Mtembu, for example, an entrepreneur in the Eastern Cape, later expressed concern that companies engaging in feedstock outgrower schemes would 'cheat the people', noting that the power dynamics involved in contractual negotiations played into the hands of bio-fuel producers and not the interests of the local community (Mtembu 2009). A key feature of how these diverse interest groups interacted with the bio-fuels debate was how they appropriated the terms and momentum of the debate to gain publicity for more specialised concerns not directly related to the draft strategy.[6] The ACB, for example, in a joint submission, paid particular attention to the negative health implications of an increased distribution of GM seed varieties, an increase that they argued would inevitably accompany growth in demand for bio-fuel feedstocks (Mayet, 2007: 10).

A more fundamental challenge was posed by Cosatu. It also questioned the socio-economic benefits of bio-fuels and expressed alarm at the proposed use of food crops for industrial bio-fuels production (Cosatu, 2007: 3–5). Rather tellingly, given the demographic distribution of its membership in skilled and semi-skilled (mostly urban) employment, Cosatu took aim at claims that the growth of the bio-fuels industry would result in job shedding in the petrol refining sector (in the region of 5 000 jobs) and job creation in the bio-fuels production and agricultural sectors (in the region of 12 000 and 48 000 jobs respectively) (Cosatu, 2007: 7). For Cosatu, the loss of skilled, better-paid jobs for the sake of employment creation in the agricultural sector 'earning lower incomes and having less formal skills' was unacceptable (2007: 7). The key bone of contention, however, was not the future bio-fuels industry *per se* but rather the broader ideological foundations underpinning the Mbeki administration's attachment to free market orthodoxy and the lack of consultation with labour unions in the development of policy. Although the draft strategy did in fact recommend an explicitly developmental role for the state, complete with price regulations and market protection, it would appear that, for Cosatu , its recommendations were not developmental *enough* or rather that the draft strategy promoted the *wrong kind* of development. The submission noted that, 'proposals that underscore a ' profits before people' and a trickle-down approach to job creation, at the mercy and whims of market forces, should be rejected with contempt' (2007: 5).

Considering the scale of investment in bio-fuels, it is understandable that the international furore around bio-fuels and food prices and the campaigning of local NGOs, activist groups and trade unions was cause for serious concern among domestic bio-fuels industry lobbyists. The challenge posed by food security campaigners and activists needed to be met with an effective and determined response. The prominent Southern African Bio-fuels Association (SABA) was eager to quash suspicions that the growth in the country's bio-fuels industry would contribute to rising food prices. In a briefing paper released in late 2007, SABA expressed concern at the way the media often misrepresented the issue, creating an unwarranted negative discourse around bio-fuels and noting that, 'many of these articles are pure hype, many simply copying the others' ideas'– a clear swipe at the way many domestic activists simply appropriated the terms of the international 'food versus fuel debate' (SABA, 2007: 12). In the paper, SABA pointed to a combination of factors contributing to higher agricultural commodity prices, including lower opening agricultural stocks (owing to policy changes in the EU and US); increased demand from China and India; widespread drought in the region; as well as market inefficiencies in South Africa to explain that year's rise in food prices (SABA 2007: 12). It explained that, because the country's commercial maize farmers received no subsidies to help them weather low commodity prices (unlike their counterparts in the EU and

US), maize prices in South Africa tended to be highly sensitive to supply and demand signals. By establishing a supportive incentive dispensation for bio-fuels, so the argument went, demand for maize would increase to approximately twelve million tonnes, which would, in the long run, stabilise maize prices (SABA, 2007: 15). Far from being the underlying cause of rising food prices, SABA argued that bio-fuels would, in fact, *improve* food security.

Similar arguments were put forward by Agriculture South Africa (AgriSA), an organisation representing commercial farmers. At the October 2007 meeting of the presidential agricultural working group in Pretoria, the lobby group had hoped to seek assurances from President Mbeki concerning the protection and support of the domestic bio-fuels industry. Another commercial farmers' organisation, Grain South Africa (Grain SA), in their official submission on the draft strategy, further emphasised how the growth of the South African bio-fuels industry would assist the country to tackle climate change and to achieve better energy security (at the time, oil prices were on the rise) (Grain SA, 2008: 2). The bulk of the submission, however, argued for greater flexibility in bio-fuel markets and improved incentives to attract potential investors. Whether or not these arguments had any effect would soon be made apparent.

THE BIO-FUELS INDUSTRIAL STRATEGY

Following the close of the official submissions process at the end of March, both pro and anti bio-fuels groups waited in earnest to hear the final outcome of the cabinet's deliberations, the product of which would be the final bio-fuels industrial strategy. Given the local and international furore surrounding bio-fuels and the intense campaigning from lobby groups from both sides of the debate, it was not surprising that the cabinet took some time to finalise its position. Although the final strategy was due to be announced by the end of June, this deadline was extended until October, and then again to December (*Engineering News*, 3 April 2007).[7] The 'food versus fuel' debate as it played out in South Africa not only represented an example of how the global discourse around bio-fuels debate translated into a domestic political context; it also shows how local actors appropriated the issue to express their own particular sector interests and concerns. This engagement on the part of civil society had a decisive, if uneven, effect on the final strategy document, as discussed below.

The bio-fuels industrial strategy, when it was released, represented a drastic departure from the government's earlier ambitions. Far from providing the financial incentives and regulatory support needed to stimulate the industry and guarantee minimal returns for investors, the government dramatically scaled back its support for the sector, much to the chagrin of the bio-fuels industry lobby. This retreat from the draft strategy's more supportive approach was clearly expressed in three key policy changes: (1) *The liberalisation of bio-fuels* uptake: from recommending that bio-fuels uptake be made a condition for the issuing of petroleum licences, the final strategy recommended that mandatory blending not be introduced, at least during the initial phases of the strategy's implementation; (2) *Reduction in market penetration target*: the official target market share for bio-fuels of the domestic liquid fuels market was revised down from 4.5 per cent to 2 per cent; (3) *Exclusion of maize*: maize was effectively banned from the bundle of feedstocks allowed for the production of bioethanol. Other changes included an increase in the exemption from the fuel tax levied on biodiesel and a (largely rhetorical) reorientation of the strategy's stated objectives from pursuing 'multiple' agendas (for example, job creation and energy security) to a more limited focus on poverty reduction and rural development. On the one hand, these changes illustrate how the food versus fuel debate was influencing policy making at a national level, something that represented a significant victory for civil society campaigners. On the other, the government's restrained regulatory and incentives regime for bio-fuels meant that AsgiSA's broader rural development aims, specifically those pertaining to employment creation and support for emerging farmers, were compromised.

Significantly reworked and reworded, the final strategy reflected a number of specific concerns raised by civil society groups during the consultation process. These include crucial issues relating to food prices and food security as well as more sector-specific concerns to do with the impact of the industry on poor farmers' access to land and the nature of the contractual arrangements guiding the interaction between farmers and wholesalers (South Africa, 2007: 15–18). However, rather than address these concerns head-on through clearly articulated regulatory interventions, the policy solutions suggested could at best be described as *laissez faire*.

First, as far as land rights were concerned, the strategy merely stated that the promotion of a bio-fuels industry in the country would assist land reform and restitution programmes 'by providing sustainable market access for farmers who benefit from these programmes' (South Africa, 2007: 15). Although emerging farmers would benefit from development projects run by state-owned enterprises (for example, the bio-fuel projects planned by the IDC and CEF), which could adopt a more 'directed' approach to feedstock procurement, the strategy did not explain how the creation of additional markets would benefit those potential land-reform beneficiaries without prior access to land. Nor indeed did it explain how present land-reform beneficiaries without adequate access to capital, or those small-scale farmers who struggled to produce a marketable surplus, would benefit from a now very limited bioethanol market. Moreover, with the reduction of financial incentives and state protection as articulated in the final strategy, it became uncertain whether the bio-fuels industry would in fact be able to create these additional markets in the first place.

Second, the way the strategy addressed the issue of contractual arrangements between farmers and wholesalers evinced a similarly 'hands off approach', papering over civil society concerns about the fairness of these contracts by presenting the mere existence of a market for feedstock contracts as a universal good (South Africa, 2007: 18). Concerns to do with the dominance of a small number of multinational corporations in the agricultural technology and supplies sector and the potential for the increased distribution of GM seed varieties (and the charge that this would result in the subsequent contamination of local plant populations) were not addressed. The impact of the reduced market penetration target on employment creation was similarly avoided. Despite having been one of the key points of reference for both the bio-fuels task team and the draft strategy (which predicted the creation of 55 000 jobs), estimations of net employment creation were conspicuously absent in the final strategy. The only quantifiable reference was the assertion that the fifty per cent bio-diesel fuel levy reduction would translate into 'R15 000 per job' (2007: 21). With the government's retreat from its earlier 'developmental' bio-fuels dispensation to a deregulated policy regime in which private sector participation in the industry seemed less secure, the prospects for large-scale employment creation in the bio-fuels refining sector appeared slim – and employment creation in the agricultural sector was set back by the fact that the small bio-fuels industry, such as it was, was unlikely to create additional demand for new sources of feedstocks (contemporary surpluses being more than adequate). It was therefore improbable that the final strategy would result in any sizeable increase in rural employment figures (2007: 21).

Nevertheless, the dropping of mandatory bio-fuels uptake and blending by petroleum wholesalers, the reduction of the bio-fuels market penetration target and, especially, the exclusion of maize from the bundle of feedstocks allowed for bio-fuels production, was a significant coup for the anti bio-fuels lobby. Their articulation of the global anti bio-fuels discourse at forums such as the civil society workshop in Durban, and their subsequent lobbying during the draft strategy submissions process – resonating as it did with the domestic food crisis – had had a powerful effect. At a press conference to launch the new strategy at the Union Buildings in Pretoria, Buyelwa Sonjika, minister for Minerals and Energy, made it clear that food security concerns were behind the government's decision to reconsider its bio-fuels ambitions. In response to a question about the viability of a future bio-fuels industry in South Africa, given the minimal incentive regime, Sonjika hinted at both local and global negative discourses regarding bio-fuels and food security.

> 'It's not only South Africa that has concerns about food security for this program. So we had to … we had to respond positively to that. But also, I mean, in a way accommodating that concern. Hence we also decided to exclude maize as a crop for feed stock. So it is really mainly about food security, that's the main reason why we decided to drop. I agree, the percentage is a little bit small. We should be a little bit more ambitious if we wanted to make an impact' (Sonjika, 2007).

The response from representatives of the bio-fuels industry and commercial agriculture, however, ranged from disappointment to plain surprise. The retreat by the government from a regulated, developmental bio-fuels policy to one that offered little in terms of market protection or subsidies had a negative impact on the industry's future growth prospects. For industry lobbyists and investors who had committed time and money on promoting bio-fuels to the government and the general public, these developments were cause for serious concern. With the narrow market envisaged in the final strategy at only two per cent of the liquid fuels market, they had good reason to be worried. The very future of private sector participation in bio-fuels production was rendered uncertain. The journalist Martin Creamer, for instance, reported in *Engineering News* that, 'at the two per cent level, only the Central Energy Fund and Industrial Development Corporation projects could be accommodated' (*Engineering News*, 12 December 2007). Compared to South Africa's foreign competitors, the lack of subsidies and support certainly ruled out the possibility of the domestic bioethanol industry producing for export. In a working document compiled for the International Institute for Environment and Development in the wake of the announcement of the final strategy, it was found that 'given the disparity between the level of support for the South African bioethanol sector and that received in potential export markets for South Africa, it is not surprising that the focus of the emerging bioethanol industry in South Africa is firmly on the domestic market'.[8]

The bio-fuels industry lobby was equally stunned at the exclusion of maize from the feedstocks available for bio-fuel production. SABA had been sure that their arguments in favour of maize during the draft consultation process had paid off. For commercial and emerging farmers alike, the exclusion of maize sank any ambitions they had had for a larger, more stable domestic market. SABA's president, Andrew Makenete, lamented that 'maize presents the greatest opportunity. Its exclusion came to us as an absolute surprise and shock' (cited in *Engineering News*, 12 December 2007). Moreover, the exclusion of maize appeared to contradict much of the evidence the bio-fuels lobby had presented in forums such as the presidential agricultural working group. Although it could not be guaranteed that the country would produce a large surplus year on year (owing to unpredictable external shocks such as drought), in an average year South Africa's maize farmers could be expected to produce a healthy surplus of three million tons over and above the eight million tons consumed locally – enough to comfortably accommodate the bio-fuels industry while also ensuring food security (Cartwright 2007: 52). Their arguments also billed maize as a particularly suitable crop for ethanol production owing to its high starch content and the drought resistance of modern varieties (*Engineering News*, 12 December 2007).

These arguments fell on deaf ears. The fall-out from the maize decision was felt most keenly in Bothaville in the Free State, at the multi-billion rand bioethanol plant that had until only recently presented itself as a development panacea for the region, 'one of the largest operations of its kind in Africa' (*southafrica.info*, 12 December 2005). Two years on and the plant was yet to be completed – its key financial backers having lost interest – while the exclusion of the region's primary feedstock, maize, meant the project was rendered all but unworkable (*Business Day*, 19 September 2008).

AFTER THE FOOD PRICE CRISIS

Almost immediately, those with a stake in the re-inclusion of maize began to lobby the minister of Agriculture and Land Affairs, Lulu Xingwana, to persuade Cabinet to review its decision. Barely days after the release of the final strategy, representatives from Grain SA, AgriSA and Nafu met with Xingwana at her office in Pretoria to reiterate their case

for the re-inclusion of maize in the bundle of feedstocks available for bioethanol production. The minister appeared to welcome their arguments, noting the possibility for the
future inclusion of maize was there, provided that farmers could produce a sizeable
surplus so as to placate the food security concerns of the cabinet (South Africa, 2007).
What ensued, however, was a veritable see-saw of policy statements and retractions, with
government appearing to simultaneously endorse the reconsideration of the maize decision while denying it in public. Following media speculation that the government was
open to reconsidering its decision – speculation that was heartily encouraged by Grain
SA – the Department of Agriculture and Land Affairs released a statement maintaining,
in no uncertain terms, that 'at no stage during the discussions did Minister Xingwana
commit government to reconsider maize for bio-fuel production. This is solely a decision
to be determined by Cabinet' (Press release: 11 January 2008).

The prospect of a policy overhaul seemed even less likely after the new president,
Kgalema Motlanthe, took office. At an African Peer Review Forum in Benin in October
2008, Motlanthe warned that the promotion of bio-fuels could exacerbate problems of
'land hunger' in Africa which would translate into less land available for food production
(*Sapa*, 27 October 2008). The following month, however, the government appeared to
have again changed its tune. Although no explicit statements were made regarding the
future inclusion of maize in the bundle of feedstocks available for bio-fuel production,
the Department of Minerals and Energy let it be known that they were reviewing the
'finer details' of the incentive regime and pointed to the possibility of increasing the fuel
levy exemption for bio-fuel producers to 100 per cent, as well as additional import and
tax incentives (*Engineering News*, 21 November 2008). The cabinet reshuffle following the
inauguration of Jacob Zuma as president in 2009 created further momentum for a reconsideration of the country's bio-fuels strategy. The new minister of Agriculture, Forestry
and Fisheries, Tina Joemat-Pettersson, adopted a conciliatory approach to commercial
farmers in general, and the bio-fuels sector and maize-producing sectors in particular. In
a speech to the Agri SA Congress in Muldersdrift in early October 2010, she stated that:

> 'Agriculture is undertaken in the context of new possibilities. It is no longer only about
> food. It is also about energy. That is why the government supports green industries
> and especially their ability to create jobs. This includes a move towards renewable
> energy and bio-fuels' (Joemat-Pettersson, 2010).

Joematt-Pettersson departed from the former minister's position by emphasising that
food security was affected by 'complex global realities' and was not a simple matter of
'food versus fuel'.[9] Her case for reviewing the lukewarm 2007 bio-fuels industrial strategy
was assisted by the fact that 2009–2010 registered South Africa's largest maize crop
(12.8 million tonnes) in over thirty years, up six per cent from the previous season
(*Business Report*, 10 February 2010). Food security was not going to excite public opinion
the way it did in 2007. Equally significant for the industry's prospects was the role outlined
for bio-fuels in minister of Economic Development Ebrahim Patel's New Growth Path

(NGP), an overarching economic development strategy designed to replace the Mbeki-era AsgiSA programme, which had since fallen out of favour. Presented to the public on 26 October after a specially convened cabinet meeting, the NGP took as its point of reference the creation of five million new jobs by 2020 'through various initiatives across the economy'(*Business Day*, 3 December 2010). It identified a number of key 'job drivers', including infrastructure development; South Africa's core economic sectors of agriculture, mining, manufacturing, tourism and services; green and knowledge economy jobs; employment opportunities arising from investing in social capital; and initiatives that support rural and African regional development (*Engineering News*, 23 November 2010). Importantly, it emphasises coordination and linkage between these sectors to achieve specific objectives, such as using the development of new 'green industries' – for example, bio-fuels – to simultaneously diversify the country's energy portfolio while creating jobs and expanding opportunities for local business procurement (South Africa, 2010).[10] Though this would appear to herald a reconsideration of the current incentives regime for the industry, a revised bio-fuels industrial strategy has yet to be drafted.

CONCLUSION

The 'food versus fuel debate' provides critical insights into how the negative international discourse concerning the relationship between bio-fuels and food price increases was expressed in a national context. It reveals how this controversial issue was interpreted and acted upon by a number of competing interest groups, including representatives from the state, business and civil society. In policy terms, the outcome of this public participations process, and the strident advocacy that accompanied it, was mixed. Bio-fuels industry lobbyists received more incentives than had existed before, but not to a degree that would enable them to compete internationally. Civil society activists ensured that the country's main food crop, maize, was dropped from the list of available feedstocks, but the reduced incentives regime also meant that many rural development projects were now no longer viable. Despite this, the avid campaigning that accompanied the development of South Africa's bio-fuels policy provides clear evidence of a vibrant culture of public participation and open debate in South Africa. This is a positive sign, but the ultimate effectiveness of civil society in influencing policy outcomes in this sphere must surely be qualified by the Zuma administration's renewed commitment to green technologies, and bio-fuels in particular. Whether the future of the bio-fuels industry in South Africa will be determined by international opinion, industry lobbying, civil society activism, or next year's agricultural statistics, remains to be seen.

NOTES

1   The Kyoto Protocol is an international agreement linked to the United Nations Framework Convention on Climate Change. Although it does not oblige developing (non-Annex 1) countries such

as South Africa to reduce their greenhouse gas emissions, it does create financial incentives for them to do so through the trading of certified emission reductions (CERs). This is known as carbon trading. See United Nations (1998) The Kyoto Protocol to the United Nations Framework Convention on Climate Change. Formulated at the World Summit on Sustainable Development in 2002, the Johannesburg Plan of Implementation committed the South African government to develop renewable energy technologies, including transport-related renewable energy sources such as bio-fuels. See United Nations (2002) Plan of Implementation of the World Summit on Sustainable Development. See also South Africa (2006) Draft Bio-fuels Industrial Strategy of the Republic of South Africa.

2   Past ANC policy held that small-scale farming had been neglected in the past and that support for a more diversified agricultural sector could 'make an important contribution to the efficiency and sustainability of agriculture and to employment creation'. See African National Congress (1994) Agricultural Policy.

3   The Basic Fuel Price is an import parity price used to determine the price of fuel in South Africa. See South Africa (2006) National bio-fuels study: An investigation into the feasibility of establishing a bio-fuels industry in the Republic of South Africa: vii–viii.

4   Note that these figures are slightly higher than the average food price increase quoted in the Draft Strategy.

5   It has been noted elsewhere that the relative smallness and undeveloped state of the South African bio-fuels industry at the time meant that links drawn between bio-fuels production and food price increases in South Africa were unwarranted. Cartwright (2007) notes that, 'these increases should not be linked to the influence of South Africa's bio-ethanol sector, which barely exists'. Biofuels trade and sustainable development: An analysis of South African bio-ethanol. Working Document, International Institute for Environment and Development: 43. On the other hand, because only fifteen per cent of agricultural land in South Africa is arable, any conversion from food crops to non-food bio-fuel feedstocks such as jatropha, switchgrass or miscanthus (used in production of second-generation bio-fuels) would have to be approached with caution. See UN (2009) Environmental Statistics Country Snapshot: South Africa.

6   A fairly obtuse example of how some NGOs co-opted the momentum behind the anti-bio-fuels movement is provided by Timberwatch, an alliance of NGOs concerned with the negative social and environmental impacts of timber plantations. In their statement submitted at the Durban conference they noted that 'similar government plans to allow the timber industry to appropriate large tracts of Eastern Cape community land for growing industrial tree plantations would compound the negative impacts of the crazy bio-fuels strategy if it was ever implemented'. See Proceedings from Civil Society Workshop to Critically Assess and Respond to the SA Biofuels Strategy 2007 Additional Statements: 6.

7   See also Spadavecchia O (2007) Bio-fuels plan should be finalised by end of October. *Engineering News*, 28 September and Hill M (2007) Final bio-fuels strategy handed to cabinet, *Engineering News*, 6 November.

8   The document noted that the estimated production cost of South African bioethanol (between US$ 0.41 and 0.46) compares unfavourably with Brazil (between US$ 0.23 and 0.27), Thailand (between US$ 0.29 and 0.45) and Australia (between US$ 0.23 and 0.38) See Cartwright A (2007) Bio-fuels trade and sustainable development: An analysis of South African bio-ethanol. Working Document. International Institute for Environment and Development: 28–29.

9   Though she cautioned though that the development of a national bio-fuels industry 'requires a national spatial plan to ensure that food is consumed closer to the point of consumption and that the bio-fuels are also cultivated as close as possible to the point of processing and refinement. This would result in 'a reduction in the cost of food and less gas emissions'. See South Africa (2010) Address by Minister of Agriculture, Forestry and Fisheries Tina Joemat-Pettersson on the occasion of the AgriSA Congress.

10   Green industries received a further boost with the announcement during President Zuma's 2011 State of the Nation address of a R20 billion investment scheme aimed at promoting the national industrial policy objectives outlined in the NGP and the industrial policy action plan. See Ensor L (2011) Zuma highlights old jobs plan in speech, *Business Day*, 14 February.

REFERENCES

African Centre for Biosafety (2007) Proceedings from civil society workshop to critically assess and respond to the SA bio-fuels strategy: Sign-on statement.

African Centre for Biosafety (2007) Proceedings from civil society workshop to critically assess and respond to the SA bio-fuels strategy: Additional statement.

African National Congress (1994) Agricultural Policy.

Business Day (February 2007 to February 2011).

Cartwright A (2007) Bio-fuels trade and sustainable development: An analysis of South African bio-ethanol. Working Document. International Institute for Environment and Development.

Cosatu (2007) Submission on the Draft Bio-fuels Industrial Strategy of South Africa.

Davenport R and C Saunders (2000) *South Africa: A Modern History*. London: Macmillan.

Der Spiegel (April 2007 to April 2008).

Earth Harmony (2007) Durban bio-fuels workshop submission.

Engineering News (May 2006 to November 2008).

Food and Agriculture Organisation (2007) Committee on World Food Security: Assessment of the world food security situation, thirty-third session.

Food and Agriculture Organisation (2008) Food, Energy and Climate: A New Equation, 2007–2008.

Grain South Africa (2008) Comment: Draft Bio-Fuels Industrial Strategy.

The Guardian (August to November 2007).

Joemat-Pettersson T (2010) Address by Minister of Agriculture, Forestry and Fisheries on the occasion of the AgricSA Congress.

Lemmer W (2009) Interview on 16 January with W Lemmer, Senior Economist at Grain South Africa.

Lodge T (2001) *Politics in South Africa: From Mandela to Mbeki*. Cape Town: David Philip.

Mather C and S Greenberg (2003) Market liberalisation in post-apartheid South Africa, *Journal of Southern African Studies* 29 (2): 394.

Mtembu N (2009) Interview on 31 March 2009.

Nafu Farmer (April 2007).

National Agricultural Marketing Council (2007) Media release: Food price trends, July 2006 to July 2007.

Mail & Guardian (August 2010).

Mayet M (2007) Opening Pandora's box: GMOs, fuelish paradigms and South Africa's bio-fuels strategy. Briefing Paper. African Centre for Biosafety.

Sapa (from 1 January 2007 to October 2008).

Sonjica B (2007) Transcript of post-cabinet media briefing on Electricity Master Plan and Bio-fuels Strategy.

South Africa (2005) Keynote speech by Minister of Minerals and Energy, Lindiwe Hendricks at Nafcoc Annual Conference.

South Africa (2006) Accelerated and Shared Growth Initiative for South Africa.

South Africa (2006b) Draft Bio-fuels Industrial Strategy of the Republic of South Africa.

South Africa (2006c) National bio-fuels study: An investigation into the feasibility of establishing a bio-fuels industry in the Republic of South Africa.

South Africa (2006) Background document, media briefing by Deputy President Phumzile Mlambo-Ngcuka

South Africa (2007) Department of Agriculture and Land Affairs press release: Door not closed for the production of bio-ethanol from maize, 14 December.

South Africa (2009) Abstract of Agricultural Statistics.

South Africa (2010) The New Growth Path: The Framework.

South Africa (2010) Cabinet statement on the new growth path.

South Africa (2010) The New Growth Path: The Framework.

South African Bio-fuels Association (2007) The impact of bio-fuel production on food security.

Sugrue A and R Douthwaite (2007) Regional Hunger and Vulnerability Programme. Wahenga Brief

United Nations (1998) The Kyoto Protocol to the United Nations Framework Convention on Climate Change.

United Nations (2002) Plan of Implementation of the World Summit on Sustainable Development.

MEDIA

4

Media transformation and the right to know

Devan Pillay

The chapters in this section address a key issue facing our country – media transformation – in the context of a perceived attack on the freedom of expression and access to information which form the bedrock of democratic rights.

Three proposed measures by the ruling party and government have raised alarm: the Protection of Information Bill, which threatens to undermine the laudable Promotion of Access to Information legislation, passed more than a decade ago, by blocking access to information that could expose corruption or negligence by government officials; the Media Appeals Tribunal, an ANC proposal to replace media self-regulation with a state-appointed body that has much stronger punitive powers, including imprisoning journalists; and a proposal to centralise all government advertising, which can be used to punish media that cast government in a bad light. Taken together, these proposals are ominous, and have given rise to the Right2Know campaign, an impressive array of civil society organisations that has the support of Cosatu as well as prominent individuals such as former minister of Intelligence, Ronnie Kasrils. Cosatu also directly partici-pates in another civil society initiative, the SOS: Support Public Broadcasting Coalition which, as Kate Skinner discusses in this section, has played a critical role in trying to ensure that the public broadcaster meets its obligations to inform and educate the country's citizens.

Media transformation is directly linked to the democratic principle of access to information, encapsulated by the public's right to know about what happens in government and in private corporations that has a direct impact on their daily lives as workers, consumers and citizens. It goes to the heart of questions of power – of those in positions of authority who usually prefer to limit access to information that might undermine their power. The mass media play a critical role in giving the public access to information and knowledge by, *inter alia*, exposing corrupt practices, negligence and incompetence, and allowing the public to hold governments and corporations to account for their actions.

In this sense, the narrow practice of 'transformation' in South Africa as increased racial (and, to a lesser extent, gender) representivity, does address some concerns about media imbalances as they relate to the white male power structure that characterised media ownership and control under apartheid.

However, as Jane Duncan points out, 'transformation' in South Africa has always meant something deeper – in addition to race and gender, it has to address the fundamental issue of class and market power, and not only in terms of representivity in ownership and control, but most crucially in the content of what media put out. It is one thing to have unions owning large chunks of media enterprises, which might generate revenue for workers' pension funds, for example, but this does not in itself mean that the content of the newspaper will change to reflect working-class concerns, if such change is perceived to 'threaten' the advertising revenue of that publication or TV station, and hence the returns on the unions' investments.

Similarly, a democratically elected government is no guarantee that the public broadcaster will remain independent and report fearlessly on issues affecting those with power. Governments everywhere have an interest in restricting access to information that could potentially embarrass them, just as do private companies that directly own media, or who are major advertisers in public or private media. The powerful will use whatever leverage they have to influence the media, unless there are clear checks and balances within individual media entities – as well as the entire media system – that allow maximum access to information and the proliferation of ideas (within the ambit of normal laws of society that restrict harmful behaviour, such as incitement to murder, and hate speech).

Like most countries, South Africa has three essential strands within its body politic that simultaneously complement and compete with each other in response to the balance of forces in society. These are the market-liberal (or market-centric), the statist-authoritarian (or state-centric) and the substantive-democratic (or society-centric) strands of discourse and practice. As the chapters in this section show, these strands feature prominently in the recent history of media transformation in South Africa, in both the broadcast and print media environments.

During the heady days of the 1990s, when the ANC began formulating its media policies, a substantive-democratic perspective was arguably dominant. The idea gained ground that the media should be as diverse as possible, and composed of three tiers – public media, non-profit community media and private commercial media. Most crucially, the SABC should become a *public* (that is, society-centric) as opposed to a *state* broadcaster – meaning complete editorial independence from both government and private interests. This could only be achieved through a secure funding stream, for example from licence fees, following the BBC model. The experiences of northern Europe, however, suggest that media diversity should be secured through limitations on private media ownership and through funding mechanisms to support community media serving a wide range of interests, in particular those in working-class communities that lack a voice in the public sphere.

In keeping with the broader realities of post-apartheid transformation, the forces of the market and the state soon overwhelmed the society-oriented, substantive-democratic perspective. Media transformation occurred mainly through the market mechanism, as the SABC sold off many of its radio stations, and the print media became less white and male dominated. The Media Development and Diversity Agency (MDDA), finally established in 2000 after protracted negotiations between government, the commercial media and the community media sector, was limited in its scope and by lack of funding to have any meaningful effect on the media landscape.

If socio-political news became more diversified, economic journalism remained firmly within the ambit of a narrow, orthodox free-market perspective. Diversity of opinion on the economy remains extremely limited, occasionally punctuated by the heterodox views of the labour movement, often cast in a negative light. In general, cost-cutting in the media, as researchers point out, has brought about lower standards of journalism, including 'the juniorisation of newsrooms, increased inaccuracies creeping into stories and poor journalistic standards' (*Mail & Guardian,* 17–23 June 2011).

The Right2Know campaign has also raised alarm about the increased concentration of media, which has a negative effect on diversity and the free flow of information. As Duncan points out, if the private media are to ward off threats to media freedom by government, it must seriously consider a transformation charter that goes way beyond narrow BEE criteria and addresses blockages to media diversity, as well as the insulation of journalists from commercial and political pressures.

As far as broadcast media are concerned, a new opportunity has opened up in the form of the broadcasting policy review process. Civil society activists are poised to push for a new vision for public broadcasting, including a new public funding model for both the SABC and community media.

True transformation in the private and public media has to be society-focused, to serve, in the first instance, the needs of democracy as opposed to the state or the market. Only concerted civil society activism will ensure that.

CHAPTER 17

The print media transformation dilemma

Jane Duncan

In 2010, legal academic Pierre de Vos argued that 'transformation' had become an empty and hollow word devoid of any meaning, captive to an elite (black and white) which, in reality, actually fears the real and deep transformation that would threaten their grip on wealth. De Vos went on to argue: 'Maybe we should ban anyone from using the word and find new words to talk about the need to change this country' (De Vos, 2010). Critics of the 'T' word, including De Vos, have directed much of their ire at black economic empowerment (BEE) as a driver of transformation. Since 2008, prominent public intellectuals, including President Jacob Zuma, have criticised BEE's tendency to empower the few while failing to raise the living standards of the many (see Lindsay in this volume; Cargill, 2010; Mbeki, 2011; SAPA, 2011). Transformation has also been criticised as a veil behind which the ruling African National Congress (ANC) hides an intention to extend its control over all aspects of state and society. But dismissing the term outright is not an option either, as it could allow existing power relations to remain unchallenged. In the absence of an alternative word, the challenge for all those committed to a true transformative vision is to struggle for a definition of transformation that captures this vision, rather than one which allows racial apartheid to be replaced by class apartheid.

Print media transformation, or the lack thereof, became a particularly contentious issue from 2009 onwards, fuelling suspicions in media circles that the 'T' word had reared its head because newspapers were being rather too effective in exposing the shenanigans of the (mainly black) elite, and the ANC wanted to reign them in.[1] Yet, there are clearly substantial concerns about the extent of print media transformation. According to a research report into print media ownership and control, commissioned by the Media Development and Diversity Agency (MDDA) in 2009, 'in post 1994 South Africa, the print media landscape has not transformed much in terms of ownership and control and is still majority owned and controlled by white shareholders. In spite of various interventions by the state through promotion of transformation processes and BEE, the majority of print media in South Africa is still owned or dominated by a few companies and individuals' (MDDA, 2009). Two related but distinct issues emerge here: the lack of racial transformation of ownership, and the lack of diversity in the print media.

The ANC has also repeatedly berated the print media for a lack of transformation, and has argued that the broadcast media are much more diverse and representative of the demographics of the country than the print media, owing to the fact that the former is state regulated, whereas where media houses have concluded BEE transactions these have not necessarily translated into a diversity of views, underlying the fact that advertising profiles and key management positions remain largely the same (ANC, 2010a). The ANC has argued, further, that white dominance, coupled with insufficient diversity, has created a mismatch between the values espoused in the media (especially the print media) and the values promoted by the ANC, including a commitment to a developmental state, collective rights, the values of a caring and sharing community, solidarity, ubuntu, non-sexism, and working together. According to the ANC, the mainstream media's ideological outlook includes, on the contrary, a commitment to neoliberalism, a weak and passive state and an overemphasis on individual rights and market fundamentalism (ANC, 2010a).

The ANC's discontent with the print media led to its calling for a parliamentary investigation into the 'transformation of the print media in respect of a BEE media charter, ownership and control, advertising and marketing and the desirability of the establishment of a media accountability mechanism, for example the Media Appeals Tribunal' (ANC, 2010b). The ANC has expressed particular ire at the Press Council of South Africa, and the Press Ombudsman's office, arguing that they are inherently biased towards the media industry, and that an independent but statutory tribunal was needed to protect basic human rights. However, more recently, the ANC's spokesperson, Jackson Mthembu, has stated that the parliamentary investigation, and the possible establishment of the tribunal, will be put on hold 'to give the media an opportunity to transform themselves' (Rossouw, 2011). The ANC has called on the Competition Commission to investigate what it termed 'the anti-competitive dynamics in the print media value chain, that is paper, printing, publishing, distribution and advertising' (SAPA, 2010). The South African Communist Party (SACP) has also criticised print media transformation, stating that the sector lacks linguistic diversity and is dominated by liberal interests, and has urged parliament to investigate 'the idea of a media tribunal as well as other transformation interventions for media diversity' (SACP, 2010).

This chapter will assess these arguments. Its main focus will be on newspapers, rather than on other sections of the print media such as magazines and books, as the controversies have focused in the main on newspaper content. It will consider some of the historical debates over the definition of transformation in the media, the print media sector status quo, their BEE credentials, changes in ownership, control and content, and will also include an assessment of the extent to which the newspaper industry has actually transformed.

RACE OR CLASS? EARLIER MEDIA TRANSFORMATION DEBATES

At the turn of the millennium, there was a lively and at times fractious debate about the extent of media transformation. Ruth Teer-Tomaselli and Keyan Tomaselli (2001) surveyed media transformation from 1994 to 2000, and argued that while significant changes had taken place in the racial composition of media ownership, class continuity was also evident. In response, Guy Berger argued (2001) that the changes to media ownership between 1994 and 2000 were, in fact, much more significant than the Tomasellis were willing to admit. Entirely new owners, drawn from the trade unions, women's movement and the development sector, had secured stakes in the media, and the emphasis on class as the most substantial concern in media transformation had led to these significant changes being undervalued (Berger, 2001). He further likened media transformation to a glass of water, which could be considered 'admirably half-full' or 'disappointingly half-empty, depending on whether one looks at the past or the future. But it indisputably contains a lot more liquid than it did before 1994' (Berger, 2001: 164).

At the time, Berger also argued for a definition that assessed the extent to which the media's normative role in deepening democracy was enhanced. This involved four elements: an assessment of the transformation of the legal environment, from a controlling one to one which allowed the media to play its democratic role unfettered by controls; changes to media ownership and control to facilitate socio-economic transformation; changes in the demographics of media to better reflect the country's racial and gender demographics; changes in content to reflect the transition to democracy and the diversity of opinion; and changes in media consumption patterns away from racially divided audiences and towards cross-racial media consumption (Berger, 1999: 82–116).

In this foundational debate, disagreements emerged about the definition of transformation. Ron Krabill and Mashilo Boloka disputed what they felt to be Berger's overemphasis on race as an indicator of transformation, which they felt all too easily lapsed into an approach that emphasised racial substitution. Successful transformation, they argued, would be achieved when the media 'reflects, in its ownership, staffing *and* product, the society within which it operates, not only in terms of race, but also socio-economic status, gender, religion, sexual orientation, region, language, etc. This is only possible if access is opened – again in ownership, staffing, and product – not only to the emerging black elite, but also to grassroots communities of all colours' (Krabill and Boloka, 2000:

76). Berger, in turn, censured them for underplaying the significance of greater racial representivity in media institutions, and argued that all tiers of society benefit from this 'transformation at the top' (Berger, 2000: 90–97).

Since these debates, the academy has largely withdrawn from engaging in general assessments of the state of media transformation, and as a result there is insufficient research that either validates or dispels the ANC's own assessment. But it has become apparent through its practices in government that the ANC has aligned itself with an understanding of transformation that emphasises racial transformation, while the definition articulated by Krabill and Boloka places greater emphasis on the need to overcome the class divide in the media and to encourage a diversity of voices. This argument, and the implications of this truncation of media transformation, will be fleshed out in the rest of this chapter.

AN OVERVIEW OF THE PRINT MEDIA SECTOR

The newspaper industry is highly susceptible to concentration. Owning several newspapers allows owners to bring the first copy costs of newspaper production down through bulk discounts that are not easily achieved by smaller competitors. Market power can also be leveraged to raise the profiles of all the newspapers in the group, procure advertising for them and distribute their products more cost-effectively. Large media groups are often vertically integrated, owning their own printing presses and distribution agencies, and are also susceptible to conglomeration, offering content across several platforms to maximise exploitation of the content. Media concentration and conglomeration are growing features of contemporary society, and South Africa is no exception to this general trend. Concentration is often considered by critical theorists, especially those in the critical political economy tradition, to be socially detrimental as it can lead to a reduction in the plurality of media outlets and diversity of opinion, the homogenisation of media content, the prioritisation of the views of an elite minority, and the dominance of commercial interests over the public interest; all these negative effects can result in a poorly informed public (Curran, 1991: 82–117; McChesney, 1999; Golding and Murdock, 1991: 15–32). Furthermore, if media owners do attempt to censor editorial content, then the risks of a misinformed public are profound, whereas the existence of a plurality of ownership mitigates this risk (The Australian Collaboration, n.d.). In South Africa, media concentration and conglomeration have taken on a racial dimension as well, as these tendencies make it more difficult for people – such as black people and women – who have historically been locked out of the market to gain access to it as barriers to entry are higher than in markets with a greater plurality of media and suppliers.

It is difficult to develop standard rules of thumb for measuring levels of concentration in the media sector, as conditions differ from country to country, but several countries are grappling with the need to develop diversity tests, which may include tests for the number of voices in a particular market, or a diversity points system. One approach suggests that if a media organisation commands more than twenty-five per cent of a single media market, then the number of media outlets in a particular market risks falling below the minimum threshold for plurality (Bilir, 2005: 22). France is one of the few countries to have legislated ownership limits for the print media, and has placed a thirty per cent circulation limit on national and regional newspapers (Carls, 2010). Eli Noam has proposed a media concentration measurement tool that defines a market with fewer than four voices,[2] with a market share of twenty per cent each, as being overly concentrated, with an 'out clause' for special circumstances (Noam, 2004).

The South African newspaper market is dominated by one large company, Media24 (owned largely by Naspers), with three smaller companies dominating the rest of the market, namely Independent Newspapers, Avusa Ltd and Caxton. According to the MDDA, Caxton, Media24 and Independent Newspapers own 47.1 per cent of the titles in circulation. Caxton alone owns 28.3 per cent of the total newspaper titles in the country. The other titles in circulation are owned by Avusa and a host of smaller publishers. Newspapers are spread unevenly across the country, with the economic powerhouse of Gauteng accounting for 50.6 per cent of titles, while the Northern Cape and North West have the lowest circulation figures, accounting for 5.6 per cent and 6.8 per cent respectively (MDDA, 2009: 83–85). While the number of radio and television stations has grown since 1991, the number of daily and weekly newspapers has remained fairly static; while some new newspapers have been launched, especially in the tabloid market, others have ceased publication.[3]

Newspapers are still read by a minority of South Africans: according to the South African Advertising Research Foundation (SAARF), 29.2 per cent of adults read daily newspapers, while 34.2 per cent read weekly papers (SAARF, 2010). According to the living standards measurement (LSM), radio has the largest penetration while television and print media tend to prioritise upper working-class and middle-class audiences in LSM 5 and above. Until the recession, South Africa bucked the global trend towards a decline in readership, with tabloids such as the *Daily Sun* introducing new readers to newspapers.

The big-four groups display high levels of vertical and horizontal integration, providing much of their own printing and distribution requirements, as well as those of other print media concerns, and Caxton and Media24 lead the pack in this regard (MDDA, 2009: 103). Media24's newspapers have the largest footprint, followed by Independent Newspapers, Caxton and Avusa. Other newspapers, independent of the four groups, account for a mere twelve per cent of circulation.

While not being nearly as concentrated a market as is Australia's (where two newspaper groups account for over ninety percent of the circulation of daily newspapers), the South African newspaper market is veering dangerously towards excessive concentration, and the dominance of Media24 should be of particular concern, especially given that its parent company repurposes the company's news content for other platforms.

Media24 is owned by multinational multimedia company Naspers, and publishes a range of mainstream dailies and weeklies.[4] Caxton CTP is the second biggest listed

Table 1: Newspaper circulation by owner

Year	Avusa	Caxton	Independent	Media24	Other
Total	133,702,360	135,913,757	204,151,961	376,503,416	98,685,251
Percentage of circulation	14%	14%	21%	39%	12%

Source: MDDA 2009 and own calculations

media company, and publishes 120 regional 'community' newspapers, either on its own or in partnership, plus the *Citizen* newspaper, and magazines. The company also undertakes commercial printing, packaging, and stationery manufacture and undertakes the distribution of its own publications in Gauteng through a network of contract drivers (Caxton CTP, 2010).

The Independent Newspapers Group was established when Independent News and Media PLC – in which Irish businessman Tony O'Reilly is the major shareholder – bought the (then) Argus Newspapers from Johannesburg Consolidated Investments in 1994. It publishes fifteen daily and weekly newspapers, principally in South Africa's main metropolitan areas, and receives about forty-eight per cent of total advertising spend in the paid newspaper market (MDDA, 2009: 40). South Africa has proved to be the most profitable of the regions in which the company has a presence, leading to accusations that it has exported profits to fund its loss-making titles elsewhere, especially in Britain (Motloung, 2009). Yet in spite of the profitability of the South African operation, speculation mounted in July 2009 that O'Reilly would have to sell his South African assets as his company was on the brink of insolvency. O'Reilly' s method of ensuring profitability has been controversial, and Independent Newspapers has been known for practicing 'piranha management' and failing to invest sufficiently in infrastructure, leading to Anton Harber's comment that 'O'Reilly has wreaked havoc and even destruction on South African journalism' (Buffet, 2009; Harber, 2009).

Avusa Ltd, formerly Johnnic Communications, has interests in digital as well as traditional media,[5] and entertainment companies such as NuMetro and Gallo. Through BDFM (*Business Day* and *Financial Mail*), it owns fifty per cent of *Business Day* and the *Financial Mail*, with the other fifty per cent being owned by the Pearson Group. Avusa also has a community newspaper division which publishes nine community newspapers. Avusa' s over-reliance on newspaper revenues, and more specifically advertising revenues, has led to the company's being heavily affected by the recession. According to its 2010 annual report, advertising revenues dropped by seventeen per cent and total circulation declined, leading to the closure of the *Weekender* newspaper, in response to which Avusa has been seeking to diversify its business (Avusa, 2010: 7).

The only national newspapers that are not owned by these four big groups are the *Mail & Guardian* and *The New Age*. The *Mail & Guardian* originally started its life as the independent *Weekly Mail*, but struggled to survive in the tough trading conditions of the South African newspaper market. It was taken over by the Guardian group in

1995, which undoubtedly saved it from closure, and the majority of its shares were then sold to Zimbabwean businessman Trevor Ncube in 2002. The *New Age* was launched in 2010 after a delay in its launch date which precipitated the departure of senior staff after one edition. The newspaper has evoked controversy, as it is owned by the Gupta group, an Indian company with close ties to the ANC, leading to suspicion that the paper was launched to sing the praises of the ruling party – a suspicion that the former editor Henry Jeffries vigorously denied. The ANC has, on numerous occasions, signalled its intention to launch its own newspaper, but has failed to do so, perhaps out of fear of the financial implications, so it remains to be seen whether the *New Age* will become an indirect way of realising this long-held ambition. While it is difficult to make out what sets the paper apart from the mainstream in terms of national coverage, it has taken a courageous editorial decision to devote several pages to regional coverage, in an attempt to redress imbalances in provincial coverage and to realise its ambitious target of servicing an extremely wide LSM group (LSM 4 to 10).

Other newspapers are owned either by regional groups such as Mooivaal Media, Tabloid Media, Sky Blue Media, Capital Media and Zoutnet, or individuals such as Danie O'Reilly, Willie Esterhuysen and Andre Coertzen (MDDA, 2009: 82–83). Many of the smaller regional groups own several titles.

THE STATE OF BROAD-BASED BLACK ECONOMIC EMPOWERMENT IN THE PRINT MEDIA

Following the demise of apartheid, there was a time when print media ownership diversified, as Berger has rightfully pointed out, but many of the early deals that saw ownership being transferred into black hands, as well as to trade unions and women's organisations, unwound because they were financed through debt rather than equity (Duncan, 2000: 34). As a result, black empowerment companies such as Kagiso media, Dynamo and New African Investment Limited and New Africa Publishers that claimed a stake in the print media pie, have withdrawn from the newspaper industry, and the print media industry reconsolidated into the four abovementioned companies. By 2004, broadcasting companies were ahead of print with regards to transformation; Primedia scored the highest points for empowerment, followed by Kagiso media. Johnnic Communications, Avusa's predecessor, scored the lowest, as its main empowerment vehicle, the National Empowerment Consortium, exited from Johnnic in 2003 when market conditions turned against it. By then, Johncom's empowerment shareholding was rated at a mere ten per cent (Newmarch, 2006).

Since the early media transformation efforts, transformation charters have been introduced to commit companies in a particular sector of the economy to achieving a set of goals, usually relating to black participation in the sector. They are largely voluntary in nature (Rumney, 2010). Even more recently, the Department of Trade and Industry has developed generic tools to measure the extent to which black people have been brought into the mainstream of the economy, in the form of broad-based black economic empowerment (B-BBEE) scorecards, which align to the B-BBEE Act' s codes of good practice.

The new B-BBEE scorecards have shifted measurement of empowerment away from ownership only, and identified seven elements of empowerment – ownership, management control, employment equity, skills development, preferential procurement, enterprise development and socio-economic development – which are weighted differently according to their importance (DTI, 2007: 4). Charters would be promulgated as sector codes only if aligned with the codes of good practice, and are vetted by the Department of Trade and Industry as contributing to sustainable black empowerment. There are no direct penalties for non-compliance, but procurement managers and buyers are enjoined to favour businesses that are compliant as it contributes to their own B-BBEE scorecards. Companies with contribution levels of three and less are considered to be fully compliant.

Charters, however, are not uncontroversial as a means of achieving sector transformation. They have also generally set higher ownership targets than sector codes, which have made them unpopular with industry (Rumney, 2010b), so it is to be anticipated that the print media industry will resist a charter. At the time of writing, there were already signs in that regard. In December 2010, the industry representative body, Print Media South Africa (PMSA) met with the MDDA to, *inter alia*, express its concern about the narrow definition of transformation adopted in the report, and noted that it has adopted the BEE scorecard as a measurement for transformation in the industry, of which ownership and control is but one element. The PMSA' s reference to the scorecard implied that, in its view, transformation was more advanced than the report suggested if all these factors were taken into account, which further implied that the PMSA felt a charter was not warranted (MDDA and PMSA, 2010).

If the print media charter becomes mired in controversy, then it may well suffer the same fate as the information and communications technology charter, which has still not been promulgated as a sector code, in spite of the fact that the charter has been seven years in development and disagreements among industry players have delayed the process enormously (Mawson, 2010). In any event, charters have worked most successfully where the government has been able to exercise licensing or buying power. While newspapers do not need licences to publish, the government could seek to exercise influence through its buying power, withholding adspend to newspapers that fail to meet transformation targets (Rumney, 2010) – but undoubtedly this practice would raise press freedom fears that advertising could be withdrawn from papers that are critical of the government. Apart from these difficulties around enforcement, charters have significant advantages in that they can encourage cooperation towards a broad transformation vision that does not necessarily have to restrict itself to the seven elements of the scorecard: the ICT charter, for instance, commits the sector to bridging the digital divide, although no specific targets are set in that regard.

The B-BBEE profile of the industry is patchy, with two of the four groups (Caxton and Independent Newspapers) being entirely white-owned (the latter by virtue of being foreign-owned).

Table 2: B-BBEE scorecards of major media houses (2010)

B-BBEE status	Weighting point	Actual points: Avusa	Actual points: Media 24	Actual points: Caxton/ CTP Limited	Actual points: Independent Newspapers
Ownership	20	17.6	12.25	0	0
Management and control	10	8.88	8.19	8.75	6.27
Employment equity	15	8.88	5.89	5.58	10.03
Skills procurement	15	5.31	2.17	6.36	7.47
Preferential procurement	20	16.48	16.75	15.54	14.05
Enterprise development	15	15.00	15.00	15.00	15.00
Socio-economic development	5	5.00	5.00	5.00	5.00
Black owned	100%	51.38%	14.55%	0%	0%
Black women owned	100%	1.48%	0.04%	0%	0%
B-BBEE contributor	Between level one (highest) and non-compliant (lowest)	Level 3	Level 4	Level 5	Level 5

Source: B-BBEE scorecards of Avusa, Caxton/ CTP Limited, Independent Newspapers and Media24.

The media organisation with the highest empowerment rating is Kagiso Media (which is not active in the print media sector), followed by Naspers. Media24 has its own scorecard, and has a level-four contribution to B-BBEE, slightly weaker than its parent company, although the company claims that it has improved on its initial scores. While it has scored full marks on enterprise development and socio-economic development, its score on ownership is not as strong as Naspers's, it is weak on employment equity and dismal on skills development. The fact that the company has any black ownership at all could be attributed largely to a share ownership scheme offered in 2006, called the 'Welkom Yizani' deal.

Media24 has a good score for management control, but the low score on skills development has been attributed to the fact that the recession had placed the company's revenues under pressure, leading it to cut spending in this area. The company also faces a particular challenge with respect to employment equity, as a number of its newsrooms are Afrikaans-speaking, which limits its ability to achieve employment equity targets:

this constraint, however, does not really exist at higher management levels as English is used as a medium of communication, as well as Afrikaans. The enterprise development category is relatively easy to score full marks in as there is a business imperative driving investment in this area, especially when it comes to developing small entrepreneurial distributors to supply titles like the tabloid *The Sun* in townships. Socio-economic development involves typical corporate social investment spend, and is calculated as a percentage of profit: so if profit declines, as happened during the recession, then this target becomes easier to meet.[6]

Avusa's management and control score is higher than Media24's, suggesting that it has enjoyed much more success in transforming this level of operations. Avusa's skills development score is also weak, suggesting that it too succumbed to the temptation to cut spending in this area during the recession. Avusa's empowerment profile improved significantly in mid-2008, when Mvelephanda Holdings, owned by Tokyo Sexwale, acquired a 25.5 per cent stake in the company from Allan Gray, which raised the company's B-BBEE ownership status to twenty per cent. The balance of the shares are owned by public shareholders (MDDA, 2009: 45).

Caxton CTP's and Independent Newspapers' empowerment ratings are much weaker than those of Naspers and Avusa. Caxton CTP has a nought per cent black ownership although it scores fairly highly on management and control and on preferential procurement. The company maintains that this is because boards and top management are easy to change rapidly, creating opportunities for BEE appointments, whereas middle and junior managers, and other staff levels, change much more slowly.[7] Its scores on employment equity and skills development are fairly weak, but it scores full marks for enterprise development and socio-economic development. Independent Newspapers' scores are slightly higher. Also with nought per cent black ownership, its senior top management is the most transformed – forty per cent of its top managers are black. Although black people are practically absent from other levels of management and as non-executive board members, they are represented to a significant extent at middle junior management levels (especially the latter). Like Caxton CTP, the company scores top marks for enterprise development and socio-economic development, both considered to be areas where compliance can be achieved fairly easily, as few people have money to buy shares, and the pool of black managers is still fairly small. However, the number of people requiring social support to become economically active was large (Mochiko, 2009).

The *Mail & Guardian* has a 87.5 per cent ownership by a historically disadvantaged individual (Trevor Ncube, who is Zimbabwean, but who has become a South African citizen), but this does not count towards ownership by historically disadvantaged individuals as owners need to be South Africans to qualify (MDDA, 2009: 88). According to its scorecard, which expired in 2009 and still needs updating, the paper is a level five contributor. *The New Age* is owned by TNA Media, which has the former director general in the Presidency, Essop Pahad, and Lazarus Zim, among its board members (De Waal, 2010a). *The Times of India* owns an undisclosed stake in the company. Out of the total of 409 newspapers in existence, forty-four per cent have black shareholding (MDDA, 2009: 86).

This overview of the B-BBEE profiles of the major media groups shows that the groups have scored extremely well on enterprise development and socio-economic development but, as has been pointed out, these targets are fairly easy to meet. In relation to enterprise development, targeted contributions can be driven by self-interest as they can assist the groups to expand their own footprints. Performance on employment equity is patchy, and it is generally poor on skills development but strong on management and control. The Achilles heel of major newspaper groups, though, is ownership; the only group that has allowed historically disadvantaged individuals to acquire a controlling stake is Avusa. In fact, it is ironic that most of the ANC's and the government's ire has been directed at the newspaper that, in terms of the B-BBEE paradigm, is fairly well transformed, namely the *Mail & Guardian*. Furthermore, as these groups are largely management-controlled, it could be argued that the industry is black-controlled – that is, that black people enjoy significant power to determine policies and operational issues. But allocative control, exercised by shareholders, can be much more fundamental to the direction of a company than operational control, exercised by directors, as shareholders have the power to appoint and remove directors if they fail to act in the shareholders' best interests. The industry is vulnerable to attack for lack of ownership transformation, as allocative control of the industry remains largely in the hands of white people.

EDITORIAL AND CONTENT TRANSFORMATION

BEE scorecards are generic, and are not designed to measure transformation in the most significant areas of the print media's operations, namely editorial content. In fact, the tools have not been developed to analyse the extent to which media transformation has enabled a diversity of content.[8] A key ANC argument about print media content is that (put crudely) much of it simply goes where the money is, leading to a reduction in the diversity of voices and opinion. In other words, it prioritises the worldviews of middle-class, mainly white and male, South Africans, whose political sympathies are not likely to be with the liberation movement which has an overwhelmingly poor, black and working-class base. The overly concentrated nature of ownership – still in largely white hands – and the commercialising influence of advertising, are to blame for these problems. The government has also expressed its displeasure with newspaper coverage on occasion, and has even suggested that it may use its substantial adspend to influence content, intimidation that started in 2007 with the threat of withdrawing advertising after the *Sunday Times's* highly critical reporting on the then minister of Health, Manto Tshabalala Msimang. A considerable portion of government's adspend on the print media goes to Avusa, especially *the Sowetan* and *Sunday Times* newspapers. More recently, the government issued a tender to assist it to centralise control of the media buying process, which has led to speculation that it will use its buying power to shift advertising to 'patriotic' media outlets like the SABC and *The New Age* newspaper (Groenewald and Sole, 2010).

In spite of these pressures, and threats of censorious legislation, such as the Protection of Information Bill, which would effectively criminalise much investigative journalism, journalists still do enjoy considerable autonomy to produce journalism in the classical watchdog mould. Newspapers remain on the cutting edge of investigative journalism, breaking far more major stories than do the electronic media.[9] Since its inception in 2006, all the winners of the Taco Kuiper awards for investigative reporting have been awarded to newspaper journalists, and of the nineteen entries to the 2010 awards selected for republication in a book on the best of investigative journalism, sixteen were newspaper journalists (Harber and Renn, 2010). Newspaper journalists dominated the 2011 awards as well. The stories are diverse, covering public and private sector corruption, the conduct of public figures, service delivery and crime. The top entries in 2010 of the Mondi Shanduka awards focused on corruption and poor service delivery in various parts of the country, and 'a general lack of accountability at many levels of officialdom' (Mondi Shanduka, 2010: 1). Newspapers that have excelled themselves in investigative journalism include the *Mail & Guardian*, *Sunday Times* and *Daily Dispatch*, while in the electronic media, *Carte Blanche* has produced a number of impressive stories. In contrast, the news organisation with the largest newsroom in the country, the South African Broadcasting Corporation (SABC), barely features on the radar of quality journalism.

The upswing in investigative journalism could be attributed to the fact that several newspapers have decided to reinvest in this strategic area to hold onto readers. In response to heightened competition in the Sunday newspaper market, the Independent Newspapers group has reinvested in the *Sunday Independent*, which was starved of resources almost since its inception. The Independent group has also established an investigative journalism unit, as has Media24, and the *Sunday Times* has also employed senior investigative journalists. In an attempt to put its investigative journalism work on a more sustainable footing, and to insulate it against commercial pressures, the *Mail & Guardian* is experimenting with a non-profit, donor-funded model, and has established a Centre for Investigative Journalism, with a grant from the Open Society Foundation of South Africa (amaBhungane, 2010). All these developments suggest a renewed commitment on the part of the newspaper groups to investing in quality news content.

However, there are also signs of print media journalists' professional autonomy operating within an ideological 'commonsense' which, in turn, places largely invisible boundaries on the news diversity. Several studies have examined how newspaper coverage reproduces and even reinforces economic and social inequalities, demonstrating a tendency to focus on stories that critique the exercise of political power, rather than economic power, while shying away from fundamental questions of policy alternatives, especially on questions of economic policy. In the process, important opinions may be shut out of the public debate (Duncan, 2009a: 2–30; Wasserman, 2006: 266; Gumede, 2005: 20; McDonald and Mahyer, 2007; Jacobs, 2005; Hadland, 2008; Lovaas, 2008; Duncan, 2009b: 216–233). The audience profiles of South Africa's major newspapers imply that they constitute a fairly elite public sphere; therefore it should come as no surprise if newspaper content tends to prioritise the worldviews of these elites.

A notable exception to this general trend is the tabloid newspapers, which entered the market in the early 2000s. The *Daily Sun* was launched in 2002 and has enjoyed phenomenal success. Other tabloids launched at the time were the Afrikaans-language *Die Son*, and the *Daily Voice*. The tabloids have been dismissed for dumbing down South African journalism and praised for revitalising a stagnant newspaper market, as well as introducing a whole new layer of working class readers to newspapers, and offering slices of everyday life (Wasserman, 2010). The *Daily Sun* identifies LSM 4–7 as its target market, or what it describes as the 'semi-skilled and skilled working class',[10] which leaves the unskilled falling within LSM 1–3 largely unaddressed by newspapers.

While the newfound commitment to investigative journalism is commendable, a more general commitment to investing in news content in the newsroom is not evident. The global recession has led to a decline in circulation figures, with English-language newspapers more heavily affected than Afrikaans-language. The decline in circulation and advertising revenues has placed pressures on newsrooms to reduce costs, and retrenchments have taken place in many newspapers, leading to even greater pressures on remaining staff. Media24 followed the lead of Independent Newspapers and centralised control of its newsrooms, retrenching several senior journalists (Harber, 2010: xxi; Niewoudt 2009), and leading to more vigorous syndication of copy across titles. Rising costs of distribution have also led to media companies cutting back their distribution in more remote areas (Niewoudt, 2009).

The usage of news agency copy appears to be on the increase. The media monitoring organisation Media Tenor has picked up an increasing reliance by English-language newspapers on copy generated by the wholesale news agency, the South African Press Agency (Sapa), suggesting that newspapers are reducing their investment in original news generation. The Afrikaans press, however, can draw on the huge news network of Media24, which reduces the need for agency copy (De Waal, 2010b: 3). Media Tenor has also expressed concern about the lack of differentiation in English-language newspapers, especially in the Independent Newspapers group that tends to run the same news in all of its titles across the country, and has expressed concern that these newspapers are out of touch with audience needs and rapidly losing relevance (De Waal, 2010b: 3).

The most dramatic example of downsizing harming the editorial integrity of newspapers involved the *Sunday Times*, where from 2008 onwards the paper gradually lost its role as the agenda-setter. A report commissioned to look into a series of editorial blunders at the newspaper tells a sorry tale of newsroom corporatisation. The organisational structure had become top-heavy, while being thin in relation to news generation, and had allowed key checks and balances to lapse (Fray et al., 2010: 79). At times, stories were rewritten and 'sexed up' into front page 'splashes', leading to sensationalism and the introduction of inaccuracies. The paper also demonstrated a tendency to withhold details about where information comes from, in the belief that this makes stories sound more authoritative – but, on the contrary, it left the paper vulnerable to the publication of incorrect information (Frayy et al., 2010).

The press ombudsman's office made adverse findings against the *Sunday Times* in a number of the cases examined by the report, and has made adverse findings against other newspapers that engage in ethically dubious practices. In fact, the ANC argument about self-regulation skewing the decisions of the Press Council towards the media is not borne out by the council's own statistics: of the cases involving government or the ANC, in sixty per cent that have been heard decisions have been found in favour of the ANC or government.[11] The council, however, is under-resourced, and forced to confine its role to hearing complaints rather than acting as a regulator of journalism standards. In order to play this broader role, the council would need to produce analyses of trends in journalism, and to identify specific problem areas and engage with the media and journalism training schools about addressing them. The council could also do much more to promote other media accountability mechanisms, and to champion press freedom. But none of these activities – which will ultimately be beneficial to the cause of good journalism – will be possible without the media industry ramping up its financial support of the council – which looks unlikely in the current economic climate.

One of the most direct ways in which owners influence editorial content is through the choice of editor. While there is little evidence of conflicts having surfaced between editors and managers or owners on the actual content of newspapers, on occasion disputes have emerged about the positioning of various newspapers and about the organisation of editorial functions. For example, *Cape Times* editor Tyrone August resigned in December 2008, reportedly around a dispute about management's plans to rationalise the group's sub-editing functions into a single national sub-editing desk (Sapa, 2008). In March 2010, *Sunday Times* editor Mondli Makhanya was 'kicked upstairs' into the position of editor-in-chief of Avusa newspapers, who would be responsible for setting up and running 'centres of excellence' to produce new content for the group's newspapers (BizCommunity.com, 2010). This move followed a serious dip in the paper's circulation, and suggested that Avusa intended to follow in the footsteps of Media24 and Independent Newspapers and centralise some editorial functions (Harber, 2010). Makhanya has championed the establishment of an isiZulu version of the *Sunday Times*, which has contributed to linguistic diversity in a newspaper market dominated almost completely by English and Afrikaans.

Editors have also found themselves in the unenviable position of attempting to maintain the quality of journalism in their papers in an environment where management are repositioning newspapers in response to commercial pressures. Ferial Haffajee was appointed editor of *City Press* to reposition the paper away from its focus on LSM 5–10 and to focus on upper LSMs (LSM 7–10 more specifically). She introduced a broader spread of content, including entertainment, in the process shifting the focus away from the political content with a Pan-African focus developed under Mathatha Tsedu's editorship (Moodie, 2010). The paper also aims to capture a cross-racial readership, especially those 'newly middle class', although this shift has seen a loss of low income readers (Gordon, 2010: 34).

While there is need for more research into trends in editorial content, there are signs that editorial quality in newspapers is highly uneven. In many instances, mainstream newspapers have excelled in investigative reporting. Yet these pockets of journalistic excellence exist in a general newsroom environment of declining resources and, furthermore, while journalistic autonomy is practised in newsrooms, this autonomy is bounded by management pressures on newsrooms to deliver content that provides returns to shareholders – which, in the current tough trading conditions, has involved a fourfold strategy of driving content towards upper LSMs, investing in investigative centres of excellence while cutting the rest of the newsroom to the barest bones, and exploiting content to the hilt, leading to a creeping homogeneity across titles in the major newspaper groups. This fourfold strategy has had negative consequences for content diversity, and hence transformation.

THE BORG LOOMS LARGE: Tensions between corporate and community media

While the circulation of the larger mass-circulation national and regional newspapers has declined, community print media circulation has grown (OMD, 2010: 23–24). In an attempt to take advantage of these trends, the four conglomerates have also entered the local newspaper market aggressively, leading to local-level wars between these groups and independent community newspapers, as the former either bought up the more commercially successful titles of the latter or engaged in practices that effectively drove them out of business (Joseph, 2005; Arenstein, 2005). In 2005, Raymond Joseph used the analogy of the Star Trek's 'borg', a nation bent on total domination and destruction, to describe the phenomenon of the big conglomerates buying up independent community newspapers. In the words of the borg, 'Resistance is futile. You will be assimilated' (Joseph, 2005).

There are structural features in the media system that disadvantage independent media. The large media companies have competitive advantages over smaller independent media, as they are able to control their own markets and manage supply chains. Furthermore, Caxton and Naspers own their own printing presses, and all four large groups can cross-sell advertising; gain easier access to capital than smaller, less well-known organisations; and can leverage the market power of their owners to raise their public profiles (Addison, 2006: 17). Clearly, strategic interventions are needed to stem the haemorrhage of grassroots publications. According to the Association of Independent Newspapers (AIP), it had a membership of 260 publications. But an audit of membership conducted in August 2010 revealed that only 127 of these publications still remain as active publishers, a fifty-one per cent decline. The AIP has attributed this drastic drop in membership to adverse publishing conditions in the light of the global recession, including shrinking advertising revenues and rising production costs (Sanglay, 2010: 3). AIP members have struggled to varying degrees with competition from the four large groups. A case in point is the *Winelands Echo*, a BEE small commercial paper which operates from Paarl and circulates in the Boland area. Advertisers have been resistant to supporting an independent newspaper as they claim that Media24 enjoys a larger footprint. Then, advertising agencies have a relationship with Media24 which, according to the *Echo*'s publisher, Joseph Bushby, makes them 'feel like the fifth wheel on the transport'.[12] While Shoprite has continued advertising with Media24, the *Winelands Echo* used their status as a BEE company to argue for support from Pick n Pay, which only chose to advertise in the paper after tough negotiations. Procuring advertising is an uphill battle, leading to churn in their sales team, even among those sales staff that the paper has invested in training. Some advertising is available from local government, but their reliance on this income stream has also led them to become cautious in their criticism of government, and to adopt what Bushby terms a 'constructive and positive approach'. Owing to the tight trading conditions during the recession, they were forced to downsize their newsroom. The newspaper used to print using Media24's printing presses, but was unhappy with the high costs and poor quality printing, and have shifted to a BEE printing company. The paper's staff undertake distribution themselves, using a network of unemployed people. In summarising the challenges they face, Bushby noted:

> The decision [made by advertisers] is not a business decision, it is a political decision. They want to use us to make business, but they don't want to support us. Black people don't want just to be consumers, but producers. We don't want to be slaves in our own country. Media24 and Independent Newspapers' tabloids are capitalising on our people's low morale, making money out of what they created in the apartheid regime … There has been twenty years to transform business. We are politically democratic, but economically we are still transforming. Government must ensure that fifty per cent of advertising goes to BEE companies …There is a loyalty of businesses to Media24 that we cannot break into. Local advertisers are cutting us, and it's getting harder every year. Media24 and the big media buyers work hand in glove to make us disappear. It's David and Goliath.

Other small commercial and community newspapers with established track records have weathered the tough trading conditions. For example, the *Soutpansberger* and *Limpopo Mirror*, published by Zoutnet and circulating in Limpopo province, have been in existence for over twenty years. The papers have a cover price which according to the publisher, Anton van Zyl, discriminates against those who cannot afford to buy the paper, but also ensures them a readership that is attractive to advertisers. Their biggest competition is from Caxton, and particularly from a newspaper published by its subsidiary, Northern Media Group, *Vhembe Herald*, a paper launched in 2005 after Caxton unsuccessfully attempted to buy Van Zyl' s papers.

According to Van Zyl, Caxton has not played fairly in entering the market, and has exercised their economies of scale, using their printing profits to subsidise the insert costs for advertisers, to undercut the Zoutnet papers. Van Zyl argued: '[When the *Vhembe Herald* was launched] they tried to lure staff members away, and gave ads virtually for free. They came in at a third or less for advertising. [It's tough when] someone takes your market, with millions in the war chest … you can't stop competition, and it's good and healthy, and keeps standards up. But not unfair competition.' Zoutnet laid a complaint with the Competition Commission about Caxton's anti-competitive practices, but withdrew the case because they could not afford the legal fees – which has led Van Zyl to conclude that small businesses are structurally disadvantaged in approaching the Competition Tribunal, as they cannot afford the legal fees necessary to mount a case (Crotty, 2006).[13]

These examples suggest that the large newspaper groups dictate the market conditions in which small publishers operate, using monopolistic behaviour, and that they can make or break these publishers by virtue of their market power. To ignore the conduct of the four big media conglomerates will simply allow practices that disadvantage grassroots media to continue. Government measures to promote diversity, primarily through the establishment and funding of the MDDA, have been inadequate and have not changed this market structure, which is hardly surprising as the mandate of the MDDA was limited to funding and commissioning research, and its eventual funding was a fraction of what was envisaged to make a significant difference to the media (Pillay, 2003: 401–420). Add to that the fact that the global recession caused the newspapers to freeze any increases to their contributions to the MDDA (PMG, 2010), and a picture emerges of an entity incapable of intervening effectively to stem the tide of closures. Furthermore, the trend towards local advertising has being undergoing a reversal. The resurgence of national advertising will undoubtedly be to the advantage of the big-four groups, as they have established relationships with the media buyers. The trading conditions for community and small commercial print media may become even harsher.

CONCLUSION: The hollowing-out of the media transformation debate

The newspaper industry of today is very different to what it was twenty years ago. Newsrooms are far more representative of the demographics of the country, as is the content of their papers. They are at the cutting edge of investigative journalism, and play a crucial role in holding those in power to account. They contribute in a measurable way to the development of black small business and corporate social responsibility. But from the available content studies (and admittedly there are few), the ANC seems to have put its finger on a problem when it argued that newspaper coverage tends to prioritise the worldviews of those with power and money who, predictably, tend to occupy the centre of the political spectrum. Geographic and linguistic diversity is still sadly lacking. Women still lack a significant voice in the media generally, with a marginal increase in the number of women sources in the past seven years (from nineteen to twenty per cent) (Rama, 2010: 9). That there are more black people and women in newsrooms has not automatically led to a transformation of content at these levels.

Apart from the investigative centres of excellence, many newsrooms are being rationalised, leading to a reduction in the diversity of news sources and to downward pressures on the quality of news. Training budgets have been slashed. These cost-saving measures are ill-advised, and may hasten the demise of South African newspapers in a global climate where the death of newspapers is now being openly spoken about. While significant improvements have been made in the management profiles of newspapers, ownership by historically disadvantaged groups has shrunk over the past decade. There are indications that foreign ownership, particularly of Independent Newspapers, has been detrimental to the quality of journalism.

Ownership concentration is a legitimate concern in the current cost-cutting climate (especially the dominance of the newspaper market by Media24, whose parent company, Naspers, is also becoming increasingly powerful in other emerging markets), as the major groups exploit content to the hilt to maximise revenue, having a negative impact on news diversity – the more concentrated the market, the more homogenous the news. The argument that fighting media concentration is akin to 'fighting yesterday's wars' (Epstein, 2010), owing to the explosion of new platforms, is dubious, as intensified news-sharing practices within the big media groups are driving homogeneity on new media platforms as well (Dwyer and Martin, 2010: 2). Small commercial and community print projects are collapsing at an alarming rate, and face an uphill battle for survival in the face of competitively dubious conduct by the big media groups. More fundamentally, the transformation that has taken place has not resulted in a diversity of forms of journalism, or even media models. The professional model of journalism and the commercial model of media remain the dominant models of media production, even in the community media sector.

Is more rigorous implementation of the B-BBEE scorecards the answer, or should the industry aspire to a transformation charter? The B-BBEE scorecard system is premised largely on changing the colour and gender of owners, managers and staff, but not on transforming the practices of the media. If this measurement of transformation is adopted, then there is no policy imperative to diversify the media. Furthermore, the B-BBEE scorecard reduces transformation to the elements on the scorecard, which are insufficient to measure it, and in addition there are indications that the scorecard system actually frustrates transformation, as businesses have no incentive to move beyond the twenty-five per cent ceiling for ownership transformation (in this regard, Jenny Cargill has noted that the most significant BEE ownership deals actually took place before the scorecards were introduced). The scorecards also allow investors to extract wealth without enhancing productivity which, in turn, can encourage rent-seeking behaviour, political patronage and even corruption (Cargill, 2010: 31–65). There is growing evidence of the more recent B-BBEE deals eschewing a broad-based approach – in which a larger spread of individuals and institutions benefit from the deals – leading to the enrichment of a small group of politically connected individuals (Rumney, 2011: 5). There ought to be a different basis for transformation in the newspaper industry, as the pursuit of transformation within the four corners of the B-BBEE scorecard only risks reproducing the very problems that have emerged in other sectors of the media.

There is merit in the ANC's calling for an investigation into anti-competitive conduct in the newspaper industry. But as things stand, the competition authority may lack the necessary tools to understand, much less intervene in, the concentration of the newspaper industry. Abuse of dominance cases are extremely resource intensive as they involve a rigorous analysis of market structure, and a complainant would need sufficient time and resources to see the process through. Alternatively, the Commission (the investigative arm of the authority) could initiate a study into the newspaper market and, on the basis of its results, initiate a complaint with the tribunal (the adjudicative arm of the authority) of its own accord. Whether the Competition Act has the analytical tools necessary to handle competition questions in the newspaper market is in doubt. Competition law has been criticised in media policy circles for not being effective in addressing social concerns about media concentration, such as the negative democratic effects of a group being able to dominate public opinion and the adverse impact on the democratic process (Bilir, 2005: 2–3); this is because competition rules apply economic criteria in the main to assessing the negative effects of dominance, rather than social criteria. For instance, competition authorities generally only intervene if dominance is abused, yet media markets consider dominance *per se* to be socially detrimental as it can lead to a reduction in the diversity of opinion.

The measurement of dominance in the print media sector should differ from the measurement of dominance in the economy generally because of the peculiar need in the sector for plurality. It is instructive to consider the different standards for measuring dominance in economic markets and in general markets. According to South Africa's Competition Act, a firm is considered to be dominant if it has at least forty-five per cent of the market, or if it has at least thirty-five per cent, but less than forty-five per cent, of that market, unless it can show that it does not have market power; or it has less than thirty-five per cent of that market, but has market power. It seems clear that, for democratic reasons, the benchmark for dominance in the newspaper industry should be lower. But even if South Africa had a greater plurality of media outlets, this may not automatically translate into a diversity of content. Media organisations are notoriously susceptible to what has become known as the 'hotelling' effect, where competitors tend to imitate one another's products if there is non-price competition between advertiser-funded media (Atkinson, 1999: 2–3). Other interventions are needed to promote diversity; they could include editorial charters negotiated at newsroom level to protect the independence of newsrooms from political and commercial pressures.

In spite of the way in which the ANC is taking up arguments for a charter – using the threat of statutory regulation in the form of a media appeals tribunal as a beating stick to *koraal* newspapers into developing a charter – there are strong arguments for the industry to develop a transformation charter to allow for the development of a broader and more inclusive definition of transformation that takes into account the specificities of the industry. Potentially, charters can be aspirational documents, outlining a vision for transformation that has become lost in the race for personal enrichment, but if the charter attempts to set targets for content transformation, such as quotas for the number of women sources, then the process may encounter opposition from the media. There should be strategies to create an enabling environment for the transformation of content to reflect a greater diversity of voices, without imposing quotas externally, as this will compromise the editorial independence of newsrooms. In any event, quotas will be a quick fix, as they will fail to address the systemic features of news production that skew coverage towards the powerful and monied in society.

But the risk is that the ANC, the government and the newspaper industry will pursue transformation within the dominant paradigm where B-BBEE is seen as unproblematically virtuous, and where race is taken to be a marker either of advantage or disadvantage. In spite of its critique of the elitism of earlier versions of black empowerment, the 'people's capitalism' of B-BBEE continues a transformation trajectory set in motion under apartheid, where the regime's objective was to create a black bourgeoisie with a stake in the system, and which would act as a buffer against more radical transformation claims (Gentle, 2006: 129). Attempts to ensure redress by keeping apartheid-style race thinking alive risks further benefiting middle-class blacks, while confining working-class and unemployed blacks to the margins of society (Alexander, 2006; Jansen, 2010). There is no reason to believe that a B-BBEE-driven transformation of the newspaper industry would have different outcomes. Would Caxton, for instance, behave differently towards independent media if it were black-owned and controlled? The recourse to B-BBEE rhetoric as a measure of media transformation, by the newspaper industry and increasingly by the ANC, represents the hollowing-out of the vision for media transformation articulated so well by Krabill and Boloka. There are real risks in allowing deracialisation to trump diversity in the transformation stakes. The concentrated nature of the newspaper market will work to the advantage of any new owner with a political agenda, as a controlling stake in any of the four major groups will automatically give the new owner control over a significant chunk of the industry, and hence over elite opinion; so it should be anticipated that the new elite will pressurise the ANC into reducing transformation to deracialisation. How the ANC will respond remains to be seen, but the facts that South Africa lacks a media diversity test for the newspaper industry, and that no serious debate about this has even been initiated, do not send out good signals about the ANC government's commitment, in practice, to diversification as a component of transformation.

The combined effect of the underfunding of the MDDA, the lack of policy to limit excessive media concentration, the shortcomings of the competition authorities in addressing diversity questions, and the reduction of transformation to B-BBEE-driven deracialisation, is that the environment has, by default, favoured media concentration, led to the destruction of much of the independent, small commercial and community press, and opened the newspaper industry up to political attack. As John Barker argued so eloquently in 2000, 'the outcome of liberalisation in Southern Africa has been an opening up of markets to private enterprise, often in a complete policy vacuum, with no regard for the promotion of diversity of ownership and information pluralism'. The lack of policies to promote media diversity plays into the hands of governments which do not want to see the expansion of a diverse media, as they and other elites risk losing control over the news agenda – a phenomenon that led him to ask rhetorically, 'is no policy a policy goal?' (Barker, 2001: 13).

Ways must be found to pursue transformation in a manner that maintains the spaces for newspapers to do what they do best: to hold those in power to account. But this watchdog role will be sustainable only if news media genuinely reflect the society in which they operate. Transformation and media freedom are two sides of the same coin: without transformation, the media will lack social legitimacy, and their freedom will be ultimately unsustainable. But transformation without freedom is no transformation at all.

NOTES

1   According to the press ombudsman, Joe Thloloe, the ANC has newspapers in its sights because they are one section of the media that the ANC does not control, and they have become a scapegoat (Stolley, 2010)
2   Noam defines a company as a voice.
3   According to OMD South Africa, the number of television stations has increased from 7 to 100 between 1991 and 2010 and the number of radio stations from 34 to 138, while the number of daily newspapers has declined from 22 to 21 and the number of major weeklies has increased from 25 to 26 (OMD South Africa).
4   These include the *Daily Sun, Die Beeld, Die Burger, Volksblad, City Press* and *Soccer Laduma.*
5   These include the *Sunday Times* and *The Times,* the *Sowetan,* the *Sunday World, Herald, Daily Dispatch,* and *Weekend Post.*
6   Discussion with Ashuk Adikare, Media24, 11 January 2011.
7   Discussion with Daphne Erasmus, 12 January 2011.
8   According to Kate Skinner, this should include a diversity of languages, styles and formats, including the voices of women, working-class and poor people, rural people, people living in geographically marginalised areas, the youth, the aged, people with disabilities, and illiterate people (Skinner, 2003: 1)
9   In the past, these included a series of stories pursued by the investigative teams in the *Sunday Times* and the *Mail & Guardian,* following story leads in *Noseweek,* on corruption in the arms deal and other government tenders. The *Mail & Guardian* also broke the 'Oilgate' story, where Imvume Holdings was accused of bankrolling the ANC's election campaign in 2004, using money received from the state oil company, Petro SA.
10 Conversation with advertising department, *Daily Sun,* 16 February 2011.
11 Information supplied by press ombudsman of South Africa, Joe Thloloe.
12 Interview with Joseph Bushby, 11 January 2011.
13 Interview with Anton van Zyl, 11 January 2011.

REFERENCES

amaBhungane (2011), About us, viewed on 15 January 2011 at http://amabhungane.co.za/page/about.
Addison G (2006) Publishing the grassroots: printing, distribution, circulation and marketing, Report for the MDDA, viewed 14 December 2010 at http://www.pressroots.co.za/REPORT_GRASS-ROOTS/0_MDDA_Report_Sections.htm on 14/12/2010.
Alexander N (2006) Racial identity, citizenship and nation building in post-apartheid South Africa. Edited version of a lecture delivered at the East London campus of University of Fort Hare, 25 March 2006, viewed on 16 December 2010 at http://www.ecsecc.org/files/publications/120307130010.pdf.
Arenstein J (2005) 'Between the borg and the big bang', *Rhodes Journalism Review,* November : 49–50.
African National Congress (2007) Resolutions: 52nd National Conference, viewed on 28 September 2010 at http://www.anc.org.za/show.php?include=docs/res/2007/resolutions.html.

African National Congress (2010a) *Media transformation, ownership and diversity.* Discussion document for National General Council meeting. Accessed from http://www.anc.org.za/docs/discus/2010/mediad.pdf on 11 December 2010.

African National Congress (2010b) Resolution of the ANC NGC meeting on media ownership, diversity and transformation. Accessed from http://www.thedailymaverick.co.za/article/2010-09-24-anc-ngc-sends-a-softer-cuddlier-media-appeals-tribunal-to-parliament on 11 December 2010.

Avusa Annual Report 2009/ 2010 (2010) Accessed from http://www.avusa.co.za/PDFs/Avusa2010AR Finalpdf.pdf on 7 December 2010.

Berger G (1999) Towards an analysis of the South African media and transformation, 1994–99, *Transformation.* Number 38: 82–116.

Berger G (2000) Response to Boloka and Krabill, *Transformation.* Number 43: 90–97.

Berger G (2001) De-recialisation, democracy and development: Transformation of the South African media, 1994–2000. In Tomaselli K and H Dunn (2001) *Media, Democracy and Renewal in Southern Africa.* Colorado Springs: International Academic Publishers.

Berger G (2010) Pluralism is a bigger priority than press ownership, *Mail & Guardian,* 2 December.

Bilir H (2005) Media ownership control: To what extent is competition law and policy sufficient to provide for diversity and plurality in the media? Unpublished paper. Accessed from http://econpapers.repec.org/paper/metstpswp/0508.htm on 12 January 2011.

BizCommunity.com (2010) 'Makhanya, Hartley, Oppelt move on up at Avusa'. Accessed from http://www.biz-community.com/Article/196/90/46048.html on 7 December 2010.

Buffet W (2009) 'Why bad newspapers can still make good profits'. Politicsweb. Accessed from http://www.politicsweb.co.za/politicsweb/view/politicsweb/en/page72308?oid=138111&sn=Detail&pid=72308 on 7 December 2010.

Cargill J (2010) *Trick or treat? Rethinking Black Economic Empowerment.* Johannesburg: Jacana Media.

Carls A-C (2011) 'France'. Press reference. Accessed from http://www.pressreference.com/Fa-Gu/France.html on 12 January 2011.

Caxton (2010) Company information. Accessed from http://www.caxton.co.za/pages/About_History.htm on 12 December 2010.

Competition Tribunal (2005) *In the large merger between Media 24 Limited and Lexshell 496 Investments (Pty) Ltd, and the Natal Witness Printing and Publishing Company (Pty) Ltd,* 17 October 2005.

Curran J (1991) Mass media and democracy. In Curran J and M Gurevitch (Eds) *Mass Media and Society.* New York: Edward Arnold.

Cranston S (2010) Peripheral but profitable, *Financial Mail,* 1 July 2010.

Crotty A (2006) Small paper stands up to Caxton's Goliath, *Business Report.* 17 July 2006.

De Vos P (2010) What do we mean when we talk about transformation? (blog). Accessed from http://constitutionallyspeaking.co.za/what-do-we-talk-about-when-we-talk-about-transformation-2/ on 18 February 2011.

De Waal M (2010a) *The New Age* launches; Underestimate it at your peril, *The Daily Maverick,* 23 July.

De Waal M (2010b) Malema, Sapa and SA English media's wire copy problem, *The Daily Maverick,* 5 October.

Department of Trade and Industry (2007) Background to, intention and application of the codes of good practice. 15 March 2007. Accessed from http://www.dti.gov.za/bee/Inside.pdf on 10 January 2011.

Duncan J (2000) Talk left, walk right: What constitutes transformation in the South African Media? In

Duncan J (2009a) The uses and abuses of political economy: The ANC' s media policy, *Transformation.* Number 70: 1–30.

Duncan J (2009b) Desperately seeking depth: the media and the 2009 elections. In *Zunami! The 2009 South African Elections.* Johannesburg: Jacana Media.

Dunn H and K Tomaselli *Media,democracy and Renewal in Southern Africa.* Colarado Springs: International Academic Publishers.

Dwyer T and F Martin (2010). 'Updating diversity of voice arguments for online news media', *Global Media Journal (Australian Edition).* Volume 4(1): 1–18.

Epstein R (2004) No need to fight yesterday's wars. Accessed from http://www.ft.com/cms/s/2/da30bf5e fa9d-11d8-9a71-00000e2511c8.html#axzz1EEQ2P1qL.

Fray P, A Harber, F Kruger and D Milo (2008) Sunday Times Review Panel (report). December.

Hadland A (2007) The South Africa Print Media, 1994–2004: An application and critique of comparative media systems theory. Unpublished PhD thesis. Centre for Film and Media Studies, University of Cape Town.

Harber A (2009) O'Reilly's travails may yet be good news for SA, *Business Day*, 22 July. Accessed from http://www.businessday.co.za/articles/Content.aspx?id=76497 on 13 June 2011.

Harber A and Renn M (2010) *Troublemakers: The best of South Africa's investigative journalism.* Johannesburg: Jacana Media.

Gedye L (2010) Caxton, Naspers go another round, *Mail & Guardian,* 27 August 2010.

Golding P and G Murdock (1991) Culture, communications and the political economy. In Curran J and M Gurevitch (Eds) *Mass Media and Society.* New York: Edward Arnold.

Gordon S (2010) The media's meerkat, *The Media.* December: 34.

Groenewald Y and S Sole (2010) Government to apply ideology to adspend, *Mail & Guardian,* 29 October 2010.

Gumede W(2005) Democracy, transformation and the media: the role of the media in strengthening democracy'. Accessed from http://www.caribank.org/events.nsf/Forum15/$File/GumedeCaribbe- anBankSpeechpdf? OpenElement on 23 May 2008.

Hlengani T (2006) Exit Molusi, defiant, *Financial Mail,* 7 August.

Jacobs S (2003) Reading politics, reading media. In H Wasserman and S Jacobs (Eds) *Shifting Selves: Post-apartheid Essays on Mass Media, Culture andIidentity.* Cape Town: Kwela.

Jansen, J (2010) Race holds us back after class, *The Times,* 9 September. Accessed from http://www.timeslive.co.za/opinion/columnists/article649353.ece/Race-holds-us-back-after- class on 16 December 2010.

Joseph R (2005) Resistance is futile, *The Media Online,* 1 December. Accessed from http://www.themedia online.co.za/themedia/view/themedia/en/page4212?oid=3930&sn=Detail on 14 December 2010.

Krabill R and G Boloka (2000) Calling the glass half full: A response to Berger's 'Towards an analysis of the South African media and transformation, 1994-1999', *Transformation.* Number 43. 2000: 75–89.

McDonald D and A Mahyer (2007) The print media in South Africa: Paving the way for 'privatization', *Review of African Political Economy.* No. 113: 443–460.

Mbeki M (2011) Only a matter of time before the hand grenade explodes, *Business Day,* 10 February.

McChesney R (1999) *Rich Media, Poor Democracy: Communication Politics in Dubious Times.* Illinois: University of Illinois Press.

Media Development and Diversity Agency (2009) Trends of ownership and control of media in South Africa. Research report produced by Z-Coms, 30 April.

Media Development and Diversity Agency (2010). Joint media statement – MDDA Board meeting with PMSA Board.

Mochiko T (2009) Independent News needs to meet state targets, *Econobee.* 14 October. Accessed from http://www.econobee.co.za/bee-articles-and-information/press-articles/independent-news- needs-to-meet-state-targets.html on 10 January 2011.

Mondi Shanduka (2010) Corruption and service delivery take centre stage. 9th Annual Newspaper Awards. Accessed from http://www.mondishanduka.co.za/MSNA%20Winners%20Booklet%20 May%202010.pdf.

Moodie J (2010) The battle for the Sunday reader, *Moneyweb.* Accessed from http://www.moneyweb. co.za/mw/view/mw/en/page304825?oid=469594&sn=2009%20Detail on 22 February 2010.

Motloung M (2009) Print: Not for sale, *Financial Mail.* 31 July..

Newmarch J (2006) The invisible media baron, *Mail & Guardian.* 12 July.

Niewoudt S (2009) 'Crisis control, *The Media Magazine.* 1 February.

Noam E (2004) How to measure media concentration, Financial Times.com. 30 August 2004. Accessed from http://www.australiancollaboration.com.au/democracy/commentaries/Media_Laws.pdf on 17 February 2011.

Omnicom Media Group (OMD) South Africa (2010) South Africa and SADC Media Facts 2010. OMD South Africa. Accessed from http://www.omdmedia.co.za/samediafacts2010.pdf on 7 December 2010.

Parliamentary Monitoring Group (2010) MDDA & International Marketing Council 2009/10 Annual & 2010/11 Midterm Reports; SA Post Office Bill; Deliberations on South African Post Office Bill; ICASA briefing on Final Call Termination Regulations. Minutes of meeting of Portfolio Committee on Communications. 24 November 2010. Accessed from http://www.pmg.org.za/report/20101124-international-marketing-council-its-2010-annual-report-performance-re on 18 February 2011.

Pillay D (2003) The challenges of partnerships between the state, capital and civil society: The case of the Media Development and Diversity Agency in South Africa, *Voluntas*, Volume 14. Number 4: 401–420.

Rama K (2010) Southern African Gender and media progress study. *Genderlinks*. Accessed from http://www.genderlinks.org.za/article/gender-and-media-progress-study-south-africa-2010-12-17 on 10 January 2011.

Rossouw M (2011) ANC backtracks on media tribunal, *Mail & Guardian*. 14 January 2011.

Rumney R (2010a) Up to a point: Ownership and media content post-1990 in South Africa. Unpublished paper delivered at a colloquium on media, democracy and transformation since 1994: An assessment, hosted by Rhodes university, 16–17 October.

Rumney R (2010b) The chink in the media's armour, *Mail & Guardian*. 3 November.

Rumney R (2011) BEE deals still on the rise at R24bn, *Business Times*. 13 February.

Sanglay M (2010) Grassroots print media and ownership in South Africa: A case study of the Association of Independent Publishers. Paper presented at a colloquium on media, democracy and transformation since 1994: An assessment. Rhodes University School of Journalism and Media Studies. 16–18 October.

Shain M (2006) *Opposing Voices: Liberalism and Opposition in South Africa Today*. Cape Town: Jonathan Ball.

Skinner K (2003) Media diversity – a draft position paper. Discussion document produced for the Freedom of Expression Institute.

South African Communist Party (2010) The liberal offensive must be defeated – SACP. Politicsweb. 24 December 2010. Accessed from http://www.politicsweb.co.za/politicsweb/view/politicsweb/en/page71654?oid=215870&sn=Detail&pid=71616 on 11 January 2011.

South African Press Association (2010) ANC questions print media's commitment to transformation, *The Times*,10 August.

South African Press Association (2009) Zuma says BEE 'not broad-based enough', *Mail & Guardian Online*. Accessed from http://www.mg.co.za/article/2009-03-11-zuma-says-bee-not-broadbased-enough on 15 February 2011.

Stolley G (2010) Ombud: ANC finds 'scapegoat' in print media, *Mail & Guardian*. 6 October 2010.

The Australian Collaboration(n.d.). Democracy in Australia – media concentration and media laws. Accessed from http://www.australiancollaboration.com.au/democracy/commentaries/Media_Laws.pdf on 17 February 2011.

Tomaselli K and R Teer-Tomaselli (2001) Transformation, nation-building and the South African media, 1993–1999. In Dunn H and K Tomaselli (Eds) *Media, Democracy and Renewal in Southern Africa: New Approaches toPolitical Economy*. Colorado Springs: International Academic Publishers.

Wasserman H (2006) Redefining media ethics in the postcolonial context: Contending frameworks in the South African media. In A Olorunnisola (Ed.) *Media in South Africa after Apartheid: A Cross-Media Assessment*. New York: Edwin Mellon Press.

Wasserman H (2010) *Tabloid Journalism in South Africa*. Indiana: Indiana University Press.

CHAPTER 18

The South African Broadcasting Corporation: The creation and loss of a citizenship vision and the possibilities for building a new one

Kate Skinner

INTRODUCTION

The SABC is the largest news operation in the country – nearly twenty million of the twenty-nine million radio listeners in South Africa tune into one of the SABC's eighteen radio stations, and the SABC's three free-to-air television channels attract more than seventeen million adult viewers each day (Open Society Institute, 2010: 125). But beyond its size and reach the SABC is important because it is the nation's public broadcaster – and as a public broadcaster it offers citizens the possibility of distinctive, reflective, quality programming, independent of major vested interests, be they government or commercial. It offers the possibility of programming specifically targeted at the deepening of citizenship and the strengthening of democracy.

For a brief moment after 1994 there was a burst of creativity at the SABC and a palpable excitement about public broadcasting and its development, information and entertainment possibilities (Du Preez, 2003; Open Society Institute, 2010). Veteran journalist Max du Preez (2003: 253) argues that, 'In 1994, it [the SABC] had the potential to be the prime agent for positive change in the new democracy'. Sadly, however, the SABC was soon dogged by crises. Since late 2007, the corporation has experienced almost perpetual governance and financial challenges. These have included problems with successive boards and CEOs and ongoing problems with the SABC's oversight structures, including the Ministry and Department of Communications, parliament and South Africa's independent regulator, the Independent Communications Authority of South Africa (Icasa).

This chapter seeks to track the reasons behind the myriad problems facing the SABC, particularly since late 2007, and seeks to put forward a number of (tentative) solutions to these challenges. The proposals outlined have been debated by independent producers, unions, NGOs, students and academics. Collectively, solutions have been debated by the civil society coalition originally known as the 'Save our SABC' campaign and then later the 'SOS: Support Public Broadcasting Coalition'. The chapter will critically examine the coalition's and broader civil society's proposals, from an insider's perspective.[1]

BRIEF HISTORY OF THE SABC'S PRESENT CRISES

To untangle the myriad problems of the SABC's recent history it is important to look back to late 2007 and the appointment of the SABC board headed by Khanyi Mkhonza. The board's appointment was mired in controversy, as ANC MPs drafted an initial shortlist which was then tampered with: ANC head office, 'Luthuli House', removed a number of the names (including that of trade unionist Randall Howard) and substituted new ones (including controversial lawyer Christine Qunta and businesswoman Gloria Serobe). This was allegedly under duress from then president, Thabo Mbeki.[2] Civil society organisations including the Congress of South African Trade Unions (Cosatu), Treatment Action Campaign (TAC) and the Freedom of Expression Institute (FXI) complained strongly about the political manipulation. They also claimed that the final composition of the board was elite and business-dominated as there were no labour or other civil society representatives, and there were no working journalists. The board thus started its tenure with its legitimacy seriously in question.

From the start, political battles in the ruling party began to play themselves out in the SABC. The board was seen to be aligned to the then president Thabo Mbeki, who made the appointments immediately after his presidential defeat at the ANC's Polokwane conference in December 2007. Management, although initially supportive of Mbeki, realigned themselves to the president-in-waiting, Jacob Zuma. An antagonistic relationship then developed immediately between the board and management. Early in 2008, a board memorandum outlining problems with CEO Dali Mpofu was leaked to the media, and by March parliament declared a vote of no confidence in the board, accusing members of leaking the memo. Although the declaration of 'no confidence' had no direct legal effect, the board was further weakened politically. It was clear ANC MPs had distanced themselves from the board, feeling that it had been imposed on them. Throughout 2008, the board continued its battles with SABC management and the CEO in particular, suspending Mpofu and re-suspending him after he was legally reinstated.

While management-board battles continued, MPs took the unusual step of introducing new legislation – the Draft Broadcasting Amendment Bill, 2008.[3] Its primary purpose was to allow parliament to remove the board as a whole, as the Broadcasting Act, 1999 only allowed for the removal of individual board members. It was at this point that the 'Save our SABC' (SOS) campaign was formed to give civil society a voice in terms of the governance crises at the SABC and in terms of the proposed amendments to the legislation. The SOS coalition looked back to the early 1990s, a time when civil society played a key role in shaping a new vision for public broadcasting. It argued that the Amendment Bill was not ideal to handle legislation in this piecemeal fashion but, given the crisis around the Board's legitimacy, MPs did need a mechanism to investigate the board and to remove it if necessary, under particular circumstances. In the medium-term, SOS called for a comprehensive green paper/white paper policy review process leading to new comprehensive legislation.

In March 2009, the Amendment Bill was passed. Although SOS had called for the Bill to deal with removal and appointment processes, it dealt solely with the removal of the board.

While board-management battles continued and the legislative process unfolded, the financial situation at the SABC deteriorated rapidly. In November 2008, the SABC tabled its annual report in parliament declaring a profit of R111.3 million (SOS, 2009: 1). At that point no indication was given that the SABC was heading for financial crisis – in fact modest profits were predicted (SOS, 2009: 1). However, at the end of January 2009 the *Sunday Independent* reported that the SABC was R500 million in deficit and at the end of February the *Mail & Guardian* declared that the deficit was in fact R700 million (SOS, 2009: 1). Finally, at the end of March 2009 the SABC broke its silence, announcing that it had 'liquidity problems'. The SABC later declared pre-tax losses of R784 million (SOS, 2009: 2).

The losses threatened unions' three-year salary agreement with the SABC. Further, the corporation defaulted on its payments to independent producers, throwing the entire independent production industry into crisis and putting the long-term production of local content in jeopardy. Calls for the board to resign – or be removed – grew increasingly strident, and members of the board *did* start to resign. In June 2009, in line with amendments to the Broadcasting Act, parliament, in a tough, contested process, then removed the board and appointed an interim board. The interim board brought some relief. It managed to avert a major strike, started work on a repayment schedule for independent producers, finalised a payout for CEO Dali Mpofu, and organised a R1.47 billion government guarantee – probably its greatest success. In its final days, it employed a new CEO, Solly Mokoetle.

In the meantime, parliament proceeded with public nominations for a new board. The SOS coalition and others played an important role in putting forward nominations; an unprecedented 200 nominations were received. In December 2009, the president announced the new board with the former minister of Arts and Culture, Dr Ben Ngubane, as chair.

In the latter half of 2009, while the interim board was moving to get the SABC's house in order, the minister of Communications, Siphiwe Nyanda, introduced new policy, a Public Service Broadcasting Discussion Document (July 2009), followed soon after by the Draft Public Service Broadcasting Bill (October 2009). The department argued that government urgently needed to introduce new policy and legislation to deal with the SABC's funding crisis, and a new funding model was the answer. However, SOS and others argued that although there were problems with the SABC's funding model, the immediate problem was a management crisis. In simple terms, Mpofu's tenure had been one of rising costs and reduced revenue. This immediate crisis could be addressed within the present legislation. A new funding model, critics argued, needed more comprehensive debate and research. This was particularly so given the fact that the SABC was moving into a new digital, multichannel broadcasting context.

The new draft Bill introduced an entirely new funding regime – it scrapped the licence fee and proposed a new broadcasting tax of up to one per cent of personal income; it proposed a central public broadcasting fund for, amongst a number of issues, signal distribution, SABC and community media programming, and public programming produced by commercial broadcasters. The independence of the fund was left undefined. The Bill then proposed the alignment of the entire broadcasting system to the goals of the 'developmental state' (the latter was also left undefined) and, finally, it introduced significant new powers for the minister to intervene in governance crises.

Although there was much unhappiness about the draft Bill, in particular the proposed new broadcasting tax, 2010 opened on a cautiously optimistic note. A new publically appointed board was now in place. However, by May 2010 the SABC had been plunged once again into crisis. This time it was around the appointment of the head of news, as the chair of the board, Dr Ngubane, made the appointment unilaterally, in violation of good corporate governance principles and the principles of the Broadcasting Act. Allegations were made that President Zuma favoured a particular candidate, Phil Molefe, and allegedly Ngubane felt compelled to deliver on this.[4] Initially board members stood up to the chair, publically declaring the move illegal, but when the oversight structures, including parliament, Icasa and the Department of Communications, refused to support them, they started to crumble – four members resigned and those who remained then eventually ratified the appointment.

Simultaneously, problems arose between the board and new CEO, Solly Mokoetle. The CEO supported Dr Ngubane's unilateral appointment of Phil Molefe as head of news, but now further problems arose from the fact that Mokoetle had not delivered on the SABC's critical turnaround strategy. The board initially suspended Mokoetle and then eventually reached a settlement and paid him out. The board thus started 2011 with four members down, and with an acting CEO. In November 2010, in a cabinet reshuffle, the minister of Communications, General Siphiwe Nyanda, was replaced by new minister, Roy Padayachie. A few weeks into Padayachie's tenure the Department of Communications called for public hearings on the Draft Public Service Broadcasting Bill; in submission after submission industry and civil society criticised it, SOS again calling for its withdrawal and for a comprehensive policy review process including a review of the broadcasting White Paper of 1998. This time the ministry and Department of Communications listened. Two weeks after the hearings the minister withdrew the

Bill, opening up the possibility of a comprehensive policy review process. Glimmers of cautious optimism were once again ignited.

A 'BLUEPRINT' FOR PUBLIC SERVICE BROADCASTING

It is important to take a few steps back from the crises and look at what international best practice says about public service broadcasting, to have a yardstick against which we can measure the SABC.

As Tleane and Duncan (2003: 73) argue, internationally there is general agreement that a public broadcaster must have certain core features and that these include universality of access to, and appeal of, its services. Simultaneously, there must be programming for special interest groups, as this is generally marginalised by the commercial sector. Further, programming should acknowledge public debate and dissent. A public broadcaster should also play a nation-building and educational role, 'serving the public interest rather than the private self-interest'. In order to achieve these, a public broadcaster has to be independent from both commercial interests and the state and it must be accountable to the public through its board, who should 'represent the broad spectrum of public opinion through a public nomination and selection process'. Board members should be accountable to the public through their public representatives in parliament.

These are some of the broad principles. Critical political economist James Curran takes these principles further and puts forward an 'ideal type' media development and diversity model. In constructing the model Curran (2000: 140) argues that it is important to 'break free from the assumption that the media are a single institution with a common democratic purpose'; he contends instead that the media should be viewed as having different democratic functions within the system as a whole. 'This calls for different kinds of structure and styles of journalism' (Curran, 2000: 140). Curran's model embraces a core public service sector which is then fed by 'peripheral media sectors that specifically facilitate the expression of dissenting and minority views'. He believes that there are several reasons for the public service media's centrality, including the fact that, traditionally, public service television has been governed by fairness and access rules, and that it has promoted public information as a central objective and has prioritised the serving of all citizens. Further, it has specifically prevented the creation of a group of second-class citizens excluded by price. Curran argues that to protect this sector from government control the following is required: 'independent funding through a licence fee, a block on unmediated government appointments to broadcasting authorities, the dispersal of power within broadcasting organisations, and a climate of freedom supported by a written constitution' (Curran, 2000: 141).

In reflecting on this model it is interesting to note how closely certain ANC perspectives in the early 1990s – particularly the ANC's strong 'substantive democratic' perspective – captured just such a vision.

MEDIA POLICY PERSPECTIVES – THE EARLY 1990S AND BEYOND

Two major media policy perspectives dominated the policy environment prior to South Africa's first democratic elections: a broad 'ANC Alliance perspective'[5] and a 'National Party/parastal'[6] perspective (Louw, 1993; Horwitz, 2001). Louw states that by the early 1990s the National Party's position had shifted profoundly, from a far-right nationalist stance which pushed for the media to play a 'lap-dog propagandistic role' to a 'central right' perspective. As the NP's power diminished they realised that their interests were better served by a pluralistic media free from government interference. Louw (1993: 17) further argues that as 'outsiders' to the existing system, the ANC Alliance demanded more fundamental changes. In general the 'ANC camp' proposed a social democratic (mixed economy) media system and this approach included an understanding that simply declaring the right to 'freedom of speech' was not enough – the right needed to be under-pinned by material resources to ensure that market forces did not *de facto* restrict this freedom to the middle class and the affluent.

The ANC's media charter, drawn up in November 1991, imagined a redistributive role for the state. Simultaneously it called for a deliberate strategy to engender a culture of open debate (Louw, 1993: 18). However, Louw notes that this open democratic stance was paralleled by elements within the ANC camp that were attracted by the potential power the SABC offered, and he argues that these elements desired 'that the SABC should serve an ANC government much as the corporation served the old NP government' (Louw, 1993: 12).

Horwitz also reflects on the early 1990s and points to the importance of civil society input in terms of the shaping of broadcast policy during this period. Two civil society campaigns were important: the Campaign for Open Media (COM) and the Campaign for Independent Broadcasting (CIB). COM played the initial role in assisting the ANC to craft its broadcasting policy (Horwitz, 2001). COM organised, hosted and co-hosted a series of workshops and conferences of which the Jabulani! Freedom of the Airwaves Conference, held in the Netherlands in 1991, was the most critical.[7] The recommenda-tions of this conference, in particular, set the terms of the debate on media transformation in the early 1990s (Horwitz, 2001: 131). According to Horwitz, the conference under-scored the differing political perspectives within the ANC and the Mass Democratic Movement on broadcast policy. Three different perspectives can be distinguished: a 'post-social democratic' approach, a 'conservative pluralist position' and a 'centralist, state broadcaster orientation'. The 'post-social democratic' approach, which had the strongest following, saw the importance of public broadcasting but was not naïve about its problems (Horwitz, 2001: 132). The approach thus championed the idea of public broadcasting as the anchor to the broadcasting system but also saw the importance of including commercial and community broadcasting as key components – but with strong public obligations. Left-wing proponents of this approach called for a commer-cial presence but ultimately campaigned for the production of as much non-state, non-commodified broadcast media as possible (Horwitz, 2001: 132). The 'conservative pluralist' proponents, by contrast, emphasised consumer sovereignty, the importance of deregulation and a reduced role for the public broadcaster. They tied the political battle of freedom of the media to the workings of the market. The 'centralist state broadcaster orientation' was the third minority orientation that called for the SABC to be 'taken over by the liberation forces' (Horwitz, 2001: 132).

After the ANC came into government in 1994, these various perspectives became competing strands in government policy (Horwitz, 2001, Pillay, 2003). In his work on media development and diversity issues, Pillay refers to these perspectives as 'substantive democratic', 'market' and 'statist', arguing that initially the 'substantive democratic' policy perspective was the most powerful but that market-orientated trends soon gained ascendancy. He argues that the strength in market approaches can be directly related to the adoption in 1996 of government's Growth, Employment and Redistribution (Gear) strategy. As argued extensively elsewhere, Gear's primary concern was to boost investor confidence by adopting the main tenets of neoliberalism. Government called for curtailing the state's role in development, prioritising the market, privatising state assets, tax relief for the middle and upper classes, and low corporate taxes. Gear assumed that economic growth would automatically lead to a redistribution of wealth (Adelzadeh, 1996; Lodge, 1999; 2002; Bond, 2000; Marais, 2001; Sparks, 2003). Pillay contends that although market influences on policy were certainly powerful this did not mean that 'substantive democratic' and 'statist' strands ceased to exist – they competed with market-oriented policies, their power waxing and waning depending on the political forces at play.

THE CREATION OF A 'SUBSTANTIVE DEMOCRATIC' VISION AND ITS MARKET REVERSAL – THE MIDDLE TO LATE 1990s

As reflected above, the process of transforming the SABC from an apartheid state broadcaster into a public broadcaster began in the early 1990s. The transformation of the SABC was seen as essential for free and fair elections (Louw, 1993; Horwitz, 2001; Open Society Institute, 2010). All parties agreed to the transformation, but for different reasons. Simply put, the National Party did not want the ANC to control the SABC *after* the elections and the ANC did not want the National Party to control the SABC *during* the elections (Horwitz, 2001; Open Society Institute, 2010), but beyond these power battles there was a genuine commitment from the ANC to ensure the SABC's independence (Horwitz, 2001) and a board that was, on balance, independent and publically nominated, was appointed (Horwitz, 2001; Open Society Institute, 2010).[8]

With the new board in place, new management was appointed. Alternative media editor and ANC veteran Zwelakhe Sisulu was appointed CEO. An active transformation unit was established and an intensive training programme for journalists, production staff and management was launched (Open Society Institute, 2010). In line with the core principles of public broadcasting internationally, the SABC committed itself to:

[...] deliver full spectrum services to all South Africans, in all parts of the country, and in each of the official languages. Programme content was aimed at protecting and nurturing South African culture and creativity, and reflecting the reality of South Africa to itself, and to the world (Teer-Tomaselli and Tomaselli, 2001: 126).

In line with this vision, the SABC set itself the following targets: extension of airtime for all official languages (other than English) on television; increases in local content programming; extension of the television footprint to reach all potential viewers; introduction of regional television slots in all provinces; equity and universal access to religious programming; provision of curriculum-based education on both radio and television; and upgrading of the African-language radio services (Teer-Tomaselli and Tomaselli, 2001).

It was also during this period that the Independent Broadcasting Authority (IBA) initiated the 'Triple Enquiry' report. Launched in 1995, this was a comprehensive and in-depth study into the protection and viability of public broadcasting, universal access and South African content. After wide consultation with stakeholders, the IBA presented its proposals to parliament. The most important proposal was a call for the public broadcaster to sell eight of its commercial regional stations and to be limited to two television stations. The SABC's third television channel was to be relicensed as a new commercial station but with significant public service obligations. The SABC was to maintain its core public African language radio channels.

While Horwitz (2001) argued that these proposals were a progressive mix of market and public interventions, Tleane and Duncan (2003) were less positive, contending that it was at this critical moment that government started to renege on its important pre-1994 promise of securing long-term public funding for the SABC. The Triple Enquiry report called for the SABC to be funded through a mix of advertising and sponsorship, licence fees and government grants but no recommendations were made as to the ratios of the different revenue streams (Open Society Institute, 2010: 170). When the Triple Enquiry recommendations were released there was significant controversy. For Horwitz (2001: 166) the important issue was the size of the SABC. He argues that many supported a large SABC because of the need to deliver broadcast programming in all the official languages but there were also 'statist, authoritarian' perspectives at play and certain groupings supported a large institution simply because they wanted to maintain the SABC's power-base. Eventually, the proponents of a 'large SABC' won. Parliament rebuffed the IBA's proposals – the SABC was allowed to retain two of its original eight radio stations and all three of its television channels (Horwitz, 2001; Open Society Institute, 2010).

In September 1996, the sale of six SABC radio channels went ahead and the SABC's sixty-year monopoly in the radio broadcasting field was broken. At this point diversity of content and ownership was enhanced – but also ironically reversed (black ownership of radio stations was enhanced and the commercial radio sector was boosted, but simultaneously the SABC was plunged into a financial crisis as it suffered loss of station income). The crisis was exacerbated by the fact that government – in line with Gear policies – retained the proceeds of the station sales. By 1997, the SABC had posted a deficit of R64 million and was predicting losses of up to R650 million (Open Society Institute, 2010: 172). With no long-term commitment to public funding in place, and a necessity to balance its books, the SABC was forced into the arms of the 'slash and burn' international change management consultants McKinsey and Associates (Tleane and Duncan, 2003).

The SABC's finances were certainly turned around, but at a serious cost. Public programming (including local content) was axed from prime time in favour of more commercially viable programmes such as international sitcoms and less costly South African programmes including game shows (Open Society Institute, 2001: 172). The use of English was increased to maximise advertising revenue (Tleane and Duncan, 2003). Further, the SABC took the radical decision to outsource all production, except news and current affairs (Open Society Institute, 2010: 172).

At the same time as the implementation of the McKinsey recommendations, new legislation was introduced. Towards the end of 1997, government launched a Green Paper on broadcasting and in 1998 it launched a broadcasting White Paper. The Green Paper asked for submissions on the 'realistic proportion of revenue from advertising, transactions and public funds' (Open Society Institute, 2001: 172). The White Paper proposed a new funding model, dependent on the division of the SABC into public and public commercial arms, with the understanding that the public commercial arm would have fewer public service obligations, would make more money and would cross-subsidise the public arm (Open Society Institute, 2001: 173). Then, in 1999, the Broadcasting Act was promulgated. It called for the corporatisation of the SABC and confirmed the separation of the SABC into public and public commercial wings (Open Society Institute, 2001: 173).

Through its corporatisation, a commercial logic and a dependence on advertising were built into the very structure of the SABC. The public commercial arm was to generate advertising and although initially it was envisaged that the public arm would generate less advertising, this was not stipulated in the legislation. All channels, therefore, became very heavily reliant on advertising. Ultimately, the model was designed to ensure that the SABC was structured to be as independent as possible from public funds.

Government's contribution to the SABC was continually cut during this period. Minister Jay Naidoo, minister of Communications at the time, announced in 1998 that government funding for the SABC would be cut by forty-one per cent from R235 million in the 1997/8 financial year to R141 million in the 1998/9 budget (Open Society Institute, 2010: 172).

Importantly (and interestingly) this corporate logic also brought with it the seeds of a 'statist' logic. A hundred per cent of the shares of the SABC were to be held by the minister of Communications, and no mention was made that this was 'on behalf of the public' (Open Society Institute, 2010: 134). Also, the minister was given a number of specific powers, including playing a key role by approving the SABC's corporate plans and appointing the SABC's executive management including the chief executive officer (also the editor-in-chief), chief financial officer and chief operations officer. The seeds of a state broadcaster logic was thus built into the SABC's new commercial legal structure (Tleane and Duncan, 2003; Open Society Institute, 2010).

MARKET DOMINANCE CONTINUES BUT NOT UNCONTESTED –
THE EARLY 2000s

As Tleane and Duncan point out, one of the major problems faced by the SABC in the early 2000s was that television was failing to implement its public service mandate, especially with respect to language. In 1999, English accounted for 86.4 per cent on SABC 1, 71.6 per cent on SABC 2 and for 99.6 per cent on SABC 3 (Tleane and Duncan, 2003: 165–166).

The portfolio committee on communications and the Department of Communications started to express serious concerns about the situation. The department engaged the SABC in a series of meetings in the early 2000s. The department espoused, in line with early 1990s media thinking, a 'mixed funding' model including direct institutional public funding for the SABC; however, to facilitate this they called for the SABC to clarify its public service remit and to develop three-year budgets. In this process the SABC's internal spending priorities became a bone of contention (Tleane and Duncan, 2003; Open Society Institute, 2010). According to Tleane and Duncan, one of the ironies of the McKinsey process was that although significant savings were made initially, in the long-term the McKinsey restructuring led to a rise in bureaucracy in the SABC and a ballooning of management costs. The management to staff ratio in the SABC in 1994 was 1:5; by 2000 it had increased to 1:3, with a ratio of one manager to every two workers in divisions like radio, television and news (Tleane and Duncan, 2003: 168). It seems the SABC was not prepared to have these issues examined (Tleane and Duncan, 2003; Open Society Institute, 2010).

In an attempt to respond to the problem of language and to challenges surrounding the SABC's corporatisation, the Department of Communications developed the Broadcasting Amendment Bill, 2002. To tackle the problem of language, the department proposed the establishment of two regional television stations, one for the north and one for the south, initially outside the structures of the SABC. The northern station would cover North West, Limpopo, Gauteng and Free State, and broadcast programmes in Setswana, Sesotho, Sepedi, Xitsonga and Tshivenda. The southern regional service would then cover Northern Cape, Western Cape, Eastern Cape, Mpumalanga and KwaZulu-Natal and would broadcast programmes in isiXhosa, isiZulu, Setswana, siSwati, Afrikaans and isiNdebele. These services were to be established as separate corporate entities, initially with the state as the sole shareholder (Tleane and Duncan, 2003: 171).

It is important to note that although the department's commitment to public funding was positive, its general approach had certain strong statist overtones. This can be seen by its proposals for the new stations. For instance, no public nomination process was proposed for their boards and no guarantees were stipulated for their independence. Further, the department put forward a set of proposals for the role of the minister. One of the key proposals, for instance, was for the minister to approve all SABC editorial and other policies. The minister was also tasked with playing a direct role in the setting up of the two boards for the public and public commercial divisions of the SABC (Tleane and Duncan, 2003).

At the portfolio committee, however, under strong civil society pressure from Cosatu and the FXI, a number of these proposals were withdrawn or reworked (Tleane and Duncan, 2003). For instance, it was agreed that the SABC board needed to ensure public participation in the development of their editorial policies. Also, new proposals around the minister and the setting up of the public and public commercial boards for the SABC were withdrawn. Further, it was agreed that the new regional services would be run by the SABC, and would therefore enjoy the same guarantees of independence and accountability as the SABC itself. Echoes of the substantive democratic vision were thus renewed.

However, the overwhelming issue was still funding. Tleane and Duncan maintain that it was not clear at the parliamentary hearings how much funding government had allocated to the regional stations:

> The fact that this information was not available at the time of the parliamentary debate caused some ire, as effectively new services were being legislated into being without a clear indication of the extent to which they needed to be funded. This meant that if sufficient funding was not forthcoming, the SABC would have to foot the shortfall, something the SABC was ill-placed to do. (Tleane and Duncan, 2003: 178)

The costs of the stations were high. I estimated in 2005 that the new channels would cost R442 million (R221 million per channel) for the first year of the licence period. In the end, government was not prepared to pay. Ultimately the proposals for the regional stations were stillborn and the department's noble attempts to deal with the language issue came to nothing.

With its reduced public mandate, the SABC's finances were turned around. In 1999–2000, government recorded a deficit of R28.1 million, and by 2001 the SABC had posted a R5.3 million surplus. In 2002, the SABC announced that it had stabilised its business, recording a R7 million profit. In 2005, it recorded an after-tax profit of R194 million and in 2006 it recorded an after-tax profit of R382 million (Open Society Institute, 2010: 177).

THE EMPTY PROMISE OF 'TOTAL CITIZENSHIP EMPOWERMENT' – STATISIM AND CONFUSION – 2005 TO THE PRESENT

Dali Mpofu's tenure as CEO at the SABC started in 2005 at the height of an advertising boom. Mpofu's predecessor, Peter Matlare, had generated significant profits. However, the political climate was shifting in the country. Significantly, the ANC as a party had started to call for greater public funding for the SABC; in 2002 the ANC had adopted a resolution at its national conference stipulating that government must 'move towards establishing a publically funded model of the public broadcaster' and must 'increase its funding of the public broadcaster' in order to reduce dependence on advertising

(Open Society Institute, 2010: 174). Then, at the ANC's national conference in December 2007, another resolution demanding an increase in public funds was passed. More specific than that taken in 2002, it stipulated that government must increase funding for the SABC from two per cent to sixty per cent by 2010–2011 (Open Society Institute, 2010: 175). The SABC's funding mix is approximately eighty per cent advertising, eighteen per cent licence fees and two per cent government funding.

In 2007, in the SABC's annual report, Dali Mpofu singled out the predominance of commercial funding as 'the single most important issue facing the corporation' (Open Society Institute, 2010: 179).

Civil society activists, who had long fought for increased public funding, were heartened by these statements. There was a clear endorsement of Mpofu's new SABC vision, a vision of 'total citizenship empowerment'. But problems soon emerged. First, it was difficult to get more than a brief explanation of Mpofu's vision, which threw its substance into question. Second, costs started to rise, with no visible improvement to public programming.

In an analysis of annual reports over the period, researcher and SABC interim board member, Libby Lloyd, points to a serious lack of financial controls. In 2007 revenue increased by eight per cent but expenditure increased by nineteen per cent. Consulting fees, for instance, increased from R41 million to R135 million. In 2008, revenue went up by nine per cent but expenses increased by fourteen per cent. Consulting fees increased by another sixty-eight per cent, and employee costs increased by thirty-eight per cent. Lloyd points to the fact that approximately 600 additional people were employed at the SABC over a period of two years, and she also points to an increase in management posts; for instance, in 2005 there were fifteen members of the executive and by 2008 there were twenty-one. Further, the salaries of management were steadily increasing. In 2007, the CEO was paid R3.8 million including allowances and performance bonuses. In 2008, the CEO received R4.5 million, an increase of nearly twenty per cent. Bonuses were paid, despite the lack of a performance management system (Lloyd, 2009).

The lack of substance of the 'total citizenship empowerment' vision (other than a commitment not to follow fiscal discipline!) was then further demonstrated during the 'blacklisting saga': on 20 June 2006 the *Sowetan* newspaper announced 'SABC bans top Mbeki critics'. The article claimed that the then head of news, Snuki Zikalala, had blacklisted political commentators critical of government, including Aubrey Matshiqi, William Gumede, Karima Brown and Vukani Mde. After strong denials from the SABC about the blacklist's existence, it was then confirmed on air by SABC talkshow host, John Perlman. Initially, with great fanfare, Mpofu announced that he would investigate to see if there was a blacklist and that 'heads would roll' if there was (*Mail & Guardian*, 2006). He appointed a commission of enquiry chaired by previous SABC CEO Zwelakhe Sisulu and promised that the final report with recommendations would be released in full.

It appears that he got cold feet. The report was never officially released and to date there is no evidence that the SABC has implemented its recommendations. The final report's evidence was damning. It stated that contrary to the imperatives of the Broadcasting

Act and the SABC's editorial policies, there *was* clear evidence of blacklisting. Further, the report was critical of Zikalala's authoritarian leadership style, arguing that it had a chilling effect on journalists' initiative (SABC, 2006). With the backing of his board, Mpofu moved to protect Zikalala and to release only certain sanitised sections of the report. However, in the meantime the full report was released on the *Mail & Guardian's* website. Mpofu threatened to sue the newspaper. In the end whistleblower John Perlman was disciplined and left the SABC. The guilty party, Snuki Zikalala, was given a rap over the knuckles and he continued as head of news.

In 2006 the FXI started its arduous legal battle to compel Icasa to ensure that the SABC implemented the commission's recommendations. After losing successive cases, the FXI finally won some reprieve. In January 2011, the High Court ordered Icasa to deal with the substantive matters of the case (FXI, 2011). Icasa's complaints and compliance committee had continuously argued that had it had no jurisdiction over the matter.

Mpofu's legacy was thus *not* one of 'citizenship empowerment' – it was one of secrecy and lack of public accountability. It was one of leadership and financial crises, and the long-term undermining of the local-content industry and the production of local programming. The perpetual crises at the SABC during his tenure, and also beyond, encouraged 'statism'. The Public Service Broadcasting Bill, for instance, called for a host of new powers for the minister to intervene in management crises (Republic of South Africa, 2009).

THE SOS COALITION'S CRITIQUE OF THE CRISES AND STEPS TOWARDS CREATING A NEW CITIZENSHIP VISION

The FXI, Cosatu, Media Monitoring Africa, the National Community Radio Forum and the Media Institute of Southern Africa are among a number of organisations that have played a critical role since 1994 in calling for the transformation of public broadcasting. From 2007, however, the intensity of the crises at the SABC necessitated coordinated action, and hence the formation of the SOS coalition in mid-2008. SOS recruited its membership from a number of sectors, including NGOs, the unions (including union federations Cosatu and Fedusa and individual unions Bemawu and Mwasa), the independent film and television production sector, academics and freedom of expression activists.

Initially, the coalition organised itself exclusively around SABC issues but later it adopted broader concerns, including community broadcasting. The coalition argued that community broadcasters should play a 'public-interest', 'citizenship' role at the local level.

Through a series of workshops, roundtables and working-group meetings, the coalition crafted a vision for public broadcasting that includes 'creating a public broadcasting system that is universally accessible and dedicated to the broadcasting of quality, diverse, citizen-orientated public programming committed to strengthening the values of the constitution' (SOS, 2011).

Four key goals inform the vision. These include strengthening all three tiers of broadcasting (public, commercial and community) and ensuring that all three have a public remit: promoting the institutional autonomy of the SABC from all major vested interests be they commercial, government or party political; strengthening the SABC's accountability to all South African communities, particularly those marginalised by other sectors of the media; and ensuring independent programming that reflects the diversity of South Africa's languages and political, economic and cultural perspectives. A key component of the coalition's work has been how to make the SABC more accountable to the public. The coalition has proposed various new structures, including the establishment of the 'office of the public editor'. The public editor would be appointed by the board to adjudicate disputes over editorial content, uphold a code of conduct on the quality and ethics of editorial material, and promote a dialogue between the public broadcaster and its audiences. SOS has called for the setting up of a national public stakeholder committee and provincial stakeholder forums to ensure ongoing, structured input on programming issues.

SOS has argued that one of the reasons for the SABC's weakness and instability has been political interference, first in the Dali Mpofu era and then in the Solly Mokoetle era and beyond. Commercial pressures have also contributed to undue interference because its funding model relies on approximately eighty per cent commercial funding. In terms of political interference, SOS has called for the transformation of the SABC into a Chapter 9 body whose independence is protected by the Constitution, and for the de-corporatisation of the SABC so as to ensure that the minister is no longer its sole shareholder. There has been much debate about the selection of the SABC board and SOS has called for the principles of maximum transparency and public participation in the nomination process and for members of the board to be barred from holding leadership positions in political parties and in government. SOS has called for the strengthening of conflict of interest clauses in new legislation to mitigate against commercial influence.

Also key to the SABC's independence has been the issue of funding. The debates in this arena have been long and fierce and although coalition members have not called for a particular funding model there is general agreement on the principle of ensuring that the SABC has long-term, assured, no-strings-attached public funding that covers both the SABC's institutional needs and public programming. In the immediate term the SABC should carry out an economic modelling exercise to ascertain its actual needs.

Finally, the SOS coalition has pointed out that one of the key problems with the SABC has been the weakness of its oversight structures – including the Department of Communications, parliament and Icasa. SOS has called for the Ministry and Department to draft policy and legislation and to secure the necessary resources for the sector's sustainability; for parliament to pass sound legislation in the public interest, hold the SABC to account in terms of its corporate plans and to monitor the SABC's finances; and for Icasa to hold the SABC to account in terms of its charter and licence conditions.

The coalition has sought inspiration from the early ANC 'substantive democratic' policy proposals. It has looked at broadcasting at a systems level; it has called for independent public broadcasting structures and independent programming; and it has motivated for public funding. It has called for strong public accountability and civil society input to restructure the broadcasting sector and to make substantive inputs into programming content.

CONCLUSION

This chapter has examined developments at the SABC in terms of three competing media policy trends, arguing that in the early 1990s the 'substantive democratic' trend was dominant, and thus the possibility to build a genuine public service broadcaster committed to the deepening of citizenship in the country was strong. However, as government's macroeconomic policies shifted towards a market orientation, the SABC was forced to cut back on its public service mandate and the 1990s saw a drive towards the commercial sustainability of the SABC.

The early 2000s was then a period of contestation – pull-backs on the mandate had been so strong that various state and public institutions, including the Department of Communications and parliament, started to ask questions. There were renewed calls for public funding and renewed calls for the SABC to fulfill its public mandate, particularly on the language front. The interplay between these trends in the 2000s is interesting: commercial trends still continued to dominate until the mid-2000s but at the same time there was a rise in dominance of statist thinking. The need for public funding was articulated but government linked these demands to greater powers for government and the minister.

The period from the mid-2000s to the present has been a particularly unstable one for the public broadcaster. The fight back against the commercialising trends in the SABC has been accompanied by a loss of control of the institution. Mpofu's tenure from 2005 to 2009 was marked by factional political battles, a lack of leadership and excessively wasteful expenditure with few accompanying improvements to programming output, and its legacy has included the destabilisation of the independent production sector, which is due to the SABC's dismal financial situation. As battles between the board and management raged, the possibilities for state intervention increased. During this period the ANC's early 1990s' 'substantive democratic' vision was buried deeper and deeper.

However, at the end of 2010 a glimmer of hope re-emerged. The minister of Communications, Siphiwe Nyanda, was dismissed from the Cabinet and a new minister, Roy Padayachie, was appointed. Minister Padayachie moved to reverse some of the problematic decisions taken under Nyanda's watch, including withdrawing the draft Public Service Broadcasting Bill. The minister has now called for a broadcasting policy review process. There are possibilities for civil society to shape a new public broadcasting agenda and for a 'substantive democratic' vision to be crafted once again. What is most important, however, is that government commits to improved levels of public funding for the SABC and – at the same time – to safeguarding the SABC's institutional autonomy and editorial independence. It is worrying that when the four new board members joined the board in June 2011, one of the original members, Peter Harris, resigned. Rumours in the media abounded that Harris's resignation was linked to his dissatisfaction with political interference on the board, specifically as regards the appointment process of the SABC's CEO.

NOTES

1   The author is the coordinator of SOS.
2   ANC MPs confirmed in parliament in November 2008 that their original shortlist had been tampered with. The SOS coordinator was present during the session.
3   Generally, departments draft legislation and then this is introduced in parliament. MPs' role is to debate the legislation once it reaches parliament.
4   The SOS coordinator discussed this with board members who indicated that Dr Ngubane had stated that the president wanted Phil Molefe to be appointed as head of news.
5   This included the Film and Allied Workers Organisation (FAWO); the Campaign for Open Media (COM); the Community Radio Working Group and the Centre for Culture and Media Studies (CCMS) (Louw, 1993: 10).
6   The parastatals included the SABC, the Electricity Supply Commission (Eskom), Human Sciences Research Council (HSRC), the Council for Scientific and Industrial Research (CSIR) etc.
7   Omroep voor Radio Freedom, an anti-apartheid Dutch coalition, played a key role in financing and convening the conference.
8   However, as Horwitz notes, this appointment was not uncontroversial. NP President FW de Klerk, contrary to the rules, tampered with the process, vetting seven of the panel's nominees including the nominee for chair, academic Njabulo Ndebele (Horwitz, 2003; Skinner, 2008).

REFERENCES

Curran J (2000) Rethinking media and democracy. In Curran J and M Gurevitch (Eds) *Mass Media and Society*, 3rd edition. London: Edward Arnold.
Du Preez M (2003) *Pale Native – Memories of a Renegade Reporter*. Cape Town: Zebra.
Freedom of Expression Institute (2011) Press statement – FXI is vindicated in blacklisting case, 25 January 2011, unpublished.
Horwitz RB (2001) *Communication and Democratic Reform in South Africa*. Cambridge: Cambridge University Press.
Lloyd L (2009) The SABC's financial crisis – what now? Powerpoint presentation to the MJ Naidoo Foundation, 16 June 2009, unpublished.
Louw PE (2003) *Studies on the South African Media – South African Media Policy: Debates of the 1990s*. Bellville: Athropos Publishers.
Mail & Guardian Online (2006) Inside the SABC Blacklist Report, 13 October 2006. http://mg.co.za/article/2006-10-13-inside-the-sabc-blacklist-report.
Open Society Institute (2010) Public Broadcasting in Africa Series, South Africa - A Survey by the Africa Governance Monitoring and Advocacy Project (AfriMAP), Open Society Foundation for South Africa (OSF-SA) and Open Society Media Programme (OSMP). Open Society Initiative for Southern Africa: Johannesburg.
Pillay D (2003) The challenge of partnerships between the state, capital and civil sciety: The case of the Media Development and Diversity Agency in South Africa, *Voluntas*, 14(4): 401–420.

Republic of South Africa (2009) *Public Service Broadcasting Bill,* 2009. Government Gazette No. 32663 of 28 October 2009

Save our SABC Campaign (2009) Memorandum – SABC Financial Issues, 8 March 2009, unpublished.

Skinner K (2005) Contested spaces: An analysis of the ANC government's approach to the promotion of media development and diversity in South Africa, with a particular focus on the policy process that led to the formation of the Media Development and Diversity Agency. Submitted as a Master's dissertation, Wits University.

Skinner K (2008) The SABC Board – proposals to ensure an independent, representative and accountable board. Unpublished research commissioned by the Freedom of Expression Institute, Johannesburg.

SOS Support Public Broadcasting Campaign (2011) Ensuring effective public broadcasting in South Africa – Vision of the SOS: Support Public Broadcasting Coalition, February 2011, unpublished.

South African Broadcasting Corporation (2008) *SABC Annual Report,* http://www.supportpublicbroad casting.co.za/library/entry/sabc_2008_annual_report/

South African Broadcasting Corporation (2006) SABC Commission of Enquiry into blacklisting and related matters, published 14 October 2006. www.mg.co.za.

Teer-Tomaselli R and K Tomaselli (2001) Transformation, nation building and the South African media, 1993–1999. In Tomaselli K and H Dunn (Eds) *Media, Democracy and Renewal in Southern Africa.* Colorado Springs: International Academic Publishers.

Tleane C and J Duncan (2003) Public broadcasting in the era of cost recovery: A critique of the South African Broadcasting Corporation's crisis of accountability. Freedom of Expression Institute, Johannesburg.

Contributors

William Attwell is an MPhil candidate in Public Law, University of Cape Town, and Fox International Fellow, Yale University.

Leslie Bank is Professor and Director of the Fort Hare Institute of Social and Economic Research at the University of Fort Hare.

Patrick Bond directs the Centre for Civil Society at the University of KwaZulu-Natal.

Imraan Buccus is Research Fellow in the School of Politics at UKZN and at the Democracy Development Program. He is also Academic Director at the School for International Training.

John Daniel recently retired as the academic director of the School for International Training in Durban.

Jane Duncan is Professor and Highway Africa Chair of the Media and Information Society, School of Journalism and Media Studies, Rhodes University.

David Fig is an honorary research associate in the Environmental Evaluation Unit of the University of Cape Town.

James Hamill is a senior lecturer, Department of Politics, University of Leicester.

Janine Hicks is a commissioner, Commission for Gender Equality.

John Hoffman is Emeritus Professor, Department of Politics, University of Leicester.

Advocate Paul Hoffman SC is a director of the Institute for Accountability in Southern Africa.

Malose Langa is a lecturer in the Department of Psychology at the University of the Witwatersrand.

Don Lindsay is a PhD candidate in the Department of Sociology, University of the Witwatersrand.

Clifford Mabhena is a post-doctoral fellow at the Fort Hare Institute of Social and Economic Research, University of Fort Hare.

Rajohane Matshedisho is a lecturer in the Department of Sociology at the University of the Witwatersrand.

Prishani Naidoo is a lecturer in the Department of Sociology at the University of the Witwatersrand.

Devan Pillay is Associate Professor of Sociology at the University of the Witwatersrand.

Haroon Saloojee, Professor, Division of Community Paediatrics, Department of Paediatrics and Child Health, University of the Witwatersrand.

Vishwas Satgar is a senior lecturer in the Department of International Relations at the University of the Witwatersrand.

Christopher Saunders is Professor Emeritus of History at the University of Cape Town.

Khadija Sharife is a visiting scholar at the Centre for Civil Society at the University of KwaZulu-Natal.

Kate Skinner is the coordinator of SOS: Support Public Broadcasting.

Roger Southall is Professor of Sociology at the University of the Witwatersrand.

Neil Southern is a senior lecturer in Politics at Sheffield Hallam University.

Karl von Holdt is Associate Professor and Director, Society, Work and Development Institute, University of the Witwatersrand.

Edward Webster is Emeritus Professor, Society, Work and Development Institute, University of the Witwatersrand.

Michelle Williams is a senior lecturer in the Department of Sociology at the University of the Witwatersrand.

Index

Printed and bound by CPI Group (UK) Ltd, Croydon, CR0 4YY

17/04/2025

14658907-0001